THE INSTITUTE FOR POLISH–JEWISH STUDIES

The Institute for Polish–Jewish Studies in Oxford and its sister organization, the American Association for Polish–Jewish Studies, who are responsible for the publication of *Polin*, are learned societies, established following the International Conference on Polish–Jewish Studies held in Oxford in 1984. The Institute is an associate institute of the Oxford Centre for Hebrew and Jewish Studies, and the American Association is linked with the Department of Near Eastern and Judaic Studies at Brandeis University.

Both the Institute and the American Association aim to promote understanding of the Polish Jewish past. They have no building or library of their own and no paid staff; they achieve their aims by encouraging scholarly research and facilitating its publication, and by creating forums for people with a scholarly interest in Polish Jewish topics, both past and present.

Each year since 1986 the Institute has published a volume of scholarly papers in the series *Polin: Studies in Polish Jewry* under the general editorship of Professor Antony Polonsky joined, in 2015, by Professor François Guesnet of University College London. Since 1994 the series has been published on the Institute's behalf by the Littman Library of Jewish Civilization. In March 2000 the entire series was honoured with a National Jewish Book Award from the Jewish Book Council in the United States. More than twenty other works on Polish Jewish topics have also been published with the Institute's assistance.

The editors welcome submission of articles for inclusion in future volumes. In particular, we are always grateful for assistance in extending the geographical range of our journal to Ukraine, Belarus, and Lithuania, both in the period in which these countries were part of the Polish–Lithuanian Commonwealth and subsequently. We also welcome submission of reviews, which are published on the website of the American Association. We are happy to translate articles or reviews submitted in Polish, Russian, Ukrainian, Lithuanian, Hebrew, or German into English. Submissions should be sent to one of the following: Dr Władysław T. Bartoszewski (email: wt@wtbartoszewski.pl); Professor Antony Polonsky (email: polonsky@brandeis.edu); Professor François Guesnet (f.guesnet @ucl.ac.uk); Professor Joshua Zimmerman (email: zimmerm@yu.edu).

Further information on the Institute for Polish–Jewish Studies can be found on its website, <www.polishjewishstudies.co.uk>. For the website of the American Association for Polish–Jewish Studies, see <www.aapjstudies.org>.

THE LITTMAN LIBRARY OF
JEWISH CIVILIZATION

Dedicated to the memory of
Louis Thomas Sidney Littman
*who founded the Littman Library for the love of God
and as an act of charity in memory of his father*
Joseph Aaron Littman
and to the memory of
Robert Joseph Littman
who continued what his father Louis had begun
יהא זכרם ברוך

'Get wisdom, get understanding:
Forsake her not and she shall preserve thee'

PROV. 4:5

*The Littman Library of Jewish Civilization is a registered UK charity
Registered charity no. 1000784*

POLIN
STUDIES IN POLISH JEWRY

VOLUME THIRTY-FIVE

Promised Lands
Jews, Poland, and the Land of Israel

Edited by
**ISRAEL BARTAL, FRANÇOIS GUESNET
ANTONY POLONSKY** and **SCOTT URY**

Published for
The Institute for Polish–Jewish Studies
and
The American Association for Polish–Jewish Studies

London
The Littman Library of Jewish Civilization
in association with Liverpool University Press
2023

The Littman Library of Jewish Civilization
Registered office: 4th floor, 7–10 Chandos Street, London w1g 9dq

in association with Liverpool University Press
4 Cambridge Street, Liverpool l69 7zu, uk
www.liverpooluniversitypress.co.uk/littman

Managing Editor: Connie Webber

Distributed in North America by
Oxford University Press Inc., 198 Madison Avenue
New York, ny 10016, usa

© Institute for Polish–Jewish Studies 2023

All rights reserved.
No part of this publication may be reproduced,
stored in a retrieval system, or transmitted, in any form or by
any means, without the prior permission in writing of
the Littman Library of Jewish Civilization

The paperback edition of this book is sold subject to the condition
that it shall not, by way of trade or otherwise, be lent, re-sold, hired out
or otherwise circulated without the publisher's prior consent in any
form of binding or cover other than that in which it is published
and without a similar condition including this condition
being imposed on the subsequent purchaser

Catalogue records for this book are available from the
British Library and the Library of Congress

ISBN 978–1–800859–92–0 *(cloth)*
ISBN 978–1–800859–93–7 *(pbk)*

Publishing co-ordinator: Janet Moth
Copy-editing: Mark Newby
Proof-reading: Andrew Kirk, Joyce Rappaport, and Julja Levin
Index: Bonnie Blackburn
Production, design, and typesetting by
Pete Russell, Faringdon, Oxon.

Printed and bound in Great Britain by
TJ Books Limited, Padstow, Cornwall

Articles appearing in this publication are abstracted and indexed in
Historical Abstracts and *America: History and Life*

This volume is dedicated to the memory of

ZBIGNIEW PEŁCZYŃSKI

*who made a major contribution to the establishment of
a democratic regime in Poland and to the improvement of
Polish–Jewish relations*

▪

This volume benefited from grants from
THE MIRISCH AND LEBENHEIM CHARITABLE FOUNDATION
TAUBE PHILANTHROPIES

Editors and Advisers

Editors

Monika Adamczyk-Garbowska, Lublin
Israel Bartal, Jerusalem
François Guesnet (co-chair), London
Antony Polonsky (co-chair), London
Michael Steinlauf, Philadelphia
Jonathan Webber, Kraków

Editorial Board

Eliyana Adler, University Park, Pa.
David Assaf, Tel Aviv
Władysław T. Bartoszewski, Warsaw
Glenn Dynner, Bronxville, NY
David Engel, New York
David Fishman, New York
Laura Jockusch, Waltham, Mass.
Ronald Liebowitz, Waltham, Mass.
Joanna Michlic, London
Elchanan Reiner, Tel Aviv

Jehuda Reinharz, Waltham, Mass.
Moshe Rosman, Tel Aviv
Szymon Rudnicki, Warsaw
Robert Shapiro, New York
Adam Teller, Providence, RI
Magda Teter, New York
Daniel Tollet, Paris
Joshua Zimmerman, New York
Steven Zipperstein, Stanford, Calif.

Advisory Board

Elissa Bemporad, New York
Andrzej Chojnowski, Warsaw
Norman Davies, Oxford
Havi Dreifuss, Tel Aviv
Michał Galas, Kraków
Frank Golczewski, Hamburg
Olga Goldberg, Jerusalem
Andrzej Kamiński, Washington DC
Hillel Levine, Boston, Mass.

Heinz-Dietrich Löwe, Heidelberg
Joanna Degler (Lisek), Wrocław
Anna Michałowska-Mycielska, Warsaw
Joanna Nalewajko-Kulikov, Warsaw
David Sorkin, New Haven, Conn.
Scott Ury, Tel Aviv
Marcin Wodziński, Wrocław
Piotr Wróbel, Toronto

Preface

VOLUME 35 OF *Polin: Studies in Polish Jewry* has as its theme 'Promised Lands: Jews, Poland, and the Land of Israel'. It seeks to examine the influence of Polish Jews, Polish Zionism, and Polish culture generally on the development of the Yishuv (the Jewish settlement in Palestine) and the State of Israel, as well as the influence of the Yishuv and the State of Israel on developments in Poland.

Among the topics covered are the early modern support for the Land of Israel and the Jewish congregations there, the connections between these congregations and Jewish communities in eastern Europe and projects for their reform, the early nationalist movement and its constituency, and the representation of the Zionist project in illustrations, posters, and engravings produced in Poland. We also examine a range of related issues: the resonances of the Polish independence movement in Jewish youth movements and the influence of Polish literary modes on the Zionist movement; the support for a revalorization and rejuvenation of Hebrew and the image of Polish Jews, both men and women, in the developing Hebrew culture of the Yishuv and the State of Israel; relations between Poland and the Land of Israel before 1948; the Zionist movement in Poland between 1944 and 1950; the 'Gomulka emigration' to Israel; the impact of Jewish models of self-government on the emerging political culture of the Yishuv; the continuities of Polish culture in Israel after 1948; and the role of travel to eastern Europe in general and Poland in particular from the 1970s, with its attempts to re-establish a connection to the former homeland. Finally, we examine mutual prejudices as well as the present crisis in Polish–Israeli relations, which we hope will have been resolved by the time this volume appears.

Polin is sponsored by the Institute of Polish–Jewish Studies, which is an associated institute of the Oxford Centre for Hebrew and Jewish Studies, and by the American Association for Polish–Jewish Studies, which is linked with the Department of Near Eastern and Judaic Studies, Brandeis University. As with earlier issues, this volume could not have appeared without the untiring assistance of many individuals. In particular, we should like to express our gratitude to Professor Ron Liebowitz, president of Brandeis University, to Mrs Irene Pipes, president of the American Association for Polish–Jewish Studies, and to David Dahlborn, treasurer of the Institute for Polish–Jewish Studies. These three institutions all made substantial contributions to the cost of preparing this volume for submission to the Littman Library, which continues to bear all the costs associated with editing and production. A particularly important contribution was that made by the Mirisch and Lebenheim Foundation, and the volume also benefited from a grant from the Taube Foundation for Jewish Life and Culture.

As was the case with earlier volumes, this one could not have been published without the constant assistance and supervision of Connie Webber, managing editor of the Littman Library, Janet Moth, publishing coordinator, Pete Russell, designer, the tireless copy-editing of Mark Newby, and the proofreading of Andrew Kirk, Julja Levin, and Joyce Rappaport.

Plans for future volumes of *Polin* are well advanced. These will focus on encounters of the Jews of Poland with Germans, German Jews, and their respective cultural traditions, and on issues of gender and body in eastern European Jewish history. We should welcome articles for these issues. As always we are grateful for assistance in extending the geographical range of our journal to Ukraine, Belarus, and Lithuania, both in the period in which these countries were part of the Polish–Lithuanian Commonwealth and subsequently.

We note with great sadness the death of Zbigniew Pełczyński, who made a major contribution to the emergence of a democratic polity in post-1989 Poland; of Henryk Samsonowicz, a major scholar of the early modern history of Poland–Lithuania and a member of the editorial board of our yearbook; of Daniel Passent, a long-standing contributor to the weekly *Polityka* and an outstanding journalist; and the former US Secretary of State Madeleine Albright, who never forgot her roots in east-central Europe and was always concerned to do what she could for the countries of that region. They will be sadly missed.

Contents

List of Contributors xii

Note on Editorial Conventions xiv

Introduction 1
ISRAEL BARTAL, FRANÇOIS GUESNET, ANTONY POLONSKY, AND SCOTT URY

1 BEFORE ZIONISM

Hasidic Communities in the Land of Israel in the Nineteenth Century 27
URIEL GELLMAN

Polish Distinctiveness in Jerusalem, Congress Poland, and Western Prussia in the Nineteenth Century 51
YOCHAI BEN-GHEDALIA

2 FROM THE BEGINNINGS OF ZIONISM TO THE SECOND WORLD WAR

Between Attraction and Repulsion, Disaster and Hope: Jews, Poland, and the Land of Israel before 1948 69
ŁUKASZ TOMASZ SROKA

Zionism in Poland, Poland in Zionism 88
ANNA LANDAU-CZAJKA

The Fourth Aliyah and the Fulfilment of Zionism in the Land of Israel 105
MEIR CHAZAN

Nalewki Street in Tel Aviv? The Political Heritage of East European Jewry in the Yishuv and the State of Israel 123
GERSHON BACON

Between Tłomackie 13, Warsaw, and Kaplan 2, Tel Aviv: The Role of the East European Jewish Press in Shaping Israeli Journalism 140
ELA BAUER

Jewish Politics without Borders: How Ben-Gurion Won the Elections to the Zionist Congress of 1933 158
RONA YONA

A Bridge between West and East: Polish Economic Policy and the Yishuv 180
KATARZYNA DZIEKAN

Palestine for the Third Time: Ksawery Pruszyński and the 203
Emergence of Israel
WIESŁAW POWAGA

3 FROM THE WAR TO THE ISRAELI DECLARATION OF INDEPENDENCE

Imagined Motherland: Zionism in Poland after the Holocaust 224
NATALIA ALEKSIUN

Between Hostility and Intimacy: Christian and Jewish Polish Citizens in 235
the USSR, Iran, and Palestine
MIKHAL DEKEL

Mordecai Tsanin: Yiddish Orphanhood in Israel and Afterlife in Poland 249
MONIKA ADAMCZYK-GARBOWSKA

4 FROM ISRAELI INDEPENDENCE TO THE END OF COMMUNISM

Art and Society between Poland and Israel: The Life and Work of 263
Henryk Hechtkopf
HANNA LERNER

Yom-Tov Levinsky, Jewish Ritual, and Exile in Israeli Culture 288
ADI SHERZER

Israel Expunged: Communist Censorship of the Polish Catholic Press, 305
1945–1989
BOŻENA SZAYNOK

Homeland, State, and Language: The Integration of Polish Jews into Israel 323
ELŻBIETA KOSSEWSKA

The Polish Exodus of 1968: Antisemitism, Dropouts, and Re-emigrants 337
in *Nowiny i Kurier*
MIRI FREILICH

5 FROM THE END OF COMMUNISM TO TODAY

Home as a Place of no Return: Journeys to Poland in the Writings of 353
Child Survivors and the Second and Third Generations
EFRAIM SICHER

Israelis? Poles? Blurring the Boundaries of Identity in Contemporary 373
Israeli Literature
SHOSHANA RONEN

Other Family Stories: The Third Post-Holocaust Generation's Journey 388
   to Poland
   JAGODA BUDZIK

Neuland, or the Displacement of an Ideal: Israel in the Work of Eshkol Nevo 399
   ALINA MOLISAK

Israel and Poland Confront Holocaust Memory 410
   YIFAT GUTMAN AND ELAZAR BARKAN

Index 435

Contributors

MONIKA ADAMCZYK-GARBOWSKA is Professor of Comparative Literature in the Department of Modern Languages at Maria Curie-Skłodowska University, Lublin.

NATALIA ALEKSIUN is Harry Rich Professor of Holocaust Studies at the University of Florida.

GERSHON BACON is Professor Emeritus in the Department of Jewish History and Contemporary Jewry at Bar-Ilan University.

ELAZAR BARKAN is Professor of International and Public Affairs and director of the Human Rights Concentration of the School of International and Public Affairs at Columbia University.

ISRAEL BARTAL is Professor Emeritus of Jewish History and the former dean of the Faculty of Humanities at the Hebrew University of Jerusalem.

ELA BAUER is associate professor in the Faculty of Arts and in the Faculty of Humanities and Social Sciences at Kibbutzim College of Education, Technology and the Arts, and also teaches at the Jewish History Department of Haifa University.

YOCHAI BEN-GHEDALIA serves as executive director of the Central Archives for the History of the Jewish People in Jerusalem.

JAGODA BUDZIK is assistant professor in the Department of Jewish Studies at the University of Wrocław.

MEIR CHAZAN is associate professor in the Department of Jewish History at Tel Aviv University.

MIKHAL DEKEL is Distinguished Professor of English at the City College of New York, where she is also the 2021–22 Stuart Z. Katz Professor of Humanities and director of the Rifkind Center for the Humanities and Arts.

KATARZYNA DZIEKAN received her doctorate in history from the University of Southampton with a dissertation entitled 'Between Anti-Semitism and Political Pragmatism: Polish Perceptions of Jewish National Endeavours in Palestine between the Two World Wars'.

MIRI FREILICH has worked at Yad Vashem and taught in Beit Berl College. She is a historian of twentieth-century Polish Jewry and has researched the Jewish community's assimilation and Polonization processes in interwar Poland and Zionist youth movements during the Holocaust.

URIEL GELLMAN is senior lecturer in the Department of Jewish History and Contemporary Jewry at Bar-Ilan University, where he holds the Marcell and Maria Roth Chair in the History and Culture of Polish Jewry.

FRANÇOIS GUESNET is Professor of Modern Jewish History at University College London.

YIFAT GUTMAN is senior lecturer in the Department of Sociology and Anthropology at Ben-Gurion University of the Negev.

ELŻBIETA KOSSEWSKA is associate professor in the Faculty of Political Science and International Studies at the University of Warsaw.

ANNA LANDAU-CZAJKA is professor at the Institute of History of the Polish Academy of Sciences and at the Department of Social Sciences of the Warsaw University of Life Sciences.

HANNA LERNER is head of the School of Political Science, Government and International Affairs at Tel Aviv University and director of the Hertog Institute for Governance and of the Brody Institute for Applied Diplomacy.

ALINA MOLISAK is assistant professor in the Department of Polish Literature of the Twentieth Century at the University of Warsaw.

ANTONY POLONSKY is Professor Emeritus of Holocaust Studies, Brandeis University, and Chief Historian of the Global Education Outreach Program at the POLIN Museum of the History of Polish Jews in Warsaw. .

WIESŁAW POWAGA was born in Poland and settled in London after the imposition of martial law in 1981. After graduating with a degree in philosophy at King's College London, he worked as a carpenter, translator, correspondent for a music magazine, and senior editor for a UK publisher. He has translated fiction, poetry, and drama and undertaken occasional scriptwriting for radio and TV.

SHOSHANA RONEN is professor in the Hebrew Studies Department at the University of Warsaw.

ADI SHERZER is Fulbright Fellow at the Helen Diller Institute for Jewish Law and Israel Studies at the University of California, Berkeley.

EFRAIM SICHER is Professor of English and Comparative Literature at Ben-Gurion University of the Negev.

ŁUKASZ TOMASZ SROKA is Professor of Humanities, chair of the History Discipline Council, and head of the Department of Nineteenth Century History at the Pedagogical University in Kraków.

BOŻENA SZAYNOK is professor in the Centre for Modern History at the Historical Institute of the University of Wrocław.

SCOTT URY is senior lecturer in the Department of Jewish History at Tel Aviv University and director of the Eva and Marc Besen Institute for the Study of Historical Consciousness.

RONA YONA teaches at Tel Aviv University, New York University in Tel Aviv, and Oranim Academic College. From 2013 to 2021 she was editor of the journal *Israel: Studies in Zionism and the State of Israel*.

Note on Editorial Conventions

Place Names

Political connotations accrue to words, names, and spellings with an alacrity unfortunate for those who would like to maintain neutrality. It seems reasonable to honour the choices of a population on the name of its city or town, but what is one to do when the people have no consensus on their name, or when the town changes its name, and the name its spelling, again and again over time? The politician may always opt for the latest version, but the hapless historian must reckon with them all. This note, then, will be our brief reckoning.

There is no problem with places that have accepted English names, such as Warsaw. But every other place name in east-central Europe raises serious problems. A good example is Wilno, Vilna, Vilnius. There are clear objections to all of these. Until 1944 the majority of the population was Polish. The city is today in Lithuania. 'Vilna', though raising the fewest problems, is an artificial construct. In this volume we have adopted the following guidelines, although we are aware that they are not wholly consistent.

1. Towns that have a form which is acceptable in English are given in that form. Some examples are Warsaw, Kiev, Moscow, St Petersburg, Munich.

2. Towns that until 1939 were clearly part of a particular state and shared the majority nationality of that state are given in a form which reflects that situation. Some examples are Breslau, Danzig, Rzeszów, Przemyśl. In Polish, Kraków has always been spelled as such. In English it has more often appeared as Cracow, but the current trend of English follows the local language as much as possible. In keeping with this trend to local determination, then, we shall maintain the Polish spelling.

3. Towns that are in mixed areas take the form in which they are known today and which reflects their present situation. Examples are Poznań, Toruń, and Kaunas. This applies also to bibliographical references. We have made one major exception to this rule, using the common English form for Vilna until its first incorporation into Lithuania in October 1939 and using Vilnius thereafter. Galicia's most diversely named city, and one of its most important, boasts four variants: the Polish Lwów, the German Lemberg, the Russian Lvov, and the Ukrainian Lviv. As this city currently lives under Ukrainian rule, and most of its current residents speak Ukrainian, we use the Ukrainian spelling unless another form is required by the context.

4. Some place names have different forms in Yiddish. Occasionally the subject matter dictates that the Yiddish place name should be the prime form, in which case the corresponding Polish (Ukrainian, Belarusian, Lithuanian) name is given in parentheses at first mention.

Transliteration

Hebrew
An attempt has been made to achieve consistency in the transliteration of Hebrew words. The following are the key distinguishing features of the system that has been adopted:

1. No distinction is made between the *alef* and *ayin*; both are represented by an apostrophe, and only when they appear in an intervocalic position.
2. *Veit* is written *v*; *ḥet* is written *ḥ*; *yod* is written *y* when it functions as a consonant and i when it occurs as a vowel; *khaf* is written *kh*; *tsadi* is written *ts*; *kof* is written *k*.
3. The *dagesh hazak*, represented in some transliteration systems by doubling the letter, is not represented, except in words that have more or less acquired normative English spellings that include doublings, such as Hallel, kabbalah, Kaddish, rabbi, Sukkot, and Yom Kippur.
4. The *sheva na* is represented by an *e*.
5. Hebrew prefixes, prepositions, and conjunctions are not followed by a hyphen when they are transliterated; thus *betoledot ha'am hayehudi*.
6. In the transliteration of the titles of works published in Hebrew, only the first word is capitalized; other than in the titles of works, names of people, places, and institutions are capitalized following the conventions of the English language.
7. The names of individuals are transliterated following the above rules unless the individual concerned followed a different usage.

Yiddish
Transliteration follows the YIVO system except for the names of people, where the spellings they themselves used have been retained.

Russian and Ukrainian
The system used is that of British Standard 2979:1958, without diacritics. Except in bibliographical and other strictly rendered matter, soft and hard signs are indicated by *y* before a vowel (e.g. Ilyich) but are otherwise omitted, and word-final -й, -ий, -ый, -ій in names are simplified to -*y*.

Introduction

**ISRAEL BARTAL, FRANÇOIS GUESNET,
ANTONY POLONSKY, AND SCOTT URY**

I crave youth, I want Palestine! Poland, where I was born, is not now my motherland. One cannot build a home on a cemetery. The blood of our dear ones calls to us from mass graves. Europe has had enough of the innocent blood of our brothers. Now we want to fertilize with our sweat and, if need be, with our blood the soil of our country. All bridges are burnt. There is no other path. Behind us is the huge army of the six million Jews murdered, gassed, and burnt in crematoria ovens. Their death shows us the path to life.

Szujka Ehrlihman, letter to her sister, 23 August 1945

We, the Polish people, have special reasons to promote the State of Israel. We have fought for too long time for a state of our own not to understand such a fight when undertaken by others. We know unfortunately better than many other nations what it means for a nation not to have a state of its own. Our nation knows the gas chambers like the Jewish nation did and our nation has not forgotten like some others, the sad lesson of this war.

Ksawery Pruszyński, speech delivered at the
United Nations as chairman of Subcommittee 1 of the
UN Ad Hoc Committee on the Palestinian Question,
25 November 1947

THIS VOLUME of *Polin: Studies in Polish Jewry* deals with two important and somewhat neglected subjects—the influence of Polish Jews, Polish Zionism, and Polish culture on the development of the Yishuv (the Jewish community in Palestine) and the State of Israel, and the impact of the Yishuv and the State of Israel on developments in Poland. The main goal of the Zionist project was to create a 'new Jew' who would be the builder of a Jewish state, preferably in the historic homeland of the Jewish people. This state would be free of the negative characteristics which, in the view of the ideologues of Zionism and other political movements which mobilized the east European Jewish communities, the Jews had developed in their long sojourn in the diaspora. Yet, inevitably, those who settled in Palestine brought with them considerable cultural baggage. A substantial proportion of the Jews who lived there before the emergence of the Zionist movement came from the territories of the Polish–Lithuanian Commonwealth, as did those who participated in the first two *aliyot* (stages of Jewish immigration to the Land of Israel) before 1914. Between November 1917 and May 1948, some 160,000 Jews from Poland entered the country, and, allowing for natural reproduction, this group probably numbered around 200,000 in 1948. At this moment it has been estimated that Jews from Poland made up at least a third of the Jewish population of the young State of Israel. Even after the substantial emigration of Jews from Arab lands and the Soviet Union, Polish Jews still constituted a major element in the country—not least because substantial territories of the post-war Soviet Union comprised formerly Polish–Lithuanian territories.[1]

Not surprisingly, this Polish Jewish presence significantly affected the political and cultural life of Jews in the Yishuv and the State of Israel. In the nineteenth century, considerable support was provided by Jews in Poland–Lithuania for the Land of Israel and the Jewish congregations there in the form of the *ḥalukah*, the organized collection and distribution of charity funds for such groups, and significant links were established between them. With the emergence of modern Jewish nationalism, Polish Jews made up a considerable proportion of its adherents, often influenced by romantic ideals about the historical mission of national collectives in general and the Polish struggle for independence in particular. It is worth remembering that Adam Mickiewicz's reflections on this matter took their inspiration from his reading of the history of Jewish exile, commanding respect, fraternity, and solidarity.[2] In addition, the struggle for Polish independence had an important impact on the development of Zionism, as did the work and ideas espoused by Polish writers from Mickiewicz to Stanisław Brzozowski, who also influenced the attitude of Poles to the Jewish national movement.

The Jewish models of self-government which had developed in Poland–Lithuania, both in the early modern period in the nineteenth century and later among the emerging Jewish political parties in the twentieth, significantly affected the political culture of the Yishuv, as did Jewish journalism and literature.[3] Poland bulked large in the world of Polish Jews who had settled in the Land of Israel, with continued cultural interaction and travel. Yet mutual prejudices persisted. Poles were seen as inveterate antisemites, and the behaviour of Polish society in the face of the German mass murder of the Jews was criticized on the grounds that the majority had been indifferent to the persecution of their Jewish fellow-citizens, that only a minority had offered assistance, that a significant number had assisted the Nazis, and that in post-war Poland antisemitic views were still held by a significant proportion of the population. Polarizing mutual stereotyping has in recent years led to a crisis in Polish–Israeli relations.

Polish connections with the Holy Land go back to the Middle Ages and are linked to the acceptance by Poland of Christianity, above all in its Roman Catholic form. In the modern period, both before and after the achievement of independence in 1918, Poles have actively supported the Zionist movement, whether because of sympathy for Jewish national aspirations or out of a desire to reduce the number of Jews in their country.

The volume is divided into five parts. The first examines the movement of Jews from Poland–Lithuania to the Land of Israel before the emergence of political Zionism and the links they maintained with the country from which they had emigrated. Uriel Gellman examines the history of hasidic communities in the Land of Israel in the nineteenth century. At this time of hasidism's rapid expansion, the movement remained confined, for the most part, to the former Polish–Lithuanian Commonwealth and the Austro-Hungarian empire. These years did, however, see the establishment of hasidim in the Land of Israel who, in Gellman's words, 'existed as a cultural enclave and a distant branch of the parent communities'. He describes the evolution of these communities in the four 'holy cities' where hasidism was centred—Safed, Tiberias, Jerusalem, and Hebron—from the beginning of the nineteenth century until about 1881, a development which led to the establishment of an Ashkenazi community in the Land of Israel. At the same time, these hasidim remained bound to *tsadikim* (the spiritual leaders of the various hasidic congregations) in eastern Europe. Important hasidic figures who emigrated to the Land of Israel did not function as *tsadikim* or establish courts for the local hasidim. While these communities remained dependent on their parent bodies in eastern Europe, they were also able to integrate themselves into the local economy. As a result, a new sort of community developed, whose members were described by a Sephardi sage in Safed: 'They have left Europe, but have not become Middle Eastern.'[4]

Yochai Ben-Ghedalia analyses the fissiparous character of the Ashkenazi community in Jerusalem in the nineteenth century. Whereas around 1800 there had been only a single, unified Jewish community in the city, on the eve of the First World War, which brought an end to the old Yishuv, there were over a hundred communities there, differentiated by the immigrants' place of origin. Ben-Ghedalia examines this process in the light of the history of Kolel Varshah, established by immigrants from Congress Poland. It was the first independent *kolel* (community) of east European Jews, and paved the way for the establishment of independent *kolelim* among other east European Jewish immigrants. He links this development with the sanctioning in 1836 of the collection of funds for the Jews in the Land of Israel by Count Ivan Paskevich, viceroy of the Kingdom of Poland. In the later part of the nineteenth century, funds were also collected for Kolel Varshah by proto-Zionist leaders in Prussian Poland, above all Rabbi Eliyahu Guttmacher of Grätz (Grodzisk Wielkopolski) and Rabbi Tsevi Hirsch Kalischer of Toruń, revealing an unexpected link between the old Yishuv and the forerunners of religious Zionism.[5]

The second part of this volume examines the period from the beginnings of modern Zionism to the outbreak of the Second World War. In his wide-ranging chapter, Łukasz Tomasz Sroka discusses the early links between Poland and the Land of Israel. As in other countries in Europe, Christianity in Poland made its adherents familiar with the geography of the Holy Land, whose place names also appeared in Polish carols. Poles had played little part in the crusades in the Middle East, but from the early modern period Christian pilgrims from Poland–Lithuania began to visit the Holy Land; their number increased in the nineteenth century, and included the insurrectionary Roman Stanisław Sanguszko and the poet Juliusz Słowacki. Increasing messianism among Jews in Poland–Lithuania in the mid-seventeenth century led to a new stress on the significance of the Land of Israel as the cradle of Judaism and induced several groups of Jews to emigrate there. One group, associated with Judah Hehasid of Siedlce (1660–1700), seems to have been an offshoot of the Sabbatians. In response to the *ḥerem* (ban) issued against it by the rabbinical court in Kraków, Judah Hehasid called for a great pilgrimage to the Holy Land to welcome the messiah. He travelled to Italy, whence he sailed to Israel, arriving in Jerusalem in October 1700. By now the number of his followers had been greatly reduced, and he himself died a few days after his arrival. Some of his followers did succeed in establishing themselves, although they were forbidden to settle in Jerusalem.

With the first and second *aliyot* the profile of the typical Jewish settler in Palestine was transformed. Pilgrims and those wishing to spend their final days in the Holy Land were replaced by those seeking to create a national homeland. Many came from the lands of partitioned Poland–Lithuania. Before the First World War the most favourable conditions for the development of the Zionist movement were to be found in Galicia, the Austrian partition. The Jews in this province had received civil equality in 1868 and also benefited from the wide-ranging autonomy granted to Galicia by the Austrian constitution of December 1867, participating extensively in the system of local government it created. Discriminatory policies pursued by the Austrian authorities before equality for Jews was granted, the connection between Jewish activists in this province and in the imperial capital of Vienna, and the prominence of progressive synagogues in Galicia were additional factors. A key role was played by Abraham Ozjasz Thon, who in 1897 was appointed rabbi of the Tempel synagogue in Kraków. Between 1919 and 1935 he was a deputy in the Polish Sejm and one of founders of the Zionist daily *Nowy Dziennik* in Kraków. It was partly the result of his influence that the Jewish lodge, B'nai B'rith, which developed rapidly from the 1890s, came to support the Zionist movement, particularly during the interwar years.

Young Jews who had benefited from the secondary and tertiary education available to them in Galicia became part of a new secular Jewish intelligentsia, many of whose members were sympathetic to Zionism. A significant number emigrated to Palestine, including some who were to play a key role as architects, among them Arie Sharon, who developed a spatial and architectural plan for Israel, and who between 1949 and 1953 was director of the Planning Office in Prime Minister David Ben-Gurion's administration. An important role in the development of kibbutzim in Israel was played by the Agricultural Academy in Dublany, not far from Lwów (Lviv).

In spite of its successes, the Zionist movement was never able to establish a dominant position in Jewish political life in Galicia and had to compete with the still influential integrationists, the Orthodox, and the socialists. However, their achievements were considerable: they have been recognized in Israel through the establishment in 1938 of the moshav Beit Yehoshua by pioneers from the Akiva movement; it is named after Thon, as are streets in the cities of Tel Aviv, Holon, Netanya, Ramat Hasharon, and Kadima-Zoran.

The Zionist movement continued to flourish in independent Poland and became one of the three principal political orientations—along with Bundism and Orthodoxy—into which Polish Jewry was split after the integrationist movement had lost traction. The Zionists were themselves divided, and the 1930s saw the increasing influence of the Revisionist Zionist party of Ze'ev (Vladimir) Jabotinsky, who stressed their ideological affinity with the regime established by Józef Piłsudski after the coup of May 1926. Thus, according to the Revisionist publication *Nasze Jutro* in

January 1939:

The Polish risings were always marked by their almost religious and fanatical zeal. Yearning for their own independent homeland was so strong among the people that all other feelings paled in comparison . . . Monism—faith in the exclusivity of one issue and one banner—the idea that several decades later became the guiding principle of Brit Trumpeldor, the avant-garde of nationalist-Jewish youth, was the driving force behind the whole of Polish society.[6]

As a consequence, between 1936 and 1939 the Revisionists reached a secret agreement with the Polish government, which granted them a loan of $400,000 to purchase weapons. In addition, Jabotinsky planned to form in Poland a 40,000-strong army which could challenge British rule in Palestine. Polish military and intelligence officers were actively involved in this somewhat unrealistic project which they attempted, unsuccessfully, to keep secret from the British authorities.

The other sections of the Zionist movement—the General Zionists, the Labour Zionists, and the religious Zionists—put much effort into training their members for agricultural settlement in Palestine. An extensive network of kibbutzim was established in the Second Polish Republic, although most were small and experimental in nature. A larger kibbutz was created in Cichy Kącik in Kraków. By 1934 the main pioneering organization, Keren Hechalutz Hamizrachi, was supporting 133 kibbutzim (*hakhsharot*) in Poland which trained not only farmers but also artisans.

Zionist ideologues saw sport as an important tool in arousing Jewish national feeling. As Jakub Selzer wrote in the *Almanach żydowski*, published in Lwów in 1937:

The aim of Maccabi is the physical and spiritual rebirth of the Jewish masses, the creation of a free and independent individual defending with dignity his own and his country's honour. Maccabi aims to connect to the wonderful heroic traditions of the Maccabees, and by adopting the symbolic name Maccabi builds a link between today and the past in the Land of Israel.[7]

All sections of the Zionist movement were affiliated with the Maccabi Jewish Gymnastics and Sports Association in Poland, part of the world-wide Maccabi movement. They participated in the first Maccabiah Games, held in Tel Aviv in March and April 1932, and the second, held in April 1935. The games planned for 1938 were cancelled because of the tense political situation and the threat of war.

Zionist groups were also represented in parliament. A key role was played by Yitzhak Grünbaum (1879–1970), a member of the Sejm from 1919 and 1932, who was one of the architects of the Minorities' Bloc in the elections of November 1922. In 1933 he emigrated to Palestine, where he became a key figure in the Jewish Agency. After 1948 he was the first minister of the interior in the government of David Ben-Gurion, although he was never elected to the Knesset.[8]

Significant numbers of Jews emigrated to Palestine from Poland in the interwar years. They did not sever all their ties with Poland, in spite of the growing antisemitism in the country. In the early 1930s a Union of Polish Jews was set up in Tel

Aviv, while associations of former residents of individual cities, such as Kraków, Łódź, Warsaw, Kielce, and Białystok, were also established. These links reflected one of the paradoxical features of Polish Zionism: the rejection of Yiddish as a 'debased' language—the product of the negative characteristics which diaspora life had imposed on the Jews—and the difficulty of acquiring Hebrew meant that Polish became the principal language of Polish Zionists. As Anna Landau-Czajka points out in her chapter, 'the call to abandon Yiddish was well received in Zionist circles, but the adoption of modern Hebrew proved much more difficult. So instead of using Yiddish many Zionists began to use Polish.' This is reflected in a poem written in 1915 by Jakub Appenszlak, later to be editor of the pro-Zionist Warsaw Polish-language daily, *Nasz Przegląd*:

> A Jew raised in Poland, I call out in Polish,
> O embody within me
> The spirit of Moses and empower me
> to transport Judah out of bondage
> And back to our ancient cradle.[9]

This commitment to Polish language and culture somewhat mitigated the accusations of dual loyalty which were levelled against Zionists. Landau-Czajka describes how many Zionists saw this dilemma: 'the Jews, even if they hoped for the establishment of a Jewish state, would remain not only loyal and law-abiding citizens but also citizens who were emotionally attached to the country in which they lived and would continue to live'. Hostility to Yiddish was a part of the profoundly ambivalent attitude of the Zionists to east European Jewry. Jewish emigration to Palestine during the British Mandate was controlled both by the British and by the Zionist Organization, which was concerned that only those Jews who could contribute to the building of a national home should be admitted to the country. Their goal was not, above all, to rescue the Jews of eastern Europe, whose situation was increasingly perilous, but rather to focus on building the Jewish national homeland in an organized and gradual manner. The Grabski Aliyah, sparked off by the negative impact on Jewish businesses of the economic stabilization plan introduced by the Polish prime minister Władysław Grabski in January 1924, led to the immigration of nearly 33,000 Jews from Poland and greatly increased the population of Tel Aviv. Its petit-bourgeois character aroused considerable apprehension. In October 1924, during a visit to Palestine, Chaim Weizmann, president of the Zionist Organization, stated bluntly that while 'our brothers and sisters from Djika and Nalevki [*sic*; streets in the heart of Jewish Warsaw] ... are flesh of our flesh and blood of our blood ... It is essential to remember that we are not building our National Home on the model of Djika and Nalevki.'[10] Although Weizmann later regretted in his autobiography that this statement had earned him the hatred of many Polish Jews, he still stood behind its general thrust. As Meir Chazan points out in his chapter, 'Weizmann's public assault against all that Nalewki and Dzika symbolized in relation to Jewish life helped define and delineate the cultural, social, and economic boundaries of Zionist activity in

Palestine.' This issue is also discussed by Gershon Bacon. Certainly, Weizmann's remarks reflected the hostility within the Zionist leadership towards the negative characteristics east European Jewry was supposed to have acquired in the diaspora, a hostility shared by such individuals as the poets Hayim Nahman Bialik and Uri Tsevi Grinberg; Moshe Glickson, editor of *Haaretz* (the most influential newspaper in the Yishuv); the literary scholar Joseph Klausner; and Arthur Ruppin, a prominent figure in the leadership of the Zionist Organization. In particular, it reflected a negative view of the way Tel Aviv was developing, which seemed to them to undermine the foundations of the Zionist ideal, in particular through the unwillingness of the new immigrants to learn Hebrew. These new settlers would need to be transformed into genuine Zionists. Accordingly, Moshe Glickson wrote: 'It is the duty [of the Zionist leadership] to *govern* this *aliyah* in accordance with our positive project and to direct it to our needs.'[11]

As Gershon Bacon points out in his chapter, the hostility to 'Nalewki' obscured the impact of Polish models on the political and cultural life of the Yishuv and the State of Israel. In his view 'in big things and in small details, the political legacy of the east European diaspora would determine the parties and politics of the Yishuv . . . The Polish model and the Polish Jewish model proved determinative for Jewish politics in the Land of Israel.' He argues that the impact of this model is to be seen, first, in the fact that most of the Yishuv's leaders reached their political maturity in eastern Europe. Among them were Yitzhak Grünbaum, whose career we have already discussed; Apolinary Hartglas, a member of the Grünbaum faction in the Polish Sejm, who served as a legal adviser to the Israeli Interior Ministry in the early years of the state; and Eliyahu Mazur, a member of Agudat Israel and former head of the Warsaw *kehilah*, who was also elected to the first Knesset. The 'new' Jewish politics of these men reflected the political and social conditions that prevailed in eastern Europe, in particular the politicization of Zionism and its entry into the local political arena. Poland retained some elements of parliamentary rule throughout the interwar period, and Zionist politicians, some of whom had already been active in the Russian Duma and the Austrian Reichsrat, honed their parliamentary skills in the Polish Sejm.

Jewish politicians may also have brought to the Land of Israel the turbulent atmosphere that characterized the Polish sejm, municipal councils, and the Jewish community boards, as well as Polish electoral campaigns.[12] Bacon argues that, alongside the fierce and uncompromising rhetoric at the ideological level, local conditions imposed on Polish Jewish politics a pragmatic side expressed in forming coalitions and in day-to-day co-operation. This tradition was also transplanted, albeit imperfectly, to the State of Israel.

Polish Zionists also brought to the politics of the Land of Israel the utopian conviction that they had the ability to reshape the Jewish nation and the individual Jew, and even the general political reality around them. In their view, politics should have a total, all-inclusive nature, with party-sponsored institutions covering all aspects of life. This was to be imparted to the next generation by youth movements, which played a key role in preparing thousands of young people for their emigration to Israel, where they were to play an important part in Israeli political life.

One important area where models established in eastern Europe clashed with those which emerged in response to the realities of life in the Land of Israel was the burgeoning press. As Ela Bauer shows in her chapter, serious efforts were made in the early twentieth century in Palestine to develop a local Hebrew press which would eschew the strongly didactic and ideological character of its east European precursors, sometimes referred to pejoratively as the 'Odessa press'. Since all cultural activity in the Yishuv should be free of 'exilic' influence, the argument went, so too the press in the Land of Israel ought to be free of such influence, concentrating, above all, on reporting rather than on ideological pronouncements, a style of journalism identified most strongly with *Do'ar hayom*, which produced its first issue in Jerusalem in August 1919.

At the same time, not all areas in the political and social life of the Land of Israel had their origins in Poland or, more generally, in eastern Europe. Other influences included the different social and ethnic composition of the Yishuv, the Ottoman legacy, and the experiences of Jews and Arabs under the British Mandate. In addition, the balance of power between the political parties in the Yishuv was different from that in Poland and Lithuania. Whereas Zionist politics in Poland were, at least until the early 1930s, dominated by bourgeois General Zionism, Labour Zionism soon became the leading element in the politics in the institutions of the Yishuv.

An important contribution to understanding the importance of the Labour Zionist dominance in Palestine for Jewish politics in Poland is provided in the chapter by Rona Yona. As she describes, in April 1933 the Labour Zionist leader David Ben-Gurion, born in Płońsk in Mazovia, came to Warsaw and was able to organize a significant victory for the previously somewhat marginal Po'alei Tsiyon Right in the elections to the Eighteenth Zionist Congress held in Prague that year. His main opponents were not the General Zionists, who had previously dominated both the world Zionist movement and Zionist politics in Poland, but the Revisionists led by Ze'ev Jabotinsky, now established in Paris. Because of Ben-Gurion's efforts, Labour won 44 per cent of the delegates to the congress and the Revisionists 14 per cent. The predominant position of Labour Zionism in the World Zionist Organization (WZO) was now established, and reflected the interaction between Zionist politics in the Yishuv and in Poland. The Revisionists, aware that they would not be able to take over the WZO, seceded from it in June 1935. At the same time, this did not mean that Labour Zionism now had the permanent support of most Polish Jews. In the local government elections of 1938, widely seen as the first stage in the return to a democratic parliamentary system, the majority of Jewish votes went to the General Jewish Labour Alliance, the Bund, considered by many to be fighting the rising tide of antisemitism more resolutely than its political rivals.

The last two chapters in this part deal with Polish involvement in the Zionist

1.2 million Jews lived in the areas of Poland occupied by the Soviets. The Polish–Soviet agreement of 30 July 1941 made provision for an amnesty of Polish prisoners, the release of prisoners of war, and the creation of a Polish army on Soviet territory. As Polish–Soviet relations deteriorated, both sides increasingly came to see that the only solution was the removal of the army from the Soviet Union. In March 1942 Stalin gave permission for Polish troops to be evacuated to Iran. From the outset Jews attempted to enlist in the army in large numbers but were, for the most part, rejected. In his memoirs Anders wrote: 'I was greatly disturbed when, at the beginning, large numbers from among the national minorities, and, first and foremost Jews, began streaming in to enlist.'[17] The impact of the policy of weeding Jews out of the army was clearly visible when the army was evacuated to Iran. Of the 78,000 Polish soldiers, barely 4,400 (20 of them women) were Jews (146 officers, 416 NCOs, and 3,839 other ranks), while Jewish civilians accompanying the forces numbered perhaps 2,500. Jews amounted to 5 per cent of the soldiers (1 per cent of the officers, 5 per cent of other ranks,) and 7 per cent of the civilians. Among the civilians were 871 Jewish children, who, because they spent some time in Tehran en route to Palestine, came to be known as the 'Tehran children'. The largest group of children, with chaperones, reached Palestine by sea, some of them arriving in February 1943, where they were ecstatically received. A number later had distinguished careers in Israel—two, Janusz Ben Gal and Hayim Erez, became generals, while Ze'ev (Włodzimierz) Schuss had a successful career as a mathematician, pianist, and translator of the dramatist, writer, and cartoonist Sławomir Mrożek.

Anders blamed the Soviets for the small number of Jews (and also Ukrainians and Belarusians) in his army, since Soviet officials had opposed the recruitment of Polish citizens who were not ethnic Poles, but it was clearly, above all, the result of his own policy of exclusion as documented in Dekel's chapter. It should also be pointed out that from March 1943 the government-in-exile had been subjected to some British pressure not to take many Jewish soldiers and civilians out of the USSR. The new base of the army was to be Palestine, and the British feared an influx of potential Jewish settlers. They were also concerned lest the Poles should encourage Zionism, whether by inducing Jews to remain in Palestine or by setting up Jewish units under their command.

Poles took advantage of the friendly environment to open schools under the supervision of the Government Delegate for Education and Schools. The Polish consulates general in Tel Aviv and Jerusalem continued to operate, as did the PKO and the delegates of the Polish Ministry of Labour and Social Security. One legacy of these years is the sections for Polish soldiers and refugees in the cemetery in Jaffa and the Catholic cemetery in Jerusalem.

The Nazi occupation left Polish Jewry devastated. Albert Stankowski has calculated that the pre-war Jewish population of Poland in 1939 numbered 3,330,000, of whom some 425,000 survived the war, a figure which some have seen as too high.[18] According to the records of the Central Committee of Jews in Poland (Centralny

Komitet Żydów w Polsce; CKŻP), the principal Jewish body in post-war Poland, 74,000 people had registered with it by June 1945. Of these, 5,500 had returned from concentration camps in Germany; 13,000 had served in the pro-communist Polish Army established in the USSR after the withdrawal of the Anders Army; about 30,000 had made their way back from the Soviet Union; 10,000 had been freed from concentration camps in Poland; and the remainder, just under 16,000, had survived on the 'Aryan side'.[19] In the next two years more than 136,000 Jews returned from the USSR, and by 1 July 1946 nearly 244,000 Jews had registered with the CKŻP.[20] By the end of the year an additional 35,000 had been repatriated from the Soviet Union.

In her chapter, Natalia Aleksiun discusses how these survivors envisaged their future. For most their hopes became increasingly tied to future emigration to Palestine, not only for themselves but also for other Jewish survivors. As one of them, Adela Hilzenrat, noted in her diary in July 1944: 'I dream about Palestine, where most Jewish survivors would want to go. There would be no obstacle for settling in Palestine. Limits on emigration would be eliminated. The White Paper would stay in the past.'[21]

As Aleksiun shows, their perception of Palestine was constructed in contrast to Poland. Poland for them was the site of their past and loss—a place filled with concrete memories, tied to pre-war images of family life and social interactions with fellow Jews, most of whom had been murdered during the war. As a result, after liberation, Poland was experienced as a profound void. Because of the persistent anti-Jewish violence, it was also a source of threat. By contrast, Palestine was a space full of possibilities, hopes not yet realized, and a potential future home. In Aleksiun's words: 'Thus, both places and spaces evoke different emotions which were closely intertwined, with Poland as a site of emotional attachment and pain and Palestine as a site of intense but vague dreams.'

Emigration to Palestine was certainly possible in the period immediately after liberation. In September 1945 Romuald Gadomski was appointed representative of the Polish government in Palestine. With the assistance of the Polish embassy in Moscow, he was granted plenipotentiary powers and provided with funds to reopen the consulate general in Jerusalem and the consulate in Tel Aviv. In the international arena, Polish diplomats, such as Ksawery Pruszyński discussed above, supported the Jews' struggle for a homeland.

The unwillingness of most survivors to live in what they saw as a Jewish cemetery, the widespread anti-Jewish violence, and the distaste for communism, which many of them had experienced during the war in the Soviet Union, led the bulk of them to emigrate, many to Palestine. Between June and September 1946, in the aftermath of the Kielce pogrom, around 100,000 Jews fled the country, and by January 1952 only around 70,000 Jews remained in Poland. Emigration continued on a more restricted scale even after Poland, under pressure from the Soviet Union, adopted a strongly hostile position to the State of Israel.

In her chapter, Monika Adamczyk-Garbowska gives an account of the trips to Poland of the Yiddish journalist Mordecai Tsanin (Cukierman). As she points out, in the immediate aftermath of the war, various Jewish organizations, institutions, and newspapers sent representatives to Poland to investigate the situation of Jewish survivors. A special place in these testimonies is occupied by that of Tsanin, whose account in Yiddish, *Through Ruins and Ashes: A Journey through a Hundred Destroyed Jewish Communities in Poland*, has never been translated into English and was only translated into Polish in 2018.[22] Tsanin, who lived in Israel but was quite critical of Zionism, was a correspondent for the New York-based *Forverts* and the author of a monumental six-volume historical novel, *Artopanos Comes Home*. Compared with the accounts of Jacob (Yakov) Pat, Shmuel Leib Shneiderman, Chaim Shoshkes, and Joseph Tenenbaum, his report is the most detailed and also the most pessimistic. He opens it with a desperate plea: 'God Almighty, give me the strength so that I can describe with my poor words what my eyes saw and my heart felt during my wandering across the rubble and ruins of the life that is no more, and so that I could uncover at least a small piece of that great epic poem that was called Jewish life in Poland.'[23]

Tsanin made several trips to Poland in 1946 and 1947, usually presenting himself as a non-Jewish English-speaking journalist in order to elicit more accurately the feelings of the population about the tragedy they had witnessed. This led him to adopt a rather negative view of the attempt to revive Jewish life in Poland. He juxtaposed memories from before the war with the present situation: the entire book, apart from chapters devoted to visits to former concentration and death camps, is constructed in such a way that images from the past are confronted with the post-war reality. He confessed that he was most afraid of visiting Warsaw and Łódź since he realized that the contrast with the pre-war situation, when large, vibrant communities had existed there, would be most painful. He was also one of the very few foreign journalists who visited most of the former death camps, including Chełmno, Majdanek, Sobibór, Treblinka, and Auschwitz-Birkenau. The last chapter of the book, 'The Gold Rush', describes the phenomenon, analysed by Jan Tomasz Gross in *Golden Harvest*, of Poles searching through human ashes in former death camps to find valuables.[24] It reflects the rather negative opinion that Tsanin had of Poles and perhaps explains his view that, from the Jewish perspective, communism was a better solution than a regime representing 'reactionary' Poland. At the same time he was also strongly critical of the Jewish institutions for insufficient involvement in commemorating the victims of the Holocaust. His final conclusion reflects his pessimism:

A Jew is travelling now across the destroyed cities and shtetls, wanders around ruins and rubble and cannot find a single untouched grave that has remained after the annihilated life. Only when you see a field grey from ashes will you know, Jew, that these are the ashes of your people. And only there can you cry out your 'Yitgadal veyitkadash'.[25]

Part 4 examines the period from 1948 to the end of communism. Two chapters deal with the cultural interaction between Jewish Poland and the State of Israel. Hanna Lerner examines the two careers, in Poland and later in Israel, of the cultural activist Henryk Hechtkopf (1910–2004). Born in Warsaw, Hechtkopf survived the war in the Soviet Union, partly as a prisoner in labour camps. On his return to Poland in late 1945, he discovered that his mother, sister, and the rest of his extended family had been murdered. In the following decade he was actively involved in attempting to document the destruction of Jewish life, above all through his drawings of the ruins of the Warsaw ghetto and his portraits of Holocaust survivors. He also played an active role in the attempts to revive Jewish culture as a board member of the Association for Jewish Culture in Poland (Żydowskie Towarzystwo Kultury w Polsce; ŻTK), and as chair of its artistic section between 1947 and 1951. Hechtkopf was also a prominent member of the Yiddish publishing house Yidish Bukh in Łódź in 1947, and provided covers and illustrations for many of its books.

He soon branched out into a new field, making a successful career in the emerging film industry of post-war Łódź. Among the films with which he was associated as assistant director were *Zakazane piosenki* (1946), an account by a Polish musician of how he set up a street orchestra during the occupation; *Dwie godziny* (1946; not released until 1957 due to political censorship), about several people who meet at a railway station after the war, who are trapped by memories of the painful past but still hope for a better future; *Żołnierz zwycięstwa* (1953) describing the life and death of General Karol Swierczewski, killed in conflict with Ukrainian partisans in 1947; and *Nikodem Dyzma* (1956), a political comedy about a hapless individual who makes a successful career in the Communist Party. He also created the scenery paintings for the film *Ulica Graniczna* (1949), the first film on the Warsaw ghetto uprising, and directed *Podhale w ogniu* (1956), an account of a seventeenth-century farmers' revolt against Polish landowners.

He clearly did not feel comfortable in the Polish People's Republic, and in 1957 emigrated to Israel with his non-Jewish wife Alicja Zielińska as part of the 50,000-strong Gomułka Aliyah. Unlike many other members of the *aliyah*, Hechtkopf was able to continue his professional career in Israel. He could not find a place in the small Israeli film industry and returned to his earlier interest in painting and book illustration. In 1958 Yad Vashem included a number of his drawings of the ruined Warsaw ghetto in the first Israeli exhibition of Holocaust artists from camps and ghettos. Two years later twenty-four of these drawings were published in a special album.

He continued to paint, mostly in the surrealist style, as part of a group of similar artists including Yigal Tumarkin, Uri Lifshitz, Samuel Bak (who later settled in the US), and Mordecai Moreh. He also attempted, in a series of aquarelles and pen-and-pencil drawings, to document the changing landscape of urban life in Israel. However, his most significant impact on Israeli culture was through the illustration of children's books, another of the fields in which he had been active in Poland. In all, Hechtkopf illustrated more than 370 books, including school textbooks and books for kindergartens, working with the leading authors and publishing houses in Israel. His achievements in this field are well documented in Lerner's chapter, based on a large range of sources culled from Hechtkopf's private archive. He also returned to his attempts to document the lost world of Polish Jewry in a series of nearly seventy black ink drawings that he produced over several decades, which depicted the various occupations pursued by Jews in pre-war Poland.

As noted above, Zionist ideology stressed the importance of the 'negation of the diaspora'. However, this was not always possible. In his chapter, Adi Sherzer examines the complex relationship between Zionism and its diasporic past through the way in which Jewish festivals were interpreted in the work of the folklorist Yom-Tov Levinsky (1899–1973). Born in Zambrów in Suwałki province in the north-east of present-day Poland, Levinsky emigrated to Palestine in 1935, and was for many years head of Yeda Am, a society for folklore research founded in Tel Aviv in 1942.

Levinsky saw his discussion of the Jewish festivals, which he promoted through radio broadcasts, newspaper articles, and anthologies, as an opportunity to stimulate interest in the Jewish culture of eastern Europe in the Land of Israel. He presented a coherent narrative which stressed historical continuity in a proto-Zionist way and emphasized the east European Jewish experience, above all in a somewhat mythologized shtetl. His narratives begin with the ancient origins of a festival, then describe its celebration in the diaspora, and conclude with the way it is observed in modern Hebrew culture. His principal work in this field is the still popular *Sefer hamo'adim*, a nine-volume anthology of sources, both religious and literary, on the Jewish festivals.

Three chapters in this part deal with how a number of key issues in this period were discussed in the Polish-language press, both in Poland and Israel. Bożena Szaynok examines how journalists in the Catholic press in Poland presented Israel and related matters between 1945 and the end of communism in 1989, and how their articles were often restricted by the communist system of censorship. As she shows, in the view of the Church, one solution to the 'Jewish question' in pre-war Poland, alongside 'assimilation by baptism' and segregation, was the emigration of Jews from Poland, and Palestine was one of the destinations mentioned in this context. At the same time, some representatives of the Church opposed the realization of the Zionist ideal in Palestine, above all because of fear of control of Christian holy sites falling into Jewish hands. The Vatican was somewhat ambivalent about the emergence of the State of Israel, and it was only in December 1993 that diplomatic relations were established. At the same time, from 1949 Moscow's original sympathy for the state shifted to hostility, which was echoed in the diplomacy of the Polish People's Republic and in the official Polish press. All references to the Middle East in the press were subject to strict censorship, which was preventative in character, so that the final form of a text was decided prior to publication.

The conflicting positions held within the Church on Israeli issues led to various views being expressed in the Catholic press in Poland, often in a garbled form because of the censorship. As Szaynok shows, the most pro-Israeli position, particularly on the Arab–Israeli conflict, was to be found in the liberal Catholic weekly *Tygodnik Powszechny*, often in articles written by the dissident figure Władysław Bartoszewski, and in the monthly *Znak*. Attempts to publish pro-Israel articles were also made by other Catholic publications. More hostile views could sometimes be found in papers like *Rycerz Niepokalanej* and *Gość Niedzielny* and were also often subject to censorship. At the same time, the coverage of the Arab–Israeli conflict in the official communist press was far more hostile to Israel; in addition, as Szaynok points out, government censorship 'inhibited the free exchange of opinion and free discussion . . . [and] inevitably impoverished discussion of important topics, among them the attitude of the Church to the State of Israel.'

In her chapter, Elżbieta Kossewska describes how the Israeli Polish-language press contributed to the linguistic integration of Polish Jews in Israel. As she shows, in the first two decades of the State of Israel over twenty Polish-language publications existed there, mostly produced by the political parties active at the time: Mapai, the Progressive Party, the General Zionists, Mapam, and the Israeli Communist Party (Maki). These party links were, however, sometimes camouflaged, but even when party control was disguised, the foreign-language press was seen by the competing parties as an important vehicle for communicating with and enlisting the support of new immigrants. At the same time, the existence of this press in a 'foreign language' was at odds with the dominant position assigned to Hebrew in Zionist ideology and to the 'sabra' in Israeli culture, something which almost all new immigrants accepted.

It was through the Polish-language press that immigrants from Poland obtained their information about the State of Israel and its political and social system. At the same time, they used it to express their ambivalent feelings about the processes of integration to which they were subjected. According to Jerzy Markiewicz, who came to Israel as part of the Gomułka Aliyah:

We found ourselves in Israel with crates full of Polish books and folk textiles from Cepelia, records of Chopin and the 'Mazowsze' and 'Śląsk' [folk troupes] . . . In the evenings, we still catch the evening news from Warsaw on 'Beethovens' or even on 'Pioneers' [radio sets]. We exchange Polish books from our personal collections. We talk—to the indignation of the *vatikim* [old-timers] and their children—all day—in shops, cafes, on the street—only in Polish.[26]

While the new immigrants were committed to adopting Hebrew, this did not in any way mean the complete abandonment of the literary tastes they had brought with them. In the second half of the 1950s interest in Polish books grew; Polish cultural events were eagerly awaited; lectures and meetings with visiting writers, scholars, and artists from Poland, among them Marek Hłasko, attracted large audiences. The Polish language did not have negative connotations for them. As one of them explained:

It was in Polish that we destroyed the world of evil and iniquity. In Polish, the language of Mickiewicz, Słowacki, and Prus, that we dreamt of the future happiness of humanity. Finally, it was in the language of Sienkiewicz and Tuwim, Orzeszkowa and Reymont, that we began to speak, cry out, and shout of Jewish injustice, of the Jewish nation, of the Jewish state. This is the language in which we described the charms of Hebrew.[27]

Whereas most of those who received permission to emigrate from Poland between 1955 and 1957 went to Israel (although some later moved on to other destinations), of the nearly 13,000 Jews who were forced to leave Poland as a result of the 'anti-Zionist' campaign of 1968, only a little over 3,000 went to Israel. In addition, a number of prominent Polish Jews who emigrated to Israel in 1968 did not remain in the country. They included the historian Szymon Szechter (1920–83) and his secretary Nina Karsov (b. 1940), the renowned sociologist Zygmunt Bauman (1925–2017) and much of his family, and the actress Ida Kamińska (1899–1980). As Miri Freilich shows in her chapter, in which she also discusses why these individuals chose not to remain in Israel, their actions aroused negative responses in the country, still euphoric in the aftermath of the victory in the Six Day War. This issue was particularly apparent in the Polish-language daily, *Nowiny i Kurier*, formed in 1957 by the merger of *Nowiny*, the Polish-language organ of the Progressive (Liberal) Party, and the *Kurier*, which was owned by Mapai. Its daily edition was small, with only six pages, but its Friday issue had sixteen pages and included opinion pieces and a supplement for cultural matters.

Among its leading journalists was Aleksander Klugman (1925–2015), a Holocaust survivor, who after the war had worked as a journalist in Poland and had been part of the Gomułka Aliyah. Another was the Warsaw-born Theodor Hatalgi (Schneeberg) (1917–2006), who had been editor of the Warsaw Irgun newspaper *Jerozolima Wyzwolona*, and who emigrated to Israel in 1947. The paper analysed extensively the 'anti-Zionist' campaign in Poland, including the human tragedies it caused. In its view, it was the result not only of the struggle over the leadership of the Polish United Workers' Party but also of the deep-rooted antisemitism of the Poles. As a Polish-language daily, *Nowiny i Kurier* also devoted considerable attention to the integration of Polish immigrants into Israeli society and was very concerned about the large number of 'drop-outs' (Jews who chose not to emigrate to Israel). Thus it felt an obligation to explain to the Israeli public why so few of those who left Poland in 1968 went to Israel and why some of the most prominent immigrants chose not to remain in the country. Criticism in the Hebrew press was certainly harsh. According to *Davar* in November 1969, 'the news of the last remnants of Polish Jewry arriving in the West and refusing to immigrate to Israel sows salt in our wounds and reveals one of the tragic episodes of contemporary Jewish history'.[28]

Nowiny i Kurier took the view that Israel was the most desirable and safest destination for the 1968 emigrants. However, it did feel a need to explain the behaviour of those Jews who felt differently. Aleksander Klugman went to Vienna, the transit point for most emigrants, in the autumn of 1968. In a series of articles, 'An Israeli in Europe',[29] he argued that the traumatic experiences of these emigrants, which recalled their sufferings in the Holocaust, made them fear that they and their children would be exposed to constant insecurity and the threat of war in Israel. In addition, he maintained that the activities of the New York-based Hebrew Immigrant Aid Society (HIAS) in Vienna undermined the attempts of the Jewish Agency to encourage Polish Jews to settle in Israel.

The final part of the volume examines developments from the end of communism to the present day. It is primarily concerned with the portrayal of Poland in Hebrew literature, which is examined in three chapters by Efraim Sicher, Shoshana Ronen, and Jagoda Budzik. A number of elements contributed to the largely negative image of Poland that had developed in the Yishuv and was strengthened by the events of the Second World War and its aftermath. Among them was the Zionist hostility to Jewish life as it had developed in eastern Europe; the view that Polish society had, with some exceptions, been indifferent to the mass murder of the Jews at German hands and the perception that some Poles had even aided the Nazis in their genocidal plans; and the belief that Poland, long one of the centres of Jewish life, was now no more than a Jewish cemetery. These views lay at the heart of Mordkhe Tsanin's account of his visits to post-war Poland described in Adamczyk-Garbowska's chapter.

Jewish society as it developed in Palestine was not only inspired by the Zionist dream but also reflected the traumas experienced by those who had emigrated in order to establish a new life. A necessary part of this process was for the places from which they had emigrated to be seen in negative terms, but there also remained a nostalgia for the world left behind. Under these circumstances, it is not surprising, as Yael Zerubavel has pointed out, that Israelis have a 'passionate interest in re-examining their collective identity',[30] or that Hebrew literature should be preoccupied with the clash between the major Zionist national narrative and a more nuanced memory of the lands from which Jews emigrated. This is reflected in a number of the works examined in this part.

In relation to Poland, the desire to challenge the accepted image was intensified by the progressive weakening of the concept of the 'negation of the diaspora' and a renewed interest in Jewish life there, and by the challenge to the role played by Holocaust education in Israeli civic culture. It was also stimulated by the largely successful transition in Poland to a prosperous consumer society and parliamentary democracy, which made it an attractive destination for Israelis, in contrast with the rather bleak character of the Polish People's Republic. Travel to Poland had become possible in the 1980s, but it was after 1989 that it became a mass phenomenon for Israelis. Many of them were now confronted by the widespread interest of Poles in Jewish history and culture in the Polish lands and the desire of some to come to terms with the negative aspects of Polish–Jewish interaction, which challenged the stereotype of deep-rooted and long-lasting antisemitism.

The changes in the perception of Poland in Hebrew and Jewish literature are explained in generational terms, with the first generation comprising the survivors, the second generation being made up of their children, and the third generation the survivors' grandchildren. Ronen, in her chapter, argues convincingly that one should, rather, use the term 'wave', and identifies two waves. The first occurred during the 1980s, when Israelis were finally allowed to travel to Poland; the second was after the collapse of the communist system in 1989. For the first wave of writers, Poland is, above all, a huge Jewish cemetery, and Poles merely exist in the background, not as partners in dialogue but as symbols of the 'Other', clearly distinct from 'us'.

Efraim Sicher continues this discussion in his examination of the literary treatment of such returns to the traumatic past. In his words:

Passing from lived memory to history and literature, the transmission of the traumatic past revisits the scene of the wound, at the risk of repeating the pain of the wound, in order to work through and to complete the process of mourning for relatives, whose story may sometimes be fragmentary or unknown but who hold the key to the narrator's personal biography and sense of self.

This is clearly the case in Paweł Łoziński's film *Miejsce urodzenia* (1992), in which the Polish Jewish writer Henryk Grynberg returns to Radoszyna, where he grew up before his family was forced into hiding during the Nazi occupation, in order to confront the local villagers and to search for his father's grave. While some of the older residents appear willing to talk, they are mostly locked in fear and shame, still afraid of retribution, though one or two openly denounce their neighbours' betrayal of Jews during the German occupation. Grynberg summed up his experiences in a long essay, *Inheritance*: 'I cannot forgive. I'm not entitled to. Let the murderers forgive, if they could... I sensed a chilly shudder facing evil. However, in some eyes, I find some warmth as well. It is essential for life.'[31]

The reportage of Yehudit Hendel and Michal Govrin also described the landscape they found in Poland as dead and empty. In Hendel's *Leyad kefarim sheketim* (Near Quiet Villages), the many places she intends, but fails, to visit are described as 'empty' and 'grey'. She repeats constantly, 'I didn't go to Kałuszyn/Krasnystaw/Krosno. What should I look for in Kałuszyn/Krasnystaw/Krosno?'[32] Similarly, Govrin sees Poland through a prism of greyness and decay.[33]

By contrast, the writers of the second wave are willing to enter into dialogue and interaction with Poles, whom they treat as subjects. In Ronen's words: 'The second-wave travellers have all this [the negative legacy of the past] in the back of their minds, but they are also distant from themselves, and they have a sense of irony as they observe the Polish reality around them.'[34]

This new understanding is reflected in the books discussed by Ronen and Budzik. Criticism of the way the Holocaust has been manipulated for political purposes in Israel is well articulated in Yishai Sarid's *Mifletset hazikaron* (The Memory Monster), which takes the form of a letter to the chairman of Yad Vashem from a guide of Israeli high-school students, soldiers, and politicians on tours to Holocaust sites in Poland. Although initially committed to his mission, as he points out in his letter, he has become convinced that the result of these trips is to instil hatred in their participants, and also admiration for the strength shown by the Nazis. In the words Sarid puts into his mouth: 'They hate the Poles, they hate the miserable Jewish victims, they hate the Palestinians, but admire the German perpetrators.'[35] As Ronen points out, it is worth noting that the book did produce a scandal in Israel and in fact articulated ideas which had been advanced in a number of academic studies.

The problems of what Sicher describes as revisiting 'the scene of the wound' are given a very different twist in two other books discussed by both Ronen and Budzik, Rutu Modan's *Hanekhes* (The Property) and Itamar Orlev's *Bandit*. *Hanekhes* recounts the journey of a young Israeli, Mika, and her grandmother Regina to Warsaw, where Regina spent her childhood and youth. The ostensible reason for the visit is to reclaim an apart-ment which belonged to the family and was appropriated during the war. From the first scenes it seems clear that Regina's war experience has left her with feelings of bitter resentment against Poland and the Poles. In her words, 'Warsaw is of no interest to me. It's one big cemetery.'[36] Yet it turns out that the real motive behind her journey is not to reclaim the property but to find her pre-war lover, a Pole, from whom she was forcibly separated by her family, a journey whose impetus lies in the death in Israel of their son, conceived before the war. Thus her anti-Polish bitterness proves to be only a facade which is gradually discarded. During their time in Poland, Mika has an affair with Tomasz, a tourist guide and graphic artist. The climactic scene of the novel, in a clear attempt to undermine the cliché of Poland as a Jewish cemetery, takes place in a Christian cemetery in Warsaw on All Souls' Day (when Poles traditionally visit the graves of their ancestors) with all four main characters present. It is now that Regina introduces Mika to her former Polish lover, who is probably Mika's grandfather. Regina and her granddaughter return to Israel, but the hope that the two couples can keep in touch means that the novel ends on an optimistic note. It also clearly critiques the discourses of Polish–Jewish relations and effectively demonstrates the shortcomings of heritage tours and calls for the restitution of property which fail to take account of the complexity of these relations.

Itamar Orlev's *Bandit* is a similar revisionist version of a visit to Poland in search of identity. It is set in the late 1980s, and its main protagonist, Tadeusz, is the son of a Jewish woman, a Holocaust survivor, who left for Israel as a result of the anti-Zionist campaign of 1968, and the Polish man who sheltered her during the war. Tadeusz travels to Poland to find his father, Stefan, with whom he has not been in touch since moving to Israel. He finds him in an old-age home for former resistance fighters in Warsaw, where he is spending his last years, in the hope of uncovering the reasons why his family's complicated life followed the path it did. After some reluctance, Tadeusz accompanies his father on an unplanned journey to the place of his birth. On this journey, his father recounts his wartime experiences: his participation in the resistance, his imprisonment in Majdanek, his escape, and the final years of the war spent in the Polish underground. He also recounts how he hid his later wife, Ewa, a Jewish woman and Tadeusz's mother. The gradual discovery of these facts transforms Tadeusz's perception of his father, whom he had seen as the principal source of his traumatic childhood. Although Tadeusz is the son of a Holocaust survivor, he does not see Poland through the prism of his mother's Holocaust experiences or of her being forced to leave Poland. These factors are present in the background, but it is his father's story that becomes the key to Orlev's description of the Polish experience. In this way, Tadeusz becomes a bridge between the Polish and Jewish worlds.

Another novel that embodies the new Israeli attitude to the diaspora is Eshkol Nevo's *Neuland* (whose title alludes to *Altneuland*, the utopian novel published by Theodor Herzl in 1902), which in 2012 won the Steimatzky Prize for Book of the Year, discussed in her chapter by Alina Molisak. A bold political parable which takes the form of an exchange of e-mails between its two principal characters, its core describes a New Age community of Israeli Jews in the heart of Argentina founded by the father of one of the novel's two protagonists. This 'Neuland' is a new version of Zionism, which can be seen as the realization of Baron Maurice von Hirsch's attempts to foster Jewish agricultural settlements in Argentina and which is free of the flaws and war-wrecked idealism which now characterize Israel itself, since it is based on the concept of the equality of all inhabitants and the Jews within it are fully secure. In the words of one of its inhabitants, it is a place where 'we stop being the persecuted Jews of the Holocaust and start being "a light unto the nations"'.[37] This idealized vision is set against the three-generational experience of those who established the State of Israel and brought it to its present situation. The novel ends with its two leading protagonists, representatives of the third generation of Israelis, surveying Jerusalem from the Dung Gate, after their return from Latin America, a landscape marked by bitter political and ethnic conflict.

The rather optimistic picture of a better understanding between Jews and Poles set out in these literary works is countered by the final chapter in this volume, by Yifat Gutman and Elazar Barkan, which examines the controversy aroused in 2018 by the amendments to the Law on the Institute of National Remembrance passed in January of that year. The most controversial of these amendments held that:

Article 55a.

1. Whoever claims, publicly, and contrary to the facts, that the Polish nation or the Republic of Poland is responsible or co-responsible for Nazi crimes committed by the Third Reich, as specified in Article 6 of the Charter of the International Military Tribunal attached to the international agreement for the prosecution and punishment of the major war criminals of the European Axis, signed in London on 8 August 1945 (Polish Journal of Laws of 1947, item 367), or for other felonies that constitute crimes against peace, crimes against humanity or war crimes, or whoever otherwise grossly diminishes the responsibility of the true perpetrators of said crimes—shall be liable to a fine or imprisonment for up to three years. The sentence shall be made public.

2. If the act specified in clause 1 is committed intentionally, the perpetrator shall be liable to a fine or the restriction of liberty.

3. No offence is committed if the criminal act specified in clauses 1 and 2 is committed in the course of one's artistic or academic activity.[38]

In a surprise move at the end of June 2018, Mateusz Morawiecki, the Polish prime minister introduced legislation in the Polish parliament which was rapidly passed, and which significantly modified the law. The cited sentences were now removed from the legislation, although the following clause was retained:

Article 53o. Protecting the reputation of the Republic of Poland and the Polish nation shall be governed by the provisions of the Civil Code Act of 23 April 1964 (Polish Journal of Laws of 2016, items 380, 585 and 1579) on the protection of personal rights. A court action aimed at protecting the Republic of Poland's or the Polish nation's reputation may be brought by a non-governmental organisation within the remit of its statutory activities. Any resulting compensation or damages shall be awarded to the state treasury.

Article 53p. A court action aimed at protecting the Republic of Poland's or the Polish nation's reputation may also be brought by the Institute of National Remembrance. In such cases, the Institute of National Remembrance shall have the capacity to be a party to court proceedings.[39]

In addition, clauses relating to the penalization of the denial of crimes 'committed by Ukrainian nationalists and members of Ukrainian units collaborating with the Third Reich' remained in the legislation.

The amendment of the legislation was accompanied by a joint statement by Morawiecki and the Israeli prime minister Benjamin Netanyahu. Later to be criticized by leading scholars of the Holocaust and much of the leadership of Yad Vashem, the agreement condemned 'every single case of cruelty against Jews perpetrated by Poles during . . . World War II' but also noted 'heroic acts of numerous Poles, especially the Righteous Among the Nations, who risked their lives to save Jewish people'.[40] In addition, it declared that:

We have always argued that the term 'Polish concentration/death camps' is blatantly erroneous and diminishes the responsibility of Germans for establishing those camps, and argued that the wartime Polish government-in-exile 'attempted to stop this Nazi activity by trying to raise awareness among the Western allies of the systemic murder of the Polish Jews'.[41]

The declaration also condemned both antisemitism and anti-Polonism and affirmed: 'we believe that there is a common responsibility to conduct free research, to promote understanding and to preserve the memory of the history of the Holocaust'.[42]

Gutman and Barkan examine why this declaration did not lead to the end of the dispute, which in their view was the result of a failure to address the more deep-rooted issues involved. In an article written in 2004, Andrzej Paczkowski observed that 'the most significant phenomenon of the last fifteen years has been the emergence, concretization (also in political life) of competing positions in the sphere of memory and in relation to the national past'.[43] This is even more the situation today. These divisions, which are clearly linked to arguments over the totalitarian experience of Poland, reflect different visions of society. One sees society as made up of different and often competing groups in which understandings of the past may differ and in which a reckoning with the negative aspects of the national history is necessary for building a pluralistic, outward-looking, and tolerant polity. It sees the nation as something which emerged in particular circumstances and whose identity can change over time. It draws on the criticism of the 'romantic-heroic' view of the Polish past that was provoked by the catastrophic failure of the 1830 and 1863 uprisings, and rejects the view of Poland as 'hero and martyr of the nations'.

The other view is centred on the nation and the community which it creates, which is seen as primordial, transcending the transient individuals of which it is made up. It strongly supports patriotism and sees its opponents as having succumbed to the lure of cosmopolitanism. It particularly values the concept of a Polish struggle 'for your freedom and ours', with its determination to continue this fight against seemingly invincible enemies, which it sees as a major factor in the survival of Poland as a nation. As Brian Porter-Szűcs has argued, for those who hold this view, history is 'the biography of the national community and the source of the traditions and values that hold everything together'.[44] In 2016 the Institute of National Remembrance, now firmly under the control of the right-wing Law and Justice Party government, defined the goal of historical study as follows:

Historical policy refers to the interpretation of facts, lives, and events and is assessed according to the interests of the society and the nation, as an element that has a long-range character and constitutes the foundation of state policies.

Historical policy is a type of history that serves to shape the historical consciousness of society, including economic and territorial consciousness, as well as to strengthen public discourse about the past in the direction of nurturing national bonds regardless of the momentary policies of the state.[45]

The issue here is not historical truth as such; instead, history is important because it is the 'long-range . . . foundation of state policies'. It is these stories that a community tells and retells in order to establish a bond between generations and to teach young people what 'we' believe. This is why historians who take a more critical stance are seen as undermining national identity.

This is not only a Polish phenomenon. A similar conflict between a self-critical historiography and one that seeks to glorify the national past can be observed in Israel and other places, including Hungary, Lithuania, and Ukraine, while the Russian government has also attempted to advance its interests through the use of a falsified patriotic history.

There is considerable common ground between these two understandings of how history should be written, and it is important not to demonize historians of whom one disapproves. There is a role both for a patriotic historiography which celebrates the achievements of the nation and for one which also points out the mistakes and wrongdoings committed in the past. For example, in both Poland and Israel, official powers have repeatedly attempted—with varying degrees of success—to appoint political figures to direct leading institutions of historical memory, including the Museum of the Second World War in Gdańsk and, most recently, Yad Vashem in Jerusalem. The English historian Edward Gibbon wrote: 'History . . . is, indeed, little more than the register of the crimes, follies, and misfortunes of mankind.'[46] In dealing with the difficult problems of the past, the careful use of primary material is essential. Governments should understand that these are complex issues. Although official support for historical study is to be welcomed, this is best carried out in universities and academic research bodies, independent of direct state intervention. Just as truth is the first casualty in war, so complexity is the first casualty in historical wars.

Ways of moving beyond narrow national frameworks need to be found. It is our hope that this volume will show the complex nature of Polish–Jewish–Israeli relations and contribute to a better understanding of both the good and the bad in this relationship. It also demonstrates how, on a number of key issues, Israeli and diaspora Jewish views have diverged. We hope in this way to encourage scholarship on the issues investigated in this volume—based on a wide range of sources, from a variety of points of view, and in different locations—which will ultimately make possible a degree of normalization in the attitudes of Poles and Israelis to the now disputed past and a reduction of the rancour with which it has been discussed in recent years.

Notes

1 See A. Stankowski, 'Nowe spojrzenie na statystyki dotyczące emigracji Żydów z Polski po 1944 roku', in G. Berendt, A. Grabski, and A. Stankowski, *Studia z historii Żydów w Polsce po 1945 r.* (Warsaw, 2000), 103–51: 104, 117–21; Israel Central Bureau of Statistics, *Statistical Abstract of Israel, 2008* (Jerusalem, 2008).

2 M. Janion, 'Mickiewicz's Jewish Legion', in ead., *Hero, Conspiracy, and Death: The Jewish Lectures*, trans. A. Shannon (Frankfurt am Main, 2014), 177–204.

3 F. Guesnet and A. Polonsky, 'Introduction', *Polin*, 34 (2022), 1–38: 31–2.

4 M. Sithon, *Kenesiyah leshem shamayim* (Jerusalem, 1874), 199; cited in R. Ambon, 'Harav shemu'el heler (1803–1884) umekomo bakehilah hayehudit', Ph.D. thesis (Tel Aviv University, 2016), 138.

5 J. Myers, *Seeking Zion: Modernity and Messianic Activism in the Writings of Tsevi Hirsch Kalischer* (Oxford, 2003).

6 H. Brandwein, 'W rocznicę styczniowego czynu', *Nasze Jutro*, 21 Jan. 1939, p. 1.

7 J. Selzer, 'Renesans sportu żydowskiego', in H. Stachel (ed.), *Almanach żydowski* (Lwów, 1937), 142.

8 S. Rudnicki, 'The Struggle in the Polish Parliament for Jewish Autonomy and the Nature of the Jewish Community', *Polin*, 34 (2022), 345–67.

9 J. Appenszlak, *Mowie polskiej* (Warsaw, 1915), 7.

10 C. Weizmann, *Trial and Error: The Autobiography of Chaim Weizmann* (New York, 1949), 301; see 'Ne'um ha-dr. ḥ. vaitsman: ba'asefah ha'amamit bete'atron "tsiyon" biyerushalayim, 11 oktober 1924', *Ha'olam*, 31 Oct. 1924, pp. 3–4.

11 M. G. [Glickson], 'Al haperek: dr. vaitsman be'erets yisra'el', *Haaretz*, 26 Sept. 1924, p. 2 (emphasis original).

12 A. Polonsky, 'Jewish Involvement in Local *Kehilot*, the Sejm, and Municipalities in Interwar Poland', *Polin*, 34 (2022), 368–86.

13 B. Hausner, 'Handel polsko-palestyński: Konferencja w C.Z.K. w sprawie eksportu do Palestyny', *Przegląd Handlowy*, 7 Sept. 1928, pp. 5–6.

14 Archiwum Akt Nowych, Warsaw, Ministerstwo Spraw Zagranicznych, 1008/1–18: Problem palestyński, 1938.

15 K. Pruszyński, *Palestyna po raz trzeci* (Warsaw, 1933).

16 Quoted in 'Biografie niezwykłe: Ksawery Pruszyński' (4 Dec. 2007): Polskie Radio website, visited 8 Dec. 2021.

17 W. Anders, *Bez ostatniego rozdziału: Wspomnienia z lat 1939–1946* (New York, 1949), 99.

18 A. Stankowski and P. Weiser, 'Demograficzne skutki Holokaustu', in F. Tych and M. Adamczyk-Garbowska (eds.), *Następstwa zagłady Żydów: Polska 1944–2010* (Lublin, 2011), 15–38.
19 J. Adelson, 'W Polsce zwanej Ludową', in J. Tomaszewski (ed.), *Najnowsze dzieje Żydów w Polsce* (Warsaw, 1993), 387–477: 388–9. The figure for those who survived in hiding is certainly too low, because many Jews either retained their new identities after the war or for other reasons did not register with the CKŻP or registered subsequently. It should probably be doubled or even trebled, which would give a figure of 32,000 to 48,000 Jews who survived thanks to Polish assistance. It may even have been higher.
20 J. Czerniakiewicz, *Repatriacja ludności polskiej z ZSRR 1944–48* (Warsaw, 1987), 12, 54, 58–9, 102–3, 130, 154–5.
21 United States Holocaust Memorial Museum, Washington DC, 2011.287.1: 'Hilzenrad Family Papers', 'Diary 1941–1944': Adela Hilzenrad, 'Kiedy bestja się budzi… Przeżycia z okresu okupacji niemieckiej. Czerwiec 1941 – sierpień 1944 r.', June 1944.
22 M. Tsanin, *Iber shteyn un shtok: a rayze iber hundert khorev-gevorene khiles in poyln* (Tel Aviv, 1952); Pol. trans.: M. Canin, *Przez ruiny i zgliszcza: Podróż po stu zgładzonych gminach żydowskich w Polsce*, trans. M. Adamczyk-Garbowska (Warsaw, 2018).
23 Tsanin, *Iber shteyn un shtok*, p. i.
24 J. T. Gross and I. Grudzińska-Gross, *Złote żniwa: Rzecz o tym, co się działo na obrzeżach zagłady Żydów* (Kraków, 2011); Eng. edn.: *Golden Harvest: Events at the Periphery of the Holocaust* (New York, 2012).
25 Tsanin, *Iber shteyn un shtok*, 313.
26 J. Markiewicz, 'Dopolszczyłam się w Izraelu', *Nowiny Izraelskie*, 1958, no. 66, p. 3.
27 S. Lebenbaum-Drzewożycki, 'Dziwny czar izraelskiej polszczyzny', *Nowiny Izraelskie*, 14 Dec. 1957, p. 3.
28 Y. Pninger, 'She'erit yehudei polin vehitlabetutam', *Davar*, 7 Nov. 1969, p. 10.
29 A. Klugman, 'Czy machnąć ręką na Żydów polskich?', *Nowiny i Kurier*, 21 Nov. 1969, p. 7; id., 'Słoń w składzie porcelany', *Nowiny i Kurier*, 7 Dec. 1969, p. 3; id., 'Alilot al aharonei hayotes'im mepolin', *Davar*, 25 Nov. 1969, p. 5.
30 Y. Zerubavel, 'The "Mythological Sabra" and Jewish Past: Trauma, Memory, and Contested Identities', *Israel Studies*, 7/2 (2002), 115–44: 115.
31 H. Grynberg, *Dziedzictwo* (London, 1993), 90.
32 Y. Hendel, *Leyad kefarim sheketim* (Tel Aviv, 1987), 47–64.
33 M. Govrin, 'Mikhtavei mimeḥozot aḥizat ha'einayim', *Iton 77*, 209 (1997), 22–42: 42.
34 S. Ronen, 'Post-Holocaust Representations of Poland in Israeli Literature', *Polish Review*, 60/3 (2015), 3–20: 7.
35 Y. Sarid, *Mifletset hazikaron* (Tel Aviv, 2017), 73.
36 R. Modan, *Hanekhes* (Tel Aviv, 2013), 15; Eng. trans.: *The Property*, trans. J. Cohen (New York, 2013), 15.
37 E. Nevo, *Neuland*, trans. S. Silverston (London, 2014), 547; Heb. orig,: *Neuland* (Or Yehuda, 2011).
38 'Full Text of Poland's Controversial Holocaust Legislation' (1 Feb. 2018): *Times of Israel* website, visited 8 Dec. 2021.
39 Ibid.
40 'The Joint Statement by Prime Minister Benjamin Netanyahu and Polish Prime Minister Mateusz Morawiecki' [27 June 2018]: International Jewish Lawyers website, visited 8 Dec 2021.

41 'Joint Statement'.
42 Ibid.
43 A. Paczkowski, 'Czerwone i czarne' (14 Mar. 2004): *Tygodnik Powszechny* website, visited 8 Dec. 2021.
44 B. Porter-Szűcs, 'Meritocracy and Community in Twenty-First-Century Poland', *Shofar* 37/1 (2019), 72–95: 87.
45 Instytut Pamięci Narodowej, 'Polityka historyczna' (n.d.): Wayback Machine website, visited 8 Dec. 2021.
46 E. Gibbon, *The History of the Decline and Fall of the Roman Empire* (London, 1776–89), ch. 3.

1. BEFORE ZIONISM

Hasidic Communities in the Land of Israel in the Nineteenth Century

URIEL GELLMAN

HASIDISM originated in Podolia and Volhynia and coalesced there as a social and religious movement towards the end of the eighteenth century; gradually, it attracted many adherents from other regions of Poland, Galicia, and Russia. Throughout the nineteenth century—the golden age of hasidism's cultural influence, demographic and geographical expansion, and political power—the movement remained within the historical boundaries of the Polish–Lithuanian Commonwealth, and, even within these boundaries, there were regions in which its presence was limited.[1] There was only one exception: the hasidic community in the Land of Israel, which was established simultaneously with the consolidation of the movement in eastern Europe and existed as a cultural enclave and a distant branch of the parent communities throughout the movement's long history. This was the only satellite community removed from the vital centres of the movement until the great migration to the west and the gradual establishment of new hasidic communities in North America and western Europe.[2]

The historiography of hasidism in the Land of Israel, which began at the same time as the study of hasidism in general, focused on the early stages of the community's development between 1777 and 1810.[3] Compared to the scholarship on the nonhasidic Ashkenazi *perushim*, disciples of the Vilna Gaon who settled in the Land of Israel at the beginning of the nineteenth century, there is little research about the history of the hasidic community in the subsequent period, when it became the central force of the Ashkenazi Old Yishuv before the Zionist *aliyot* (migrations to the Land of Israel) beginning at the end of the nineteenth century. Although a number of important studies have recently been written on the later period, there is still a need for continued research on its full historical, social, and cultural contexts.[4] Orthodox hasidic historiography has certainly dealt with this later era extensively but, despite the importance of these works, which are based on important sources and include much new information, they cannot serve as a substitute for critical historical research.[5]

The story of the hasidim in the Land of Israel is important not only in its specific context, as the hasidim were a dominant sector of the large population of east European Jews who established new communities far from their cultural centres. Despite the obvious differences between these remote communities and their communities of origin, they had a great deal in common and a shared sense of belonging, and hence should also be discussed in the context of the history of east European Jewry. This is a unique case of a society of immigrants that aspired to preserve its original culture in a new, different, and very challenging setting. A complete study of the history of hasidism in the Land of Israel can draw on rich and varied new source materials: letters from hasidim and their leaders;[6] population censuses;[7] archives of Jewish organizations, government institutions, and European consulates;[8] travelogues and missionary journals;[9] *pinkasim* (Jewish community record books);[10] autobiographies;[11] and newspapers.[12]

This chapter will provide a general description of the hasidic communities in the four 'holy cities'—Safed, Tiberias, Jerusalem, and Hebron (the presence of hasidim elsewhere was negligible)—from the early nineteenth century until about 1881. It is not possible to provide a comprehensive history of even one of these communities within the constraints of this chapter, which will therefore serve as a 'road map' with a wide perspective and will not address all the important aspects of this topic, in the hope that they will be clarified in future studies.

The Hasidic 'Old Yishuv'

Hasidism was a supra-local diasporic movement rooted in the cultural landscape of east European Jewry. It included its own spatial perception that was based on spiritual dimensions and the map of numerous hasidic courts headed by charismatic leaders, whereas 'the Holy Land' became primarily a spiritual symbol.[13] Despite the marginal standing of the actual Land of Israel in the history of the hasidic movement, hasidim developed connections to the region by way of financial support for their fellow hasidim who moved there.

The first *aliyah* of hasidim in 1777 was unusual in its scope and marked the beginning of a demographic shift that brought about the establishment of a sustainable Ashkenazi community in the Land of Israel and the growth of the Jewish population in the nineteenth century from a few thousand to approximately 26,000 before the Zionist *aliyot*.[14] Like other groups in the Old Yishuv, which was perceived as an exclusive religious elite by diaspora Jews, the hasidim were also dependent on *ḥalukah* funds: money collected in their countries of origin.[15] The hasidic centres in eastern Europe organized support for the immigrants, and letters and emissaries maintained a continuous connection between them. In this way, the leadership maintained its authority over the distant hasidim, who continued to belong to their original group. The *ḥalukah* funds established the image of the Old Yishuv as a passive, impoverished, and idle society. In reality, however, the financial survival of the Ashkenazi Yishuv, and especially that of the hasidim, depended on involvement in the local economy alongside the unique and predominant 'community of learners' whose livelihood depended on donations from abroad.[16]

The organizational structure of the Yishuv was based on the *kolel*, which served as a substitute for the traditional *kahal*, or community, in the diaspora. The *kolel* provided a variety of social and financial services and oversaw the distribution of the *ḥalukah* funds to its members, based on financial standing, *yiḥus* (pedigree), and Torah learning. Individuals became very dependent on their communities, and, as a result, local *kolel* appointees enjoyed great authority in all social matters and could interfere in personal matters. For the immigrants, the *kolel* served also as a social and cultural framework, and they aspired to preserve their particularistic identity through it. The hasidic *kolelim* became a decisive factor in maintaining social and ideological distinctions between the different groups, precisely at a time when community institutions were being weakened or completely eliminated by governments in their countries of origin. Like the hasidic court, which also performed functions that used to be the responsibility of the local Jewish communities, the *kolel* became integrated into the organizational hasidic system and into the Orthodoxization processes that shaped it in the nineteenth century.

There were three forces which sought to control the hasidic communities in the Land of Israel. First, chronologically, were the *tsadikim* and rabbis in eastern Europe, whose involvement in the support of the Yishuv gave them the power to appoint the collectors of funds and influence over the communities in the Land of Israel. Second was the Pekidim Va'amarkalim (Treasurers and Administrators) in Amsterdam, led by Tsevi Hirsh Lehren (1784–1853). This was a centralized Orthodox organization which collected funds for the Yishuv in central and western Europe and aspired to shape it into a 'society of learners' and a model of conservatism.[17] Finally, there was Moses Montefiore (1784–1885), who stood for intercession, philanthropy, and the rise of a new Jewish politics, and accordingly worked to advance economic productivity and modernization initiatives in the Yishuv.[18] The hasidim had to manoeuvre between these patrons and their conflicting agendas.[19]

Every Jew in the Yishuv belonged to a *kolel*, which defined their financial, social, and religious status. Thus, while in their countries of origin there were no formal boundaries between hasidim and *mitnagedim*, in the Yishuv there were clear social, cultural, and organizational divisions between the hasidim and the *perushim* and between members of different hasidic courts. The very distance from the courts of the *tsadikim* made identification with the group more meaningful and encompassing. This organizational difference was also visible in the status of women in local hasidic society. Even assuming, as some scholars do, that women did not take an active part in the hasidic courts, at least in the Land of Israel, they were official members of the community, certainly with regard to financial matters.[20] In the various censuses, women were included in the lists of members of the hasidic *kolelim*, which recorded significantly more widows than in their communities of origin. They expressed their piety in unique ways—for example, praying and performing religious rituals at holy sites—but did not participate in the exclusive 'society of learners' and did not fulfil any official functions. For the most part, in the Middle Eastern context, they could not continue to work in the typical occupations of Jewish women in eastern Europe, such as peddling, market trading, and storekeeping.[21]

The geographical distance and separation of the society of emigrants from the main arena of hasidism required the creation of alternative social infrastructures. The leaders of the first *aliyah* in 1777, Rabbi Menahem Mendel of Vitebsk (1730?–1788) and Rabbi Avraham of Kalisk (1741–1810), were renowned *tsadikim* before their emigration. Their efforts to continue to lead their hasidim in Belarus by means of letters were doomed to failure because of the lack of an unmediated connection between the hasidim and their *tsadik* that had always formed the basis of the hasidic experience. They were forced, in the end, to appoint Rabbi Shneur Zalman of Liady (1745–1812), founder of Habad hasidism, as leader in their place.[22] From that point, and throughout the nineteenth century, there were no hasidim in eastern Europe who maintained an attachment to a *tsadik* who had moved to the Land of Israel. The hasidim in the Land of Israel were subject to the *tsadikim* in eastern Europe, and important hasidic figures who emigrated to the Land of Israel ceased to function as *tsadikim* and did not establish hasidic courts. Instead of the models of hasidic leadership built on *yihus* and kinship, local leadership was based on personal qualities and organizational abilities.

The identity of every hasid was based on membership of a specific court or dynasty. At first the hasidim in the Land of Israel were united in a single organizational framework, Kolel Vohlin (or Kolel Hahasidim), whose centres were in Jerusalem and Safed. Over the years, the *kolel* split due to disagreements and claims of unfair distribution of the *halukah* funds. Changes in the balance of power between centres of hasidism abroad, controversies between or within hasidic courts, and the emergence of new hasidic dynasties all influenced the structure of the community in the Land of Israel. Sometimes hasidim from the same court belonged to different *kolelim*, but usually each *kolel* represented a single geographical region of origin or a particular hasidic court (some of the splits will be discussed below).

The ongoing conflicts between groups and within *kolelim* at the local level caused further shifts in the status, size, and importance of the communities, and there were strong forces that determined their fates. Frequent plagues, natural disasters, and political uprisings, on the one hand, and improvements in the means of transportation and communication on the other were fateful for the hasidic community.[23] Naturally, the political and financial situations in their countries of origin also influenced the pace of immigration, as when the Russian and Austrian governments limited the transfer of money to the Ottoman empire.[24] An important turning point in the history of the community occurred under the Egyptian rule of Muhammad Ali in the Land of Israel (1831–40). He was liberal towards Christian and Jewish minorities, implemented financial reforms, and improved the level of security.[25] The enhanced conditions brought about an increase in immigration that persisted even after the return of Sultan Abdulmejid's rule in 1840, as the Ottomans were now committed to the new reforms, including equality for non-Muslim subjects.[26]

With the greater involvement of the European powers in the Ottoman empire in the 1840s, the Land of Israel increasingly occupied Jewish media, as prominent Jewish individuals and organizations increased their political interaction with the region.[27] With the 'capitulations' (agreements between the Ottoman empire and the European powers), European consulates extended their protection to the European immigrants in the Yishuv, thus improving their legal and political status. These events influenced the ethnic structure of the Yishuv, further increasing the predominance of the Ashkenazi community.[20] Most of the hasidim had arrived from the tsarist empire, but tsarist bureaucrats showed a lack of interest in their subjects, so many of them moved to the protection of the British or Austrian consulates.[29] In general, the Ottoman authorities granted freedom of religion to the various ethno-religious groups, and the remaining legal restrictions that affected the communities were primarily those concerning the construction of synagogues and other public structures.[30] This was very different from the situation of the hasidim in their countries of origin, where they were constantly compelled to struggle for recognition and group status within their communities and were subject to state authorities who imposed a variety of restrictions on them. In addition, the cultural conflict between the hasidim and the maskilim, which took different forms throughout this period, had less impact on the hasidim of the Land of Israel, although they too had to fight for the preservation of the traditional cultural character of their community. The local hasidim lived alongside immigrants from other countries in a totally different ethnic and religious environment. Despite the organizational separation and financial competition among the groups, the encounter between them had a significant influence on the daily life, customs, clothing, language, and finances of the hasidim. At the same time, the hasidim managed to preserve their unique culture within the community framework which was part of Ottoman law.[31] The Orthodoxization of hasidism, which accelerated in the second half of the century, unfolded differently in the Land of Israel than in Europe but was part of the same campaign of cultural defence. The hasidim of the Yishuv contended with a more moderate version of modernization than their European counterparts, one largely imported by European cultural agents, and most of the hasidim chose the cultural segregation that later evolved into religious extremism in the face of Jewish nationalism.

During this entire period there was limited migration of hasidim to the Land of Israel, due to the distance from their major centres and the exceedingly difficult financial and social challenges they faced. Despite this, as Table 1 illustrates, the hasidim constituted the majority of the Ashkenazi Yishuv throughout this period. Most of the non-hasidic Ashkenazim were members of Kolel Perushim and lived predominantly in Jerusalem, the centre of the Old Yishuv, while most of the hasidim lived in Safed or Tiberias and established much smaller communities in Jerusalem and Hebron.

The demographic growth of the hasidic community in the Land of Israel was attributable primarily to immigration, whereas natural population growth was slow relative to that in their communities of origin.[32] The population was elderly, with a comparatively large number of widows, widowers, and families without children, despite the prominence of family units among immigrants from eastern Europe. The fertility rate was low, largely as a result of malnutrition and poor sanitary conditions.[33] Over time, however, the number of hasidim born in the Land of Israel increased, and leaders from this group operated effectively in the local political and

Table 1 Hasidim in the four 'holy cities'

Year	City	Hasidim N	Hasidim %	Non-hasidic Ashkenazim N	Non-hasidic Ashkenazim %	Total Ashkenazim N	Total Ashkenazim %	Percentage of hasidim among Ashkenazim %
1839	Jerusalem	38	3.4	417	88.2	455	28.9	8.4
	Safed	543	49.2	28	5.9	571	36.2	95.1
	Tiberias	379	34.3	0	0.0	379	24.0	100.0
	Hebron	144	13.0	28	5.9	172	10.9	83.7
	Total	1,104	99.9[a]	473	100.0	1,577	100.0	70.0
1855	Jerusalem	696	24.1	1154	95.7	1,850	45.2	38.0
	Safed	1246	43.2	52	4.3	1298	31.7	96.0
	Tiberias	803	27.8	0.0[b]	0.0	803	19.6	100.0
	Hebron	142	4.9	0.0	0.0	142	3.5	100.0
	Total	2,887	100.0	1206	100.0	4,093	100.0	71.0
1880	Jerusalem	2,088	28.0	4708	96.7	6,796	55.0	31.0
	Safed	3,890	52.1	170	3.3	4,060	32.9	96.0
	Tiberias	1,000	13.4	0.0[b]	0.0	1000	8.1	100.0
	Hebron	489	6.5	0.0[b]	0.0	489	4.0	100.0
	Total	7,467	100.0	4878	100.0	12,345	100.0	61.0

Source: N. Karlinsky, 'Haḥevrah haḥasidit shel tsefat bamaḥatsit hasheniyah shel hame'ah hatesha esreh keḥevrat mehagerim: hebetim demografiyim vegibush ḥevrati', in I. Etkes, D. Assaf, and Y. Dan (eds.), *Meḥkerei ḥasidut* (Jerusalem, 1999), 151–96: 156.

[a] Due to rounding error.
[b] Regarding the figures for Tiberias in 1855 and 1880 and Hebron in 1880: the total number of Ashkenazim is known from reliable sources, but there is no reliable information on how many of them were hasidim. Since all other sources say that there were most likely no non-hasidic Ashkenazim there at the time, it can be assumed they were all hasidim (see Karlinsky, 'Haḥevrah haḥasidit shel tsefat bamaḥatsit hasheniyah shel hame'ah hatesha esreh keḥevrat mehagerim', 152, 156–7).

cultural realms for the welfare of the community. There was no pool of potential converts to hasidism in the Land of Israel, so the group was made up entirely of migrants from Europe and their descendants.

Communities in Galilee: Safed and Tiberias

Among the few members of proto-hasidic circles to arrive in the Land of Israel were the Ba'al Shem Tov's brother-in-law, Rabbi Gershon of Kitev, who arrived in Jerusalem in 1747, and two of his associates, Rabbi Menahem Mendel of Premishlan (Peremyshlany) and Rabbi Nahman of Horodenka. They settled in Tiberias in 1764.[34]

They arrived as individuals without a distinct 'hasidic' identity and were assimilated into the existing community. Only after the famous hasidic *aliyah* of 1777 is it possible to speak of a true hasidic community.³⁵ The immigrants, under the leadership of followers of the Magid of Mezritsh, arrived in Safed, which enjoyed special status by virtue of its mystical and messianic heritage and its proximity to the gravesites of the sages in Galilee. Because of tensions between them and the local community, most of the hasidim moved to Tiberias.³⁶ With the spread of hasidism to new areas, the emigration of hasidim from Ukraine and Galicia also increased, including several renowned personalities such as Rabbi Ya'akov Shimshon of Shepetovka (1794) and Rabbi Ze'ev Wolf of Cherniostrov (1798). Conflicts in the Tiberias community led some of the hasidim to move back to Safed, where most of the Ashkenazim in the Yishuv lived. Other immigrants joined them at the beginning of the nineteenth century, among them well-known hasidim such as Rabbi David Shelomoh Eybeschütz (1809) and Rabbi Hayim Tyrer of Chernovits (1813). Safed gradually became the 'capital' of the hasidim, while the community in Tiberias, which formally separated from it in 1831, remained in its shadow throughout the period.³⁷

The competing factions of the Jewish communities in Galilee caused constant tension. Gershon Margaliot, the former rabbi of Skalat in Galicia, who was appointed leader of Kolel Vohlin after arriving in Safed in 1811, frequently got into disagreements with other groups in the city and with the heads of the Pekidim Va'amarkalim, and was accused of dubious handling of the *ḥalukah* funds.³⁸ The increase in *aliyah* in the 1830s brought new energy to the troubled community. In 1831 Yisra'el Bak (1797–1874) emigrated from Berdichev to Safed and established a printing press that employed dozens of workers. He and his son Nisan (1815–89) contributed greatly to the development of the community in Safed and later in Jerusalem through their business activities.³⁹ Two years later, Rabbi Avraham Dov of Owrucz (1765–1840), who had been rabbi of Zhitomir and acted as a 'secondary *tsadik*' under the hegemony of the famous Ukrainian *tsadikim*, Rabbi Yisra'el of Ruzhin (1797–1850) and Rabbi Mordekhai of Chernobyl (1770–1837), came to Safed and quickly became the lively and admired leaders of the hasidim.⁴⁰ Rabbi Avraham Dov established a hasidic *beit midrash* (house of study), which benefited from the contributions of Moses Montefiore and served as a gathering place for the hasidim of Safed. He imported social patterns based on those of the hasidic courts to Safed and served as a spiritual leader to his congregation and as an influential community activist.⁴¹

As opposed to the strained relationship between the hasidim and the *perushim* in Jerusalem (see below), in Safed a relationship was established that allowed them to live together despite economic competition. Prior tensions between Ashkenazim and Sephardim in the city contributed to this arrangement, but the pragmatic leadership of the head of the Kolel Perushim in Safed, Rabbi Yisra'el of Shklov (1770–1839), a disciple of the Vilna Gaon who emigrated to the Land of Israel in 1809, enabled them to overcome their ideological struggles and build strong relationships with the local hasidim.⁴² There are indications of a deep and ongoing friendship between Rabbi Yisra'el and Rabbi Avraham Dov: 'and even the Rav, Rabbi Yisroel, who is of the *perushim*, sent him a *kvitl* [petitionary note] with his own name and his mother's name, requesting him to pray on his behalf, and also sent him a *pidyon* [a donation for Avraham Dov to pardon his soul] when he was ill, may the All-Merciful protect us'.[43] Rabbi Yisra'el conducted negotiations with the hasidim regarding the *ḥalukah* funds, achieving compromises that enabled the expansion of both communities, and even served as an arbitrator in disputes between the hasidic *kolelim*.[44]

The 1830s were exceedingly challenging for the Jews of Galilee. In the summer of 1834 a peasant revolt against Muhammad Ali erupted, including riots against the Jews during which their property was looted.[45] In the midst of these horrifying events, the hasidic community in Safed split: some remained with Gershon Margaliot, while Rabbi Avraham Dov and his supporters were expelled from the city.[46] Following these events, and because of allegations of corruption—related to compensation money obtained with the intervention of foreign consuls—levelled against Margaliot and his faction, the conflicts between the Russian and Galician Jews intensified and caused the Pekidim Va'amarkalim to formally appoint Rabbi Avraham Dov as the leader of the hasidic *kolel*.[47]

On 1 January 1837 a massive earthquake destroyed Safed and Tiberias, doing immense damage to their Jewish communities.[48] Among the thousands of dead were approximately 800 hasidim.[49] Restoration efforts went on for a long time, and *tsadikim* from Russia and Poland provided moral support and increased fundraising to help the hasidim. At the end of the decade the Jews of Galilee suffered a drought and a recession, and in the summer of 1838 there was more violence in the Druze uprising against Egyptian rule. The repeated disasters that befell the Jews of Galilee shifted the demographic balance in the Yishuv: most of the members of Kolel Perushim moved to Jerusalem, and Safed became a hasidic stronghold. The Ashkenazi community in Tiberias, which constituted about half the Jews of the city during this entire period, also became almost entirely hasidic.

The death of Rabbi Avraham Dov began an extended battle for the leadership of the Safed community between Rabbi Ya'akov Dov of Roman (1794–1858), a close associate of Rabbi Yisra'el of Ruzhin and father-in-law of Nisan Bak, and Rabbi Shemu'el Heller (1803–84), who arrived in Safed as a child and did not belong to any specific hasidic court.[50] The rivalry reflected the complicated political structure of the Yishuv and its patrons: Rabbi Heller was supported by the Pekidim Va'amarkalim and the religious leaders of the Sephardi community in Safed, while Rabbi Ya'akov Dov was supported by his *rebbe* and received backing from Moses Montefiore. The ongoing dispute between them destabilized the financial situation of the hasidic *kolel*, while the two rabbis received *ḥalukah* funds from different sources.[51] Despite efforts to calm the situation, the tension between the factions persisted and was conspicuous during Moses Montefiore's visit to Safed in the summer of 1849, when they vied for his support and presented two separate censuses of the community.[52] When Kolel Varshah was established in 1848, Heller was appointed as its head and won the support of rabbis and *tsadikim* in Poland.[53]

Because of his organizational and political skills Heller was recognized as head of the Ashkenazi community, and combined traditional rabbinical leadership, magical healing abilities, and ideological guidance. Heller's leadership symbolized the strengthening of an independent 'native' stratum that was part of the culture of the Land of Israel from the beginning, and he knew how to manoeuvre in the complex political landscape and reinforce the security and the Orthodox character of the community.[54]

The pragmatism of Heller and his people resulted in the Safed community (more than any other) advocating for productivity and working the land alongside their opposition to modernization in any other domain. On each of Montefiore's visits to Safed (the last one was in 1875), he received requests from groups of local Jews for his help in advancing economic initiatives, most of which were never realized.[55] With the growth of the population, and as a result of a new law permitting non-citizens to buy land, settlement initiatives began again in the 1870s. The first settlement attempts in Ein Zeitim and Gai Oni (1874) were made with the support of the heads of the *kolelim* and anticipated the development of the Rosh Pina colony upon the arrival of the First Zionist Aliyah (1882–1903).[56] An interesting phenomenon in Safed was the involvement of the hasidim in the production and sale of alcoholic beverages, an economic sector imported from eastern Europe into a Muslim environment that prohibited it. The culture of drinking deteriorated at times into addiction and violence, and the community was forced to regulate the industry.[57]

After several relatively quiet years, a number of disputes erupted during the 1870s and 1880s. Members of the younger generation challenged Heller's leadership, and Jewish newspapers were soon filled with their critical reports and polemical articles about events in the Land of Israel. The latter are important historical sources for the social challenges that developed in the community before the Zionist *aliyot*.[58] These battles, which I cannot explore in detail here, were theoretically separate but in fact reflected the cultural changes that penetrated the Old Yishuv and revealed the flaws of the old politics. The critique exposed the intrigues in the *kolelim* and the social problems associated with the *ḥalukah* system.

The political tension and critique of the leadership were accompanied by a general tension that caused additional atomization in the system of *kolelim*. At the end of the 1860s Kolel Ostriyah, to which migrants from Galicia transferred in 1851, split into three (Kolel Lemberg, Kolel Kosov, and Kolel Vizhnits).[59] Members of Kolel Vohlin and Kolel Ostriyah took opposite sides in the dramatic intra-hasidic Sanz–Sadagora dispute about the extravagant lifestyle led in the courts of the House of Ruzhin. The founder of the Sanz dynasty, Rabbi Hayim Halberstam (1797–1876), a righteous man, a scholar, and a zealot, saw this lifestyle as a departure from the original hasidic way and called for the *ḥerem* (excommunication) of the Ruzhin courts. The tension between the local supporters of the two camps and the participation of some of the hasidim in the counter-*ḥerem* placed upon Rabbi Hayim of Sanz tore the community apart and led to episodes of considerable violence which created further divisions.[60] For instance, the hasidic courts of the Chernobyl dynasty, which predominated in

Ukraine, started sending their contributions directly to their hasidim in Safed, bypassing the established distribution mechanisms, and their followers were able to establish several small prayer houses. The tension between them and the hasidim of Sadagora caused them to split off from Kolel Vohlin and establish Kolel Zhitomir.[61] In 1877 immigrants from Romania established Kolel Moldavyah Vevalakhyah.[62]

The *perushim* and the Habad hasidim, two small and relatively marginal groups within the Galilean Ashkenazi communities, were affiliated with their own *kolelim* in Jerusalem and Hebron. A number of the descendants of Bratslav hasidism, which was at that time a small and isolated hasidic group, migrated to Safed and Tiberias, but there is no evidence that they joined together as a group before the beginning of the twentieth century.[63] The splitting of the communities was a result of social and cultural fissures and was reflected on the ground in the growing number of prayer houses named after hasidic courts in Ukraine and Galicia to which the specific hasidic factions belonged. As S. Y. Agnon wrote, 'there is no *tsadik* outside of the Land of Israel who doesn't have a prayer house in Safed'.[64]

Little is known about the community in Tiberias. It did not have famous leaders such as those in Safed,[65] and was dominated by 'Lithuanian hasidism'—hasidic courts from the southern regions of Belarus—which gave it a cultural distinctiveness. The *tsadikim* of the Karlin–Stolin dynasty encouraged their hasidim to emigrate to the Land of Israel, and excelled in their organization of fundraising for Kolel Vohlin. The first group of Karlin hasidim settled in Tiberias in the 1830s, in the days of Rabbi Aharon the Second (1802–72), the grandson of the founder of the dynasty, who was among the patrons of the *kolel*.[66] Some of the hasidim of Tiberias belonged to Kolel Varshah and Kolel Ostriyah. The hasidim of Kobrin and Lachowicz (Belarusian courts) belonged to Kolel Reisen, which was established around 1855.[67] In subsequent years, the hasidim of Rabbi Avraham Weinberg of Slonim (1803–83) joined this *kolel* as well, and it became the dominant group in Tiberias. Eventually some of Weinberg's close family members followed them there. The Slonim community in Tiberias developed into a distant alternative to the court towards the end of the nineteenth century, in the days of Rabbi Shemu'el Weinberg (1850–1916), who himself visited Tiberias several times.[68]

In the 1860s the Karlin hasidim purchased the building that housed the synagogue established by Rabbi Menahem Mendel of Vitebsk, which had been damaged in the 1837 earthquake. In 1869 the renovation of the synagogue was completed, and it was renamed Beit Aharon.[69] In 1874, after constant complaints of discrimination in the distribution of the *ḥalukah* funds, the hasidim of Karlin split off from Kolel Vohlin and established Kolel Karlin.[70] Their independence was apparently intended, inter alia, to establish the status of their new leader, Yisrael Perlov of Stolin (1868–1921) the *yenuka* (child prodigy), who became *tsadik* when he was less than 5 years old, after his father's death.[71] The move positioned the Karlin hasidim as a central force in Tiberias.[72] This is an interesting case, because by breaking off and establishing their own institutions the Karliners ultimately raised the status of their *tsadik* and reconsolidated the group around his court back in eastern Europe. By 1880 there were approximately 1,000 hasidim in Tiberias, with seven synagogues in addition to those established by the first immigrants.[73]

Jerusalem and Hebron

In contrast to Galilee, which enjoyed relative stability until the beginning of the nineteenth century, in Jerusalem the Jews' life was extraordinarily difficult. The few Ashkenazim were perceived by the authorities as descendants of Rabbi Judah Hehasid's Sabbatian group that had arrived in the city in 1700, and thus responsible for the payment of debts left behind by the group after its dissolution in 1720.[74] Therefore, while the hasidic communities in Galilee had kept on developing since the hasidim first arrived in 1777, a similar community did not develop in Jerusalem, and occasional visitors to the Land of Israel rarely went to Jerusalem. Rabbi Nahman of Bratslav (1772–1810), for example, when he visited in 1798, did not go to Jerusalem even though he apparently initially intended to do so.[75] Presumably the economic or security situation in the city discouraged visitors, but it is also clear that the hasidim as a group did not invest in the development of an Ashkenazi community in Jerusalem.[76] For the first three decades of the nineteenth century the presence of the hasidim was so marginal there that the heads of the Pekidim Va'amarkalim, who knew even the smallest details regarding the Jewish communities in the Land of Israel, thought there were no hasidim at all in Jerusalem.[77]

Hasidim avoided living in the city because of the debts of the Sabbatians (a problem that was eventually solved) and because of tensions with the *perushim*, whose leader in Jerusalem was Rabbi Menahem Mendel of Shklov (d. 1827), a close disciple of the Vilna Gaon, a great mystic and an ideological opponent of hasidism.[78] After about eight years in Galilee, he went to Jerusalem in 1816 and revitalized the Ashkenazi settlement there.[79] As long as he was alive there was no possibility of establishing even a small hasidic community in Jerusalem, and the few hasidim who did settle there often quarrelled with the *perushim* on ideological and economic grounds.[80] The rivalry between the groups prevented any possibility of co-operation, as was reported by Joseph Wolff, representative of the London Society for Promoting Christianity Amongst the Jews, in 1822: 'The Polish Jews themselves, residing in Jerusalem, are subdivided into three parties . . . The enmity between those parties is so great, that the Pharisee strives to prevent the settlement of the Polish party in Jerusalem; and accuse even each other to the Turkish Governor.'[81]

A true hasidic community appeared in the city only after 1838, following the arrival of Rabbi Aharon Moshe Migeza-Tsevi of Brody (1775–1845), a disciple of the Seer of Lublin. At first the group's financial situation was very grave.[82] According to Montefiore's 1839 census, approximately 2,500 Jews lived in Jerusalem, including an Ashkenazi minority of 417 *perushim* and 38 hasidim. Some of the hasidim worked for a living, but they, too, were dependent on *ḥalukah* funds, which they received through the established community in Safed, until a separate hasidic *kolel* was established despite the opposition of their patrons, who thought that a separate organization would be reckless and counterproductive.[83]

In Jerusalem, as in Galilee, sub-groups evolved, each aligned with a different hasidic court. The most dominant group was made up of followers of Rabbi Yisra'el of Ruzhin (1796–1850), patron of Kolel Vohlin since the 1830s.[84] Ruzhin's influence in Jerusalem grew until the 1837 earthquake in Galilee drove many Jews to Jerusalem, among them the Bak family, which moved in 1840/1. The family supported building and development initiatives and re-established their printing press.[85] Under the leadership of the Bak family, the hasidim, in co-operation with the Sephardim, also supported the establishment of a Jewish hospital in Jerusalem, and in 1856 Nisan Bak was among the supporters of the Lämel School. The *perushim* of Jerusalem objected to the establishment of both institutions, which demonstrates that the hasidim had achieved independent standing in the Ashkenazi community.[86] At the suggestion of Nisan Bak, Rabbi Yisra'el of Ruzhin appointed Montefiore president of the hasidic *kolel*. Rabbi Yisra'el of Ruzhin believed in Montefiore's tremendous influence, and this effort fitted in with his endeavours to harness the philanthropist's generosity for the benefit of Russian Jewry.[87]

By the end of Rabbi Yisra'el of Ruzhin's life, his hasidim constituted a majority of the hasidim in Jerusalem.[88] Under the leadership of his son, Rabbi Avraham Ya'akov of Sadagora (1819–1883), support for the hasidic settlement in the Land of Israel increased, and Kolel Vohlin widened its influence and grew steadily. Members of the Bak family, who were Austrian subjects, headed Kolel Vohlin, while other hasidim from Galicia and Bukovina joined Kolel Ostriyah. As in Galilee, the members of these *kolelim* took opposite sides in the dispute that raged among the hasidim in Galicia, and the hasidim of Sadagora in Jerusalem declared a *ḥerem* on Rabbi Hayim of Sanz.[89]

With the arrival of hasidim from Galilee and the stream of immigrants that continued throughout the 1840s, the community continued to grow. Still, in 1844 there were only two hasidic synagogues: in the private homes of Rabbi Aharon Moshe and Yisra'el Bak:

The Peroshim have two synagogues ... and they are about to rebuild another of some magnitude, which has long been lying in ruins ... The Khasidim are reckoned at about 100, including some visitors from Safed and Tiberias, where the members of their sect principally reside. They have two small synagogues, one of which is the house of Rabbi Israel, an influential member of their community.[90]

The *perushim*'s efforts to build a grand synagogue on the ruins of Rabbi Judah Hehasid's court roused the hasidim to build their own synagogue to signify their presence in the city. A plot of land was purchased in 1843, funded by the Sadagora court, and at the end of 1844 Rabbi Yisra'el of Ruzhin sent a letter to the leaders of the hasidim in Jerusalem in which he exhorted them to build their own synagogue:

And it will restore my soul, that God, Blessed be He, brought success to my heart's yearning, for this is my wish and desire, that there be a special synagogue where the whole community of hasidim pray, from their greatest to their smallest, together . . . and that is why I have come with this letter to spur you to immediately see fit to exert yourself in the building of a synagogue with alacrity.[91]

Rabbi Yisra'el provided an initial sum of money, and his hasidim began to collect donations. However, the start of construction was delayed for many years. It was difficult to get a building permit from the Turkish authorities, and not until 1859, after the intervention of the Austrian consul, was one obtained. Stopping in Jerusalem on his way to attend the opening of the Suez Canal in November 1869, Emperor Franz Josef visited the site of the synagogue and made a contribution.[92] The impressive Tiferet Yisra'el Synagogue was finally dedicated in a festive ceremony in 1872, and became the symbol of the city's hasidim.[93]

This was the first major architectural project intended specifically as a public hasidic building: previously all hasidic community structures had functioned within the courts. There were certainly impressive hasidic synagogues in eastern Europe, but these were traditional community buildings and had not been initially established as exclusive hasidic centres. Political but not ideological or messianic significance was attributed to the Tiferet Yisra'el Synagogue. It confirmed the centrality of Sadagora hasidism (and then Boyan) within the hasidic world, and strengthened Sadagora's position in the controversy with Sanz hasidim. The hasidim now had a large and respectable building that served as a cultural focal point and community centre.[94] The synagogue's tall dome, prominent on the Jerusalem skyline, was an expression of the blossoming of hasidism in eastern Europe and competed with the impressive dome of the *perushim*'s synagogue, the Hurva, and with the much older domes of the other religions in Jerusalem.

Despite its demographic growth and organizational sophistication, the Jerusalem hasidic community remained in the shadow of the *perushim* until the end of the nineteenth century. About a year after the dedication of the synagogue, a Jerusalem hasid complained: 'I can testify that here in the Holy City there are many *perushim*, and all the *tsadikim* of awesome name, all the holy ones since the Besht, are like a monkey and as nothing in their eyes . . . and the *perushim* are the majority and the hasidim are few.'[95] The relative inferiority of the hasidim was also reflected in the religious-judicial field. The Ashkenazi *beit din* (religious court) in Jerusalem operated in the Hurva Synagogue from 1841 and was an important political centre. A hasidic *beit din* established in 1855 did not last long, and there were no more hasidic *dayanim* until 1863.[96] The new *beit din* was of no consequence to the *perushim*, and it too ceased to operate after a short time. Only in 1892 was a stable hasidic *beit din* established under the auspices of the Habad rabbi, Shneur Zalman Fradkin of Lublin. In the same period the hasidim were also allocated a separate burial plot in the Mount of Olives cemetery.[97]

In 1862, Yehiel Brill, Mikhel Hacohen, and Yoel Moshe Salomon opened a printing press that broke the Bak family's monopoly, and started printing *Halevanon*, a newspaper that became the organ of the *perushim* in Jerusalem.[98] As a countermeasure, the Bak printing press started the *Ḥavatselet* newspaper, edited by Yisra'el Dov Frumkin, who supported the hasidim and the Sephardim, and was critical of Kolel Perushim.[99] *Ḥavatselet* called for increased migration and support for the Yishuv. It reported on the progress of the Tiferet Yisra'el Synagogue and served as an incentive to its completion a few years later. However, only five issues were published before the Turkish authorities closed both presses in the spring of 1864.[100] *Halevanon* migrated to Paris, and *Ḥavatselet* only came out in Jerusalem again in 1870. In the following decades, the press of the Land of Israel played an important role in bringing information to world Jewry, and served as a platform for cultural struggles over the character of the Yishuv.

Besides the members of Kolel Vohlin, there were several other hasidic groups in Jerusalem. Towards the end of 1850 Rabbi Moshe Biderman of Lelov (1777–1851) arrived. He was the son of the Polish *tsadik* David Biderman, the founder of the Lelov dynasty, and the son-in-law of Rabbi Ya'akov Yitshak, the 'Holy Jew' of Pshiskhe (Przysucha). He died soon thereafter, and in the following years his descendants became dominant in the hasidic community. The Ohel Moshe Synagogue, founded by his sons Yitshak David (1815–87) and Elazar Menahem Mendel (1827–83), who headed a tiny hasidic group, was named after him.[101] After the death of his sons, the leadership passed to his grandsons. They opened the Hayei Olam Yeshiva in 1886, which provided elementary education for the children of those *kolelim* that broke off from the 'general council' of the Ashkenazi *kolelim*, which was controlled by the *perushim*. The Hayei Olam institutions challenged the dominance of the *perushim*'s Ets Hayim institutions, and some of Poland's great rabbis, among them Rabbi Hayim Elazar Waks of Piotrków and Rabbi Yehoshua Trunk of Kutno, extended their patronage to the hasidic institutions.[102] David Tsevi Shelomoh Biderman was notably active in Kolel Varshah, and towards the end of the nineteenth century led an initiative to build a new neighbourhood outside the walls of the Old City of Jerusalem for immigrants from Poland: Batei Varshah.[103] Under Rabbi Moshe Biderman's grandsons, Lelov hasidim became close to the Karlin hasidim, who were dominant in Tiberias but had also established a synagogue in Jerusalem, and ultimately were fully absorbed into Karlin. It was rare for a hasidic dynasty to join another one and accept its customs, and it was only the unique social structure in the Land of Israel that made the union of a Polish group and a Lithuanian group with a quite different spiritual and social ethos possible.

In the last quarter of the nineteenth century the hasidim further divided on the basis of geography and dynastic identity. At the end of the 1870s *Halevanon* counted twelve Ashkenazi *kolelim* in Jerusalem, many with hasidic members.[104] A few additional *kolelim* eventually joined these. In the old Kolel Vohlin there were frequent struggles for power and control. For example, after the death of Rabbi Avraham Ya'akov of Sadagora in 1883, the leadership of the *kolel* was handed over to his son Rabbi Yitshak of Boyan (1850–1917); however, in 1891 a struggle broke out between several *tsadikim* for the position, which was a symbol of status and prestige in the hasidic community.[105]

Demographic growth and social changes within the Old Yishuv led the hasidim to move outside the walls of the Old City of Jerusalem. A small neighbourhood, Kiryah Ne'emanah, also known as Batei Nisan Bak, was established north of the Damascus Gate in 1878.[106] Gradually, the hasidic presence in the Old City declined, causing the decline of the pride of the hasidim, the Tiferet Yisra'el Synagogue.

The Jewish community in Hebron was the smallest of those in the four 'holy cities', and until the hasidim arrived only very few Ashkenazim lived there.[107] The history of the Hebron hasidic community is tied to Habad hasidism and its proximity to Jerusalem. Differences between the Habad hasidim and all the other hasidic groups caused them to remain separate even after their arrival in the Land of Israel. The dispute between the founder of Habad, Rabbi Shneur Zalman of Liady, and the leader of the hasidim in Tiberias, Rabbi Avraham of Kalisk, which began at the end of the eighteenth century, also contributed to the isolation of the Habad hasidim, leading them to move to Safed in about 1800 and arrange separate funding for themselves.[108] In Habad more than in other hasidic groups, there was a connection between the organizational patterns of the court and the mechanism for collecting funds for hasidim in the Land of Israel.

In 1822 more Habad hasidim started moving to Hebron on the instructions of Rabbi Dov Ber of Lubavitch (1773–1827), Shneur Zalman's son. Like his father, Dov Ber was very involved in organizing support for the hasidim of the Land of Israel, and he was even arrested by Russian authorities for sending funds to the Ottoman community.[109] The first mention of a *pushke*, a special box for the collection of *halukah* funds, is in one of his letters from about 1815. The *pushke* encouraged individuals to donate domestically and was hence an expression of the growth and establishment of the system of support.[110] He prevailed on some of the greatest rabbis in Europe and the Pekidim Va'amarkalim to found an independent collection system for his hasidim in Hebron.[111] During this entire period, only a few non-Habad hasidim settled in Hebron, and the community's uniform Habad character meant that the frequent schisms and bitter conflicts that occurred in other communities were avoided.

A number of prominent Habad hasidim settled in Hebron, among them the printer Yisra'el Yoffe of Kapust (who printed the first hagiography concerning the Ba'al Shem Tov's life and the origins of hasidism, *Shivḥei habesht*, in 1814), Moshe Maizlish, a follower of Shneur Zalman, and Shimon Menashe Haikin, the rabbi of the community. The three of them led the Habad hasidim.[112] They embodied a new layer of leadership that enjoyed prestige within Habad and formed close personal connections with the *tsadik* and his court. During this period, the Habad community was based primarily on internal migration from Galilee and less on arrivals from the Habad strongholds in the northern parts of the Pale of Settlement or the regions of New Russia.[113]

Due to a reorganization of the Lubavitch court at the time of Rabbi Menahem Mendel Schneersohn (1789–1866), the third leader of Habad, who came to power in 1828, the number of Habad hasidim emigrating to the Land of Israel grew. This included several members of his extended family, among them his sister in-law, the daughter of Dov Ber, Menuhah Rahel (1798–1888), her husband Ya'akov Slonim, and their family, who became central figures in the community. Family members of Moshe (1784–1853), the youngest son of Shneur Zalman, who was mentally unstable and ultimately abandoned his faith in 1820, came to Hebron in 1843, and a few years later moved with other hasidim to Jerusalem.[114]

The Habad community in Jerusalem grew at the expense of the community in Hebron, which suffered financial and social hardships. In 1849 approximately thirty Habad families lived in Jerusalem, and they requested Moses Montefiore's assistance in building their own synagogue where they would be able to pray according to their unique customs.[115] Only in 1858 did they succeed, with the support of the Sassoon family of India, in establishing the Beit Menahem or Tsemah Tsedek Synagogue, named after their leader.[116] Among the first Habad hasidim in Jerusalem were Baruch Mordechai Etinger of Bobruisk and Eliyahu Yosef Rivlin of Płock, who was representative of the community until his death in 1865. He was an important rabbinical figure, who, because of his friendship with the leaders of the *persushim*, occasionally participated as judge in their *beit din*.[117]

The poverty of the Hebron community also stemmed from tensions with the Muslim majority in the city, especially in the 1850s during the days of the local ruler, Abdul Rahman, whom the Jews called 'the Black Rabbi'. The community was forced to pay excessive protection money, which undermined their already dire financial situation.[118] This situation did not change in the years following. The editor of *Havatselet*, Yisra'el Dov Frumkin, wrote:

My heart turns over inside me seeing the state of our brothers, the inhabitants of this city, and the many hardships that they endure every day, inflicted by the nations amongst whom they dwell . . . The situation of the Jews in Hebron is worse by far than the situation of a Jew in the other cities of Palestine.[119]

He described harsh economic competition, lack of personal safety, violent struggles between Jews and Muslims, and weak protection from the foreign consuls in Jerusalem or the coastal cities.[120] In the early years, the Habad hasidim gathered in a wing of the Sephardi Avraham Avinu synagogue, and they did not establish their own synagogue until 1853.[121] At approximately the same time, they established an educational institution in Montefiore's name, but unlike the Sephardi children in the city, who were taught general studies, the Habad children were not. The Habad leadership joined the conservative forces in the Yishuv who battled against any change in traditional education.[122]

Kolel Habad, consisting of only about 100 people, was established in 1872 and grew at a slower rate than other *kolelim*.[123] Despite the economic competition and social tension between them, the hasidim managed to reach a compromise with the Sephardi community and even to send joint emissaries to other Jewish communities in the Middle East and Europe.[124] Under the leadership of Menahem Mendel, Habad fundraising became an authoritative supra-communal institution, which even continued after his death in 1866 and the subsequent division of Habad hasidism into various courts established by his sons. Later, tensions arose between the hasidim in Hebron and those in Jerusalem, which reflected profound sociocultural divergences between newcomers, who settled mostly in Jerusalem, and the more established members in Hebron, who were already accustomed to local political realities, similar to those in Safed at the time. The struggles over the fundraising system reflected the decline of the Lubavitch court under Rabbi Shemu'el Schneersohn (1834–82), as his brother's activities (mainly in the courts of Kapust and Liady) overshadowed his own and weakened his court. It was his son, Shalom Dov Ber (1860–1920), who managed to rehabilitate the court in Lubavitch, in part through his reinvolvement in the Yishuv, which was combined with his extremist anti-Zionist ideology, but that goes beyond the chronological scope of this chapter.[125]

Conclusion

This brief review of the history of hasidic communities in the Land of Israel shows that they were a microcosm of the hasidic centres in eastern Europe and that the changes that shaped hasidism in the nineteenth century had a decisive impact on their development and their social and cultural character. The hasidim experienced themselves as belonging to a hasidic court and living under the patronage of a *tsadik*. In the words of Israel Bartal:

The hasidim of Kolel Vohlin—their bodies are in Safed, Tiberias, or Jerusalem, but their eyes are on Ruzhin or Sadagora. The different groups in the Land of Israel do not integrate into a whole 'nation'; rather, each group retains its uniqueness . . . in other words, the diasporas survived in the [holy] land.[126]

At the same time, the geopolitical contexts in Ottoman territory, the economic conditions, the ethnic and religious environment, the demographic structure, and everyday challenges all gradually shaped a complex and unique culture. As one of the Sephardi rabbis in Safed defined the community in his city: 'They have left Europe, but have not become Middle Eastern.'[127] This model of a distant community that preserved its way of life in new contexts influenced the development of Jewish Orthodoxy in the following years, as it faced increasingly greater challenges from accelerated processes of secularization, the nationalist movement, migration to the West, and more.

The hasidic presence in the Land of Israel was marginal and demographically insignificant compared to that of east European Jewry and the waves of migration that were to come. At the end of the period discussed here, they numbered only about 7,500. They were perceived, however, both at the time and in historical consciousness, as a significant factor in the introduction of the Land of Israel into the discourse about the future of the Jews and of Judaism. With the First Aliyah from 1881 to 1903, Jewish settlement in the Land of Israel entered a new era. The political and cultural campaign over the character of the Yishuv created a whole new world of images in which the society of previous immigrants and their descendants became the 'Old Yishuv', a feeble, anachronistic entity. It seems that the call for greater engagement with the history of the old will foster a better understanding of the new, as well as providing tools for a renewed and more balanced assessment of the differences between them.

Translated from the Hebrew by Naomi Stillman

Notes

1. M. Zalkin, '"Mekomot shelo matsah adayin haḥasidut ken lah kelal"? bein ḥasidim lemitnagedim belita bame'ah hatesha esreh', in I. Etkes, D. Assaf, I. Bartal, and E. Reines (eds.), *Bema'agalei ḥasidim: kovets meḥkarim lezikhro shel mordekhai wilensky* (Jerusalem, 1999), 21–50; S. Stampfer, 'How and Why did Hasidism Spread?', *Jewish History*, 27 (2013), 201–19.
2. M. Wodziński and U. Gellman, 'Toward a New Geography of Hasidism', *Jewish History*, 27 (2013), 171–99; M. Wodziński, *Historical Atlas of Hasidism* (Princeton, NJ, 2018), 22–4, 34–51.
3. S. Dubnow, 'Haḥasidim harishonim be'erets yisra'el', *Pardes*, 2 (1894), 201–11; S. A. Horodezky, 'Haḥasidim be'erets yisra'el', *Hashilo'aḥ*, 8 (1902), 486–97; I. Halpern, *Ha'aliyot harishonot shel haḥasidim le'erets yisra'el* (Jerusalem, 1947); B. Dinur, *Bemifneh hadorot* (Jerusalem, 1955), 69–79.
4. The state of research on hasidism in the Land of Israel in the nineteenth century is reflected in the absence of a chapter on the topic in the comprehensive book on the history of hasidism, of which I was a co-author (D. Biale, D. Assaf, B. Brown, U. Gellman, S. C. Heilman, M. Rosman, G. Sagiv, and M. Wodziński, *Hasidism: A New History* (Princeton, NJ, 2017)).
5. D. Assaf, 'Kevod elokim hester davar: perek nosaf bahistoryografyah ha'ortodoksit shel haḥasidut be'erets yisra'el', *Cathedra*, 68 (1993), 57–66; N. Karlinsky, 'The Dawn of Hasidic-Haredi Historiography', *Modern Judaism*, 27 (2007), 20–46.
6. Many letters have been published in hasidic books and periodicals, and many more are held in private and public collections. On letters of the hasidim as historical sources, see N. Karlinsky, *Historyah shekeneged. igerot haḥasidim me'erets yisra'el: hatekst vehakontekst* (Jerusalem, 1998).
7. Sir Moses Montefiore's censuses are an extremely important source in the history of the Jews of the Land of Israel ('Censuses': Montefiore Endowment website, visited 31 Mar. 2021; see M. Ben Ya'akov, 'Mifkedei montifyori veḥeker hayehudim be'agan hayam hatikhon', *Pa'amim*, 107 (2006), 117–49; D. Kessler, 'The Jewish Community in Nineteenth Century Palestine: Evidence from the Montefiore Censuses', *Middle Eastern Studies*, 52 (2016), 996–1010).
8. See e.g. A. Cohen, *Yehudim beveit hamishpat hamuslimi: ḥevrah kalkalah ve'irgun kehilati biyerushalayim ha'otomanit—hame'ah hatesha esreh* (Jerusalem, 2003); M. Eliav, *Britain and the Holy Land, 1838–1914: Selected Documents from the British Consulate in Jerusalem* (Jerusalem, 1997). A precise examination of the scope of relevant material in east European archives has not yet been carried out.
9. A. Yaari, *Masa'ot erets yisra'el* (Ramat Gan, 1976); I. Kalinowska, *Between East and West: Polish and Russian Nineteenth-Century Travel to the Orient* (Rochester, NY, 2004), 61–142; Y. Ben-Arieh, *The Making of Eretz Israel in the Modern Era: A Historical–Geographical*

Study (Jerusalem, 2020), 51–98; Y. Perry, *British Mission to the Jews in Nineteenth Century Palestine* (London, 2003); A. Jagodzińska, '"For Zion's Sake I Will Not Rest": The London Society for Promoting Christianity among the Jews and Its Nineteenth-Century Missionary Periodicals', *Church History*, 82 (2013), 381–7.

10 For example, the *pinkas* of the Pekidim Va'amarkalim contains important data about the history of the Jewish communities; however, only limited use has been made of it so far (*Pinkas pakuam*: Yad Izhak Ben-Zvi website, 'Resource Material: The Administrators and Clerks of Amsterdam—in Hebrew', visited 31 Mar. 2021; see also Allard Pierson website, visited 31 Mar. 2021).

11 A. Yaari, *Zikhronot erets yisra'el* (Jerusalem, 1983); Z. Aner, *Sipurei mishpaḥot: sipuran shel ḥamishim mishpaḥot betoledot hayishuv* (Tel Aviv, 1990).

12 D. Assaf, 'Press', in M. Wodziński (ed.), *Studying Hasidism: Sources, Methods, Perspectives* (New Brunswick, NJ, 2019), 164–77.

13 M. Idel, 'Erets yisra'el hu ḥayut mehabore b"h', in A. Ravitzky (ed.), *Erets yisra'el bahagut hayehudit ba'et haḥadashah* (Jerusalem, 1998), 256–75; U. Gellman, *Hashevilim hayotse'im milublin: tsemiḥatah shel haḥasidut bepolin* (Jerusalem, 2018), 105–21.

14 Y. Ben-Arieh and I. Bartal (eds.), *Hahistoryah shel erets yisra'el: shilhei hatekufah ha'otomanit (1799–1917)* (Jerusalem, 1983), 194–6.

15 See C. Bloom, 'The Institution of Halukah: A Historical Review', *Jewish Historical Studies*, 36 (1999–2000), 1–30.

16 For the proportions of individuals fully engaged in Torah study among the Ashkenazi Yishuv based on the Montefiore censuses, see Kessler, 'The Jewish Community in Nineteenth Century Palestine', 1005–6; on the *halukah* funds, see I. Bartal, *Kozak uvedui: am ve'erets bale'umiyut hayehudit* (Tel Aviv, 2007), 170–87.

17 A. Morgenstern, *Ge'ulah bederekh hateva: talmidei hagera be'erets yisra'el, 1800–1840* (Jerusalem, 1988), 389–409; I. Bartal, *Galut ba'arets: yishuv erets yisra'el beterem hatsiyonut* (Jerusalem, 1994), 64–73.

18 I. Bartal, 'Moses Montefiore: Nationalist before His Time or Belated Shtadlan?', *Studies in Zionism*, 11 (1990), 111–25; A. Green, 'Rethinking Sir Moses Montefiore: Religion, Nationhood, and International Philanthropy in the Nineteenth Century', *American Historical Review*, 110 (2005), 631–58; Y. Ben-Ghedalia, 'Empowerment: Tzedakah, Philanthropy and Inner Jewish Shtadlanut', *Jewish Culture and History*, 19 (2018), 71–8.

19 D. Assaf, *The Regal Way: The Life and Times of Rabbi Israel of Ruzhin* (Stanford, Calif., 2002), 187–211.

20 See A. Rapoport-Albert, *Hasidic Studies: Essays in History and Gender* (Liverpool, 2018), 318–67; M. Wodziński, *Hasidism: Key Questions* (New York, 2018), 43–86; T. Kauffman, 'Hasidic Women: Beyond Egalitarianist Discourse', in A. E. Mayse and A. Green (eds.), *Be-Ron Yahad: Studies in Jewish Thought and Theology in Honor of Nehemia Polen* (Boston, Mass., 2019), 223–57.

21 No study has yet been written exclusively about women or gender issues in hasidic society in the Old Yishuv. For women in the Yishuv in general, see M. Shilo, *Princess or Prisoner? Jewish Women in Jerusalem 1840–1914* (Waltham, Mass., 2005). Among hasidic women in Jerusalem, Khane-Rokhl Werbermacher, 'the Maiden of Ludmir', who arrived in Jerusalem around 1859, became famous, but she was definitely an exceptional case (see N. Deutsch, *The Maiden of Ludmir: A Jewish Holy Woman and Her World* (Berkeley, Calif., 2003), 190–211).

22 I. Etkes, *Rabbi Shneur Zalman of Liady: The Origins of Chabad Hasidism* (Waltham, Mass., 2014), 9–21.

23 A. Morgenstern, *Hastening Redemption: Messianism and the Resettlement of the Land of Israel* (Oxford, 2006), 51–76.
24 Morgenstern, *Ge'ulah bederekh hateva*, 112–91; A. Morgenstern, *Hashivah liyerushalayim: ḥidush hayishuv hayehudi be'erets yisra'el bereshit hame'ah hatesha esreh* (Jerusalem, 2007), 245–62; R. Manekin, 'Maskilei lemberg ve'erets yisra'el: al parashah lo yeduah mishenat 1816', *Cathedra*, 130 (2008), 31–50.
25 S. Karagila, *Hayishuv hayehudi be'erets yisra'el bitekufat hakibush hamitsri (1831–1840)* (Tel Aviv, 1990).
26 Bartal, *Galut ba'arets*, 41–8.
27 J. Frankel, *The Damascus Affair: 'Ritual Murder', Politics, and the Jews in 1840* (Cambridge, 1997), 109–84.
28 A. J. Brawer, 'Reshit hashimush bizekhut hakapitulatsyot al yedei yehudim be'erets yisra'el', *Zion*, 5 (1940), 169–91; I. Friedman, 'Mishtar hakapitulatsyot veyaḥasah shel turkiyah le'aliyah ulehityashevut, 1856–1897', *Cathedra*, 28 (1983), 47–62; M. Maoz, 'Changes in the Position of the Jewish Communities of Palestine and Syria in the Mid-Nineteenth Century', in id. (ed.), *Studies on Palestine during the Ottoman Period* (Jerusalem, 1975), 142–63.
29 J. Finn, *Stirring Times: or, Records from Jerusalem Consular Chronicles of 1853–1856*, 2 vols. (London, 1878), i. 112–13; ii. 57; J. Hoffman, 'A Memorandum from the Russian Jews in Safed and Tiberias to Sir Moses Montefiore (1863)', *Nordisk Judaistik*, 6 (1985), 75–83.
30 R. Kark, 'Changing Patterns of Landownership in Nineteenth-Century Palestine: The European Influence', *Journal of Historical Geography*, 10 (1984), 357–84.
31 See e.g. I. Harari, '"The Arab Clothes of Our Forefathers": Articulating Ashkenazi Palestinian Jewish Identity through Dress and Language', *Contemporanea*, 20 (2017), 569–86.
32 N. Karlinsky, 'Haḥevrah haḥasidit shel tsefat bamaḥatsit hasheniyah shel hame'ah hatesha esreh keḥevrat mehagerim: hebetim demografiyim vegibush ḥevrati', in I. Etkes, D. Assaf, and Y. Dan (eds.), *Meḥkerei ḥasidut* (Jerusalem, 1999), 162–71.
33 U. Schmaltz, 'Kavim meyuḥadim bademografyah shel yehudei yerushalayim bame'ah hatesha esreh', in Y. Ben-Porat, B. Z. Yehoshua, and A. Kedar, *Perakim betoledot hayishuv hayehudi biyerushalayim*, 2 vols. (Jerusalem, 1973–6), ii. 52–76; H. N. Shiff, 'Hademografyah shel hakehilah ha'ashkenazit bitsefat: mifkedei montefiori bishenat 5609 (1849)', *Cathedra*, 146 (2012), 67–100.
34 H. Shteiman-Katz, *Reshitan shel aliyot haḥasidim* (Jerusalem, 1987), 11–20; A. J. Heschel, *The Circle of the Baal Shem Tov* (Chicago, 1985), 44–112.
35 D. Assaf, 'Sheyatsa shemuah sheba mashiaḥ ben david: or ḥadash al aliyat haḥasidim bishenat 5537', *Zion*, 61 (1996), 319–46. Many studies have dealt with the motivations for the immigration of these hasidim (see I. Etkes, 'On the Motivation for Hasidic Immigration (Aliyah) to the Land of Israel', *Jewish History*, 27 (2013), 337–51; A. Morgenstern, 'Hameni'im la'aliyot haḥasidim le'erets yisrael', *Zion*, 76 (2011), 127–38).
36 M. Wilensky, *Hayishuv haḥasidi biteveryah* (Jerusalem, 1988).
37 Karlinsky, 'Haḥevrah haḥasidit shel tsefat', 158–9.
38 D. Assaf, 'Mivoḥlin litsefat: deyokeno shel avraham dov me'ovrutsh kemanhig ḥasidi bemaḥatsit harishonah shel hame'ah hatesha esreh', *Shalem*, 6 (1992), 223–79. On immigration from Galicia, see N. M. Gelber, 'Aliyat yehudim mibohemyah vegalitsyah le'erets yisra'el', *Meḥkarei erets yisra'el*, 4 (1953), 243–51.
39 Morgenstern, *Ge'ulah bederekh hateva*, 439–49; on the initiatives of the Bak family, see I. Bak, 'Et ledaber', *Ḥavatselet*, 11 Jan. 1872, pp. 1–2; Bartal, *Galut ba'arets*, 119; E. R. Malachi, 'Letoledot beit ha'arigah shel montifyori', in S. Belkin (ed.), *Abraham Weiss Jubilee Volume* (New York, 1964), 441–59.

40 M. M. Boim, *Korot ha'itim liyeshurun* (Vilna, 1839), 19; see also Assaf, 'Mivohlin litsefat'.
41 Assaf, 'Mivohlin litsefat', 252–6.
42 U. Gellman, *Sefer ḥasidim: ḥibur ganuz bigenutah shel haḥasidut* (Jerusalem, 2007), 25–9.
43 Montefiore Library, London, Ms. 575, 34g: anon., letter to Moses Montefiore (n.d.); cited in Assaf, 'Mivohlin litsefat', 255.
44 *Tikatev zot ledor aḥaron* (Jerusalem, 1845).
45 S. Karagila, 'Igeret r. shemu'el bar yisra'el perets heler be'inyan bizat tsefat bishenat 5594 (1834)', *Cathedra*, 27 (1983), 109–16; M. Abir, 'Hamered bitsefat vehaperaot bakehilah hayehudit (1834)', *Ariel*, 208 (2015), 86–90.
46 I. Ben-Zvi, *Meḥkarim umekorot* (Jerusalem, 1969), 114–18.
47 Assaf, 'Mivohlin litsefat', 149–51.
48 I. Ben-Zvi, 'Me'oraot tsefat mibizat 5594 ve'ad meridat hadruzim bishenat 5598', *Sefunot*, 7 (1963), 275–322; M. Eliav, 'Edut re'iyah al moraot hara'ash bitsefat 5597', *Cathedra*, 79 (1996), 53–78.
49 For varying estimates of the number of dead, see Morgenstern, *Hastening Redemption*, 87–8.
50 See R. Ambon, 'Harav shemu'el heler (1803–1884) umekomo bakehilah hayehudit', Ph.D. thesis (Tel Aviv University, 2016).
51 Ibid. 82–92.
52 Shiff, 'Hademografyah shel hakehilah ha'ashkenazit bitsefat'; R. Ambon, 'Ta'alumat ha-mifkad hakaful: madua hegishah hakehilah ha'ashkenazit bitsefat lemontifyori be 5609 (1849) shenei mifkadim?', *Cathedra*, 149 (2013), 153–66.
53 See E. Davidson, 'Me'ah shenot pe'ilut "kolel varshah" biyerushalayim ha'atikah (1848–1948)', in I. Rozenson and Y. Spanier (eds.), *Minḥat sapir* (Rehovot, 2013), 423–46.
54 Ambon, 'Harav shemu'el heler', 126–48.
55 Y. Kaniel, *Bema'avar: hayehudim be'erets yisrael bame'ah hatesha esreh* (Jerusalem, 2000), 228–42; Bartal, *Galut ba'arets*, 100–60.
56 Ambon, 'Harav shemu'el heler', 190–217.
57 Ibid. 181–6, 215–16.
58 See ibid. 251–324.
59 See D. Assaf, *Hetsits venifga: anatomyah shel maḥloket ḥasidit* (Haifa, 2012), 232–3.
60 Ibid. 239–51.
61 Ibid. 232; G. Sagiv, *Hashoshelet: beit tshernobyl umekomo betoledot haḥasidut* (Jerusalem, 2014), 172–7.
62 Y. Geller, 'Kolel moldavya vevalakhyah be'erets yisrael', *Cathedra*, 59 (1991), 56–82.
63 Very little is known about Bratslav hasidism in the Land of Israel before the end of the nineteenth century. In 1894 Rabbi Avraham Hazan (1849–1917) settled in Jerusalem. He was an important connection between the Bratslav community in Ukraine and the one in Galilee (see D. Assaf, *Breslav: bibliyografyah mu'eret* (Jerusalem, 2000), 13).
64 S. Y. Agnon, *Temol shilshom* (Jerusalem, 1969), 500–1; see also Assaf, *Hetsits venifga*, 240; A. Zederbaum (Erez), 'Ed beshaḥak ne'eman', *Hamelits*, 14 Nov. 1870, pp. 1–4; M. Eilbaum, *Erets hatsevi* (Jerusalem, 1982), 74–5; Y. Stepansky, 'Batei keneset ha'ashkenazim bitsefat bame'ot hashemonah esreh vehatesha esreh: meḥkar rishoni', *Al atar*, 19 (2017), 57–89.
65 B. Panteliat, 'Ḥakhamim verabanim bakehilah ha'ashkenazit biteveryah', *Kovets ḥitsei giborim*, 9 (2016), 875–92.
66 W. Rabinowitsch, *Haḥasidut halita'it* (Jerusalem, 1961), 76–8; A. Shor, *Ketavim: pirkei toladot ve'iyun bemishnat karlin–stolin* (Jerusalem, 2018), 14–27.

67 A. Suraski, *Yesod hama'aleh: divrei hayamim leyishuv hahasidim be'erets yisra'el*, 2 vols. (Benei Berak, 1991), i. 239–53; see also Assaf, 'Kevod elokim hester davar'.
68 Suraski, *Yesod hama'aleh*, i. 321–79.
69 A different synagogue, which served Rabbi Avraham of Kalisk, had already been renovated in the 1840s, and a Karlin synagogue was established in Safed in 1870 (see Shor, *Ketavim*, 1–6, 14–41, 47–49; B. Brown, *Kisefinah mitaltelet: hasidut karlin bein aliyot lemashberim* (Jerusalem, 2018), 95–6, 98–100).
70 The appointees of Kolel Vohlin submitted an irate letter against the Karlin hasidim to Montefiore (see Shor, *Ketavim*, 160).
71 Shor, *Ketavim*, 152–60; G. Sagiv, 'Yenuka: al tsadikim viyeladim bahasidut', *Zion*, 76 (2011), 154–5.
72 Y. D. Frumkin, 'Eharat hamol', *Havatselet*, 14 Mar. 1878, p. 3. In an independent census conducted by the new *kolel* in 1875, forty-five families were counted (eighty people in Tiberias and approximately sixty in Jerusalem), most of them from Polesie (see Shor, *Ketavim*, 164–80).
73 Y. D. Frumkin, 'Od pa'am beharei hagalil', *Havatselet*, 12 Sept. 1889, p. 2. For more on cultural battles in hasidic Tiberias, see I. Freidin, 'Nisyonot rishonim lahakamat beit-holim biteveryah bame'ah hatesha esreh', *Cathedra*, 22 (1982), 91–112; E. R. Malachi, *Mineged tireh* (Jerusalem, 2001), 289–314.
74 E. Ben Shimon-Pikali, 'Hurvat rav yehudah hehasid biyerushalayim: mibinyan lehurban, 1622–1720', in R. Gafni, A. Morgenstern, and D. Cassuto (eds.), *Hahurvah* (Jerusalem, 2010), 11–31; J. Barnai, *The Jews in Palestine in the Eighteenth Century: Under the Patronage of the Istanbul Committee of Officials for Palestine* (Tuscaloosa, Ala., 1992), 109–47.
75 A. Green, *Tormented Master: The Life and Spiritual Quest of Rabbi Nahman of Bratslav* (Woodstock, Vt., 1992), 63–94. His student, Rabbi Natan of Nemirov, also did not visit Jerusalem during his visit in 1822.
76 On the hasidic community in Jerusalem in the nineteenth century, see U. Gellman, 'Hahasidim biyerushalayim bame'ah hatesha esreh', in R. Gafni, Y. Ben-Ghedalia, and U. Gellman (eds.), *Gavoha me'al gavoha: beit hakeneset tiferet yisra'el vehakekilah hahasidit biyerushalayim* (Jerusalem, 2016), 11–30.
77 *Igerot hapekidim veha'amarkalim me'amsterdam*, ed. Y. Y. Rivlin and B. Rivlin, 2 vols. (Jerusalem, 1965–70), i. 195; see also A. L. Frumkin, *Toledot hakhmei yerushalayim*, 3 vols. (Jerusalem, 1929), iii. 153; B. Landau, 'Hayishuv hahasidi biyerushalayim mereshito', *Mahanayim*, 58 (1961), 70–81.
78 M. Wilensky, *Hasidim umitnagedim* (Jerusalem, 1990), 314–18.
79 Frumkin, *Toledot hakhmei yerushalayim*, iii. 138–9; Morgenstern, *Hashivah liyerushalayim*, 11–49.
80 *Igerot hapekidim veha'amarkalim me'amsterdam*, i. 86–7.
81 *The Jewish Expositor and Friend of Israel*, 7 (1822); cited in Morgenstern, *Hashivah liyerushalayim*, 39.
82 See Rabbi Aharon Moshe's letters (Naftali Zvi of Ropshits, *Imrei shefer* (Lemberg, 1884), 15b; M. Y. Gutman, *Migiborei hahasidut: rabi dov mileova* (Tel Aviv, 1952), 35).
83 H. Assouline, *Mifkad yehudei erets yisrael, 1839* (Jerusalem, 1987), 169–70; Y. Ben-Arieh, *Ir bire'i tekufah: yerushalayim bame'ah hatesha esreh. ha'ir ha'atikah* (Jerusalem, 1977), 305–8. A few years later approximately a hundred hasidim were counted in Jerusalem, but this number includes an unknown number of visitors from Galilee (see J. Wilson, *The Land of the Bible Visited and Described* (Edinburgh, 1847), 455).

84 For Rabbi Yisra'el of Ruzhin's activity on behalf of the hasidic settlement, see Assaf, *The Regal Way*, 202–12. The regard and admiration for him can be seen in a letter from Rabbi Aharon Moshe in which he describes a mystical–messianic experience he had in 1840 in which Rabbi Yisra'el appeared (see D. Rabinowitz, 'Perakim betoledot beit hakeneset tiferet yisra'el', *Tiferet yisra'el*, 20 (1988), 19–20). On messianic anticipation in 1840, see Morgenstern, *Ge'ulah bederekh hateva*, 23–50.

85 I. Bak, *Moda'at zot* (Jerusalem, 1841); P. M. Grajewsky, *Beit hadefus harishon biyerushalayim* (Jerusalem, 1939); M. Benayahu, 'Beit defuso shel r. yisra'el bak bitsefat vereshit hadefus biyerushalyim', *Areshet*, 4 (1986), 271–95; S. Halevy, *Sifrei yerushalayim harishonim* (Jerusalem, 1976), 15–26.

86 Morgenstern, *Ge'ulah bederekh hateva*, 307–26; Y. Ben-Ghedalia, '"Lo miduvshaikh velo miuktsaikh": pulmus lemel (5616) kinekudat mifneh beyahas haperushim letikunim behinukh', in I. Rozenson and Y. Rivlin (eds.), *Talmidei hagera be'erets yisra'el: historyah, hagut, re'alyah* (Jerusalem, 2010), 68–71.

87 Assaf, *The Regal Way*, 192; Morgenstern, *Hashivah liyerushalayim*, 320.

88 Josef Pizzamano, Austrian consul in Jerusalem, memo, 31 Dec. 1849, in *Österreich und das Heilige Land: Ausgewählte Konsulatsdokumente aus Jerusalem, 1849–1917*, ed. M. Eliav (Vienna, 2000), 118.

89 Assaf, *Hetsits venifga*, 234–51.

90 Wilson, *The Land of the Bible*, 454–5; see also H. Horwitz, *Ḥibat yerushalayim* (Jerusalem, 1844), 40a; 'Shelom yerushalayim', *Ḥavatselet*, 26 July 1872, p. 1. Before the establishment of Tiferet Yisra'el, there were a few small hasidic synagogues (see M. N. Kahanov, *Sha'alu shelom yerushalayim* (Jerusalem, 1878), 7–11; I. Goldman, 'Hashkafah kelalit al matsav benei yisra'el be'erets hakodesh', *Ha'asif*, 3 (1887), 84).

91 Yisrael of Ruzhin, *Igerot harav hakadosh miruzhin uvanav*, ed. D. B. Rabinowitz, 3 vols. (Jerusalem, 2003), ii. 86–7.

92 'Shelom yerushalayim', *Ḥavatselet*, 7 Oct. 1870, p. 2.

93 'Ḥanukat beit hakeneset hamefo'ar tiferet yisra'el', *Ḥavatselet*, 23 Aug. 1872, pp. 1–3.

94 Educational institutions were also opened there (see *Sefer haḥukim leḥevrat hatalmud torah viyeshivat ḥukei ḥayim beveit keneset tiferet yisra'el* (Jerusalem, 1887)).

95 Y. L. Orenstein, *Tal yerushalayim* (Jerusalem, 1873), 21.

96 'Et besorah', *Ḥavatselet*, 30 July 1863, p. 3; *Kunteres emet umishpat* (Jerusalem, 1863), 21.

97 Frumkin, *Toledot ḥakhmei yerushalayim*, iii. 248.

98 R. Beer, *Al ḥomot haneyar: iton halevanon veha'ortodoksyah* (Jerusalem, 2017), 38–43.

99 Malachi, *Mineged tireh*, 98–212.

100 Z. Ilan, 'Reshitah shel haḥavatselet' (5623) im giluyam shel ḥameshet hagilyonot harishonim', *Cathedra*, 7 (1978), 7–47.

101 'Shelom yerushalayim', *Ḥavatselet*, 9 Aug. 1872, p. 1; U. Gellman, 'Chasydyzm Lelów w Ziemi Izraela', in M. Galas and M. Skrzypczyk (eds.), *Wieża Dawida: Chasydzi lelowscy* (Kraków, 2018), 29–37.

102 *Zot torat habayit* (Jerusalem, 1929), 5–13; Y. Salmon, 'Haḥinukh ha'ashkenazi be'erets yisra'el bein "hayashan" la"ḥadash" (1840–1906)', *Shalem*, 6 (1992), 281–301.

103 'Mikerev ha'arets', *Hatsevi*, 9 July 1886, p. 1; Y. Ben-Arieh, *Ir bire'i tekufah: yerushalayim haḥadashah bereshitah* (Jerusalem, 1979), 264–6.

104 They were Hod (Holand Vedaytshland), Varshah, Suvalk, Vilnah Vezamoshtsh, Horodnah, Slonim, Minsk, Reisen, Shomerei Hahomot (Hungary), Vohlin, Ostriyah, and Habad (Ben-Arieh, *Ir bire'i tekufah: yerushalayim haḥadashah bereshitah*, 404).

105 See *Ḥok olam: mishpetei tsedek mipesak beit din hagadol shebiyerushalayim* (Jerusalem, 1892).
106 L. Shreiber, *Ḥasid shel erets yisra'el: sipur ḥayav shel r. nisan bak* (Jerusalem, 2018), 134–47.
107 M. Ish-Shalom, 'Al hayishuv hayehudi beḥevron lefi mekorot notṣeriyim', in M. Benayahu (ed.), *Sefer zikaron le yitsḥak ben-tsevi* (Jerusalem, 1964), 337–59.
108 Shneur Zalman of Liady, *Igerot kodesh, admor hazaken*, ed. S. D. Levine (Brooklyn, 2012), 375; I. Lurie, *Milḥamot lubavitsh* (Jerusalem, 2018), 128–32.
109 S. D. Levine, *Ma'asar uge'ulat admor ha'emtsa'i* (Brooklyn, 1998).
110 Dov Ber Schneersohn, *Igerot kodesh, admor ha'emtsa'i*, ed. S. D. Levine (Brooklyn, 2013), 117; S. Stampfer, *Families, Rabbis and Education: Traditional Jewish Society in Nineteenth-Century Eastern Europe* (Oxford, 2010), 102–20.
111 Dov Ber Schneersohn, *Igerot kodesh*, 169–71, 220; Y. Mondstein, *Migdal oz* (Kfar Habad, 1980), 526–7.
112 Y. Gur-Aryeh, *Ḥasidut ḥabad beḥevron: mereshit hayishuv be'erets yisra'el ad shenat 1866* (Lehavot Habashan, 2001), 26–65.
113 Lurie, *Milḥamot lubavitsh*, 134–6.
114 S. D. Levine, *Toledot ḥabad be'erets hakodesh* (Brooklyn, 1988), 78; D. Assaf, *Untold Tales of the Hasidim: Crisis and Discontent in the History of Hasidism* (Hanover, NH, 2010), 40; Lurie, *Milḥamot lubavitsh*, 136–40. According to Amram Blau, the family went directly to Jerusalem (A. Blau, 'Yaḥasei hagomelin bein haḥasidim vehaperushim talmidei hagaon mivilna biyerushalayim uve'erets hakodesh', *Heikhal habesht*, 25 (2009), 143–4).
115 Levine, *Toledot ḥabad be'erets hakodesh*, 195.
116 S. Z. Mendelovich, *Zikhron yerushalayim* (Jerusalem, 1876).
117 In 1875 there were about 300 Habad hasidim in Jerusalem and they extended their synagogue ('Layesharim na'avah tehilah', *Ḥavatselet*, 11 July 1879, pp. 3–4; see also Blau, 'Yaḥasei hagomelin', 145–6).
118 Gur-Aryeh, *Ḥasidut ḥabad beḥevron*, 189–90.
119 Y. D. Frumkin, "Ḥevron', *Ḥavatselet*, 27 Oct. 1876, p. 3.
120 On the involvement of the British and Austrian consuls, see Gur-Aryeh, *Ḥasidut ḥabad beḥevron*, 193–211.
121 Mendelovich, *Zikhron yerushalayim*, 9; Levine, *Toledot ḥabad be'erets hakodesh*, 87.
122 See e.g. E. Y. Rivlin, *Ohalei yosef* (Jerusalem, 1868), 17–18; *Lahat haḥerev* (Jerusalem, 1873).
123 *Igerot hapekidim veha'amarkalim me'amsterdam*, i. 176; Assouline, *Mifkad yehudei erets yisra'el*, 183–7; O. Avissar, 'Mifkad toshavei ḥevron hayehudim 1855, 1866, 1875', in id. (ed.), *Sefer ḥevron* (Jerusalem, 1970), 77–8; Levine, *Toledot ḥabad be'erets hakodesh*, 44–6.
124 M. Shapira, 'Adat ḥasidei ḥabad beḥevron', in H. Z. Hirschberg (ed.), *Vatikin* (Ramat Gan, 1975), 116–67; Levine, *Toledot ḥabad be'erets hakodesh*, 58–61; Gur-Aryeh, *Ḥasidut ḥabad beḥevron*, 48–57.
125 On the later period of Habad, see Lurie, *Milḥamot lubavitsh*, 140–79.
126 Bartal, *Galut ba'arets*, 15.
127 M. Sithon, *Kenesiyah leshem shamayim* (Jerusalem, 1874), 199; cited in Ambon, 'Harav shemu'el heler', 138.

Polish Distinctiveness in Jerusalem, Congress Poland, and Western Prussia in the Nineteenth Century

YOCHAI BEN-GHEDALIA

Introduction

In the nineteenth century the Yishuv, the Jewish population of the Land of Israel, was made up primarily of first-, second-, and third-generation immigrants who preserved ideological, social, and financial ties with their communities of origin. The financial bond was especially significant, given that a substantial portion of the Yishuv's economy was based on donations from diaspora communities and individuals. Donations were distributed by means of community structures known as *kolelim*. On the eve of the First World War, which ultimately brought an end to the Old Yishuv, there were over a hundred *kolelim* in Jerusalem alone, differentiated by the immigrants' city or region of origin, such as Kolel Pinsk or Kolel Minsk.

A hundred years earlier the situation in Jerusalem was very different, with only a single, unified Jewish community in the city. Much has been written about the division of east European Jewish communities into two or three communities, primarily against the backdrop of differing religious tendencies. The fragmentation of the Jerusalem community, especially its east European elements, into over a hundred communities similar in religious practice demands explanation.

The focus of this chapter is on the establishment of Kolel Varshah in Jerusalem by immigrants from Congress Poland. This was not the first *kolel* to take an independent turn, but it opened the floodgates for the establishment of independent *kolelim* among east European Jewish immigrants.[1] The first part of this chapter will address the establishment of Kolel Varshah and the crisis it faced only a few years afterwards. While the rise and (temporary) fall of Kolel Varshah occurred in Jerusalem, it was the result of administrative decisions made in Congress Poland. I will then consider, in the light of the crisis of Kolel Varshah, whether there was such a thing as Polish particularism and whether outside observers, in this case the Jews of England, were able to identify such particularism. I will show that the Jews of the British Isles did not see the crisis as specific to the *kolel* but rather as a problem throughout the Yishuv or even as part of the international crisis at the height of the Crimean War. In the third and final part of the chapter I will examine the 'Polishness' of Jewish Orthodoxy in western Prussia (Prussian Poland) approximately sixty years after the last partition of Poland, as revealed in the crisis of Jerusalem's Kolel Varshah.

The Rise and (Temporary) Fall of Kolel Varshah

The Land of Israel in the nineteenth century was an anomalous immigration destination for European Jews. Although the number of immigrants was not negligible, it was tiny compared to internal migrations to urban centres, and certainly so compared to migration to the New World. The main difference between these migrations, however, was their motive. A significant number of *olim* (Jewish immigrants to the Holy Land) had no financial motivation to immigrate; they moved to the Holy Land for religious reasons. Many devoted their lives to prayer and Torah study in proximity to the holy sites, in a Yishuv that was a vestigial island of piety in a changing world. Still, even these *olim* needed financial support, and, like their counterparts in the Christian world, they received it by way of contributions from abroad, known as *ḥalukah* funds. The *ḥalukah* system represented a significant source of income for the Yishuv. Some migrants to the Holy Land secured a source of personal income before immigrating, but most of the community's financial support was transmitted to the *kolelim*; the *kolelim*, in turn, distributed the funds to their members and institutions. This was how the *ḥalukah* system functioned, and, in doing so, it bound the Jews of the Holy Land to their co-religionists in Europe.

Funds originating in the Russian empire had to circumvent tsarist laws to reach their intended recipients in the Yishuv. As would be expected of an economy based on mercantilist principles, the tsarist empire forbade the transfer of money abroad. Transferring it to the Jewish settlement in the Land of Israel was especially problematic, as it was part of the Ottoman empire, Russia's enemy. Because of the ban, Jewish fundraising networks operated secretly throughout the nineteenth century.[2] A significant change occurred in 1836 in Congress Poland, which was part of the Russian empire, when Count Ivan Paskevich officially sanctioned the collection of funds for the Jews in the Land of Israel.[3] A formal fundraising programme was established in Warsaw, and a network of collectors fanned out across Poland. The centre submitted reports of its activities to the Ministry of Religious Denominations and Public Enlightenment, and reported contributions of thousands of roubles annually. Other sources, including government authorities, estimated that the sums of money collected were even greater.[4]

The authorization to collect funds brought an increase in donations to the Yishuv, but Count Paskevich's ruling had another consequence of greater impact on the Ashkenazi community in the Land of Israel which changed the structure of the Yishuv. At the beginning of the nineteenth century the Jewish population in the four holy cities of the Land of Israel was predominantly Sephardi. Their representative body, Kolelot Hasefardim, was part of the fabric of local government under the Ottoman empire. The few Ashkenazi Jews in the cities were absorbed into the Sephardi *kolel* system. Donations were sent by fundraising emissaries and centres in Istanbul and, later, Amsterdam, and delivered to Kolelot Hasefardim. During the first third of the century, thanks to the protection they received from various European consuls, the Ashkenazi Jews broke away from the Sephardi community and formed an alternative system. As subjects of foreign governments, the Ashkenazi Jews were no longer *rayah*, non-Muslim subjects of the Ottoman empire. Once excluded from the Ottoman system, they were not obliged to belong to the Sephardi community. They created an alternative system, on a voluntary basis, which was also called a *kolel*. Despite the shared name, the two frameworks were entirely different from one another—one traditional and part of a corporate structure; the other more recent in origin and a product of a secular society.[5]

The initial divisions among the Jews from eastern Europe naturally and organically reflected the familiar religious and social division between hasidim and *mitnagedim*. The transition to voluntary membership in *kolelim*, however, soon encouraged the establishment of new *kolelim* whenever financial or other considerations justified it.[6] The first was Kolel Hod (Holand Vedaytshland), founded by Jews from Holland and Germany, who left their original *kolelim* at the end of the 1830s and established a new one to control the funds received from central Europe.

The establishment of an organized and official fundraising centre in Congress Poland after Count Paskevich's authorization encouraged the founding of another voluntary *kolel*—Kolel Varshah—in 1848. This *kolel* was established for utilitarian purposes, and, as can be seen from the composition of the group, it did not reflect the usual religious and social divisions. It included hasidim and *mitnagedim*, whose common ground was their region of origin. These regions, in turn, corresponded to the regions from which the funds were collected. Religiously and socially, the *mitnagedim* and the hasidim continued to function separately, praying in their distinct synagogues and retaining their separate administrative structures. Arie Morgenstern notes the relatively good relations between the money-collecting centres of the *perushim* (disciples of the Vilna Gaon who settled in the Land of Israel at the beginning of the nineteenth century) and the hasidim in Congress Poland, a relationship that culminated in the establishment of the joint fundraising centre in Warsaw. He attributes the collaboration between *perushim* and hasidim in Kolel Varshah to this relationship. He also ascribes the creation of a separate Kolel Varshah to the Polish immigrants' sense that the *perushim* favoured the Lithuanian Jews and did not distribute funds equitably.[7] It is quite possible that the relative tolerance in Warsaw planted the seeds for the co-operation between the hasidim and the *perushim* and that the Polish immigrants, feeling that they were not treated fairly, intensified their push to create a separate *kolel*. I would argue, rather, that the main reason for the establishment of Kolel Varshah was to gain control over regional funds and to create a bond between the fundraising centre in Europe and the *kolel* in Jerusalem.

Morgenstern mentions an earlier attempt by the three Levi brothers, Rabbi Asher Lemel of Galin, Rabbi Nahum of Szadek, and Rabbi Ya'akov Yehudah Leib of Ślesin, to guarantee their own financial survival in Jerusalem before they migrated there in 1845. All three later became prominent members of Kolel Varshah. While the practice of arranging financial support before immigration was not a new one, the Levi brothers were unique in aiming to establish a new community framework known as

Kolel Galin. They were unsuccessful, but their initiative demonstrates the strategy of the immigrants from Poland splitting off from the traditional *kolelim*.[8]

Kolel Hod was the first *kolel* to be established on a regional basis, but it was Kolel Varshah that paved the way for the development of the many small regional *kolelim* among east European immigrants, while there were no further divisions among the central European immigrants, with the exception of the Hungarians. Thus, on the eve of the First World War there were over a hundred *kolelim* in Jerusalem, many tiny and barely viable. As mentioned, these divisions were made possible because Ashkenazi immigrants were not subjects of the Ottoman empire and therefore were not answerable to the official Ottoman agency for Jewish matters, the Kolelot Hasefardim.

Additional evidence can be gleaned from a comparison of the Ashkenazi and the Sephardi communities. While the Ashkenazi community continued to divide and subdivide, among the Sephardi Jews, only groups that were not part of the Ottoman empire broke off—these included North African (French or Moroccan), Persian, Bukharan, and Georgian Jews.

In the early nineteenth century, the main centre for the collection of funds, the Pekidim Va'amarkalim (Clerks and Administrators), was based in Amsterdam. It waged a battle, without great success, against the regionalization of the *kolelim*. From its point of view, the Jews of the Land of Israel formed a single entity and the collection of funds should be concentrated in one place and then divided proportionately between the communities. The Pekidim Va'amarkalim did not oppose the private support of individuals by their families or communities of origin, but when other groups tried to claim funds intended for the Land of Israel it objected. Despite the Pekidim Va'amarkalim's sympathy for the Jews from Warsaw in Jerusalem, and the ideological affinity between the two ultra-Orthodox entities, it deliberately avoided using the term *kolel* for the Warsaw initiative, referring to it instead as the *anshei varshah*, 'the people of Warsaw'. In addition, the Pekidim Va'amarkalim could not transfer designated funds to the new organization until the writing of a new *pesher*, an agreement updated approximately every decade dealing with the distribution of funds among the *kolelim*. Until the new agreement became operative, the immigrants from Warsaw continued to receive their funds from Amsterdam via the *kolelim* of the hasidim and the *perushim*.[9] In addition to the ideological principle of the unity of the Jews of the Land of Israel and the Pekidim Va'amarkalim's wish to control the donations, the Dutch bankers, Lehren, who headed the agency, were guided by financial considerations of risk management, and the wish not to depend on fundraising from a single source.

The Pekidim Va'amarkalim's strategy was soon proved right. In 1848 two fundraising emissaries from the Polish Jews in Jerusalem—Rabbis David Tevia Yellin and Ya'akov Yehudah Leib Levi—arrived in Warsaw. Their mission was to discuss with the fundraising centre the possibility of establishing a *kolel*. Soon after, Rabbi Samuel Salant, an emissary of Kolel Perushim, arrived in Warsaw to thwart their plan. The argument between the emissaries, and the controversy that ensued, were probably responsible for the formation of an investigative committee by the Polish Government Commission for Religious Denominations and Public Enlightenment to examine the issue of fundraising for the Jews of the Land of Israel. It is also possible that informants from the Yishuv were involved in fomenting opposition to the idea of Kolel Varshah.[10] The committee was established on 3 November 1851 and submitted its report in March 1853. This expressed surprise that authorization had been granted to collect funds for the Yishuv, claiming this was damaging to the Russian economy. The report's recommendations were unequivocal: to annul the authorization to collect funds and impose sanctions on those disobeying the new edict. On 18 November 1853 Count Paskevich accepted the recommendations of the report and forbade the collection of funds for the Jews of the Land of Israel. The Jewish community of Warsaw publicized an announcement to this effect on 13 December 1853.[11]

The edict seriously undermined the young *kolel*. With the fundraising centre in Warsaw shut down, the attempt to unite and establish a *kolel* for immigrants from Poland ended in the loss of the Polish immigrants' livelihoods. The official permission to raise funds, which was in effect in Congress Poland until 1853, had shown itself to be a two-edged sword. Unlike the collection network in the rest of the Russian empire, which carried out its mission without the knowledge or approval of the authorities both before and after 1853, the collection system in Poland operated openly and officially and was well known to the authorities until the ban. The Polish system was then completely paralysed, whereas elsewhere in Russia the unauthorized network continued to operate surreptitiously.

The plight of Kolel Varshah was dire, but one of its options was to roll over its loans. The *kolel* would take a loan, then take another loan to repay the previous one, and so on indefinitely. This method, which the Sephardi Jews in the Yishuv had perfected, was extremely problematic, as interest payments soon became the bulk of the *kolel*'s debts.[12] This method was not foreign to Kolel Varshah, as demonstrated in one of their letters of appeal: 'Until now we borrowed and gave a meagre monthly allowance to the wretched poor, and in our yearning we hoped for God's help to return the matter to its former situation ... as we know the rules of the Land of Israel are to repay the old and borrow anew.'[13]

In contrast to the longstanding Sephardi *kolel*, which owned considerable property that could serve as collateral for the debts, the new *kolel*'s only equity was the regular income from Warsaw. News of the ban on the collection of funds in Poland significantly undermined the ability of the *kolel* to borrow money, as it emphasized in one of its letters:

And when the bad news came and reached the ears of our lenders, we despaired of finding a gateway, for all were locked before us and our creditors oppress us and pressure us, saying that, God forbid, our hope is lost and our expectations are ruined, since we will not receive money from our country as is customary from year to year.[14]

Another option was to send emissaries to raise funds. In an unusual move, the small *kolel* sent three emissaries in the same week, among them two of its leaders: Rabbi

Ya'akov Yehudah Leib Levi left for Europe,[15] and Rabbi Eliyahu Yehudah Deiches left, with Hayim Hakohen, for France, England, and America.[16]

Dispatching emissaries, like rolling over debt, proved expensive. Travel costs were high and required a significant initial investment. The financial situation of Kolel Varshah was so bad that it had difficulty finding the resources to support the fundraising trips intended to help pull it out of the crisis: 'And how many difficulties we had, until we obtained a loan to cover the expenses of the emissary's journey, and it was a miracle! The compassion of one person was aroused and he loaned us a small sum, may it be sufficient for the ocean voyage, may God repay his kindness to us.'[17]

The fundraising documents reveal the alternatives explored by the *kolel*. It turned to wealthy Jewish communities in western Europe and North America. Since few Jews emigrated to the Yishuv from these communities, they did not have their own regional *kolelim* or individuals to support. In addition, there was no internal Jewish ban on fundraising emissaries—even if the communities were not always happy to receive them—and the distribution of donations from western Europe and North America was not subject to the *pesher*.

Along with sending emissaries, members of Kolel Varshah wrote letters to Amsterdam and threw themselves on the mercy of the Pekidim Va'amarkalim. They asked it to publicize the *kolel*'s predicament, which it did, with dozens of letters and announcements in the Jewish press. More important, and more challenging, was the request to transfer direct support from the body to those *kolelim* that were not officially recognized. This was in opposition to the status quo that saw the Polish Jews in Jerusalem as part of the established system of east European *kolelim* of *perushim* and hasidim. Despite its sympathy for their situation, the Pekidim Va'amarkalim's hands were tied. It was able to forward funds that were specifically designated for the *anshei varshah* or for individuals within it, but it could not contravene the established agreement between the *kolelim*.[18]

According to the Pekidim Va'amarkalim's annual report, it could not even transfer the funds from the special appeal for the *kolel*—'A New Donation for Bread for the Hungry'—that it made in 1854 after publicizing the *kolel*'s distress, as they were considered general funds and were distributed only among the officially recognized *kolelim*.[19] The organization transmitted significant contributions assigned to the *kolel*, but these were listed in a separate section of the report.[20]

The fate of the *anshei varshah* should have confirmed the Pekidim Va'amarkalim's fears of regional divisions. Although their crisis occurred relatively early, it failed to prevent future splits. The various efforts of the *anshei varshah* were only marginally successful in easing the crisis. However, a few years later, in 1857, fundraising in Poland was again permitted, under state supervision.[21] The *kolel* was significantly strengthened by the arrival of Meir Auerbach of Kalisz in 1859, and it eventually became one of the central *kolelim* in Jerusalem.[22]

The Pekidim Va'amarkalim did not encourage the independence of the *anshei varshah*; instead, it took advantage of their troubles to undo the agreement between the *kolelim* in order to completely sever the *kolelim*'s connection to their countries of origin. In a letter to the rabbis of southern Germany it wrote:

After all, the conditions of the agreement were established only on this basis, that the other Ashkenazi *kolelim* receive for themselves alone the collected funds in the lands of their birth, Poland and Russia ... What is it to us if the people came from the Netherlands and Germany or Poland and Russia? After all, they left the land of their birth without intending to return, in order to settle in the Holy Land (may it be rebuilt and re-established), and the law of settlers of the land now applies to all of them equally and they are no longer identified by the land that they left. And it is not the purpose of those who give charity to the poor of the Land of Israel to support the poor of their own city, because if that was their purpose they would not have to send their money to a faraway land, rather they could give the money to their local poor themselves.[23]

The halakhic principle that 'the poor of your own city have precedence' prioritizes giving charity to those closest to you and was used frequently against the Pekidim Va'amarkalim, which collected funds for Jews living far away. Regional *kolelim* provided a possible response to such criticism. Kolel Varshah was the distant outpost of Warsaw in Jerusalem; Kolel Vilnah, for its part, was 'the Vilna of the Land of Israel'.

The Pekidim Va'amarkalim's outlook was also based in Jewish law. This held that anyone who leaves a city and moves elsewhere becomes a full resident of their new home. They are obligated to follow local customs and break with their original traditions. An immigrant to the Land of Israel therefore became a resident there, and their community of origin was irrelevant.

Although the Pekidim Va'amarkalim's approach had a firm religious basis, it was not well suited to the nature of immigration in the second half of the nineteenth century, which was not one of individual movement from place to place but rather of mass migrations that created transnational communities with the transfer of entire communities to new destinations. Like the Spanish expulsion that led to the establishment of congregations of Jews in the Ottoman empire in which the exiles banded together on the basis of their community of origin and preserved their original customs, resisting the adoption of local custom, so too the second half of the nineteenth century and the first half of the twentieth saw the establishment of regional *kolelim* in the Land of Israel and *landsmanshaften* (immigrant aid societies) on the other side of the Atlantic Ocean that boasted of preserving their original culture and community. In both cases, the attempt to transplant the original community culture had to contend with a tendency towards assimilation in the new home. The story of the establishment of Kolel Varshah suggests that, in the case of the *kolelim* of the Land of Israel, the effort to maintain a connection with the community of origin may have been driven more by financial considerations than by an effort to preserve society and culture.

The case of the Kolel Varshah is very revealing of the changes in the organizational and financial structure of the Yishuv in Jerusalem. Its story also extended beyond the borders of the Land of Israel. On the one hand, contemporary outside observers (such as the Jews of England) were unwilling to recognize the division into *kolelim*;

instead, they understood the crisis as affecting all of the immigrants from eastern Europe, which led to an unprecedented rallying in support of the Jews of Jerusalem and even became part of an international crisis. On the other hand, the attempt to separate the Polish Jewish community in Jerusalem from the rest of the east European Jews, and especially its temporary failure, provides a glimpse of the preservation of particular identity in other regions approximately sixty years after Poland's last partition.

The Ukase That Wasn't

On 15 May 1854 Sir Moses Montefiore sent a personal appeal, along with letters he had received from Jerusalem, to Rabbi Nathan Marcus Adler, chief rabbi of the British empire. Montefiore described the appalling financial distress that had befallen the Yishuv and implored Adler to petition the Jews of Britain and America to relieve the situation and prevent its recurrence. By 1854 Montefiore had already made three visits to the Land of Israel (out of a total of seven), which established him as the Yishuv's main contact and as the authority on the Land of Israel in Britain and the entire Jewish world. Rabbi Adler responded on 18 May, writing that although he believed Montefiore was better suited to send out such a petition, he would nonetheless heed his request and issue a 'pastoral letter'. This was published that same day and publicized the next day in the Jewish press in Britain.[24] On 20 May it appeared in the London *Times* and other leading newspapers.[25]

The letter told of horrifying hunger and even of a father attempting to sell his son to 'the stranger' (implying the Anglican mission) for a loaf of bread. The distress described in the letter was not in fact worse than that described in countless fundraising letters disseminated, with little success, by centres of support for the Yishuv; however, Montefiore's campaign, backed by Adler's pastoral letter, was phenomenally successful. It raised close to £20,000 from thousands of people, Jewish and non-Jewish, in the English-speaking world. The letter led to unprecedented interest in the fate of the Jews in the Land of Israel, expressed in the Jewish and non-Jewish press, at well-attended gatherings, and in dozens of programmes for the improvement of the Yishuv.

Abigail Green contends that the success of Adler's pastoral letter was based on the three principles that she sees as the root of Montefiore's activism—religion, a British romantic view of the exotic oriental lands, and a humanitarian commitment to the universal rights of man.[26] In my view, the secret of the letter's success lay in its timing, and in its surprising fit with public sentiment in Britain. Montefiore shrewdly took a standard charity-seeking letter and added a sentence to the English translation that did not appear in the original, informing readers that donations from Jews in the Russian empire to their brethren in the Land of Israel were now banned by an edict of the tsar (ukase). Thus the success of the letter is probably related not to the Yishuv or to Montefiore; rather, Montefiore's extra sentence fed into the anti-Russian sentiment of the British public on the eve of the Crimean War, and contributed greatly to the success of the campaign.[27]

Hostility to the tsar is a persistent theme in all publications related to the campaign in both the Jewish and the general press. The edict that stopped the flow of contributions from the tsarist empire to the Ottoman empire (with which it was at war) was interpreted as a tyrant's harassment of his erstwhile subjects. The general press saw the Jews of Jerusalem as victims of Russian oppression;[28] *Lloyd's Weekly Newspaper* described the tsar's symbolic arrival at the gates of Jerusalem, if not in the person of his monks and soldiers, then in the form of the hunger that he imposed upon the local Jews.[29]

In newspaper articles, letters to the editor, and Jewish and Christian sermons published in the two Jewish newspapers in England, Tsar Nicholas I was reviled with names drawn from the pantheon of enemies of the Jews through the ages, among them the 'Northern Pharaoh' (the subjugation of the tsar's subjects and the conscription of Jewish children into the army depicted as crueller than pharaoh's decree to throw children into the Nile);[30] Goliath (alluding to the monumental size of the Russian army);[31] Sennacherib and Nebuchadnezzar[32] (kings of Assyria and Babylon and, like Russia, enemies from the north);[33] Haman;[34] and even Genghis Khan (the barbarian ruler whose expansionist goals were met by a united Muslim and Christian front from the south and west, just as in the Crimean War England and France joined the Ottoman empire against Russia).[35]

Abraham Benisch, editor of the *Hebrew Observer*, was among the first to connect the condition of the Jews of the Land of Israel to the war. He claimed that the Crimean War had broken out because of a dispute over Jerusalem, in which the opposing sides—the tsarist and Ottoman empires—had the largest Jewish populations in the world. Benisch described the tsar with the epithets listed above, and pronounced Russia a barbaric semi-civilization. The tsar was a despotic tyrant who expelled entire nations from their lands and snatched children from their mother's breast for his army. Even his edict to modernize Jewish attire, which was supported and advanced by the maskilim, was criticized by Benisch as an objectionable interference in the Jewish way of life.[36]

An expression of the mood in England can be found in Rabbi Henry Pereira Mendes's sermon in the synagogue in Birmingham on Humiliation Day, a day of prayer proclaimed by Queen Victoria in response to the situation. Mendes spoke of the Russian tsar in the words of Ezekiel:

Turn ye, brethren, to the prophet Ezekiel, and let his 38th chapter arrest your thoughts:

'Son of man, set thy face against Gog, the land of Magog, Prince of Rosh, Meshech, and Tubal, and prophesy against him . . .'

Now the words Gog and Magog have no other affinity, save to the single word *gag*—a roof, a conception which was most likely to have originated a name for the country that is literally the roof of the then-known world. But to confirm the reference, the Prophet speaks of the monarch of Magog as being the Prince of Rosh, Meshech, and Tubal, easily recognized as the three primitive districts of Russia, viz., Russia proper, Muscovy—or Southern Russia, Tobolsky—or Asiatic Russia.[37]

While the German-language Jewish newspapers stressed what Ludwig Philipson, editor of *Die Allgemeine Zeitung des Judentums*, called 'the Eastern Jewish Question' during the Crimean War, in Britain the war was conceived not as an east–west confrontation, but as a north–south one: 'from the north will come the evil'.[38] The proclaimed enemy was the Russian tsar, and he was perceived as attacking the Yishuv. The British public awaited the day when the aggressor would pay for his actions with the Danubian principalities, the Crimean peninsula, and Jerusalem.

A similar atmosphere prevailed in France, Britain's ally across the Channel, which also joined the Turks in the war against Russia. The Consistoire Central des Israélites de France, in a public letter to Napoleon III, assigned personal blame to the tsar for the humanitarian crisis in Palestine. In the letter, the consistory noted that the tsar had issued an edict forbidding Jews in his lands to send money to the Jews of Israel.[39] These views have also influenced the historiography of the Yishuv, which has portrayed the Yishuv's distress in the 1850s as a direct result of the Crimean War, during which the tsar forbade the transfer of *ḥalukah* funds from Russia to Jerusalem.[40]

The consistory accused the tsar of issuing a special edict against the Jews of Jerusalem, but no such edict has been found in the laws pertaining to the Jews collected by Levanda in the imperial archives in tsarist Russia, even though the archive includes many other laws from the war years dealing with taxation, conscription into the army, and the observance of Jewish ritual in the army.[41] In the anti-Russia atmosphere of the Jewish press during the war, several news items were published about the attitude of the despotic tsar towards the Jews, including the publication of various decrees. Most had no basis in reality. Among them were an alleged decree against praying for the tsar's well-being[42] and another against distributing Moses Montefiore's picture among the Jews of Poland.[43] The claim that a blanket prohibition against fundraising was in place is refuted also by the fact that, in most of the Russian *kolelim* in the four holy cities, of both *perushim* and hasidim, there are no accounts of an unusual need for funds during the war, certainly not at a level indicating there had been a complete cessation of the transfer of donations.

In fact, Nicholas I never imposed a sweeping ban on fundraising on behalf of the Jews of the Ottoman empire during the Crimean War: the ban pre-dated the war. The withdrawal of permission by low-ranking bureaucrats to raise funds locally in Congress Poland was all that occurred, and the Pekidim Va'amarkalim realized this first. As the body co-ordinating the transfer of funds from Orthodox communities around the world, the Pekidim Va'amarkalim was always best informed about what was happening in the Jewish east. Early in 1854 leaders of the collection centre in Warsaw had notified the body that they were no longer permitted to raise funds in Congress Poland:

We find it fitting to inform your honourable eminences that approximately three weeks ago the permit for the collection of charity on behalf of the poor of the Holy Land was withdrawn, and from now on there is no further hope for the impoverished to be supported by us, because we will not, God forbid, do anything to resist the directive, and we must give thanks and praise for the good and the kindness that they received for sixteen years and the Blessed One will support them from His generous hand.[44]

In an urgent letter to the leaders of the fundraising centre for the Land of Israel in southern Germany, the Pekidim Va'amarkalim emphasized that the cessation of contributions affected only Congress Poland but expressed its concern that the edict would soon be broadened:

We have received tidings and are very agitated that—as appears inevitable—a proclamation will be made against the collection of funds for the impoverished of the Land of Israel (may it be rebuilt and re-established) in other lands of the tsar of Russia; in Vilna, Reisen [Belarus], and in the other territories under his rule their hands will be tied and they will be able to do nothing for those who dwell in the Holy Land, and the tree from which the *kolelim* of the *perushim* and the hasidim in all the holy cities (may they be rebuilt and re-established) were sustained until now, has been cut down, and the spring from which the channels of abundance emerged for the *kolelim* has dried up, for the waters of the Shiloah[45] have been blocked and the hand of those who love them cannot save them.[46]

It quickly became evident that the Pekidim Va'amarkalim's fears were unfounded and that the new edict was purely local, affecting only Kolel Varshah. But Jewish public opinion in western Europe remained ignorant of this fact. In the eyes of west European Jewry, all the Jews of eastern Europe were one, and they judged the humanitarian crisis by the interests of the countries where they lived. From their point of view, this event did not represent the decision of local authorities to annul an existing agreement but rather the tsar's personal harassment of the Jews of Jerusalem as part of general Russian aggression during the Crimean War. The war succeeded in turning the crisis of a marginal Jewish organization in Jerusalem into a Yishuv-wide humanitarian crisis, and the problem of the Jews of Jerusalem into part of the larger narrative of the war.

This is the secret of the success of the Montefiore–Adler campaign. It allowed British Jews to feel they were part of the war effort with a symbolic contribution of sixpence. The campaign on behalf of starving Jews in the Land of Israel was experienced as a personal battle against the tsar, who was supposedly harassing the Jews of Jerusalem. Ironically, Kolel Varshah, whose crisis led to the success of the charity campaign, did not derive greater benefit from the campaign than other *kolelim*, and perhaps even less than the others as it was not yet officially recognized.

Posen: Liminal Identities

The crisis that Kolel Varshah experienced was caused by the ruling of local authorities in Congress Poland that brought fundraising practices there into conformity with those in the rest of the Russian empire. Across the border, on lands that were annexed to Prussia with the partitions of Poland, a cultural, religious, and political battle raged between the Prussian government and the German minority, on the one hand, and the majority Polish population on the other. The Jews were positioned between the Poles and the Germans, and scholars are divided as to the extent of Germanization of the Jewish population of Posen and Pomerania in the first half of the nineteenth century.[47] The crisis experienced by Kolel Varshah in faraway Jerusalem provides an additional perspective from which to assess the degree of 'Polishness' of the Jews in this part of Prussia, approximately sixty years after the last partition of Poland.

The loss of income from Congress Poland forced Kolel Varshah to dispatch emissaries throughout the world as part of an emergency campaign. Two emissaries went to the new and affluent Jewish centres in Europe and North America. A third, Ya'akov Yehudah Leib Levi, was sent to Posen (Poznań), according to a letter from the Pekidim Va'amarkalim to Rabbi Moshe Landsberger of Posen in which it tried to determine whether the emissary had arrived. The short letter also mentions a much wider correspondence, carried on through it between Rabbi Landsberger and Rabbi Nahum of Szadek, Levi's brother and another of the *kolel*'s leaders.[48]

The collapse of the collection network in Congress Poland compelled Kolel Varshah to turn to those districts of Posen and Pomerania which had belonged to Poland–Lithuania before its partition. The mission was a result of the *kolel*'s great need, but the affinity between the prominent figures of Kolel Varshah and Posen had earlier roots. Rabbi Avraham Posner, father of the Levi brothers, had been a student of Akiva Eger, the rabbi of Posen.[49]

I will not cover this topic at length and much more research is required to examine the connections between Kolel Varshah and the central Jewish communities in the Grand Duchy of Posen. I will, however, point out some of these connections. A key figure in this complex relationship was Elijahu Guttmacher, the rabbi of Grätz (Grodzisk Wielkopolski). Guttmacher was a proto-Zionist and member of the Society for the Settlement of the Land of Israel (Hevrat Yishuv Erets Yisra'el), which he led together with Rabbi Tsevi Hirsch Kalischer, who also lived and was active in the border areas of Prussia. Alongside his nationalist activity, attributable to what he saw as the 'new Jewish age', Guttmacher continued to be active as the '*nasi* [prince] of the Holy Land', responsible for fundraising for the Yishuv through traditional channels. As documents in the National Library of Israel show,[50] Guttmacher was in regular contact with the leaders of the *kolelim* in Jerusalem, including key figures of Kolel Varshah.

An 1866 letter from the head of the Pekidim Va'amarkalim, Akiva Lehren, reveals the complexity of Guttmacher's association with the *kolelim*. Guttmacher divided the funds that he raised into three equal parts. One-third was sent to Kolel Perushim, the first Ashkenazi *kolel* in Jerusalem. Guttmacher had apparently begun sending money to the Ashkenazi *kolel* before the new *kolelim* broke off from it and continued to do so because of the precedent. How he distributed the remaining funds testifies to the duality with which he contended. Another third went to the German–Dutch Kolel Hod, and the remaining third to Kolel Varshah.[51] Obviously Rabbi Guttmacher felt a need to support representatives of both German and Polish Jewry in the Land of Israel.

With the cessation of contributions from Congress Poland, Kolel Varshah made Posen its support base, leveraging both a shared heritage and existing networks. A letter written to Guttmacher in 1857 states that there were 'standing orders' from both individuals and communities for regular donations to Kolel Varshah, dating from Rabbi Levi's visit. Rabbi Levi urged donors to designate their contributions exclusively for Kolel Varshah.[52] His mission also led to the publication of a book, *Affection for Zion and Love for Jerusalem*, promoting the Land of Israel and singing its praises. Its publisher, Wolff Alexander, wrote:

And it happened that a delightful man, my associate and acquaintance, our teacher the rabbi, Rabbi Ya'akov Yehudah of Jerusalem, came to my home a few days ago and showed me precious things the likes of which I have never seen and never heard, letters he has in his possession, and I saw their contents, filled with all that is good, and I was inspired by the divine spirit, and I said they are worthy to be distributed to Jacob and to be circulated to Israel, so that the entire House of Israel will know the standing and situation of the Holy Land.[53]

Revenue from sales of the book were dedicated to the Jewish poor in the Land of Israel.

The relationships that were established during Rabbi Levi's trip were not limited to financial matters. The Levi brothers, who led the Yishuv's opposition to reform in education, used the relationships they built to publicize their opinions to the Jewish communities of Prussian Poland and the Congress Kingdom. In one instance, they used Hayim Nathansohn of Wreschen (Września), one of the fundraisers whom Ya'akov Yehudah Leib met during his visit, to distribute a fiery pamphlet outlining their opposition to the establishment by Ludwig August Frankl of the Lämel School in Jerusalem, which was perceived as the first modern school in the city.[54] Nathansohn also served as an intermediary between Kolel Varshah and Rabbi Guttmacher and others.[55]

In a letter to Guttmacher, Nathansohn wrote:

And they sent to me the *Igeret hakolelet* mentioned above to copy in many copies and to send them to the rabbis in Poland and also in our land to gather and stand up against the enemy oppressor... And I have already written letters to Poland, as I have sent them letters that were sent to them through me, to rouse them and to awaken them to this great cause, and I stand ready to compose many more letters to the rabbis around me.[56]

Thus the Polishness of the Jews of the north-western provinces of Prussia was not limited to support for Kolel Varshah in Jerusalem: they preserved close ties with Jewish population centres beyond their borders. This was the situation at the beginning of the nineteenth century, when funds collected in the Posen region were transferred via the centre in Warsaw to the Land of Israel, until Rabbi Solomon Eger abolished this practice in 1842 and established an independent centre.[57] Nonetheless, multiple connections continued to exist even after the suppression of the 'Spring of Nations' in Posen in 1848 that brought an intensification of the Prussian authorities' efforts towards Germanization.

Current research about the Jews of Posen and Pomerania concentrates on the extent of their support for the Prussian government, on the one hand, and for the majority Polish population on the other, or examines the spread of German language and culture in the Jewish population and the adoption of religious reform and Wissenschaft des Judentums as indicators of support for the German and Polish orientations within the community.[58] Support for the communities of the Yishuv provides a different perspective on this matter. The Jews of the region, or at least the rabbinic elite and conservative institutions, identified themselves with both the German Kolel Hod and the Polish Kolel Varshah, and preserved extensive connections with the Jews of Congress Poland even some sixty years after the last partition of Poland.[59]

This duality is also reflected in the person of Rabbi Kalischer, albeit in a slightly different way. Kalischer saw himself as 'one of the survivors in the land of Ashkenaz who fear and tremble before the word of God and the love of that which is holy burns in their heart',[60] that is, as an authentic remnant of the pre-modern, pious German Jewry which pre-dated the Haskalah and the Reform movement. His tragedy was that he directed his activity to a German-speaking society of which he hoped to become an integral part. In reality, however, he was a liminal figure, a hybrid of east and west. Along with Guttmacher, he became involved with the Society for the Settlement of the Land of Israel, founded by Hayim Luria in Frankfurt an der Oder, and published widely in Jewish German newspapers. He also established a branch of the Alliance Israélite Universelle in Thorn (Toruń) in Pomerania, where he lived, and maintained an extensive correspondence with the organization.[61] Despite all this, his proto-nationalist ideas were not widely accepted in Germany and France. Kalischer did succeed in creating an impressive network of activists for the settlement of the Land of Israel, but it was based mostly in Prussian Poland and the lands to the east of it; his influence in the west remained limited.[62]

Another expression of this east–west gap can be seen in a different activity. Guttmacher was known as the *tsadik* of Grätz and received thousands of *kvitlekh* (personal notes requesting blessings or advice). Marcin Wodziński examined approximately 7,000 of them from Guttmacher's final years (1873–4) that are preserved in the YIVO archive in New York. The majority (87 per cent) originated in Poland, and only 2 per cent were from nearby territories under Prussian rule.[63] Wodziński claims that residents of these adjacent regions did not have to resort to mailing their *kvitlekh* because they lived near the *tsadik*, but I believe that the difference lies in the cultural and religious changes experienced by the Jews of Posen. As a result of these changes, Guttmacher lost his standing in his own country while remaining important in the Polish regions.

In faraway Jerusalem, members of Kolel Varshah knew well what rabbis Guttmacher and Kalischer refused to understand—that although Kalischer and

Guttmacher were born after the annexation of Posen to Prussia, they lived in an area where the traditions of Polish Jewry were still strong, a border region between Prussia and Poland. To a certain extent their activity in this liminal space is part of the reason for their success beyond Congress Poland. Guttmacher received *kvitlekh* from western Galicia and even from Grodno, whereas Kalischer's activity allowed him to share his proto-nationalist ideas with the Jews of the tsarist empire and to plant the seeds of the Hibat Tsiyon movement.

Translated from the Hebrew by Naomi Stillman

Notes

1. A. Morgenstern, *Hashivah liyerushalayim: ḥidush hayishuv hayehudi be'erets yisra'el bereshit hame'ah hatesha esreh* (Jerusalem, 2007), 352.
2. Ibid. 52–4.
3. Archiwum Główne Akt Dawnych, Warsaw, 1/190 'Centralne Władze Wyznaniowe Królestwa Polskiego', 1463, fos. 4–5: Golovin, Government Commission for Religious Denominations and Public Enlightenment, to Szmule Pinosu, 25 Nov. 1836. There is extensive documentation about this matter in 'Centralne Władze Wyznaniowe Królestwa Polskiego', 1463 (see also Central Archives for the History of the Jewish People, Jerusalem (hereafter CAHJP), HM2-6889: microfilm copy of 'Centralne Władze Wyznaniowe Królestwa Polskiego', 1463). The file is described in detail by Morgenstern and much of this chapter is based on his research (see Morgenstern, *Hashivah liyerushalayim*, 70–81).
4. Morgenstern, *Hashivah liyerushalayim*, 76–7.
5. On the secularization of community structure in the Land of Israel in the nineteenth century and the differences between Galilee and Jerusalem, see Y. Ben-Ghedalia, 'Filantropyah yehudit-eiropa'it biyerushalayim bizeman milḥemet kerim', Ph.D. thesis (Hebrew University of Jerusalem, 2013), 31–50.
6. I. Bartal, *Galut ba'arets: yishuv erets-yisra'el beterem tsiyonut: masot umeḥkarim* (Jerusalem, 1994), 54–6.
7. Morgenstern, *Hashivah liyerushalayim*, 348–9.
8. Ibid. 349.
9. Pekidim Va'amarkalim, letter to *anshei varshah*, Jerusalem, 4 July 1854, *Pinkas pakuam*, bk. 13, p. 261: Yad Izhak Ben-Zvi website, 'Resource Material: The Administrators and Clerks of Amsterdam—in Hebrew', visited 31 Mar. 2021.
10. Morgenstern, *Hashivah liyerushalayim*, 76–7. It seems from the words of the Pekidim Va'amarkalim scribe that a Jewish physician, Bernhard Neumann, was the informant. See also Jacob Roos, letter to Rabbi Natan Coronel, Hamburg, 31 Oct. 1855, *Pinkas pakuam*, bk. 13, p. 296; E. Selig Hausdorf, letter to the editor, 22 May 1853, *Die Allgemeine Zeitung des Judentums*, 27 Jun. 1853, p. 332; repr. in *Hebrew Observer*, July 1853, p. 14.
11. Morgenstern, *Hashivah liyerushalayim*, 76–81. A similar description from the *anshei varshah* appears in Eliyahu Yehudah Deiches and Hayim Hakohen, fundraising letter, July 1854; reproduced in A. Etz-Hadar, *Ilanot: letoledot hayishuv be'erets yisra'el, 1830–1920* (Tel Aviv, 1967), 48–9, pls. 10–11.
12. Y. Hashash, 'Iskei halvaot: nihul kaspei hakehilah hasefaradit biyerushalayim bame'ot hashemonah esreh vehatesha esreh le'or mismakhim ḥadashim', *Zion*, 78 (2013), 501–26; I. Bartal, 'Berurim beshulei tazkir: kolel hasefaradim biyerushalayim mishenat 1855', *Zion*, 43 (1978), 97–118.

13 Deiches and Hakohen, fundraising letter.
14 CAHJP, IT-Ts-161: Kolel Varshah, Jerusalem and Safed, letter to the Trieste community regarding Ya'akov Yehuda Leib Levi's mission, 8 July 1853.
15 Ibid.
16 Deiches and Hakohen, fundraising letter; Eliyahu Yehudah Deiches, fundraising letter, July 1854; reproduced in Etz-Hadar, *Ilanot*, 50, pl. 12; Pekidim Va'amarkalim, letter to Rabbi Jacob Ettlinger of Altona, 26 July 1854, *Pinkas pakuam*, bk. 13, p. 272.
17 Kolel Varshah, letter to Trieste community, 8 July 1853.
18 Pekidim Va'amarkalim, letter to *anshei varshah*, Jerusalem, 4 Sept. 1854, *Pinkas pakuam*, bk. 13, p. 278.
19 CAHJP, AHW-858a-1: Pekidim Va'amarkalim, *Ot emet*, 3 (1855), 24.
20 A 'certain rich man from Mainz' donated 200 gold coins for the 200 members of Kolel Varshah (Pekidim Va'amarkalim, letter to *anshei varshah*, 14 July 1854, *Pinkas pakuam*, bk. 13, p. 266).
21 Morgenstern, *Hashivah liyerushalayim*, 416 n. 163. For a list of members of Kolel Varsha, see Archiwum Główne Akt Dawnych, 'Centralne Władze Wyznaniowe', 1463, fos. 482–6: accounts of the fundraising centre in Warsaw, July 1859.
22 E. Davidson, 'Me'ah shenot pe'ilut "kolel varshah" biyerushalayim ha'atikah (1848–1948): iyunim historiyim vege'ografiyim leregel gilui kelei kesef mibeit hakeneset "ohel ya'akov"', in I. Rozenson and Y. Spanier (eds.), *Minḥat sapir* (Elkana, 2013), 423–46.
23 Pekidim Va'amarkalim, letter to rabbis Seligman Baer Bambarger of Würzburg and Lazarus Ottensoser of Hoechberg, 13 Jan. 1854, *Pinkas pakuam*, bk. 13, p. 196.
24 *An Appeal on Behalf of the Famishing Jews in the Holy Land* (London, 1854); 'An Appeal on Behalf of the Famishing Jews in the Holy Land', *Jewish Chronicle*, 19 May 1854, p. 284 and supplement; 'An Appeal on Behalf of the Famishing Jews in the Holy Land', *Hebrew Observer*, 19 May 1854, pp. 374–5. The printing of the appeal on a Thursday and its urgency required the printing of a special supplement. The rush to print also caused a delay in printing the next issue (see 'Notice', *Hebrew Observer*, 26 May 1854, p. 377).
25 'An Appeal on Behalf of the Famishing Jews in the Holy Land', *The Times*, 20 May 1854, p. 6.
26 A. Green, *Moses Montefiore: Jewish Liberator, Imperial Hero* (Cambridge, Mass., 2010), 235.
27 For the original version, see 'Dimat ha'ashukim', *Shomer tsiyon hane'eman*, 175 (7 Apr. 1854), 349; E. Selig Hausdorf, 'Im Auftrage der sefardischen und deutsch-holländischen Gemeinden', *Die Allgemeine Zeitung des Judentums*, 17 Apr. 1854, p. 196.
28 'Appeal on Behalf of the Jews in the Holy Land (from the *Hampshire Independent*)', *Hebrew Observer*, 9 June 1854, p. 399.
29 'The Czar in Jerusalem (from *Lloyds' Newspaper*)', *Hebrew Observer*, 9 June 1854, p. 395.
30 [A. Benisch], 'The Eastern Question', *Hebrew Observer*, 10 Feb. 1854, p. 260; 'Western Synagogue, St. Alban's Place', *Hebrew Observer*, 21 Apr. 1854, pp. 341–2; Ben Japhet, 'The Famishing Jews in the Holy Land', *Hebrew Observer*, 1 June 1854, pp. 386–7; 'The Distress of the Jews at Jerusalem', *Hebrew Observer*, 9 June 1854, p. 399.
31 'Day of Humiliation', *Jewish Chronicle*, 12 May 1854, p. 272.
32 'Day of Humiliation: Sermon by Rev. Dr. Adler', *Hebrew Observer*, 5 May 1854, pp. 356–7.
33 [A. Benisch], 'The Eastern Question', 260.
34 Ibid.
35 [A. Benisch], 'The Eastern Question and the Jews', *Hebrew Observer*, 17 Mar. 1854, p. 300.
36 [A. Benisch], 'The Eastern Question', *Hebrew Observer*.

37 'Birmingham: Day of Humiliation', *Hebrew Observer*, 5 May 1854, pp. 353–4; 'The Recent Day of Humiliation', *Jewish Chronicle*, 5 May 1854, p. 261. For an early reference to the tsar as 'the Scythian Gog and Magog', see [Benisch], 'The Eastern Question', 260. It is interesting to note that the British consul in Jerusalem, James Finn, attributes a similar tradition to the Jews of Jerusalem (J. Finn, *Stirring Times, or: Records from Jerusalem Consular Chronicles of 1853 to 1856*, 2 vols. (London, 1878), ii. 48). For the identification of the three main regions of Russia with Ezekiel's end-of-days vision in the eschatological writings of the nineteenth century, see M. Saperstein, *Jewish Preaching in Times of War, 1800–2001* (Oxford, 2008), 126.

38 Ben-Ghedalia, 'Filantropyah yehudit-eiropa'it biyerushalayim bizeman milḥemet kerim', 96–116. For east–west/north–south axes, see L. Wolff, *Inventing Eastern Europe: The Map of Civilization on the Mind of the Enlightenment* (Stanford, Calif., 1994).

39 S. Cahen, 'Intervention du Consistoire Central des Israélites de France en faveur de Israélites de la Turquie', *Archives Israélites*, 15 (1854), 228–30; id., 'Du Consistoire Central des Israélites de France en faveur de Israélites de la Turquie', *L'Univers Israélite*, 8 (1854), 341–4.

40 See e.g. A. Schischa, 'The Saga of 1855: A Study in Depth', in S. L. Lipman and V. D. Lipman (eds.), *The Century of Moses Montefiore* (Oxford, 1985), 269–70; Green, *Montefiore*, 232.

41 V. O. Levanda (ed.), *Polnyi khronologicheskii sbornik zakonov i polozhenii, kasayushchikhsya evreev, ot Ulozheniya tsarya Alekseya Mikhailovicha do nastoyashchego vremeni, ot 1649–1873 g.: Izvlechenie iz polnykh sobranii zakonov Rossiiskoi imperii* (St Petersburg, 1874).

42 'Foreign Intelligence (from the *Daily News*)', *Hebrew Observer*, 30 June 1854, p. 421.

43 'The Emperor of Russia's Last Liberal Move', *Jewish Chronicle*, 31 Mar. 1854, p. 225.

44 Pekidim Va'amarkalim, letter to rabbis Seligman Baer Bambarger of Würzburg and Lazarus Ottensoser of Hoechberg, 13 Jan. 1854.

45 Shiloah is the name of a spring in Jerusalem (see Neh. 3: 15), but also a play on the Hebrew root *sh-l-ḥ*, 'to send'.

46 Pekidim Va'amarkalim, letter to rabbis Seligman Baer Bambarger of Würzburg and Lazarus Ottensoser of Hoechberg, 13 Jan. 1854.

47 S. Kemlein, *Die Posener Juden, 1815–1848: Entwicklungsprozesse einer polnischen Judenheit unter preussischer Herrschaft* (Hamburg, 1997); K. Makowski, 'Poles, Germans and Jews in the Grand Duchy of Poznań in 1848: From Coexistence to Conflict', *East European Quarterly*, 30 (1999), 385–94; E. Sariel, '"In the East Lie My Roots; My Branches in the West": The Distinctiveness of the Jews of Posen in the First Half of the Nineteenth Century', *Leo Baeck Institute Year Book*, 58 (2013), 175–92.

48 Pekidim Va'amarkalim, letter to Rabbi Moshe Landsberger, Posen, 25 Aug. 1854, *Pinkas pakuam*, bk. 13, p. 275.

49 Morgenstern, *Hashivah liyerushalayim*, 349.

50 National Library of Israel, Jerusalem (hereafter NLI), Arc. 4* 1069, Rabbi Elijahu Guttmacher Archive.

51 M. Hildesheimer, 'Yishuv erets-yisra'el behaguto uvefo'alo shel harav eliyahu gutmakher', in A. Yedidya (ed.), *Harav tsevi hirsh kalisher vehitorerut letsiyon* (Jerusalem, 2014), 103–29: 121.

52 NLI, Arc. 4* 1069, Box 24: Lazer son of Rav Dov Hakohen of Gniewkowo, letter to Rabbi E. Guttmacher, 1857.

53 W. Alexander, *Ḥibat yerushalayim va'ahavat tsiyon: di traye anhanglikhkeit tsu yerushalayim und di libe tsu tsion; dershtelungen in yerushalayim, fun der gebridern rotshild neygegrunderten hospitals (erleitert fun zalman levinzon)* (Wollstein, 1855), 6.

54 NLI, Arc. 4* 1069: Nahum of Szadek, and Yaakov Yehuda Leib of Ślesin, 'Igeret hakolelet', 12 June 1896; S. Halevy, 'Igeret hakolelet neged yisud beit-sefer "Lemel"', *Cathedra*, 5 (1977), 198–209.

55 See e.g. NLI, Arc. 4* 1069: Hayim Nathansohn, letter to Rabbi Elijahu Guttmacher, 3 Nov. 1856.

56 E. R. Malachi, 'Letoledot beit hasefer lemel', *Ramah*, 3/5 (1940), 194–9; repr. in id., *Mineged tireh* (Jerusalem, 2001), 411–17: 415–16. The letter had accompanied a copy of the pamphlet; however, Malachi was unaware of that, as the pamphlet wasn't published until later. He deciphered the signature as Hayim son of Natan Schor of Wreschen, whom he was unable to identify. It is clear that he erred and that the writer was Nathansohn (Library of the Admor of Karlin-Stolin, ha-Rav Shochet, Jerusalem, Israel Ms. 108: Hayim Nathansohn, 4 letters to Rabbi Elijahu Guttmacher, 1856–9; Institute of Microfilmed Hebrew Manuscripts, NLI, F46291: copy of Hayim Nathansohn, 4 letters to Rabbi Elijahu Guttmacher, 1856–9). On the connections between Nathansohn and the heads of the rabbinical courts in Galin and Warsaw, see Hayim Nathansohn, letter to Rabbi Elijahu Guttmacher, 3 Nov. 1856.

57 Morgenstern, *Hashivah liyerushalayim*, 349.

58 See Kemlein, *Die Posener Juden*; Makowski, 'Poles, Germans and Jews in the Grand Duchy of Poznań in 1848'; Sariel, '"In the East Lie My Roots; My Branches in the West"'.

59 See also Sariel, '"In the East Lie My Roots; My Branches in the West"'.

60 Zvi Hirsch Kalischer, letter to Rabbi Alinke Krantinger, 1863, in *Haketavim hatsiyonim shel harav tsevi kalischer*, ed. I. Klausner (Jerusalem, 1947), 216.

61 A. Yedidya, 'Merotshild lekremyeh: "nedivei vesarei yisra'el" bemishnato uvefo'alo shel harav tsevi hirsh kalisher', *Cathedra*, 155 (2015), 47–72; see also J. Myers, *Seeking Zion: Modernity and Messianic Activism in the Writings of Tsevi Hirsch Kalischer* (Oxford, 2003).

62 A. Yedidya, 'Hayahadut ha'ortodoksit begermanyah veyaḥasah le'erets-yisra'el le'or po'alo shel harav kalisher', in id., *Harav tsevi hirsh kalisher vehitorerut letsiyon*, 191–205.

63 M. Wodziński, *Historical Atlas of Hasidism* (Princeton, NJ, 2018), 99–101.

2. FROM THE BEGINNINGS OF ZIONISM TO THE SECOND WORLD WAR

Between Attraction and Repulsion, Disaster and Hope

Jews, Poland, and the Land of Israel before 1948

ŁUKASZ TOMASZ SROKA

Introduction

Current Polish–Israeli relations can only be understood in their broader historical context. This has to take into account the fact that the State of Israel only came into existence in 1948, although Jewish involvement in the Land of Israel clearly persisted from the destruction of the Second Temple until the founding of the state. Similarly, pre-partition Poland–Lithuania contained areas which are today part of Lithuania, Belarus, Ukraine, and Russia, and Poland did not exist as a state during the 123 years of the partitions. For the purposes of this chapter I regard as Israeli those lands that are today within Israel's borders. As for Polish lands, I understand them to be the territory of the Polish–Lithuanian Commonwealth prior to the first partition. This is not an ideal solution since today other countries occupy part of that area. In addition the western lands of present-day Poland, which ended up within its borders after the Second World War, are excluded. However, this takes into account the fact that Jews, who for centuries had lived in places such as Breslau (Wrocław) or Stettin (Szczecin), identified themselves as German Jews or, if they had been assimilated, as Germans. A similar situation existed in places such as Lwów (Lviv), Drohobycz (Drohobych), Wilno (Vilnius), and Grodno. Jews there spoke Yiddish or Polish, and sometimes after 1772 one of the languages of the partitioning powers, but not Lithuanian, Belarusian, or Ukrainian. The long-established community of Polish Jews extended hundreds of kilometres east of Poland's present-day borders.

The subject of the relationship between Poland and the Land of Israel before 1948 is very broad and its analysis could easily fill, if not several volumes, then at least one very large one. I do not wish to restrict myself to the academic formula of 'introducing the subject',[1] so I intend here to adopt a new approach to this problem: elucidating the dilemmas set out in the title of this chapter. I focus above all on the position of the Jews. Polish Jews found themselves in a situation in which they were affected both by the forces attracting them to the Land of Israel and the factors pushing them away from Poland—antisemitism and the related widespread economic distress. Of course, similar processes were at work more or less throughout Europe.

All this was accompanied by despair and hope. The ultimate fate of the Jews in Poland proved disastrous. They had established in Poland a large and diverse community but also frequently experienced considerable injustice (not always at the hands of Poles), in the form of legal restrictions, actual maltreatment, and sometimes even pogroms. In this context, the Land of Israel, embedded in Jewish religious ritual as a place of longing, represented an alternative, arousing hope for an improvement in their lot and for the establishment of their own homeland. This double phenomenon is linked to the fact that Poles too, especially after independence, looked to Palestine as a potential way to ease Polish–Jewish relations. The twenty years between 1918 and 1939 saw not only continually growing tension in Polish–Jewish relations but also growing Jewish impoverishment and unemployment. The governments of the Second Republic hoped that the emigration of Jews to the Land of Israel would help to solve both problems.

Poland and the Land of Israel before 1948

Relations between Poland and the Land of Israel have their roots in the Middle Ages, when the foundations of Polish nationhood were laid. Over time Christianity (mainly the Roman Catholic faith), to which the rulers of Poland had converted in 966, became the most numerous and influential religion in Poland. Because of the importance of Catholicism in Polish culture and customs, many elements appeared connected to the biblical tradition and topography of the Land of Israel. The architecture of the churches spread thickly throughout Poland derives to a lesser or greater extent from that of the Temple in Jerusalem: for instance, the internal division between the nave and the choir, taken from the Temple of Solomon with its Holy Place and Holy of Holies.[2] The names of various places in the Land of Israel, especially those mentioned in the New Testament, appear in many religious songs, especially Christmas carols. Poles took part in the crusades in the Middle Ages, although, compared to other European countries, their involvement was small. Over the centuries, the number of Christian pilgrimages to the Holy Land grew, especially during the nineteenth century with the advent of railways and steamships. Among the more celebrated nineteenth-century pilgrims were Ignacy Domeyko (1802–89), geologist, mining engineer, and explorer of South America; Prince Roman Stanisław Sanguszko (1800–81); and Juliusz Słowacki (1809–49), a leading poet. According to the calculations of the Franciscan Father Anzelm Szteinke, 1,195 Poles visited the Holy Land between mid-1862 and the end of 1888. Over the following two years there were as many as 1,286 Polish pilgrims.[3] This lively interest in the Holy Land and biblical history did not, however, lead to an improvement in Polish–Jewish relations. Christian Poles making pilgrimages to the Holy Land, as emerges from their many memoirs, visited almost exclusively those places commemorating events and persons associated with their religion. Sites important for Jews, although also contributing to the creation of the Christian heritage, were for the most part avoided, or at best elicited an unfeeling or indifferent response. This was not, however, exclusively a Polish reaction, since similar behaviour characterized other European pilgrims.

Starting in the second half of the nineteenth century and up to the outbreak of the Second World War, alongside the pilgrimages, tourist travel developed. Polish consular representation was established soon after the creation of Mandatory Palestine and was seen as a high priority by the Polish Foreign Ministry, as can be seen in diplomatic documents held in the Archiwum Akt Nowych in Warsaw.[4] On 1 January 1923 the Polish consulate was opened in Jerusalem, and two years later it was elevated to a consulate general. In 1927 a consulate was established in Tel Aviv, and in 1936 the network of Polish diplomatic missions in Palestine was completed by an honorary consulate in Haifa.[5]

Economic relations also increased significantly and formed a solid basis for relations between Poland and the Yishuv, the original Jewish community in the Land of Israel. To a great extent this was connected to the emigration of Polish Jews to Israel.[6] In 1938 Poland exported to Palestine mainly plant-based products worth 286,000 zlotys; animals and animal products worth 1,930,000 zlotys; food products and tobacco worth 92,000 zlotys; chemical and pharmaceutical products worth 94,000 zlotys; raw materials and textiles worth 293,000 zlotys; timber, cork, and associated products worth 5,229,000 zlotys; paper and paper products worth 125,000 zlotys; base metals and metal products worth 545,000 zlotys; and transport equipment worth 138,000 zlotys.[7] Palestinian exports to Poland were also considerable.

Jews in Poland and the Land of Israel before the Zionist Movement

It was only with the Zionist movement, which emerged during the second half of the nineteenth century, that the lofty words in the Hebrew Bible about returning to the Land of Israel began to be put into action. Nonetheless, despite later Orthodox criticism of the Zionist movement, this could not have developed without the heritage that observant Jews had created and nurtured. Melchior Wańkowicz (1892–1974), a Polish journalist, commentator, and columnist, described the importance the Hebrew Bible played in developing knowledge of the Land of Israel among Jews:

Zionism came spontaneously to a boy ... in ḥeder; it was not taught, it was not organized, it came together with religion. Reading the Tanakh, the impressionable youngster imagined for himself the landscape of the Promised Land ... In a moment of inattention on the part of their teacher young boys would tear themselves away from the mechanical chanting of texts and would ask one another 'What does an olive look like? What kinds of camels did the Amalekites ride? Does the Promised Land still exist? Is it still the land in which all your dreams will come true?'[8]

Polish Jews had been emigrating and going on pilgrimages to the Land of Israel long before the development of the Zionist movement. Unfortunately, the extant source materials do not reveal the precise beginnings or extent of this phenomenon or what percentage of Polish Jews arriving in Israel returned, stayed, or moved on. It seems clear that such migration was not a mass phenomenon, but in the modern period it acquired an organized dimension. The concept of ḥalukah had existed as early as the sixteenth century and supported pilgrims heading for the Land of Israel. It was a kind of tax, which was collected in the local Jewish communities. Each community had its own committee that supervised its collection, and it was then handed over to a central committee. The person heading the committee had the honorific title of 'Lord of the Holy Land' or 'Prince of the Land of Israel'.[9] In the second half of the eighteenth century these committees ceased their activities as a result of changes in the organization of local Jewish committees. The ḥalukah now lost its status as a tax and became a voluntary donation. As a result, the *tsadik* Menahem Mendel of Vitebsk, who had settled in Tiberias, proposed a new system of gifts for the Land of Israel. His intention was that the funds thus collected should be used to defray the costs for Jews of settling in the land. Within a short time, this idea became the *grosz palestyński* (grosz for Palestine) donated to support pious old men in the Land of Israel, who devoted the final years of their lives to prayer and penance. From the start of the nineteenth century charitable confraternities were established in Jewish communities and sent money every year through a special emissary to their co-religionists in Israel.[10]

The Khmelnytsky uprising, the Swedish invasion, and wars with Russia in the mid-seventeenth century stimulated Jewish emigration, some of which went to the Land of Israel. The popularity of such emigration was increased by messianic movements that underlined its significance as the cradle of Judaism.[11] One of these was associated with Judah Hehasid of Siedlce. Given that its members drew inspiration, at least in part, from Sabbatai Zevi they were seen as yet another heretical Sabbatian group. The rabbinical court in Kraków issued a *ḥerem* (excommunication ban) against them. As Jan Doktór writes:

In response Judah Hehasid called for a great pilgrimage to the Holy Land to greet the messiah. The hasidim set off in two groups through central Europe and Italy to the Holy Land. Their messianic propaganda was met almost everywhere with enthusiasm. More and more people joined the hasidim, so supposedly the number of pilgrims grew to 1,300 and, according to some sources, to 1,500. One group, led by Hayim Malakh and consisting of 150 people, sailed down the Danube to the Black Sea and from there to Jaffa. A second, larger group, led by Judah Hehasid, travelled to Italy whence it sailed in two groups to the Holy Land. Judah Hehasid arrived with his group in Jerusalem on 14 October 1700. The number of pilgrims had fallen greatly on the way mainly owing to illness and death. Some sources state that of the 1,500 people who set out for the Holy Land, 500 pilgrims died en route, mainly in the group led by Judah Hehasid, who himself died a few days after arriving.[12]

After the group reached Jerusalem its problems were not over. The rabbis of Istanbul issued a *ḥerem* against them.[13] Nevertheless, some of its members stayed in Israel, even if they had to leave Jerusalem for a time.

The partitions of Poland at the end of the eighteenth century created a further impulse for emigration. Initially they resulted in the deterioration of the situation of

Jews in all three partitions and motivated some to leave. However, it is not known how many left or what percentage migrated to Israel.

Zionism in the Polish Lands before 1918

Emigration to the Land of Israel changed drastically with the development of Zionism. Key proto-Zionist figures included Rabbi Tsevi Hirsch Kalischer (1795–1874) of Toruń (Thorn) and Rabbi Eliyahu Guttmacher (1796–1874) of Grätz (Grodzisk Wielkopolski). In 1832 Rabbi Kalischer issued a proclamation asserting that even before the coming of the messiah there should be a large community of Jews in the Land of Israel. During a conference of rabbis in Toruń in 1860, concrete steps were proposed to set up agricultural settlements. In the wake of these initiatives the Hovevei Tsiyon (Lovers of Zion) movement was formed,[14] whose chief ideologist was Leon Pinsker (1821–91). This was followed by the emergence of political Zionism and the personalities of Natan Birnbaum and Theodor Herzl. In 1892 Birnbaum proposed the name 'Zionism' for the new movement.

As a result of the activities of the proto-Zionists and political Zionists the profile of the typical Jewish settler in the Land of Israel underwent an important change. Pilgrims and those wishing to spend their final days there were replaced by those who had chosen Israel as a place in which to build a life and recreate a national homeland. This new type of immigration occurred in distinct stages: the First Aliyah—immigration to the Land of Israel within the context of a programme to build a Jewish national homeland—began in 1881 and lasted until 1903. The Second Aliyah took place between 1904 and 1914. The new emigrants were for the most part young and middle-aged and often displayed exceptional courage and resourcefulness to attain their goals.

The new situation is well captured in an editorial which appeared in the Warsaw periodical *Izraelita* in 1890:

Apart from a small handful of locals [the country's] previous inhabitants had been almost exclusively pilgrims from various corners of the earth, who had come to end their days amidst prayer and memories and to leave their bones in the land of their forefathers. Today the population comprises for the most part working people leaving mainly our lands to till the soil of the land of their forefathers. Over the last twenty-five years the Jewish population has more than quadrupled. The following cities have more than 35,000 inhabitants: Jerusalem, Safed, Tiberias, Jaffa, Hebron, Sidon, Haifa, Acre, Nablus, and Gaza. Around 10,000 or so are scattered across the country in small settlements, while several thousand live in large colonies of, as we said, emigrants from our parts, who have come to till the land of their forefathers with their own hands. Thanks to their industry and dedication and despite many obstacles erected by the Turkish government and little support from their European co-religionists, they have succeeded in making some of their communities flourish within a short time . . . The products of the colonies in the Land of Israel are usually exported to Europe. We should recall too that some of the larger settlements mentioned, such as Petah Tikva, Zikhron Ya'akov, Rosh Pina, and others, are in terms of culture, properly established with their own synagogue, schools, almshouses, and other institutions, so that they represent fully formed little Jewish religious communities.[15]

Up to the end of the First World War the best conditions for the development of the Zionist movement on the Polish lands were to be found in Galicia. The large community of Jews there displayed considerable energy in the social, political, economic, cultural, and academic fields. In 1857 Jews, 448,973 in number, represented nearly 10 per cent of the total population. By 1910 this number had almost doubled, reaching 871,895, nearly 11 per cent of the total population.[16] The Jews, like the Poles and the Ukrainians, felt the positive effects of the liberal reforms that culminated in the constitution of December 1867, which granted the province wide-ranging autonomy. Within its framework, local economic political entities were established in the form of trade and industrial chambers of commerce, while territorial local government was revived. Thanks to their participation in local government, Jews gained a great deal of experience in political activity. It was precisely in these Galician political bodies that an impressive group of Zionist leaders developed, some of whom emigrated at different times to the Land of Israel, while others remained in Galicia but worked with the Yishuv.

In Galician local government Jews learned to overcome individualism and to work as a collective, which was very important from the point of view of creating Zionist political groupings and gaining support for them. A powerful spur to the general development of the Jewish community in Galicia was the granting of equal rights, which were achieved in 1867 on the strength of the December constitution. In the Kingdom of Poland, equal rights for Jews had been introduced in 1862, and in the Prussian Partition in 1869, while they were never formally granted in the Russian partition outside the Kingdom of Poland. As in the tsarist empire, the authorities supervised them carefully, but did not interfere in their work and did not take action against their members. In these conditions it was Galicia that became an important centre of the Zionist movement and even, as some claim, a 'mother of Israel'.[17] Its members did not have an easy time. They found it difficult to overcome local Jewish indifference, described in a letter dated 27 February 1895 from the village elder of Bohorodchany to the Galician viceroy: 'The majority of the Israelite community, which is very poor, is completely indifferent to this issue [Zionism], since, having no property to dispose of, it sees no way of emigrating, while the more prosperous among them have no intention of leaving something certain for vague promises.'[18]

A number of interlocking factors explain the strength of the Zionist movement in Galicia. During its first stage, Habsburg rule had not led to an improvement in the situation of the Jews. On the contrary, the government in Vienna tried to limit their numbers and imposed additional taxes on them, which heightened their sense of difference. The movement was also greatly strengthened by the fact that the Jews in Galicia quickly learned to work with their co-religionists in Vienna. This was not easy: on the Galician side there was a great fear of becoming dominated by outside liberal influences, while among Viennese Jews there was a strong prejudice against their 'backward' brothers from the north-eastern province.[19] Nonetheless channels of communication were opened for political and philanthropic co-operation that were later successfully used by Zionist activists.

A key factor in the emergence of the Zionist movement in Galicia was the community of progressive Jews. They were open to German and Polish cultural influences and to secular education, while retaining ties to their own people and religion. Towards the end of the nineteenth century Abraham Ozjasz Thon (1870–1936) became a leading figure in this community and in 1897 was appointed rabbi at the Tempel synagogue in Kraków. That same year he helped Theodor Herzl organize the First Zionist Congress in Basel. Between 1919 and 1935 he was a member of the Polish Sejm. He helped found *Nowy Dziennik*, one of the Polish Zionists' leading publications, which appeared from 9 July 1918 to 2 September 1939.

Thon also became an important intermediary between Zionist communities and the rapidly growing Jewish lodge, B'nai B'rith. On 15 October 1892, on the basis of an edict of the viceroy in Lwów, the association B'nai B'rith Solidarność was formally registered in Kraków.[20] In Lwów itself the local 'Leopolis' lodge was registered at the viceroy's office on 5 October 1899.[21] Thon for a time chaired B'nai B'rith in Kraków. It was partly under his influence that the lodge dropped its hostile attitude to the Zionist movement. B'nai B'rith sought to build links between acculturated Jews, who often had to interact on a day-to-day basis with the non-Jewish community, and also sought to serve their spiritual and intellectual development. Its members were mainly the intelligentsia and representatives of the professions and entrepreneurs. The selection of speakers and the subjects of the lectures given at lodge meetings show that an interest in the Land of Israel, its history and culture, and in the rebirth of a Jewish community there, was growing among these people. Between the wars the B'nai B'rith lodges in Poland provided financial support to Jewish settlements in Israel. Initially these were small donations collected, above all, in the blue and white tins of the Jewish National Fund (Keren Kayemet Leyisra'el). Subsequently, under the influence of growing antisemitism, members of B'nai B'rith significantly increased their material aid to Jews emigrating to Israel. In this manner enduring ties of solidarity began to be formed. In 1932, twenty or so members of the Leopolis lodge set off for the first time on a trip to Israel. According to the report they prepared, 'the party received an exceptionally warm reception from the lodges in the Land of Israel. They were greeted by delegates of the great lodge in Jerusalem, received by the lodge in Tel Aviv, and on the return journey by delegates of the lodge in Cairo.'[22]

Academic secondary schools with high standards were a feature of life in Galicia. As a result of the granting of equal rights, the number of Jews attending such schools grew continuously. Subsequently, growing numbers of Jews attended local institutions of higher learning, especially the Jagiellonian University in Kraków and the University of Lwów. By the end of the nineteenth century nearly a fifth of the Jagiellonian University's law students were Jewish. In the academic year 1896/7 Jews made up over a quarter of the students in the Faculty of Medicine.[23] Studying in Vienna was also popular among the Jews of Galicia. At the University of Vienna, according to a survey of 1899, there were 45 Jewish medical students out of 494 matriculants, 45 law students out of 538, and 2 out of 141 philosophy students.[24] As a consequence, in Galicia, as throughout the whole Habsburg empire, a new Jewish elite in the form of a secular intelligentsia began to develop. A great many Galician Jews, educated in well-known schools and colleges on Habsburg lands, played an important part in Zionist organizations and subsequently in building the State of Israel. The leaders of the Zionist movement were also able to take advantage of the skills of some of those who had no formal connection with it. A number of eminent architects, who went to the Land of Israel from Galicia, stand out. They include Dow Kutchinsky (Kuczyński) (1866–1933) from Kraków, a graduate of the Kraków Polytechnic School of Architecture; Pinchas Hütt (1888–1949) from Lwów, who graduated from the School of Architecture at the Polytechnic in Chernovtsy; Jacob Pinkerfeld (1897–1956) from Przemyśl, a graduate of the Higher Technical School in Vienna; Yosef Neufeld (1899–1980) from Monasterzyska, who studied in Vienna and Rome; Carl Rubin (1899–1955) from Śniatyn, a graduate of the Technical School in Vienna; and Arie Sharon (1900–84) from Jarosław, who studied at the German Higher Technical School in Brno and the Bauhaus school in Dessau under Walter Gropius. Each of them played an important role in the history of Jewish architecture. One of the most outstanding was Arie Sharon, who was not only an architect but also developed a spatial and architectural plan for Israel. Between 1949 and 1953 he was director of the Planning Office in Prime Minister David Ben-Gurion's administration. He produced a plan to divide Israel into twenty-four zones of settlement, as well as plans for new towns, settlements, roads, freeways, bridges, and viaducts.[25]

The Agricultural Academy in Dublany, located not far from Lwów, also played a little-known role in the development of the kibbutz movement. It was established in 1856, running a three-year agricultural course, and in 1872 became the Higher School of Agriculture. In 1901 it was renamed the Agricultural Academy. In addition to young Poles, young Jews also started to attend it, acquiring in this way a training which was to be useful in the Land of Israel. Many of the agricultural instructors at the numerous kibbutzim established in Galicia had studied at the academy.

The activity of Zionist groups was not limited to propaganda and encouraging migration to Israel. Although building a state in the Land of Israel was the main goal, it was realized that Jews needed to advance in education, culture, and social matters in order to achieve this. This is reflected in the official correspondence. In a report dated 6 April 1898 to the office of the viceroy of Galicia in Lwów, the village elder of Rohatyn described the work of the Bnei Zion association in the area:

The aim of the aforementioned association in Rohatyn is to promote education among the Israelites, to support Hebrew and German newspapers, and to arrange lectures on various branches of knowledge. The association is also involved in improving the lot of poor Israelites, especially taking care of and providing for people of the Mosaic faith who have been expelled from Russia and Romania.[26]

Only at the end of the letter did he note:

The aim of the association is also to take care of emigrants to the Land of Israel and Syria, where the organization 'Zion' of Vienna has already purchased in the Land of Israel land valued at 100,000 francs, and by way of a deposit has paid B[aron] Rothschild 20,000 francs, the rest to be paid off in instalments.[27]

Contrary to general opinion, the Zionist associations were neither dominant in the Jewish community nor particularly wealthy. Most of those in Galicia covered the costs of their statutory activities with difficulty. In 1898 the village elder of Rzeszów reported to the Galician authorities that the local Hovevei Tsiyon association that had been in existence since 1891 and whose membership he estimated at 130 had an annual income of 500 to 600 zlotys, which covered 'rent, firewood, light, and daily papers, with rarely any significant surplus'.[28] The elders of Stanisławów and Tarnopol sent similar letters. The latter commented that it cost 4,000 zlotys for a single family to emigrate to Israel, whereas the annual income of the Bnei Zion association, active in Tarnopol since 1894, was 400 zlotys.[29] Given this situation, the financial support of Zionist organizations in the West, which had decidedly larger budgets, played a key role. It should be noted too that after 1918 the circumstances of Zionist associations in Poland improved, but here too the assistance of co-religionists in the West was not insignificant, especially the fundraising carried out in the USA by Ozjasz Thon on behalf of Jewish settlements in the Land of Israel. Thon has been appropriately commemorated in Israel: the moshav Beit Yehoshua, located on the plain of Sharon and founded in 1938 by pioneers from the Akiva movement, is named after him, and so are streets in the cities of Tel Aviv, Holon, Netanya, Ramat Hasharon, and Tzoran-Kadima.

Zionism in Poland from 1918 to 1939

After 1918 Zionist groups were able to function successfully in the reborn Second Republic, although Polish–Jewish relations were marked by considerable tension.[30] Among Zionist groups, which were an important part of the Jewish political scene, it was the right-wing Revisionist Zionists who developed the best relationship with the authorities. The reason for this was not only agreement that Jews ought to emigrate from Poland (from the point of view of the Polish government Palestine was not the only option, others being Angola, Kenya, Uganda, Argentina, Brazil, Ecuador, Guatemala, Colombia, Australia, and Birobidzhan);[31] an important role was also played by the group's ideological affinity with the Polish government, led after May 1926 by Józef Piłsudski. The leader of the Revisionists, Vladimir (Ze'ev) Jabotinsky (1880–1940), was much influenced by the nineteenth-century Polish nationalist uprisings fuelled by Romanticism and the person of Piłsudski, and maintained very good relations with Polish political and military circles. When forming the youth organization Betar, Jabotinsky drew inspiration from Piłsudski's Rifleman's Association. Thanks to negotiations he conducted between 1936 and 1939, the Revisionists reached a secret agreement with the Polish government which granted them a loan of $400,000 to purchase weapons. Fearful of the reaction of the British, who were administering Palestine, the delivery of weapons, ammunition, and explosives took place in conditions of extreme secrecy. The Polish side also delivered to the Revisionists aircraft supposedly for sporting uses, but in fact with every intention that they be used for military purposes. In addition, Jabotinsky planned to form in Poland a 40,000-strong army capable of mounting an assault on the British authorities in Palestine with the aim of seizing control. One of the ways that the men were to get there was on the Polish ship, the *Polonia*. Polish military and intelligence officers were actively involved in the project. In the spring of 1939 top-secret training for leaders of this assault was held in the mountainous region of Andrychów. Its students were Irgun fighters who had travelled to Poland from Palestine. Abraham Stern (1907–42), born in Suwałki, the founder and leader of the Zionist paramilitary organization Lehi, also played an important part in underground operations and in the organization of secret training.[32]

The Zionist organizations active in Poland from the end of the nineteenth century contributed greatly to building up Jewish settlement in the Land of Israel. Zionist activists succeeded in encouraging wealthy Jews to support their poorer brethren who wanted to emigrate to Israel, even if they did not wish to do so themselves. This not only helped to facilitate emigration but also contributed to building links between the new inhabitants of Israel and their benefactors in the Polish lands and in other parts of Europe. The Zionist organizations also undertook large-scale action to prepare emigrants as well as possible for the journey and for life and work in the Land of Israel. To that end organizations from Zionism's left wing focused mainly on agricultural and professional training for Jews. In the Polish lands, as throughout Europe, the overwhelming majority of Jews were urban, and a large percentage of them were involved in professions connected with trade and the handling of money, or worked as craftsmen. In most cases they were self-employed. Hence planning for the establishment of a Jewish state involved teaching Jews how to work as a collective in agriculture, something they had little experience of.

Both of these tasks were entrusted to the numerous kibbutzim established in the Polish lands. Degania, the first kibbutz in the Land of Israel, was established in 1910, but there is a lack of evidence regarding the founding of the first kibbutz in Europe, and it is quite possible that this might have been one of the Polish kibbutzim. Certainly the network of kibbutzim in the Second Republic between the wars was denser than that in the Land of Israel. However, most of them were experimental in nature and small, with only a few instructors and students (for the most part school and university students), who on small plots of land (often in the courtyards of apartment buildings) learned to grow plants and raise animals. There was a larger kibbutz in Kraków in Cichy Kącik on a slice of land between modern Błonie and the stadium of the Wisła Kraków football team.[33] The pioneers were not only taught farming skills but also crafts—tailoring, carpentry, weaving, locksmithing: trades which were needed in building a new state. By 1934 Keren Hehaluts Hamizrahi in Poland was supporting 133 training kibbutzim, which had their own workshops and crafts cooperatives, and thousands of people were being trained there.[34] Much of this work was carried out by instructors from Israel. They shared their knowledge and practical skills on the weather, geology, and local conditions. Various educational and informational materials would make their way from the Land of Israel to the Polish lands, including the reasonably regular delivery from Jerusalem of newssheets and organizational materials sent to all the major Zionist centres around the world.

The right-wing Zionist organizations placed greater emphasis on self-defence and the study of Hebrew. Their work led to a rise in the popularity of Hebrew, which in the Land of Israel had already been adopted for everyday use. In 1922 it attained the rank of one of the three official languages of Mandatory Palestine. The Zionist left and right were linked by an attachment to sport, which played a large part in arousing Jewish national feeling. Jakub Selzer wrote in the *Almanach żydowski*, published in Lwów in 1937:

The aim of Maccabi is the physical and spiritual rebirth of the Jewish masses, the creation of a free and independent individual defending with dignity his own and his country's honour. Maccabi aims to connect to the wonderful heroic traditions of the Maccabees, and by adopting the symbolic name Maccabi builds a link between today and the past in the Land of Israel.[35]

The beginnings were none too easy:

In this work young people encountered extraordinary obstacles, both from the Orthodox, who saw gymnastics as a threat to the Jewish spirit, as well as from the older progressive generation, who regretfully watched this 'wasting' of time on 'games' and physical exercise. The first Jewish sports clubs in Poland were formed at the turn of the nineteenth and twentieth centuries in the Austrian and Prussian partitions.[36]

Many sports clubs were linked to specific political parties, and the non-Zionist parties also had their own. Organizations associated with the Bund set up a network of clubs called Jutrzenka in Polish and Morgenstern in Yiddish. The Zionist movement's clubs were affiliated with the Maccabi Jewish Gymnastics and Sports Association, which was part of the world-wide Maccabi movement. The Maccabiah Games organized by the movement played an important part in its development. The first games were held between 28 March and 6 April 1932 in Tel Aviv, with teams from eighteen countries taking part. The Polish contingent, consisting of sixty-six athletes, won the team event, beating teams from Austria and the United States. This success led to the Polish Maccabi Association being entrusted with the preparations for winter games. The first winter Maccabiah Games were held in Zakopane between 2 and 5 February 1933, with the Polish team repeating its Tel Aviv success and winning the team event. The Second World Maccabiah Games were held in April 1935. The games planned for 1938 did not take place owing to the tense political situation and the threat of war. The event was revived in 1950 in independent Israel.

After 1918 Zionism became one of the leading political forces among Polish Jews. Zionist groups were represented in parliament. One of their leading figures, the lawyer Yitzhak Grünbaum (1879–1970), was a member of the Sejm between 1919 and

1932, and was instrumental in setting up the Minorities Bloc in the elections of November 1922. In 1933 he emigrated to the Land of Israel where he was one of the leaders of the Jewish Agency. He used the knowledge and experience gained in the Polish Sejm when working on the creation of the Israeli parliament, the Knesset, although he himself was never elected to it. However, he was the first minister of the interior in the government of David Ben-Gurion.

Zionist activists in Poland did not primarily use fear of antisemitism or poverty to encourage Jews to emigrate. They attempted, above all, to convince Jews of the attractiveness of the Land of Israel, expatiating on its religious, historical, and cultural attributes, and even its scenery. Thus the dominant message was positive, even if perhaps propagandistic, since difficult topics were often avoided, such as the low cultural level, the shortage of drinking water, and the harsh climate. The issues of antisemitism and economic problems in the diaspora were secondary. Naturally, this state of affairs changed with the rise to power of the Nazi party in Germany and the widespread growth of antisemitism in Europe.

Despite the often repeated criticism of Zionist groups of lacking interest in the situation of the Jews in Poland, their activities were not limited to propaganda for emigration. While their priority was building a state in the Land of Israel, their members realized that to facilitate this Jews first of all needed support in the areas of education, culture, and social affairs. Nevertheless, encouraging migration to the Land of Israel was central to all parts of the Zionist movement.

The Third Aliyah (1918–23) was begun in October 1918 by six boys who set out from Będzin in Silesia. Keeping their intentions secret from their parents they travelled only with rucksacks, which they filled with clothes and food. They journeyed through Kraków, Przemyśl, and Lwów all the way to Odessa, where they stayed with Hayim Nahman Bialik, reaching Jaffa on 12 December 1918. In the Land of Israel they were described as the 'Boys from Będzin'.[37] Although most Polish Jews travelled by rail to the ports of Trieste, Constanța, or Odessa, where they transferred to ships, there were also cases of rather more original modes of transport. In 1932 a group of young Jews from Poland rode to Trieste on bicycles manufactured by the Łucznik company in Radom and then transferred to a ship for Haifa.[38] Tens of thousands of Polish Jews travelled to Palestine between the wars, ostensibly as tourists, in an attempt to evade the limits put on Jewish immigration by Great Britain.

Successive *aliyot* by Polish Jews were spurred by dreams of a better life in the Land of Israel, a consequence, among other things, of the difficult living conditions and tense political situation in Poland. The exchange-rate reform introduced by Prime Minister Władysław Grabski in 1924 had serious consequences. While the reform was essential from the economic point of view, it was mainly the Jewish middle class that bore the brunt of the hardships it imposed. According to statistics compiled by Zionist organizations, 32,536 Polish Jews emigrated to the Land of Israel between 1924 and 1926.[39] They made up the Fourth, or Grabski, Aliyah, whose middle-class character aroused a negative response from the Zionist leadership. An even greater number of Jews emigrated to the Land of Israel between 1931 and 1939.

The emigration of Polish Jews to Israel fits into the context of breaking with the diaspora and returning to the former homeland. Nevertheless, some doubt should be cast on the appropriateness of the words 'breaking with' (especially if they are understood to mean a complete rupture) in terms of links with Polish culture. An expression of the vital links with Poland retained by Polish Jews was the numerous patriotic associations that they established. The Union of Polish Jews was set up in Tel Aviv at the start of the 1930s.[40] In addition, Polish Jews also created associations of former residents of specific cities, such as Kraków, Łódź, Warsaw, Kielce, and Białystok. For example, in 1925 the Związek Krakowian w Izraelu (Association of Cracovians in Israel) was formed in Tel Aviv and soon acquired a significant membership.[41] Towards the end of the twentieth century Aleksander Klugman listed over 180 active Polish patriotic associations in Israel. They provided common values, memories, and social and cultural events for their members. Among their legacies are the memorial books that they produced. They were dedicated to the towns and villages formerly inhabited by the associations' members.[42] Putting it simply, Polish Jews were extremely proud of their former 'little homelands'—the towns and villages where they had as often as not spent their childhood—as opposed to Poland itself, towards which they nursed many grievances, the result, for example, of government policy. Furthermore, Poland had been partitioned for 123 years, which in this instance was also not uninfluential. Many Jews left the Polish lands before the rebirth of the Second Republic in 1918, or shortly thereafter.

1939–1948

The arrival of further waves of immigrants was interrupted by the outbreak of the Second World War. During the war Polish–Jewish relations, in the context of the Land of Israel, underwent a great change but were not severed. First of all, disturbing news started to reach Israel of the Polish Jews' tragic fate. Zionist activists did not, however, have the resources to confirm this information immediately nor, above all, to respond to it effectively. Couriers were despatched to Europe, but most of them were traced and killed by the Germans and their allies' forces and intelligence agencies. However, Jews living in the Land of Israel were not unaware of what was taking place in occupied Poland. Even less is it true that they were indifferent to the fate of their compatriots living under Nazi rule. Echoes of the tragic events taking place in Europe affected the imagination of the inhabitants of the Land of Israel. The Warsaw ghetto uprising that broke out on 19 April 1943 and lasted until mid-May became one of the founding myths of the State of Israel. The insurgents' courage was compared to the Maccabees' heroic struggle. In 1943 the Yad Mordechai kibbutz, named in honour of Mordechaj Anielewicz, was established.[43] Then, in 1948, Holocaust survivors established the Lohamei Hageta'ot (Ghetto Fighters) kibbutz. Among the founders of this kibbutz were insurgents from the Warsaw ghetto, including Yitzhak Zuckerman and his wife Zivia Lubetkin.

An event of great significance was the arrival in the Land of Israel of General

Władysław Anders' army, which was accompanied by a very large number of civilians, including children. Among the 77,000 soldiers, who, together with Anders, left Soviet captivity, there were around 6,000 Jews, including over 4,401 soldiers (20 of them women)—146 officers, 416 NCOs, and 3,839 other ranks.[44] In the Land of Israel a number of them abandoned the army, while others fought on into Europe, evidence of which can be seen in the Jewish graves in the military cemetery at Monte Cassino. Those Jews who remained in the Land of Israel found employment in civilian occupations, but a great many of them also joined Jewish self-defence groups such as the Haganah, Irgun, and Lehi. Their knowledge and experience made them invaluable to the Jewish combat organizations. Among them was Menachem Begin (born in Brześć nad Bugiem in 1913), who had been released from an NKVD jail and who in 1977 became the first right-wing prime minister of modern Israel. According to various sources, between around 800 and 1,000 Jewish children were among those exiles who left the Soviet Union. Their path had led through Tehran, leading to the name 'Tehran children'. The largest group of children with chaperones reached the Land of Israel by sea, some of them arriving in February 1943. A number of the children saved by General Anders grew into Israeli military, intellectual, and artistic personalities. Among them were Avigdor 'Janusz' Ben-Gal (born in Łódź in 1936), who became a distinguished soldier, division commander, and hero of the Yom Kippur War, and Ze'ev (Włodzimierz) Schuss, an acclaimed mathematician, pianist, and translator. Historians are more or less in agreement that the exiles who helped form General Anders' army undoubtedly saved their lives by doing so, since in the Soviet Union they were faced with death from overwork in labour camps, inadequate food, and the inhospitable climate. However, there is a serious difference of opinion as to whether the leadership of the Anders Army treated Poles and Jews who expressed an interest in being evacuated equally. There is plenty of evidence that Poles were helped first, and there are no grounds for questioning the numerous accounts by Jews who themselves encountered obstacles and difficulties or witnessed others encountering them.[45] There are also testimonies in which the Poles received glowing praise from the Jews. An example of this is a letter from Rabbi Israel Halberstam of Kraków addressed to General Władysław Sikorski, prime minister of the Polish government-in-exile in London.

As one of those rabbis evacuated from Russia I, together with my brother Leib Halberstam, feel it my duty to convey our deepest gratitude to you, esteemed sir, as the head of the Polish government for the care and assistance afforded us by the Polish authorities during our time in the USSR. I see it as repayment of a moral duty if I state that the whole of Ambassador Kot's term of office in Kuibyshev, and especially the care that the government delegates, Professor Heitzman in Samarkand, Mr. Szyszkowski in Bukhara, and, during the evacuation, Mr. Jenicz in Yangi-Yul, devoted to us allowed us to survive the painful and difficult year that we endured after our release from camps and places of exile. This is not the time to describe in detail the kind attention we received in Russia from our own relief agencies. Taking no account of national or religious differences, our Polish authorities took care of all citizens, interceded whenever the release of a Polish citizen was at stake, provided financial and moral support for everyone in need. I believe that I speak for all Polish Jews, especially those 'residing' in Uzbekistan, when I say that it this aid alone that we have to thank for having survived so far, and I express the hope that our esteemed Polish government will continue to take care of our brethren, who unfortunately have remained in the USSR. With expressions of our deepest gratitude.[46]

Apart from the Jews accompanying Anders, on the whole during the Second World War only fugitives and those pretending to be non-Jews using so-called 'Aryan papers' succeeded in reaching the Land of Israel

The Anders Army's stay in the Land of Israel also played an important role in the lives of the Poles in the army. Now, for the first time since leaving Polish territory, they encountered a large group of people speaking their language, tens of thousands of Jews, often their own former friends, acquaintances, and neighbours. There was no lack of tension though. Some Poles, despite the wartime tragedies, were unable to shed their prejudices towards Jews. Nevertheless, Polish–Jewish relations in the Land of Israel were generally harmonious. The Poles encountered a great deal of goodwill on the part of the Jews, who were in the dominant position. There are a great many comments in the accounts of Polish exiles on the subject of the help and kindness shown them by the Jews. For example, Polish children often received free meals, juice, and clothing.[47] Polish troops felt safe in the Jewish environment. It even happened that British troops, who were often attacked by Jewish fighters, decked out their vehicles with Polish emblems and flags to afford them greater protection, in the conviction that the Jews did not attack Poles. Thus, the Poles found in the Land of Israel favourable conditions to stop for a moment, take control of the situation in the ranks, heal the sick, and set up schooling for their children. With this in mind, a number of Polish schools were opened. The Government Delegate for Education and Schools worked effectively. Polish soldiers and civilians conducted an ambitious publishing programme: the dailies *Gazeta Polska*, *Ochotniczka*, and *Przez Lądy i Morza* appeared, as did the weekly *Orzeł Biały* and the fortnightly *W Drodze*. Additionally, the Polish consulates general in Tel Aviv and Jerusalem continued to operate, as did the PKO Bank and the delegates of the Polish Ministry of Labour and Social Security. A Polish Information Centre in the East was opened, which supported the Polish Telegraph Agency in Jerusalem, publishing in English a newssheet called the *Polish Digest*. There is also a section of the cemetery in Jaffa dedicated to Polish exiles.[48]

With the end of hostilities came an opportunity for a fresh start in relations between Poland and the Land of Israel. The first decisions of Poland's communist authorities were not indicative of later problems and the complete breakdown of relations. On 21 September 1945 Romuald Gadomski was nominated as representative of the Polish government in Palestine. With the help of the Polish embassy in Moscow he was provided with plenipotentiary powers and funds to open a consulate general in Jerusalem and a consulate in Tel Aviv.[49] In the international arena Polish diplomats supported the Jews' striving for their own homeland. However, shortly after the proclamation of Jewish independence, Poland, under orders from Stalin, radically cooled its relations with Israel. Furthermore, in Poland itself a number of unfortunate events and incidents affected Polish–Jewish relations very negatively.[50]

Of the approximately 3.5 million Polish Jews, no more than around 10 per cent survived the Holocaust. The conviction of the need to build an independent Jewish state was growing, which made emigration attractive. Owing to various legal technicalities, and later when the Polish communist authorities closed the borders, most Jews emigrated from Poland illegally, assisted by the underground Zionist organization Berihah. Forces of repulsion, such as feelings of loneliness after the Holocaust, memories of traumatic experiences in Poland, and the association of Poland with the graveyard where their families, acquaintances, and friends had met their deaths now began to work fully on the Jews. No less a force of repulsion was the post-war atmosphere of lawlessness and violence which, while indeed general, was not short of incidents aimed specifically at Jews. Many of them, having survived the Holocaust, were afraid to return to their homes. For some Jews attempts to recover their homes and property ended in tragedy, injury, or death, and news of this spread rapidly. The pogrom in Kielce of 4 July 1946, in which at least forty Jews died and double that number were injured, came as a great shock. The communist authorities felt obliged to come to an agreement with representatives of the Jewish community, on the strength of which they agreed to allow organized groups of Jews to leave the country. Altogether more than 100,000 Jews left Poland, of whom a significant number headed for the Land of Israel.

Conclusion

The relationship between Poland and the Land of Israel dates back to the Middle Ages. It includes pilgrimages by Poles and Jews to the Holy Land, tourist visits, Jewish migrations, economic and cultural exchanges, and diplomacy. The overall result is positive, although it is cause for sorrow that successful relations between Poland and the Land of Israel did not have a positive effect on Polish–Jewish relations overall.

The Land of Israel exercised a significant influence on both Christians and Jews. Yet while for Christians this was an issue of religion, for Jews it was also an issue of statehood. The Zionist movement, which postulated rebuilding a national homeland for Jews, was born in the nineteenth century. While various locations were considered, the decision was quickly taken to make the Land of Israel the Jewish homeland. Its great power of attraction for Jews was taken into account. In addition to Jews' natural ties to the Land of Israel and centuries of longing, the spread of antisemitism in Poland (and indeed throughout Europe) and economic difficulties contributed to the development of Zionism. These factors were forcing Jews to leave Poland. However, not all emigrants chose the Land of Israel as the (final) destination of their journey. The largest percentage of Jews emigrated to western Europe or the United States. Therefore, Zionist activists made a great many efforts to motivate Jews not only to emigrate but to choose the Land of Israel. Furthermore, even after the proclamation of the independence of Israel on 14 May 1948, not all Jewish emigrants headed there. Even those who had imagined the State of Israel as the place where they could at last feel themselves to be at home did on the whole realize that life there was none too easy. In this regard things began to change only when the Israeli economy began to grow and the standard of living to improve appreciably.

The Second World War brought an end to large-scale Jewish life in Poland. Yet it was events that took place later that led to the definitive rupture. The protests against the Polish regime in March 1968 led to an antisemitic witch hunt, which forced many of the remaining Polish Jews to leave the country. Thus the heritage of the Polish Jews and the tradition of rich Polish–Israeli relations were ruptured in an exceptionally unfortunate way. Leaving Poland for the Land of Israel and later for independent Israel, Jews had a great many reasons to remember Poland in the worst possible way. The fact that nevertheless a large group of Polish Jews in Israel have begun to nurture their memories of Poland and the traditions associated with it should be recognized as an unusual phenomenon, and one which needs to be supported.

Translated from the Polish by Jarosław Garliński

Notes

1 I have already published an article following this convention (Ł. T. Sroka, 'Relations between Poland and Erets Yisrael before 1948', in Ł. T. Sroka and B. Brutin (eds.), *Polish–Israeli Cooperation Experience: From Zionism to Israel* (Kraków, 2017), 109–23). The project was financed by a grant from National Science Center/Poland/(UMO-2015/19/B/HS3/02116).

2 J. Kowalczyk, 'Elementy Świątyni Salomona w kościołach nowożytnych w Polsce', in P. Paszkiewicz and T. Zadrożny (eds.), *Jerozolima w kulturze europejskiej* (Warsaw, 1997), 395–406: 395; see also T. Zadrożny, '*Dei templum est, Dei structura est, Dei aedificatio est*, czyli o niektórych aspektach recepcji idei Świątyni Jerozolimskiej w nowożytnej architekturze sakralnej', in Paszkiewicz and Zadrożny (eds.), *Jerozolima w kulturze europejskiej*, 407–20.

3 A. J. Szteinke, *Polscy bracia mniejsi w służbie Ziemi Świętej 1342–1995* (Poznań, 1999), 19.

4 Archiwum Akt Nowych, Warsaw, 2/322, 'Ministerstwa Spraw Zagranicznych w Warszawie', 2279, 2282, 2285, 2292, 2304, 2305, 10543, 10550.

5 J. Dyduch, 'Stosunki polsko-izraelskie: Próba analizy czynników je kształtujących', in E. Waszkiewicz (ed.), *Współcześni Żydzi – Polska i diaspora: Wybrane zagadnienia* (Wrocław, 2007), 155–95: 156–7.

6 J. Łazor, 'Żydowska emigracja a polskie stosunki gospodarcze z Palestyną w okresie międzywojennym', in J. Skodlarski and A. Pieczewski (eds.), *Rola Żydów w rozwoju gospodarczym ziem polskich* (Łódź, 2014), 189–202.

7 J. Łazor, *Brama na Bliski Wschód: Polsko-palestyńskie stosunki gospodarcze w okresie międzywojennym* (Warsaw, 2016), 176.

8 M. Wańkowicz, 'Do Erez Izrael', *Kultura*, 13 (1948), 60–8: 61.

9 I. Schiper, 'Dzieje sjonizmu na ziemiach polskich (do 1918 r.)', in I. Schiper, A. Tartakower, and A. Hafftka (eds.), *Żydzi w Polsce Odrodzonej: Działalność społeczna, gospodarcza, oświatowa i kulturalna*, 2 vols. (Warsaw, 1932–3), i. 518–30: 519.

10 Ibid.

11 Schiper, 'Dzieje sjonizmu na ziemiach polskich', i. 518.
12 J. Doktór, 'Formowanie się chasydyzmu polskiego', in M. Galas (ed.), *Światło i słońce: Studia z dziejów chasydyzmu* (Kraków, 2006), 39–59: 42–3.
13 Ibid. 43.
14 J. L. Myers, 'Zevi Hirsch Kalischer and the Origins of Religious Zionism', in F. Malino and D. Sorkin (eds.), *From East and West: Jews in a Changing Europe, 1750–1870* (Oxford, 1990), 267–94.
15 See Z. Borzymińska, *Dzieje Żydów w Polsce: Wybór tekstów źródłowych. XIX wiek* (Warsaw, 1994), 107–8.
16 K. Zamorski, *Informator statystyczny do dziejów społeczno-gospodarczych Galicji: Ludność Galicji w latach 1857–1910*, ed. H. Madurowicz-Urbańska (Kraków, 1989), 70–1.
17 See E. Gawron, 'Matka Izraela / The Mother of Israel', trans. I. Reichardt, *Herito: Dziedzictwo, Kultura, Współczesność*, 21 (2015), 48–57.
18 Tsentral'nyi derzhavnyi istorychnyi arkhiv Ukrayiny, Lviv (hereafter TsDIAL), f. 146, op. 58, spr. 3046: Bohorodchany village elder, letter to viceroy of Galicia, 27 Feb. 1895.
19 See G. Kohlbauer-Fritz (ed.), *Zwischen Ost und West: Galizische Juden in Wien* (Vienna, 2000).
20 Archiwum Narodowe w Krakowie, 29/557, 'Związek Żydowskich Stowarzyszeń Humanitarnych "B'nei B'rith" w Krakowie 1892–1938', 1: 'Statut Stowarzyszenia Humanitarnego "Solidarność" w Krakowie', 15 Oct. 1892.
21 TsDIAL, f. 701, op. 2, spr, 1022: Statut Towarzystwa 'Leopolis' (B'nei B'rith) we Lwowie, 5 Oct. 1899.
22 Archiwum Narodowe w Krakowie, 29/557/387, 'Żydowskie Stow. Hum. "Leopolis" BB we Lwowie (Loża Leopolis)'.
23 M. Kulczykowski, *Żydzi – studenci Uniwersytetu Jagiellońskiego w dobie autonomicznej Galicji (1867–1918)* (Kraków, 1995), 34–5.
24 J. Holzer, 'Żydzi galicyjscy na Uniwersytecie Wiedeńskim w okresie zaborów', in A. K. Paluch (ed.), *The Jews in Poland*, i (Kraków, 1999), 181–5: 184.
25 See B. Świątkowska (ed.), *Adrichalim – architekci: Leksykon pochodzących z Polski architektów działających w Palestynie i Izraelu w XX wieku* (Warsaw, 2016).
26 TsDIAL, f. 146, op. 58, spr. 3046: Rohatyn village elder, letter to the viceroy of Galicia, 6 Apr. 1898.
27 Ibid.
28 Ibid.
29 Ibid.
30 See T. Gąsowski, 'The Second Republic and Its Jewish Citizens', in S. Kapralski (ed.), *The Jews in Poland*, ii (Kraków, 1999), 125–36.
31 Z. Trębacz, *Nie tylko Palestyna: Polskie plany emigracyjne wobec Żydów 1935–1939* (Warsaw, 2018), 67.
32 See J. Łazor, 'Wywóz polskiego sprzętu wojskowego do Palestyny w okresie międzywojennym', in T. Głowiński and K. Popiński (eds.), *Gospodarka i społeczeństwo a wojskowość na ziemiach polskich* (Wrocław, 2010), 217–20.
33 A. D. Pordes and I. Grin, *Ich miasto: Wspomnienia Izraelczyków, przedwojennych mieszkańców Krakowa* (Warsaw, 2004), 117, 181.
34 B. Łętocha, A. Messer, A. Cała, and I. Jabłońska, *Palestyna w żydowskich drukach ulotnych wydanych w II Rzeczypospolitej: Dokumenty ze zbiorów Biblioteki Narodowej* (Warsaw, 2009), 67.

35 J. Selzer, 'Renesans sportu żydowskiego', in H. Stachel (ed.), *Almanach żydowski* (Lwów, 1937), 140–4: 142.
36 Ibid. 141.
37 J. Lasker, 'Shishah ḥalutsim rishonei ha'aliyah hashelishit', in *Pinkas bendin*, ed. A. S. Stein (Tel Aviv, 1959), 222–3.
38 'Szlakiem rowerowej aliji' (24 June 2013): Virtual Shtetl website, visited 9 Jan. 2022.
39 E. Mendelsohn, *The Jews of East Central Europe Between the World Wars* (Bloomington, Ind., 1983), 60.
40 The organization survived until the start of the twenty-first century. Its last president was the lawyer Arie Adelist.
41 Organizacja Żydów z Krakowa w Izraelu website, visited 19 Apr. 2021. It is still active and is headed by Lili Haber.
42 A. Klugman, *Polonica w Ziemi Świętej* (Kraków, 1994), 120–3. The largest collections of memorial books are located in the USA (YIVO Institute for Jewish Research, New York; Jewish Theological Seminary, New York; Brandeis University, Waltham, Mass.; and the Library of Congress, Washington DC) and in Poland (Żydowski Instytut Historyczny, Warsaw, and to a lesser extent the Biblioteka Narodowa, Warsaw) (see M. Adamczyk-Garbowska, 'Żydowskie księgi pamięci', *Akcent: Literatura i Sztuka*, 2003, no. 3, pp. 67–76).
43 The kibbutz played an important military role during the first Arab–Israeli war in 1948. For a time it managed to tie down large Egyptian forces heading for Tel Aviv, while the citizens of Tel Aviv were preparing an effective defence.
44 D. Levin, 'Alija "waw"': Masowa dezercja żołnierzy żydowskich z Armii Polskiej w Palestynie w latach 1942–1943', in id., *Żydzi wschodnioeuropejscy podczas II wojny światowej*, trans. E. Balcerek (Warsaw, 2005), 117–40: 122.
45 Yad Vashem Archives, 03/1852, 03/1365, 03/2502; see Levin, 'Alija "waw"', 118–22.
46 Narodowe Archiwum Cyfrowe, Warsaw, sygn. 000272: digitized copy of Rabbi Israel Halberstam of Kraków, Tehran, to General Władysław Sikorski, prime minister of Poland, 5 Oct. 1942 (original in Hoover Institution, Stanford, Calif.).
47 See H. Chudzio and A. Hejczyk (eds.), *Pokolenia odchodzą: Relacje źródłowe polskich Sybiraków z Wielkiej Brytanii. Nottingham* (Kraków, 2014).
48 See A. Patek, *Polski cmentarz w Jafie: Z dziejów Polonii w Izraelu* (Kraków, 2016).
49 *Stosunki polsko-izraelskie (1945–1967): Wybór dokumentów*, ed. S. Rudnicki and M. Silber (Warsaw, 2009), 55–6.
50 B. Szaynok, *Z historią i Moskwą w tle: Polska a Izrael, 1944–1968* (Warsaw, 2007).

Zionism in Poland, Poland in Zionism

ANNA LANDAU-CZAJKA

THIS CHAPTER focuses not on the history of Zionism in Poland but on the attitudes towards Poland of Zionists and the way these were expressed in Zionist ideology. It is based above all on a broad review of Jewish Polish-language publications from the interwar period,[1] as well as on the memoirs and reminiscences of Polish Jews, often written years later. Thus it presents not so much detailed descriptions of ideological concepts as the views of specific individuals or newspapers, concentrating above all on what was actually happening as opposed to what was proposed.

Zionism emerged in Poland long before the country regained its independence. The movement's first centres were to be found in the 1880s mainly in Warsaw and Łódź and in several smaller towns, such as Kalisz and Piotrków.[2] Before 1918 the Yiddish-language Zionist daily *Haynt* tried to convince Jews that they were a separate nation able to act 'on their own behalf' and not just a religious minority.[3] The movement developed quickly, although it soon split into different parties and factions, united by the hope of regaining the Land of Israel as a homeland but divided in their views on religion and on social and economic issues.

In 1918 Poland regained its independence. Over 3 million Jews lived there, and Jewish political life flourished. The Zionists constituted a very significant force on the Jewish political scene: the movement was relatively recent and attractive to young people, presenting a vision of the future in which the Jews would acquire their own homeland and would cease to be a persecuted minority. In addition, because of their political strategy, the Zionists were represented in the Polish parliament, something the large and otherwise effective socialist Jewish General Workers' Alliance (the Bund), for example, never succeeded in attaining.

In a Poland that was by degrees becoming more hostile towards them, Jews had several ideological options. Setting to one side the traditional and devout Jews, for whom secular life was subordinate to religion and who thus voted, above all, for Agudat Yisrael, the rest of the community had in essence three options: assimilation, Zionism, or left-wing politics—whether social-democratic or communist. Given the increasing bankruptcy of assimilation, the real alternatives were either Zionism, leading to emigration and the start of a new life somewhere else, or attempting to rebuild existing society so that Jews, too, would have a place in it, through the overthrow or reform of capitalism and the creation of a socialist state. According to Jerzy Surdykowski:

Communism provided a different answer from Zionism to the same painful dilemma of a persecuted race having no land and no country of its own, condemned either to disappear or to the miserable and humdrum daily life of the ghetto. The Zionists proposed a radical solution—emigration . . . the communists a no less radical one—the destruction of an unjust world through revolution. Alienated through the cold hostility of their Christian surroundings, Jews found in the fire of world revolution the long-desired warmth of a new community, connected not by ties of race or narrow nationalism, but by an all-embracing ideology.[4]

However, revolution and the destruction of the existing social order had only minimal support. For those who wished to be treated as equal citizens, there remained social democracy as embodied in the Bund and the Polish Socialist Party and Zionism. As was the case elsewhere, the Zionist movement in Poland was not monolithic: it embraced the spectrum of political parties from the left to the right, from the religious to the secular, from the radical to the moderate.

Patriotism

However, the position of the Zionists on Polish territory had one specific feature. Both before 1918 and afterwards they had to face an extremely important issue that did not exist in countries with a solid and well-established sense of their statehood. Given that the Poles had been compelled to regain their independence through force of arms and then to rebuild and hold on to their statehood, the loyalty of all citizens probably counted for more than in other countries. This presented the Zionists with a difficult problem. They found themselves in a situation in which loyalty towards one state was automatically considered treachery towards another. In 1918 and during the Polish–Soviet war the Zionists had to convince their own supporters that while the Jews' future and real homeland was in the Land of Israel, at the same time the newly emerging Poland should also be treated as their homeland or, at the very least, as a country with which they were linked by ties of citizenship and a resultant loyalty and, even more, by an emotional attachment since it was the land of their birth. This remained the situation until the Second World War.

The Zionists in the east of the country during the Polish–Ukrainian war found themselves in the most difficult position. *Chwila*, the Polish-language Zionist daily published in Lwów (Lviv), a town which was contested in late 1918 and early 1919 by the Polish Republic and the West Ukrainian People's Republic, took the view that unambiguous support for either the Poles or the Ukrainians could have negative consequences. Thus, in October and November 1918, some of the Jewish political parties (principally the Zionists at the Zionist Congress of Eastern Galicia in Lwów on 27 October 1918), together with the administrative organization of the Jewish community of Lwów, took the decision that the Jewish population would observe neutrality in the Polish–Ukrainian conflict.[5] This meant not supporting either side and not getting involved in military operations. *Chwila*'s Zionist columnists argued that the Jews were a separate nation and should not involve themselves in other people's conflicts. Since both sides saw the conflict as a national struggle against foreign rule, they should not contribute to the victory of either. They would support whatever government established itself in the area. According to *Chwila* on the eve of the elections to the Constituent Sejm in January 1919:

The Jews here have no land of their own and it is not their role to draw international borders. It is not the Jews' place to create a state here, rather is to be good citizens of whatever state is created... When the guns fall silent, when the borders are established, the Jews will willingly give their all, not excluding blood, for it and the defence of its borders.[6]

Although this argument was meant to convince Poles of the Jews' future positive role in the Polish state, it was double-edged. The *Chwila* columnists did not seem to have realized that, in asserting the Jews' loyalty towards any future state, they were also asserting that, in the event of Poland's defeat, the Jews there would become devoted citizens of Ukraine and would even fight for it; in other words, they would take the side of Poland's enemies. Claiming (in Polish) that the Jews might in future become faithful Ukrainian citizens inevitably aroused hostility and suspicion and, indeed, large-scale anti-Jewish violence after the area came under Polish rule. It is thus not surprising that a section of the Lwów Zionists had earlier come out strongly against the policy of neutrality, claiming that Jews were linked to Polish rather than to Ukrainian culture and that many of them had Polish patriotic feelings.[7]

In 1920, during the Polish–Bolshevik war, neutrality was out of the question. The Zionist politician Apolinary Hartglas perhaps best summed up the feeling among the Zionists, arguing that while 'our national ideal, the future of our nation is not in Poland... we are Polish citizens and, as for us, as only a part of the Jewish nation, we wish to share Poland's life. We wish to rejoice at its happiness and lament its sorrows.'[8] In a situation where the Polish nation was in danger, 'we must demonstrate our complete commitment to our civic duties'.[9]

Chwila, which had proclaimed neutrality in the Polish–Ukrainian war, now came down unambiguously on the Polish side, which was in line with its statements that the Jews would be loyal citizens of the country to which eastern Galicia was assigned. It initially published articles explaining that when soldiers shed blood for their country, the rest of society should at least offer financial support. By 15 July 1920 it was no longer a question of peace and money, and *Chwila* published two calls to arms on its front page. They were similar, and both recalled the unequal treatment of citizens in the Polish state and the injustice and repression that had affected the Jews. Nevertheless, they called for all Jews to defend their homeland, irrespective of any grievances they might feel against Poland. Many Zionist newspapers published the dramatic appeal by Zionist members of parliament:

Jews! Poland is in Danger... A powerful voice rings out throughout the land calling to the people, to every citizen to defend the country, its freedom and independence. Together with all citizens we, the Jews, have also answered the call to do our duty. We have not heard any words... that would cause us to forget all the injustices we have suffered, which would enable us to feel true unity with this country... On the contrary, we still continue to hear from different sides words of hatred and are the objects of continual calumny and slander. Jews! Let us not forget what we owe to this country in which we live and for whose building and development we too have worked. Let us remember just one thing: the country is in peril and needs the disinterested assistance of its sons and daughters . . . Jews, do your civic duty! Let each of you bring his necessary sacrifice, be it of blood, or life, or treasure! Let no one fail to come to the defence of the Polish state's freedom and independence![10]

It emerged unambiguously from this appeal that Poland was the homeland of the Jews, the country with which they were linked and to which they owed an obligation. It was easy to see that this was a clear contradiction of the recent assertion of the neutrality of the Jews as a nation not linked by ties to any other country.

Admittedly, Zionists were in agreement that Poland, as the land of their forefathers, was the homeland of Polish Jews, but it could not be the only one, since their real homeland was the Land of Israel. Was it possible to have two homelands and, if so, did they have equal standing? It is hard to find a more characteristic illustration of this dilemma than the short statement printed on the front page of *Tygodnik Żydowski* on 10 July 1920 as the Bolshevik forces were approaching Warsaw. 'Since some of the editorial staff have gone to attend the Zionist Congress in London and others have left to join the army, we shall therefore be temporarily suspending production of the paper.'[11] However, the patriotic fervour of the Jews, including that of the Zionists, subsided when it turned out that Jewish volunteers, instead of being sent to the front, were being interned in a camp at Jabłonna.

A similar problem emerged during the first years of the Second Republic, when national autonomy for the Jews was being fought over. It was hard to explain at the same time to readers (some of them Polish) that Jews were just as good patriots as Poles and yet also wanted to maintain a separate national identity. According to Sabina Kwiecień, Jewish journalists in the Galician press emphasized that

the aim of maintaining a separate national identity and building an independent Palestine, as advocated by the Zionists, did not conflict with the interests of the Polish state and the Polish working classes . . . The negative attitude of the authorities and Polish society towards granting the Jews national autonomy was explained as the result of the 'traditional contempt, hatred and aversion' Poles felt for the Jewish population in the country.[12]

Rafael Scharf has maintained that in the Polish-language Zionist press it was difficult to reconcile the battle for Jews' rights in the lands of the diaspora with encouragement to leave for the Land of Israel in order to build their own country there.[13] There were certainly Jews who claimed that two patriotisms were impossible in Poland and that one needed to choose just one—Polish. In an interview published in 1927 in *Dziennik Warszawski*, the historian Aleksander Kraushar argued that French Jews could be both good citizens of France and devoted to Jewish matters. He added, however, that 'this is not possible here in Poland, since in order to participate in the life of contemporary Poland, one has to be devoted to Poland alone. I belong to the generation that fought for, lived, and will live with the greatest love for Poland in our hearts.'[14] We should, however, recognize that these were the views of a freedom fighter from the time of the January uprising, of an assimilationist, a convert, and certainly not in line with the paper's pro-Zionist position.

This was not the view of the Zionists, and for them there was no conflict between a defence of civil rights in one's place of residence and encouraging people to build their own homeland. They were, however, caught up in a deeper contradiction. The Jews were supposedly bound by a dual loyalty—to the Land of Israel, as the future homeland of their dreams, and to Poland, as their current homeland. These two patriotisms were very different from one another, which is precisely what the assimilationists (and often even more vehemently the Poles) pointed out. Love of the Land of Israel was the duty of all Zionists, whereas it was loyalty, 'political patriotism', rather than true feeling that bound them to Poland. This was spelled out explicitly, perhaps out of fear of giving substance to the frequent criticism that Jews had no feelings for Poland and that they changed loyalty with the change of frontiers. Especially during the post-war years such accusations were often made against the Jewish community, and the Zionists felt the need to answer them.

Some Zionists distinguished their Jewish and Polish loyalties in a different way. They proclaimed their loyalty to Poland as the country of which they were citizens and would fulfil all their obligations to it, remembering, however, that their primary duty was to cherish their own national traditions. Their obligations towards Poland were, in their view, inextricably tied to the rights of the Jewish minority, and were to be fulfilled only on condition of full civil rights.

Ozjasz Thon expressed this point of view in *Nowiny Codzienne*, a newspaper which claimed to have no political affiliation, although it expressed similar views to the those of the Zionists and was above all hostile to assimilation:

We are only too conscious of the fact that the symbiosis of Jews with the undoubted rulers of Poland, with the Polish people on this land, is a historical necessity, the result of a historical process which has lasted many centuries. We in no way wish to be helots in this country. We do not want to be upper-class citizens just as we don't want to be forced into self-destruction.[15]

Here too, however, there was no unanimity among the Zionists. The contention that Poland was their temporary homeland, with which Jews ought to be connected by both loyalty and a conscientious fulfilment of their obligations, but not by emotion, aroused the opposition not only of the assimilationists but also of some prominent Zionists. From the very earliest days of the Second Republic there was resistance to the idea that the Jewish community's obligations towards Poland were the result solely of laws that bound all citizens.[16] Hartglas stated emphatically in 1922 in *Nowiny Codzienne* that:

I have always maintained and still maintain that a citizen is bound by more than a perfunctory passive loyalty. Loyalty to one's country does not mean, as our assimilationists have argued in their journal, *Nasz Kurjer*, loyalty towards the state in whose power this country currently lies. Rather loyalty is owed towards the people that has the moral and historical right to create its own state in a given country, which is creating this state's history, which is the overlord of this land. Loyalty cannot be just passive. Civic loyalty requires action and sacrifice if needed, it requires sympathy and a feeling for the dominant nation, it requires dedication at moments when this nation is threatened with the loss of its lawful rights. Of course, this sympathy and this feeling, the degree of our civic engagement, depend to a great extent on how this dominant nation treats us, but this is the domain of feeling and not political calculation.[17]

Many years later, in 1937, *Przegląd Zachodni* expressed itself in a very similar fashion. The writer, Samuel Druck, emphasized that the creation of a Jewish state would not mean that all Polish Jews would move there. Thus, even the establishment of a national homeland in Palestine would not actually change the situation of the Jews in the diaspora. Jews were citizens of the states in which they lived and would continue to live:

Jews should enjoy full and equal civil rights in the Polish state, and their legal and civil status will not change after the establishment of a Jewish state in Palestine. Palestine will be unable to absorb all the Jews scattered throughout the world, including all the Jews in Poland and [the creation of a Jewish state there] should not in any way change their legal status.[18]

In other words, Jews, even if they hoped for the establishment of a Jewish state, would remain not only loyal and law-abiding citizens but also citizens who were emotionally attached to the country in which they lived and would continue to live.

However, this was not the only position adopted. In Zionist publications, especially in those of associations focused on preparing young people to settle in Palestine, right up to the end of the interwar period only one patriotism dominated—love for the future Jewish state. Poland and its problems did not as a rule figure at all in these publications, which concentrated exclusively on the struggle for the Land of Israel and preparing young people for the hard life on a kibbutz and to fight the Arabs. In addition, the conclusion can be drawn that, in these publications, the Land of Israel was the Jews' only homeland not from any explicit discussion of the issue but rather from the complete absence of Poland and Polish subjects.

The situation changed in the last years before the outbreak of war. It was clear at this time that publications that exclusively stressed Zionist patriotism needed to modify their position. Faced with the imminent threat to the country, efforts were made to convince readers even of strongly Zionist publications that love for the Land of Israel need not be exclusive, that there was no contradiction between an attachment to both Jewish and Polish cultures and societies. Thus, Zionists were supposedly bound by two patriotisms and two loyalties in equal measure, towards the old, as well as the new, homeland. After several years of concentrating exclusively on cultivating support for Jewish settlement in the Land of Israel, the magazine *Betar* unexpectedly began to explain to its readers that they were children of two homelands and that devotion to only one of them was desertion or betrayal. An extensive article was devoted to this issue, since such a drastic change of line needed to be justified to the readers of a publication that had been unusually radical in its exclusive Zionism and anything but supportive of Poland. The paper explained that maintaining that the Jews' only homeland was the Land of Israel and that Jews were its 'spiritual' citizens, waiting only to leave, was simply antisemitic slander. The claim that Jews were willing to sacrifice themselves only on behalf of their promised land was also hostile propaganda. This had been the basis for the papers of the Obóz Narodowo-Radykalny, a leading fascist group which claimed that Jews were foreigners in Poland. Until the situation deteriorated and the citizens of Poland were called upon to make sacrifices for their country and to contribute to defence loans, it was difficult to refute such claims. This changed when Jews demonstrated enormous generosity in contributing to a loan for anti-aircraft defences, which was a cause of some pride for Polish Jews, who thus had proof that they were not merely foreigners in the country. Jews were now also clearly willing to sacrifice their own lives fighting for Poland. The claim that the Jews were exploiting such actions to curry favour with the Poles was attacked as the invention of 'twisted minds'. Such people could not understand simultaneous love for and loyalty towards two homelands. This, it was claimed, was borne out by history—no one, it was argued, accused Jan Henryk Dąbrowski of shirking his obligations towards the First French Republic when forming the Polish Legions in Italy in 1797.

However, for Jewish publicists, although Polish Jews had to be willing to make sacrifices for Poland, this could not be their only sacrifice. They ought to contribute to both Polish and Jewish causes. Just as one ought to contribute to the National Defence Fund (Fundusz Obrony Narodowej; FON),[19] helping Jewish causes was also categorical and mandatory:

We are conscious that we are greatly superior in every respect to those who are trying to deny our right to fulfil our elementary obligations towards the country, with whom we have been linked for centuries . . . This Polish readers should know. There is, however, something that the Jewish reader must consider and, once he has done that, will realize that every Jew has the same right and duty to contribute to the Polish FON—his country's fund—as he does to Keren Tel Hai—the fund of the emerging Jewish State in Palestine . . . He who will not be mobilized and grudges every penny for the Polish cause, which is after all guarantee of the safety of his own person, of his wife, his children must be regarded as a deserter. But he who simultaneously does not see on his own Jewish banners the calls for defence of the nation is a base traitor, he who ignores the Jewish FON.[20]

This article clearly sought to explain to its readers, Jewish as well as Polish, the possibility of being loyal to two homelands, while at the same time hierarchizing this loyalty. Above all, it denied that Zionists had an exclusive love for the Land of Israel while ignoring Poland. In other words, love for Poland was a virtue and undermining it was a serious error.

Throughout the whole of the interwar period there was competition between the followers of specific Jewish groups to demonstrate their loyalty to Poland and to induce the Polish government to see them as an appropriate partner. It might be thought that the Zionists, given their commitment to rebuilding their own country and to emigration, would not proclaim themselves fervent Polish patriots. Yet this is how they too, at times, saw themselves, although it should be admitted that such patriotic declarations were more typical of smaller, local, papers. The Zionist *Nasz*

Głos in Kołomyja, an ethnically mixed area, declared in June 1924, still in a rather restrained fashion: 'There is no division in Poland between Jews who have a Polish orientation and those who have a non-Polish orientation. Everyone, Zionists first in line, stand solidly and immovably in support of Polish statehood.'[21] In this way they stressed their identity as good Polish patriots, similar to the representatives of other groups. Ten years later, in September 1934, the Zionist *Nasz Głos* in Stanisławów, another ethnically mixed area, went further, attacking Jewish politicians and commentators for declaring their patriotism and love of country but not backing this up with action:

It has become fashionable to outbid one another in loyalty, as if Polish Jews had not already proved a hundred times over that they are, without exception and reservation, devoted to the Polish state and Polish concepts of statehood, and as if patriotism manifests itself not in positive and creative work for the state and society but in attempts to curry favour with the authorities. The goal that must shine through a rational and honest Jewish national policy should be to turn Jews into citizens and upholders of state values, in the sense that a means should be found for Jews to contribute actively and creatively to building a great Poland.[22]

The phrase 'to curry favour' does not appear here accidentally and was intended to draw attention to the competition for favour between various Jewish groups. The article's argument was that in order to turn Jews into citizens, what was needed was a single organization that would unite all Jews and work closely with the Polish government.

Polish Models

Without regard for the state of politics at the time, Polish–Jewish relations, and the growth of antisemitism, particularly in the 1930s, the Polish nation's struggle for freedom during the partitions was presented to supporters of Zionism as a model. It was an example of a heroic national struggle, which, despite the seemingly hopeless situation and a great many defeats, had been crowned with unexpected success. Thus, according to the Revisionist publication *Nasze Jutro* in January 1939:

The Polish risings were always marked by their almost religious and fanatical zeal. Yearning for their own independent homeland was so strong among the people that all other feelings paled in comparison . . . Monism—faith in the exclusivity of one issue and one banner— the idea that several decades later became the guiding principle of Berit Trumpeldor, the avant-garde of nationalist-Jewish youth, was the driving force behind the whole of Polish society . . . It was solely that strong and resolute will of the Polish people to gain their freedom and their own country that, despite the defeats and failures, allowed them eventually to achieve their goal. We Jews should under these circumstances take a moment to reflect on the methods that allowed the Poles to achieve such glorious results. We should realize that one's country is won with great struggle and sacrifice.[23]

In this narrative Marshal Józef Piłsudski played the role of leader and saviour—for whose counterpart the whole Jewish people were still waiting. In the eyes of some

Zionist journalists, he was not only the personification of a great Pole, the liberator of Poland from slavery, and (less often) a supporter of equal rights, but was also a model to be followed by those who wished to rebuild a Jewish state in the Land of Israel. The convergence here was noted: Piłsudski had freed his country after years of bondage and despite the scepticism of most of society. Poland arose, not thanks to a general rising, but thanks to the will and dedication of a minority. Lack of freedom is demoralizing, therefore someone must be found who will drag society out of the swamp. Poles, after little more than a century of bondage, had lost a great deal, not only materially but also morally. The Jewish people, though, had been living for two thousand years without a homeland. As the Zionist periodical *Naród* argued in 1928:

The idea of an Independent Poland first had to drain within its own community the stinking swamp of general cynicism, of vulgar, general egoism, base materialism, and hatred for one's brother. Zionism too must first fight and destroy on the Jewish street the disgusting cynicism, the vile prevailing cheap materialism, the poisonous hatred by the slaves of *golus* [the diaspora] towards a resurrected Judea ... A resurrected Poland was the work of heroic warriors who achieved it with their own blood. A resurrected Judea will be the work of our 'madmen', our fanatics for the national idea.[24]

In a piece after Piłsudski's death, a columnist in *Cel* expressed his deep sorrow at the death of the creator of independent Poland, a living legend, the object of 'unbounded worship' for thousands of little people, the model of honour and patriotism. Poland had suffered an irreparable loss. The Jews were united in grief with the whole Polish people, and not just because they were citizens. Because for them, as Jews, Piłsudski had been an example they should emulate: 'And for us, who are still fighting for the Jewish people's freedom and are slowly forging the foundations of our future country, the radiant figure of Józef Piłsudski will remain always as a model and an example of an indomitable warrior for the nation's freedom and independence.'[25] Other Zionist publications, such as *Trybuna Narodowa*, maintained that the Jewish people owed much to Piłsudski: 'However, he will have a hundredfold greater significance for us as a living example teaching us how to serve one's country, how to suffer for one's country, how to conquer for one's country and how to free one's country by the sweat of one's own brow and despite insurmountable obstacles.'[26]

It appears that in this case Zionist publications reflected relatively faithfully their readers' feelings. Memoirs also contain testimony that Piłsudski was seen as a model for Jews wishing to see the rebirth of their nation. According to Pinhas Adler:

Father was a devoted citizen of the Polish republic as well as one of the ideologues of the Zionist Revisionist Party, which promoted and believed in the return of the Jewish people to their own homeland in the Land of Israel ... The history of Polish insurrections, and above all the figure of Marshal Józef Piłsudski served to some extent as a model.[27]

Aleksander Hertz noted that Zionism had adopted a great many of Piłsudski's philosophical concepts: 'There is a story that Ben-Gurion was an avid reader of Józef Piłsudski's writings. Even if this is only a legend, it is highly characteristic!'[28]

Language

There is also the importance of language. Although of course there was the Yiddish daily *Haynt*, which supported Zionism, other pro-Zionist dailies such as *Nasz Przegląd* and *Chwila*, and the major weeklies, used Polish. Zionists did not try to justify their use of Polish—for them Yiddish was the language of the diaspora and not worth retaining. Hebrew, quite simply, was not widely used. That left Polish, literary and idiomatic Polish at that, with Polish cultural references. *Nasz Przegląd* (which did not support Zionism officially, although it promoted it warmly) was an important source of news on the Zionist movement. Marian Fuks described it as a 'bourgeois Warsaw daily'.[29] It provided its readers with information on all manner of subjects—Polish and foreign politics, Zionism, and Palestine, but also book and theatre reviews, sports news, and health and beauty tips. According to Marta Ciesielska, the daily was 'close to the moderate Zionist grouping, Et Livnot . . . supporting Jewish aspirations, not only those of the organized Zionist movement to establish a national base in Palestine but also the establishment of national and cultural autonomy in the diaspora, in association with the culture and social life of the Jews' country of residence'.[30] *Nasz Przegląd*, like most Zionist publications, was geared towards readers living in Poland, who for the most part saw their life's goals being realized in that country.

There was, however, a large group of smaller, usually low-circulation Zionist publications, aimed at young people who were considering emigrating to the Land of Israel. These had Hebrew and occasionally Yiddish titles, although they were usually published only in Polish and covered exclusively or almost exclusively events in Palestine. Among them were *Olamenu* (1921–8), *Gedud* (1922), *Hakefir* (1924), *Kefir* (1924), *Hano'ar* (1925), *Hamakabi* (1933–6), and *Oyfgang* (1937). Some of them had Polish titles, such as *Nasza Palestyna* (1925) and *Cel*, published between 1934 and 1937 in Lwów, which, as its subtitle proclaimed, was 'a paper devoted to Jewish issues and the rebuilding of a Jewish State in Palestine'.[31] All these publications were geared towards Polish-language readers, but Poland, Poles, and Polish affairs were only very rarely, if at all, covered in them.

One of the most striking phenomena of the interwar period was the linking of far-reaching assimilation (or indeed acculturation) with Polish patriotism and Zionism. Such was the case of the Feldblum family, who had served Poland with distinction. There are a great many similar accounts of children from Zionist families who were also assimilated. According to Ruth Eldar, 'Father made sure we were brought up as loyal Poles while we also lit sabbath candles. A longing for Israel, hope associated with the Promised Land made him a supporter of the Zionist movement of the day.'[32] Describing in 1992 the work of Jakub Appenszlak, editor of *Nasz Przegląd*, Joanna Godlewska observed with surprise that 'it is hard to see . . . as an average Jew and a typical Zionist . . . a young blond boy with blue eyes [who wrote] a youthful poem: "O Polish language! The language of Mickiewicz and Norwid | You are my language too."[33] Yet, in the light of other memoirs, he turns out to be a not untypical Zionist.

It is perhaps worth quoting here a few poems that are proof that many Zionists were deeply assimilated Polish patriots, torn between love for an old homeland and the homeland of their dreams. In 'Wyznanie moje', Maurycy Schlanger wrote:

> Today I write in Polish
> For the day greets me in a bright Polish undertone
> the muse plays in Polish on a Aeolian harp
> lilac withers in Polish, the scent of rye is Polish
>
> . . . .
>
> One day, in a year or two, soon I shall bid you farewell
> I shall bid you farewell, white birch trees and irises
> I shall go there to the East...
> Torn today between two cultures
> cursed today with two languages
> tomorrow I shall kiss the moss of the Holy Wall,
> tomorrow I shall enjoy my native tongue.
> Yet while the palms do not spread the shade of the menorah
> over my head that is filled with joyful labour,
> I shall be sad and sick
> I—a Polish poet and a Hebrew mute.[34]

Similarly Maurycy Szymel, in 'Dwie ojczyzny':

> Two homelands—two lands and two skies
> Fate sent the heart on a penitential voyage—
> One must choose only one, one
> For haughty labour, for a proud hard life...
> Yet although the jeremiad's voice calls out at night,
> The dewy dawn makes me a musical shepherd—
> The land of the Piasts has given me the sweetness of language
> And small Polish forget-me-nots.
> But I know that I shall go and build a small white dwelling,
> Where a Polish maple will grow beside the vineyards;
> Should I fall into a wild thicket of memories,
> Let the shadow of the white Piast pass by at night.[35]

Even children who were meant to grow into settlers in the Land of Israel were educated at times in Polish culture and language. Before the war, Stanisław Vincenz was shocked when, during a visit to a Jewish Zionist orphanage, he discovered that the children, although all speaking excellent Hebrew, used Polish amongst themselves and with guests, 'and to cap it all one of the pupils declaimed one of his own visionary poems about the land of Israel in Polish, of course ... I spoke to Dr. Schaff: "Where are we then? What nationality is everyone?"'[36] Children from Jewish schools produced little magazines in Polish. One of them published on the front page a poem about the Land of Israel beginning with the words 'There our homeland lies'.[37] Another announced that the publication would tackle, above all, Jewish issues, despite the fact that it was entirely in Polish.[38]

Readers of Zionist publications were often required to possess a perfect knowledge of Polish language and culture. These publications, including provincial ones, used the language with faultless and often astonishing accuracy. *Nasz Przegląd* was not alone in requiring a command not just of basic but of literary Polish. Quotations from Polish literature often appeared in such periodicals, which assumed a good knowledge of Polish culture. *Opinia* criticized a number of submissions to a literary competition which it organized in 1934 for their poor Polish and stated that it expected such works to be written without grammatical errors.[39]

Much of the mass-circulation daily press, with a few exceptions, such as *5-ta Rano*, was geared towards the Jewish intelligentsia, usually in the large cities, although it was of course read in smaller towns too. However, the provincial press usually reached readers of only a specific region, and most publications produced material of a decidedly lower quality; some of them, especially those that focused on local Jewish life, appear to be have been aimed at readers with little education. Yet the papers published in Polish also assumed an excellent knowledge of the language, which means that they were targeting readers with an above-average education or who had been significantly Polonized. This acculturation sometimes seems to have gone beyond the abilities of its readers. A periodical with the Hebrew title *Hakefir*, published in Kalisz, which was devoted exclusively to life in the Land of Israel and the problems of emigration, had the subtitle: 'A *kefir* [village] publication produced by the *alizim gedud kefir* [happy activists of the village group]'. In its first issue, it contained an appeal to its reader written in a mangled Polish marked by Jewish and peasant usages:

Well, when I go round to sign up for Hashomer, it was so nice and comfortable that I not want to leave ... But at their confabs when the big boss starts to gab, he never ends ... And I have to scram to get home for lunch because otherwise my Mom rips me up saying, 'Adyk, don't go back to that slum'. I try to calm her down and say, 'Mom, Adyk won't go there more'. And Mom then says I can go again. So I go and go and go again, because once you is hooked, you don't want to give it up.[40]

The rest of the paper is written in good Polish, but the use of idiomatic language proves that its target audience included readers who used Polish at home, to whom Polish was not something strange, learned at school, or used only with the neighbours. A Jew who spoke the local dialect had not only to be in contact with Poles but also to have learnt the language at home. At the same time the paper's subject matter focused almost exclusively on Jewish issues, irrespective of how deeply its readers were rooted in Polish culture.

Likewise, *Nasz Przegląd*, while it stigmatized Jews' failure to study their 'own' languages, expected its readers to have a perfect knowledge of Polish, including dialect.

It invited groups from Zakopane to perform using mountain dialect. What is perhaps even odder is that it expected its readers to recognize Góral (highland) names like Sabała and Bartuś Obrochta, without any explanation.

Even *Nowe Słowo* (with its subtitle 'The Organ of National Jewry in Poland'), a publication which unquestionably took even less interest in Polish affairs than *Nasz Przegląd*, the only Poles appearing in its pages being politicians and antisemites, expressed indignation at the failure of Jews to speak Polish correctly and began a campaign for pure Polish. A journalist who went for a walk through the town could not conceal his irritation on seeing shop signs with mistakes. The Warsaw City Council, he suggested, when accepting bids from new firms, should focus on the correct spelling of their names and should under no circumstances accept those not written in correct Polish. If this were done, he concluded, 'we would be most grateful'.[41] This suggests that Polish was not only known and used but was clearly being treated as a native tongue to which the paper's writers were emotionally attached. Like *Nasz Przegląd*, *Nowe Słowo* accepted as given that its readers would have an excellent knowledge of Polish literature. Its Polish theatre reviews give the impression of having been written for a Polish public. They took for granted a knowledge not only of the Polish classics but also of new playwrights (such as Jerzy Szaniawski) and Polish actors.

Acculturation, Assimilation, Zionism

This dualism is also evident in memoirs. Diarists, writing of their pre-war choices, can no longer themselves understand how they were able to combine two quite different emotions: an attachment to Poland, its language, and culture, and to Zionism with its dreams of the Land of Israel. According to Miriam Akavia: 'My views were not fully developed. On the one hand I wanted to study Polish language and literature, I thought that I would read for a degree in Polish after finishing school. On the other hand, though, I wanted to go to Israel. I have no idea how I was planning to combine the two.'[42] Zionism as the political choice of people from assimilated families was not as surprising as it may seem. As the commentator who wrote under the pseudonym Józef Grabiec maintains, 'in place of the "tired and the weary" assimilationists the Zionists, those foes of assimilation, appeared and promoted their slogans . . . in Polish . . . This was the greatest triumph of assimilation.'[43] Bohdan Halczak wrote of Zionism's complex impact:

> The factor hindering the Jewish population's assimilation was the strong influence of Zionist groups. The impact of this factor was, however, complex. The Zionists opposed Orthodox Jewish tradition. They contributed indirectly to reducing the differences between the Polish and Jewish communities . . . Those individuals with the strongest sense of their own nationality emigrated. More conventional individuals with a weaker sense of their national distinctiveness were more willing to remain in Poland and they formed the core of those who supported the process of assimilation.[44]

Leszek Hońdo emphasized even more strongly the influence of Zionism on assimilation: 'The growing signs of identification with Polish culture existed even among Zionists.' He quoted as proof a 1914 declaration testifying to the Zionists' Polish patriotism:

Finally, the time has come when the Jewish people can display their great love and admiration for the Polish people, who took up the fight for a free and independent Poland . . . We follow with bated breath the course of events and we look with admiration at the Polish soldiers marching triumphantly . . . With all our hearts we wish this heroic campaign success and good fortune.[45]

As Jolanta Żyndul claimed in her introduction to the memoirs of Apolinary Hartglas, the road from assimilation to Zionism was very typical for the first generation of Zionist activists, and not just in Poland.[46] Hartglas himself had his own explanation for the willing acceptance of Zionist ideas by assimilated Jews: they were the most Europeanized and intelligent of the Polish Jewish community and thus were better able to understand the necessity of having one's own homeland.[47] In the face of growing antisemitism and a sense of rejection, Jews were looking for somewhere they would be fully accepted. Parents often did not approve of such choices, not really understanding why their children wanted to return to a world from which they had with difficulty escaped. Józef Lewandowski's parents, who came from a hasidic environment and were perhaps not fully assimilated, although they were clearly Polonized (his father subscribed to *Kurjer Poranny* and knew the whole of *Pan Tadeusz* by heart), sent their son to a school for Jewish children with Polish as the language of instruction. Lewandowski, when recalling his world, stated that 'Zionism ruled almost alone among the younger generation. The idea that Poland was our native land was on the way out.'[48] Rachel Fleischman-Seidman, a young girl from another largely assimilated family where Polish was spoken and the family frequently attended performances at the Słowacki Theatre, joined a Zionist organization at the age of 13, and her brother obtained a law degree and left for the Land of Israel.[49]

A great many assimilated parents opposed Zionism and even forbade their children to join Zionist organizations. One young girl, Mira Slowes, was invited to Hashomer meetings. Even though she really liked them and became committed to Zionism, her parents forbade any further involvement.

At the meetings I learned that I come from an ancient cultured people, that members of my faith have achieved high office and have had a great influence in science and culture. The country of our future was to be Palestine . . . My parents came from devout families, but at home there was an assimilationist spirit. Mother claimed that going to organizational meetings was a waste of time.[50]

At times the turn towards Zionism was a simple accident. A friend belonged to the organization and suggested joining; someone read an advertisement and met with some supporters of a Zionist organization. It happened that such accidental encounters led to deep commitment. As Anka Grupińska wrote about one of the participants in the ghetto uprising: 'Henoch (Heniek) Klajnwajs... was born in 1917 in Warsaw. He grew up in a wealthy assimilated family. Quite by chance he ended up in Gordonia and became a fervent supporter of the Land of Israel.'[51]

To this day a great many people wonder what could have caused such astonishing and indeed contradictory political choices. In an interview conducted by Anis Pordes, Shoshana Adler provided a convincing answer. In her view, the cause of the spread of Zionism among assimilated Jews might quite simply have been foresight. These people realized that they were standing on the edge of a catastrophe, that eventually there would come some kind of explosion, and either they themselves prepared to emigrate, or they educated their children in that way of thinking.[52] Another, perhaps the most plausible, explanation was the dislike that people who chose assimilation and Zionism had of being a minority. Miriam Akavia describes how some of her acquaintances in pre-war Kraków recalled their aunt:

Auntie Hania used to go to Jordan Park... When we were sitting there... she absolutely did not want to be taken for a Jew... Absolutely! And yet... she was a Zionist! She was an 'either/or' kind of person. Either one lives in one's own country, or if not, then one assimilates.[53]

Another diarist, Tulo Schenirer, explained his father's fervent patriotism (he recalled that there were two flags at home, which were hung out on the balcony on all state occasions) and his membership of a Zionist organization by the lack of any real contradiction between the two options.[54] The State of Israel did not yet exist, and so there was no question of there being a conflict of belonging or of national loyalty.

It may also be that certain tenets of Zionism led to assimilation without this having been the intention. One such element could have been the call to abandon Yiddish for Hebrew. The reality was that the large majority of Jews had only a scanty knowledge of Hebrew and this was in its liturgical Ashkenazi form rather than the modern Hebrew associated with Zionism, which was spoken by few Jews in Poland. In these circumstances the call to abandon Yiddish was well received in Zionist circles, but the adoption of modern Hebrew proved much more difficult. So instead of using Yiddish many Zionists began to use Polish. A significant number of Zionist schools used Polish as the language of instruction. In other words, fighting Yiddish by the Zionists could lead to Polonization.

One way or another, strange though it may seem, in many cases assimilation, acculturation, Polish patriotism, and a love of the Land of Israel went hand in hand. Those people who were Polish-speaking Zionists, closely linked to Polish culture (although not necessarily to Polish society), and who also dreamed of leaving and working for the Land of Israel did not feel—at least not then—any inner contradiction.

Translated from the Polish by Jarosław Garliński

Notes

1 See A. Landau-Czajka, *Polska to nie oni: Polska i Polacy w polskojęzycznej prasie żydowskiej II Rzeczypospolitej* (Warsaw, 2015).
2 N.A. [Aleksiun], 'Syjonizm', in *Polski słownik judaistyczny: Dzieje, kultura, religia, ludzie*, ed. Z. Borzymińska and R. Żebrowski, 2 vols. (Warsaw, 2003), ii. 591–2.
3 J. Nalewajko-Kulikov, *Mówić we własnym imieniu: Prasa jidyszowa a tworzenie żydowskiej tożsamości narodowej (do 1918 roku)* (Warsaw, 2017).
4 J. Surdykowski, *Duch Rzeczypospolitej* (Warsaw, 2001), 242.
5 W. Jaworski, *Syjoniści wobec rządu polskiego w okresie międzywojennym* (Sosnowiec, 2002), 10–11.
6 'Z okazyi wyborów sejmowych', *Chwila*, 20 Jan. 1919, p. 1.
7 e.g. T. Askenase, 'Gdybym był syjonistą!', *Chwila*, 23 Jan. 1919, p. 1.
8 A. Hartglas, '3 maja 1916 – 3 maja 1920 r', *Tygodnik Żydowski*, 14 May 1920, p. 5.
9 A. Hartglas, 'W chwili istotnego niebezpieczeństwa', *Tygodnik Żydowski*, 9 July 1920, p. 5.
10 'Odezwa', *Tygodnik Żydowski*, 10 July 1920, p. 1.
11 Ibid.
12 S. Kwiecień, 'Krakowska polskojęzyczna prasa żydowska w latach 1918–1939 wobec społeczeństwa polskiego', in B. Kosmanowa (ed.), *Prasa dawna i współczesna*, 5 vols. (Poznań, 2000–4), ii. 31–50: 34.
13 R. Scharf, 'Polacy i Żydzi – podsumowanie dyskusji', *Kultura*, 386 (1979), 115–23.
14 C. Nescher, 'Co mówią o sobie, Polsce i żydostwie pisarze polscy pochodzenia żydowskiego', *Dziennik Warszawski*, 6 Jan. 1927, p. 5.
15 O. Thon, 'Dla kogo?', *Nowiny Codzienne*, 12 Oct. 1922, p. 1.
16 Tobiasz Askenase argued that Jews cannot freely 'choose' (T. Askenase, 'Gdybym był syjonistą!', *Chwila*, 23 Jan. 1919, p. 1–2).
17 A. Hartglas, 'Blok i lojalność', *Nowiny Codzienne*, 19 Oct. 1922, p. 2.
18 S. Druck, 'Hands Off!', *Przegląd Zachodni*, 16 July 1937, p. 1.
19 The National Defence Fund was for military expenditure. It was established in 1936 by presidential decree and depended partly on voluntary donations from the public.
20 S. Liwa, 'Dwie ojczyzny', *Chad-Ness*, May 1939, pp. 12–13.
21 'W interesie prawdy', *Nasz Głos* (Kołomyja), 20 June 1924, p. 2.
22 XX, 'O nową orientację polityki żydowskiej', *Nasz Głos* (Stanisławów), 15 Sept. 1934, p. 1.
23 H. Brandwein, 'W rocznicę styczniowego czynu', *Nasze Jutro*, 21 Jan. 1939, p. 1.
24 J. Zineman, 'Zmartwychwstanie Polski a Zmartwychwstanie Judei', *Naród*, 1928, no. 2, pp. 18–19.
25 J.K., 'Józef Piłsudski', *Cel*, 15 May 1935, p. 1.
26 'Nad trumną Józefa Piłsudskiego', *Trybuna Narodowa*, 17 May 1935, no. 20, p. 1.
27 P. Adler, 'Rodzina humanistów i wojskowych', in A. Czesław Dobroński (ed.), *Białostoccy Żydzi*, 4 vols. (Białystok, 1993–2002), iii. 55–66: 56.
28 A. Hertz, *Żydzi w kulturze polskiej* (Warsaw, 1988), 192.
29 M. Fuks, '"Mały Przegląd" Janusza Korczaka', *Biuletyn Żydowskiego Instytutu Historycznego*, 105 (1978), 3–28: 6.
30 M. Kopczyńska-Ciesielska, *Jerzy Abramow – redaktor 'Małego Przeglądu'* (Warsaw, 2003), 3.
31 *Cel: Pismo poświęcone problemom Żydostwa i odbudowy Państwa Żydowskiego w Palestynie*.

32 R. Eldar, *Wstrząsnąć filarami świątyni* (Łódź, 2004), 14.
33 J. Godlewska, 'Polski Żyd: Jakub Appenszlak jako krytyk teatralny', *Pamiętnik Teatralny*, 1992, nos. 1–4, pp. 127–134: 127.
34 M. Schlanger, 'Wyznanie moje', in *Międzywojenna poezja polsko-żydowska: Antologia*, ed. E. Prokop-Janiec (Kraków, 1996), 456.
35 M. Szymel, 'Dwie ojczyzny', in *Międzywojenna poezja polsko-żydowska*, 264.
36 S. Vincenz, *Tematy żydowskie* (Gdańsk, 1993), 47–8.
37 'Tam ojczyzna nasza leży', *Z Ławy Szkolnej: Miesięcznik młodzieży żydowskiej szkół średnich we Włocławku*, 1922, nos. 3–4, p. 1.
38 *Życie Uczniowskie: Pismo żydowskiej uczącej się młodzieży* (Lublin, 1922).
39 M. Cyankiewicz, 'Oblicza życia kulturalnego żydowskiej społeczności miejskiej Zagłębia Dąbrowskiego i jego żydowsko-polskich związków w świetle polskiej prasy regionalnej okresu międzywojnia', in D. Rozmus and S. Witkowski (eds.), *Z dziejów Żydów w Zagłębiu Dąbrowskim* (Sosnowiec, 2006), 76–87: 79.
40 'Winc jak jo ci przysłam do ty izby, żeby się tu zapisać do 'Haszomiru', to już mi się nie kciało wyleźć, tak ci tam miło i psyjemnie ... A na zbiórkach jak kwecierowa zacnie gadać, to już bez końca i miary, tak ci goda i goda ... Ale jak nie psyjdę rychtyn na obiad, to matula, jak mi nie zacnie zwymyślać: "Adyk nie pójdziesz ta wincy do ty chałupy". A jo jak nie zacne pseprasać i gadać: "Adyk matulu już wincy nie byde", tak zarok matula kążum nazad łazić. I tak łażę i łażę i ciągle byde łaziła, bo jak tam ktoś wlizie, to już mu się nie kce wyleźć' (Marycha kw. Zmiroth, 'Jo w "Haszomirze"', *Hakefir*, 1924, no. 1, p. 3). It is hardly surprising that this publication did not prove lasting.
41 'Barbarzyńskie neologizmy', *Nowe Słowo*, 29 June 1931, p. 3.
42 'Miriam Akavia i Lea Shinar', in A. D. Pordes and I. Grin, *Ich miasto: Wspomnienia Izraelczyków, przedwojennych mieszkańców Krakowa* (Warsaw, 2004), 32–66: 58.
43 J. Grabiec [Dąbrowski], 'Wilhelm Feldman, jako publicysta i działacz społeczny', in *Pamięci Wilhelma Feldmana* (Kraków, 1922), 60–104: 72.
44 B. Halczak, *Publicystyka narodowo-demokratyczna wobec problemów narodowościowych i etnicznych II Rzeczypospolitej* (Zielona Góra, 2000), 77.
45 L. Hońdo, 'Stosunki polsko-żydowskie na przykładzie rady miasta Tarnowa 1867–1918', in B. Breysach, L. Hońdo, and W. Jaworska (eds.), *Ze sobą, obok siebie, przeciwko sobie: Polacy, Żydzi, Austriacy i Niemcy w XIX i na początku XX w.* (Kraków, 1995), 151–166: 165.
46 J. Żyndul, 'Wstęp', in A. Hartglas, *Na pograniczu dwóch światów* (Warsaw, 1996), 5–19: 7.
47 Hartglas, *Na pograniczu dwóch światów*, 51.
48 J. Lewandowski, *Cztery dni w Atlantydzie* (Konin, 1996), 64.
49 'Rachel Fleishman-Seidman', in E. Isakiewicz, *Ustna harmonijka: Relacje Żydów, których uratowali od Zagłady Polacy* (Warsaw, 2000), 145–54.
50 M. Slowes, *Moje trzy życia* (Tel Aviv, 1994), 15–16.
51 A. Grupińska, *Odczytanie Listy: Opowieści o powstańcach żydowskich* (Kraków, 2003), 86.
52 'Shoshana Adler [Rozalia Kühnreich]', in Pordes and Grin, *Ich miasto*, 11–31: 23.
53 'Miriam Akavia i Lea Shinar', 63.
54 'Tulo Schenirer', in Pordes and Grin, *Ich miasto*, 270–9: 276.

The Fourth Aliyah and the Fulfilment of Zionism in the Land of Israel

MEIR CHAZAN

Introduction

During a visit to Palestine in October 1924 Chaim Weizmann, president of the Zionist Organization, stated bluntly that, while 'our brothers and sisters from Djika and Nalevki are flesh of our flesh and blood of our blood', the national homeland should not be modelled on these Warsaw streets.[1] Years later, in his autobiography, Weizmann confessed that this statement earned him the hatred of many Polish Jews, a hatred that he was never able to overcome. Although he noted in his memoirs that he perhaps should have been more careful in his choice of words, even in his old age Weizmann stood behind the general thrust of his observation.[2] Like other characteristic catchphrases in the history of the Yishuv, the Jewish community in the Land of Israel, such as Vladimir (Ze'ev) Jabotinsky's 'Iron Wall' and David Ben-Gurion's 'We must assist the British in the war as if there were no White Paper, and we must resist the White Paper as if there were no war', Weizmann's reference to Nalewki and Dzika was a concise and penetrating formulation of a central principle in dealing with the challenges of the time. The argument of this chapter is that Weizmann's public assault against all that Nalewki and Dzika symbolized in relation to Jewish life helped define and delineate the cultural, social, and economic boundaries of Zionist activity in Palestine.

Weizmann's denigration of Nalewki and Dzika was not the product of chance but rather a direct outcome of his deep misgivings about the negative influence that the way of life of a considerable segment of east European Jewry might have on the future character of Jewish society in Palestine.[3] His statement represented one more layer —dramatic in terms of its significant and concrete implications for shaping the Zionist reality of the Yishuv—of the continued ambivalence harboured by significant portions of central and west European Jewry towards east European Jews. Their way of life and behaviour were perceived as impeding the Jews both individually and collectively in adapting to the modern world. Weizmann's profound knowledge of the shtetl and the 'Jewish spirit' it reflected aroused in him not only an emotional identification with the wellsprings of his culture but also feelings of aversion towards its ghetto-like essence.[4] In the writings of this period, Weizmann's remarks about those Warsaw streets are often mentioned, frequently in the same breath as similar statements by other personalities.[5] However, to understand them fully it is necessary to outline systematically the circumstances in which they were uttered and their significance in the context of the concrete historical reality of those times.

The 'Nalewki and Dzika' affair described below occurred—historically speaking—on the very eve of the opening of the cultural centre which Weizmann saw as having the most important role in shaping the character of Jewish society: the Hebrew University of Jerusalem, which was due to be inaugurated in April 1925. This institution, of tremendous importance for the national and cultural revival of the Jewish people in the twentieth century, was, in the view of Weizmann, 'the Third Temple'. Establishing the dominance of Hebrew culture in the modern Jewish society taking shape in the Land of Israel was intended, among other things, to help create a social and economic existence different from that of the Jewish society of eastern Europe. The outcomes in the various milieus (political, economic, and cultural) responsible for the structuring of the new Hebrew society would exemplify the new Zionist ideals. They would nourish the process of revolutionary national revival and determine what would be legitimate and suitable to include within the Zionist framework.[6]

In order to map the process by which Polish Jewish immigration became fixed in the public imagination at this time, I will describe and analyse Weizmann's visit to Palestine in September and October 1924. In my estimation, this visit constituted a central and decisive historical crossroads for the consolidation within the cultural reality of the Yishuv of the negative image of Polish Jews and the problems of their assimilation into the Zionist project. This occurred not only because of Weizmann's words in and of themselves but also because some of the most prominent shapers of public opinion in the Yishuv held similar beliefs and actively propounded them. In this group, which Yaacov Shavit called 'the cultural ideologues' of Hebrew national culture,[7] were Hayim Nahman Bialik; Moshe Glickson, editor of *Haaretz* (at the time the most influential newspaper in the Yishuv); Joseph Klausner, editor and literary scholar; Arthur Ruppin, sociologist and member of the leadership of the Zionist Organization; and the poet Uri Tsevi Grinberg. They were joined by Yitshak Laufbahn, editor of *Hapo'el hatsa'ir*, the leading publication of the Labour movement in Palestine. Their opinions were voiced at a time when the shared consensus in the Zionist movement was that its immediate goal was not to save the Jewish nation in an immediate sense but to focus on building the Jewish national homeland in an organized, calculated, and gradual manner. To this end, Zionist policy advocated the immigration of people who could participate in the establishment of a social and economic infrastructure geared towards national revival and settlement in accordance with the country's absorptive capacity and the changing political circumstances.[8]

The Fourth Aliyah: The Demographic Dimension

During the years of British rule over Palestine, from November 1917 until May 1948, some 160,000 Jews from Poland entered the country. Allowing for natural reproduction, a cautious estimate would suggest that this group numbered some 200,000 people in 1948—a little less than a third of the Jewish population of Palestine at the time. Polish Jews thus constituted one of the largest groups of immigrants in the Yishuv.[9] Within this period, immigration from Poland between June 1924 to June 1926 had a profound impact on the history of Mandatory Palestine. Contemporaries, and later the historiography of the Yishuv, called this wave of immigration the Fourth Aliyah.

On 26 May 1924 the Johnson–Reed Act was passed in the US Congress, radically limiting immigration to the United States, including Jewish immigration from eastern Europe.[10] Less than a month later a small notice on a back page of the Zionist Organization publication, *Ha'olam*, stated:

Increase in the immigration from Poland to the Land of Israel—the *aliyah* from Poland to Erets Yisra'el is increasing on a daily basis. On 11 June, thirty families from Warsaw arrived and the following day, 200 people. The government of Palestine is sending a special envoy to Poland to oversee the progress of this immigration.[11]

In all, 771 Jews from Poland immigrated in June, compared to 340 in April and 359 in May, an impressive increase of 115 per cent, following a group of only 140 in March.[12]

The Fourth Aliyah was the first mass *aliyah* in the history of Zionism. It was dubbed the 'Bourgeois Aliyah', 'Polish Aliyah', or 'Grabski Aliyah' (after the Polish prime minister Władysław Grabski, whose economic policies led many Jews whose financial situation had worsened to emigrate to Palestine).[13] According to the official records of the Zionist Organization, Polish Jews made up 41 per cent of Jewish immigrants to the Yishuv in 1924 (6,674 of 16,297), 50 per cent in 1925 (18,632 of 36,933), and 52 per cent in 1926 (7,605 of 14,656).[14] During these years, immigration from Poland amounted to 48 per cent of the total (32,911 of 67,886). This was the period when the Polish Jewish middle class first began to emigrate to Palestine in large numbers and in a co-ordinated fashion. However, this phenomenon should not be exaggerated. Those with financial assets and their family members constituted only a quarter of the immigrants, whereas more than half were defined as 'labourers'. Despite this, the mood and outlook that this group of immigrants brought with it to the country had an enduring impact on the tone and mood of the period, both at the time and in the collective memory and historiography. Most of those with private capital came from the lower middle class (small merchants, artisans and cottage industry workers, brokers), and only a few were wealthy industrialists or well-to-do merchants.[15]

Images of the Immigrants and the Ordeal of Disembarking

One of the most significant sociocultural motifs in the history of Zionism, although its first appearance pre-dates the movement's emergence, is that of the 'new Jew'. The revolutionary call to create the new Jew became 'an ideological and political battle cry' in Palestine with the arrival of the Fourth Aliyah.[16] One of the central issues on the agenda of the Zionist movement and of the Yishuv was which types of Jew were the most desirable candidates—in terms of realizing Zionist ideals—for immigration to the Land of Israel, where, of course, they would reap the material rewards for their labour and achievements as well as accruing social and national prestige.

In the historical study of the Yishuv it is customary to divide the Jewish influx to Palestine into waves of immigration. Naturally, the cultural, economic, and human encounter between the veterans and the immigrants engendered competition, tensions, anxiety, and sometimes even hatred and aversion. The background to such encounters was differences in everyday behavioural norms, modes of dress, and even aesthetics. A host of images and stereotypes, usually negative, was attributed to each wave of immigrants, which to some degree reflected how they were perceived and the challenge or threat that they presented to various circles within the Yishuv. Thus, for example, Yemenite Jews who arrived during the Second Aliyah (1904–14) were described as 'natural labourers'; the pioneers of the Third Aliyah (1918–23), who came from the Soviet Union, were described as revolutionaries and Bolsheviks; members of the Fifth Aliyah (1932–5), arriving from Germany, were derogatorily named *yekes* as an expression of their rigidity and fastidiousness; and immigrants who came from Morocco in the early 1950s were seen by those who wanted to foster their absorption as primitive, savage, and ignorant.[17]

Immigrants in every wave, in Palestine and around the world, experienced the ordeal of quarantine, which was depicted vividly by Aharon Vardi at the height of the Fourth Aliyah:

At the moment of disembarking at the Jaffa port you take off your clothes, which are tossed into an iron vat for laundering. During the wait, you take a shower and the supervisor pours a murky, watery fluid on your head on the way out. The following day personal belongings are disinfected and cleaned, then tied to the back of a camel which transports them outside of the disinfecting yard. When you ask: 'All these sufferings, to what end?! Will you treat us like impure negroes?' then someone responds: 'Who invited you to come here?!'[18]

In a similar vein, Eliezer Steinman (born in the Pale of Settlement in the Russian empire), who emigrated to Palestine from Warsaw in 1924, wrote shortly after his arrival that 'the word "new immigrant" in Palestine has a familiar enunciation—heavy, derisory, and alienating. Until one pays a sort of "acclimatization tax", for days, weeks, and months on end it is illegitimate to "ask questions, complain, or call attention to dysfunctions".'[19] His words did indeed express a rather common experience of migration to a new country, but at the same time they conveyed the considerable surprise of Jewish immigrants, who assumed they would be received warmly and with open arms by their predecessors, on the basis of the shared Zionist political and ideological purpose which they were striving to achieve.

The immigrants of the Fourth Aliyah were not perceived as appropriate participants in the Zionist revolution, which sought to create a new brave, heroic, and manly Jew, able to overcome any physical and mental challenge, who with his own hands (the ideal was essentially male) would establish a new and productive society. They were not considered as idealized Zionist 'new Jews' but rather as typical of the long-established, exilic, petit-bourgeois, weak, Yiddish-speaking Jews. They aspired to liberate themselves from the chains of religion and tradition and to blend into the Middle Eastern landscape, and all their actions were guided by personal utility.[20] Tel Aviv, the first Hebrew city, was the crucible of the encounter of these immigrants with the Zionist dream, and the confrontation that resulted underscored these tensions.

Tel Aviv as Allegory

The Fourth Aliyah was seen as radically different from the first three—which were understood as pioneering, productive, and the result of careful selection—above all as its impact was not felt in the countryside or in the agricultural domain but rather in the city, especially in Tel Aviv, and in the development of commerce and urban family life. Tel Aviv experienced dramatic growth during the period of the Fourth Aliyah, from 21,610 inhabitants in 1924 to 34,200 in the following year, an increase of 58 per cent.[21] Even if the majority of the new immigrants were destined to become the rank and file of the labour force, the dominant social type was someone who took up residence in the city and made a living from the urban trades. For the first time in the history of the Yishuv, the city became a dynamic and active factor within Zionism at the expense of the various types of rural life.[22] With deep concern, Ben-Gurion, then secretary of the General Federation of Labour, wrote in his diary on 7 November 1924 that only 7 per cent of the members of the Fourth Aliyah had joined the federation.[23]

A central indicator of Tel Aviv's growth was the large number of stores that opened. In 1921 there was one store for every 113 people; by mid-1924 the city had one store for every 45 inhabitants. Of the 750 stores in Tel Aviv in 1924, 43 were kiosks, since the sale of carbonated drinks and ice-cream did not require a large initial investment and 'many jumped at [this opportunity]'.[24] Tel Aviv was often compared to 'a remote shtetl in the diaspora, where most of the inhabitants led a parasitical life and made a living off each other'.[25] Simultaneously, the lifestyle that began to develop in Tel Aviv in the 1920s was perceived as reflecting a hedonistic ethos that valorized material, consumer culture: the desire for luxury items, spendthrift leisure habits, and the carefree patronizing of street cafes and the pleasures of the seaside. All these were presented as undermining the frugality, asceticism, and sacrifice on behalf of the general public whose unique purpose was the realization of the Zionist dream.[26] It was also a melange of east and central European Jewish Ashkenazi folkloristic traditions, which chafed against the Zionist cultural hegemony. It became a microcosm of human, cultural encounters that were Western and modernist in appearance, but were in fact often permutations of Western cultural elements that had been absorbed in haphazard fashion in the cities of the tsarist empire (such as Moscow, Warsaw, and Odessa) in the late nineteenth and early twentieth centuries.[27]

Above all, the Fourth Aliyah was the harbinger of a new element in Jewish public life in Palestine. While fizzy drinks, commerce, construction and consumption, the store and the workshop, the noise and the crowd were some of the unmistakable identifying marks of this *aliyah* and of the transformation it wrought in the Land of Israel, the most conspicuous public novelty it brought was the 'street'. The 'street' had already existed in the colonies of the First Aliyah (such as Petah Tikva, Rishon Lezion, and Rehovot) and in the four holy cities (Jerusalem, Tiberias, Safed, and Hebron), and of course in Haifa, Jaffa, and the fledgling Tel Aviv, but before this point its presence and influence had not become a factor in the lives or imaginations of the general Zionist public in Palestine. In his classic article about the Fourth Aliyah, Chaim Arlosoroff, one of the leaders of the Hapo'el Hatsa'ir party, accurately pointed to its contribution, 'which turned the street-scene within the communities of the new Yishuv into a common sight'.[28] This state of affairs was open and visible to all. The critics who attempted to summarize the character and impact of the Fourth Aliyah specifically targeted the nascent Tel Aviv 'street', its substance, appearance, images, and meanings, comparing them with behavioural patterns familiar from Jewish Warsaw.

Nalewki Horrors in Palestine

On 24 September 1924 Weizmann arrived in Palestine on the visit he routinely made every eighteen to twenty-four months. In a speech he delivered at the reception prepared for him that day, he said: 'Conditions need to be created that will be economically receptive to the new elements, especially now', when one needed to 'lay the foundations of the [national] home, so that God forbid no rot should enter its foundations.'[29]

What was Weizmann referring to when he spoke about 'rot entering its foundations'? A biting and explicit answer can be found in a series of articles published by Moshe Glickson, editor of *Haaretz*, in advance of Weizmann's visit.[30] In his articles, Glickson aimed to depict—for Weizmann's benefit and of course also for the paper's readership—the appearance of the country that he was about to encounter. In practice, Glickson wished to outline for Weizmann, a fleeting visitor, the co-ordinates by which he ought to observe and examine the reality of the Yishuv and thus to shape the insights and conclusions that he would formulate from his tour. His principal demand was that the Zionist leadership become involved in guiding the middle-class Jews arriving with the Fourth Aliyah, just as it had assisted the *ḥalutsim* (agricultural pioneers) during the days of the Third Aliyah. Responding in the appropriate manner to the new type of immigrant was crucial. The Zionist leadership should not 'ignore the *aliyah*, if it does not want it to become, in part, a pitfall and a curse'.[31] Glickson pointed out that in numerical terms the immigrants who had arrived in the previous few months were fulfilling Weizmann's hopes in terms of the rate of *aliyah* required for the building of a national homeland during its first years, not only from a quantitative point of view but also 'in terms of the human material: it has brought to us good and desirable elements from among our Sephardi brethren, from Bulgaria, Greece, and other countries'.[32] However, there were also among these new immigrants some who constituted 'difficult and oppositional material, in terms of public, national discipline'.³³ Glickson was referring to their refusal to adopt the Hebrew language, which was considered Zionism's greatest national and political asset. In the concentrations of these immigrants in Tel Aviv—in hotels, restaurants, shops, and elsewhere—there was no hint of Hebrew. At this point Glickson abandoned his non-specific reference to the provenance of these immigrants and aimed his barbs directly at Polish Jewry. The latter, in response to the demand that they speak Hebrew, replied: 'Do not speak "Turkish" to me.' In this reference to Hebrew as Turkish, he saw a clear sign that these circles of Polish immigrants might, during a crisis, join forces with 'extremist haters of Zionism' (the ultra-Orthodox who opposed the revival of Hebrew) and thus weaken its hold in Palestine. This was the source of Glickson's demand of Weizmann and the leadership of the Zionist Organization which he headed: 'If the Zionist executive does not want this *aliyah* of our middle class to bring us a new Nalewki in the Land of Israel—and a Nalewki without the Jewish tradition and without the livelihood of the Warsaw Nalewki—it is its obligation to *control* this *aliyah* . . . and to direct it to our needs.'³⁴ In effect, Glickson was the progenitor of the image of the immigrants of the Fourth Aliyah as importers of the spirit of Nalewki and Dzika Streets to Tel Aviv, and it is from this article that Weizmann borrowed the image.

The next day Weizmann wrote to his wife Vera, who had remained behind in London, and described to her the impression that Tel Aviv had left on him following his three-day visit. After commenting on the large amount of buildings, bustle, and crowding that had recently developed in the city, he arrived at his main point:

This is the gate through which all the despoiled, oppressed and injured are crowding in. It makes a depressing impression in many respects. There's much that is unattractive and noisy. Nalewki transplanted to Palestinian soil or, to be more correct, a mixture of Nalewki with the pseudo-American, poorer of course than New York and not so spacious, but when real immigration begins this kind of phenomenon is obviously unavoidable.³⁵

Not a day, then, had gone by since Glickson's comparison of Tel Aviv to Nalewki was published before Weizmann adopted it to depict forthrightly the reality that presented itself to him in the first Hebrew city.

These were the days of the Jewish holiday season of 1924, and on the second day of Rosh Hashanah, 30 September, the General Zionist party held a banquet in honour of Weizmann on Rothschild Boulevard in Tel Aviv. An excited crowd gathered outside the banqueting hall and greeted the leader with loud and effusive hurrahs. The keynote speakers were the poet Hayim Nahman Bialik and Weizmann. Bialik, who had migrated to the country six months earlier (on 26 March), felt, according to Avner Holtzman, both a desire and a duty to become involved in public affairs and to make an impact on the cultural life that was taking shape in the Land of Israel. The poet had become fixed in the minds of his generation as the most outstanding citizen of Tel Aviv.³⁶ In his speech, Bialik focused on the prevailing culture of the Yishuv. He declared that the current wave of immigration had led to 'the arrival of people of the kind that we had not wanted to have among the immigrants; our organizations responsible for their absorption, in particular the cultural ones, have difficulty absorbing and swallowing such a crude element'. Bialik did not explicitly name the immigrants from Poland, but his audience had no doubt whom his words were referring to when he proclaimed: 'Let us not be afraid of the masses. If we are afraid, then one must fear that a wave of filth will sweep away our labours in a single day.'[37]

The harsh and demeaning imagery of Bialik's language, which had been preceded by Weizmann, on the day of his arrival in Tel Aviv, speaking of 'rot', became thenceforth a pattern of speech that was given public legitimacy in the Yishuv's internal struggles over how the Fourth Aliyah was to be absorbed. Weizmann was well aware of the value of Hebrew and its significance for shaping the Zionist way of life in the Yishuv. In his speech, which followed Bialik's, he commented that it might have slipped the minds of many of those currently arriving, but it was crucial to remember that every step taken there, every word spoken or written there, was scrutinized by the entire world. Therefore, the appearance of the Yishuv, including its use of language, was an important political factor. He warned that if the Yishuv became merely a receptacle for exilic Jews, it would not be taken seriously.[38] Thus the cultural representatives of Zionism took advantage of the tremendous impact that their utterances would have throughout the Jewish world in order to stigmatize the immigrants from Poland for damaging the most sacrosanct foundations of the national movement.

The national character of the Yishuv, as *Ha'olam* hastened to explain to its readers on the basis of the speeches of Bialik and Weizmann, would be a product of whatever transpired in the cultural field. The new immigrants from Poland, most of whom had arrived devoid of national aspirations or knowledge of Hebrew, must 'surrender' to the Hebrew life of the Land of Israel 'instead of trying to impose their cultural hegemony on it'.[39] Joseph Klausner, editor of *Hashilo'ah*, who in a few months would be appointed head of the Department of Hebrew Literature at the Hebrew University in Jerusalem, published in *Ha'olam* on 3 October an annual review article on social and cultural life in Palestine. In it he argued that the municipality in Tel Aviv was facing obstinate opposition to the creation of a new Hebrew society on the part of old-fashioned exilic Jews who were adhering to the life of Polish–Lithuanian ghettos in spite of having been ejected from the diaspora to the Land of Israel.[40]

In the executive meeting of the Zionist Organization on 10 October, Weizmann reported his impressions from his visit to Palestine. He expressed concern that the Fourth Aliyah would precipitate a major crisis in the Yishuv and the Zionist movement, and remarked that, unlike the immigrants from Bulgaria, who made an excellent impression, urgent and grave warnings should be sent to the Zionist movement in Poland to avoid facilitating irresponsible immigration. The loud conversations on the streets of Tel Aviv, the raucous singing in foreign languages in the city's squares, had left him with an uneasy feeling. Arthur Ruppin, one of the main architects of Jewish settlement in Palestine, concurred, and noted that precautions needed to be taken lest immigration from Poland become a problem for the Yishuv, since the newly arrived Polish Jews despaired easily and in due time might generate a mood of despondency that would affect the entire Yishuv. The unequivocal conclusion of the Zionist executive was that under no circumstances should Polish Jews be encouraged to emigrate to Palestine.[11]

On Saturday night, 11 October, Weizmann gave a public speech at a mass convention at the Zion Theatre in Jerusalem. Over a thousand people filled the auditorium while thousands more remained outside and crowded at the entrance doors. His speech reached a climax when he shifted the focus of his remarks from the reality in the Jezreel Valley and the colonies of the First Aliyah to what he had seen in the streets of Tel Aviv and Jerusalem:

> The rising stream of immigration delights me, and I am delighted, too, that the ships should bring these thousands of people who are prepared to risk their life's savings in the Jewish National Home. Nor do I underrate the importance of this immigration for our work of reconstruction. Our brothers and sisters of Djika and Nalevki . . . are flesh of our flesh and blood of our blood. But we must see to it that we direct this stream and do not allow it to deflect us from our goal. It is essential to remember that we are not building our National Home on the model of Djika and Nalevki. The life of the ghetto we have always known to be merely a stage on our road; here we have reached home, and are building for eternity.[42]

Basing himself on the public legitimacy that Weizmann had accorded to derisive remarks about the immigrants from Poland, Yitshak Laufbahn, the most sharp-tongued and outspoken columnist in the Yishuv, wrote:

> Today it is not just the shop from Dzika and Nalewki, with its miserable economic tradition and its distorted way of life, that is entering the Land of Israel, but more particularly its shopkeeper. For him, the homeland's landscape is merely something divided into *dunams* [a measurement of land] that carry a monetary value and from which profit can be made. This shopkeeper behaves like a domestic animal that gazes at the landscape and takes it all in as if it were fodder; thus for the shopkeeper from the streets of Warsaw, the advantage which a human being has over such an animal is that he, the shopkeeper, has a speculative mind—'What will it cost and how much will I make?'[43]

Uri Tsevi Grinberg, who arrived in Palestine in December 1923, was also deeply affected by the 'lamentable' character of the Polish Jews. As he put it a year after his arrival: 'If the dark hour has arrived in which the pedlars from Poland have finally remembered the Land of Israel, this is a sign that all hope is lost.'[44]

Nalewki Horrors in New York

As opposed to the young poet, who cursed and reviled, Weizmann, being a seasoned politician, chose to communicate different messages about the Fourth Aliyah to different audiences. The arena he chose for praising and valorizing it during its early months was that of American Jewry. The central political struggle in which Weizmann was caught up during this period was for the establishment of the Jewish Agency,[45] which he saw as providing the crucial leverage needed to acquire the monetary resources and political support for the Jewish people in order to realize the

Zionist dream. Upon his return from travels to Palestine, Geneva, and London, and in advance of his forthcoming trip to the United States, Weizmann wrote enthusiastically to Louis Marshall, his non-Zionist partner in the effort to create the Jewish Agency: 'People come with money, with machinery, with their foremen; Salonika and Lodz are shifting bodily into Palestine, with the result that cotton spinning [and] silk weaving [have] taken a development promising to make out of Jaffa and Haifa important industrial centers on the Mediterranean Coast.'[46] At the same time, Weizmann admitted to his associates among American Zionist groups that the Zionist Executive knew how to handle pioneers, but was at a loss when it came to people arriving with 1,000 to 1,500 pounds sterling (£60,000–£90,000 today), and didn't know how to help them.[47]

The manner in which Weizmann politically manipulated the immigration issue is most apparent in the detailed description that he sent to Marshall concerning the immigration data for June to October 1924. He camouflaged the fact that, of the approximately 10,000 arrivals during these five months, some 4,000 had come from Poland, and presented a false picture of a veritable *kibuts galuyot* (ingathering of the exiles) involving Jews from around the world (the Balkans, Iraq, Morocco, Tunisia, Uzbekistan, India, Germany, and other countries).[48] A month later, in a letter to Albert Einstein, Weizmann boasted about the noteworthy 'psychological fact' that, in contrast to the past, when immigrants belonged predominantly to the classes lacking financial means, a significant proportion of the current arrivals were small traders and skilled craftsmen who believed that there were already sufficient opportunities for the successful settlement of people of their class.[49]

These statements should not be understood to mean that Weizmann had changed his mind about the immigrants arriving in Palestine. In February 1925 he travelled to the United States to participate in a conference organized by non-Zionists regarding the establishment of the Jewish Agency.[50] On 16 February, a week after his arrival in New York, he gave the first public speech of his visit at a fundraising convention that had been organized by Keren Hayesod in Carnegie Hall. In the course of it he again made reference to Dzika and Nalewki, and did not hold himself back. According to a description in the *New York Times* the day after the convention, 20,000 people came to the hall but only 5,000 could be admitted, filling every vacant space in the auditorium. The audience was enthusiastic, and Weizmann was welcomed with long bursts of applause.[51] Buoyed by the intensity, it is hardly surprising that he set aside his written notes and delivered an impassioned, impromptu speech.

Dzika and Nalewki Streets, he explained to his audience, were not comparable to New York's Fifth Avenue. Fifty per cent of the new immigrants remained in Tel Aviv and the city was growing disproportionately, upsetting the balance between rural and urban life, in the same aberrant manner in which the Jewish neighbourhoods of New York, Brooklyn and Borough Park, developed. From this point, he proceeded to speak about the uniqueness of the Zionist project in the light of current Jewish existence: 'In the Jewish ghetto throughout the world, we became typical urban dwellers. The land, the soil, the country—and therefore the entire civilization based on the countryside—the language, the tradition, and the land were not ours, and that is what took place in Poland.'[52]

If the same were to occur in Tel Aviv, the very same fatal outcome that befell the Jews of Warsaw and of Poland generally would also be the fate of Tel Aviv. In Palestine 'Zionism is ascendant and guides the process of building', and, therefore, though it may be uncomfortable to hear, it was 'a sacred duty' to prevent the development of an imbalance between the land, the village, the town, and the city.[53] In Palestine one could not build skyscrapers, Weizmann pointed out to the Jews of New York, drawing on familiar images from their everyday lives: 'They would collapse over our heads and crush us. I am warning you about Dzika and Nalewki just as I would warn against Fifth Avenue . . . A private person usually resides in a city. He must reside there . . . The pioneers whose glories we have been singing for so many years are creating the foundations upon which a city will rise, and will rise solidly at that.'[54]

On the level of policy, Weizmann's speech about Dzika and Nalewki left no doubt in the minds of his audience about his view of the immigrants that were required for the development of the Jewish homeland. While Weizmann made sure to emphasize the agricultural pioneer which the Zionist leadership tended to idealize in diaspora settings, Laufbahn's observations had a more down-to-earth character. Free-market competition and unorganized labour, he claimed, were surely more advantageous from the perspective of the 'superior person' from Nalewki Street or New York's East Side, than for a worker with a socialist ideological consciousness who desired a Hebrew culture and the development of an independent, non-private, national economy. In his view, 'the Hebrew homeland' would be built by the labour and economic activity of the worker in the rural and urban areas or it would not be built at all. Any alternative would mean 'that what will be built will be neither a homeland nor speak Hebrew, but rather be a squalid, Levantine alleyway of a Jewish country in Asia Minor'.[55]

Basing itself on Weizmann's speech, *Hado'ar*, the Hebrew-language weekly published in New York, expanded on the derisive and undesirable image of the Jewish immigrant from Dzika and Nalewki, in a style borrowed from the Yiddish writers Mendele Moykher Sforim (Sholem Yankev Abramovitsh), Yitskhok Leybush Peretz, and Sholem Aleichem:

What is the nature of the people of 'Nalewki' and 'Dzika' who have become a byword, and I would say 'proverbial' in our conversations? These people are 'extremely wise' [Prov. 30: 24]; they are nimble and quick-witted. Always they are occupied [with something]: whether running after someone or running away from someone. By day and by night they build castles in the air, devising the strangest of plans about all sorts of mixtures, amalgamations, and 'combinations'. Whether of a species with its own kind or a species with not of its own kind. And what is the *nafka minah* [the practical consequence]? Their brains are a large storeroom of all sorts of commercial dealings and industries. And in some cases, there is neither this nor that, and their minds are full of useless vain illusions. Their one concern: how to turn a profit? And not necessarily because they are poor. No! Because of their delight in the affair: 'pigeon racing' [an activity associated with liars and thieves (*San.* 25a–b)], 'buying and selling, obtaining the two hundred dinar he lacks, after he already has one hundred'. These people have no world but this: concluding a deal. And there is no interest for them in life, except for this one and only point of leverage. And they have no connection with life, except by these spider-webs that they spin all the time ... There are cases in which such people ... jump onto a ship and sail to the Land of Israel. They and all that is in their brains ... In their view 'What do I care whether I am here and there? A skilful person will find his way even among mountains of sand.' With his innovations and inventions using the word 'trade' he conjures up actual worlds. And here the Land of Israel is in the process of being built. And here he takes off and here he arrives.[56]

As opposed to this undesirable stereotype, Weizmann presented a single scene that was revealed to his eyes during his visit to Tel Aviv. It was with this image that he concluded his speech at the Keren Hayesod convention and also the description of the Fourth Aliyah in his autobiography. American Jewry, he observed defensively in his refined rhetoric, treated the ḥalutsim and their path with a degree of suspicion, not only because they were not keen on the American individualistic ideal of profit-seeking but also because of their excessively secular character. The ḥalutsim were not religious according to the manner of religious communities in Brownsville or Yorkville, he said, but on the evening of Yom Kippur he saw the way thousands of ḥalutsim were gathering near the synagogues in Tel Aviv. Seventeen thousand of the city's 25,000 residents went to hear the Kol Nidrei prayers, he reported proudly.[57] He did not bother to share with his American Jewish audience the fact that these same ḥalutsim carried him and Bialik aloft on their shoulders through the city's streets, dancing and singing holiday songs.[58] But it was this fact more than any derogatory term alluding to Jewish streets in Warsaw that revealed the nature of the unmediated and organic connection between the political-cultural approach taken by the Zionist movement and the public upon which it placed its hopes to realize their shared vision in the real world, upon them and not upon 'others' from Nalewki and Dzika and the like.

Three weeks after Weizmann's speech in Carnegie Hall, at a place far distant from New York, another Jew danced and other Jews shed tears of emotion. On 7 March, 600 Jews left Warsaw by train on their way to the Land of Israel. Some 25,000 people gathered at the city's station. According to the Warsaw paper *Hayom*,

At the time of parting, heart-rending scenes took place that made a strong impression on everyone in the large crowd ... One Jew, a shop-owner from Nalewki Street, departed with his entire family to the Land of Israel ... Suddenly this Jew took to the streets in a happy dance. This scene brought to tears all the men and women who saw the Jew dancing for joy.[59]

The Jew in question was not dancing because of the monetary profit awaiting him in Palestine, and this was not the reason the onlookers shed emotional tears. The fervent hope for revival and national independence had become the centre of the dreams of certain portions of Polish Jewry, and they imagined them to have a concrete character that could be realized here and now.

The Image of the Nalewki and Dzika Immigrants Reconsidered

A growing awareness and tortuous admission that the terminology used to describe the immigrants from Poland was perhaps exaggerated and not conducive to a welcoming attitude was articulated by Moshe Glickson towards the end of October 1924. He remarked that there was no place for the suspicion they aroused, which made it seem as if the arrival of Polish Jewry was being opposed, and that no one should believe that 'the homeland would not be built by an "aristocracy" either of the bourgeoisie or of labourers'.[60] The journal *Hayishuv*, which had just been launched and was a vehicle for the bourgeois middle class, declared vehemently that 'this is not the way—we should not divide the land's [Jewish] citizens into "privileged citizens" and "second class citizens"!'[61] For his part, Shemu'el Czernowitz, a member of *Haaretz*'s editorial board, pointed out that 'speaking slanderously and mockingly about Tel Aviv in general and about the Jews of Dzika and Nalewki in particular' was to forget the fact that just a year ago 'we sat and wept over the ships leaving the land' which carried Jews who had decided to abandon it and return to the diaspora. Those now arriving, he admitted, were opening shops, selling fizzy drinks, and speculating on land deals, but 'this is the nature of the people, whether we like it or not'. The shopkeeper mentality of the new arrivals was a problem, but Jews who had arrived in earlier waves of immigration had had a similar mentality which they had not yet shed, even though they were now beating their chests and proclaiming: 'We are the sons of the land!'[62] Eight months later, Czernowitz had also reached the conclusion that the 'Menahem Mendels of Nalewki had imported negative currents'. Years later, Amos Oz would claim that the Labour movement had never been able to rid itself of its obsession with the 'petit-bourgeois malady' which sought to detach itself from the world-view of the *ḥaluts* and its ascetic priorities and the ethos of sacrifice on behalf of the collective.[63]

Indignation at the profiteering and speculating which allegedly characterized the Jewish immigrants from Poland and—according to this view—their unproductive character which was now affecting the social and cultural atmosphere of the Yishuv did not cease throughout the period of the Fourth Aliyah. The finishing touches of this group's profile in the collective memory of Zionism and the Yishuv were added towards the end of 1925 by Yosef Aharonovitz, the director of Bank Hapo'alim and leader of the Hapo'el Hatsa'ir party. He described them as 'a very large mass' of 'people whose livelihood was based on wheeling and dealing', who 'opened stores upon stores and restaurants and cafes, leaving no room to spare'. The hope that over time they would adapt to the prevalent Zionist ethos had proved vain.[64] However, the visible presence of businessmen and merchants in the corridors of the Fourteenth Zionist Congress that took place in Vienna in 1925 was an innovation that demonstrated that the exilic Jews immortalized by Mendele Moykher Sforim and Sholem Aleichem were becoming an inseparable part of the Zionist scene.[65] For a single historical hour in the life of the Jews, those seeking an opportunity to make a profitable living crossed paths with the proponents of a Jewish national homeland. A decade later, Yitzhak Dov Berkowitz, Sholem Aleichem's son-in-law, gave delightful literary expression to this encounter. His novella *Menahem Mendel in the Land of Israel* evaluated the new immigrants positively: 'Everyone lends a hand to the building of the land ... for we speculators and middlemen are the first to engage in the construction work—if we did not supply the plots, that is land for construction, on what would they build the land?'[66] Thus the classical figure of the Polish Jew who excels at *luftgesheft*, a product of Sholem Aleichem's observation and inspiration, transformed its identity while sticking to its former occupation. The difference was that this time Menahem Mendel was no longer the exilic idler, but was presented rather as making a vital contribution to implementing the national vision. This recognition began to prevail in Yishuv society when the momentum of the Fourth Aliyah gradually slowed during the first half of 1926.

Bialik set out his contradictory views on this topic during a visit to New York. He began by observing, 'I am sorry to see Nalewkis in the Land of Israel.' Young Jews going out dancing at the Tel Aviv Casino and Jewish middlemen had made a very negative impression on him, he admitted. Nevertheless, he thought that 'peace ought to be made' with the middle class, because without its contribution it would be impossible to build the land. However, his conclusion that, even if it were 'possible to bring two million Jews from the exile to the Land of Israel on the wings of eagles', it should not be done,[67] sheds disconcerting light on the way leading Zionists saw the problems facing the Jewish people in those critical years. Bialik clearly believed that the Land of Israel and Zionism would be unable to cope with the challenge of absorbing masses of Jews whose identity and character were products of the Jewish life of streets like Nalewki and Dzika in Warsaw.

Conclusion

A crucial event in the history of Zionism took place in the second half of 1924. Laufbahn described it candidly: 'Today it is no longer a pipe-dream, the Jews are indeed clamouring at the gate of the Land of Israel.' For a brief moment it appeared to those involved in the historical drama described in this article that an earthquake in the life of the Jewish people was under way and that the Zionist dream was no longer a 'make-believe fantasy'.[68] But as Uri Tsevi Grinberg declared at the beginning of 1927, when the Fourth Aliyah had lost its momentum and the number of those leaving the country equalled the number of arrivals, 'the ultimate [fate] of these immigrants proves to us, that it was not a [Zionist] *vision* that had been kindled in their hearts commanding them to rise up and go [to Palestine]'.[69] From the perspective of Weizmann, Bialik, and the other figures who shaped Hebrew national culture, the majority of the Jewish masses who seemed to be steering their course towards Palestine were not 'fit and worthy of it. They are not [meant] for the land, nor the land for them.'[70] In this respect, Weizmann remained firm in his beliefs, and in his speech at the Fourteenth Zionist Congress he declared: 'I too am part of Nalewki and Dzika—a bit more remote: from Pinsk [the town to which he moved at the age of 11]—and indeed we all became Zionist through the negation of Nalewki.' In other words, 'Nalewki' for him was the current essence of the parasitic exilic condition and of the lack of Jewish sovereignty. He added: 'We know that the hidden powers of Dzika are immense, but if the Land of Israel were to submit to these powers—our Zionism would lose all of its value. Zionism is a protest against Dzika and our only aspiration is to turn Nalewki and Dzika into what we call "Erets Yisra'el".'[71]

At a public self-reckoning conducted by Martin Buber in April 1926, when the crisis of the Fourth Aliyah had already become the talk of the day in Zionist circles, the philosopher argued that the institutions of higher learning that had been inaugurated (the Hebrew University in Jerusalem and the Technion in Haifa), admirable as they were, should not become the be-all and end-all of what was termed 'Jewish culture in Erets Yisra'el'. What was most important was cultural work geared towards the education of the people. Buber expressed doubts over whether the Zionist movement had been able to respond effectively to questions posed by the Fourth Aliyah: 'What sort of people does the Land of Israel need, and what people does it have? How can one transform those who are not attuned to its goals so that they can contribute to building the Land? How can a group of random settlers become *a people*?' If the leaders of Zionism and its spokespersons did not recognize the duty incumbent upon them in this respect, he argued, then 'we will stand powerless, shaken and frightened' in the face of a convenient lodging-house 'named Zion', which was nothing but a branch of the large 'Hotel Exile'. He concluded: 'It is still up to us whether after a hundred years the Zionist project will be seen as elevated and lofty in character, or whether people will shake their heads in wonderment over its false realization and its folly, and say, "Clearly, such a project could not be sustained."'[72] With these words Buber indicated the historical perspective necessary to examine what Weizmann had hoped to achieve when he condemned the phenomenon of 'Dzika and Nalewki' in Palestine. Nearly a century has passed since then. Nalewki and Dzika are still preserved in this manner in the Israeli collective memory, but from the point of view of world Jewry, the crucial factor is that these Jewish streets themselves no longer exist.

Translated from the Hebrew by Ilana Goldberg

Notes

1 C. Weizmann, *Trial and Error: The Autobiography of Chaim Weizmann* (New York, 1949), 301; 'Ne'um ha-dr. ḥ vaitsman: ba'asefah ha'amamit bete'atron "tsiyon" biyerushalayim, 11 oktober 1924', *Ha'olam*, 31 Oct. 1924, pp. 3–4.

2 C. Weizmann, *Masah uma'as* (Jerusalem, 1949), 296–7.

3 I. Kolat, 'Aliyat manhiguto shel ḥayim vaitsman', *Avot umeyasedim* (Tel Aviv, 1975), 1–22: 15; Y. Gorny, *Shutafut uma'avak: ḥayim vaitsman utenuat hapo'alim be'erets yisra'el* (Tel Aviv, 1976), 73.

4 See e.g. S. E. Aschheim, *Brothers and Strangers: The East European Jew in German and German Jewish Consciousness, 1800–1923* (Madison, Wis., 1982), 89–91; Y. Weiss, *Etniyut ve'ezraḥut: yehudei germanyah viyehudei polin, 1933–1940* (Jerusalem, 2001), 32–5.
5 See e.g. E. Mendelsohn, *Hatenuah hatsiyonit bepolin: shenot hahithavut 1915–1926* (Jerusalem, 1986), 239–43; A. Halamish, *Bemeruts kaful neged hazeman: mediniyut ha'aliyah hatsiyonit bishenot hasheloshim* (Jerusalem, 2006), 428; R. Schoenfeld, 'Avot uvanim: ha'aliyah mipolin bashanim 1924–1932 be'einei hador hashelishi', *Gal-ed*, 15–16 (1997), 213–14.
6 Y. Shavit, 'Ma'amadah shel hatarbut betahalikh yetsiratah shel ḥevrah le'umit be'erets yisra'el: emdot yesod umusegei yesod', in Z. Shavit (ed.), *Toledot hayishuv hayehudi be'erets yisra'el me'az ha'aliyah harishonah: beniyatah shel tarbut ivrit be'erets yisra'el* (Jerusalem, 1998), 9–29; J. Reinharz, *Ḥayim vaitsman: baderekh el hamanhigut* (Jerusalem, 1987), 404–33; C. Weizmann, *Devarim*, 4 vols. (Tel Aviv, 1936–7), ii. 349–52.
7 Shavit, 'Ma'amadah shel hatarbut', 14.
8 See M. Lissak, 'Aliyah, kelitah, uvinyan ḥevrah be'erets yisra'el bishenot ha'esrim (1918–1930)', in M. Lissak, A. Shapira, and G. Cohen (eds.), *Toledot hayishuv hayehudi be'erets yisra'el me'az ha'aliyah harishonah: tekufat hamandat haberiti*, ii. (Jerusalem, 1995), 213–45; A. Halamish, '"Aliyah selektivit" bara'ayon, bama'aseh uvahistoryografyah hatsiyoniyim', in A. Shapira, J. Reinharz, and Y. Harris (eds.), *Idan hatsiyonut* (Jerusalem, 2000), 185–202.
9 A. N. Polack, 'Yehudei polin be'erets yisra'el', in I. Bartal and I. Guttman (eds.), *Kiyum veshever: yehudei polin ledoroteihem*, 2 vols. (Jerusalem, 1997–2001), i. 400.
10 H. M. Sachar, *A History of the Jews in America* (New York, 1993), 322–4.
11 'Batenuah hatsiyonit', *Ha'olam*, 20 June 1924, p. 12 (emphasis in original).
12 *Din veḥeshbon ha'ekzekutivah shel hahistadrut hatsiyonit lakongres ha-14* (London, 1925), 234–5; *Din veḥeshbon ha'ekzekutivah shel hahistadrut hatsiyonit lakongres ha-15* (London, 1927), 209.
13 D. Giladi, *Hayishuv bitekufat ha'aliyah harevi'it (1924–1929): beḥinah kalkalit upolitit* (Tel Aviv, 1973).
14 *Din veḥeshbon ha'ekzekutivah shel hahistadrut hatsiyonit lakongres ha-14*, 234–5; *Din veḥeshbon ha'ekzekutivah shel hahistadrut hatsiyonit lakongres ha-15*, 212.
15 Giladi, *Hayishuv bitekufat ha'aliyah harevi'it*, 40–1.
16 A. Shapira, 'Hamitos shel hayehudi heḥadash', in ead., *Yehudim ḥadashim, yehudim yeshanim* (Tel Aviv, 1997), 155–74: 158.
17 See e.g. M. Lissak, 'Dimuyei olim: stere'otipim vetiyug bitekufat ha'aliyah hagedolah bishenot haḥamishim', *Cathedra*, 43 (1987), 125–44; H. Shoham, 'Meha'aliyah hashelishit la'aliyah hasheniyah uveḥazarah: hivatserut haḥalukah litekufot lefi ha'aliyot hamemusparot', *Zion*, 77 (2012), 189–222.
18 A. Vardi, 'Al saf hamoledet', *Haaretz*, 11 Aug. 1925, p. 2.
19 E. Steinman, 'Mipinkaso shel "ḥadash"', *Haaretz*, 5 Dec. 1924, p. 5. Steinman would be awarded the Israel Prize for literature in 1963.
20 Y. Yunes-Dinovich, 'Bein hishtalevut litelishut: hamehagerim mipolin le'erets yisra'el bein shetei milḥamot ha'olam bemifgash im "kur hahitukh hatsiyoni"', M.A. thesis (Hebrew University of Jerusalem, 2004), 56–66.
21 W. Preuss, 'Pirkei statistikah shel tel aviv', in A. Droyanov (ed.), *Sefer tel aviv* (Tel Aviv, 1936), 321–410: 341.
22 C. Arlosoroff, 'Leha'arakhat ha'aliyah harevi'it', *Hapo'el hatsa'ir*, 11 May 1925, pp. 3–6.
23 Ben-Gurion Archive, Sde Boker, Diaries, item ID 79631: Ben-Gurion Diary 1915–1971, 7 Nov. 1924. Ben-Gurion was secretary of Histadrut from 1921 to 1935 and one of the leaders of the Labour movement.

24 Z. Smilansky, 'Tel aviv ufarnasoteiha', *Ha'olam*, 31 Oct. 1924, pp. 4–7.
25 Ibid. 7.
26 A. Helman, *Or veyum hikifuha: tarbut tel avivit bitekufat hamandat* (Haifa, 2007), 116–21; M. Azaryahu, *Tel aviv ha'ir ha'amitit: mitografyah historit* (Kiryat Sde Boker, 2005), 41–2; L. R. Halperin, *Babel in Zion: Jews, Nationalism, and Language Diversity in Palestine, 1920–1948* (New Haven, Conn., 2014), 44–9, 72–5.
27 I. Bartal, *Tangled Roots: The Emergence of Israeli Culture* (Providence, RI, 2020), 49–58.
28 Arlosoroff, 'Leha'arakhat ha'aliyah harevi'it'. At the time Hapo'el Hatsa'ir was the second-largest party in the Labour movement after Ahdut Ha'avodah led by Ben-Gurion and Berl Katznelson. Arlosoroff was head of the political department of the Jewish Agency from 1931 to 1933 as a representative of Mapai (after the two parties united in 1930) and was a central figure in the confrontation over hegemony in the Zionist movement between the Labour movement and the Revisionist movement. Arlosoroff was assassinated in June 1933 while walking on the beach in Tel Aviv with his wife.
29 'Kabalat penei manhigeinu betel aviv', *Do'ar hayom*, 26 Sept. 1924, p. 3.
30 M.G. [Glickson], 'Al haperek: dr. vaitsman be'erets yisra'el', *Haaretz*, 24 Sept. 1924, p. 2; 26 Sept. 1924, p. 2; 5 Oct. 1924, p. 2; 6 Oct. 1924, p. 2.
31 Ibid., 26 Sept. 1924.
32 Ibid.
33 Ibid.
34 Ibid. (emphasis in original).
35 Chaim Weizmann, letter to Vera Weizmann, 27 Sept. 1924, in *The Letters and Papers of Chaim Weizmann*, Series A: *Letters*: xii: *August 1923 – March 1926*, ed. J. Freundlich (Jerusalem, 1977), 240–1.
36 A. Holtzman, *Ḥayim naḥman bialik* (Jerusalem, 2009), 200–1. The General Zionist party reflected the outlook of liberal urban groups, business people, and owners of capital in the Yishuv.
37 'Mishteh likhev[od] haprof[esor] vaitsman betel aviv', *Do'ar hayom*, 1 Oct. 1924, p. 2.
38 Ibid.
39 'She'elot ha'aliyah', *Ha'olam*, 7 Nov. 1924, p. 3.
40 J. Klausner, 'Haḥayim haḥevrutiyim-ruḥaniyim be'erets yisra'el', *Ha'olam*, 3 Oct. 1924, pp. 8–10. From the late 1920s Klausner's writing would become an outstanding source of inspiration to the right-wing Revisionist circles within the Yishuv and the Zionist movement generally.
41 Central Zionist Archive, BK\65756\62: Central Office of the Zionist Organization, 'Minutes of Meetings of the Executive Committee in London, 1.1.1924 – 19.12.1924', 10 Oct. 1924.
42 Weizmann, *Trial and Error*, 301; see 'Ne'um ha-dr. ḥ. vaitsman', 3.
43 Y. Laufbahn, 'Hama'amad habeinoni', *Hapo'el hatsa'ir*, 27 Nov. 1924, pp. 4–5.
44 U. T. Grinberg, 'Manifest le'bitui', *Sadan*, 1–2 (Dec. 1924), 3; see P. Ginosar, 'Uri tsevi grinberg ve'aliyat grabski', *Iyunim bitekumat yisra'el*, 1 (1991), 523–46: 526. Four years later Grinberg would join the Revisionist movement and be counted as one of its most radical members.
45 Y. Eilam, *Hasokhnut hayehudit: shanim rishonot, 1919–1931* (Jerusalem, 1990), 52–71.
46 Chaim Weizmann, letter to Louis Marshall, 8 Nov. 1924, in Weizmann, *Letters*, xii. 246–7.
47 Chaim Weizmann, letter to Morris Rotenberg and Emanuel Neumann, 9 Nov. 1924, in Weizmann, *Letters*, xii. 251.

48 Weizmann, letter to Marshall, 8 Nov. 1924.
49 Chaim Weizmann, letter to Albert Einstein, 12 Dec. 1924, in Weizmann, *Letters*, xii. 285.
50 Eilam, *Hasokhnut hayehudit*, 68–70.
51 'Ovations by Zionists to Dr. Weizmann', *New York Times*, 17 Feb. 1925, p. 14; 'Pirtei asefat ha'am benyu york', *Haaretz*, 17 Mar. 1925, p. 2.
52 Yad Chaim Weizmann, Rehovot, Weizmann Archives, 2-986: 'Address of Doctor Chaim Weizmann Delivered at Carnegie Hall', 16 Feb. 1925.
53 Ibid.
54 Ibid.
55 Y. Laufbahn, 'Hasitnah', *Hapo'el hatsa'ir*, 21 Aug. 1925, pp. 7–8.
56 S. Rosenfeld, 'Aliyah sheyesh imah yeridah', *Hado'ar*, 27 Feb. 1925, pp. 3–4.
57 Weizmann, letter to Marshall, 8 Nov. 1924; 'Address of Doctor Chaim Weizmann Delivered at Carnegie Hall'; Weizmann, *Masah uma'as*, 298.
58 'Dr. vaitsman be'erets yisra'el', *Ha'olam*, 10 Oct. 1924, pp. 12–13.
59 'Varshah: aliyat sheyarah gedolah bat 600 ish le'erets yisra'el', *Hayom*, 9 Mar. 1925, p. 4.
60 M.G. [Glickson], 'Ha'aliyah veproblemoteiha', *Haaretz*, 27 Oct. 1924, p. 2.
61 Halodzai, 'Lo zo hi haderekh!', *Hayishuv*, 29 Jan. 1925, pp. 9–10. These remarks were written in the spirit of the famous article by Ahad Ha'am about the path to rebuilding the land in the time of the Hibat Tsiyon movement (Ahad Ha'am (Asher Zvi Ginsberg), 'Lo ze haderekh', *Hamelitz*, 15 Mar. 1889, p. 1).
62 S. Czernowitz, 'Sihot', *Haaretz*, 5 Dec. 1924, p. 6. Czernowitz was the father of the Israeli diplomat Jacob Tsur and the grandfather of the historian and pre-eminent philosopher of the kibbutz, Muki Tsur.
63 S.Cz. [Czernowitz], 'Hane'elavim', *Haaretz*, 17 Aug. 1925, p. 2; A. Oz, 'Hamahalah haze'eir burganit', in id., *Be'or hatekhelet ha'azah* (Tel Aviv, 1978), 125–30.
64 Y. Aharonovich, 'Hametsiut kemo shehi', *Davar*, 2 Dec. 1925, p. 2.
65 M. K. [Kleiman], 'Agav', *Ha'olam*, 28 Aug. 1925, p. 14. Moshe Kleiman was the editor of *Ha'olam*.
66 Y. D. Berkowitz, 'Menahem mendel be'erets yisra'el', in *Kitvei y. d. berkowitz*, 12 vols. (Tel Aviv, 1951–66), i. 224.
67 B. Zuckerman, 'Bialik bezivo', *Davar*, 15 Mar. 1926, p. 2.
68 Y. Laufbahn, 'Miproblemot ha'aliyah', *Hapo'el hatsa'ir*, 29 Aug. 1924, pp. 5–6.
69 U. T. Grinberg, 'Mimegilat hayamim hahem', *Davar*, 14 Jan. 1927, pp. 2–3 (emphasis in original).
70 Y. Tahon, 'Hayahadut hapolanit vegoralah', *Ha'olam*, 23 Apr. 1926, pp. 8–10.
71 'Ne'um hateshuvah shel vaitsman', *Ha'olam*, 4 Sept. 1925, pp. 1–4.
72 M. Buber, "Heshbon hanefesh', *Ha'olam*, 23 Apr. 1926, pp. 3–6 (emphasis in original).

Nalewki Street in Tel Aviv?
The Political Heritage of East European Jewry in the Yishuv and the State of Israel

GERSHON BACON

Polish Jewry: Metaphor and Reality in the Eyes of the Zionist Movement

During the Fourth Aliyah (1924–6) the population of the Yishuv in the Land of Israel underwent a great quantitative and qualitative change. Thousands of businessmen and shopkeepers made their way from Poland to the cities of Mandatory Palestine, using so-called 'capitalist' visas issued by the British authorities and not the 'certificates' issued under the aegis of the Jewish Agency and the Zionist federations to young pioneers. These newcomers contributed greatly to the development of commerce and industry and especially to the growth of the city of Tel Aviv. In 1924, with the imposition of the quota system for immigration to the United States, Polish Jews seeking to emigrate turned to Palestine as the best alternative, and for the first time the number of Jewish immigrants from Poland to Palestine surpassed that of Polish Jews emigrating to America. Yet almost from the outset, what should have been the fulfilment of Zionist dreams, the arrival of thousands of immigrants, became a matter of controversy. In the eyes of many Zionist leaders, the timing and social makeup of this wave of migration was deeply problematic and represented no less than a threat to the long-term aspirations of the Zionist enterprise as a whole.[1] This wave of immigration quickly received the sarcastic nickname the 'Grabski Aliyah' after the Polish premier and finance minister who imposed a series of decrees on the middle class as part of his successful currency stabilization programme. For many Zionist leaders, these Polish Jewish newcomers were not what the country needed at this stage of its development, as they perceived them as mere immigrants rather than ideologically motivated *olim*. Writing in *Haaretz* on the eve of the regular, periodic visit to Palestine by Chaim Weizmann, chairman of the Zionist Organization in September and October 1924, editor Moshe Glickson presented a stark portrayal of the potential damage that the newcomers from Poland could bring about: 'If the Zionist executive does not want this *aliyah* of our middle class to bring us a new Nalewki in the Land of Israel—and a Nalewki without the Jewish tradition and without the livelihood of the Warsaw Nalewki—it is its obligation to *control* this *aliyah* . . . and to direct it to our needs.'[2] Thus was born a negative metaphor for the nature of Polish Jewry, where Nalewki, the busy street in the Jewish quarter of Warsaw,[3] became a metonym for certain attributes of Polish Jewry as a whole. This metaphor was quickly taken up by Weizmann himself in his speeches during the visit to Palestine and in subsequent writings and presentations. In his speech in Jerusalem in October 1924, Weizmann made the contrast clear:

Our brothers and sisters from Djika [another street in the Jewish quarter of Warsaw] and Nalevki are flesh of our flesh and blood of our blood. But we must see to it that we direct this stream and do not allow it to deflect us from our goal. It is essential to remember that we are not building our National Home on the model of Djika and Nalevki. The life of the ghetto we have always known to be a stage on our road; here we have reached home, and are building for eternity.[4]

Thus, Nalewki Street and similar streets in Warsaw and other Jewish metropolises in eastern Europe became the symbol of what the Jewish people had to overcome if it wished to rebuild itself in the historic homeland. Weizmann shared his view on the matter numerous times, as in his remarks a year later at the Fourteenth Zionist Congress: 'the great immigration movement to Palestine is the result of our five years of activity. We have all become Zionists because we have rejected the Nalewki and Dzika atmosphere. I say that though I have myself come out of the Nalewki environment, and that is what is urging us to insist on the transformation of the Jews in Palestine.'[5] Some months earlier, in the run-up to the Fourteenth Zionist Congress, Dr Ozjasz Herschdörfer presented an unembellished picture of what was at stake in an article in the Kraków daily *Nowy Dziennik*, tellingly entitled 'The Problem of Mass Immigration', in which he warned that importing the spiritual level of what he termed 'the outlook of Nalewki and Kazimierz [the Jewish district of Kraków], the spiritual level of hucksters, merchants, and *luftmenschen*, for whom *parnasah* [making a livelihood] is the sole and exclusive ideal of life' to Palestine stood in opposition to the much-needed spiritual regeneration of the Jewish people in the land of the patriarchs.[6] Through Weizmann and a number of opinion makers and journalists in the early stages of the Fourth Aliyah, this image would become integral to the discourse surrounding the *aliyah* for years to come. This characterization of Polish Jewry did not go without criticism at that time, however. Yehoshua Gottlieb, leader of the Et Livnot faction of the General Zionists in Poland, responded that the attacks by Socialist Zionists on the Nalewki Jews of Tel Aviv echoed the attacks by Polish antisemites on the Nalewki Jews of Poland.[7]

Weizmann and those who shared his views remained firm in their stance.[8] As economic distress struck the Yishuv in 1926 and immigration slowed to a trickle, with some of the immigrants even returning to Poland, those who were sceptical from the outset regarded it as proof that the middle-class *aliyah* had been premature. As Yitshak Grünbaum, leader of the Al Hamishmar faction of the General Zionists, put it, the Land of Israel first had to be built up by pioneers willing to sacrifice their personal comfort for the cause, even if the factory owner in Tel Aviv may have contributed no less and perhaps even more to the immediate development of the Yishuv. At some point in the future the Land of Israel could and should become a land of immigration, but that time had not yet arrived.[9] Only those pioneers who succeeded in shedding the qualities of the diaspora and became 'new Jews' would be able to build up and consolidate the Yishuv. The metaphor of Nalewki provided a powerful counter-example to what Weizmann, Grünbaum, and others envisioned for the Yishuv.

But the question remains: were Glickson, Weizmann, Grünbaum, and others carried away in the heat of the polemic? Was it necessary, or even possible, to rid themselves of Nalewki or of Poland writ large? In many areas, especially in the political field, quite a few of the attributes of the so-called new Jews had their roots in the same Jewish society in eastern Europe, and this cannot be presented as a polar contrast between two worlds. In the approach of Grünbaum and his colleagues there was much of the historical experience of Nalewki and similar streets in the cities of Poland, Lithuania, Latvia, and other east European countries. In big things and in small details the political legacy of the east European diaspora would determine the parties and politics of the Yishuv. Despite the protestations and disclaimers of the politicians of that generation, it is impossible to ignore the impact of their east European background and their exposure to Polish language, culture, and history. Often the very language of protest and criticism of Polish Jewry reflected the symbols, ideals, and political strategies that characterized Polish history and Polish Jewish history. The Polish model and the Polish Jewish model proved determinative for Jewish politics in the Land of Israel.

In this chapter, I will survey those areas in which the impact of the east European Jewish political heritage on the development of political life in the Yishuv and later in the young State of Israel is prominent.

The Personal Dimension: Poland as Birthplace and Formative Influence

First and foremost, there is the personal and biographical dimension. Most of the Yishuv's leaders were born and bred in eastern Europe. A generational factor was also at work, with some of the leaders of the Zionist youth movements in Poland only later becoming senior political figures in Israel, such as Ya'akov Hazan[10] and Meir Ya'ari.[11] Their attitude to many issues, such as the status of religion, language, and women, were addressed by the leaders of the Yishuv in ways that were influenced by their family, cultural, and religious backgrounds in the cities and towns of Russia and Poland. Even when they consciously rebelled against their parents' tradition and culture, that rebellion was directed against the east European version of Judaism and Jewish culture and not an abstract construct bereft of concrete social context. Some of the political elite of Zionist Poland never arrived in Israel: some, such as Yehoshua (Ozjasz) Thon of Kraków,[12] the leader of the General Zionists in western Galicia, died in the 1920s and 1930s; and many were murdered in the Holocaust. Even those who arrived in Israel did not always continue to serve in the Zionist leadership of the Yishuv in positions comparable to those they held in the diaspora. Thus there was continuity in leadership but not necessarily direct continuity.

Some Jewish politicians from eastern Europe participated actively and directly in formulating parliamentary and governmental life in the Yishuv and in the State of Israel. These include Yitshak Grünbaum,[13] the former Polish Sejm deputy and General Zionist leader in Congress Poland, who held many positions in the Jewish Agency executive and served as a minister in the Provisional Government of the State of Israel; Apolinary Hartglas,[14] former Sejm deputy and a member of the Grünbaum faction in Poland, who served as a legal adviser to the Israeli Interior Ministry in the early years of the state and, among other things, prepared the legal infrastructure for local government in the country; Mordechai Nurock,[15] the Mizrachi leader and deputy in the Latvian parliament for more than a decade, who was elected to the Knesset several times and also served as a cabinet minister in the Israeli government; and Eliyahu Mazur, a member of Agudat Yisrael and former head of the Warsaw community, who was also elected to the first Knesset.[16] They were among the few politicians who had previous parliamentary or governmental experience in addition to their activity within the Zionist movement or in the bodies of the organized Yishuv.

Eastern Europe: The Birthplace of the 'New' Jewish Politics

The new Jewish politics of the Yishuv and of the State of Israel in its early years reflected the political and social conditions that prevailed in eastern Europe. In an article summarizing Jewish politics at the beginning of the twentieth century, Grünbaum himself saw the roots of the new politics in opportunities that opened up following the failed Russian revolution of 1905, which for the first time allowed underground or semi-legal organizations to surface and function as fully fledged political parties.[17] Writing almost a century after Grünbaum, Scott Ury also emphasized the crucial impact of the post-1905 era for the subsequent development of Jewish politics both in Poland and in the Land of Israel, stressing the symbiotic relationship between the emerging Polish and Jewish national movements:

Time and again, developments in the Polish political sphere exerted an immeasurable degree of influence over the course of Jewish politics as predominant concepts of community and belonging among Jews were repeatedly shaped by parallel conceptualizations of these key social and political constructs in the Polish political sphere . . . Under the influence of the National Democrats' language and rhetoric as well as critical changes in the Jewish public sphere, Jewish organizations began to construct their own brand of nationalism that was both democratic and exclusive. In this sense, the roots of what should be referred to as 'Jewish National Democracy' can be traced back to turn-of-the-century eastern Europe and not, as has been argued by some scholars, to the twentieth-century Middle East. While separated by only several decades, it is critical to note that Jewish politics and nationalism were angry and exclusive long before they were transplanted and transformed in Ottoman and then British Palestine.[18]

At the beginning of the twentieth century, the Zionists stood out as a leading political movement in the diaspora. The Zionist movement in Russia, at its famous

1906 conference in Helsingfors (Helsinki, Finland, then part of the Russian empire), had taken the decision to adopt the concept of *Gegenwartsarbeit* or *avodat hoveh* (work in the present) as one of its guiding principles. According to this doctrine, the Zionist movement saw the struggle for Jewish national rights in the diaspora as a legitimate part of its activities. The Russian Zionists thus rejected the contrary principle of *shelilat hagolah* (negation of the diaspora), which saw the bringing of Jews to Israel as the central, almost exclusive, role of the Zionist movement. According to this latter view, political activity in the diaspora only distracted from the main goal of Zionism. It is noteworthy in this context that two of the main spokesmen who advocated the idea of *avodat hoveh* at Helsingfors were none other than Grünbaum, then a young lawyer, and a young journalist named Ze'ev (Vladimir) Jabotinsky, each of whom would leave his mark on the Zionist movement.[19]

Thus the very politicization of Zionism and its entry into the local political arena are part of the legacy of east European Jewry. Similarly, the emergence of factions and sub-movements within Zionism also first developed among east European Zionists (whether in eastern Europe itself or among east European students located in western Europe), a phenomenon that was looked at askance by Herzl, the father of political Zionism.[20] This new political tradition would have numerous influences on the politics of the Yishuv, in form and content, in style, and in essence.

The political parties in the Yishuv were for the most part transplants of those in the diaspora: General Zionists, Socialist Zionists, Revisionist Zionists, and those opponents of Zionism who also came to the Land of Israel—communists and the Orthodox Agudat Yisrael. Perhaps the balance of power was not the same as it was in eastern Europe, but for those immigrants who came from there, the political landscape was at least familiar in its general contours.

Notwithstanding the often problematic status of the Jewish minority in Poland and other east European countries between the two world wars, parliamentary democracy in those countries, even if it was nationalist, limited, and short-lived, nevertheless allowed Jews to develop a level of political activity unparalleled in Jewish history in the diaspora. In eastern Europe, Zionist politicians received their political 'baptism of fire', including fully fledged parliamentary service, both in the Russian duma and the Austrian Reichsrat before the First World War and in the parliaments of the successor states in eastern Europe in the interwar period. These few deputies tried, with generally limited success, to protect the rights of the Jewish minority in general and to address the problems of private citizens who suffered discrimination. This political experience, along with the ongoing political tradition within the Jewish communities and Zionist congresses, served as the training for many of the leaders who would influence the political life of the Yishuv. Beyond the practical importance of parliamentary activity and election campaigns, such activity made a decisive contribution to raising the Jewish national question on the political agenda in the international arena, thus promoting the Zionist claim to a Jewish national homeland in Palestine. This was Grünbaum's answer to those who disputed the doctrine of *avodat hoveh* as distracting from the main objectives of Zionism.

On the contrary, he claimed, Jewish national politics in the diaspora strengthened Jewish national consciousness, thus fulfilling one of the principles of the Basel plan, the original programme of political Zionism as formulated by Herzl himself, simultaneously strengthening the Jewish claim for national rights everywhere, in the diaspora and in Palestine. While not denying the central importance of migration to the Land of Israel in the concept of political Zionism, Grünbaum argued that political activity in the diaspora would prepare the people for immigration and also advance the interests of Zionism. The appearance of the proud Jewish politician, who rejected the old political tradition of *shtadlanut* (intercession) as humiliating, made it clear to all, Jews and non-Jews alike, that a new type of politician spoke on behalf of a people desirous of taking its rightful place as an equal member of the nations of the world.[21] The new Jewish politicians from eastern Europe also convinced Jewish leaders from the West, such as the American Louis Marshall, who had opposed the notion of Jews as a national group in the United States, to support the demand of east European Jews for national rights at the peace conference after the First World War.[22]

This revolution did not begin in Palestine but in the political struggles of the Jewish parties in the diaspora and especially in eastern Europe. It was the debut of the new Jewish politics. In his criticism of the Fourth Aliyah, Grünbaum noted that the Yishuv needed symbolic heroes like Trumpeldor rather than a Tel Aviv factory owner. But in eastern Europe political figures like Grünbaum himself were the heroes for thousands of Jews in Poland and other countries, and they inspired the Jewish public no less than the heroic figures of the Yishuv.

It would be incomplete, however, to limit the political heritage of east European Jewry to the internal Jewish dynamic alone. Poland, Polish history and culture, and Polish politics played a significant role as well in the concretization of that political heritage. For example, in an autobiographical sketch of his childhood, Grünbaum recalled the influence of Polish history and Polish (and French) literature in his formative years, both in school and at the literary evenings in their home conducted by his mother, where the poetry of Mickiewicz and Słowacki was recited: 'They enriched my general knowledge of the history of Poland and France and of the wars for freedom of oppressed peoples. Their heroes captured my soul, arousing in me affection for the Poles who fought for their rights, and for the French, happy in spirit and lovers of freedom, influencing my dreams and my aspirations.'[23]

The story of the Polish nation that lost its independence, struggled for long decades in various ways to restore it, and ultimately succeeded constituted both an inspiration and a usable historical model for young Polish Jews like Grünbaum, raised on both Polish and Jewish culture, who developed a modern Jewish nationalist stance. As Ezra Mendelsohn has written:

There is ample room here for a positive attitude towards at least one aspect of Polish history—namely the Polish heroic struggle, against all odds, for national freedom. Indeed, one can say that an essential lesson of Polish-Jewish history is the necessity for Jews to emulate the Polish national model . . . In short, integral nationalism of the Polish variety, while in some ways obviously 'bad for the Jews', was helpful in providing them with a heroic model of action.[24]

The impact of Polish culture and education on the younger generation of Jews became even more profound in the interwar period, when the vast majority of Jewish students were educated in Polish public schools.[25] The required curriculum, even for students in private Jewish school networks, had a significant component of Polish language and literature, geography, and history, all taught in Polish. In newly independent Poland, the school was one of the main tools for state-building and inculcating a national identity.[26] Despite discrimination, antisemitism, and doubts about whether there was any chance for their eventual acceptance as part of the Polish nation, numerous testimonies attest to the growing Polonization of the younger generation and to the influence of the Romantic portrayal of Poland's history on the minds of Jewish youngsters in the interwar period. An excellent example is the autobiography of 'Esther', a 19-year-old woman from a Gerer hasidic family, submitted to the youth autobiographies competition sponsored by the YIVO Institute in Vilna in 1939:

I was then in the seventh grade of public school. I kept a diary in Polish. I was becoming more and more immersed in the Polish language. I especially loved Polish literature. I idolized the Polish Romantic poets Mickiewicz and Słowacki. Polish history was also a subject I loved and learned easily. I was enthralled by everything connected with Polish history. I was consumed with the great martyrdom of Polish heroes in their struggle for Poland's independence. I venerated Marshal Józef Piłsudski.[27]

Jewish nationalist activists, left and right, whether in youth movements or educational streams, similarly drew inspiration from the Polish national tradition. The Socialist Zionist youth movement Hashomer Hatsa'ir owed much to the model of the Polish scouting movement and attracted many young men and women from Polish-speaking homes who were educated in Polish gymnasia. These young people, who joined a movement that demanded of its members a personal commitment to emigrate to the Land of Israel and work on a kibbutz, often had little or no knowledge of Hebrew or Yiddish sources. Their Jewish nationalism was nourished more by Polish Romanticism than by acquaintance with Bialik or Tchernichowsky.[28] The curriculum of the Tarbut school network, a network devoted to Hebrew and Zionism, directed its teachers to identify links between the Polish and Zionist national liberation struggles.[29]

Of all the Zionist parties, though, the Revisionist Zionists and their Betar youth movement were most influenced by the model of Polish nationalism, its symbols and ceremonies. What is more, Jabotinsky, now the leader of the Revisionists, was himself directly affected by his encounter with young Polish Jews during a visit in 1927, when he saw how Poland and Polish nationalism exerted a profound influence on their self-image as Zionists. Their attitudes were inspired by the newly established Sanacja regime and the authoritarian leadership style of Piłsudski. As Daniel Heller put it, 'the young Polish Jewish adherents of Revisionism, many of whom drew inspiration from elements of Polish nationalism, did not simply accept a political vision imposed from above but played an active role in shaping it as well'.[30] The Revisionists found much to emulate in the nationalist vision and nation- and state-building they witnessed around them:

> Much of Revisionist literature and code of behaviour is modelled on Polish history, Polish values, and the Polish ethos and national existence. During the 1930s Poland was not only considered by Revisionists as a great and valuable political and military ally of Zionism, but it also became a model of inspiration to the ideology and praxis of political terrorism, armed underground struggle and political revolution.[31]

Like its Polish counterparts, Betar offered a blend of scouting and military training, yet insisted that these activities reinforce the Jewish identities of its members. It was the only Jewish youth movement with such paramilitary trappings and regularly participated in Polish national celebrations alongside Polish scouts and Polish soldiers and adopted the choreography of Polish youth and military groups for its own national celebrations.[32] The secular messianic approach of Betar, as evidenced, for example, in the writings of the young Betar activists Menahem Begin and Yitzhak Shamir, both future prime ministers of Israel, strongly resembled the Polish version of sacrifice for the sake of the nation, an approach developed during Poland's century of statelessness.[33] Finally, the connection between the Zionist right in Poland and Palestine expressed itself graphically in the symbol and slogan adopted by the military wing of the Revisionists in Palestine, the Irgun Tseva'i Le'umi. This symbol, featuring a hand grasping a rifle on the background of a map of the original land allotted to Mandatory Palestine, which included both banks of the Jordan, and bearing the slogan 'Rak kakh!' ('Only thus!'), which harked back directly to 'Tylko tak!', the slogan of the Polish legionnaires, first appeared in a Polish-language bi-weekly published by Polish Jewish intellectuals in Warsaw sympathetic with Revisionism and the Irgun.[34]

The ideology of the Zionist right wing and its attitude to the use of military force, even terrorism, for the achievement of national goals was forged in a Polish context no less than by events on the ground in Palestine and, with the rise to power of Menahem Begin and the Likud in 1977, has exerted a direct influence on Israeli policy ever since.[35]

The Political Style of East European Jewry

Among the features of the political tradition brought by Jews from eastern Europe was the raucous, even violent, atmosphere that characterized the Polish Sejm, the municipal councils, and the Jewish community *kehilah* boards. In the Sejm chamber, Jewish delegates were targets of particularly blunt antisemitic insults and catcalls, and they, too, could respond with taunts of their own. In the conference rooms of the Jewish community councils, the opposing parties directed insults and, sometimes, physical objects at each other. For example, in a particularly violent meeting of the

Warsaw *kehilah* board in October 1931:

Ellenberg announced that the Zionist faction would not put up with the present situation in the *kehilah*. It would use the 'obstruction' method and would interfere with the meeting. Before he finished his speech, members of the Zionist faction, who had been waiting in a nearby room, entered the conference hall, and an unrestrained disturbance began. Yitshak Schipper pulled off the tablecloth covering the chairman's table, and as a result glasses, pitchers of water and documents fell to the ground. Chairs, inkwells, and anything that could be moved were thrown about the hall. The hall became a battlefield of shouts, insults, and scuffles . . . Mazur [chairman of the *kehilah*, from Agudat Yisrael] was wounded in the head by a chair thrown at him, and a shard of glass struck his eye. Bleeding, he was transferred to a nearby clinic and given first-aid treatment. After they had bandaged his head and his eye, he returned to the community building to adjourn the stormy session.[36]

A few years earlier, the Warsaw *kehilah* building was occupied by Orthodox Jews protesting a plan to set up a dormitory for (usually secular) Jewish university students on a plot of land near an area of synagogues and study houses in the capital's Praga suburb. This demonstration was also accompanied by violence, numerous wounded and arrested, and extensive property damage.[37]

The rhetoric in election campaigns was no less harsh, as when Grünbaum spoke of the need to deal a 'death blow' to his Orthodox opponents from the Agudat Yisrael party. In the fierce competition between the Socialist Zionist camp and its rivals in the socialist Bund and the Communist Party, or between Revisionists and other Zionists, acute disagreements and aggressive political vocabulary and sometimes physical violence were a common feature. It is not surprising, then, that the political style that developed in the Land of Israel was also not particularly gentlemanly in its behaviour. The same style characterized the press, which did not abjure any means to attack ideological or political enemies.

Ezra Mendelsohn pointed to another feature of the political style of Polish Jewry: the tendency to alternate between periods of exaggerated euphoria and periods of deep despair, and this is also evident in the status of the various political organizations in Polish Jewry, which saw periods of sudden numerical growth and then almost absolute collapse, when neither euphoria nor despair were completely justified by the realities on the ground.[38]

Political Pragmatism alongside Ideological Opposition

Alongside the fierce and uncompromising rhetoric at the ideological level, east European Jewish politics had a pragmatic side expressed in forming coalitions and in day-to-day co-operation in the various political arenas. Ultimately, both Zionist and Jewish politics in general in east European countries were 'big tent' politics. Only those parties that, for ideological reasons, decided to separate themselves from the community at one point or another were out of this consensus. A notable example of this was the socialist Bund, which withdrew from *kehilah* politics for a full decade, from the mid-1920s to the mid-1930s, even refusing to co-operate with 'bourgeois' parties in demonstrations against Nazi Germany, preferring instead to march with Polish socialists in a separate demonstration. In 1935 the Revisionist Zionists also resorted to separate and independent politics as they withdrew from the Zionist Organization and formed the New Zionist Organization. But these were exceptions. Therefore, despite talk of death blows to political rivals and the like, the typical political situation in interwar Poland was a state of alliances and coalitions between the Zionists and Agudat Yisrael in *kehilah* councils, running for parliament together in the 'Minorities Bloc' with members of other national minorities in 1922, and working together in the Jewish faction (Koło Żydowskie) in the Polish Sejm. The same east European norm of co-operation despite sharp political and ideological disagreements also became part of the evolving political norms in the Yishuv and the State of Israel, as, for example, in the struggle within the Agudat Yisrael branch in Mandatory Palestine between members of the Old Yishuv and new arrivals. From the mid-1930s, members of the Polish Aguda who immigrated to Israel began to change the nature of the local organization. Unlike members of the Old Yishuv, who exhibited strong separatist tendencies, Polish Agudists did not oppose participation alongside Zionist parties in most of the Yishuv's institutions.[39] The pragmatic approach was in evidence at the Third Kenesiyah Gedolah, Agudat Yisrael's 1937 world gathering in Marienbad. When the conference discussed the Peel Commission's proposals to divide the Land of Israel into a Jewish state and an Arab state, many of the leaders of the Polish Aguda supported the plan as long as sufficient guarantees were given that the Jewish state would abide by the laws of the Torah. Even the Polish rabbis who opposed the plan expressed more opposition to a state led by secular Zionists than to the idea of partition per se.[40] The pragmatic trend is also reflected in an abortive attempt to bring about a union between the Po'alei Agudat Yisrael Labour movement and the Hapo'el Hamizrahi religious Zionist Labour movement.[41] The decision to co-operate with the Yishuv institutions had far-reaching consequences, which eventually enabled Agudat Israel and the Jewish Agency to sign the 'status quo agreement' of 1947, regulating the status of religion in the emerging Jewish state. Agudat Yisrael then supported the United Nations Partition Plan for Palestine and participated in the first elections for the Knesset and the Israeli government in a United Religious Front together with the religious Zionists.[42] All these moves, accompanied by no small hesitations on the part of Zionists and Agudists, were a direct continuation of the pragmatic political tradition of east European Jewry.

Principled ideological struggles, deep to the point of political stalemate, were also expressed in heated debates in the *kehilah* council chambers, but ultimately all parties were forced to compromise and acknowledge the divided reality of the Jewish public. The same ideological stalemate could have resulted in a budgetary stalemate and paralysis of the various auxiliary party organizations, such as schools, youth groups, and cultural institutions. Each party saw its role as increasing the allocations to its own institutions and minimizing allocations to those of its rivals. Thus, in discussions of support for educational and cultural budgets, unusual temporary coalitions were formed, such as the Bund and Agudat Yisrael representatives joining forces to prevent budgets for Zionist institutions, Zionists and Bund people together opposing budgets for Aguda institutions, and Aguda and the Zionists voting against budgets for Bund institutions. There were some cases where such paralysis led to the intervention of the Polish authorities. Usually, though, after the heated debate and the 'principled' votes, spirits calmed down, and, in a re-vote, all the proposed allocations would go through. Everyone was aware that the means for support of Jewish education were meagre because government support for Jewish educational institutions under the terms of the Minorities Treaty never materialized and support from overseas Jewish organizations was limited, as was the ability of parents to pay tuition fees, thus support of the education systems by the *kehilot* was critical to their existence.[43]

The same pragmatic approach was expressed in the sensitive area of the relationship between religious and secular Jews. From the very beginning of religious Zionism, some of the Mizrachi leaders expressed the view that in the Land of Israel, when Jews overcame the distortions imposed on their lives during the long exile, the religious life of the Jewish people could adopt forms of expression that were not possible under diaspora conditions. However, the reality was different, and religious life continued more or less in its traditional ways both in the diaspora and in the Land of Israel. The devastating potential of the gap between religious and secular was obvious to both groups from the early days of the Hibat Tsiyon movement in the 1880s, and so the movement adopted a strategic policy of putting off any attempt to reach a final resolution of the religious–secular debate that could jeopardize the unity of the young movement and threaten its very existence.[44] Leaders like Grünbaum may have believed in a 'cultural war', but in the realm of ongoing political activities they did not engage in a fight to the finish. Grünbaum was willing to give modernity time to act on Jewish society, and in the long run the problem would solve itself in the desired direction, or so he believed. The same strategy of delay continued in the Yishuv in the form of interim arrangements, the culmination of which was the aforementioned 'status quo' agreement of 1947, signed, with no small irony, by none other than Yitshak Grünbaum the Zionist and Yitshak Meir Levin of Agudat Yisrael, two bitter rivals from Poland.

Another particularly important contribution of the east European heritage to the political discourse in the Yishuv and the State of Israel was the very conception and definition of the constitutive terms, 'religious' and 'secular'. The two sides to this debate, the two lifestyles that developed in the Yishuv, arose against the background of the situation in eastern Europe. The inroads of secularization may have led to considerable attrition of the traditional society in Poland, but a significant segment of that society still remained in the period between the wars. Those aspiring to preserve tradition and those rebelling against it spoke the same language, both literally and figuratively, and had a common cultural heritage, expressed in common concepts and symbols. The two sides understood each other and the differences between them. However, the vocabulary of the religious–secular debate in the Land of Israel was largely incomprehensible to Jews who came from Islamic countries and to Jews who immigrated from western Europe or North America. For better or worse, the argument that began during the Hibat Tsiyon period continued in the factional disputes in the Herzl era, moved to the party struggle in eastern Europe between the wars, finally found its expression later in the Yishuv, and has largely not changed since.

Political Ideals and Political Idealism

Jewish political activists in eastern Europe held the sincere belief that they had the ability to reshape the Jewish nation and the Jewish individual and even the general political reality around them. An example of the latter is the attempt by Jewish politicians to make Poland a 'state of nationalities', an idea that stood in direct contradiction to the views of most Polish parties, right- and left-wing alike, and opened the Jewish minority to accusations that it wished to undermine hard-won Polish independence that had been restored after a prolonged period of occupation and oppression.[45] Also on the inner Jewish front, the idealism of the politicians encountered the stubborn reality of a Jewish people that did not change in the way they recommended. The path to the realization of the promises and hopes of diaspora Zionists and diaspora socialists alike was neither quick nor clear. Such a complex reality could be expected to alternately lead to euphoria or despair, but it could also lead to the political pragmatism discussed above in trying to achieve the possible in the real world.

Another component of east European Jewish political tradition was its total, all-inclusive nature, with party-sponsored institutions from kindergartens and schools to banks and sick funds, youth movements and sports organizations, and of course a party press, accompanying a person throughout their life. The 'membership booklet' politics in the Yishuv and in the young State of Israel also had its roots in the Jewish life of eastern Europe.

Even one of the most sacred ideals and founding myths of the Yishuv had east European roots: the symbol of the Jew with weapon in hand to protect his people, a symbol derived from Jewish self-defence groups (Zionist and socialist) against east European pogroms no less than from the activities of the Hashomer militia in the Land of Israel. The poem 'Song of the Terrorists' by Ya'akov Cahan, with its well-known refrain 'By blood and fire did Judea fall, by blood and fire will Judea rise', was written in Bern, Switzerland, following the pogrom in Kishinev in 1903, and was adopted by the Hashomer group as its anthem and in the interwar period by Revisionist youth groups in Poland and in Palestine.[46]

And finally, another facet of the political ideals and the attempt to impart these ideals to the younger generation was the ramified network of Jewish youth movements in eastern Europe. The autobiographies of teenagers at the time and memoirs written many years later attest that, in their confrontation with a confusing and turbulent world, the youth movements supported their members by providing a separate world away from the stresses of family and day-to-day concerns about education and making a living. Zionist youth movements played an important role in preparing thousands of young Jews for immigration to the Land of Israel and also served as the first political stage for a young leadership cadre, which would later be among the leaders of the Yishuv and the State of Israel.

Conclusion

The Jewish political tradition of eastern Europe made its mark on the political and social life of the Yishuv and the young State of Israel. Of course, there were equally notable differences between the two places, reflecting the different social and ethnic composition of the Yishuv, the Ottoman legacy, and the experiences of Jews and Arabs under the British Mandate. Additional factors shaped politics in the Yishuv, such as the socialist tradition, the ongoing development of Zionism and Zionist ideology, the Holocaust, and the struggle with the Arab population. The balance of power between the political parties in the Yishuv was very different from that in Poland or Lithuania and Latvia, even within the Zionist camp, where Socialist Zionism dominated politics in the Yishuv's institutions, as opposed to bourgeois General Zionism that was the majority movement in the Polish diaspora. This is reflected ironically in the personal political fate of Yitshak Grünbaum. Grünbaum opposed the relocation of Warsaw's Nalewki Street to Tel Aviv, as noted at the beginning of this chapter. He was ready to accept the rise of a Jewish bourgeoisie and petty bourgeoisie in the Land of Israel but only at a later stage. In the formative period of the Yishuv, though, he believed priority should be given to the agricultural pioneers, the *halutsim*. The time had not yet come to see emigration to the Land of Israel as just another example of migration, as in all other countries. Grünbaum's principle, while idealistic, was politically to his detriment, since those middle-class Jewish people whom Grünbaum wished to keep out were the backbone of political support for him and his General Zionist party. Those masses of Polish Jews never reached Palestine, and thus Grünbaum, the prominent leader of millions of Jews in Poland, found himself neutralized by David Ben-Gurion and other leaders in the Yishuv, and never achieved the political importance he enjoyed in Poland. In his particular case, he could actually have benefited from a bit more of Nalewki Street in Tel Aviv.

According to Ezra Mendelsohn, the political heritage of east European Jewry

has played an important role in making the Jewish people a people committed to democracy. The majority of Jewish political organizations in pluralistic Eastern Europe enthusiastically entered parliamentary politics and educated their constituencies in its ways and advantages. This is a matter of no small importance, and it is one explanation for the victory of political democracy in the successor state of Eastern European Jewry, the State of Israel.[47]

Mendelsohn did note, however, that for some contemporary Israeli politicians, the Polish Jewish case was a cautionary tale as well: 'I have little doubt that when such leading Israeli politicians as Shimon Peres (also Polish-born) voice their tremendous apprehension concerning the demographic relationship between Jews and Arabs in Israel they are thinking of the Polish case.'[48] The experience of interwar Polish Jewry demonstrated the potential conflicts, both moral and political, in the relationship between nationally conscious majority and minority groups.

From the beginning of the twentieth century, east European Jewry underwent a process of initiation into parliamentary democracy of a kind not completely identical with the liberal regimes in England, France, and the United States. East European democracies between the two world wars were ethnic democracies, where the majority people in each country was given clear practical advantages and minority groups were forced to wage an endless struggle for their status and rights. Sami Smooha expressed reservations regarding this tradition of ethnic democracy transferred from eastern Europe to Israel. From his analysis, a less than flattering picture of Israeli democracy emerges, with this time the Jews being the majority, dominant ethnic group ruling a national minority of Arabs. For immigrants who arrived in the country from eastern Europe the situation was familiar, but the roles were reversed.[49]

The assessments of Mendelsohn and Smooha may differ slightly, but they agree that the democratic political tradition made the transition from the busy streets and meeting halls of Warsaw, Łódź, Vilna, and Riga to the political life of the Yishuv. Part of Nalewki Street continued to live on in Tel Aviv.

Notes

This is an expanded and updated version of G. Bacon, 'Reḥov nalewki betel aviv? al hamoreshet hapolitit shel yahadut mizraḥ eiropah bayishuv uvimedinat yisra'el', in A. Gal (Goldberg), G. Bacon, M. Lissak, and P. Morag-Talmon (eds.), *Baderekh hademokratit: al hamekorot hahistoriyim shel hademokratyah hayisra'elit* (Beer Sheba, 2012), 153–68. My thanks to Ela Bauer, Ezra Mendelsohn z"l, and Sammy Smooha, whom I consulted in the preparation of the original article.

1 For a broader discussion and numerous examples of the negative image of the Fourth Aliyah in general and Nalewki in particular, see M. Chazan, "Ḥayim vaitsman vehivatserut dimuyah shel ha'aliyah harevi'it bereshit yameha', *Zion*, 76 (2011), 459–67; see also P. Ginosar, 'Uri tsevi grinberg va'aliyat grabski', *Iyunim bitekumat yisra'el*, 1 (1991), 523–46.

2 M.G. [Glickson], 'Al haperek: dr. vaitsman be'erets yisra'el', *Haaretz*, 26 Sept. 1924, p. 2 (emphasis in original).

3 For the factories and other businesses on Nalewki Street on the eve of the Second World War, see Z. Pakalski, *Nalewki: Z dziejów polskiej i żydowskiej ulicy w Warszawie* (Warsaw, 2003); for a recent fascinating portrait of another typical Jewish street in Warsaw, see B. Mer, *Smocza: biografia shel rehov yehudi bevarshah* (Jerusalem, 2019).

4 C. Weizmann, *Trial and Error: The Autobiography of Chaim Weizmann* (New York, 1949), 301.

5 'Weizmann's Reply to the Debate', *Palestine Bulletin*, 4 Sept. 1925, p. 2.

6 O. Herschdörfer, 'Problem masowej imigracyi', *Nowy Dziennik*, 16 May 1925, p. 5.

7 'Great Day at Zionist Congress', *Palestine Bulletin*, 21 Aug. 1925, p. 1. See also the slightly

hedged defence of Nalewki Jews and the critique of the anti-religious kibbutzim by Mizrachi leader Meir Berlin (Bar-Ilan) (M. Berlin, 'Heated Debate in Financial Committee', *Palestine Bulletin*, 24 Aug. 1925, p. 1)

8 In his memoirs written decades later, Weizmann noted that his speech in Jerusalem earned him the lasting hatred of many Polish Jews. In retrospect, he remarked, perhaps he could have stated his views more tactfully, but even with the perspective of time he remained convinced of the danger posed by the social makeup of the Fourth Aliyah (see Weizmann, *Trial and Error*, 301).

9 See his speech at the convention of the Polish Zionist Federation, reproduced in 'Yeshivot hamo'etsah hamiflagtit shel hahistadrut hatsiyonit bepolin', *Hatsefirah*, 2 Nov. 1926, p. 1.

10 See Z. Tzahor, *Ḥazan – tenuat ḥayim: hashomer hatsa'ir, hakibuts ha'artsi, mapam* (Jerusalem, 1997).

11 See A. Halamish, 'Me'ir ya'ari: biyografyah kibutsit', *Yisra'el*, 3 (2003), 69–96; id., 'Manhig meḥapes tsibur: darko shel me'ir ya'ari lehanhagat hashomer hatsa'ir, 1918–1927', *Iyunim bitekumat yisra'el*, 12 (2002), 99–121; id., *Me'ir ya'ari: biyografyah kibutsit. ḥamishim hashanim harishonot, 1897–1947* (Tel Aviv, 2009).

12 See N. M. Gelber, 'Dr. yehoshua thon', in *Sefer krako: ir va'em beyisra'el*, ed. A. Bauminger (Jerusalem, 1959), 355–7; N. Rost Hollander, *Jehoshua Thon: Preacher, Thinker, Politician* (Montevideo, 1966); S. Ronen, *A Prophet of Consolation on the Threshold of Destruction: Yehoshua Ozjasz Thon, an Intellectual Portrait* (Warsaw, 2015).

13 See R. Frister, *Lelo pesharah* (Tel Aviv, 1987); Y. Grünbaum, *Ne'umim basejm hapolani* (Jerusalem, 1963); id., *Milḥamot yehudei polanyah: 5673–5700* (Jerusalem, 1941).

14 M. A. Hartglas, *Shilton atsmi mekomi (hatsa'ah)* (Jerusalem, 1950); see also E. Bauer, *Hashorashim hapolaniyim shel hademokratyah hayisra'elit* (Haifa, 2007), 2–3. Hartglas's autobiography was written in the early 1950s but only published four decades later (Hartglas, *Na pograniczu dwóch światów* (Warsaw, 1996)).

15 See Y. Goldshlag, 'Nurok, mordekhai', in Y. Raphael (ed.), *Entsiklopedyah shel hatsiyonut hadatit*, 6 vols. (Jerusalem, 1968–2000), iv. 32–6; 'Mordechai Nurock' (n.d.): Knesset website, visited 3 Apr. 2021. Nurock had a unique experience for a Jewish member of parliament in the diaspora when he was asked to form a new governing coalition in Latvia, after he had organized a vote of no confidence in the sitting government in 1927.

16 See D. Tidhar, 'Eliyahu mazur', in id., *Entsiklopedyah lehalutsei hayishuv uvonav*, 19 vols. (Tel Aviv, 1947–70), iv. 1621; 'Eliyahu Mazur' (n.d.): Knesset website, visited 3 Apr. 2021.

17 Y. Grünbaum, 'Di yidishe politik in poyln in di letste yortsenten', in *Haynt 1908–1928/5668–5688: yubilei-bukh*, ed. S. Y. Yatskan (Warsaw, 1928), 64–5.

18 S. Ury, *Barricades and Banners: The Revolution of 1905 and the Transformation of Warsaw Jewry* (Stanford, Calif., 2012), 267–8.

19 Y. Maor, *Hatenuah hatsiyonit berusyah* (Jerusalem, 1974), 315–19.

20 Ibid. 160–2, 181–5, 195–6.

21 On the polemics about the politician as *shtadlan*, see G. Bacon, *The Politics of Tradition: Agudat Yisrael in Poland, 1916–1939* (Jerusalem, 1996), 228–33.

22 See O. I. Janowsky, *The Jews and Minority Rights (1898–1919)* (New York, 1933), 263–8; M. Levene, 'Britain, a British Jew, and Jewish Relations with the New Poland: The Making of the Polish Minorities Treaty of 1919', *Polin*, 8 (1994), 14–41.

23 Y. Grünbaum, 'Yalduti', in H. Barlas, A. Tartakower, and D. Sadan (eds.), *Entsiklopedyah shel galuyot*, xii: *Varshah*, iii (Jerusalem, 1973), 45–64: 55.

24 E. Mendelsohn, *The Ambiguous 'Lessons' of Modern Polish-Jewish History* (Oxford, 1995), 9.

25 See G. Bacon, 'National Revival, Ongoing Acculturation: Jewish Education in Interwar Poland', *Jahrbuch des Simon-Dubnow-Instituts*, 1 (2002), 71–92; I. Bassok and A. Novershtern, 'Ma'arkhot haḥinukh liyehudei polin bein shetei milḥamot ha'olam', in I. Bassok, *Alilot ne'urim: otobiyografiyot shel benei no'ar yehudim mipolin bein shetei milḥamot ha'olam* (Jerusalem, 2011), 736–40.

26 On general issues of schooling, curriculum, and nation-building in interwar Poland, see D. Wojtas, *Learning to Become Polish: Education, National Identity and Citizenship in Interwar Poland, 1918–1939* (Cologne, 2009).

27 'Esther', in *Awakening Lives: Autobiographies of Jewish Youth in Poland before the Holocaust*, ed. J. Shandler (New Haven, Conn., 2002), 321–43: 326.

28 M. Kligsberg, 'Di yidishe yugnt-bavegung in poyln tsvishn beide velt-milkhomes (a sotsiologishe shtudye)', in J. Fishman (ed.), *Shtudyes vegn yidn in poyln, 1919–1939 / Studies on Polish Jewry, 1919–1939* (New York, 1974), 137–228: 208–9.

29 D. Kupfert Heller, *Jabotinsky's Children: Polish Jews and the Rise of Right-Wing Zionism* (Princeton, NJ, 2017), 17.

30 Ibid. 30.

31 Y. Shavit, 'The Influence of Polish National Heritage on Modern Jewish Nationalism', in M. Misztal and P. Trojański (eds.), *Poles and Jews: History, Culture, Education* (Kraków, 2011), 19–28: 25–6; see id., 'Politics and Messianism: The Zionist Revisionist Movement and Polish Political Culture', *Studies in Zionism*, 6 (1985), 229–46.

32 Heller, *Jabotinsky's Children*, 144.

33 T. Snyder, *Black Earth: The Holocaust as History and Warning* (New York, 2015), 64.

34 *Jerozolima Wyzwolona*, 1/5 (11 Nov. 1938), p. 1 (which tellingly appeared on the twentieth anniversary of Polish independence); see also Y. Shavit, 'Bein pilsudski lemitskevitch: mediniyut umeshiḥiyut barevizyonizm hatsiyoni baheksher shel hatarbut hapolitit hapolanit vezikato lepolin', *Hatsiyonut*, 10 (1985), 7–32: 27. On the background and subsequent development and use of the symbol, see O. Gruweis Kovalsky, '"Rak kakh": yad oḥezet beroveh o shetei gadot layarden? liveḥinat hasemel shel ha'irgun hatseva'i hale'umi', *Cathedra*, 166 (2018), 119–46. In 1971 Rabbi Meir Kahane, a Betar member in his youth, used the same symbol for his newly founded Kakh party in Israel. Only when requested to desist by Irgun and Betar veterans did Kahane change the party's symbol to the more familiar clenched fist on a Star of David background.

35 Heller, *Jabotinsky's Children*, 27.

36 A. Guterman, *Kehilat varshah bein shetei milḥamot ha'olam: otonomyah le'umit bekhavlei haḥḥok vehametsiut 1917–1939* (Tel Aviv, 1997), 307–8; see also 'Kehile-rat farurtaylt oyfn sharfster ofn dem onfal fun a tayl tsiyonistisher parnosim oyfn prezes mazur', *Yidishe togblat* (Warsaw), 17 Mar. 1932, p. 5.

37 See Guterman, *Kehilat varshah*, 152–4; R. Żebrowski, 'Budowa domu akademickiego w Warszawie i jej miejsce w dziejach warszawskiej gminy wyznaniowej', *Kwartalnik Historii Żydów*, 216 (2005), 467–80; for contemporary reports, see 'A hamon fanatiker pogromirt di gmine', *Haynt*, 26 Nov. 1923, p. 1; 'Nekhtiger shturm fun ortodoksen oyf der gmine', *Der moment*, 26 Nov. 1923, p. 1.

38 E. Mendelsohn, 'Jewish Politics in Interwar Poland: An Overview', in Y. Gutman, E. Mendelsohn, J. Reinharz, and C. Shmeruk (eds.), *The Jews of Poland Between Two World Wars* (Hanover, NH, 1989), 10–11. For a sober evaluation of the changes in support for the contending parties in the *kehilah* elections, see R. M. Shapiro, 'The Polish *Kehillah* Elections of 1936: A Revolution Re-examined', *Polin*, 8 (1994), 206–26.

39 M. Friedman, *Ḥevrah vadat: ha'ortodoksyah halotsiyonit be'erets yisra'el, 5678–5686* (Jerusalem, 1977), 364–6; G. S. Schiff, *Tradition and Politics: The Religious Parties of Israel* (Detroit, 1977), 73. On the complex relationship between Zionists, religious Zionists, and Agudists in Poland, see G. Bacon, 'Reluctant Partners, Ideological Opponents: Reflections on the Relations between Agudat Yisrael and the Zionist and Religious Zionist Movements in Interwar Poland', *Gal-ed*, 14 (1995), 67–90.

40 S. L. Dotan, *Pulmus haḥalukah bitekufat hamandat* (Jerusalem, 1979), 197–200; S. Eliash, 'Ha'emdah hadatit tsiyonit velo-tsiyonit letokhnit ḥalukat erets yisra'el, 5697–5698', in M. Avizohar and Y. Friedman (eds.), *Iyunim betokhnit haḥalukah, 1937–1947* (Beer Sheba, 1984), 55–74.

41 See Y. Avneri, 'Heskem shelo butsa: tiud ha'masa umatan bein hapo'el hamizraḥi lefo'alei agudat yisra'el bishenot hasheloshim al hakamat tenuat po'alim meshutefet', in M. Eliav (ed.), *Bishevilei hateḥiyah meḥkarim batsiyonut hadatit*, 3 vols. (Ramat Gan, 1983–8), ii. 167–99; A. Gebel, *Ḥaredim ve'anshei ma'aseh: po'alei agudat yisra'el, 1933–1939* (Jerusalem, 2017), 71.

42 M. Friedman, 'Ve'eleh toledot hastatus kuo: dat umedinah beyisra'el', in V. Pilovsky (ed.), *Hama'avar miyishuv limedinah* (Haifa, 1990), 47–79.

43 'Di linke ongehoybn a kampf gegn der kehile', *Der yud*, 21 Dec. 1927, p. 3; 'Di subsidiyes fun der kehile far di yudishe kulturele institutsyes', *Der yud*, 8 July 1928, p. 4; R. M. Shapiro, 'Jewish Self-Government in Poland: Lodz 1914–1939', Ph.D. thesis (Columbia University, 1987), 295; L. S. Dawidowicz, *From that Place and Time: A Memoir, 1938–1947* (New York, 1989), 156.

44 See E. Luz, *Parallels Meet: Religion and Nationalism in the Early Zionist Movement* (Philadelphia, 1988).

45 See Mendelsohn, 'Jewish Politics in Interwar Poland', 12–13.

46 Y. Cahan, 'Shir habiryonim'. For the words of the poem and melodies to which it was sung, see the Zemereshet website, visited 7 July 2020.

47 E. Mendelsohn, 'Reflections on East European Jewish Politics in the Twentieth Century', *YIVO Annual of Jewish Social Science*, 20 (1991), 23–37: 35–6.

48 Mendelsohn, *Ambiguous 'Lessons'*, 14.

49 S. Smooha, 'Is Israel Western?', in E. Ben-Rafael and Y. Sternberg (eds.), *Comparing Modernities: Pluralism versus Homogeneity. Essays in Homage to Shmuel N. Eisenstadt* (Leiden, 2005), 413–42: 438–9; id., 'The Model of Ethnic Democracy: Israel as a Jewish and Democratic State', *Nations and Nationalism*, 8 (2002), 475–503.

Between Tłomackie 13, Warsaw, and Kaplan 2, Tel Aviv
The Role of the East European Jewish Press in Shaping Israeli Journalism

ELA BAUER

ON 3 APRIL 1957, at a ceremony attended by Yitzhak Ben-Zvi, president of the State of Israel, and its prime minister, David Ben-Gurion, Beit Ha'itona'im al Shem Sokolow (the Sokolow Journalists' House) on 2 Kaplan Street, Tel Aviv was inaugurated. The decision to name it after the journalist and Zionist leader Nahum Sokolow (1859–1936) was made as early as 1945. As Chaim Weizmann, at that time leader of the Zionist Organization, then observed, it was both fitting and self-evident that the future home of journalism in the Land of Israel should be named after Sokolow.[1] The name of Tel Aviv itself was derived from his Hebrew translation of Herzl's utopian novel *Altneuland*.[2] In addition, Sokolow, whom Weizmann described as a friend and companion, had laid the foundations for the daily Hebrew press and dedicated his efforts to journalism in Hebrew.[3]

It was Yosef Heftman (1888–1955), head of the National Association of Journalists in the Land of Israel (Ha'igud Ha'artsi Shel Ha'itona'im Be'erets Yisra'el), who had suggested naming the building after Sokolow. In the 1940s and 1950s Sokolow was a household name in the Yishuv because of his journalism and activities on behalf of the Zionist movement.[4] However, most of his journalism was not published in Israel, where the key roles were played by others, such as Eliezer Ben-Yehuda (1858–1922) and his son Itamar Ben-Avi (1882–1943),[5] but in Poland.[6] However, even if Sokolow's journalistic achievements were not associated with the press of the Yishuv in British Mandate Palestine, those who cherished his memory were determined that he be memorialized in Tel Aviv.[7] Heftman and other members of the National Association of Journalists saw themselves as his disciples, continuing Sokolow's tradition of the Jewish press from eastern Europe in the young State of Israel.[8] After the Second World War, the memorialization of Sokolow became linked not only with his journalism but also with the commemoration of Polish Jewry as a whole. In 1945 it had been argued that:

> There is reason for concern that because of the annihilation of east European Jewry and particularly after the destruction of Polish Jewry—out of which Nahum Sokolow grew, from which he drew sustenance, in which he spent his most creative years, and where his name is cherished with pride and admiration—that his memory might fade into obscurity.[9]

Thus the name Beit Sokolow emphasized the connection between the Jewish press in eastern Europe and Hebrew journalism in the Land of Israel. This emphasis, however, was at odds with attempts in the early twentieth century to distinguish the local Hebrew press in Mandate Palestine from the east European Jewish press with its strongly didactic and ideological character.[10] Since all cultural activity in the Land of Israel was to be free of 'exilic' influence, the argument went, so too ought the press to be free of such influence and concentrate above all on reporting.[11] However, despite this declaration, in 1948 and the years immediately after the establishment of the State of Israel, at a time when local creativity was heavily favoured over that produced in the diaspora, the Jewish press of eastern Europe still exercised a major influence on the development of the Hebrew press in Israel.

In this chapter, I wish to examine some of the links between the press in the Land of Israel and the Jewish press that had thrived in eastern Europe. The journalism of eastern Europe influenced the character of newspapers in the Yishuv during the British Mandate period and also during the early years of the State of Israel. In addition, the various activities organized by the Association of Jewish Writers and Journalists (Yidishe Literatn un Zhurnalistn Farayn) in Warsaw throughout the 1920s and 1930s had an impact, albeit in the late 1950s, on those who were responsible for determining the activities at Beit Sokolow. I will also investigate what can be learned from the process of integration (or lack of integration) of journalists from eastern Europe into the Hebrew press in the Yishuv during the 1930s and 1940s and the different ways in which the Jewish journalism of eastern Europe influenced that of the Land of Israel. Above all, I will describe the ongoing conflict between a more elevated form of journalism, concerned with shaping opinion, which was derived from Jewish journalism in eastern Europe, and a more popular form of reporting, which sought to expose scandals and reform society.

The National Association of Journalists began life in the 1930s as Agudat Ha'itona'im Betel Aviv (the Tel Aviv Journalists' Association), a trade union whose goal was to ensure fair employment conditions, to assist members who encountered financial difficulties, and to help immigrant journalists find employment on local papers in Palestine.[12] The two figures who consolidated its influence in the journalistic community of the Yishuv and who stood behind the initiative to establish Beit Sokolow were Heftman and Moshe Ron (Dancygekron, 1909–85).[13]

Heftman served as chairman of the association from the early 1940s until his death in 1955. Between 1936 and 1955 he was editor of *Haboker*, a newspaper associated with the General Zionist party.[14] His path within the world of Jewish journalism had begun during the first decade of the twentieth century, when his articles began to appear in *Hashilo'aḥ*. He also wrote for *Hatsefirah*, the Warsaw-based Hebrew daily, under the pseudonym 'Josipon'. Between 1921 and 1925 Heftman was editor of *Hayom*, another Warsaw-based Hebrew newspaper, and in June 1926 he was appointed editor of *Hatsefirah*.[15] From 1912 until he left Poland, articles he wrote under the pseudonyms 'A. Mentsh' and 'Emanuel' were published in Yiddish in the popular Warsaw daily *Der moment*.[16] On 24 March 1916 Heftman participated in the founding meeting of the Association of Jewish Writers and Journalists which was held in the auditorium of the Jewish musical society Hazamir on 2 Długa Street in Warsaw. At this assembly, he was elected to the association's managing board and appointed its secretary.

Moshe Ron immigrated to Palestine in 1935. His career as a journalist had started in *Haynt* in Warsaw, where he had been one of the paper's junior reporters.[17] Unlike Heftman, who was active in the Association of Jewish Writers and Journalists in Warsaw, Ron had a different relationship with the union. His wife was the daughter of one of the partners of the Metropolin restaurant that operated on the ground floor of the building on 13 Tłomackie Street, where the association was based. After their wedding, the young couple lived in the building.[18] Between 1935 and September 1939 Ron was the distributor of the Yiddish daily *Haynt* in Palestine and also, from time to time, submitted articles to the paper. For a short time after the establishment of the State of Israel, he wrote for the Hebrew newspaper *Yediot aharonot*. But he was more of a communal activist, someone engaged in public affairs, than a journalist.[19] In addition to his role as secretary of the National Association of Journalists, he was one of the founders of the Israeli Editors' Committee.[20] He also had a role in establishing the World Association of Jewish Journalists.

Heftman's and Ron's activities in the National Association of Journalists were influenced by the way the Association of Jewish Writers and Journalists in Warsaw had functioned.[21] At its foundation, the National Association of Journalists numbered around one hundred members. Only some wrote regularly for local newspapers. Heftman and Ron strictly enforced the restriction of membership to professional journalists, as had been the case with the Warsaw-based organization.[22] Just as the home of the Association of Jewish Writers and Journalists at 13 Tłomackie Street had been a central force in Warsaw's Jewish cultural life, so too, in Tel Aviv, Heftman and Ron would later invest much effort in ensuring that Beit Sokolow played a significant role in Israeli public life.[23]

The Association of Jewish Writers and Journalists in Warsaw was intended for those who wrote in Hebrew and Yiddish. According to its by-laws, only those with considerable writing experience or who were regularly employed by a newspaper could become members.[24] The reputation of the association stemmed not only from the fact that it concerned itself with the working conditions of its members and defended their professional interests[25] but also from the various activities, official and informal, held at its headquarters, which played an important role in making Warsaw the centre of Jewish literary and journalistic life in Poland in the interwar period. Anyone who wished to belong to the literary and journalistic milieu in Warsaw could not afford to ignore the social, literary, and cultural activities taking place at 13 Tłomackie Street,[26] including birthday celebrations for authors, memorial events for writers and journalists who had died, receptions for visitors from abroad, literary soirées and discussions, launches of new books by association members, and fundraising events to support the association's many activities.[27]

The association has been the subject of considerable scholarly attention and its activities are also described in considerable detail in the memoirs of its regular patrons.[28] Tłomackie Street was a small street near Warsaw's crowded and busy Jewish district,[29] not far from the headquarters of *Der moment* at 38 Nalewki Street and of *Haynt* on Chłodna Street, as well as the offices of other Jewish newspapers.[30] For a fee of 500 zlotys per month, the association rented apartment 4 on the first floor of a three-storey building. The building was vibrant and always packed.[31] The offices of the Mizrachi youth movement occupied a separate flat in the same building, and, as mentioned, the Metropolin restaurant was on the ground floor. According to Bashevis Singer, to the chagrin of the representatives of Mizrachi and the association's management, there was even a brothel in the building's basement, whose owner, unlike the rest of the building's residents, actually paid his rent regularly and on time.[32]

Like apartment 4 at 13 Tłomackie Street in Warsaw, Beit Sokolow on Kaplan Street in Tel Aviv also hosted a large number of social activities, meetings of association members with important overseas visitors and embassy representatives, and receptions for press delegations. Members enjoyed special screenings of films not yet shown in commercial cinemas.[33] Those interested could study foreign languages, especially English and French; see shows by artists and entertainers such as Shimon Dzigan and Yisroel Schumacher, which were arranged exclusively for members; and their children could participate in various activities, such as the annual Purim party.[34] The venue did not serve merely as a social club for association members: it was intended as a meeting place for all members of Jewish society in Israel, open to the public at large.[35] From the early years of the establishment of the state, many Israeli public buildings had clear political affiliations; however, Beit Sokolow took great pains to present itself as having none.

Unlike Beit Sokolow, the centre for writers and journalists in Warsaw was not named after a journalist or an author. Yet, even if this was not made explicit, the connection of 13 Tłomackie Street to the Yiddish writer Yitskhok Leybush Peretz was known to both the regular and casual patrons of the centre. Many of those who frequented Tłomackie Street began their literary careers in Peretz's apartment, seeking his blessing. Some likened this to a rabbinic 'ordination' bestowed by Peretz on the next generation of Yiddish writers.[36] To those who obtained it, such an ordination earned them a place of honour at Tłomackie Street and throughout Warsaw's Jewish literary milieu.[37] A large portrait of Peretz hung in one of the rooms of 13 Tłomackie Street. Under his watchful gaze, members played chess, read newspapers, argued, gossiped, ate, listened to music, and sometimes even danced.[38] To Melech Ravitsch (Zekharye Khone Bergner), the association's secretary, and Hersh Dovid Nomberg, one of its founders, it was important that the intellectual activities at the association's headquarters serve as a direct continuation of those in Peretz's apartment at 1 Ceglana Street and should recall activities in which Peretz participated,[39] such as the literary salon held around his dinner table until 1905 or the literary soirées hosted there until the outbreak of the First World War.[40]

By naming the home of journalism in the Yishuv after Sokolow, Heftman and his colleagues sought to endow Sokolow with a degree of recognition similar to that which Peretz had received at Tłomackie Street. Sokolow's own journalistic activity had not been given any special recognition at Tłomackie Street, although when he had resided in Warsaw his role had been appreciated by his literary and journalistic colleagues. *Hatsefirah*'s editorial bureau at 40 Królewska Street was one of the first venues in the city where Sokolow met writers and journalists who came to Warsaw.[41] For those who did not live in Warsaw, such trips were akin to visits by hasidim to the courts of *tsadikim*.[42] Part of the intellectual circle that surrounded Peretz also included Sokolow's loyal readership, and some of the regular participants in the gatherings at Peretz's apartment were also regulars at the gatherings at Sokolow's home.[43] Some, like Heftman, viewed themselves as Sokolow's disciples. As a consequence, perpetuating the memory of Sokolow in Tel Aviv was a matter of great importance to them.[44]

In addition to memorializing Sokolow and commemorating the east European Jewish press prior to 1939, Heftman and others hoped that 'the spirit of Tłomackie 13 . . . in Warsaw would be present in Beit Sokolow in Tel Aviv'.[45] There soon developed a clear agenda, which should also be seen as a response to widely held reservations among many journalists in the Yishuv about the east European Jewish press, which manifested themselves in an attempt to establish a new, local, style of journalism and to break with the traditions of the Hebrew press in eastern Europe, which had been dubbed by its critics 'Odessa journalism'.[46]

There were several reasons for this nickname. Unlike other cultural and literary centres in eastern Europe, such as Vilna and Warsaw, Odessa was remote from the typical Jewish environment of the shtetl. Despite its peripheral location, a large number of intellectuals, writers, public activists, scholars, and Zionist leaders lived in the city in the late nineteenth century. Thanks to them, Odessa became an important Jewish cultural centre.[47] The Society for the Promotion of Culture Among the Jews (Obshchestvo dlya rasprostraneniya prosveshcheniya mezhdu evreyami v Rossii; OPE) was active there, as were modern Jewish educational institutions. During the final decades of the nineteenth century proto-Zionist activity was added to the cultural menu. As early as the 1860s, a number of important newspapers were published in Odessa, including *Rassvet* and *Den* in Russian and the Hebrew paper *Hamelits*. In 1869 *Hamelits* published a Yiddish supplement, *Kol mevaser*, which soon evolved into an independent weekly. Several publishing houses, producing a considerable number of books in Yiddish and Hebrew, also operated in the city, including Moriah, established at the beginning of the twentieth century by Hayim Nahman Bialik and a number of his associates. The city has been memorialized in several important Jewish literary works.[48] Yet, Dan Miron's assertion that at the end of the nineteenth century Odessa, alongside Warsaw, was a Jewish literary capital notwithstanding,[49] by the early twentieth century its status had somewhat declined.[50] Despite continuing attempts to start new Hebrew journals in Odessa, a significant number of journalists moved to St Petersburg or Warsaw.[51]

Within Hebrew literature there had developed a school of writing that was identified with Odessa and which survived even after it was no longer a significant Jewish cultural centre.[52] Thanks to this literary tradition, the city came to be identified with east European Jewish journalism, even if more Hebrew newspapers and journals were published in other places.[53] Odessa's renown as a centre of Hebrew journalism was due to the newspaper *Hamelits*, which was regarded as the principal journalistic platform of Russian Jewry, in which modern, maskilic, and nationalist trends were promoted.[54] This was in spite of the fact that, of the forty-one years of the paper's activities (1863–1904), *Hamelits* was published in Odessa for only fifteen (1863–78). From 1878 to 1904 *Hamelits*'s editorial bureau was based in St Petersburg. Moreover, in the final decade of the nineteenth century and until it ceased publication in 1904, the paper's prestige waned among the east European Jewish public as it came to be seen as increasingly old-fashioned. None of this, however, undermined the association of the paper with Odessa. In the Palestine of the 1920s, the critique of and reservations about Odessa journalism and the east European Hebrew press were manifest in the confrontation between the Hebrew newspapers *Haaretz* and *Do'ar hayom*.

Haaretz initiated its activity in Jerusalem in 1919.[55] In 1923 the paper's headquarters moved to Tel Aviv.[56] *Do'ar hayom*, under the editorship of Itamar Ben-Avi, produced its first issue in Jerusalem in August 1919.[57] When *Haaretz* first began publication in Jerusalem, efforts were made, without success, to recruit Eliezer Ben-Yehuda and Itamar Ben-Avi to its staff of writers. However, the members of *Haaretz*'s editorial board, on the one hand, and Ben-Yehuda and Ben-Avi, on the other, represented different approaches to journalism.

Moshe Glickson (1878–1939), editor of *Haaretz* between 1922 and 1937, and the paper's regular writers—Nissan Turov, Mordechai Ben Hillel, Abraham Ludvipol, Joseph Lurie, and Ze'ev (Vladimir) Jabotinsky—had connections with the Jewish newspapers published in Odessa, Vilna, and St Petersburg. They maintained that a Hebrew newspaper in the Land of Israel should be no different in form from the Hebrew newspapers published in eastern Europe prior to the First World War.[58] Like many writers in the east European Jewish press, the journalists of *Haaretz* thought that it was their job to lead their readers to the 'correct' position on major topics.[59] They believed that a good newspaper article should not be assessed according to the facts it marshalled but by the way in which it guided and educated its readers in matters of culture and ideology.[60]

Ben-Avi, born in Jerusalem, and his co-editors at *Do'ar hayom* sought to create a new kind of Hebrew press, modelled on the newspapers published in Britain and France. It was no coincidence that the name of their newspaper was a literal translation of the popular London newspaper, the *Daily Mail*.[61] At *Do'ar hayom*, the emphasis was on news and information. These were areas which received relatively little attention in most Hebrew newspapers in eastern Europe.[62] In several sensationalist and popular newspapers in France and England, critical and biting news reporting ensured that they were viewed as an important element in the democratization process. This was different from the situation in tsarist Russia, where both the Jewish and non-Jewish press operated under severe restrictions and where critical news reporting could hardly flourish. Despite the limitations on freedom of speech, articles which expressed strong views and satirical feuilletons were published in the newspapers of the region and had the potential to promote public discourse and social and cultural reforms.[63]

The editors of *Haaretz* regarded journalists as spiritual leaders whose opinion pieces should guide readers towards the correct path. For Ben-Avi, the model was the journalist who exposed wrongdoing and sounded a clarion call to rouse society to action.[64] Even if in the early years the editors of *Haaretz* could claim credit for numerous journalistic scoops, the editorial board did not think it worthy or honourable to chase after them. A scoop, in their thinking, was a kind of 'swollen wart that bursts after a day'.[65] Ben-Avi and his co-editors at *Do'ar hayom* took a different view and regarded scoops as the very heart of their journalistic work.[66]

Hence the two newspapers articulated very different journalistic styles. *Haaretz* was a broadsheet, while *Do'ar hayom* was a tabloid. According to the editorial board of *Haaretz*, the polemic was between a paper that viewed itself as 'serious' and one that 'merely sought to provoke sensation'.[67] In response to *Haaretz*'s self-proclaimed respectability, Itamar Ben-Avi asserted that while *Haaretz* might be respectable, it was not a newspaper, whereas *Do'ar hayom* might not be respectable, but it was indeed a newspaper.[68] He sought to revolutionize Hebrew journalism, aware that he was facing a challenge and that his journalistic style differed from that of other Hebrew news-papers published in Palestine and elsewhere.[69] *Do'ar hayom* was presented as a paper for those born in the Land of Israel who wished to be free of any so-called exilic influences. 'We too, the native-born of the young Erets Yisra'el wish to take part [in this process of liberation] . . . and our newspaper is but a first step on our ascending path.'[70]

The divergent approaches of those who believed that the Hebrew journalism in Israel should be no different from east European Hebrew journalism and those who felt that it should make a clear break with it were also manifested in the attitude towards the feuilleton sections, which occupied a respected place in many Jewish newspapers in eastern Europe.

Hamelits was the first Hebrew newspaper in which a feuilleton section appeared—in 1867.[71] The writers of feuilletons in *Hamelits* over the years included Judah Leib Gordon, Elhanan Leib Lewinsky, Yisra'el Hayim Tawiow, Reuben Brainin, and even Sholem Aleichem.[72] The importance of the feuilleton in east European Jewish journalism and the feuilletonist's writing style developed not only because of *Hamelits* and other Hebrew newspapers like *Hatsefirah* but also thanks to Yiddish newspapers, especially *Haynt* and *Der moment*.[73]

In addition to *Haaretz*, there were other newspapers in the Yishuv in which feuilletons were valued. This was true of *Davar*, established by Berl Katznelson in 1925 to provide the Histadrut (the General Federation of Labour) with a paper that was both informative and educational and which would provide quality opinion pieces to workers in the Yishuv, eschewing large and sensational headlines.[74] Similarly, *Haboker*, a Hebrew paper founded in 1935, gave a central place to its feuilleton section. The editors presented the newspaper to its readers as seeking to fulfil their spiritual, cultural, and intellectual needs.[75] Thus, despite the local reservations about Odessa journalism, during the British Mandate period many newspapers in the Yishuv continued the trends that had developed in the east European Jewish press.[76]

However, over time, and especially after the first generation of writers gave way to the next, it is possible to discern a change within some of these newspapers. Even if they did not adopt the sensationalist and provocative style of writing characteristic of *Do'ar hayom*, they began to change their attitude to the feuilleton and opinion pieces,[77] and more importance and space were given to news reporting and other feature articles. The dominant style of Israeli journalism moved further and further away from that of the east European Hebrew press. It seems that the goal that Ben-Avi had formulated in the early twentieth century, to differentiate journalism in the Land of Israel from that which he described as 'exilic', was achieved shortly after his death.

One of the journalists and editors whose career followed the transformation of journalism in the young State of Israel, especially in relation to the position of the feuilleton and opinion pieces, was Ezriel Carlebach (1908–56), the first editor and founder of *Maariv*. Carlebach, a native of Leipzig, began to write for *Haynt* in 1934. Before his arrival in Palestine in 1937, his articles also appeared in the Polish-language newspapers *Nowy Dziennik* in Kraków and *Chwila* in Lwów.[78] David Lazar wrote that, after moving to Poland, Carlebach took the local Jewish press by storm. The average Jewish newspaper reader, his fellow journalists, and public figures like Yehoshua Ozjasz Thon saw Carlebach as Sokolow's heir.[79] Carlebach later became one of the central figures in Israeli journalism as a result of what came to be known as 'the great putsch'—his departure in February 1948 from *Yediot aharonot*, where he had served as editor, taking with him almost all the other journalists who had worked with him.[80]

The confrontation between Carlebach and the publisher of *Yediot aharonot*, Yehuda Mozes, an industrialist and a native of Kalisz, who in 1924 together with other entrepreneurs had established the Lodzia textile factory in Tel Aviv, had its roots in the two different styles of journalism described above. *Yediot aharonot* was an evening paper that offered its readers large, bold headlines without much analysis or commentary. While *Yediot aharonot*'s style was popular and sensationalist without indepth opinion pieces,[81] other newspapers published in Palestine at that time were commentary-heavy, especially on matters of ideology and politics. The editors of these papers believed that it was their duty to provide their readers with in-depth analysis, especially during the Second World War and its aftermath, when it became clear that fateful decisions regarding the future of Palestine were taking place.

This was also the view that Carlebach embraced when establishing *Maariv*. From its first issues, he wrote a weekly column under the pseudonym Ipkha Mistabera, a talmudic phrase, usually translated as 'on the contrary, it appears that . . .'. It was a weekly feuilleton written in a style reminiscent of those that had appeared in the Hebrew and Yiddish newspapers in eastern Europe. However, despite its success, during the 1950s it became clear, even to Carlebach, that Israeli newspapers had to alter their style, and that news reporting would need to take the place of the feuilleton. He expressed this clearly in the speech he gave on Sukkot 1954 at the first award ceremony for an Israeli journalist (which in 1956 would be renamed the Sokolow Prize).[82]

The co-operative management and ownership model of the Warsaw newspapers *Haynt* and *Der moment* was also adopted by Carlebach and his co-founders at *Maariv*: David Giladi, David Lazar, Ouri Kessary, Shalom Rosenfeld, and Shmuel Schnitzer. At the end of 1930, after *Der moment* had run into financial difficulties and following a long strike stemming from a conflict between the paper's management and the trade unions, one of the newspaper's owners, Eliezer Zilberberg, suggested to the employees the possibility of managing it on a co-operative basis. In 1931 a co-operative named Nasza Prasa was established, in which there was a representation of employees from all of the newspaper's different departments. The paper's editor-in-chief, Tsevi Pryłucki, retained his position. Alongside him a rotating committee was appointed, whose members included Hillel Zeitlin, Yosef Heftman, and Yehoshua Gottlieb. Until 1937 the co-operative attempted to pay off its debts by increasing the paper's revenues, number of subscribers, and overall readership. However, ultimately Nasza Prasa was unable to meet its financial obligations. In order to prevent the paper from going bankrupt, the court appointed Marek (Meir) Kohan as its business manager. In the wake of this appointment, the Revisionist party took over the paper, and the Nasza Prasa co-operative ceased to exist.[83] In the eyes of many, the way in which the Revisionist party took over *Der moment* was reminiscent of its takeover of *Do'ar hayom* in Jerusalem in 1928.[84]

In 1932, following a financial crisis, ongoing conflicts between the owners of *Haynt* and the paper's employees, and a six-week-long strike, ownership of the paper was transferred to its employees. The co-operative they founded was named Alt Nay, and the paper's management included representatives of the typesetters, the administrative staff, and the journalists.[85] While the co-operatives established at *Haynt* and *Der moment* were the result of economic crises, the one at *Maariv* arose because Carlebach and other journalists wished to create a newspaper that would be independent of the economic interests of its owners.[86] Nevertheless, the *Haynt* and *Der moment* co-operatives, and especially Alt Nay, served as sources of inspiration for Carlebach and his colleagues. It seems that the modus operandi of both the papers also affected how Carlebach and his partners managed the transition from the editorial board of *Yediot aharonot* to the editorship of *Maariv*. *Maariv* was presented to its readers as the first Hebrew newspaper in the Land of Israel run by a journalists' co-operative. According to the paper's editorial board, this was the only way to guarantee its independence from private proprietors and political parties.[87] Journalists, Carlebach noted, are not scribes for hire: 'the only people to whom they are accountable is the public and not to any private person, whoever he might be'.[88]

Carlebach had first-hand acquaintance with the operations of the *Haynt* editorial board, including the fierce competition between *Haynt* and *Der moment* for the Polish Jewish readership, and was familiar with how senior journalists could move from one paper to another,[89] and the various efforts made by editorial boards to increase their readership and to recruit specific journalists.[90] Carlebach was also familiar with the contribution of different parts of the paper to the popularity of *Haynt*, especially that of serialized novels, a practice which dated from the paper's earliest years and which was still rare in the Jewish press.[91] In *Maariv*'s first issue, there appeared a chapter of a novel whose previous instalment had been published in *Yediot aharonot* on 13 February 1948.[92] The practice of serializing novels in the Israeli daily press was, however, not long-lived. The more the Israeli press, including *Maariv*, became news-oriented, the more the serial publication of novels seemed outmoded.[93] Nevertheless, the adoption of this journalistic practice taken from the popular Yiddish press of interwar Warsaw is noteworthy, since it took place at a time when Yiddish, the language and culture identified with east European Jewry, did not enjoy the blessing of the Zionist leadership in Israel. Indeed, attempts to publish Yiddish newspapers encountered much opposition.[94]

The daily newspapers published in Warsaw during the interwar years—*Haynt* and *Der moment*—were regarded with disdain by the Jewish intelligentsia in Poland, which saw them as popular and sensationalist.[95] However, Peretz had welcomed the development of the press in Yiddish, as he saw the existence of popular journalism as a testament to normal societal development where a variety of journalistic forms existed to meet the needs of different sectors of society.[96] Sokolow also recognized the importance of the popular Yiddish press, and in January 1906 began to publish *Der telegraf*, which was favourably received by the Jewish newspaper-reading public.[97] Nevertheless, he disapproved of the sensationalist and tabloid style that developed in many Yiddish papers in Poland in the interwar years.[98] Although he published a fair number of articles in *Haynt*, he observed the development of the Yiddish press in Warsaw with concern, regretting what he saw as the transformation of the 'beautiful folk tongue' of Yiddish into a vulgar language of the marketplace.[99] In Palestine, many of those associated with journalism were similarly uncomfortable with the sensationalist Hebrew press. These reservations, however, did not prevent them from adopting the practices of the sensationalist Yiddish press, as *Maariv* did. It is quite likely that the close acquaintance of journalists like Heftman and Carlebach with the daily Yiddish press in Warsaw and with other papers was also a factor contributing to the adoption such practices.[100]

In the 1940s those journalists who emigrated to Palestine from eastern Europe hoped to find employment with local newspapers, especially those in Tel Aviv. One journalist who integrated successfully was Yohanan (Jan) Bader, who, before becoming a Knesset member representing the right-wing Herut party, wrote for *Hamashkif* and the *Palestine Tribune*. During 1948 and 1949 he was editor of *Herut*.[101] In Poland in the 1930s Bader had edited *Trybuna Narodowa*,[102] whose readers included supporters of the Revisionist movement (especially the young) and Polish politicians and journalists who wished to broaden their knowledge about the Revisionist movement in Poland and elsewhere.[103] Like other writers in Jewish newspapers in eastern Europe, Bader did not see his journalist role as limited to scoops or interviewing politicians and leaders. While still in Poland, he took pride in the fact that his articles in *Trybuna Narodowa* were read by senior officials of the Polish government who took them into account in formulating policy. After his emigration to the Land of Israel, Bader claimed his journalistic writing helped liberate the land from foreign domination. He was also proud of the fact that in the Yishuv his essays were read not just by colleagues and supporters but also by political adversaries and senior British officials.[104] Bader's approach was not unlike that of other east European Jewish journalists, who argued that journalism's main role was not to report on events taking place in the Jewish and non-Jewish worlds; Jewish journalism should strive, rather, to become a significant factor in Jewish public life and shape the world-view of its readers.[105]

However, not all the journalists in the diaspora were successful at finding a place for themselves in Israel. Among those who had a difficult time was Moshe Bunem Justman, one of the best-known and most popular journalists of the Yiddish press. To his readers in Poland, he was known as 'Jaushzun' or 'Itshele'. Between 1920 and 1925 he was a regular contributor to *Der moment* under the latter pseudonym. His column 'Politshe brive', which appeared every Friday, was greatly appreciated by the newspaper's readers.[106] In 1925 he moved to *Haynt*, *Der moment*'s competitor. During the first week in which Justman's column appeared in *Haynt*, the newspaper's circulation increased by 5,000. According to various estimates, ultimately some 10,000 of *Der moment*'s subscribers followed Justman to *Haynt*.[107] He was greatly admired by his readers and colleagues for his ability to combine high and low styles in his writing.

After the outbreak of the Second World War, Justman managed to reach the Land of Israel but did not succeed in securing a place in the local Hebrew press. For journalists in the Yishuv who were familiar with his writing and aware of his prestige among readers of the popular Yiddish press, his exclusion from local journalism was painful. They found it difficult to accept that a journalist who had enjoyed such a high status in Warsaw and beyond was unable to find a place for himself in Israel.[108] In Poland, Justman had presented news commentary through a broad Jewish lens on a weekly basis. In the Land of Israel, this kind of observation and analysis was considered 'exilic', something that journalists and newspapers should not engage in.[109] Those who were not among his loyal readers argued that there was no room for this kind of journalism in the new Israeli public sphere.[110]

Another journalist who did not succeed in finding a foothold in local journalism was Benzion Katz. Before the First World War Katz had written for the Hebrew press in Vilna and St Petersburg. The Hebrew newspaper *Hazeman*, which he founded and edited, began to appear in St Petersburg in January 1903, and at the end of 1904 its editorial board moved to Vilna, which served as the paper's headquarters until 1915.[111] Like other writers and editors in the Hebrew east European press, Katz adopted an intellectual style.[112] After arriving in the Yishuv in 1931 he became one of the founders of *Haboker* and also published various articles in *Haaretz*. However, he never became part of the local journalistic milieu. His journalistic activity in the Land of Israel did not reflect the status and reputation he had attained in eastern Europe.[113] In a long obituary, Getzel Kressel described him as having a contentious character and never hesitating to criticize those with whom he disagreed. He also expressed opinions and positions that were either unpopular or diverged from those of the Zionist hegemony, as in 1934 during the trial of the suspected murderer of Chaim Arlosoroff (1899–1933), the head of the Jewish Agency's political bureau.[114] His failure to find an appropriate place in journalism in Israel was not, however, the result of his political opinions. As with Justman, it was the result, rather, of the ever-widening gap between the journalistic style that was developing in Israel and that of the east European Jewish world.

Nevertheless, despite the growing reservations about the style of journalism in eastern Europe, as well as Israeli society's ostensible rejection of all that was seen as being 'exilic', east European Jewish journalism was clearly a source of inspiration for journalism in the Land of Israel for decades. Even though, during the British Mandate period and the formative years of the State of Israel, there was a relatively strong attempt to differentiate the local press from the east European Jewish press, journalists and editors who gained their early journalistic experience in east European Jewish newspapers often found a place in the Israeli press. Some of them even held central positions on editorial boards, while others took an active role in the attempt to develop a new, Israeli journalistic style. As a result, the style of east European Jewish journalism faded rather quickly from the Israeli press. At the same time, these journalists and editors were also involved, primarily after 1945, in different attempts to commemorate the east European Jewish press in the Israeli public sphere.

Translated from the Hebrew by Ilana Goldberg

Notes

1 C. Weizmann, 'Beit sokolow', *Davar*, 1 Apr. 1945, p. 1.
2 T. Herzl, *Tel aviv*, trans. N.S. [Sokolow] (Warsaw, 1902).
3 Weizmann, 'Beit sokolow'. Although Weizmann declared that Sokolow was his friend and companion, throughout the years of their acquaintance and joint activities there was frequent friction between them, as for example during the First World War in the run-up to the Balfour Declaration. In 1931 Sokolow was elected president of the Zionist Organization, replacing Weizmann. Sokolow served until 1935.
4 H. Shurer, '40 shanah ba'itonut', *Sefer hashanah shel ha'itona'im*, 1960, pp. 273–7: 273.
5 See I. Ben-Avi, *Im shaḥar atsma'utenu: zikhronot ḥayav shel hayeled ha'ivri harishon* (Jerusalem, 1961), ch. 122.
6 S. Asch, 'Nahum sokolow karakteristikah', in Y. Heftman (ed.), *Lenaḥum sokolow ore'aḥ yehudei-polanyah: kovets ma'amarim, reshimot, zikhronot* (Warsaw, 1923), 5–7.
7 'Until now Sokolow's name has not been properly commemorated in our country' ('Ha'itona'im nigashim lehakamat beitam', *Haboker*, 6 May 1946, p. 4).
8 M. Ron, *Darki bamamlakhah hashevi'it* (Tel Aviv, 1981), 286; I. Remba, 'Ezraḥ ha'olam hagadol', *Sefer hashanah shel ha'itona'im*, 1955, pp. 18–21: 19.

9 'Prospekt al beit sokolow', facsimile in M. Ron, *Darki bamamlakhah hashevi'it*, 276.
10 G. Kressel, *Historyah shel itonut ivrit be'erets yisra'el* (Jerusalem, 1964), 121.
11 I. Ben-Avi, 'Tokhnitenu', *Do'ar hayom*, 8 Aug. 1919, p. 2.
12 A. Shamir, 'Tena'ei ha'avodah shel ha'itona'i', *Sefer hashanah shel ha'itona'im*, 1955, pp. 190–3: 191; A. Paz, 'Divrei hayim 1' (4 July 2015): Agudat Ha'itona'im Betel Aviv website, visited 23 Apr. 2021.
13 S. Samet, 'Yamim veleilot be"ha'arets" ve"davar" de'az: reshamim ishiyim bimelot 50 shanah le"ha'arets"', *Sefer hashanah shel ha'itona'im*, 1969, pp. 347–51: 350.
14 B. Kara, 'Hasofer ha'itona'i', *Sefer hashanah shel ha'itona'im*, 1955, pp. 11–15: 11; Y. Eisenberg '30 shanah u-3 ḥodashim beveit haboker', *Haboker*, 31 Dec. 1965, p. 3. On the newspaper, see M. Naor, 'Haboker: iton hamerkaz vehaḥugim ha'ezraḥiyim', *Kesher* (Tel Aviv), 29 (2001), 44–55.
15 I. Remba, 'Ha'itonut hayomit ha'ivrit bepolin bein shetei milḥamot ha'olam', in Y. Gothelf (ed.), *Itonut yehudit shehayetah* (Tel Aviv, 1973), 20–6, 27–30.
16 H. Bareket-Glanzer, *Hayomon beyidish der moment, 1910–1939: ofen hatsagat eru'e hatekufah bepolin me'al dape ha'iton* (Jerusalem, 2018), 25.
17 Ron, *Darki bamamlakhah hashevi'it*, 5–23.
18 Ibid. 26.
19 Ibid. 319–24.
20 On the Editors' Committee, see Z. Lavie, 'Va'adat ha'orekhim mitos umetsiut' (1 Sept. 2016): Agudat Ha'itona'im Betel Aviv website, visited 23 Apr. 2021.
21 Ron, *Darki bamamlakhah hashevi'it*, 242.
22 Ibid. In Palestine the association only included journalists and not writers.
23 Jabotinsky Institute, L14-1/11, Tel Aviv, Herut Editorial Board, Correspondence with Association of Israel Journalists, National Association, 1957–1963: 'Beit ha'itona'im al-shem sokolow' (n.d.).
24 N. Cohen, *Sefer, sofer ve'iton: merkaz hatarbut hayehudit bevarshah, 1918–1942* (Jerusalem, 2000), 18.
25 I. Bashevis Singer, 'Figuren un episoden fun literaten farayn', *Forverts*, 20 July 1979, p. 3.
26 Cohen, *Sefer, sofer ve'iton*, 18; id., 'Igud hasoferim veha'itona'im hayehudim bevarshah beḥayav uveyetsirato shel yitsḥak bashevis-singer', in H. Shmeruk and S. Verses (eds.), *Bein shetei milḥamot olam: perakim miḥayei hatarbut shel yehudei polin lileshonoteihem* (Jerusalem, 1988), 247–64: 249.
27 M. Ravitsch, 'Tłomackie 13: agudat hasoferim veha'itona'im hayehudim', in Y. Gothelf (ed.), *Itonut yehudit shehayetah* (Tel Aviv, 1973), 233.
28 N. Cohen, 'Tłomackie 13: The Heart and Soul of Jewish Literary Warsaw', in E. Bergman and O. Zienkiewicz (eds.), *Żydzi Warszawy: Materiały konferencji w 100. rocznicę urodzin Emanuela Ringelbluma* (Warsaw, 2000), 91–8; Cohen, *Sefer, sofer ve'iton*, 18–31; id., 'Igud hasoferim veha'itona'im'; Bashevis Singer, 'Figuren un episoden fun literaten'; id., 'Demuyut ve'epizodot mibeit agudat hasoferim veha'itona'im bevarshah', *Kesher* (Tel Aviv), 10 (1991), 4–20; M. Ravitsch, *Dos mayse bukh fon mayn lebn* (Tel Aviv, 1975); id., 'Tłomackie 13'; R. Auerbach, 'Bapa'am ha'aḥaronah ba'agudat hasoferim veha'itona'im bevarshah', in Gothelf (ed.), *Itonut yehudit shehayetah*, 219–36.
29 Tłomackie Street was also famous for the Wielka Synagoga and for the library, which first operated in the synagogue before relocating to a separate building (see A. Guterman, *Meḥitbolelut lile'umiyut: perakim betoledot beit hakeneset hagadol hasinagogah bevarshah, 1806–1943* (Jerusalem, 1993); H. Nussbaum, *Szkice historyczne z życia Żydów w Warszawie*

(Warsaw, 1881), 106–8; E. Bergman, 'Nie masz bóżnicy powszechnej': Synagogi i domy modlitwy w Warszawie od końca XVIII do początku XXI wieku (Warsaw, 2007)).
30 See J. S. Majewski, Żydowski Muranów i okolice (Warsaw, 2012); J. Leociak, Biografie ulic. O żydowskich ulicach Warszawy: Od narodzin po Zagładę (Warsaw, 2018).
31 Ravitsch, 'Tłomackie 13', 219.
32 Bashevis Singer, 'Demuyut ve'epizodot mibeit agudat hasoferim veha'itona'im bevarshah', 4.
33 Jabotinsky Institute, L14-1/11: M. Ron, general secretary of the National Association of Journalists, letter to I. Remba, editor of Herut, 15 Jan. 1958; D. Landwer and M. Ron, letters to I. Remba, 5 Nov. 1958; 13 Feb. 1959.
34 Jabotinsky Institute, L14-1/11: National Association of Journalists, general report, 6 Oct. 1959. In the 1950s Heftman and his colleagues were not the only ones who wanted to establish a cultural centre in Tel Aviv that would be similar to the one at Tłomackie Street. There was also interest in founding Yiddish theatre (see R. Rojanski, Yiddish in Israel: A History (Bloomington, Ind., 2020), 113–14). However, Beit Sokolow was affiliated with the Israeli establishment, while in the 1950s the Israeli Yiddish theatre was not.
35 E. Carlebach, 'Beit sokolow lamah, mikhtavim lama'arekhet', Al hamishmar, 27 Apr. 1945, p. 3; 'Ha'itona'im nigashim lehakamat beitam'.
36 M. Justman, 'Avi', in id. (ed.), Yehoshua yustman; B. Jaushzun, Lezikaron (Jerusalem, 2005), 11–35: 16–17.
37 Cohen, Sefer, sofer ve'iton, 3–4 .
38 Cohen, 'Igud hasoferim veha'itona'im', 251. 'My brother led me to another, larger room, whose walls were covered with some kind of brown cloth. There were pictures hanging from the wall. The one above the piano was of Peretz' (I. Bashevis Singer, Hasertifikat (Tel Aviv, 1993), 168).
39 Cohen, 'Igud hasoferim veha'itona'im', 222; Y. Y. Trunk, Di yidishe proze in poylin in der tekufa tsvishen beyde velt-milhamos (Buenos Aires, 1949), 46.
40 E. Bauer, 'From the Salons to the Street: The Development of a Jewish Public Sphere in Warsaw at the End of the 19th Century', Jahrbuch des Simon-Dubnow-Instituts, 7 (2008), 143–59; S. Niger, Y. l. perets: zayn lebn (Buenos Aires, 1952), 462–3.
41 S. Mintz, 'Shetei tekufot', in Y. Heftman (ed.), Lenaḥum sokolow ore'aḥ yehudei polanyah (Warsaw, 1923), 16–17: 16.
42 P. Lahover, 'Ha'agadah sokolow', in Heftman (ed.), Lenahum sokolow ore'akh yehudei polania, 10–11: 10; S. Y. Yatzkan, Kitei zikhronot, in Heftman (ed.), Lenahum sokolow ore'akh yehudei polania, 19–20: 19.
43 At the turn of the twentieth century, parallel to the salon at Peretz's home, similar gatherings took place in Nahum Sokolow's home at 2 Maryańska Street (see Bauer, 'From the Salons to the Street'; Niger, Y. l. perets, 463–4).
44 Ron, Darki bamamlakhah hashevi'it, 286.
45 Gothelf, 'Mavo', in id., Itonut yehudit shehayetah, 7–12: 11.
46 Kressel, Historyah shel itonut ivrit be'erets yisra'el, 134; U. Elyada, 'Itonut "tsehubah" mul itonut "hagunah": ha'imut al itsuv demutah shel ha'itonut ha'arets yisre'elit bishenot ha'esrim', Kesher (Tel Aviv), 26 (1999), 37–48: 37.
47 S. J. Zipperstein, The Jews of Odessa: A Cultural History, 1794–1881 (Stanford, Calif., 1985), 80–4.
48 Mendele Moykher Sforim (Sholem Yankev Abramovitsh), Sefer hakabetsanim (Tel Aviv, 1988); id., Masot binyamin hashelishi (Tel Aviv, 1950); P. Smolenskin, Hato'eh bedarkhei

haḥayim (Warsaw, 1929). On Odessa in Hebrew and Yiddish literature, see O. Menda Levy, *Likro et ha'ir: haḥḥavayah ha'urbanit basifrut ha'ivrit, me'emtsa hame'ah ha-19 ve'ad emtsa hame'ah ha-20* (Tel Aviv, 2010), 69–91.

49 D. Miron, *Bodedim bemo'adam* (Tel Aviv, 1988), 299.
50 N. Cohen, *Yidish bestman keriah: mileshon dibur lisefat tarbut* (Jerusalem, 2020), 246–9.
51 Among the periodicals that continued to be published in Odessa were *Kaveret*, edited by Ahad Ha'am, and *Pardes*, edited by Yehoshua Hana Ravnitzky.
52 Y. D. Berkowitz, *Kitvei* (Tel Aviv, 1964), 285–9 .
53 M. Gilboa, *Leksikon ha'itonut ha'ivrit bame'ah hashemonah-esreh vehame'ah hatesha-esreh* (Jerusalem, 1992), 471 .
54 See ibid. 137–57; S. Leib Zitron, 'Reshimot letoledot ha'itonut ha'ivrit', *Ha'olam*, 11 Feb. 1913, pp. 10–12; 1 Apr. 1913, pp. 10–12; 8 Apr. 1913, pp. 11–12; 18 Apr. 1913, pp. 20–2; 27 May 1913, pp. 12–14; 24 June 1913, pp. 8–10; 1 July 1913, pp. 10–12; 31 July 1913, pp. 6–8; 7 Aug. 1913, pp. 8–10; 22 Oct. 1913, pp. 8–10; 6 Nov. 1913, pp. 11–13; 13 Nov. 1913, pp. 10–12; 27 Nov. 1913, pp. 10–12; 4 Dec. 1913, pp. 8–10; 11 Dec. 1913, pp. 9–10; 9 Jan. 1914, pp. 15–17; 26 Feb. 1914, pp. 10–12; 9 July 1914, pp. 13–15; 23 July 1914, pp. 15–17, 30 July 1914, pp. 9–11.
55 The newspaper began to appear in Jerusalem after the Zionist philanthropist Isaac Leib Goldberg (1860–1935) purchased *Ḥadashot ha'arets*, which had been founded by the British authorities and was published in Cairo. *Haaretz* was not the first paper with which Goldberg was connected: he was also involved in the publication of several Hebrew papers in St Petersburg and Warsaw. Similarly, he was involved in the publication of the first Hebrew daily, *Hayom*, which was initially published in St Petersburg in 1886 and by the Ahiasaf publication house in Warsaw, and in the publication of several journals which Ahiasaf helped print, including the weekly *Hador*, edited by David Frishman from 1901 in Warsaw, and with the journal *Hashilo'aḥ*. Goldberg was also associated with the Hebrew journal of the Zionist movement, *Ha'olam*. See 'Y. L. goldberg ben shivim', *Davar*, 13 Feb. 1930, p. 1.
56 For the early years at *Haaretz*, see Kressel, *Toledot ha'itonut ha'ivrit*, 18–152; M. Naor, 'Hashanim harishonot shel iton "ha'arets"', *Kesher* (Tel Aviv), 5 (1989), 78–86.
57 See 'Do'ar hayom' (n.d.): National Library of Israel website, 'Historical Jewish Press', visited 23 Apr. 2021.
58 Kressel, *Historyah shel itonut ivrit be'erets yisra'el*, 121 .
59 'Devar hama'arekhet', *Haaretz*, 18 June 1919, p. 1.
60 S. Samet, 'Yamim veleilot be"ha'arets" ve"davar" de'az, 348.
61 On the history of the *Daily Mail*, see J. Simkin, 'The Daily Mail 1896–1940' (1997; updated 2020): Spartacus Educational website, visited 3 Apr. 2021.
62 Elyada, 'Itonut "tsehubah" mul itonut "hagunah"', 40.
63 On the non-Jewish press in tsarist Russia, see D. Balmuth, 'Origins of the Russian Press Reform of 1865', *Slavonic and East European Review*, 47 (1969), 369–88; C. A. Ruud, *Fighting Words: Imperial Censorship and the Russian Press, 1804–1906* (Toronto, 2009); L. McReynolds, *The News Under Russia's Old Regime: The Development of a Mass Circulation Press* (Princeton, NJ, 1991). On the Hebrew press in eastern Europe and its handling of Russian censorship, see inter alia M. Gilboa, *Leksikon ha'itonut ha'ivrit*, 31–8; I. Bartal, 'Mevaser umodia le'ish yehudi; ha'itonut hayehudit ke'afik shel ḥidush', *Cathedra*, 71 (1994), 157–65; D. Elyashevich, 'A Note on the Jewish Press and Censorship during the First Russian Revolution', in S. Hoffman and E. Mendelsohn (eds.), *The Revolution of 1905 and Russia's Jews* (Philadelphia, Pa., 2008), 49–54: 49.

64　Elyada, 'Itonut "tsehubah" mul itonut "hagunah"', 43.
65　Kressel, *Toledot ha'itonut ha'ivrit*, 139.
66　Ben-Avi, *Im shaḥar atsma'utenu*, ch. 85.
67　'Hefkerut', *Haaretz*, 17 Aug. 1921, p. 3.
68　Ben-Avi, *Im shaḥar atsma'utenu*, ch. 85.
69　O. Kessary, 'Ha'orekhim sheli', *Sefer hashanah shel ha'itona'im*, 1969, pp. 289–92: 287.
70　I. Ben-Avi, 'Tokhnitenu', *Do'ar Hayom*, 8 Aug. 1919, p. 2.
71　A.E. 'Aleh nidaf', *Hamelits*, 5 (17) Jan. 1867, p. 2.
72　See S. Verses, 'Tseloḥit shel filiton vesamaneha, al omanut hafiliton shel yehudah leib gordon', *Meḥkarei yerushalayim besifrut ivrit*, 2 (1983), 105–25.
73　J. Nalewajko-Kulikov, '"Hajnt" (1908–1939)', in J. Nalewajko-Kulikov, G. P. Bąbiak, and A. J. Cieślikowa (eds.), *Studia z dziejów trójjęzycznej prasy żydowskiej na ziemiach polskich (XIX–XX w)* (Warsaw, 2012), 61–75; K. Weiser, '"Der Moment" (1910–1939)', in Nalewajko-Kulikov, Bąbiak, and Cieślikowa (eds.), *Studia z dziejów trójjęzycznej prasy żydowskiej na ziemiach polskich*, 77–88.
74　B. Katznelson, 'El kore'einu', *Davar*, 1 June 1925, p. 1. On *Davar*, see inter alia M. Gilboa, 'Reshit "davar"', *Kesher* (Tel Aviv), 16 (1994), 80–91; Y. Gothelf, 'Mikets 45 shanah ledavar', *Iyunim beve'ayot ḥevrah ḥinukh vetarbut*, 3 (1971), 172–82; A. Shapira, *Berl biyografyah* (Tel Aviv, 1980), 241–70.
75　M. Dizengoff, 'Iton ḥadash', *Haboker*, 11 Oct. 1935, p. 2; see also Naor, 'Haboker'.
76　Kara, 'Hasofer veha'itona'i', 11.
77　Eisenberg, '30 shanah u-3 ḥodashim'.
78　See K. Steffen, '"Polska – to także my!" Prasa polsko-żydowska (1918–1939)', in Nalewajko-Kulikov, Bąbiak, and Cieślikowa (eds.), *Studia z dziejów trójjęzycznej prasy żydowskiej na ziemiach polskich*, 129–46.
79　D. Lazar, 'Ezriel karlebakh', *Maariv*, 12 Feb. 1956, p. 2. Lazar was the grandson of Shimon Menahem Lazar (1864–1932), editor of *Hamitspeh*, a Hebrew weekly published in Galicia from 1904 to 1915 and from 1917 to 1921. See also M. Ungerfeld, 'Al hamitspeh', *Davar*, 25 July 1969, p. 8.
80　M. Naor, 'Haputsch hagadol, milḥemet yediot aḥaronot – ma'ariv: hahatḥalah', *Kesher* (Tel Aviv), 33 (2003), 3–15; A. Markuze-Haas, *Ha'iton: vesipur hamishpaḥah sheme'aḥorav* (Jerusalem, 2012), 66–73.
81　Markuze-Haas, *Ha'iton*, 68–70.
82　National Library of Israel, Jerusalem, Shalom Rosenfeld Archive, ARC 4* 1854/6/1: Ezriel Carlebach, article about the awarding of the Journalism Prize for 1954 (MS).
83　A. Zack, '"Der moment" bein shetei milḥamot ha'olam', in Gothelf (ed.), *Itonut yehudit shehayetah*, 102–9; Bareket-Glanzer, *Hayomon beyidish der moment*, 35–47. On the Revisionist party's takeover of *Der moment*, see Zack, '"Der moment"', 107–10; M. Kahn, 'Pirkei zikhronot', in Gothelf (ed.), *Itonut yehudit shehayetah*, 7–126.
84　Jabotinsky Institute, A1-4/21, Ze'ev Jabotinsky Collection, Miscellaneous Documents: 'Iton do'ar hayom 1928–1929'; U. Elyada, 'Do'ar hayom harevizionisti', *Kesher* (Tel Aviv), 17 (1995), 73–86.
85　Nalewajko-Kulikov, '"Hajnt"', 71–2.
86　Although from the outset, *Maariv* had two outside investors, Oved Ben Ami and Shemu'el Hefetz, who between them owned 50 per cent of the newspaper.
87　E. Carlebach, D. Giladi, D. Lazar, O. Kessary, S. Rosenfeld, and S. Schnitzer, 'Tsurah ḥadashah', *Yediot maariv*, 15 Feb. 1948, p. 4. This statement appeared at the bottom of the last page.

88 R. Ipkha Mistabera, 'Lamah yatsanu', *Maariv*, 20 Feb. 1948, p. 2.
89 Such as the move by Yehoshua Justman from *Der moment* to *Haynt*.
90 H. Bareket-Glanzer, 'Yaḥasei aḥim! ahavah, kinah viyerivut, hama'avakim bein ma'arekhet ha'iton der moment uma'arekhet ha'iton der haynt', *Kesher* (Tel Aviv), 46 (2014), 100–6.
91 Cohen, *Yidish besiman keriah*.
92 S. Warshai, 'Roman "yulah yotset mehamaḥaneh, binetiv hayisurim shel ha'akurim be'eiropah"', *Maariv*, 15 Feb. 1948, p. 2.
93 The Yiddish press was of course not the only press in the first half of the twentieth century that understood the potential of the publication of serial novels to turn casual readers into regular ones. In the 1930s Gramsci wrote: 'The serial novel is a way of circulating newspapers among the popular classes ... Hence the newspaper looks for that novel, that type of novel which the people are "certain" to enjoy and which will assure a permanent and "continuous" clientele' (A. Gramsci, 'Concept of "National-Popular"', in *The Gramsci Reader: Selected Writings 1916–1935*, ed. D. Forgacs (New York, 2000), 364–70: 365).
94 See R. Rojanski, *Yiddish in Israel: A History* (Bloomington, Ind., 2020), 48–101.
95 Note the criticism voiced by Yitshak Dov Berkowitz in 1910 in a Yiddish pamphlet published in the form of a Passover Haggadah, entitled 'A Haggadah of Farce'. The targets of the criticism were the editors of *Der fraynd*, *Haynt*, *Undzer leben*, and *Di naye velt* and their attempts to increase their readership. See Berkowitz, *Kitvei*, 244–45; Cohen, *Yidish besiman keriah*, 198–9.
96 Cohen, *Yidish besiman keriah*, 199.
97 Central Zionist Archive, Jerusalem, A18/579: Sokolow, letter to his wife Regina, 3 Mar. 1905; A18/75: Sokolow's diary, 12, 13 Nov. 1905. In the summer of 1906, after Sokolow left Warsaw and moved to Cologne, publication of the paper ceased.
98 N. Sokolow, 'Masa lepolanyah bishenat 1934', in *Ketavim nivḥarim*, ed. G. Kressel, 3 vols. (Jerusalem, 1958–61), iii. 240–335: 241–3; id., 'Bameh tezakeh ha'itona'ut et orḥah? al leidat barvazot itona'iyot', in *Ketavim nivḥarim*, iii. 543–65.
99 Sokolow, 'Masa lepolanyah', 243.
100 Joseph Lurie, who was a member of *Haaretz*'s editorial board, was also the editor of *Der jude*, a bi-weekly magazine published in Warsaw by the Ahiasaf publishing company.
101 Bader was a member of the Knesset from its first term (Feb. 1949) until the end of its eighth (June 1977), representing the Herut party, which later became part of the Likud party.
102 Shalom Rosenberg, who later became the editor of *Maariv*, also began his journalistic career at *Trybuna Narodowa*.
103 Y. Bader, *Darki letsiyon* (Jerusalem, 1999), 142.
104 Ibid. 393–6.
105 M. Asaf, 'Yosef heftman kavin', *Davar*, 11 Jan. 1956, p. 2.
106 Justman, 'Avi', 21.
107 S. Netzer, 'Hakore'im avru le'iton hamithareh', *Kesher* (Tel Aviv), 29 (2001), 128–31.
108 E. Steinman, 'Bekhi al holekh', *Davar*, 20 Feb. 1942; Y. M. Neiman and B. Jaushzun, "Ḥamesh shanim lemoto', *Davar*, 5 Mar. 1947; D.L. [Lazar], 'Ben ya'ush', *Maariv*, 25 Mar. 1966, p. 19.
109 Justman, 'Avi', 23.
110 Y. Yatziv, 'Kav lekav', *Davar*, 27 Mar. 1942, p. 8.
111 See 'Hazeman' (n.d.): National Library of Israel website, 'Historical Jewish Press', visited 23 Apr. 2021.

112 See e.g. Benzion Katz, *Or nogah al shemei hatalmud* (Warsaw, 1895); id., *Lekorot hayehudim berusyah, polin velita bame'ot hashesh-esreh vehasheva-esreh* (Berlin, 1899).
113 Jabotinsky Institute, L14-4/7: I. Remba, letter to Benzion Katz, 11 June 1957.
114 G. Kressel, 'Ben tsiyon kats z"l', *Moznayim*, 6/29 (1958), 208–9.

Jewish Politics without Borders
How Ben-Gurion Won the Elections to the Zionist Congress of 1933

RONA YONA

IN APRIL 1933 David Ben-Gurion arrived in Warsaw and took the Zionist world in Poland by storm. Although he came as a member of a marginal Polish Jewish party (Po'alei Tsiyon Right[1]), he managed to win a landslide victory in the elections to the Eighteenth Zionist Congress which convened in Prague that year. Within three months he had united the Labour Zionist movement in Poland, which in the decades to come redefined Zionism in Poland, the Yishuv, and the Jewish world as a whole.

The election for the Zionist congress in Poland in 1933 was a transformative moment in Zionism generally and in Polish Zionism in particular. The campaigns, which succeeded in mobilizing large segments of the Jewish public, were led by two outsiders: Ze'ev (Vladimir) Jabotinsky, a Russian exile from Odessa who was living in Paris, and David Ben-Gurion, a Labour leader from the Land of Israel. Although Ben-Gurion was born in Płońsk, in Mazovia, not far from Warsaw, in his political education he was more Russian than Polish. His political world had been formed by the 1905 revolution in the tsarist empire.[2] These two were competing to inherit the leadership of the World Zionist Organization, after the sudden resignation of Chaim Weizmann, who had been the unchallenged leader of the General Zionists since the First World War: Ben-Gurion from the left and Jabotinsky from the right. This chapter thus explores the increasing transnational dimension of Zionist politics and the growing influence of the Yishuv on Polish Zionism in the 1930s.

Although studies of the historic victory of Mapai[3] in the election for the Eighteenth Zionist Congress have noted that Poland was the centre of gravity in those elections, they have focused on the power dynamics within the Yishuv.[4] No study to date has examined Mapai's power base in Poland or asked how the elections affected Zionism in Poland. Conversely, scholars of Polish Zionism have not yet concerned themselves with the rise of the Labour movement as a central factor in Jewish political life in Poland in the 1930s. In this chapter I examine how these elections transformed the Zionist establishment and what it was that brought the Labour movement to the centre of the Zionist stage in Poland and in the Zionist Organization as a whole.

The Missing Dimension in the Study of Zionism in Poland

Polish Zionism has usually been described as having two axes: the non-Jewish Polish context and *aliyah* (immigration to the Land of Israel) as seen from a Polish Jewish perspective.[5] Ezra Mendelsohn designated the period between 1915 and 1926 as 'the formative years', which occurred during an era of political freedom that began with the German occupation of central Poland and ended with Józef Piłsudski's coup of May 1926.[6] However, Polish Zionism in the 1930s had undergone profound transformations and new elements gained ascendancy—the Labour movement on the left and Revisionist Zionism on the right. After Piłsudski's ascent to power and the crisis of the Fourth Aliyah (1924–6), the focus of public interest in Zionist political activity shifted from the Polish parliament to the Zionist congresses, seven of which were held between 1926 and the outbreak of the Second World War. This was Zionism of a different kind, which was reflected inter alia in the strengthening of Zionist parties that were not active in Polish parliamentary politics but participated in local government and negotiations with the Polish government.[7] The main source of their strength was their engagement in nation-building efforts in the Yishuv and in the Zionist Organization.

Failure to take into account these extra-Polish contexts leaves several questions that are crucial to the understanding of Zionism unanswered. Among them is how the immigration quotas set by the British government in Palestine affected Zionist life in Poland. Another is why the world's largest Zionist movement, that in Poland, did not become the leading force in Zionism. The Polish Zionist leadership, headed by Yitzhak Grünbaum, was in conflict with the leadership of the Zionist Organization, headed by Chaim Weizmann—an issue that has not yet been researched by historians. David Engel, who has studied the ideological differences between the General Zionists in Poland and the world Zionist leadership, argued that the Polish leadership adopted the political strategy of a national minority and saw as its goal the establishment of a multinational state in Poland—something that could not be reconciled either with Polish nationalism or with the ideal of a Jewish nation state in Palestine.[8] However, as Marcos Silber has shown, the focus of the leading liberal current of Polish Zionism regarding equal rights in Poland after it formed a separate Polish Zionist Federation in 1916 and became autonomous from Russian Zionism was itself the result of German Jewish influence.[9]

Labour Zionism was initially a marginal factor in Polish Jewish politics but succeeded in gaining ascendancy in the Zionist movement in the mid-1930s. The reasons for this should be sought outside Poland, in developments in the Yishuv and the Zionist congresses. The classical approach has examined Polish Zionism in the non-Jewish Polish context and through an analysis of emigration to the Land of Israel. New scholarly perspectives broaden this approach and reveal Zionist activity in Poland as operating within three interrelated spheres: Polish politics (including Polish Jewish politics), the Zionist congresses, and immigration to the Land of Israel (including the Yishuv's perspective on the latter). The Labour Zionist movement hardly took part in national Polish politics. Parts of it, such as Hehaluts,[10] focused on migration and settlement in the Land of Israel and withdrew, in early 1921, from the Polish Zionist Organization and became affiliated with the Histadrut[11] in the Yishuv.

Others like Hashomer Hatsa'ir[12] had no ties with the Polish Zionist Organization from the outset.[13]

Throughout the 1920s the Labour Zionist movement had created a wide institutional network that linked its various sections across the Jewish diaspora, in Poland and other countries and the Land of Israel. These included political parties, youth movements, co-operatives, kibbutzim in Palestine, and a fundraising apparatus led by Jewish workers' organizations in the United States.[14] Since the 1930s the Labour Zionist movement had engaged in intensive activity in the elections to the Zionist congresses, which contributed to the rise of Labour Zionism in Poland, as well as in the Zionist Organization.

Poland: 'The Great Unknown'

On the eve of Passover 1933, 10 April, Ben-Gurion arrived in Warsaw.[15] He immediately met the main Labour Zionist emissaries from Palestine in Poland who were part of the inner circle of activists: the leaders of Hehaluts, Gershon Ostrowski and Feivish Bendori (emissaries of Hakibuts Hame'uhad[16]); Melech Neustadt, the head of the League for Labour Palestine (the emissary of the Histadrut); and Baruch Zuckerman, the emissary of Po'alei Tsiyon in the United States, who was in Poland on Keren Hayesod[17] business.

Ben-Gurion had come to Poland to conduct what he hoped would be a victorious election campaign to the Eighteenth Zionist Congress and to assume the leadership of the Zionist movement.[18] He believed this was possible because of the failure of Chaim Weizmann to be re-elected to the presidency of the Zionist Organization at the previous congress in Basel in June and July 1931. Another envoy, Hayim Shurer, a former member of Hapo'el Hatsa'ir,[19] had gone to Eastern Galicia.[20] Before leaving the Land of Israel, Ben-Gurion told the Mapai Central Committee that Poland was both the 'centre of gravity' of the elections and 'the great unknown'.[21] In a letter to Melech Neustadt he explained his political strategy in Poland: 'I am primarily interested in *destroying Revisionism among the youth and the masses*.'[22] Elsewhere he spoke about 'a crusade against Revisionism'.[23] In his pocket journal, he recorded the results of the recent congresses in Poland and in eastern and western Galicia, all part of the Polish state but organized separately in the Zionist movement.[24] 'The issue will be decided in three countries', he wrote to Israel Merminsky, a Histadrut envoy to the United States, 'the Land of Israel, Poland, America'.[25] These were the locations in which most of the voters for the Zionist congress lived, but the situation in each was different. In Palestine, Mapai, which had been established three years earlier, had become the largest party in the most recent elections to the Elected Assembly of the Yishuv, and there the Labour movement was better organized and incomparably stronger than the relatively new Revisionist movement. Palestine was also the location of the movement's central institutions and leadership. In the United States, Zionism was still, for the most part, a general movement, Labour Zionism was relatively weak, and the Revisionists had not yet taken root. The largest group of voters in the three centres was in the Polish Republic where both competing movements enjoyed broad support. The situation there was therefore the most fluid. In Ben-Gurion's words: 'the main battle will be in Poland and the two Galicias; there we will confront a dangerous enemy'.[26]

Poland was also the main source of migration to Palestine, accounting for some half of all immigrants in this period, and elections there would determine the demographic composition of the Yishuv, since the victorious party would control immigration through the Jewish Agency offices in Warsaw for the following two years—something that would increase the number of supporters of the victorious group in the Yishuv (immigrants) and in Poland (prospective emigrants) alike.

Because of the increase in the number of members of the Zionist movement since the last elections in Poland, it was clear that the victory would not be decided by redividing the pie but by winning new supporters. 'We must build upon increasing our own strength and not rely on our enemies' weakness', wrote Ben-Gurion concerning the schism in the Revisionists.[27] For this he could count on the rapid growth of Hehaluts—since the last congress, 25,000 members had joined movements with ties to the Histadrut and this trend was continuing.

Establishing the Labour Zionist Bloc

When Ben-Gurion arrived in Poland, the Revisionist movement was in the midst of a split between Jabotinsky's Hatsohar[28] party and the movement's veteran leadership led by Meir Grossman who established Mifleget Hamedinah Ha'ivrit (the Jewish State Party). However, the situation in his own camp was no better. Members of the movements and various organizations tied to the Histadrut were not organized as a single political body like the Revisionists and there was no single element coordinating them. A united party had not been established in Poland and the attempt by the Histadrut in the Yishuv to create a merger in the form of the League for Labour Palestine (Histadrut Erets Yisra'el Ha'ovedet) had failed. He could only create a joint list for the elections. By focusing on the struggle against the Revisionists, Ben-Gurion hoped to consolidate his camp's support around the goal of 'conquering Zionism'.

The leadership of Mapai in the Yishuv had its reservations about this ambitious goal. Ben-Gurion thus presented his plan to Hehaluts, Po'alei Tsiyon, and Hitahadut in Poland: 'The members are sceptical', he wrote in his diary. 'They say that it is difficult to sell a shekel [membership of the Zionist Organization], it costs 1.2 zloty, and that is a huge sum in Poland. The Mizrachi and the Revisionists are distributing shekels free. If we had money, we could become the majority.'[29] The shekel was equivalent to a full day's wages or two days' subsistence,[30] which was beyond the reach of many Jews. The leaders of Hehaluts presented the question of elections in Poland as a matter of funding and placed the responsibility on Ben-Gurion to raise the funds necessary to purchase shekels so its members could join the Zionist Organization and vote.

In Palestine, the merger of the Labour parties had proved successful and in the elections on 5 January 1931 for the Third Assembly of the Yishuv, Mapai had achieved its first major victory. In the diaspora, the merger process was encountering severe difficulties, especially in Poland. Because of the opposition of Po'alei Tsiyon and Hitahadut,[31] the decisions of the First Mapai Convention in October 1932 on 'conquering Zionism' were not even published there.[32] Emissaries from the Yishuv were meant to assist with the unification process but were not, in the end, sent.[33] In administratively separate Eastern Galicia, the merger was successful thanks to local initiatives,[34] but, in central Poland, the two parties stressed their separate identities. The Hitahadut party prepared to celebrate the twenty-fifth jubilee of its precursor, Hapo'el Hatsa'ir, which no longer existed, and no agreement was achieved regarding the distribution of mandates between it and Po'alei Tsiyon.[35] The rivalry persisted until the Second World War when the merger was finally accomplished in Vilna, after the Nazi occupation of Poland.[36]

Ben-Gurion's list had won the largest number of votes in the elections to the Seventeenth Zionist Congress in Poland in 1931, as support for the General Zionists there had virtually disappeared. But the Revisionists were the fastest growing party between 1929 and 1931, growing threefold, whereas Labour only maintained its size. The gap between the rival camps amounted to 2,000 votes, and, with Mizrachi,[37] the Revisionists were close to achieving a majority in Poland.[38]

Upon his arrival, Ben-Gurion initiated a series of meetings with the heads of the organizations connected with the Histadrut.[39] Warsaw became the site for the headquarters of Poland's Labour Zionist bloc (Gush Ha'avoda), or, according to its official title, Blok Erets Yisra'el Ha'ovedet (the Bloc of the Working Land of Israel) for the Eighteenth Congress,[40] which included all of the above organizations except Hitahadut, which ran on a separate ticket, and Po'alei Tsiyon Left, which continued to boycott the Zionist Organization. Ben-Gurion decided to focus on central and eastern Poland. He also embarked on one tour of Eastern Galicia (Lwów (Lviv) and its environs), where the Labour Zionist movement was strong and where a special emissary from Mapai was active, and visited Lithuania and Latvia. In Western Galicia (Kraków and its environs), the Labour camp was weak, and he decided it was not worth campaigning there.

Ben-Gurion later met with the leaders of Labour Zionist youth movements. Hashomer Hatsa'ir was the largest Jewish youth movement in Poland, but its leaders had a negative attitude to politics and did not encourage its members to join political parties or to have any part in the election process. In order to gain a majority, Ben-Gurion needed to unite all the organizations connected to the Labour movement in Palestine and to mobilize their members. He was isolated in pursuing this goal. 'The only person I have found until now who understands the situation is Neustadt.'[41]

The means available to Ben-Gurion were rather limited. He did not have a daily newspaper at his disposal that might serve the Labour list's campaign among the wider public. The most popular Yiddish daily, *Haynt*, was controlled by the General Zionists and the radicals (Yitshak Grünbaum, a leading General Zionist in Poland,

and Yehoshua Gottlieb, a well-established journalist and General Zionist), and Ben-Gurion was able to publish in it only about once a month.[42] Its rival, *Der moment*, was a long-time opponent of Labour Zionism, and the Revisionists enjoyed a great deal of influence over it, with Jabotinsky a regular contributor.[43] From the beginning of 1933 Melech Neustadt pressed for the establishment of a Yiddish daily affiliated with Labour Zionism in Poland,[44] but Ben-Gurion was concerned that such a project was too ambitious and that its influence on public opinion would come too late while draining resources required for the elections themselves.[45]

Ben-Gurion decided to rely on the existing means at his disposal. Two days after his arrival, it was decided to transform Hehaluts's Yiddish monthly *Yedies* into a weekly, which, together with Po'alei Tsiyon's newspaper *Bafrayung*, would serve as the left's propaganda organ.[46] *Yedies*, which until then had focused on *hakhsharah* (pioneer training) and *aliyah*, now declared that 'the campaign has begun'. It acquired new political features and relentless calls to fight 'Jewish Hitlerism', Ben-Gurion's derogatory term for Revisionism.[47] This was the start of the intensive politicization of Hehaluts.

From an organizational standpoint, Ben-Gurion decided that 'the spearhead in the war [would be] Hehaluts'[48] and the youth movements, because of their size, their direct connection with the Histadrut (the leadership of all the groups was located in Palestine), and the fact that the Labour Zionist parties in Poland were small and in conflict with one another. When he arrived in Poland, Hehaluts was the largest adult organization at his disposal, and due to the appeal of emigration to the Land of Israel, was growing rapidly. In April Hehaluts had nearly 30,000 members; thousands were joining every week and the decision was made to authorize thousands of immigration applications even before the quotas for the spring and summer of 1933 were announced. Ben-Gurion's decision to expedite emigration to the Land of Israel in order to demand from the British government an increase in entry permits also contributed to the accelerated pace of immigration and of enlistment in the Hehaluts movement.[49] This decision was apparently influenced by political considerations in advance of the elections to the congress, since the relatively disappointing schedule which had been published in April aroused concerns within Mapai that the Revisionists would acquire thousands of additional votes.[50]

In addition to Hehaluts, there were another 50,000 members of leftist Zionist youth movements: Hashomer Hatsa'ir, numbering 20,000; Hehaluts Hatsa'ir (Hakibuts Hame'uhad), 11,000; Freiheit (Po'alei Tsiyon), 10,000; Gordonia (Mapai–Hever Hakevutsot), 8500; Dat Va'avodah (religious Histadrut members) 1,000; as well as the small organizations Herzliyah and Akiva.[51] The members of the youth movements could not vote, but their impact on the Jewish public sphere in the shtetls was considerable. Ben-Gurion gave them an active role in the election campaign. According to his calculation, if each member brought in half a shekel, this would amount to an additional 25,000 votes, and together with Hehaluts and the party it would be possible to reach the target he had set of 75,000 votes in Poland, more than three times the number attained in previous elections. Only pressure of a personal nature could achieve this result, and this element was found in the desire to leave Poland.[52]

The political use of entry permits by the workers' camp was clear to their rivals and aroused their indignation. But the Labour movement benefited from the advantageous timing of the renewal of immigration because of the seats they held on the Zionist executive and on the immigration committees and their control of the allocation mechanism during the period between the decline of the General Zionists and the coalescence of the new power arrangements within the Zionist movement that the Eighteenth Congress brought into effect. It is most probable that the other Zionist groupings (Betar,[53] Mizrachi, and the General Zionists) would not have behaved differently had they had the power. In fact, the leaders of Mapai exercised a degree of restraint in their distribution of entry permits and did not exploit it solely for the benefit of their supporters but also used it to appeal to other groups. The Zionist movement was a voluntary organization lacking powers of coercion, and this necessitated consensual politics in the relations between political rivals and caution in pushing things too far, which might lead to the breakup of the organization. This policy created conflicts within the Labour movement between Ben-Gurion and the leaders of Hehaluts, who demanded an increase in their portion of the quota. According to Yitshak Grünbaum, Ben-Gurion was 'too "Zionist" and too little of a Hehaluts patriot'.[54] Added to this was the opposition of the leaders of Hakibuts Hame'uhad, headed by Yitshak Tabenkin, to taking over the leadership of the Zionist movement. Tabenkin was worried that appealing to the masses would reduce the influence of the kibbutz movement in the Yishuv.[55]

Nevertheless, Hehaluts had many advantages: it was the largest organization on the Zionist left in Poland, it was an organization of adults with voting rights, its members were dependent on the Central Committee in order to go on *hakhsharah*, and it was widely dispersed geographically. The Zionist public in Poland was spread out over hundreds of towns: in the large cities, support was weak. 'Dispersion makes action more difficult', complained Ben-Gurion. 'We are dealing with 600 to 700 towns, and with a multitude of competing organizations.'[56] 'Instructors for these locations are needed', he wrote, 'people who will travel to all these towns and mobilize the members.'[57] Hehaluts had a presence in almost every shtetl. It had branches and kibbutzim in 600 cities and towns throughout Poland, almost as many as the Jewish National Fund, which was the Zionist organization with the widest distribution, numbering some 700 branches. Dispersion 'opens up tremendous opportunity, and and if we are well organized it will have a large impact', Bendori argued.[58] In Neustadt's view, 'the crux of the entire war: [paying] visits to different locations' and direct encounters with members. Seasoned by his years with the League for Labour Palestine in Poland, he explained that propaganda materials are easily distributed, but 'the main thing: direct visits to places. The letters and circulars will not fulfil this need by any means.' Neustadt argued that this was how the Revisionists had built their movement. 'We don't visit—and our members' commitment is weakened.'[59]

The Leader and the Public

During the first week of his stay in Poland, Ben-Gurion went on a three-day tour of lectures, assemblies, and meetings with movement members in Mława and Białystok. In both places he appeared before large crowds, which often spilled out of the auditoriums. He meticulously collected data on all the organizations in the province, including figures on membership in the Zionist Organization, results of previous elections, and estimates of the number of votes anticipated in the upcoming elections.

During his first weekend, he lectured in Łódź and Warsaw, where again the crowds could not all fit into the venues. However, there was internal strife between Labour Zionist groups and violent clashes with Revisionists, following confrontations in Palestine and Berlin. In Warsaw, a heavy object that was hurled at the stage was first suspected to be a bomb but was later revealed to be a stink bomb thrown by a Betar member in response to a violent attack by Labour activists on Betar youths in Tel Aviv.[60] At the end of the first week in Poland, Ben-Gurion made the following evaluation: 'We are the largest force in Polish Jewry—stronger than all the other Zionist parties as well as the other [Jewish] workers' parties'. The main problem was that 'there is a lack of cohesion, and a lack of leadership and sufficient guidance'. Waxing lyrical, he summed up: 'Our country is vast and wide—but it has no order.'[61] The public assemblies gave him a taste of the stormy Polish Jewish political atmosphere, its tendency to degenerate into violence, and the vociferous and belligerent attitude to external and internal rivals. He witnessed the tremendous thirst for information from the Yishuv, for emigration, and the lack of knowledge about these topics and the Labour movement there.

Ben-Gurion and Hehaluts

At the end of the first week, Ben-Gurion held a meeting in Warsaw at the European election campaign headquarters of the Labour Zionist bloc, in which thirty activists from the various component movements worldwide participated, most of them veteran emissaries from the Yishuv.[62] Ben-Gurion and Shurer were at this point the only two emissaries from the Land of Israel who had come with the express purpose of dealing with the elections. The main part of the discussion focused on Poland, and in its course a conflict erupted between Ben-Gurion and the leaders of Hehaluts (the outgoing Feivish Bendori and the incoming Gershon Ostrowski). Bendori, who had led Hehaluts in Poland for the previous two years, reviewed the political situation and the swift growth of Hehaluts, claiming proudly that 'to the credit of the Polish Hehaluts one can say that, more than any of the other movements, it has succeeded in building on the [Zionist] awakening [in Poland] and this was due to our methods of action'. He expressed uncertainty in regard to the elections: 'It is hard to imagine what will occur as the congress approaches. The battle will be harsh. We must make use of means of mass mobilization. Revisionism has yet to draw from their sheaths its many weapons.'[63] In his diary, Ben-Gurion recorded his statement: 'It will be a war of fists and knives.'[64] Concerning Betar, Bendori said that it 'has not grown at the rate that we have. [It] has not taken advantage of the interest in the Land of Israel as we have. Its members also lack the inner confidence that was there a year ago. Nevertheless, the Jewish masses ... hold Jabotinsky in esteem.'[65]

Bendori declined to commit the organization entirely to the election campaign: 'We cannot neglect our ongoing activity for the sake of the issue of the congress', he said, alluding to the Hehaluts kibbutzim, which were the pride and joy of the emissaries of Hakibuts Hame'uhad.[66] Ben-Gurion claimed that the key to the hearts of the masses rested on one simple thing—'work in the Land [of Israel]'.[67] This is what would secure the immigrants' hold on the soil. This was what the Jewish public was yearning and hoping for, although it was not for the most part composed of 'workers'. In his view, it was this element that would furnish a majority for Labour Zionism. The remaining question was that of executing this policy and here he identified two dangers: 'fear of major undertakings and disdain for details'.[68] The Labour movement was used to seeking limited objectives, he argued, and it lacked the courage and vision that was required for the leadership of the Zionist movement. At the same time, there was a lack of proper respect for the individual, as demonstrated by Bendori's contemptuous words about the small Dat Va'avodah organization and the constant conflicts between the kibbutz movements within Hehaluts. The failure to foster individual members could lead to the loss of thousands of votes. In his view, 'when there is no appreciation for small things—there is no capacity for great things'.[69] At any given time, the main objectives must be identified. He told the headquarters' staff and the heads of Hehaluts who had their own reservations that 'right now, the main point is the battle of the congress'.[70]

After these opening remarks, Ben-Gurion attacked the leaders of Hehaluts. He stated that 'there [was] no need to be under any illusions' regarding the rapid growth of Hehaluts and refuted Bendori's claim that Hehaluts's success was due to *hakhsharah*. It was not Hehaluts that attracted them, but rather the land:

The masses are not flocking to our ideology; they are pushed toward the Land of Israel. They are coming to us because they see us as a conduit for immigration. If we do not become that conduit, they will flock elsewhere. Our ideas attracted the youth in previous years. At the moment, a completely different factor [is at play]: *aliyah*. And these [people] will go wherever the control of [*aliyah*] happens to be. Those who are hesitant to be devoted entirely to the work of the congress [and] only care about Hehaluts proper—are mistaken.[71]

Ben-Gurion explained the importance of the oncoming elections, which had nothing to do with Revisionism but rather with the historical and unique opportunity that had been created by the tragedy of German Jewry, which could be leveraged for the sake of *aliyah* and settlement to a degree not yet encountered. He explained that Labour's claim for hegemony must be based on Jewish mass migration to Palestine, not just on pioneer migration.

The previous congress had determined that the composition of the local Jewish Agency offices in each country would be set according to the outcome of the elections to the congress there and not the composition of the coalition, but the reality was different: 'Either we shall be the people of the Zionist Organization and the ones issuing the entry permits or we shall not see any permits or budget. That is the main issue for the next five years.'[72] Victory would depend on the complete dedication of Hehaluts's leaders in Poland to the elections.

Following Ben-Gurion's speech it was decided to require Hehaluts members to purchase a shekel, without which they would not be able to go on *hakhsharah* and emigrate to Palestine.

According to Shurer, Ben-Gurion's speech and the establishment of the headquarters had given 'the campaign a good push.'[73] It was decided that Hehaluts and the youth movements would be completely at the disposal of the party and would focus on the elections; that a Department for Shekel Distribution would be created at Hehaluts; and whoever failed to purchase a shekel would be expelled from the movement. The members of the youth movements were given the task of recruiting parents, brothers, sisters, and other relations, and the Hehaluts kibbutzim were designated as propaganda hubs. The members of the central committees of Hehaluts, the youth movement, and the parties would visit the local branches and organize regional assemblies and mass rallies.[74] This resolved the issue of how to sell shekels as well as the question of having activists visit hundreds of towns.

At the end of the meeting Ben-Gurion wrote with satisfaction: 'I realized that we have a broad movement'. His main conclusion was that success hinged on organization and not on propaganda, as he initially thought. 'There is a large camp that will go with us . . . if only we know how to register it to the ZO [Zionist Organization] and bring it to the polls.'[75] In another letter he explained: 'The main condition for the success of our campaign is to distribute shekels among our friends and their relatives, and in Poland, with its large population and six or seven hundred shtetls this is no trifling matter and a huge organizational operation is required to put the best of our members into action.'[76]

He then travelled to Lithuania and Latvia for a series of meetings and lectures, similar to his tour in Poland, and returned to Warsaw exhausted but satisfied with the mission. Next he travelled to his home town of Płońsk to rest, but, there too, the stream of visitors did not cease, especially petitions for assistance with emigration, and he returned to Warsaw earlier than planned.[77] One lesson he drew from the tours and lecture circuit was to insist that he pre-approve every meeting, assembly, or party that had been planned for him, so that he could conserve his strength.[78] He intended to devote most of his energy and attention to the distribution of shekels at the Warsaw headquarters.

The Department for Shekel Distribution

Upon his return to Warsaw on 9 May 1933 Ben-Gurion went to the Department for Shekel Distribution in the Hehaluts offices.[79] The campaign budget was invested in a systematic operation of visiting hundreds of towns in order to urge members to purchase and distribute shekels[80] to sign up as many members as possible for the Zionist Organization. During the first years of the Zionist congress, shekels were distributed by a general non-political Zionist committee, but, in the 1930s, above all in Poland, membership registration was carried out by the various parties and movements within the Zionist Organization.

Central and eastern Poland was divided into twenty-five provinces, each of which contained forty-five 'points' (cities and towns), involving some 1,000 locations. An instructor was responsible for the activity in each province.[81] Ben-Gurion met with the first ten instructors, rejecting those who could not commit to full-time activity and allocating the remainder to the different provinces.[82] He told them to build local teams of three to five members in each town and to organize assemblies for both older and younger sympathizers. He outlined for them what they should speak about and provided propaganda materials on four topics: *aliyah*, labour relations in the Yishuv, settlement, and Jabotinsky's position on the Jewish Legion, which was meant to undermine his reputation.[83] On the following day, he left for a ten-day tour of six cities in Eastern Galicia.

The third and final stage of Ben-Gurion's stay in Poland began on 29 May and lasted around two months. This was the longest and most important part of his mission. He stayed in Warsaw until the elections were over and only occasionally left to give speeches in other cities in order to generate revenue for the Central Committee.[84] When he returned to Warsaw, the deadline for shekel distribution in Poland was approaching (ultimately it was extended for another month). Ben-Gurion was glad to forgo the travel and the speeches, which, in his view, were of limited value and wore him out. Poland's size and the dispersal of the Zionist public did not facilitate contact with significant portions of the population of the kind he had been able to achieve in the intensive tours of the large cities of Lithuania, Latvia, and Eastern Galicia. This seems to be the main reason that he gave so few lectures in Poland.

Ben-Gurion made use of the momentum that had been created in Hehaluts ranks in the spring of 1933, when the movement's numbers surged following a significant increase in migration quotas to Palestine. His acute political instincts identified the possibility of generating a large number of supporters at this time. In view of the weakness of Po'alei Tsiyon and the League for Labour Palestine and the political marginality of the youth movements, the mobilization of the members of Hehaluts was a huge success. The election campaign gave tens of thousands of new members of the movement a specific cause to which they could devote their youthful enthusiasm.

Victory

Ben-Gurion's decision to base his strategy on personal contact with tens of thousands of members and fieldworkers through the Central Committee's activists and to 'entrust the young members' with this operation created a special atmosphere within Hehaluts.[85] Whereas Betar relied on Jabotinsky's charisma, popular esteem, and public appearances, Hehaluts appeared to its members as a 'movement'. Dozens of young activists encountered the members of Hehaluts as equals. These encounters fashioned a different political culture from that of the hierarchical militarism of Betar. Hehaluts had acquired hierarchical and anti-democratic features with time, like the termination of its biannual conventions in 1925.[86] During the 1933 campaign it again became a cohesive movement of equals, in which each member could take an active part, if only briefly. This was one of the reasons for the success of Hehaluts's shekel operation. In a letter to Ben-Gurion, the young activist who co-ordinated the instructors' work cited letters from the Hehaluts branches which attested to 'sincere dedication' and local initiative. One branch wrote:

Our members are putting together their pennies to purchase the shekel. Our branch is made up of the most destitute of our people and the task is difficult, but we are making every effort in our power so that not a single person will be unable to purchase a shekel with his own means or with the help of the branch. We have also taken upon ourselves the duty to purchase shekels for members of the kibbutz branch in our town.[87]

In another branch, the shekel committee organized a special fund whose sources of income were 'the work method. All members of the branch go out to work' and thus purchase shekels and distribute additional shekels among people they trust.[88]

The potent appeal of the elections to the movement was attested by the secretary of the Hehaluts branch in Lubartów near Lublin. Velvl (Wolf), who came from a very religious family with no Zionist background, decided to join on the day he turned 18, when his father beat him for combing his hair during prayers and again after he refused to attend prayers subsequent to the incident. Every day he stole fifty groschen from his father's shoe store, where he worked, to travel to the Land of Israel and in January or February 1933, he joined Hehaluts. His father kicked him out of the house when he found out, and Velvl was forced to sleep at the Hehaluts branch. At first, he had a difficult time getting accustomed to the presence of young women. After Passover, he became an activist, serving as secretary and treasurer of the branch and managing the distribution of shekels. He was soon sucked into ceaseless activity, neglecting his work at his parents' shop and dropping out of night school. For several months he devoted himself exclusively to the election. 'Because of my political fanaticism', he admitted frankly a year later, 'I was constantly getting beaten up for tearing down the election posters of the rivals. But I accepted this as an honour. I was proud of getting beaten up by a fascist.' His father was appalled that he had become one of the 'Reds, the Bolsheviks'.[89] Children of the well-to-do bourgeoisie—secular students who were attracted to the movement—similarly aroused the anger of their parents who bitterly opposed their joining the 'Bolsheviks' and the 'mob'.[90]

At the beginning of June Ben-Gurion was impressed by the data streaming into Hehaluts headquarters: 'Something is starting to catch fire',[91] he noted. He estimated that 'chances are not bad',[92] but continued to press the leaders of Hehaluts, demanding that they meet with him urgently, in an official letter in which he berated them for the feebleness of their operation, even though they shared an office. 'I still do not sense urgency either at the headquarters or in the branches',[93] he wrote. The data that arrived at headquarters by 6 June, two weeks before the first deadline for the distribution of shekels, covered only one tenth of the branches in which members of Hehaluts had purchased 2,000 shekels, 6 per cent of the movement's membership. The registration rate in those branches came to 37 per cent, similar to the low rate of the previous congress. Ben-Gurion claimed that if there was a failure in the election it would be the responsibility of the Central Committee and not of the Hehaluts members, 'who were strongly committed to this campaign'. He demanded the cessation of all other activity, the mobilization of all the Central Committee members and the students at the movement's seminary in Warsaw, 'in order to save the situation', and an intensification of the personal pressure on the activists.[94] He knew that many purchased shekels in instalments and that a full picture would emerge only after the operation was complete.[95] But he also knew how to goad the Central Committee into action. The following day there were fifty instructors at his disposal.[96]

In June the shekel operation reached its peak. From now on Ben-Gurion monitored the data on a daily basis.[97] During the final three weeks, the pressure on the members began to show results. A week after his letter of rebuke, data from a third of the branches arrived and the rate of registration had risen to 60 per cent. Ben-Gurion estimated that Labour would win around half of the votes, depending on the number of shekels distributed, but he continued to maintain a target of 60 to 70 per cent of the votes.[98]

At the high point of the campaign, on 16 June 1933, Chaim Arlosoroff, a Labour Zionist leader, was assassinated in Tel Aviv. The murder caused a public storm that did not subside for a long time. The day before the murder, in view of the success of the shekel operation in Poland, Ben-Gurion feared that the Revisionists or the Mizrachi would attempt to sabotage the elections 'because they are getting more and more panicky' and that the shekel operation would go to waste.[99] Eleven days were left to conclude the operation and the elections in Poland were about a month away. A fierce propaganda war broke out regarding the murder.[100] The movement's lack of a daily newspaper in Poland was now even more sorely felt. In response, *Yedies* began to appear in the middle of the week as well.[101]

After the shekel distribution was concluded, the focus shifted to propaganda. In the month remaining before the election it was necessary to make sure that everyone who had purchased shekels actually voted, since not all eligible members did so. Ben-Gurion stayed in Poland to supervise this. Most members of the movement were new, and some of them had previously been members of rival movements. The Central Committee of Hehaluts had insisted that they purchase a shekel but could not oblige them to vote. It was therefore decided finally to establish the daily newspaper that had been discussed for many years, while carrying on with the programme of visits and assemblies.[102] Two and half weeks before the elections, on 5 July, *Dos vort*, the Yiddish daily of the Labour camp, appeared in Warsaw. It was edited by Ben-Gurion and Shneur Zalman Rubashov, who came specifically from Palestine for the purpose.[103] Ben-Gurion wrote for the newspaper on an almost daily basis, harshly attacking the Revisionists and Jabotinsky. Half of the first issue was dedicated to Arlosoroff and his murder and to attacks on the Revisionists.[104] News about Hehaluts disappeared almost entirely from the paper.[105] The swallowing up of Hehaluts's paper by the party signals the completion of the politicization of the movement, which had begun with Ben-Gurion's arrival.

By a conservative estimate, along with the other branches and kibbutzim, the number of Hehaluts shekels totalled some 70,000, compared to a mere 4,000 at the previous congress, accounting for two thirds of all the shekels distributed by the Labour Zionist bloc in Poland.[106] In all, around 250,000 shekels were sold in Poland in the lead-up to the elections, three times more than at the previous congress (86,500), and far more than anticipated in the initial forecasts.[107] Together with 200,000 shekels in eastern and western Galicia, close to half a million shekels were sold in the Second Polish Republic.[108] On election day 215,000 people voted in central and eastern Poland, almost 10 per cent of its Jewish population. This figure comprised 40 per cent of all voters to the Zionist Congress that year, and 60 per cent with Galicia. This was far more than the 60,000 people (11 per cent of the total voters) who voted in Palestine. Outside of the main cities, the levels of excitement were almost hysterical. In a small town of 1,800 Jews on the outskirts of Równe (Rivne), for example, 500 shekels were distributed.[109]

The Labour Zionist bloc in Poland won 91,000 votes (42 per cent), compared to 22,000 (31 per cent) at the previous congress, an increase of some 70,000 votes, nearly all of them members of Hehaluts. The Revisionist vote increased by only 29,000, with a total of 49,000 votes (23 per cent) compared to 20,000 (28 per cent) in 1931. The gap between the two sides rose to 40,000 votes (from 3 per cent to 19 per cent). Mizrachi came in third place, followed by the General Zionists, who received only minimal support. The parties that did not join the large blocs (Hitahadut and Mifleget Hamedinah Ha'ivrit) earned only a few thousand votes.[110] In total, Labour won 44 per cent of the seats at the Eighteenth Zionist Congress and the Revisionists 14 per cent.[111] It is difficult to estimate the impact of Arlosoroff's murder on the election, because the purchase of shekels in instalments meant that the tallying of their number was delayed. The final number of shekels purchased approximately matched the estimates that had been gathered before by Hehaluts—around 45 per cent for the Labour Zionist bloc and around 20 per cent for the Revisionists—so it seems that Arlosoroff's murder merely entrenched the position of the two groups and did not significantly change the balance between them.[112]

Conclusion

The Labour Zionist movement did not win an absolute majority in Poland (nor worldwide), but the victory of the Histadrut list led by Hehaluts was overwhelming. They blocked the Revisionists and diminished their power. The striking similarity between the election results in Poland in 1933 and the results of the elections for the Elected Assembly in January 1931 (43 per cent for Mapai; 21 per cent for the Revisionists)[113] raise the question of the link between developments in the Yishuv and in Poland. Did the elections in Poland somehow reflect the power dynamics in the Yishuv on the eve of the Fifth Aliyah (1932–5)? Election patterns during periods of high emigration were different to those during periods of low emigration, since in periods of high emigration voting was determined by immediate interests. In Poland it would seem the key issue in the elections was the question of emigration and absorption into the Yishuv. In his memoirs, written years later, Ben-Gurion claimed that it was the growing strength of the Labour movement in Palestine in the 1920s which created 'an effective lever for establishing the movement in diaspora' and not the other way round.[114] Clearly, when it came to absorbing immigrants without capital, the Labour Zionists enjoyed a significant advantage, which was the result of their long years of institution-building in the Yishuv.

The success of the 'conquest of Zionism' is even more remarkable in comparison with the election held in 1925 (the Fourteenth Zionist Congress) during the Fourth Aliyah. In 1925 Labour's strength in the congress, which had been stable throughout most of the 1920s, diminished due to the expansion of Zionist organizations in Poland and the flow of immigrants to the Yishuv. But after the establishment of Mapai, and particularly in 1933, candidates from the Labour Zionist list considerably increased their presence at Zionist congresses and consolidated their dominant position.[115]

The decline in 1925 was a result of the largely middle-class character of the Fourth Aliyah. Most immigrants possessed the required financial means to migrate without a permit and they organized the Et Livnot faction in order to demand the assistance of the Zionist Organization in their absorption into the Yishuv. By the 1930s the majority of Polish Jews who sought to emigrate to Palestine fell below the economic criteria set by the British because of impoverishment and a doubling of the personal capital required. In the elections to the Eighteenth Congress, the Et Livnot faction disappeared almost entirely, and the Labour Zionists and the Revisionists competed for the allegiance of the increasingly impoverished lower middle class. Through Hehaluts,[116] the leadership of Labour Zionism successfully reached out beyond its narrow circle in order to incorporate members of this group into its ranks and to build its own strength on its path to leadership of the Zionist Organization.

The 1933 election to the Zionist congress was a crucial moment in the establishment of the hegemony of the Zionist left. Its victory strengthened the position of the Labour movement in the Yishuv and in the Zionist immigration apparatus and gave it a significant advantage during the peak period of *aliyah* from the 1930s to the Second World War, an advantage that enabled it to consolidate its dominance and to win subsequent elections.

The Revisionists were left behind and broke away from the Zionist Organization in June 1935. The decisive outcome of the electoral contest in 1933 raises the question of what the position of the Revisionists would have been had they joined the Zionist Executive in 1931 after the resignation of Weizmann, as seemed possible.[117]

What opportunities might have opened up for them had they obtained control of immigration during this period?

Hehaluts in Poland was the central building block of Mapai's ascent to leadership. Its members brought it tens of thousands of votes and provided the key support in Poland both publicly and organizationally. Unlike the Labour Zionist parties, Hehaluts embodied the general Histadrut-like quality that Ben-Gurion favoured and attracted support among those who did not identify with Po'alei Tsiyon's Marxism, with the radical Hebraism of the Hitahadut, or with party politics in general. Hehaluts afforded Histadrut a dedicated cohort of activists and an impassioned public, while the leadership in its entirety came from the Yishuv. Hehaluts and the youth movements created the link between the workers' leadership from the Yishuv and the Jewish public in Poland.

The pressure exerted on the members of Hehaluts to distribute shekels does not in itself explain the success of the election campaign and the genuine excitement that swept over its members. In the spring and summer of 1933 Hehaluts continued to grow despite the fact that immigration did not expand and even slightly contracted in the half-yearly quota published by the British in April 1933. After his return to Palestine, Ben-Gurion depicted the mass mobilization of tens of thousands of impoverished Polish Jews who cast their votes in the election to the Zionist Congress, in order to explain the mutual dependence of the Yishuv and the diaspora. 'How much will, how much passion' was demonstrated by these people living 'in that dreadful poverty'. He had no choice but to 'be cruel to them'. 'The emotional cost on me was awful. I said [to them]: Eat half [of what you habitually eat] and purchase the shekel. I had bitter feelings about doing this, because I knew that I was able to eat day in and day out.' People in the Yishuv did not always appreciate the diaspora, he argued. 'Our duty to them is to invest great energy in building the Yishuv, which hundreds of thousands look to in hope. Whatever we in the land do on behalf of these people is what unites us!'[118]

The Jewish public in Poland was prepared to participate in election campaigns and to do so with great passion. However, the willingness and the ability to engage on a daily basis in mundane projects which could fulfil the Zionist vision, such as studying Hebrew, fundraising and providing assistance to the Yishuv, were low. The crucial election of 1933 to decide who would lead the Zionist movement was a transformative moment in Zionism, which shaped it for a decade, if not decades, to come. But when the storm died down there remained the very real problems that Polish Jews faced, apart from the tens of thousands who were fortunate enough to emigrate.

Translated from the Hebrew by Ilana Goldberg

Notes

1 Po'alei Tsiyon (Workers of Zion) was a Marxist Zionist party founded in Russia in 1905, as well as in other countries. Following the Russian Revolution and the Balfour Declaration (1917) Po'alei Tsiyon split into a pro-Soviet left wing (Po'alei Tsiyon Left), which left the

party and the Zionist Organization, and a right wing (Po'alei Tsiyon Right), affiliated to the Second International. In Palestine Po'alei Tsiyon Right formed the Ahdut Ha'avodah party in 1919.

2 Ben-Gurion claimed that he never learned Polish, only Russian. A. Shapira, 'Berl, tahenkin uven-guryon veyahasam lemahapekhat oktober', in id., *Hahalikhah al kav ha'ofek* (Tel Aviv, 1997), 258–92; S. Ury, 'The Generation of 1905 and the Politics of Despair: Alienation, Friendship, Community', in S. Hoffman and E. Mendelsohn (eds.), *The Revolution of 1905 and Russia's Jews* (Philadelphia, 2008), 96–110.

3 Mapai (Mifleget Po'alei Erets Yisra'el; Workers' Party of the Land of Israel) was a Labour Zionist party formed in 1930 by the merger of Ahdut Ha'avodah and the non-Marxist Hapo'el Hatsa'ir and linked with the Histadrut, the major Zionist labour federation.

4 A. Shapira, 'Historyah medinit shel hayishuv, 1918–1939', in M. Lissak, A. Shapira, and G. Cohen (eds.), *Toledot hayishuv hayehudi be'erets yisra'el me'az ha'aliyah harishonah tekufat hamandat haberiti*, 4 vols. (Jerusalem, 1988–2008), ii. 1–171: 119–21; Y. Goldstein, *Mifleget po'alei erets yisra'el: goremim lehakamatah* (Tel Aviv, 1975), 137–40; id., *Baderekh lehegmonyah: mapai–hitgabeshut mediniyutah (1930–1936)* (Tel Aviv, 1980), 168–82; Z. Tsahor, *Hahazon vehaheshbon: ben-guryon bein idiologyah lefolitikah* (Tel Aviv, 1994), 77–122. For the other main streams within Zionism and their political relations, see e.g. Y. Gorny, *Shutafut uma'avak: hayim weizman utenuat ha'avodah hayehudit be'erets yisra'el* (Tel Aviv, 1976); Y. Eilam, *Hasokhenut hayehudit: shanim rishonot* (Jerusalem, 1990); A. Kaniel, *Yomrah uma'as: hamizrahi bepolin bein shetei milhamot ha'olam* (Ramat Gan, 2011); R. Robinson, *Se'arah mesaya'at: hatenuah harevizyonistit bashanim 1925–1940* (Jerusalem, 2011); Y. Shavit, *Merov limedinah* (Tel Aviv, 1977); D. K. Heller, *Jabotinsky's Children: Polish Jews and the Rise of Right-Wing Zionism* (Princeton, NJ, 2017).

5 See E. Mendelsohn, *Zionism in Poland: The Formative Years, 1915–1926* (New Haven, 1981), 55; Y. Gorny and S. Netser, 'Avodat hahove hamurhevet', in E. Tzur (ed.), *Olam yashan, adam hadash: kehilot yisra'el be'idan hamodernizatsiya* (Sde Boker, 2005), 87–119.

6 Mendelsohn, *Zionism in Poland*, 7.

7 Po'alei Tsiyon Right participated in the municipal elections in Poland and achieved some limited gains. At the end of the 1930s both the Labour movement and the Revisionists conducted secret negotiations with the Polish government in order to train Haganah and Etsel activists in Poland, and the Revisionists led a public initiative to settle hundreds of thousands of Polish Jews in Palestine. See L. Weinbaum, *A Marriage of Convenience: The New Zionist Organization and the Polish Government, 1936–1939* (New York, 1993).

8 D. Engel, '"Hameser hakaful": hatsiyonut hakelalit bepolin lenokhah medinat hale'om', *Gal-ed*, 20 (2006), 55–79.

9 M. Silber, *Le'umiyut shonah, ezrahut shavah! hama'amats lehasagat otonomyah liyehudei polin bemilhemet ha'olam harishonah* (Tel Aviv, 2014), 9.

10 Hehaluts was a Zionist pioneer movement formed in eastern Europe during the First World War which promoted emigration to the Land of Israel and manual labour. It was associated with the Histadrut and promoted kibbutz life.

11 The Histadrut (Hahistadrut Haklalit Shel Ha'ovdim Be'erets Yisra'el; General Organization of Workers in Israel) is the national organization of trade unions in Israel. It was established in 1920 by Ahdut Ha'avoda, Hapo'el Hatsair, and Hehaluts. David Ben-Gurion was elected its secretary, and it soon became one of the most powerful organizations in the Yishuv.

12 Hashomer Hatsa'ir (The Young Guard) was the largest Zionist youth movement in interwar Poland. It promoted emigration to kibbutzim in the Land of Israel.

13 I. Oppenheim, *Tenuat heḥaluts bepolin, 1917–1929* (Jerusalem, 1982), 170 n. 78. Those pushing for a split were apparently Labour Zionists of Russian origin within Hehaluts who had led a similar move in their own party in 1919 (Mendelsohn, *Zionism in Poland*, 154).
14 The process began with the establishment of the World Union of Po'alei Tsiyon in the Hague in 1907 and of Kupat Po'alei Erets Yisra'el in the United States in 1909.
15 See S. Tevet, *Kine'at david: ḥaye ben-gurion*, 4 vols. (Jerusalem, 1976–2004), iii. 32–55.
16 Hakibuts Hame'uhad (United Kibbutz) was formed in 1927 by the union of several kibbutzim and was associated with Po'alei Tsiyon and Hehaluts Hatsa'ir, the Hehaluts youth movement.
17 Keren Hayesod (The Foundation Fund) raised money for the Zionist movement from around the world.
18 Ben-Gurion, letter to Mapai Central Committee, 1 Apr. 1933, in *Igerot ben-guryon*, 3 vols. (Tel Aviv, 1971–4), iii. 216–17.
19 Hapo'el Hatsa'ir (The Young Worker) was a non-Marxist workers' movement active in Palestine from 1905 until it united with Ahdut Ha'avoda in 1930 to create Mapai.
20 Yosef Sprinzak was meant to go but did not show up, and the visit of Chaim Arlosoroff, head of the Political Department of the Jewish Agency, was cut short by events in Germany (Israeli Labour Party Archives, Beit Berl (hereafter ILPA), 2-101-1933-13: Mapai Central Committee, minutes, 10 Jan. 1933; 2-023-1933-4: Melech Neustadt to Berl Locker, 28 May 1933).
21 Mapai Central Committee, minutes, 27 Oct. 1932 (D. Ben-Gurion, *Zikhronot*, 4 vols. (Tel Aviv, 1971–87), i. 540, 586).
22 Ben-Gurion Archive, Sde Boker (hereafter BGA), Correspondence, 01/01/1933–31/03/1933, item ID 263514: Ben-Gurion, letter to Melech Neustadt, 5 Jan. 1933 (emphasis in original).
23 Ben-Gurion to Mapai Central Committee, 21 Mar. 1933 (Ben-Gurion, *Zikhronot*, i. 592).
24 BGA: Diaries, item ID 80034: Ben-Gurion Pocket Journal, 4 Apr. 1933.
25 Ben-Gurion, letter to Israel Merminsky, 5 June 1933, in *Igerot ben-guryon*, iii. 297.
26 Ben-Gurion, letter to Hashomer Hatsa'ir, 1 Apr. 1933, in *Igerot ben-guryon*, iii. 220.
27 Ben-Gurion, letter to Eliyahu Dobkin, head of Mapai Overseas Department, 11 Apr. 1933, in *Igerot ben-guryon*, iii. 229.
28 Hatsohar (Hatsionim Harevizionistim; Revisionist Zionists) was a right-wing Zionist party founded in 1925. It emphasized revising Zionist policy to create a Jewish state on both sides of the River Jordan and establishing an army.
29 Ben-Gurion, *Zikhronot*, i. 525.
30 'Ben-guryon al mifal arlosorof', *Davar*, 22 Oct. 1933, pp. 1, 5.
31 Hitahadut was a Labour Zionist party established in 1920 in Poland and other countries, which was affiliated with Hapo'el Hatsa'ir in Palestine. In 1932, following the establishment of Mapai in Palestine, it united with Po'alei Tsiyon to form Ihud Olami (World Union), except in Poland where it remained separate.
32 BGA, Diaries, item ID 79631: Ben-Gurion Diary 1915–1971, 19 Apr. 1933.
33 ILPA, 2-023-1933-4: Benyamin Vest (*sic.*) and Eliyahu Dobkin, statement at Mapai Central Committee, 10 Jan. 1933.
34 A merger assembly was held in Lwów (Lviv) in January 1933 (ILPA, 2-101-1933-13: Executive Committee of Hitahadut in Eastern Galicia, letter to Mapai Central Committee, 21 Dec. 1932).

35 ILPA, 2-101-1933-13: Hitahadut Central Committee, letter to Mapai Central Committee, 24 Dec. 1932; Hayim Shurer, letter to Mapai Central Committee, 21 Apr. 1933.
36 Hitahadut also opposed teaching Yiddish in Hebrew schools. The merger took place in early 1940 (N. Kantorovich, *Di tsionistishe arbeter bavegung in poyln 1918–1939* (New York, 1968), 36).
37 Mizrachi was a religiously Orthodox Zionist party, founded in Vilna in 1902 to promote religious values and observance in the Zionist Organization and the Yishuv.
38 Ben-Gurion, *Zikhronot*, i. 754.
39 The meeting of 19 April 1933 included representatives from Poland, Latvia, Eastern Galicia, Romania, and Germany (Ben-Gurion, *Zikhronot*, i. 604, 614).
40 ILPA, 2-023-1033-4: Central Bureau letterhead, Melech Neustadt, letter, 18 May 1933.
41 Ben-Gurion, letter to Dobkin, 11 Apr. 1933.
42 The first article was published in the Friday issue (D. Ben-Gurion, 'In kampf for yidisher arbayt', *Haynt*, 14 Jan. 1933, pp. 9–10), followed by six more until Arlosoroff's murder.
43 After the schism in the Revisionists, Grossman moved to *Haynt* (H. Bareket-Glanzer, *Hayoman beyidish der moment (1910–1939): ofen hatsagat eru'e hatekufah bepolin me'al dape ha'iton* (Jerusalem, 2018), 217).
44 YIVO Archives, New York, RG28, Box 13, folder 395: Po'alei Tsiyon Central Committee, letter to Po'alei Tsiyon, Warsaw, Jan. 1933.
45 Ben-Gurion, letter to Neustadt, 5 Jan. 1933; ILPA 2-101-1933-13: announcement to the members of the League for Labour Palestine in Poland, 'In Favour of a Daily Newspaper', 24 Dec. 1932; 'Far an aygener tag-tsaytung', *Yedies*, 15 Jan. 1933, pp. 2–3.
46 As well as the League for Labour Palestine's special publications and its revamped newspaper (D. Ben-Gurion, 'Tsum kamf kegn der hitleristisher mageyfa!', *Dos arbetende erets yisro'el*, Apr. 1933, p. 1).
47 *Yedies*, 28 Apr. 1933.
48 Ben-Gurion, *Zikhronot*, i. 611.
49 ILPA 2-101-1933-13: Pinhas Rashish, letter [to Mapai Central Committee?], 30 Apr. 1933.
50 Shurer, letter to Mapai Central Committee, 21 Apr. 1933. On expediting the schedule, see BGA, Correspondence, 01/04/1933–31/05/1933, item ID 263879: Eliyahu Dobkin, letter to Ben-Gurion, 26 Apr. 1933.
51 Bendori's estimate (Ben-Gurion Diary, 19 Apr. 1933). In the census of 1 April 1933 there were 22,455 Hehaluts members in 443 branches, and according to some estimates, the 121 branches not included in the census had at least another 3,500 members. An additional 4,135 members on *hakhsharah* in 160 kibbutzim were counted, and 4,448 were registered. According to this data, Hehaluts numbered between 26,500 and 30,500 members. 'Hehaluts in tsifern, 1 april'', *Yedies*, 2 June 1933; 'Haḥsharah', *Yedies*, 23 June 1933; 'Hehalutz in tsifrn', 23 June 1933.
52 Ben-Gurion Diary, 19 Apr. 1933.
53 Betar (Berit Yosef Trumpeldor; Joseph Trumpeldor Alliance) was a youth movement affiliated with the Revisionists. Originally founded in Riga in 1923 it became one of the largest Zionist youth movements in interwar Poland, combining Polish nationalism with Zionism.
54 Ben-Gurion, letter to Mapai Central Committee, 1 Apr. 1933, in *Igerot ben-guryon*, iii. 217.
55 Tevet, *Kine'at david*, iii. 24–35, 40–1.
56 BGA, Correspondence, 01/04/1933–31/05/1933, item ID 263937: Ben-Gurion, letter to Mendel Zinger, activist (Vienna), 16 May 1933.
57 Ben-Gurion, letter to Levi Eshkol, Mapai head of finance, 15 May 1933, in *Igerot ben-guryon*,

iii. 261; BGA, Correspondence, 01/04/1933–31/05/1933, item ID 263921: Ben-Gurion, letter to 'Eisenstadt', 13 May 1933.
58 Ben-Gurion Diary, 19 Apr. 1933; Ben Gurion, *Zikhronot*, i. 609, 613.
59 Ben-Gurion Diary, 19 Apr. 1933; Ben-Gurion, *Zikhronot*, i. 609, 613.
60 Ben-Gurion Diary, 21 Apr. 1933.
61 Ibid.
62 There are three versions of the minutes of this meeting: the official version that was sent to the Mapai Central Committee by Hayim Shurer (ILPA, 2-101-1933-13: Labour Zionist bloc, minutes of emissaries' meeting, 19 Apr. 1933; enclosed with Shurer, letter to Mapai Central Committee, 21 Apr. 1933); one in Ben-Gurion's diary, which covers the entire meeting except for his own speech (Ben-Gurion Diary, 19 Apr. 1933); and one in Ben-Gurion's memoirs which is probably based on the official minutes with some editing (Ben-Gurion, *Zikhronot*, i. 604–18).
63 Labour Zionist bloc, minutes of emissaries' meeting, 19 Apr. 1933.
64 Ben-Gurion Diary, 19 Apr. 1933.
65 Labour Zionist bloc, minutes of emissaries' meeting, 19 Apr. 1933.
66 Ibid.; Ben-Gurion Diary, 19 Apr. 1933.
67 Labour Zionist bloc, minutes of emissaries' meeting, 19 Apr. 1933.
68 Ibid.
69 Ibid.
70 Ibid.
71 Ibid.
72 Ibid.
73 Shurer, letter to Mapai Central Committee, 21 Apr. 1933.
74 Ben-Gurion, *Zikhronot*, i. 758.
75 Ben-Gurion, letter to Berl Locker, 22 Apr. 1933, in *Igrot ben-guryon*, iii. 235.
76 Ben-Gurion, letter to 'Eisenstadt', 13 May 1933.
77 Ben-Gurion, letter to Eliyahu Dobkin, 7 May 1933, in *Igerot ben-guryon*, iii. 246; Ben-Gurion Diary, 9 May 1933.
78 Ben-Gurion, letter to Hitahadut–Po'alei Tsiyon in Eastern Galicia, 7 May 1933, in *Igerot ben-guryon*, iii. 247.
79 Ben-Gurion Pocket Journal, 6 May 1933 (before his trip to Płońsk); meeting of Gush Ha'avodah (Ben-Gurion Diary, 9 May 1933 (after his return from Płońsk)).
80 BGA, Correspondence, 01/04/1933–31/05/1933, item ID 263887: Ben-Gurion, letter to Dobkin, 3 May 1933; Ben-Gurion, letter to Dobkin, 8 May 1933, in *Igerot ben-guryon*, iii. 248; Ben-Gurion, letter to Shkolnik (Levi Eshkol) (Ben-Gurion Diary, 15 May 1933).
81 Ben-Gurion, letter to head of [Mapai] Department for Shekel Distribution, 16 May 1933, in *Igerot ben-guryon*, iii. 267–8. For an example of a regional convention in Równe in which Aryeh Tartakower participated, see Ghetto Fighters' House Archive, 25696: League for Labour Palestine, circular, 15 May 1933.
82 Ben-Gurion Diary, 9 May 1933.
83 Ibid., 18 May 1933; see also ILPA, 2-101-1933-13: 'Aseret hadiberot la'irgun' (n.d.); 'Aseret hadiberot leta'amulah' (n.d.).
84 Ben-Gurion, letter to Yosef Bankover, Mapai Central Committee, 2 June 1933, in *Igerot ben-guryon*, iii. 291. Of his day lecturing in Równe, for example, he wrote: 'One of the most tedious days I had' (Ben-Gurion Diary, 11 June 1933). He lectured in Będzin (31 May), Brześć nad Bugiem (Brest) (9 June), and Równe (11 June), and began a tour of Vilna,

Grodno, and Daugavpils, which was cut short because of Arlosoroff's murder, and then lectured in Warsaw (1 July).
85 C. Dan, *Revadim: pirkei iyun vezikaron* (Tel Aviv, 1985), 44.
86 The last convention was officially held in 1929, but it was more of a technicality as it was effectively controlled by envoys from the kibbutz movements in the Yishuv.
87 BGA, Correspondence, 01/04/1933–31/05/1933, item 263975: Chaim Fish, letter to Ben-Gurion, 26 May 1933.
88 Ibid.
89 YIVO Archives, RG 4 (Autobiographies of Jewish Youth in Poland), Autobiography 3715, 61–6. To his great disappointment, when he requested to go on *hakhsharah* at the end of 1933, he was passed over in favour of a member who had belonged to Po'alei Tsiyon Left for many years. According to him, when he discovered that the member was chosen because he had invited the members of the committee for beers he left the movement.
90 Autobiography of Ludwig Stockel, who joined the Hitahadut–Po'alei Tsiyon party (J. Shandler (ed.), *Awakening Lives: Autobiographies of Jewish Youth in Poland before the Holocaust* (New Haven, Conn., 2002), 190–1).
91 Ben-Gurion Diary, 29 May 1933.
92 Ben-Gurion, letter to Yosef Bankover, Mapai Central Committee, 2 June 1933.
93 BGA, Correspondence, 01/06/1933–30/06/1933, item ID 264158: Ben-Gurion, letter to Hehaluts Central Committee, 6 Jun. 1933.
94 Ben-Gurion, Diary, 6, 13 June 1933. The members of the youth movements were charged a fee of half a shekel to finance the operation, and later pressure on the kibbutzim was intensified.
95 BGA, Correspondence, 01/04/1933–31/05/1933, item ID 263975: Hehaluts Central Committee, letter to Ben-Gurion (in Galicia), 26 May 1933.
96 Ben-Gurion, letter to Shkolnik, 7 June 1933, in *Igerot ben-guryon*, iii. 299. A few days earlier he had demanded another twenty instructors (Ben-Gurion, letter to Yosef Bankover, 2 June 1933).
97 BGA, Correspondence, 01/06/1933–30/06/1933, item ID 264173: Ben-Gurion, letter to League for Labour Palestine, Piotrków, 7 June 1933; item ID 264181: Ben-Gurion, letter of praise to Z. Kinros, 8 June 1933; summary of the first reports (Ben-Gurion Diary, 20 May, 2 June 1933); ILPA, 2-101-1933-13: Ben-Gurion, letter of rebuke about 'horrific reports' to the League for Labour Palestine, Bendin (Będzin), 6 June 1933.
98 BGA, Correspondence, 01/01/1933–31/03/1933, item ID 264269: Ben-Gurion, letter to Dobkin, 15 June 1933 (mistakenly catalogued under 15 Mar. 1933); Correspondence, 01/06/1933–30/06/1933, item ID 264316: Ben-Gurion, letter to Yehuda Reznichenko (Erez), 15 June 1933.
99 Ben-Gurion, letter to Dobkin, 15 June 1933.
100 See e.g. Ben-Gurion, 'Ikh bashuldik', *Yedies*, 25 June 1933, p. 1; 'Ani ma'ashim', *Davar*, 7 July 1933, p. 2.
101 After the murder special editions of *Yedies* appeared on 19 and 20 June 1933 ('Hed haretsaḥ bagolah', *Davar*, 29 June 1933, p. 1; B. H. [Habas], 'Ha'evel bepolin', *Davar*, 29 June 1933, p. 2).
102 Ben-Gurion Diary, 9 July 1933. See e.g. an announcement about an assembly a day before the vote in Ludmir (Volodymyr-Volynsky) in which 'Revisionism was placed on trial by the people' with the active participation of a young activist from Hehaluts who was described as a 'representative from Warsaw' (Ghetto Fighters' House Archive, 25696: poster for an assembly in Ludmir [22 July 1933(?)]).

103 BGA, Correspondence, 01/06/1933–30/06/1933, item ID 264353: Ben-Gurion, letter to Reznichenko, 3 July 1933; Kantorovich, *Di tsionistishe arbeter bavegung in poyln*, 26–7, 49–59; C. Ya'ari, 'Dos vort, dos naye vort, folksvort', in Y. Gotthelf (ed.), *Itonut yehudit shehayta* (Tel Aviv, 1973), 165–79.

104 See e.g. D. Ben-Gurion, 'Vi men vil raynvashn', *Dos vort*, 7 July 1933, p. 2. For the responses in the Revisionist press in Poland and in *Haynt*, see Heller, *Jabotinsky's Children*, 201–4.

105 Regular reporting was renewed only after the election (*Dos vort*, 7 Aug. 1933).

106 Ben-Gurion Diary, 3 July 1933.

107 535,113 votes were cast, while Mapai's forecasts in October 1932 estimated that there would be between 250,000 and 300,000 (Ben-Gurion, *Zikhronot*, i. 540).

108 Shapira, 'Historyah medinit shel hayishuv', 120; 'Hekher 250 toyzend shkalim', *Haynt*, 3 July 1933, p. 5; 'Tsiyonistishe ekzekutive', *Haynt*, 6 July 1933, p. 2.

109 Ghetto Fighters' House Archive, 23870: Yisrael Otiker, report on Zdolbuniv, 17 June 1933. There are five more similar reports in the same file.

110 Y. Shavit, 'Erets yisra'el vepolin kema'areḥet politit meshulevet', *Medina, mimshal veyaḥasim be'inle'umi'im*, 25 (1981), 148–60: 149.

111 Ben-Gurion, *Zikhronot*, i. 385.

112 Ben-Gurion Diary, 27 June 1933.

113 'Herkev asefat hanivcharim', *Davar*, 1 Jan. 1931, p. 1.

114 Ben-Gurion, *Zikhronot*, i. 337, 385.

115 In 1921 they took 8 per cent of the vote; in 1923, 21 per cent; in 1925, 18 per cent; in 1927, 22 per cent; in 1929, 26 per cent; in 1931, 29 per cent; in 1933, 44 per cent; in 1935, after the Revisionists left the Zionist Organization, 50 per cent; and in 1937, 46 per cent (ibid. 385; Gorny, *Shutafut uma'avak*, 16).

116 A similar organization called Ha'oved was used in 1935, following the demise of Hehaluts.

117 Shapira, 'Historyah medinit shel hayishuv', 106–7; Y. Goldstein, *Baderekh lehegemonia, mapai–hitgabshut mediniyutah, 1930–1936* (Tel Aviv, 1980), 37–51.

118 'Ben-guryon al mifal arlosorof'.

A Bridge between West and East
Polish Economic Policy and the Yishuv

KATARZYNA DZIEKAN

> Poland's *raison d'état* is legitimately based on emigrants, as they are not only the pioneers of Polish colonial thought in Palestine, but they also pave the way for Poland's economic expansion.
>
> Samuel Stendig, *Polska a Palestyna*

ON WEDNESDAY morning, 27 September 1933, the passenger ship SS *Polonia* left the Black Sea port of Constanţa in south-east Romania on its maiden voyage to Palestine a few months after the Polish Transatlantic Shipping Company had made the decision to establish its first Levantine route.[1] As the establishment of a Polish maritime link to Palestine was almost entirely linked with the Jewish settlement there, the day of the ship's departure was extensively reported in both Polish and Jewish newspapers. Among the passengers were prominent Polish politicians and journalists.[2] The day after its departure, Mirosław Arciszewski, head of the Polish legation in Bucharest, stated at a press conference that extensive diplomatic efforts had gone into the establishment of the new shipping route. Bernard Hausner, a politician affiliated with the Mizrachi Zionist Organization and the Polish consul-general in Tel Aviv, who was viewed as a 'spiritual father of the idea of establishing a new shipping route', briefly presented the recent developments in Polish–Palestinian trade relations.[3] Samuel Wołkowicz, the editor of *Nasz Przegląd*, in turn pointed out: 'Gentlemen, you speak about the new shipping route as ships. But you forget something. You forget that for us, Jews, these are not ships. For us it is a bridge. A bridge between Poland and Palestine.'[4]

The vessel, with several hundred passengers on board, anchored three days later, on Sunday morning, in Haifa. The Polish diplomats were officially welcomed by Tel Aviv's mayor, Meir Dizengoff, the mayor of Haifa, Hassan Bey Shukri, and the highest government officials. In a celebratory speech, Dizengoff emphasized the importance of the new shipping route in enhancing and developing economic relations between Poland and Palestine.[5] He also recalled that the Polish authorities had supported the Balfour Declaration and Zionist nation-building aspirations. After the playing of 'Mazurek Dąbrowskiego'—the Polish national anthem—Arciszewski gave a speech in which he stated that 'besides the commercial reasons for the new service, it has been prompted by the harmonious relations between the Polish and Jewish peoples'. 'The Jewish people', he continued, 'are establishing their national home, advancing towards an independent existence, and the sentiments of the Polish nation are with them. The new steamship line shows that the Polish government is anxious to ensure that its Jewish citizens sail to their homeland under appropriate conditions.'[6] On behalf of the Polish cabinet, Arciszewski expressed his great admiration for 'the enormous constructive activity' of Jews in Palestine and concluded his speech with 'long live the Land of Israel'.'

This chapter examines the economic interactions between Poland and the Yishuv, the Jewish community in the Land of Israel, before the Second World War. Particular attention is given to the connection between the emigration of Polish Jews to Palestine and the intensification of trade. By placing Polish–Zionist interactions within the wider context of deteriorating political and economic circumstances in Poland, Poland's deflationary policies, and its economic interests in the Middle East, it makes clear the deep interest of the different elements within Józef Piłsudski's Sanacja regime following the coup of May 1926 in establishing close commercial relations with the emerging Jewish Palestine. The chapter also examines how and to what extent the Sanacja regime's pro-Zionist attitudes were influenced by economic factors.

The Changing Perception of the Yishuv

At the end of the First World War the newly re-established Polish state faced daunting economic problems.[8] Uniting the country's regions and introducing a single set of economic norms proceeded slowly. Under such circumstances, promoting Polish trade abroad was of secondary importance. However, in the second half of the 1920s as the country began to experience a relative economic upturn, Warsaw directed its efforts to finding new outlets for the goods it produced. Not surprisingly, Palestine, with its growing number of Jewish immigrants from Poland, now became a viable economic partner. Successive waves of immigration not only shaped the socio-demographic pattern of Palestine but also had a profound impact on the perception of the region in the eyes of the governing elites in Warsaw. Recent studies on the economic effects of migration have shown that it has a positive influence on commercial relations between the country of settlement and the country of origin. Complementing the research of Jerzy Łazor, this chapter argues that this was certainly the case for the interwar migration of Polish Jews to Palestine.[9] The official view was that Palestine was not so much a territory like others as a region with a substantial number of Jews of Polish origin. Within the ruling circles in Poland these developments came to constitute an unparalleled opportunity to enhance foreign trade. Consequently, from 1926 to 1939 successive cabinets in Warsaw, regardless of their political persuasion, actively promoted exports to Palestine.

The economic revival which took place in Palestine was inextricably linked with the large influx of Jewish immigrants from Europe and found its full expression in the economic statistics of the country. During the interwar years approximately 362,000 immigrants moved to Palestine, of whom some 40 per cent came from Poland. As a result, its Jewish population grew from 83,790 in 1922 to 445,457 in 1939.[10] The accelerating process of immigration and the rapid growth of per capita Jewish national income raised the overall demand for various goods, raw materials, and other products.[11] As the statistics show, the rise in imports largely corresponded to the increase of the Jewish population—approximately 37 per cent in 1925.[12] Since Palestine, unlike the other countries in the region, had eliminated all exchange restrictions, its market became extremely attractive for European exporters.[13] Throughout the interwar period the Jewish economy in Palestine experienced an annual rate of growth of 4.8 per cent. With trade growth of 516 per cent between 1928 and 1948, Palestine became the most vibrant economy in the Middle East.[14]

On 14 February 1923 Aleksander Skrzyński, the minister for foreign affairs, proposed the establishment of a Polish consulate in Jerusalem. In his explanatory statement he wrote:

The substantial increase in emigration from Poland to Palestine means that we need to obtain comprehensive information about the political situation in Palestine and to maintain direct contact with the relevant institutions in order to assist Jewish emigration, which will be beneficial for the Polish state . . . Moreover, Palestine and Egypt are significant as economic entities, as sources for raw materials, and as important market outlets for Polish goods.[15]

A month later, on 16 March, the Polish Council of Ministers appointed Jerzy Adamkiewicz, a former secretary of the Polish legation in London, consul to Palestine.[16] Shortly after his appointment, in an interview with the Jewish Telegraphic Agency, Adamkiewicz affirmed: 'The promotion of commercial relations between Poland and Palestine is my principal purpose'.[17] He also stated that he would seek to co-operate with all Jewish institutions in general and, in particular, with the Jewish Agency.

Adamkiewicz quickly confirmed the economic potential of the region. In a report to Warsaw he wrote:

In the whole Middle East, not only in Palestine but also in Egypt, Syria, Transjordan, Arabia, Mesopotamia, and Turkey, we have done nothing. Everything, however, suggests that our commercial expansion has a great future in these countries. With adequate energy, consistency, and skills we can find here an unlimited demand for our goods.[18]

Despite various diplomatic efforts, Polish exports to Palestine, based predominantly on small and medium-sized enterprises, remained extremely small until the late 1920s. To a large degree, this situation stemmed from the Polish state's economic difficulties and the fiscal crisis that lasted until early 1926. The adoption of a pro-Palestine policy, indirectly triggered by the need to find new outlets for exports, intensified in the second half of the 1920s, after the Grabski Aliyah, which brought to Palestine approximately 35,000 Polish Jews, mostly merchants, shopkeepers, and artisans.[19]

Both Jerzy Tomaszewski and Jerzy Łazor note that 1927 was a watershed year for the shaping of bilateral relations.[20] After Piłsudski's *coup d'état* of May 1926 mutual economic co-operation was given a new dimension by appointments in the Polish consular service. In January 1927 the decision was made to transfer Titus Zbyszewski from Leipzig to Palestine. Soon after his appointment, in a conversation with the editor of the *Palestine Bulletin*, Zbyszewski admitted that despite being 'only at the beginning of his work, he [was] thinking of preparing some definite plans for extending the trade connections between Poland and Palestine'.[21] The second appointment took place in mid-May 1927, when Aleksander Skrzyński appointed Bernard Hausner Polish commercial councillor in Haifa.[22] The nomination, widely commented on in Poland and abroad, was referred to as 'a bold and calculated political move'.[23] The Polish and Jewish press speculated as to who might have made the decision to appoint a Jew affiliated with the Mizrachi movement to the Polish consular service. Within Jewish circles, it was believed that Piłsudski had insisted on it.[24] Certainly, in appointing Hausner the Sanacja leaders made explicit their support for Jewish national interests and their eagerness to develop further economic relations with the Yishuv.[25] In an interview with the *Jewish Telegraphic Agency*, Hausner stated:

> The Polish government has made this appointment knowing the facts and after careful consideration. It was not the ordinary appointment of a consul. I am fully aware of the responsibility of my post. I shall have to represent the double interests of Poland and of reviving Palestine, the interests of the Polish immigrants who form the largest part of the immigrant stream, and also the interests of the Polish State. I trust that the Polish government circles will as a result be convinced that it is possible to be a devoted Zionist and also to safeguard the interests of the Polish state no less than if one is an assimilationist. I regard the action of the Piłsudski Government in making this appointment as a blow to assimilationism and an expression of confidence in Zionism.[26]

Since Palestine was supposed to serve as a hub for international trade, the Zionist leadership viewed these nominations as a step of great importance for the further development of trade relations. In spite of some friction and misunderstanding, Zbyszewski and Hausner immediately began to look into ways of strengthening the economic relationship between Poland and Mandatory Palestine, preparing a draft scheme for opening branches of a Polish bank in Tel Aviv, Jaffa, and Beirut.[27]

Palestine's 'Polish Jewish Diaspora' and Its Economic Significance

Polish diplomats now began to point to the enormous potential of Jewish emigrants in developing exports to Palestine. In September 1928 Hausner argued that 'Jewish immigrants from Poland frequently manifest their sympathy and deep attachment to their country of origin', and therefore Poland had 'an unprecedented chance to use those people to take additional shares of the Palestinian and other Middle Eastern markets'.[28] Over the next few years this theme became the main argument in official reports submitted to Warsaw for stimulating commercial relations between the two countries.

The large-scale 'commercial use' of former citizens who had settled in Palestine became part of the wider context of Polish trade policy.[29] Stanisław Głąbiński, a prominent publicist, wrote: 'establishing proper commercial relations with emigrants and through them with the colonial power will not only reduce our dependence on primary raw materials but can also improve our balance of payments'.[30] From this vantage point, the size of Palestine's Polish Jewish population became the crucial determinant of bilateral trade. This rhetoric received considerable support from the Sanacja regime in the early 1930s with the revival of Polish Jewish migration to Palestine.[31] Tadeusz Nieduszyński, an economic adviser to the Ministry of Foreign Affairs, considered the Yishuv a crucial overseas market for Polish products. In an article devoted to the question, he claimed that 'by virtue of their deep emotional attachment to Poland, Polish Jews are becoming the ultimate element of our economic expansion to the region. Every effort should be thus made to further develop cultural and economic co-operation between Poland and Palestine.'[32]

Polish Zionists also shared such views. Menachem Kirschenbaum, in a letter to the Polish Ministry of Foreign Affairs, wrote: 'Thousands of Polish citizens emigrate every month to Palestine, creating a majority here and maintaining close contact with Poland on the level of family, citizenship, and financial and commercial activity, at the same time extending their commercial influence throughout the whole of the Near East. This factor is undoubtedly of economic and political importance for Poland.'[33] In the eyes of both Polish Zionists and Sanacja elites, Palestine was perceived as 'the Middle East's fertile granary' and a gateway to other countries in the region. It was this that required the Palestine market to be taken seriously.[34]

Accordingly, Polish Jews were considered a bridgehead for developing economic co-operation between Poland and Palestine. This approach was inextricably intertwined with Sanacja ideology. Unlike right-wing groups, the Sanacja regime did not view Jews as having a negative attitude to Poland. Between 1926 and 1935 the ruling elites effectively embraced a policy of 'state consolidation' that envisaged uniting all citizens, including ethnic minorities, in loyalty to the state.[35] This significantly affected economic policy, strengthening the Sanacja regime's pro-Zionist approach. The large-scale development taking place in Palestine and the role played by Polish Jews in its reconstruction confirmed their beliefs. As a consequence, politicians and intellectuals around Piłsudski repeatedly emphasized the impressive involvement of Polish Jews in the process of building up Palestine and the importance of maintaining close ties with them. The strong and well-organized community of Polish Jews came to be seen as an important partner in opening the doors of the Middle East to Polish trade and industry. Thus the creation of the 'Polish Jewish diaspora' in Palestine not only closely corresponded with the Polish economic agenda but also essentially underpinned Sanacja ideology between 1926 and 1935.

Polish Jews participated actively in Palestine's economic life, becoming productive and creative members of a modern society.[36] Many of them found entrepreneurial activity to be an accessible niche in Palestine's market. At the same time, they were intimately familiar with Polish products and eager to promote them both in Palestine and in neighbouring countries.[37] Moshe Shertok, head of the Political Department of the Jewish Agency, argued:

It is obvious that Poland stands in a special relationship to the Jewish work of reconstruction in Palestine. The majority of the recent Jewish immigrants have hailed from Poland and they naturally still maintain close contacts with their native land. It is significant for instance that Poland is the only foreign state which maintains in Palestine a branch of its Postal Savings Bank [Polska Kasa Oszczędności; PKO], through the agency of which very considerable sums are transmitted every year by Jewish residents in Palestine to their relatives in Poland. On the other hand, Poland is doing a very profitable export trade with Palestine. Large consignments of Polish cattle, eggs, furniture, and glassware are being exported every year to Palestine. Finally, the Polish government, by virtue of its membership of the League of Nations and by the most important positions it holds therein as a member of the council, is able to support and assist the Jewish efforts of the national reconstruction in Palestine.[38]

Jewish immigrants were, indeed, eager to maintain close ties with their country of origin. Their knowledge of Polish markets, ability to speak the language, and business connections provided solid foundations for bilateral trade co-operation. *Nasz Przegląd* proclaimed:

A significant part of Palestine's population is tied to Poland by the ties of the past, and above all by the knowledge of our economic relations and opportunities, which is a serious asset for the future and which should cause a natural turn of Palestine's foreign trade towards Poland.[39]

In a similar vein, Jakub Appenszlak, editor-in-chief of *Nasz Przegląd*, wrote:

Ties between Poland and Palestine are vital, organic, emotional and economic, as they stem from the fact that the builders and pioneers of the Jewish National Home are mostly Jews, Polish citizens, whose spiritual and economic ties with the country of their ancestors, with the centre of the diaspora, with the land soaked with their sweat and blood of their brothers who had fallen in defence of Polish freedom did not weaken after emigration.[40]

Similar opinions were frequently expressed in the pages of *Palestyna i Bliski Wschód*.[41]

The Yishuv as a New Commercial Partner

As the Great Depression began to affect Poland's economy, the governing elites started to draw attention not only to the need to find new outlets for exports but also to the necessity of accelerating emigration.[42] Seeking to obtain the most beneficial outcome for the national economy, the Sanacja regime looked to the Yishuv. In 1929 Gustaw Załęcki, a member of the Institute for Emigration and Colonization Research, wrote: 'overseas policy has become crucial for Poland as a newly re-established state . . . Our exports choke within Europe's post-war political order.'[43] Although the exchange of goods with continental partners played a dominant role in Poland's foreign trade, there was a serious risk in depending solely on European markets. For this reason, in the early 1930s the Polish government advanced a strategy of establishing close commercial relations with the emerging markets of the Middle East, such as that of Palestine, where economic activity showed an upward trend in the midst of a worldwide economic depression. Fishel Rotenstreich, a member of the Trade and Industry Department of the Jewish Agency, described Palestine as 'an island in the sea of world economic crisis'.[44] In 1933 *Palestyna i Bliski Wschód* reported that, 'as opposed to almost all other countries affected by severe economic crisis, Palestine offers a safe haven, far from economic storms and catastrophes'.[45]

Throughout the 1930s, both 'British Palestine' and 'Jewish Palestine' were major consumers of Polish goods. In 1931 Jews accounted for 25 per cent of Palestine's total population and their share of imports steadily increased, reaching 60 per cent at the beginning of the 1930s.[46] Polish exports increased after the mid-1920s along with the huge influx of Polish Jewish immigrants to Palestine. The numerous export promotion activities, initiated in the late 1920s, facilitated bilateral exchange, resulting in stronger economic relations between Poland and the Yishuv. Between the wars, the Yishuv leaders and activists, anxious to promote settlement in Palestine, were frequent visitors to Poland. They travelled across the country encouraging local Zionist organizations, and met Polish authorities, who were particularly keen to initiate talks with the Zionists. These increasingly frequent interactions soon brought the results that both sides were hoping for. In August 1930 David Bloch-Blumenfeld, a former mayor of Tel Aviv, organized a conference in Jaffa promoting commercial relations between Poland and the Yishuv. It was agreed that it was in the interests of both sides that 'Poland as a country actively seeking export opportunities in the Middle East should exploit the Yishuv as an intermediary'.[47] A few weeks later, Arthur Ruppin, a member of the Zionist Executive of the Jewish Agency, went to Warsaw to confer with the Ministry of Industry and Trade about commercial exchange and the migration of Polish Jews to Palestine. As a result, in January 1930 the Palestine–Poland Immigrant Bank was established in Tel Aviv with a share capital of £10,000. Its main purpose was to facilitate commercial exchange between the two countries and to grant loans for the import of Polish products.[48] Furthermore, the Polish government agreed to approve the budget of every Jewish institution which included subsidies for Palestine's institutions.[49]

From 1931 onwards Polish exports to Palestine steadily increased, reaching their highest level in 1935. During this period Polish exports increased fourteenfold, whereas Palestine's exports to Poland only increased sixfold. Palestine, which now took approximately 10 per cent of all Polish exports, became, after the United States, the second-largest importer of Polish goods.[50] According to official statistics, in 1932 Palestine imported Polish goods with a value of £101,355. This constituted a striking rise in imports from 1931 when such goods were valued at £38,499. The timber, steel, and textile industries were of particular interest to importers, including raw materials and semi-finished goods. The 1933 boycott of German products and services was initially seen by the Polish authorities as an unprecedented opportunity to enhance commercial relationships between Poland and the Yishuv, and it undertook widespread diplomatic action against German products. However, in 1935 it decided to stop supporting the boycott on the grounds that it was contrary to the official policy of limited détente towards Germany.[51]

Table 1 Imports into Palestine, 1932–1938

Year	Imports	Imports from Poland	
	£	£	%
1932	7,768,920	101,355	1.3
1933	11,123,489	289,718	2.6
1934	15,152,781	475,375	3.1
1935	17,783,493	778,789	4.4
1936	13,979,023	368,367	2.6
1937	14,292,633	428,779	3.0
1938	14,472,724	419,709	2.9

Source: Department of Customs, Excise and Trade (Palestine), *Annual Report for the Year 1933* (Jerusalem, 1933), 48–9; Department of Statistics (Palestine), *Statistics of Imports, Exports and Shipping* (Jerusalem, 1936), 54–5; J. Thon, 'Polsko-Palestyńska wymiana towarów w roku 1937', *Palestyna i Bliski Wschód*, 1938, no. 4, pp. 74–80: 74.

In 1935 Japan and Germany left the League of Nations and therefore lost the right to unrestricted trade with Palestine. Since their products were in direct competition with Polish goods, the Ministry of Foreign Affairs saw this as a further opportunity to enlarge Poland's sphere of economic influence over the Middle East.[52] In January 1936 Leon Lewite, president of the Polish–Palestine Chamber of Commerce and Industry, wrote: 'we wish to draw attention to these opportunities and the need to prepare the Polish economy to be in a position to provide substitutes for the exports from these countries'.[53] This was confirmed by Shlomo Jaffe, director of the Levant Fair, who emphasized that the economic potential and the favourable economic conditions in Palestine had not yet been fully exploited by Warsaw.[54]

Whereas commercial exchanges between Poland and its European partners were decreasing, relations with countries outside Europe flourished.[55] After a temporary drop by approximately 53 per cent in 1936, the import of Polish products to Palestine began to stabilize, reaching £419,709 in 1938 (see Table 1).[56] In 1937 Poland ranked seventh among Palestine's suppliers.

Throughout the interwar years capital continued to flow from Poland to Palestine. This state of affairs met with fierce opposition from the right-wing Endeks. Although they were in favour of the Palestine project, viewing it as a means of realizing their primary goal, 'the dejudaization of Poland', their principal organ, *Dziennik Narodowy*, attacked what it described as the irretrievable withdrawal of large sums of capital from Poland by the Jews. The daily claimed that approximately 37 per cent of the capital brought into Palestine in 1936 came from Poland, against only 34 per cent from Nazi Germany. In this way, *Dziennik Narodowy* reinforced the prejudices of the ethno-nationalist segments of Poland's population. The *Palestine Post* commented:

The Endek organ chooses to forget the large sums sent from Palestine to Poland in support of relatives left behind, over ten million zlotys in 1935 alone, and the fact that during 1935

Polish exports to Palestine aggregated 14,398,000 zlotys against only 4,026,000 zlotys for Palestinian exports to Poland . . . Palestine is becoming one of Poland's most important markets, which will be lost if the Endek journal's suggestion is carried out, that Polish Jews should be allowed out of Poland—but their money left behind [57]

Polish currency restrictions did succeed in reducing the export of capital to Palestine, but the clearing agreement that came into force in May 1937 made such capital transfers easier.[58] A few months earlier Fishel Rotenstreich had come to Warsaw to discuss the terms of the agreement.[59] An expert on economic issues and a former member of the Polish senate Budget Commission, Rotenstreich, like Grünbaum, a prominent Zionist leader and former member of the Sejm, expressed reservations about the clearing agreement with Poland. In his July 1936 column for *Haaretz* he commented:

Since we want to enable Polish Jews to immigrate into Palestine, we are compelled to agree to such arrangements, which we would not do under different conditions. This does not mean that we accept all conditions and demands . . . We are prepared to purchase Polish goods, only if Polish dumping remains limited by the rules of competition, as it was formerly . . . Thanks to us, the Polish government has established commercial relations with the countries of the Middle East, and without our assistance these relations would not have taken concrete form. We, the Jews, and Jews from Poland in particular, contributed to the economic expansion of this Poland . . . If the Jews, emigrants from Poland are, to a great extent, in favour of Polish exports, we also have a right to demand a proper approach from the Polish government.[60]

Eventually, in January 1937, after long negotiations between the Polish Ministry of Foreign Affairs and the directorate of the Jewish Agency, the transfer agreement was signed. Overall, it was supposed to follow the pattern of the transfer agreement signed with Germany in 1933, and particular attention was given to the export of Jewish capital to Palestine. In accordance with the document, prospective Jewish emigrants were allowed to export their capital up to the value of £1,000, in the form of Polish goods which they were obliged to purchase. In contrast to the one with Germany, this agreement was supposed to be reciprocal and to provide a long-term basis for commercial exchange between Poland and the Yishuv. After the opening of a clearing office in May 1937 both imports and exports significantly increased.[61] As a result, before the outbreak of the Second World War Jewish emigrants deposited large sums in clearing banks in Poland which were then transferred to banks in Palestine. According to Maksymilian Friede, vice president of the Polish–Palestine Chamber of Commerce and Industry, the clearing agreement had a profound significance for commercial relations between the two countries.[62]

Although Palestine's export trade was relatively small in comparison with the value of its imports, its vitality and expansionist character made it of great importance. Throughout the interwar period the United Kingdom was Palestine's biggest supplier, while Palestine's exports also mainly went to the United Kingdom. Poland was far behind, with imports from Palestine mostly unchanged at around £17,000 at the beginning of the 1930s.[63] In 1933 Palestine imported Polish goods to the total value of £289,718, and in exchange sent goods to Poland of the value of £15,122. As the figures suggest, the balance of trade was distinctly favourable to Poland throughout the interwar years. The huge discrepancy can be explained by the specific nature of Palestine's international trade. In accordance with British Mandate provisions, all members of the League of Nations as well as the United States benefited from the same rights concerning trade in goods with Palestine. Palestine was therefore disqualified from imposing protective tariffs or practising compensatory trade.[64]

Over the next few years, Palestine's exporters initiated various export-promoting activities.[65] Within influential circles in Palestine the Polish market was seen as very important and of great potential.[66] It was hoped that Poland would became a major customer for Palestine's products. The Zionist leadership in the mid-1930s argued that 'Poland could greatly assist the Jewish work in Palestine by fostering the increased importation of Palestinian products'.[67] As Moshe Shertok put it in 1935:

Certain alleviations have recently been granted in this respect but much still remains to be done under this head and we have every confidence that Polish sympathy for our work in Palestine will in growing measure find expression in the absorption of the products of Palestinian agriculture and industry.[68]

Export-promoting initiatives succeeded in achieving their goals. As indicated in Table 2, Palestine's exports to Poland increased more than fourfold between 1934 and 1935. These developments were largely attributed to the relatively strong state of Palestine's economy, close commercial co-operation between the authorities in Warsaw and the Yishuv, and the increased quota for the import of citrus fruit from Palestine permitted by the Polish government.

Table 2 Exports from Palestine, 1932–1938

Year	Exports £	Exports to Poland £	%
1932	2,381,491	16,499	0.7
1933	2,591,617	15,122	0.6
1934	3,217,562	31,990	1.0
1935	4,215,486	122,245	2.9
1936	3,500,000[a]	136,406	3.9
1937	5,800,000[a]	135,406	2.3
1938	5,000,000[a]	133,981	2.7

Source: P. Waserman, 'Rozwój gospodarki palestyńskiej w roku 1934', Palestyna i Bliski Wschód, 1935, no. 1, pp. 2–12: 10; Department of Customs, Excise and Trade (Palestine), Annual Report for the Year 1936 (Jerusalem, 1936), 54–5; id., Annual Report for the Year 1939 (Jerusalem, 1939), 45–6, 54.

[a] Approximate figures.

Growing Interest in the Zionist National Project

The Zionist project attracted considerable interest among political activists and publicists affiliated with the Sanacja regime. Polish consuls repeatedly visited settlements established by Jewish immigrants, expressing their satisfaction at the rapid progress made by Zionists in Palestine and at the substantial role that Jews from Poland played in it.[69] Among the Sanacja elite, Polish Jews were seen as 'builders of Palestine'. With great respect and interest it was observed how Zionists were building their national homeland and developing both industry and agriculture. According to Antoni Paprocki, head of the Research Section of the Ministry of Foreign Affairs:

The Jews with their persistence, work, and capital turn the wasteland into flourishing areas. The sphere of Jewish influence is moving from the sea to the east and is gradually encompassing a large part of the territory of Palestine, which suggests that this process cannot be slowed down and even in the event of fierce political resistance this Jewish sphere of influence will take over Palestine, first economically, then politically.[70]

It was frequently emphasized that enhanced economic co-operation between the two countries was based on strong ideological foundations. Marian Turski, director of the State Export Institute, wrote:

We are fully aware both in Poland and in Palestine that the ideological basis for economic co-operation between our countries is much broader than with other countries. Our co-operation is the result of much more than merely economics. The commercial relationship between Poland and Palestine does not stem solely from economic circumstances . . . the fact is that the question of Palestine's revival arouses universal interest in Poland and Palestine's exports are particularly popular. This is the result of much deeper causes.[71]

The government press expressed its admiration for both the urban and rural development of the Yishuv. Attention was also given to the creation of educational institutions and the change in profile of Jewish emigrants from Poland. B. Mohuczy, a correspondent for *Gazeta Polska*, who travelled on the *Polonia* in October 1933, described emigrants travelling on board. 'All of them were passionate and full of hope. There were many with secondary education qualifications, many students who had dropped out of universities and headed to Palestine to work the land.'[72] All these developments, both ideological and socio-economic, led the editors of *Gazeta Polska* to conclude: 'Jewish Palestine serves as the best evidence that prosperity produced by the application of science and diligence can reshape a land that was badly neglected for many generations.'[73]

The numerous articles on Mandatory Palestine in the Polish press suggest that the Palestine question attracted not only official but also public attention in the 1930s. In the early spring of 1933 Ksawery Pruszyński, a young and promising Polish publicist, travelled to Palestine as a correspondent of Vilna's maverick conservative journal *Słowo*, edited by Stanisław Cat-Mackiewicz, in order to trace the sociopolitical prospects of the 'new Jewish Palestine'.[74] His detailed and highly sympathetic reportage addressed to the general Polish public was subsequently published in *Słowo*. Its huge nationwide success, along with the increased interest of Polish elites in the Yishuv, resulted in the publication of *Palestyna po raz trzeci*, which established enduring paradigms for Polish perceptions of Zionism.[75] While religious pilgrims gravitated to Palestine to visit the holy sites, others—mainly journalists and reporters —came to investigate the 'Zionist experiment' and the phenomenon of the 'new Jew', and to experience at first hand the development of the country.[76] The orientalist Bogdan Richter appraised the industrial and economic achievements of the Zionists —Haifa harbour, land acquisition, the Haifa–Mosul pipeline, and the rapid expansion of urban centres.[77] Józef Brodzki in *Kurjer Poranny* expressed his awe at the idealism of young Zionists, praising modern Tel Aviv, where 'Berlin's Kurfürstendamm Avenue could be found alongside Mała Ziemiańska [a Warsaw coffeehouse]'.[78] Interestingly, the political opposition to the Sanacja regime also shared the opinion that Poland should maintain close trade links with the Yishuv. Stanisław Stroński, a vocal opponent of Piłsudski affiliated with the right-wing *Stronnictwo Narodowe*, emphasized that commercial relations with Palestine would continue to improve since the governing elites of Poland were aware that Polish economic expansion to the Middle East was possible only through Palestine.[79]

Pro-Palestine Institutions and Initiatives

Establishing close commercial relations with the Yishuv would not have been possible without the assistance of professional institutions and committees. In September 1927 the State Export Institute was established, modelled on American and French commercial institutions. A subsequent step in developing economic links was the establishment of the Polish–Palestine Chamber of Commerce and Industry in Warsaw, its sister organization in Tel Aviv, and the Polish–Palestine Bank of Warsaw. The chambers of commerce served as particular intermediaries in business contacts between Polish and Palestinian entrepreneurs. The number of proposals and offers clearly suggests that merchants in both Poland and Palestine were greatly interested in mutual trade. Michael Rozenzweig, a former Polish citizen, opened the Palestine and Near East Trading House in Tel Aviv and approached the Polish–Palestine Chamber of Commerce and Industry in 1932, which provided him with detailed information about Polish firms willing to export their products to the Middle East. Another Jewish immigrant from Poland asked the chamber to provide connections with Poland's biggest meat producers. Interestingly and surprisingly, his aim was to export 'Polish ham to the Middle East'.[80] General Gustaw Orlicz-Dreszer, who had promoted the development of the Polish merchant marine in close co-operation with Nahum Sokołow, and Zdzisław Lubomirski initiated the establishment of a pro-Palestine section within the Polish Maritime and Colonial League.[81] In early 1934, after two years of negotiation between Polish officials and Sokołow, the Pro-Palestine Committee was founded in Warsaw.[82] The opening session took place in the Polish senate in January 1934 in the presence of many prominent politicians and representatives of the army and universities.

According to its programme, the committee aimed at the promotion of Jewish national endeavours in Palestine throughout Poland. Among its members were prominent representatives of Polish political and intellectual elites—Orlicz-Dreszer, Tadeusz Schaetzel, Tadeusz Gwiazdowski, Antoni Ossendowski, Zofia Nałkowska, and others. The crucial support of the Polish Ministry of Foreign Affairs was reinforced by the membership of former foreign minister August Zaleski, and the undersecretary of state, Jan Szembek. This long list of influential personalities, representing every shade of politics and ideology, reflected Poland's ongoing support for Jewish national aspirations in Palestine. Prince Lubomirski, in the inaugural speech, emphasized that Poland shared pro-Zionist sympathies since 'Palestine was a fulfilment of Jewish dreams about a state of their own'. Sokołow, in turn, expressed the hope that the establishment of the committee would 'solidify Poland's sincere approval for Jewish national development'. He continued: 'Jewish Palestine has faith in Poland, because the Second Polish Republic embraces national idealism in harmony with human idealism'.[83] The establishment of the committee was seen as the result of effective Zionist propaganda activities in Poland and the sympathy of Polish officials towards Jewish national aspirations in 'the new Palestine'.[84] The publicist Samuel Stendig saw its establishment as 'a sign of the development of the political thinking of the Polish government and its particular interest in the Jewish national ideology'.[85] Jakub Appenszlak described the establishment of the committee as a result of 'the powerful, organic connection between the new Poland and the new Palestine'.[86] As the main instrument for promoting Poland's policy towards the Yishuv domestically, the committee argued that Warsaw's political and economic interests were best served by acting in favour of Zionism and the Jewish colonization of Palestine.

A crucial role in stimulating commercial exchange was also played by the Polish–Palestine Chamber of Commerce and Industry, whose local branches served as intermediaries in business contacts between Polish and Palestinian entrepreneurs. Over the interwar period, its chamber in Warsaw, along with the local branches in Łódź and Poznań, had 385 permanent members, while its sister organization in Palestine had over 82. The number and nature of its departments, which dealt with trade, fairs and exhibitions, emigration, tourism, the press, and fiduciary matters—clearly reflect its extensive activity. It took numerous initiatives seeking to improve trade connections between Poland and the Yishuv, the great majority of which were subsidized by the Polish Ministry of Industry and Trade. The chamber's executive and members regularly participated in international conferences and met with the leading politicians in Poland. In consequence Jewish companies in both Poland and Palestine could take advantage of the widespread opportunities for promotion, including trade fairs and commercial missions. From the Zionists' point of view, the institution thus played a crucial role in promoting *totseret ha'arets* (products of the Land of Israel).

To facilitate currency exchange between Poland and Palestine the PKO, one of the largest Polish banks, established a branch in Tel Aviv. As its circulation of capital rose—in 1934 this amounted to £300,000—it decided to establish a branch in Haifa.[87] According to the official figures from 1935, former Polish citizens who had emigrated to Palestine sent £387,000 to their relatives in Poland via the branch in Tel Aviv.[88] Unfortunately, there is no precise data as to what proportion of the private capital of Polish Jews was transferred to Palestine between the two world wars.

Transportation Facilities and Levant Fairs

The growth of economic relations between Poland and Palestine brought with it, as noted at the beginning of this chapter, the need to improve transport facilities between the two countries. In 1933 Polish Jews in Palestine complained that the Romanian shipping services were not sufficiently frequent and that the establishment of a direct and cheap steamship connection along with transport by air was necessary.[89] At the beginning of 1932, when commercial exchanges between Poland and the Middle East and emigration to Palestine began to increase, the Polish authorities initiated direct negotiations with the Jewish Agency in order to establish a new passenger service between Constanţa and Haifa. Soon afterwards, the idea was endorsed by the State Export Institute as 'a significant improvement of Polish-Levantine freight transportation'.[90]

Facilitated by an agreement between the Polish government and the Immigration Department of the Jewish Agency, the *Polonia* service, the first voyage of which I have already described, was mainly used by passengers. However, as Mieczysław Fularski, chairman of the Maritime and Colonial League, asserted, 'the inclusion of the *Polonia* in the Polish Romanian Levantine environment will lead to an increase in the exchange of goods'.[91] Indeed, the establishment of the first national deep-sea service to Palestine was proof that the Polish authorities were keenly interested both in enhancing export to the region and in the establishment of close relations with the emerging Jewish polity.[92] The ship was the largest on the Constanţa–Haifa route. Launching this line was the result of the unarguable success of Polish diplomacy in the region. Between September 1933 and November 1934 *Polonia* carried 21,462 people. Overall, in 1933 she made six trips between Constanţa and Palestine's ports with a total cargo of 27,114 tonnes.[93] In the following year, the number of trips increased to twenty-four, with a total cargo of 108,456 tonnes. Along with the renewed flow of migration to Palestine, it was clear to the Jewish Agency that existing rail and shipping services were insufficient to cope with the growing number of passengers.[94] In October 1935, as Jewish emigration was about to reach its peak, a second Polish vessel, the SS *Kościuszko*, able to carry 700 passengers, was transferred to the route. Both ships sailed regularly once a fortnight between Constanţa and the ports of Palestine until the beginning of 1936, when the *Kościuszko* was withdrawn from service. In October 1936 the *Polonia* was also withdrawn; however, the Ministry of

Foreign Affairs decided to resume its operation due to its political importance and pressure from Zionists. The *Polonia* returned to service in spring 1937.[95]

At the same time, a project for an air service between Poland and Lydda (Lod) airport was initiated. Samuel Stendig emphasized that establishing a regular air link between the two countries was necessary to facilitate economic transactions (in particular by facilitating postal communication) and to encourage exports. It was also suggested that air transport might serve up to 10 per cent of the total number of passengers travelling between Poland and Palestine.[96] Eventually, in April 1937, the Polish LOT service started to operate flights between Warsaw and Lydda, the fourth air service from Palestine. The flight, with refuelling stops in Lwów, Bucharest, Sofia, Thessaloniki, Athens, and Rhodes, took approximately twenty-seven hours.[97] This regular service not only improved passenger transport but also provided a basis for further development of commercial relations. As Palestine ranked second in the world in the quantity of postal traffic with Poland, the establishing of air transport was significant. Planes were supposed to carry mail three times a week to a number of places: Poland, Russia, Latvia, Lithuania, Estonia, Finland, Bulgaria, Romania, Turkey, Greece, Yugoslavia, and Rhodes.[98] Since the question of transportation was of paramount importance, the establishment of these new routes was seen as an international success. In Stendig's words, 'whereas the Consulates in Tel Aviv and Jerusalem represent the Second Polish Republic in Palestine and the Levant, [SS *Polonia*] became an unofficial Polish "consul" at sea for the south-east'.[99]

Since the quantity of imported goods to Middle Eastern countries totalled over £80,000,000 every year, Polish entrepreneurs sought new opportunities to enlarge the sphere of their commercial activity. Because of the progress of colonization and the development of suburban and rural areas, exports to Palestine steadily increased in volume.[100] The Levant Fair organized from 1926 onwards was supposed to serve as a platform for European manufacturers and exporters to establish and enhance their commercial relations with Middle Eastern partners. These fairs aimed at 'restoring to the Near East the economic status it enjoyed in ancient times'. Over time, however, Arabs began to boycott them, viewing them as a British Jewish initiative.[101] Although Arab participation was decreasing, the Polish government continued to see the events as providing a significant economic stimulus.

The Exhibition and Trade Fair held in April 1932 in Tel Aviv was planned on a far larger scale than the previous event, which had a local rather than an international scope. Siegfried Hoofien, president of the Jaffa and District Chamber of Commerce, emphasized that 'the development of these Fairs as a permanent institution may open up for Jaffa and Tel Aviv a new vista and give them new significance in the life of the Near East generally as the appropriate meeting ground between the commerce of the East and West'.[102] The fair was indeed a great success, attracting dozens of foreign participants and making Tel Aviv into a commercial centre of the Middle East.

The Polish authorities developed a keen interest in the event. Since Palestine had become a crucial trade area, participation in the fair was seen as a special opportunity to develop commercial relations with Middle Eastern partners. Ferdynand Zarzycki, the Polish minister of industry and commerce, expressed his hope 'that the Levant Fair will contribute to the intensification of commercial and cultural relations between Poland and the countries of the Near East'.[103] Thus intensive activities were undertaken by the Polish–Palestine Chamber of Commerce and Industry in close cooperation with the Ministry of Industry and Trade, the Ministry of Foreign Affairs, and the Association of Industrial and Trade Chambers in order to prepare the Polish pavilion. Lewi Lewin-Epstein became the honorary representative of the fair, for which tickets could be bought in the Palestine office of the Jewish Agency in Warsaw. Special facilities were afforded for visitors from central and east European countries: Polish railways for instance offered fare reductions of 25 per cent and a reduction of 50 per cent on freight.[104]

The Levant Fair was the first far-reaching attempt to promote Polish goods in the Middle East. Forty-seven Polish companies, representing over thirty sectors and industries, displayed their products at the 1932 fair. The 1934 fair provided the opportunity to celebrate the twenty-fifth anniversary of the founding of Tel Aviv, and attracted 227 firms from Poland, which was the fourth-largest exhibitor after Palestine, the United Kingdom, and France.[105] For this purpose, the Polish–Palestine Chamber of Commerce and Industry built a 400 square metre brick pavilion, along with two other provisional show pavilions. Overall, over 1,000 square metres were given to Polish entrepreneurs, representing chiefly textiles, chemicals, and the food industry.[106] The central pavilion was almost entirely dedicated to public and government institutions. Among the exhibitors were the PKO bank and the Polish Overseas Mercantile Society. Gdynia-America Shipping Lines and the Polish harbour authorities were also given display stands. Until 1934 the fair was mainly informative in character, but the 1936 fair was devoted to the acquisition of new customers. On this occasion, as at earlier fairs, Polish exhibitors were offered free transport for their goods from Poland to Palestine, and the Polish pavilion was one of the most interesting and best organized.[107]

The event had not only a commercial but also a political character and accordingly attracted tourists, entrepreneurs, and influential figures from Poland.[108] The significant involvement of Polish elites in the event clearly indicates the importance of Jewish Palestine in Polish economic policy. According to Stanisław Świsłocki, a Polish Jewish journalist, 'the Levant Fair could act as a stimulus to further economic exchange between Poland and Palestine'.[109] *Der moment*, for its part, wrote about the possibilities of Poland acquiring new markets and expanding economically into the Middle East.

Conclusion

Throughout the interwar period, migration to Palestine continued to be a highly important economic force. Jewish emigrants' ties to Poland not only had an important impact in fostering bilateral trade links but also significantly shaped Polish officials' perceptions of Palestine and consequently of Zionism. Being aware of the scale of

Polish Jewish emigration to Palestine, the Sanacja elites maintained close relations with the leadership of the Yishuv on the assumption that the two sides shared a set of common interests. As this chapter has demonstrated, this point of view was characteristic of Sanacja ideology between 1926 and 1935. In the eyes of the governing elites, Polish Jews, because of their knowledge of the language, familiarity with local products, and business contacts, were in a position to establish successful companies exporting Polish merchandise. Co-operation with emerging Jewish Palestine became an unparalleled opportunity, not only to enhance Polish exports but also to promote national products in the region. According to this perception, Polish Jews who sought to establish a state of their own in the Land of Israel were invaluable as pioneers for Polish commercial expansion in the Middle East.

Given their significance to Polish political and economic life, Jewish emigration and Polish–Palestine relations became vital questions in the interwar years. Members of successive Polish cabinets and prominent publicists observed with admiration the political and economic development of Jewish Palestine. Since the Zionists were seen as having brought prosperity to this backward former Ottoman province, co-operation with them became a matter of strategic importance for Poland. Existing evidence clearly suggests that the cultivation of commercial relations between Poland and the Yishuv developed over the interwar period and became an integral part of Poland's trade policy at the beginning of 1930s. Apart from wide-ranging diplomatic activity, the Sanacja elites embarked on an extensive campaign to promote commercial exchange between the two countries. In the eyes of the Polish authorities, the Yishuv was an important political partner, while co-operation with the Zionists also created unparalleled economic opportunities.

Notes

1 'Sherut aniyah polani le'erets yisra'el', *Do'ar hayom*, 26 July 1933, p. 1.
2 'Polonyah: erets yisra'el vepolin', *Davar*, 3 Oct. 1933, p. 4.
3 W. Berkelhammer, 'Pod polską banderą do żydowskich brzegów…', *Nowy Dziennik*, 10 Oct. 1933, p. 2.
4 W. Filochowski, *Ziemia dwakroć obiecana: Notatki z podróży do Palestyny* (Pelplin, 1937), 40–1.
5 'Polonyah'.
6 'Celebrated on SS the Polonia', *Palestine Post*, 2 Oct. 1933, p. 5.
7 'Polish–Palestine Steam-Ship Service Opened', *Palestine Post*, 2 Oct. 1933, p. 5.
8 It is estimated that over 80 per cent of territories subsequently included in the Second Polish Republic had been affected by the destruction of the First World War, upsetting its socio-economic infrastructure from the very beginning (B. Slay, *The Polish Economy: Crisis, Reform, and Transformation* (Princeton, NJ, 1994), 14).
9 J. Łazor, *Brama na Bliski Wschód: Polsko-palestyńskie stosunki gospodarcze w okresie międzywojennym* (Warsaw, 2016), 151–4.
10 D. Gurevich, *Statistical Handbook of Jewish Palestine* (Jerusalem, 1947), 18.
11 J. Metzer, *The Divided Economy of Mandatory Palestine* (Cambridge, 1998), 11, 19.

12 K. Grunwald, 'Foreign Trade of Palestine in 1925', *Palestine and Near East Economic Magazine*, 1 (1925), 126–34: 126–8.
13 The 'open-door' provision was set forth in article 18 of the Mandate for Palestine: 'The Mandatory shall see that there is no discrimination in Palestine against the nationals of any State Member of the League of Nations ... as compared with those of the Mandatory or of any foreign State in matters concerning taxation, commerce or navigation, the exercise of industries or professions, or in the treatment of merchant vessels or civil aircraft. Similarly, there shall be no discrimination in Palestine against goods originating in or destined for any of the said States, and there shall be freedom of transit under equitable conditions across the mandated area.

Subject as aforesaid and to the other provisions of this mandate, the Administration of Palestine may, on the advice of the Mandatory, impose such taxes and customs duties as it may consider necessary, and take such steps as it may think best to promote the development of the natural resources of the country and to safeguard the interests of the population. It may also, on the advice of the Mandatory, conclude a special customs agreement with any State the territory of which in 1914 was wholly included in Asiatic Turkey or Arabia' (League of Nations, *Mandate for Palestine*, British Command Paper 1785 (Dec. 1922), art. 18; see D. Danon, *Israel: The Will to Prevail* (New York, 2012), 197).
14 C. Issawi, *An Economic History of the Middle East and North Africa* (New York, 1982), 16–17, 83.
15 Archiwum Akt Nowych, Warsaw (hereafter AAN), 438/21: Protokoły posiedzeń Rady Ministrów Rzeczypospolitej Polskiej, 14 Feb. 1923.
16 AAN, Konsulat Generalny Rzeczypospolitej Polskiej w Nowym Jorku, 493/274: Akt ustanawiający etatowy konsulat I klasy RP w Jerozolimie, Warszawa, 16 Mar. 1923; 'Akt ustanawiający etatowy konsulat I klasy RP w Jerozolimie', *Dziennik Urzędowy MSZ*, 5 (1923), 68; Protokoły posiedzeń Rady Ministrów Rzeczypospolitej Polskiej, 14 Feb. 1923.
17 'Polish Consul to Cooperate with the Jewish Agency', *Jewish Telegraphic Agency*, 31 May 1923.
18 J. Adamkiewicz, *Stan gospodarczy Palestyny w 1923 roku* (Warsaw, 1924), 25.
19 Z. Landau and J. Tomaszewski, *Gospodarka Drugiej Rzeczypospolitej* (Warsaw, 1991), 226–34.
20 J. Łazor, *Brama na Bliski Wschód: Polsko-palestyńskie stosunki gospodarcze w okresie międzywojennym* (Warsaw, 2016), 154; J. Tomaszewski, 'Druga Rzeczpospolita wobec Palestyny', *Almanach Żydowski*, 16 (1999–2000), 7–17: 10.
21 Given that Poland was one of the 'cheapest countries in the world, authorities in Warsaw expected that extensive export promotion would bring about a reduction of prices in Palestine. [Zbyszewski] believes that the two countries can help each other. Poland can export to Palestine timber, cement, agricultural and textile products, while Palestine can export to Poland fruits: particularly oranges and wine' ('Polish Consul on Palestine-Polish Relations', *Palestine Bulletin*, 25 May 1927, p. 3).
22 After a few months the Polish diplomatic post was moved to Tel Aviv. This was requested by Bernard Hausner who pointed to the economic importance of the Polish Jewish community in the city and Jaffa port (AAN, Ambasada Rzeczypospolitej Polskiej w Londynie (hereafter ARPL), 1213/84–5, 87: Titus Zbyszewski, letters to Ministry of Foreign Affairs, 10 Jan., 2 Feb. 1928; 1213/88–9: Ministry of Foreign Affairs, letter to Konstanty Skirmunt, 28 Feb. 1928; 1213/11: Tomaszewski, 'Druga Rzeczpospolita Polska wobec Palestyny').
23 'Sjonista konsulem Rzeczytpospolitej Polskiej', *Nasz Głos*, 27 May 1927, p. 3; see 'Pierwszy żyd konsulem Rzplej Polskiej', *Rzeczpospolita*, 13 May 1927, p. 1; 'Sjonista konsulem Polski',

Głos Wileński, 3 July 1927, p. 1; 'Żydzi w Polsce', *Kurjer Warszawski*, 29 June 1927, p. 16; 'Hatsir hausner: konsul hapolani batel-aviv', *Hatsefira*, 12 May 1927, p. 2.

24 'Appointment of Deputy to Palestine Consular Service Widely Commented on in Poland', *The Sentinel*, 10 June 1927, p. 16.

25 Within Warsaw political circles Hausner was well known for his deep engagement in strengthening economic bonds between Poland and Jewish Palestine. In late 1926, for instance, he initiated a wide-ranging campaign, promoting the export of textile goods manufactured in Łódź to Palestine and from there to other countries of the Middle East ('Sprawy palestyńskie: O rozszerzenie eksportu towarów łódzkich do Palestyny', *Nasz Przegląd*, 15 Sept. 1927, p. 5).

26 'News Brief: Interview with Dr. Bernard Hausner, Lemberg, 16 May 1927', *Jewish Telegraphic Agency*, 2 June 1927.

27 According to Jerzy Łazor, Titus Zbyszewski's irritation was motivated by the fact that he was not consulted about the appointment of Bernard Hausner. In addition, the post in Haifa was supposed to be fully autonomous (Łazor, *Brama na Bliski Wschód*, 96; AAN, ARPL, 500/48–9: Titus Zbyszewski, letter to Ministry of Foreign Affairs, 2 Aug. 1927).

28 'Handel polsko-palestyński: Konferencja w C.Z.K. w sprawie eksportu do Palestyny', *Przegląd Handlowy*, 7 Sept. 1928, pp. 5–6; AAN, Ministerstwo Spraw Zagranicznych (hereafter MSZ), 10039/2: T. Zbyszewski, report on political situation in Palestine, 8 Jan. 1929.

29 In 1925 the Ministry of Foreign Affairs had published a circular obliging Polish diplomatic missions abroad to promote all initiatives aiming to enhance export through emigration ('Okólnik z dn. 3.09.1925 r. w sprawie wyzyskiwania emigracji dla celów ekspansji gospodarczej', *Biuletyn Urzędu Emigracyjnego*, 1925, nos. 9–11, 56–7: 56).

30 S. Głąbiński, *Emigracja i jej rola w gospodarstwie narodowem* (Warsaw, 1931), 16.

31 In 1931 immigrants from Poland constituted 20 per cent of the total Jewish population of Palestine, amounting to 35,775 people. Over the next five years their number rose to between 40 and 50 per cent.

32 T. Nieduszyński, 'Palestyna – nasz czołowy rynek zamorski', *Palestyna i Bliski Wschód*, 1936, no. 4, pp. 197–200: 199.

33 Central Zionist Archives, Jerusalem (hereafter CZA), S25/5742, fos. 44–50: copy of E. J. Kirschenbaum, letter to Polish Ministry of Foreign Affairs, Apr. 1933, enclosed with S25/5742, fo. 39: E. J. Kirschenbaum, letter to Political Department of Jewish Agency, 20 July 1933; S25/5742, fos. 40–3: English translation of E. J. Kirschenbaum, letter to Polish Ministry of Foreign Affairs, Apr. 1933, enclosed with Kirschenbaum, letter to Political Department of Jewish Agency, 20 July 1933.

34 M. Friede, 'Palestyna jako brama wypadowa na Bliski i Środkowy Wschód', *Palestyna i Bliski Wschód*, 1937, no. 5–6, pp. 192–3; S. Standig, 'Brama wypadowa na Bliski Wschód', *Lektura*, 18 Mar. 1934, p. 2.

35 Waldemar Paruch distinguished two phases in the development of Sanacja attitudes to national minorities. The first phase, 'state consolidation' (*konsolidacja państwowa*), lasted from 1926 to 1935, the second, 'national consolidation' (*konsolidacja narodowa*), was implemented after Piłsudski's death and lasted from 1935 to 1939. During the state consolidation phase, the Sanacja regime did not perceive emigration as an end in itself but rather as a complementary process to assimilation; during the national consolidation phase assimilation lost its appeal amongst the Sanacja elites (see W. Paruch, *Od konsolidacji państwowej do konsolidacji narodowej: Mniejszości narodowe w myśli politycznej obozu piłsudczykowskiego (1926–1939)* (Lublin, 1997), 24–35).

36 Ł. T. Sroka and M. Sroka, *Polskie korzenie Izraela: Wprowadzenie do tematu; Wybór źródeł* (Kraków, 2015), 309–21.

37 In 1927 Polish diplomats throughout the Middle East pointed out that Jewish immigrants from Poland and Russia were keenly concerned with developing commercial relations between Poland and Palestine (AAN, ARPL, 290–2: reports submitted by Polish diplomatic posts in the Middle East, 1927; 1213/87: Titus Zbyszewski, letter to the Ministry of Foreign Affairs, 2 Feb. 1928).
38 CZA, S25/2262-7: Moshe Shertok, letter to Stanley Philipson, editor of *Codzienna Gazeta Handlowa*, 2 July 1935.
39 H. Strasburger, 'O właściwą politykę gospodarczą Polski wobec Palestyny', *Palestyna i Bliski Wschód*, 1936, no. 4, p. 13.
40 J. Appenszlak, 'Misterje polsko-palestyńskie', *Lektura*, 14 Jan. 1934, p. 1.
41 e.g. L. Lewite, 'Palestyna i Bliski Wschód', *Palestyna i Bliski Wschód*, 1932, no. 1, pp. 2–3; id., 'Palestyna z punktu widzenia polskiej ekspansji gospodarczej', *Palestyna i Bliski Wschód*, 1934, nos. 4–5, pp. 11–13.
42 Landau and Tomaszewski, *Gospodarka Drugiej Rzeczypospolitej*, 239.
43 G. Załęcki, *O polską politykę zamorską* (Warsaw, 1929), 6.
44 F. Rotenstreich, 'O fachową politykę gospodarczą w Palestynie', *Palestyna i Bliski Wschód*, 1932, no. 3, pp. 142–6: 142.
45 L. Lewite, 'Żydzi z Polski – budowniczymi Palestyny', *Palestyna i Bliski Wschód*, 1933, no. 7, pp. 370–2.
46 S. Jaffe, 'Widoki rozwoju polsko-palestyńskich stosunków handlowych', *Palestyna i Bliski Wschód*, 1935, no. 3, pp. 130–9: 130.
47 'W sprawie obrotu polsko-palestyńskiego', *Gazeta Polska*, 17 Aug. 1930, p. 7.
48 Archiwum Państwowe w Poznaniu, 53/707 Izba Przemysłowo – Handlowa w Poznaniu, Stosunki z Palestyną, 773/3: Palestinian–Polish Chamber of Commerce and Industry in Tel Aviv to the Polish–Palestine Chamber of Commerce and Industry in Poznań, 26 Jan. 1930.
49 'Polish Government Subscribes £1,000 Towards Share Capital of Palestine Poland Immigrant Bank', *Jewish Telegraphic Agency*, 23 Jan. 1931.
50 *Rocznik Handlu Zagranicznego Rzeczypospolitej Polskiej i Wolnego Miasta Gdańska 1935* (Warsaw, 1936), 10–11; Landau and Tomaszewski, *Gospodarka Drugiej Rzeczypospolitej*, 388–91.
51 J. Tomaszewski, 'Bojkot towarów niemieckich w Polsce w latach 1933–1935', *Acta Oeconomica Pragensia*, 7 (2007), 448–59.
52 AAN, MSZ, 1572/2: 'Materiały na 90-te posiedzenie Ligi Narodów, Dr T. Lubaczewski, Raport o współpracy gospodarczej z Palestyną', 11 Jan. 1936.
53 L. Lewite, 'Znaczenie i rola Targów Lewantyńskich w Tel-Awiwie dla ekspansji gospodarczej Polski', *Palestyna i Bliski Wschód*, 1936, no. 1, pp. 2–5.
54 S. Jaffe, 'Zadania Targów Lewantyńskich, ich rozwój i znaczenie', *Palestyna i Bliski Wschód*, 1936, no. 4, pp. 207–10.
55 This tendency was remarked on by Henryk Floyar-Rajchman, who served as minister for trade and industry between 1934 and 1935. At a meeting of the Sejm budget committee, he emphasized that in 1934 Poland's trade with the Middle East increased significantly (Landau and Tomaszewski, *Gospodarka Drugiej Rzeczypospolitej*, 389–90).
56 The decline of 1936 was partially caused by the tense international situation. The Italian invasion and conquest of Ethiopia caused panic among exporters, and the political situation in Palestine had a negative impact on the flow of trade. As Stanisław Łukaszewicz, the consul in Tel Aviv, reported to his colleagues in Warsaw, several Polish companies decided to stop the further dispatch of their products. Moreover, the Polish government

decided to introduce currency restrictions in mutual exchange, which had a particularly adverse impact on trade (AAN, MSZ, 6274/136: Stanisław Łukaszewicz, letter to the State Export Institute, 21 Oct. 1935).

57 'Polish Palestine Trade Heavily in Poland's Favour', *Palestine Post*, 1 Apr. 1936, p. 11. In 1935 one pound sterling was worth 26 zlotys. The Palestine Jews, therefore, transferred around £400,000 to support their relatives in Poland in 1935.

58 *Bulletin of the Economic Research Institute of the Jewish Agency for Palestine*, 1 (1937), 7.

59 'Polish-Palestine Transfer', *Palnews*, 8 Sept. 1936, p. 4.

60 F. Rotenstreich, 'Musagim yatsivim', *Haaretz*, 2 July 1936, p. 2.

61 'Chamber of Commerce: Stimulating Effect on Trade', *Palestine Post*, 24 Dec. 1937, p. 8.

62 Friede, 'Palestyna jako brama wypadowa na Bliski i Środkowy Wschód'.

63 'Trade in 1932', *Palestine and Near East Economic Magazine*, 8 (1933), 184–5: 184.

64 P. Waserman, 'Rozwój gospodarki palestyńskiej w roku 1934', *Palestyna i Bliski Wschód*, 1935, no. 1, pp. 2–12: 10.

65 'Current Topics: Agriculture', *Palestine and Near East Economic Magazine*, 8 (1933), 125–6: 125.

66 I. Benari, 'Continental Markets for Jaffa Oranges', *Palestine and Near East Economic Magazine*, 4 (1929), 47–8.

67 Moshe Shertok, letter to Stanley Philipson, 2 July 1935.

68 Ibid.

69 In June 1927 Zbyszewski paid a visit to Rishon LeZion and Benei Berak. During a banquet organized by the Organization of Polish Jews in Tel Aviv Zbyszewski expressed his delight at the rapid development of Tel Aviv and the prominent part the Polish Jews had played in it ('Bikur hakonsul hapolani heḥadash', *Davar*, 20 June 1927, p. 4).

70 AAN, MSZ, 1008/1–18: Problem palestyński, 1938.

71 M. Turski, 'Naturalne związki gospodarcze', *Palestyna i Bliski Wschód*, 1936, no. 4, pp. 194–5.

72 B. Mohuczy, 'Pod polską banderą do Palestyny', *Gazeta Polska*, 13 Oct. 1933, p. 3.

73 Although the semi-official organ of the government agreed that Jewish immigration to Palestine was advisable since the influx of foreign capital stimulated the economic development of the region, the newspaper also emphasized that it should serve the interests of both Jewish and Arab communities ('Kłopoty palestyńskie: Dlaczego Arabowie są niezadowoleni?', *Gazeta Polska*, 23 July 1930, p. 3).

74 As Adolf Bocheński, Pruszyński's close friend from neo-conservative circles, described him, 'he was not an ordinary tourist and not an ordinary reporter. He simply lived Palestine . . . He crossed the Jezreel Valley on foot, dug ditches through the swamps, helped penniless immigrants swim to the shore, every step of the way arguing hotly against the perils of communism and belligerent materialism. No, he was no ordinary tourist' (A. Bocheński, 'Palestyna po raz trzeci', *Słowo*, 7 Nov. 1933, p. 1).

75 K. Pruszyński, *Palestyna po raz trzeci* (Warsaw, 1933). The title, 'Palestine for the Third Time', refers to what Pruszyński saw as the third emergence of Palestine onto the world stage: the first occurred during the biblical period, the second during the Crusades.

76 Andrzej Strug wrote: 'I did not head for Palestine for tourist impressions and experiences . . . I went there because I simply wanted to encounter all these things I had read about before. I wanted to see for myself the transformation of Jewish people in Palestine, all spiritual changes and prevalent joy. I encountered all these things' (A. Strug, 'Renesans duszy żydowskiej', *Czarno na Białem*, 10 Apr. 1938, p. 7).

77 B. Richter, 'Skarbnica świata', *Gazeta Polska*, 1 Oct. 1933, p. 3; id., 'Skarbnica świata', *Trybuna Narodowa*, 5 Oct. 1933, p. 7.

78 J. Brodzki, 'Nowe miasto na prastarej ziemi', *Kurjer Poranny*, 18 Oct. 1933, p. 3. After returning from his trip to Palestine Brodzki wrote: 'In Kibbutz Ein Hahoresh, I saw both unusual people and their unusual work. With my own eyes I saw the advantages gained by them and the striking progress, which shaped the desert earth into fertile soil full of joy and wealth' (J. Brodzki, 'Przez pustynię do tych, co budują Nową Palestynę', *Kurjer Poranny*, 30 Oct. 1933, pp. 3, 7: 3).

79 'Poylens interes in a yidisher erets yisra'el', *Der moment*, 16 Jan. 1934, p. 4.

80 Archiwum Państwowe w Poznaniu, 53/707 'Izba Przemysłowo – Handlowa w Poznaniu', 772/16: Michael Rozenzweig, letter to the Polish-Palestine Chamber of Commerce, 20 Nov. 1932; see also 771–3: requests submitted from Palestine, 1930–1933.

81 The Maritime and Colonial League was founded in October 1930 and aimed to prepare the Polish market for the further development of exports and the exclusion of foreign middlemen. Before the outbreak of the Second World War it was one of the largest and most influential organizations in Poland. As a mass and social organization, the league aimed to educate Poles about maritime issues and develop the merchant fleet and navy and called for granting Poland overseas territories for settlement. See T. Białas, *Liga Morska i Kolonialna: 1930–1939* (Gdańsk, 1983).

82 Janusz Makarczyk, the first chairman of the committee, in an interview given to *Der moment* described the scope of the committee's activity and prerogatives in broad terms, ranging from information and advisory activities to organizing exhibitions and trips to Palestine. In February 1934, for instance, the committee asked the Jewish Agency to co-organize a trip of young Poles to Palestine in order to show that 'the flowering of the desert has resulted from a love of the homeland' ('Wycieczka polskich dzieci szkolnych do Palestyny', *Nowy Dziennik*, 28 Feb. 1934, p. 5; see 'Poylens interes in a yidisher erets yisra'el', *Der moment*, 27 Dec. 1933, p. 4; CZA, S25/1381-68: Janusz Makarczyk, letter to the Jewish Agency regarding Wiesław Czermiński travelling to Palestine, 3 Sep. 1934).

83 'Ukonstytuowanie się Komitetu Propalestyńskiego w Polsce', *5-ta Rano*, 9 Jan. 1934, p. 2; 'Mowa N. Sokołowa', *Gazeta Polska*, 9 Jan. 1934, p. 2.

84 See L. Lewite, 'Komitet Pro-Palestyna w Polsce', *Palestyna i Bliski Wschód*, 1934, no. 1, pp. 5–6; S. Stendig, *Polska a Palestyna: stosunki wzajemne w dobie obecnej* (Warsaw, 1935), 13–15; 'Polski Komitet Propalestyński', *Gazeta Polska*, 9 Jan. 1934, p. 2.

85 Stendig, *Polska a Palestyna w dobie obecnej*, 13–15.

86 Appenszlak, 'Misterje polsko-palestyńskie'.

87 The official ceremony took place in May 1933 and was attended by members of consular corps, prominent bankers, and business representatives. Addressing the gathering, the Polish consul reiterated Polish political and economic interest in the building-up of the Jewish national homeland in Palestine ('Polish Bank Opens in Tel Aviv', *Jewish Telegraphic Agency*, 15 May 1933).

88 'Palestine Residents Support Relatives in Poland', *Palestine Post*, 24 Mar. 1936, p. 5.

89 Kirschenbaum, letter to Polish Ministry of Foreign Affairs, 20 July 1933.

90 Łazor, *Brama na Bliski Wschód*, 130.

91 'Maritime and Colonial League and the Palestine Problem: Report of an Interview with Major M. Fularski', *Palestyna i Bliski Wschód*, 1934, nos. 4–5, pp. 13–14.

92 'Polonyah'; N., 'Polska-Lewant', *Gazeta Polska*, 25 Aug. 1935.

93 Department of Customs, Excise and Trade (Palestine), *Annual Report for the Year 1933* (Jerusalem, 1933), 106.

94 L. Lewite, 'W sprawie komunikacji lotniczej między Polską a Palestyną', *Palestyna i Bliski Wschód*, 1934, no. 10, pp. 370–3.

95 AAN, MSZ, 2508/118–21: Notatka z konferencji u dyrektora Dep. Morskiego MPiH w sprawie utrzymania linii palestyńskiej, Feb. 1937.
96 Stendig, *Polska a Palestyna w dobie obecnej*, 29.
97 'Rishmei masa polin', *Davar*, 7 July 1937, p. 2.
98 'Polish–Palestine Air Line Initiated', *Palestine Post*, 6 Apr. 1937, p. 1.
99 Stendig, *Polska a Palestyna w dobie obecnej*, 24.
100 'Levant Fair 1932, Tel Aviv', *Palestine and Near East Economic Magazine*, 6 (1931), p. 186.
101 A. Helman, *Young Tel Aviv: A Tale of Two Cities* (Waltham, Mass., 2010), 53.
102 'Palestine: The Economic Position', *Palestine and Near East Economic Magazine*, 7 (1932), p. 11.
103 F. Zarzycki, 'Minister of Trade and Industry on Levant Fairs', *Palestyna i Bliski Wschód*, 1934, nos. 4–5, p. 3.
104 'List of Railway, Motor and Steamship Reductions accorded in connection with the Levant Fair 1932, Tel Aviv, to Holders of Fair Permanent Tickets', *Palestine and Near East Economic Magazine*, 7 (1932), p. 17.
105 'Rozwój stosunków gospodarczych pomiędzy Polską a Palestyną: Wywiad z prezesem L. Lewite', *Czas*, 23 Jan. 1936, p. 14.
106 'The Levant Fair, 1934', *Palestine Commercial Bulletin*, 11/9 (1934), 267–79: 274; L. Lewite, 'Wystawa polska na Targach Lewantyńskich w Tel-Awiwie', *Palestyna i Bliski Wschód*, 1934, no. 2, pp. 66–9.
107 'Bezpłatny przewóz eksponatów na Targi Lewantyńskie', *Biuletyn Gospodarczy*, 26 Mar. 1936, p. 6.
108 Among those who came to Palestine especially for this occasion were Minister Aleksander Bobkowski; Henryk Gruber, director of the PKO bank and head of the Polish Institute for International Co-operation; M. Sokołowski from the Ministry of Foreign Affairs; and J. Wojstomska, the Ministry of Industry and Trade's delegate. Lewite and Friede represented the Polish Zionist community.
109 S. Świsłocki, 'O pomarańcze i tytoń z Palestyny', *5-ta Rano*, 15 Mar. 1934, p. 1.

Palestine for the Third Time
Ksawery Pruszyński and the Emergence of Israel

WIESŁAW POWAGA

IN A SCENE from Natalie Portman's film *A Tale of Love and Darkness*, based on Amos Oz's book of the same title published in 2003,[1] a group of Jews, adults and children, mill around anxiously in the dark backyard of a Jerusalem townhouse listening to a radio broadcast from New York. They are waiting for news of the vote on Resolution 181 which is taking place at the United Nations. When the result finally comes through, the crowd in the backyard erupts in joyous celebrations—the world has formally recognized the right of the Jewish people to self-determination and their own state. The celebrations quickly spill across the town, across the country, across the world.

It was 29 November 1947. Few people at the time knew that the man responsible for shaping that resolution and navigating it successfully to its final vote was a Polish diplomat, journalist, and writer, Ksawery Pruszyński, the chairman of Subcommittee 1 of the UN Ad Hoc Committee on the Palestinian Question. It was the committee's report and its recommendations for the legal basis and borders of a new Jewish state that formed the backbone of Resolution 181. Perhaps Pruszyński's impassioned speech in support of it delivered at the General Assembly was also broadcast in Jerusalem. Perhaps there were even a few people in that crowd who knew his name. But even though 29 November 1947 is as important in Israeli history as the date of the actual founding of the state, 14 May 1948, Ksawery Pruszyński's name has quickly faded, washed over by the joy of celebrations, the blood spilt in the ensuing wars, and the sweat shed on building sites. Even the official record of his speech has disappeared and is nowhere to be found, not in the archives of the United Nations, not in the archives of the Polish Foreign Office, and not even in the Central Zionist Archives in Israel.

Pruszyński was invited to work on the committee on the strength of a book he had written some fifteen years previously as a budding journalist. The book, a collection of his reportage from Mandatory Palestine, was published in Poland in 1933 under a title which seemed to be anticipating the vote of 29 November 1947, *Palestine for the Third Time*.[2] He seemed to be a perfect fit for the job. The book and the name of its author were well known to Poles and Polish Jews at the time, not only in Poland but in Jerusalem and New York.

When Ksawery met Mojżesz

Ksawery Pruszyński (4 December 1907–13 June 1950) was one of the leading Polish journalists of the first half of the twentieth century. According to Ryszard

Kapuściński, who regarded him as one of his masters, Pruszyński opened a new era of reportage, 'reportage which not only describes the world but also tries to explain it'.[3] He was born into an aristocratic Polish family in what is now Ukraine, but the Bolshevik revolution forced the family out of their estates, and, greatly impoverished, they settled in newly independent Poland. His widowed single mother, in spite of financial difficulties, managed to send both Ksawery and his brother Mieczysław to the Jagiellonian University, where they studied law.

It was there that they met Mojżesz Pomeranz as members of the conservative student organization, Myśl Mocarstwowa. Formed in the 1920s, Myśl Mocarstwowa was a political movement active in academic centres across Poland with a largely upper- and middle-class membership. Like today's think tanks, it sought to set out a political agenda for the new Polish state which its young elites would develop and implement. While its main goal was to build a strong modern state, at the same time it idealized the old Jagiellonian Polish–Lithuanian Commonwealth, which it believed had functioned as a multi-ethnic and multi-national state. Unlike its rival Endecja, which wanted to fuse the ethnic and the national as the core of Polish identity and the foundation of the state, Myśl Mocarstwowa's leading thinkers (such as Rowmund Piłsudski, a distant relative of Marshal Józef Piłsudski, and Jerzy Giedroyc) proposed an inclusive civic platform encompassing all ethnic groups within the structure of the state. At the international level, it aimed at a modern commonwealth, a federalist structure comprising the former nations of pre-partition Poland, such as Lithuania and Ukraine, and those of the Caucasus, such as Georgia. This new formation of a string of independent states was supposed to create a secure buffer for Poland in its difficult geographical position between Russia and Germany.

The standard-bearing periodical in which the group debated ideas was the tellingly titled *Bunt Młodych* ('Rebellion of the Young'), edited by Giedroyc, who after the Second World War would go on to edit the major émigré monthly, *Kultura*. As well as Giedroyc and Pruszyński, the periodical's other leading authors were Pruszyński's brother Mieczysław and the Bocheński brothers, Józef Maria, Aleksander, and Adolf. Pruszyński's and Giedroyc's common political roots and common political evolution seem remarkable today, when the two names are hardly ever mentioned in the same breath, but they raise an intriguing question: had it not been for Pruszyński's early death, would those paths have continued to run as closely despite their contrasting attitudes towards the political order of post-war Poland?

One key difference between Myśl Mocarstwowa and Endecja was the latter's unashamed antisemitism. It was not only their official policy: it often took the form of displays of aggression that led to street fights. It was such a fight with Endek activists, in which Pruszyński was injured, that cemented his friendship with Mojżesz Pomeranz. Some years later, when Mieczysław followed in his brother's footsteps, Pomeranz mobilized the support of Jewish students, and they all, together with Myśl Mocarstwowa and other democratic organizations, successfully campaigned in the elections to the Library Society of Law Students, which, governed by the Endecja's All-Polish Youth, was planning to bar and expel Jewish students. This victory was especially satisfying, as only a few months earlier Hitler had come to power in Germany. Ousting the Endek leadership significantly limited their previously undisputed influence within the Jagiellonian University.

Pruszyński and Pomeranz's friendship continued outside the lecture halls, with Ksawery and his brother often visiting the Pomeranz family, and after graduation. Pruszyński got a job at the daily *Czas* in Kraków, where he went from proofreading to reporting to writing his first book—*Sarajevo 1914, Shanghai 1932, Gdańsk 193?*[4]— an early example of his prophetic gift, warning of the possible outbreak of the next world war. At the same time, Pomeranz opened his own legal practice and became increasingly interested in the Zionist idea of creating a state for the Jews.

By the early 1930s Zionism had emerged as one of the main topics of political debate among Jews and non-Jews, and naturally between Pruszyński and Pomeranz. Since they were both deeply committed to the idea of the state as an intellectual and political construct—as distinct from the Endecja's stress on the primacy of the nation as defined by ethnicity—it did not take long for Pomeranz to persuade Pruszyński of the value of on-the-ground reporting from the Zionist front lines in Mandatory Palestine.

Ksawery Pruszyński thus went to Palestine on a mission, to find out whether the Zionist dream of creating a modern state in the Land of Israel had any chance of realization. He convinced Stanisław Cat-Mackiewicz, editor of the Vilna newspaper *Słowo*, of the value of a series of articles on Zionist activities in the Land of Israel, and Cat-Mackiewicz furnished him with the necessary accreditation and gave him his blessing but not much more. Pruszyński had to borrow from friends to finance the trip, hoping he could recoup the costs by publishing his reportage in what he described to his mother as 'a great book everyone will want to read'.[5]

He left Poland in spring 1933, travelling to Haifa on the Romanian ship *Dacia* from Constanţa. He returned ten weeks later, in early May, when his correspondence from Palestine, a series of twenty-two articles, had already started to appear in *Słowo* (23 April–8 July). As planned, he turned these articles into a book, *Palestine for the Third Time*. The title alluded to the three periods in which the area had had an impact on world history: the biblical kingdom of David, during the Crusades, and—possibly —the present. This all happened in the space of ten months. Pruszyński's commitment and focus was total, although the book betrays some signs of haste, as he wanted to produce it as fast as he could to pay off his debts.

To understand Pruszyński's interest in Palestine requires an understanding of his formative years. Pruszyński's background had a profound and lasting influence on his thinking as he evolved and matured into a leading reporter of pre-war Poland, a popular writer and broadcaster, and a diplomat participating in world-changing events. It was essentially the same mindset that made him interested in Mandatory Palestine and led him to throw in his lot, tragically—some say fatally, given the persistent rumours surrounding his tragic death in a car accident[6]—with the new communist regime of post-war Poland: that of an idealistic yet pragmatic supporter of the idea of the state as the force which creates the nation.

Pruszyński was born in Wolica Kierekieszyna (Volytsya-Kerekeshyna) in Volhynia to an old aristocratic family with an admixture of Ruthenian and Tartar stock but cultivating patriotic Polish and Roman Catholic traditions. After several decades of ruthless Russian suppression—political, cultural, and economic—under the governor general of Vilna Province, Mikhail Nikolaevich Muravev, known as 'the Hangman', the idea of Poland's resurrection had begun to revive and circulate. For most Poles, who over the years had succumbed to Russification, these ideas were at best pipe dreams, but they could have dangerous consequences. Nevertheless, they were again on the rise, not just because they were anti-Russian but also anti-tsarist or, as we would say today, anti-systemic. They were a natural complement to the other idea that was coming to the boil: socialist revolution.

Pruszyński grew up surrounded by different nationalities—Ukrainians, Belarusians, Russians, Baltic Germans, and Jews. Such cultural pluralism was not unusual in Europe at the beginning of the twentieth century, when the borders imposed by the old nineteenth-century order were already showing signs of strain, and national and irredentist aspirations were rising throughout the continent—from Ireland, Brittany, and Catalonia in the west, to Poland, Ukraine, and Belarus in the east; from the Balkans to Scandinavia. The specific though not uncommon ethnic and religious mix of Volhynia engendered deep awareness of other cultures and their national aspirations. It was all held in place by the Russian imperial administration, for the time being.

However, while the Polish nobility and intelligentsia were indeed succumbing to Russification, making careers in the state apparatus, the army, and academia, there were still those who clung to the old romantic notion of Polish independence. The most rebellious of them eventually gathered under one banner, forming in 1892 in Paris the Polish Socialist Party (Polska Partia Socjalistyczna; PPS), which sought both national independence and socialist revolution. However, it quickly became apparent that these disparate goals could not be contained within a single organization. A year later the PPS split and its two main ideological components went their separate ways: the socialists, Rosa Luxemburg, Karl Radek, and Feliks Dzierżyński, took the Marxist path (later merging with the Bolsheviks); and the patriots, with Józef Piłsudski, held on to their dream of Polish independence. By 1906, following more internal struggles and further splits, the PPS had evolved from a few hundred anarchic dreamers into a major political force, tens of thousands strong, commanding popular support in all parts of partitioned Poland. By 1914, on the eve of the First World War, Piłsudski's Revolutionary Faction of the PPS began to form a military force, the Polish Legions, ready to fight for Poland's resurrection as a sovereign state, capturing the imagination of the young and laying the foundation for the Piłsudski legend. It was also at this time that Piłsudski articulated his main political ideas of 'Prometheism', aimed at dismembering the Russian empire into its ethnic and national components, and 'Intermarium', a federation of states between the

Baltic Sea and the Black Sea able to withstand the imperial pressures of Russia and Germany. These geopolitical projects, visionary and ultimately short-lived, had nevertheless a fundamental influence on Piłsudski's younger followers, such as Pruszyński, Giedroyc, Adolf Bocheński, and Anatol Mühlstein. It was this vision, first articulated by Piłsudski in his memorandum to the Japanese government in 1904 on the eve of the Russo-Japanese war, that informed and inspired the political thinking of Pruszyński's generation. It was also Pruszyński's direct inspiration in joining Myśl Mocarstwowa. Soon, together with Mieczysław and Adolf and Adam Bocheński, Pruszyński became not only a regular contributor to Giedroyc's *Bunt Młodych* but also an activist fully involved in academic politics.

Meeting Pomeranz was the second decisive factor behind Pruszyński's expedition to Palestine. Pomeranz, a young Zionist, and Pruszyński, a young conservative and supporter of Polska Mocarstwowa ('great power' Poland), must have made an unusual pair, yet their friendship survived the war and lasted until Pomeranz's death in 1949. The stone thrown by the Endek hoodlum as Pruszyński stood up to defend his Jewish colleagues on the steps of Collegium Novum initiated a lifelong friendship, not just between the two students but also between their families: Pruszyński's mother helped Pomeranz's family in Kraków under German occupation.

It was also an intellectual friendship. Pruszyński and Pomeranz began a discussion that continued long after their student years, as they established their professional careers throughout the 1930s in Poland and even during the war when they both met in Palestine where Pomeranz had moved just before the war and Pruszyński and his brother were stationed with General Anders' army.

What brought the two friends together was a shared admiration for Piłsudski and an interest in the ideas of statehood and nationhood. But while they shared the same political platform they came from disparate backgrounds and their thinking ran in different directions—Pruszyński's towards Piłsudski's Prometheism and a federation of states comprising different ethnic and national components, and Pomeranz's towards Zionism and the building of a new Jewish state in Palestine. When they met, the Zionist project was still in its early stages of development, yet it was riding high on the cusp of the Second Aliyah (1904–14), the wave of Jewish migration to the Land of Israel from Ukraine, Belarus, and Lithuania. Just as the idea of Poland's independence had a profound influence on Pruszyński, so did the idea of a return to Zion have on Pomeranz. And just as the programme of Polska Mocarstwowa harked back to the Jagiellonian commonwealth, the Zionist programme had even more distant roots in the historic Land of Israel.

The two ideas, which emerged at the same time and place and produced politically fruitful and popular movements, grew in parallel. Interestingly it was newly independent Poland that offered a platform where the two could confront each other and it was there that the minds of Pruszyński and Pomeranz met. There is too little information on the life and work of Mojżesz Pomeranz to allow a detailed analysis of his arguments for Zionism or how he envisaged the new State of Israel. He emigrated to Palestine just before the outbreak of the war and the family he left behind in

Poland perished in the Holocaust. He did establish a new family in Palestine, but after his death they Hebraized their names and by now all traces of them are lost.

There is, however, one significant document setting out Pomeranz's views: an article 'Israel Calls for Justice' written in 1933 and published in *Bunt Młodych*. The article appeared in February, with the following introduction by the editors:

Wanting to throw clear and objective light on the Jewish question in Poland we thought it only appropriate to ask for the opinion of the interested party. We have therefore invited a leading proponent of the Zionist movement in academic circles, Mr Mojżesz Pomeranz, MA, whose article we present below.[7]

In the article Pomeranz set out his arguments for the Zionist cause, opening with a comparison of the fate of the two nations, Poles and Jews:

Jewry has survived two thousand years without a fatherland. It has survived rivers of spilt Jewish blood, uncountable autos-da-fé, crusades, inquisitions, Khmelnytsky massacres, and Kishinev pogroms. Are we responsible for these sufferings? To us our survival seems rather the result of unparalleled heroism, a phenomenon, a miracle. But for the enemies of Israel—and the Hitlerites of all countries agree on this—what kept us alive was our drive to rule the world. Is this not also said by hostile critics of Poland? That the country survived bondage dreaming about conquering the world? We do not accept either argument. Jews survived 2000 years of servitude, Poles 150 years, only because they are living nations. Because they refused to be sent to the Hades of History...

Nevertheless our life is abnormal. This abnormality is just what constitutes 'the Jewish question'. It has two sides—the material, that is the economic, and the spiritual, or cultural.[8]

Pomeranz then considered these two aspects, setting out first the problems that beset Jews living in host nations under the pressures of modern economic developments and then discussing the other side of the Jewish question, an 'even sadder' problem— 'tragic to the core'—assimilation.

For many Jews, assimilation had been a natural and long-accepted consequence of their active participation, for many generations and in all social classes, in different areas of social, political, and economic life. Apart from specific instances of religious movements like Frankism or the different shades of secular and religious integration advocated by the Haskalah (the Jewish Enlightenment), the extent of assimilation had depended largely on individual circumstances. However, by the turn of the century with the emergence of Zionism, the Jewish world had clearly split into two camps—assimilators and the rest, which included such disparate groups as Zionists, autonomists, hasidim, and mitnagedim, who all sought to cultivate their Jewish religious and cultural heritage.

The prospect of an independent Poland renewed the discussion of assimilation and put it in a new, for some even hopeful, light. Assimilation in the Russian empire, given the restrictions of the Pale of Settlement and aggressive antisemitism as manifested in pogroms and Black Hundreds, was not only difficult, expensive, and dangerous but also morally dubious. Perhaps the new Poland, shaking off the shackles of the imperial system and emerging into the new world of modern democracy, would now offer its ethnic minorities economic and cultural room in its newly emerging social order.

In a booklet, *Assimilation, Politics, and Progress*, published in Warsaw in 1913, Anatol Mühlstein, another fervent supporter and later a close co-operator and friend of Piłsudski, analysed the 'Jewish question' specifically from the point of view of the interests of the Polish state. He focused on the choice between 'progressives'—supporters of the socialist option—and 'assimilators'. He criticized both sides as working against Poland's best interests, but, being an assimilator himself, his criticism of his own faction was particularly harsh. He accused his fellow-assimilators of turning their backs on the uneducated ghettoized Jewish masses and selfishly pursuing their own aspirations and ambitions. He urged the 'enlightened' assimilators to launch a long-term educational programme which would show their fellow-Jews the benefits of assimilation and the right way to achieve it. It was necessary to talk to them in their own language, Yiddish, and to make clear that there was more to assimilation than short-term material benefits. In the last chapter of the booklet, bearing, like Lenin's pamphlet, the title 'What Is To Be Done?', he wrote:

So far we have been unsparingly hard on the assimilators. We have shown their powerlessness and inertia with merciless frankness and prodded the open wounds inflicted on them by recent events. But the time has come to move beyond criticism. For despite their many political errors, despite their widely adopted mistakes they are the only force which can set the Jewish question on the path towards practical solution.[9]

Assimilationist and integrationist views did have some support among Polish Jews. They hoped that Piłsudski's overwhelming political and military victories, culminating in the resurrection of the Polish state, sealed in the 1918 treaty of Versailles, and confirmed in the treaty of Riga of March 1921, would create a more favourable climate for such initiatives. The Polish–Jewish Agreement reached in July 1925 seemed a favourable omen. Aleksander Skrzyński, minister for foreign affairs and later prime minister, described this during a visit to the United States on which he was accompanied by Mühlstein:

I must with regret admit that several years after the war there was a great antisemitic movement in Poland . . . [However] the Polish-Jewish-Agreement comes at a time when the antisemitic movement in Poland is growing weaker and it is my firm conviction that the day is not distant when antisemitism in our country will, thanks to this agreement, entirely disappear.[10]

Another favourable omen was Piłsudski's 1926 decree granting immediate and unconditional Polish citizenship to 600,000 Jews from the Pale of Settlement, an unprecedented act on a scale not matched anywhere in the world until the new State of Israel.

Pomeranz put forward the arguments for assimilation, which he described as a 'third way':

Tertium datur: to seek a solution in the full granting of equal rights and respect for national character of the Jewish nation in Poland. A healthy Jewish society is one of the guarantors of Poland's power status. We give Poland our blood, our labour and all that it demands of us, so let it treat us as citizens. Our nations should reach not so much an 'agreement', which involves mutual claims on each other, but a Polish–Jewish union. Two nations united in the common goal—the good of the Polish Republic.[11]

However, by the time he wrote this article, the government of Skrzyński had been succeeded by the May coup and the new regime of Piłsudski. This had been initially sympathetic to Jewish demands, but the impact of the Great Depression and the rise of the Nazis in Germany undermined support for the integration of the Jews. As a result, Pomeranz's call for Polish–Jewish unity and the assimilation this would bring about was more of a rhetorical exercise than practical politics. As if answering Mühlstein's argument of twenty years before, Pomeranz explicitly rejected assimilation along with political radicalism:

The Jewish question cannot be solved either by communism or by assimilation. And mentioning them in one breath is not accidental. Essentially they boil down to the same thing. 'White assimilation' argues: Jewish poverty will disappear when you blend in with the surroundings. Speak Polish, think Polish, just keep your faith. Experience, however, teaches us that those who in the process of blending reach that last boundary, faith, cross it like a Rubicon, without stopping. The communists argue along similar lines: join the ranks of the proletariat—Polish, Russian, or any other—and you will find your place. But with that place comes the culture of that proletariat, which starts by divesting you of your old one. Thus all we really have to choose between is either 'white' or 'red' assimilation. For us in the end it is immaterial if we are asked to assimilate into German culture and the German bourgeoisie or proletarian culture, whatever that happens to be now, just as it does not matter to the man condemned to death whether he dies by the bullet or electric chair. The Jews do not want to assimilate.[12]

Pomeranz's article in *Bunt Młodych* was an extension of the discussions he began with Pruszyński ten years before. But now the time had come to move beyond words. And a plan was hatched.

Palestine for the Third Time

Pruszyński, by now a young reporter with his first book under his belt, decided to take a closer look at the Zionist project. Just how close a look he meant to take was revealed straight away on the first leg of his journey when, together with young Romanian immigrants, he found a berth for himself in the lower decks of a ship from Constanța to Haifa.

In his five-week trek across Palestine he visited places and met people which now make up a historic landscape and the heroes' gallery of modern Israel. He saw the ancient Land of Israel acquire the trappings of a modern state, with up-to-date agriculture and industry, new ports and cities. He talked to people from all walks of life, Jews and Arabs. He saw how the old generation, which had grown up in tsarist Russia and in contact with the Polish nobility, had adapted successfully to a new life and how the new generation of sabras was being raised. He could see for himself how the people lived and how theories were transformed into practice. He visited a number of kibbutzim, including Ein Harod and Degania Alef, which formed the ideological backbone and became the legend of the new state. He spoke to people who were later recorded in the history of the State of Israel as its shapers and the major contributors to its material and cultural substance, such as Hayuta Bussel, Meir Ya'ari, and Eliezer Peri. At the same time, as a Catholic keenly aware of the religion at the core of his national identity, he made a pilgrimage to the Christian holy places and saw them as the living source of his faith.

Adolf Bocheński, also a writer and journalist who later wrote one of the first (not entirely favourable) reviews of *Palestine for the Third Time*, remembered Pruszyński's visit to his parents' estate in Ponikwa (Ponykva), near Brody in western Ukraine:

I saw him on his way back from Constanța when he visited us in the country. The Mongolian face he had inherited from the Pruszyńskis (grandmother née Czeczel of Tartar stock) burnt by Palestine's fearsome sun, covered with scabs, was a sight to behold, unique. He was not an ordinary tourist and not an ordinary reporter. He simply lived Palestine ... He crossed the Jezreel Valley on foot, dug ditches through the swamps, helped penniless immigrants swim to the shore, every step of the way arguing hotly against the perils of communism and belligerent materialism. No, he was no ordinary tourist.[13]

Bocheński noted Pruszyński's conviction that the emergence of the State of Israel was not a mere possibility but a practical certainty. This conviction was borne out after the Second World War and was put to work when in 1947 he became the chairman of Subcommittee 1 of the UN Ad Hoc Committee on the Palestinian Question set up to establish the legal basis and draw up borders for the State of Israel carved out of the Palestine he had visited fourteen years before. The experience of the war and the fate of millions of Jews killed in the Holocaust could only have strengthened his conviction of the need for such a state. But it is important to bear in mind that its seed was sown during his discussions with Mojżesz Pomeranz as they searched for their own solution to the question Mühlstein posed in 'What Is To Be Done?' It is easy, with the hindsight of eighty years, to praise Pruszyński for his sound judgement and all his efforts to act on it, but the question remains, which Bocheński also raised, whether Pruszyński's enthusiasm was not simply a fusion of 'emotional filosemitism and political antisemitism'?[14]

As a representative of Poland, there was little new or surprising in Pruszyński's support for the new State of Israel. In fact it could be argued that he was simply continuing the policy of Poland's pre-war government which happily collaborated with Jabotinsky and Begin in their Zionist programme for the large-scale emigration of Jews from Poland to the point of actively helping to protect the Jewish settlements against the Arab revolt by providing military training and equipment for the Haganah and Betar. It might be argued that Poland's new communist regime had no problem in continuing the policy of facilitating Jewish emigration as a way of solving the 'Jewish question' through the departure of most of the remaining Jews. Allowing visa-free migration to Mandatory Palestine in 1947, while the 1939 White Paper restrictions on Jewish emigration from post-Holocaust Europe were still in force, might be seen as an expression of that policy, even if it was at odds with the new one—hostility to the State of Israel—gradually being adopted by the Soviet authorities as part of a general ideological, anti-capitalist—anti-British—turn in the direction of the Cold War.

It would be interesting at this juncture to compare Pruszyński's position and arguments for the State of Israel with those of Anatol Mühlstein. As a fellow admirer and biographer of Piłsudski, political thinker, Polish diplomat, and behind-the-scenes representative of France at the United Nations, Mühlstein must have closely observed Pruszyński's work for the Ad Hoc Committee on the Palestinian Question.

After holding various offices at the Polish embassy in Belgium, Mühlstein moved to France where, with direct support from Piłsudski, he became minister plenipotentiary at the Polish embassy in Paris. After Piłsudski's death in 1935 he apparently lost the support of the new foreign minister, Józef Beck, and ended his career in Polish diplomacy, settled in France, and devoted himself to working on a biography of Piłsudski. While still dedicated to Piłsudski and his political thought, he became, like Giedroyc and Pruszyński, increasingly critical of the policies pursued by his successors.

Mühlstein and his family managed to escape from France in 1940 and settled in New York, where he continued to refine his political ideas, reworking and adapting Piłsudski's idea of Prometheism to the new circumstances, publishing in 1942 *United States of Central Europe*.[15] Throughout the war he was also involved with the life of the Polish and Jewish diaspora in the US, fundraising for the Society for Trades and Agricultural Labour, and helping fellow writers like Julian Tuwim.

In 1942, as if as an addendum to his grand political vision of the *United States of Central Europe*, Mühlstein delivered a lecture in New York, 'The Future of Central Europe and the Jewish Question'. It sounds like another voice in the discussion started by Pomeranz and Pruszyński. Mühlstein articulated in it all his earlier arguments on Jewish nationhood, the progress of assimilation, the rise of antisemitism, and the prospects of Palestine as a practical solution to the Jewish question. He considered the situation of east European Jewry to have been significantly different from that of Western Jews, whose assimilation in the Western nations had progressed without major obstacles until the rise of Hitler. The difference became apparent when after the First World War the collapse of the three large empires which dominated eastern Europe and the emergence of thirteen new states not only imposed new borders limiting the free movement of goods and people but often led to the emergence of political entities which sought to consolidate their existence on the foundation of ethnic identity. While praising the achievements of the Zionist project, he still thought that it could not offer a permanent and stable solution, primarily because of the sheer number and diversity of the Jews. As a result he stressed the importance of civic—rather than ethnic—nationalism of the kind which had emerged over a protracted period in Western nations which allowed ethnic, cultural, and religious diversity to exist within the state and to be an integral part of the fabric of the nation. Conscious of the power of economic integration as an assimilatory force, he argued for allowing it to take its course.

All this was not dissimilar to the hopes and arguments of Pruszyński and Pomeranz. However, the text of the speech, written before the full extent of the Nazi genocide was properly absorbed in the West which meant that all discussion of the 'Jewish question' had to be seen in a radically new light, was not published until much later.[16] Might Mühlstein's 'Quo vadis, Israel?'[17] have in 1947 evoked a different, more definitive answer? There are rumours that David Ben-Gurion offered him the position of foreign minister in the first government of the new State of Israel but he turned it down. Sadly, there seem to be no reliable documents confirming Ben-Gurion's offer, nor in fact any other public record of what he actually thought then, when the utopian possibility of resurrecting the State of Israel had so unexpectedly been turned into political reality.

Mühlstein moved in the same social and diplomatic circles as Pruszyński in postwar Paris and New York, even establishing friendships with Pruszyński's old friends Giedroyc and Józef Czapski and contributing to their newly founded journal *Kultura* until his untimely death in 1957. Yet, intriguingly, Pruszyński and Mühlstein—diplomats, writers, and political thinkers, leading such similar lives and thinking along similar lines—apparently never met to swap notes on the Palestine coming back to life for the third time.

When delivering his speech at the United Nations in support of Resolution 181, apart from grand political visions, Pruszyński was also keenly aware of more compelling arguments. Polish antisemitism, exacerbated by the Nazi occupation, was still a powerful force, even if some sections of the population were sympathetic to the Jewish plight. The many cases of anti-Jewish violence, from small, unprovoked 'spontaneous' outbursts occurring every day across the country to large-scale pogroms reminiscent of the 1930s, like those in Kraków or Kielce, also created a powerful incentive to emigrate to Palestine. In these circumstances, the policy of the state, at least as presented in Pruszyński's speech, and the large numbers of distraught and traumatized survivors seemed to be pushing in the same direction.

Yet, while the official and unofficial state policies of the pre- and post-war Polish governments might indeed be seen as political antisemitism—that is, as an attempt to solve 'the Jewish question' by encouraging the emigration of Jews to the Land of Israel—Pruszyński's support for the Zionist project had roots deeper than mere political expediency. As the title of his book clearly implies, his was a vision of a return of a homeless nation to its native land, the source of its unique culture, the beginning of the unbroken line of its history. He saw this as a way to right the wrongs and injustices heaped on a people who lacked the protection of their own state, and perhaps, in the grander scheme of things, reviving some part of the world of those ancient civilizations which had produced the pyramids, the Bible, and the classics.

That was the essence of the speeches delivered at the United Nations as the chairman of Subcommittee 1 of the UN Ad Hoc Committee on the Palestinian Question, a call to grant this vision another chance in the aftermath of total destruction.

However it appears today, it is undeniable that Pruszyński's belief and Pomeranz's dream have been realized, and their efforts to bring them about are justified by the seventy-four years of continuous existence of the State of Israel. Whether they would feel satisfied with the form their dream has taken is another issue. Yet Pruszyński's book can certainly serve as a witness of that dream in the making.

■

Palestine for the Third Time is without doubt a very special book. Written 'on the knee', under the pressure of the need to file regular dispatches, it may not be a polished piece of writing. Nevertheless, and perhaps because of this, it reflects the moment and manifests the enthusiasm of an eyewitness account. Stylistically, it is an interesting mixture of old and new: the old-fashioned Polish of the *fin-de-siècle* literary movement, Młoda Polska, at times poetic, full of elaborate metaphors and comparisons, pressed into the service of modern reportage with unvarnished immediacy. At times peppered with economic and technical jargon, showing off the solid research characteristic of modern journalism, but also littered with references to Greek and Roman history.

More intriguingly, *Palestine for the Third Time* captures not just the early years before the formation of the State of Israel. It is not merely a report from a building site, even if it dutifully shows Tel Aviv rising from the desert sand or paints a panorama of new road networks and describes plans for a modern bustling sea port. Pruszyński's open mind and heart, his enthusiasm and sympathy for his fellow travellers, his burning curiosity to learn more about them are deeply moving and bring the whole scene to life. The book must be one of the earliest records of modern Israel's founding myths, collected years before the actual founding of the state. Here are the stories and iconic images which feature later in Oz's *A Tale of Love and Darkness* as the defining moments of Israeli history. From the sight of hasidim praying in the morning mist aboard the *Dacia* sailing from Constanța, on which Pruszyński had a fourth-class ticket, to the vista of the Promised Land in the morning from the *Constanza*, on which Oz's Auntie Sonia travelled third class;[18] from the vignette of a dark, book-lined room in a Jerusalem house, where Pruszyński is transported via a brittle page back to 'Szyszkowce and tenants farms, contracts in Dubno, transports from Odessa', to Równe, 'an important railway junction', with its undulating fields and wooded hills, where Auntie Sonia took little Amos down memory lane to Dubieńska Street, describing it 'precisely and in detail';[19] from Pruszyński's hailing of the supremacy of the Palestinian citrus industry and its new interest in grapefruit over that of California to Arieh's eulogy to Jaffa oranges.[20]

Amazingly, Pruszyński's *Palestine for the Third Time* and Oz's *Tale of Love and Darkness* seem also to intermingle outside the text, in Pruszyński's claim in the Afterword that 'Communism as an idea cannot be vanquished by police measures; it can only be defeated by another idea' and Oz's that 'Hamas is not just a terrorist organisation. Hamas is an idea ... To defeat an idea you have to offer a better idea';[21] or when the historical fact of Pruszyński delivering his speech before the vote on Resolution 181 blends into the image in Oz's book of the Jews milling around the backyard listening to the radio, waiting for the results of that vote.[22] All this some seventy years before Amos Oz turned them into yarns of yore and wove them into the mythic fabric of the nation.

Ksawery Pruszyński at the United Nations

Palestine for the Third Time was Pruszyński's first truly successful book, and, if it did not make him quite the household name he later became, it certainly advanced him into the first rank of journalists in pre-war Poland. It had a broad, if mixed, reception: ambivalent and contradictory in the Polish press; curious, even enthusiastic, in Jewish forums of all political groups. Following his return from Palestine and the book's publication, Pruszyński embarked on a number of tours, mostly to the eastern borderlands, from Vilna, through Lublin to Lwów (Lviv), drawing fascinated audiences everywhere, mostly but not exclusively Jewish. The popularity of the book among Jewish readers is attested to by a number of reviews, such as Heszel Klepfisz's 'Pruszyński on Happy Island'.[23] Leon Weinstock, editor-in-chief of the Polish-language Zionist newspaper *Chwila* published in Lwów, wrote: 'Palestine, as seen and described by Ksawery Pruszyński, has an important explanatory and publicity mission to fulfil, in both Jewish and Polish homes. That series of reportage from Palestine is certainly among the best. It fully deserves to be read in every home in Poland.'[24]

The book was not Pruszyński's last word on the Zionist project or Polish–Jewish relations. It was followed by articles like 'Przytyk i stragan' about the pogrom in a small town near Radom in March 1936, and short stories such as 'Karabela z Meschedu', about a Jew who joined the Anders Army to fight Hitler.[25] But in summer 1936 Pruszyński's attention was captured by the Spanish Civil War and in the autumn he set off for his next journalistic assignment, which resulted in another masterpiece of reportage, *W czerwonej Hiszpanii*.[26]

That might have been the natural end of his Palestinian adventure and preoccupation with the Zionist project. Then came the war and the Holocaust and, in one of those strange twists of fate, Pruszyński found himself again involved in the Zionist project and this time not only as an observer but quite instrumentally.

In 1947, while in New York working as an adviser to the Polish mission at the United Nations, he was invited by Oskar Lange, the ambassador of the new communist Polish People's Republic to the United States, to join the Ad Hoc Committee for the Palestinian Question, a newly formed part of the UN Special Committee on Palestine (UNSCOP). As mentioned, it was on the strength of *Palestine for the Third Time* that he was considered an expert on this question. But it was also his experience as a diplomat during the war—when posted in the Soviet Union and working with General Sikorski who was negotiating with Stalin—that made him uniquely qualified for the job. By now, Pruszyński's political position had evolved from the idealistic conservatism of Myśl Mocarstwowa through an increasingly critical and ultimately openly hostile attitude towards the post Piłsudski colonels' regime, to pragmatic centre-left statism. Following his experience of the Spanish Civil War and the deep disappointment of the Yalta conference, which reduced Poland to a Soviet satellite state to which many of his friends decided not to return, he agreed to work with Poland's new communist regime—for the good of the (next) new state.

Pruszyński was elected head of one of the subcommittees—Subcommittee 1, tasked with preparing the legal groundwork and drawing up the geographical borders for the new state which was to emerge following the termination of the British Mandate for Palestine. He committed himself wholeheartedly to the work, believing that the Jews deserved a state of their own, while fully aware that the festering Arab–Jewish conflict required some kind of guarantee for the rights of the Palestinians. The final recommendation of his subcommittee was two separate states—one Arab, the other Jewish. He worked tirelessly in support of this plan; according to historical records, he had great negotiating skills, dealing with pressure from different, often directly opposed, directions, and always with the clear aim of bringing about the creation of a Jewish state. This is best illustrated by the two speeches he delivered as chairman of Subcommittee 1: the first at the final, closing session of the Ad Hoc Committee on the Palestinian Question, where he explained in detail the complexities of the proposal and why it was still the best possible in the circumstances; the second on 29 November before the General Assembly's vote on Resolution 181, when he passionately argued for the creation of a Jewish state. The mechanics of the vote were less straightforward, but nevertheless it has gone down in history as a defining moment in the history of the State of Israel, which was founded later in May 1948.

■

In November 1947 Mojżesz Pomeranz wrote to Pruszyński:

I cannot express in this letter the admiration and enthusiasm inspired by both of your speeches. Someone said that if you came to Palestine, people would greet you with flowers, like another Balfour, only with greater love. Anti-Polish sentiments which are undoubtedly present in Jewish society in Palestine ... are today fading away and doubtless it is thanks to Ksawery Pruszyński, who is saving the good name of the Polish nation and enhancing that of Poland.[27]

Amidst the ensuing frantic protests of the Arab delegations and the increased arm-twisting of the Jewish one, Pruszyński was quietly removed from his position by his superiors, perhaps alarmed by his determined support for the Jewish state while Stalin was still weighing his options. Nevertheless, in that final speech on the day of the vote he reiterated his—and what he believed to be Poland's—official position:

[Poland] was the closest living witness of the terrifying mass murder carried out by Germany on the Jews ... and this is why the fate of the Jews has shaken Poles to the core ...

No other nation understands like the Polish nation the longing for one's own land, the land that belonged to one's ancestors, where one would not have to suffer the fate of an intruder or pilgrim.[28]

This moving conclusion was clearly the product, at least in part, of his experiences in Palestine. *Palestine for the Third Time* thus not only provides a fascinating vignette into what the Zionist dream was in the early 1930s and invites us to reflect on what has become of it now. It is also one of the factors which led to the realization of that dream.

Appendix: Ksawery Pruszyński's Speeches at the United Nations

As chairman of Subcommittee 1 of the UN Ad Hoc Committee on the Palestinian Question, Pruszyński gave two important speeches. Unfortunately, neither of these speeches have been archived in any official records of the UN or the Polish Foreign Office, and their full original texts have remained unknown for over seventy years.

The first speech was delivered on 25 November 1947 at the closing session of the Ad Hoc Committee, when the subcommittee delivered its final report. In his speech, Pruszyński addressed questions and issues raised by the other members of the committee, explaining the difficulties involved in arriving at the final version of the proposal and defending it as the only possible, if flawed, compromise. The text presented here is a faithful transcription of Pruszyński's handwritten version, preserving his original style and slightly flawed English. The manuscript was only discovered in December 2019 in the private archive of Mieczysław Pruszyński. It is the first publication of the English original *in extenso*.

The second speech was delivered on 29 November 1947 when the proposal of Sub-committee 1 was put to the vote before the General Assembly as Resolution 181. The text presented here is an extract from that speech prepared by the author for publication in the Polish-language Zionist paper *Opinia* in 1948. It appeared there as 'Poland and the Land of Israel'.[29] Here it is published for the first time in English.

Ksawery Pruszyński, Speech at the Closing Session of the UN Ad Hoc Committee on the Palestinian Question, Lake Success, 25 November 1947

Mr. President,
I would like to try, with your most kind permission to proceed to a summing up of what has been said during these last three days, when, as we all remember, two different reports and two different draft resolutions were presented to this committee. You have both in front of you, and you have already heard during that debate, different views and different opinions. Listening to them all, I realised the very important difference existing between the draft resolutions as presented by the Sub-committee No. 2 and that one which has been presented by the Subcommittee No. 1 of which I had the most unexpected and most certainly undeserved honour to be

the acting chairman. That very important difference is that the members of Subcommittee No. 2, or, speaking otherwise, of the Arabic Subcommittee, are all feeling extremely enthusiastic and extremely sure that their project, elaborated during a couple of days, is a perfect and excellent work, done easily and promptly.

We of the Subcommittee No. 1, or, with other words, the Subcommittee of Partition, have never congratulated ourselves for our work. It took us several weeks of time, during which we were working hard, as the honourable representative of Syria has already pointed out. Twice we had to apologise before you, Mr. Chairman, and before this illustrious assembly for the slowness and delay of our work. When coming here, we presented you with a solution about which we were far from being enthusiastic. Quite on the contrary. We all pointed out and stressed the difficulties, the complications even the many dangers of our own plan. We never denied that we presented you with a solution complicated because the situation, the reality of the land we were concerned with is difficult, troubled, complicated and divided. The plan of Subcommittee No. 2, that of our distinguished concurrents [*konkurenci*, i.e. rivals] is easy and straight. That which is the product of wishful thinking, of what we would like to see, not what actually exists, is always extremely easy, and childishly straight.

It has been said, and I think that the honourable delegate of Syria has said it, that just work is easy and simple while a work which is not just is—as ours was—hard and long. Mr. Chairman, honourable Delegates, please, look at that map you have in front of you. Look at this complicated difficult map. This map with corridors, with enclaves, with so-called points of intersection. Why [is] this map so complicated? This map is so complicated just because the Jews, when settling, came to what have been the worst land. They came to those barren, desolated sand hills along the coast from Haifa to Jaffa, where there was nothing but sand and where now is nothing but an orchard. They came to that long valley, linking Haifa with the Jordan, where once more there was nothing but marshes and malaria. They left the whole hilly land, settled, inhabited and cultivated by the Arabs—to the Arabs. Always in history, invaders took the best land for themselves. The Jews took what was the worst, they paid for it. Not only with money, but with sweat, tears and blood they paid many times its value.

This map, gentlemen, like the report of the Subcommittee No. 1, like all the work of that Subcommittee No. 1, represents a compromise. Its boundary line goes between what the Arabs possessed from centuries and what the Jews acquired by an effort as great as not many nations have ever effectuated. Once more, an effort quite unique.

Yes, Mr. Chairman, we are very far from proposing you a solution which we would call easy or simple or straight. What we are proposing is—as the representative of Canada said—a best possible solution in a difficult, particularly difficult, situation. There was not a single word by which we ever tried to diminish the danger of the question, nor the responsibilities of the UN. But just because it is a *cas unique*, just because it is danger, just because it is difficult, just because responsibility is involved, we felt and we feel that it is the task, the duty—yes, the duty of the United Nations—to deal with this situation. We feel, that in that case we need a very strong cooperation of all of us. Of the Mandatory Power, of all the United Nations, of the Palestinian population.

I have heard many angry words on the part of the Arab delegations. I am not at all surprised. I am not at all angry for it. I am just sorry for two things.

First, that a political partition of Palestine was inevitable; secondly, that it could not be proceeded to in a better mutual spirit. You all remember that the Arabs have refused all participation in the work of the United Nations Special Committee on Palestine, that the last chance of conciliation, initiated by you Mr. Chairman, was similarly and most unfortunately lost. One of the first steps of the Subcommittee No. 1 was to invite to its meetings a representative of the Arab High Committee. Once more they refused. I can very frankly assure you of one thing. During all our dealings we had no bad feelings against the Arabs. I had just the best feelings for them. They are a proud race, they are a valiant race, and perhaps similarly to the Poles, they were in the last two hundred years at least an unhappy race. I think I may say, that the foreign policy of my country, Poland, has supported in the past and will support in the future all the justifiable claims of Arabic nations. We voted for the introduction to the UN of several Arabic States, although we were not always completely sure they were complying quite exactly to all the required conditions.

We, Polish people, have special reasons to promote the State of Israel. We have fought for too long time for a state of our own not to understand such a fight, when done by others. We know unfortunately better than many other nations what it means for a nation to have a state of its own. Our nation knows the gas chambers like the Jewish people did and our nation has not forgotten, like some others, the sad lesson of this war.

In our opinion we all have a common debt towards the nation which gave so much to the world and was so badly repaid, and it is now the moment to repay this thousand-year-old debt.

Ksawery Pruszyński, Speech at the UN General Assembly before the Vote on Resolution 181, Lake Success, 29 November 1947

Some states, whose representatives are present here in this room, have asked why Poland, of all nations, why this new Poland, so actively supports the Jewish cause in Palestine, the partition of Palestine, the establishment in Palestine of a national sovereign Jewish state.

The present Polish government has always and still strives to explain to the United Nations all its political decisions. Those responsible for the implementation of Polish foreign policy have always endeavoured to clarify and explain Poland's position so that it can be fully understood by international society. I am therefore especially keen to try and answer those questions relating to our position on the question of Palestine, to explain what it has always been and still is.

First, let me turn to our interest in Palestine in general. This interest is, in Poland, despite its geographical distance, very lively and takes many forms. For the Polish nation, Catholic in its overwhelming majority, where the traditions of faith and national identity are closely linked, this land is for us—just as it is for many nations represented in this assembly—the Holy Land, swathed in all the glory of Christendom. In addition, it is a land closely linked to the Arab world, the world of the Islamic Orient; and although we have in the past been involved in military conflict with this world, these battles have not poisoned later relations between our nations, just as the old Anglo-French antagonism does not darken current relations between France and Great Britain.

From history we remember now not so much the wars we fought against each other but more the period which at the end of the eighteenth century began the process of twilight and eclipse for Poland and for the world of Islam, the time of decline and bondage.

The struggle for national independence and sovereignty, which many Arab nations have fought, or are still fighting against the colonial powers, has always found the warmest feeling of sympathy among Poles—and in Polish foreign policy, many, even quite recently, material manifestations of active support.

We are genuinely pleased to see representatives from Syria, Lebanon, Egypt, Pakistan, and Saudi Arabia, Iran and Yemen in this international forum, and we welcome the entry of representatives of other ancient Arab nations into international life. The more so since we can now hear them speak with the voice of their own nations and not that of foreign powers. It is in this same spirit that we have tried, as far as possible, not to divide Palestine in such a way that the borders drawn up now will become insurmountable walls in the future. This is why we have supported the most recent, seemingly hopeless, attempts to reach a direct understanding between Arabs and Jews. This is why in our plan of partition we have tried to draw up borders, infrastructural links, and interconnections, so that a future agreement between the two sides, perhaps still far off, but which never should be ruled out, will discover more bridges than obstacles.

Yet it is also true that Poland has a particular Jewish interest in Palestine. This issue has been raised by some Arab representatives here, but—in my view—they have missed the point. So please allow me now to set it straight.

Yes, Poland has a historical interest in supporting the creation of a Jewish state in Palestine—this is true. However, the reasons for this interest are altogether different from those assumed by these Arab representatives. They are wrong to think that Poland views a Jewish state in Palestine as a kind of reservoir into which it can channel its own 'inconvenient' Jewish population. I understand why they might think that. First, they assume that Poland in 1947 is still the same Poland of 1939, and secondly that the country still has its large Jewish minority. However, between 1939 and 1947 the largest war in human history rolled over Poland with all its deadly weight. The overwhelming majority of the Jewish population of Poland has been murdered; the small fraction that has survived is, by the force of circumstances, being assimilated. Antisemitism, which unfortunately also survived, thus outliving those it was originally meant to harm, is actively fought by the Polish government today in a way rarely seen in history and never before in Poland.

However, perhaps it is precisely because of that antisemitism and the sense of guilt for our sins in the past that the Jewish cause lies so near our heart. My nation was the closest living witness of the terrifying mass murder carried out by Germany on the Jews; my country was the place of those executions—and this is why the fate of the Jews has shaken us to the core. It is that past and that fate which has stirred in us this conviction that a nation for centuries deprived of its motherland has to have a motherland to return to, that it has to find its HOME. In our view the Jewish nation is the most tragic nation in the world. And it is also the nation, in my view, to whom the world owes the most.

It is to the Jews that we owe the idea of the one God—Judaism is the root of Christianity. The holy books of this nation constitute that source from which the world's nations have drawn more than from any other vessel of human thought. This nation has given us an example how a small nation ought to—and can—resist the violence of the stronger, how David defeated Goliath, how the Maccabees went to their death. It was their poetry that sounded for the first time—and loudly—the note of longing for the land of forefathers, sung over the rivers of Babylon.

In their diaspora, they have shown an invincible will to survive; from within their midst, people who have served the whole of humanity, like Spinoza and Heine, Mendelssohn and Marx, have emerged. All of us in this room, including those from the Arab nations, are in debt—yes, in debt—to this pauper who has now claimed his rights to the land from which he was banished by force. Shall we send him back with nothing?

Gentlemen, you are right to claim that in this whole matter Poland has demonstrated more concern than other nations about the fate of Israel. We accept these—presumably sarcastic—words as the highest praise for our foreign policy. This is the case. We have defended the cause of the Spanish people; we have, and will, defend the freedom of the Greeks; and we support Indonesia in its fight for independence. We have defended and will always defend any just cause, which is why we have been defending, and will defend, the Jewish cause. We are defending it because of all those thousands of threads that bind us to those Jewish people who came looking for refuge in medieval Poland—even then, in the Middle Ages, fleeing persecution from Germany. We are defending it now for we feel humbled by the guilt of the weighty sins we committed against this nation in the sad, and still not so distant, past.

But there is yet another reason why we defend it. No other nation understands better than the Polish nation the longing for one's own land, the land that belonged to one's ancestors, where one should not have to suffer the fate of an intruder or a pilgrim. This is the reason why the Polish nation understands the struggle of Palestinian Jewry. The right each nation has to sovereign existence on the land of its ancestors—that is the international rule supported by the Polish nation. Independence, the right to one's own national state—this is a need which we Poles understand perhaps better than others, which is why today we understand the demands and aspirations of the Jews in Palestine and beyond, just as we understand every thirst for freedom, every struggle for freedom.

Notes

1 N. Portman (dir.), *A Tale of Love and Darkness* (Focus World, 2015); A. Oz, *Sipur al ahavah vehoshekh* (Jerusalem, 2003); Eng. trans.: *A Tale of Love and Darkness*, trans. N. de Lange (London, 2004).
2 K. Pruszyński, *Palestyna po raz trzeci* (Warsaw, 1933); Eng. trans.: *Palestine for the Third Time*, trans. W. Powaga (Boston, Mass., 2020).
3 R. Kapuściński, *Lapidarium*, 5 vols. (Warsaw, 1990–2002), ii. 18.
4 K. Pruszyński, *Sarajewo 1914, Szanghaj 1932, Gdańsk 193?* (Warsaw, 1932).
5 A. Pruszyńska, *Między Bohem a Słuczą*, ed. M. Pruszyński (Wrocław, 2001), 240.
6 C. Miłosz, 'Ksawery, Jane i inne', *Kultura*, nos. 7 and 8 (Paris, 1985); J. Czapski, *Swiat w moich oczach* (Paris, 2001), 144–5; and S. Swieniewicz, *W cieniu Katynia* (Łomianki, 2016), 438.
7 [J. Giedroyć], introduction to M. Pomeranz, 'Izrael woła o sprawiedliwość', *Bunt Młodych*, 36 (Feb. 1933), p. 7.
8 Pomeranz, 'Izrael woła o sprawiedliwość'.
9 A. Mühlstein, *Asymilacja, Polityka i Postęp* (Warsaw, 1913), 32.
10 'Polish Foreign Minister in US; Talks about Jews', *Wisconsin Jewish Chronicle*, 24 July 1925, pp. 1, 8.
11 Pomeranz, 'Izrael woła o sprawiedliwość'.
12 Ibid.
13 A. Bocheński, 'Palestyna po raz trzeci', *Słowo*, 7 Nov. 1933, p. 1.
14 Ibid.
15 A. Mühlstein, *United States of Central Europe* (New York, 1942).
16 A. Mühlstein, 'Pamiętnik', *Zeszyty Historyczne*, 1978, no. 43, pp. 44–101.
17 A. Mühlstein, *Dziennik: Wrzesień 1939 – listopad 1940* (Warsaw, 1999), 194.
18 Pruszyński, *Palestyna po raz trzeci*, 17; id., *Palestine for the Third Time*, 6; Oz, *A Tale of Love and Darkness*, 190.
19 Pruszyński, *Palestyna po raz trzeci*, 133; id., *Palestine for the Third Time*, 87–8; Oz, *A Tale of Love and Darkness*, 145, 150–1.
20 Pruszyński, *Palestyna po raz trzeci*, 25–6, 111–14, 135–6; id., *Palestine for the Third Time*, 13–14, 74–6, 92–3; Oz, *A Tale of Love and Darkness*, 195–6.
21 Pruszyński, *Palestyna po raz trzeci*, 202; id., *Palestine for the Third Time*, 140; A. Oz, 'Israeli Force, Adrift on the Sea', *New York Times*, 2 June 2010, p. A25.
22 Oz, *A Tale of Love and Darkness*, 342.
23 H. Klepfisz, 'Pruszyński na Szczęśliwej Wyspie', in *Przedwojenny świat przez pryzmat młodego Żyda polskiego* (Tel Aviv, 1999), 105–10.
24 L. Weinstock, 'Polak na drogach pracy żydowskiej w Erec Izrael', *Chwila*, 22 Sept. 1933, pp. 7–8.
25 K. Pruszyński, 'Przytyk i stragan', *Wiadomości Literackie*, 1936, no. 30, p. 1; id., 'Karabela z Meschedu', in *Karabela z Meschedu: Opowiadania* (Warsaw, 1948).
26 K. Pruszyński, *W czerwonej Hiszpanii* (Warsaw, 1937).
27 Pruszynski Family Archives: Mojżesz Pomeranz, letter to Ksawery Pruszyński, 28 Nov.

1947; facsimile in Pruszyński, *Palestine for the Third Time*, 9; see M. Pruszyński, *Mojżesz i Ksawery* (Warsaw, 1999); B. Szaynok, *Poland – Israel 1944–1968: In the Shadow of the Past and of the Soviet Union*, trans. D. Ferens (Warsaw, 2012).

28 K. Pruszyński, 'Polska a Erec', *Opinia*, 28 (1948), 1; repr. in K. Pruszyński, *Publicystyka*, ed. G. Ryka and J. Roszko, 2 vols. (Warsaw, 1990), ii. 402–5.

29 Ibid.

3. FROM THE WAR TO THE ISRAELI DECLARATION OF INDEPENDENCE

Imagined Motherland
Zionism in Poland after the Holocaust

NATALIA ALEKSIUN

IN THE SUMMER OF 1944 Adela Hilzenrad eagerly awaited the arrival of the Red Army. Having survived in hiding on the outskirts of Drohobycz (Drohobych), she likened the sound of Soviet cannon to the 'heavenly music that was supposed to give us freedom and life'.[1] On the brink of freedom, Hilzenrad's hopes became increasingly tied to her future emigration to Palestine, not only for herself and her immediate family but also for other Jewish survivors. Her hopes were as political as they were general—future-oriented and at the same time immediate. As she noted in her diary:

I dream about Palestine, where most Jewish survivors would want to go. There would be no obstacle for settling in Palestine. Limits on emigration would be eliminated. The White Paper would stay in the past. I believe that when I will finally step out of this house it will still be summer. For the first time in many months I'll be able to smell the wonderful scents of gardens and fields. I will be able to hug the trees and be happy to be alive.[2]

In diaries, early testimonies, and memoirs, Polish Jews—men, women, and children—documented the hopes and dreams that began to manifest themselves—though cautiously—as thinking about the future became possible. Beginning with a close reading of Adela Hilzenrad's account and including other early personal accounts, this chapter seeks to examine visions of the future that she and other Holocaust survivors formulated on the eve of liberation or shortly afterwards: in particular, if and how they wrote about their hopes for a future in Palestine. How did that country emerge as a 'promised land'? Did the survivors allude to it as either a political solution to Jewish suffering, a national revival, or a place for new, personal beginnings, with only a vague ideological tie to a specific party or movement? Their desires and emotions encapsulate the central dilemma that nearly all survivors faced: how to rebuild their lives after the Holocaust.

For those who had long been active in the Zionist movement, the moment of liberation indicated a clear call for action on behalf of their organization, party, and the Zionist ideologues who would take charge of their collective future. For example, a leading activist of the left Zionist Hehaluts Hatsa'ir and member of the Jewish Fighting Organization in the Warsaw ghetto, Yitzhak Zuckerman (1915–81), recalled a conversation with a Po'alei Tsiyon Left leader Adolf Berman (1906–78) and his wife

Batya Temkin-Berman (1907–53) shortly before the outbreak of the Warsaw uprising in August 1944. By allowing themselves to talk about the future for the first time, they realized the strategic difference of opinion concerning the role of the Zionist movement in Poland, which would shortly be controlled by the Soviet Union.[3] After Warsaw was liberated, Zuckerman continued to think about the future of the movement and the practical steps that needed to be taken:

The day the Red Army entered Warsaw, we felt like orphans; we had a sense that there was no Jewish people anymore. We had no estimate, we didn't know how many were left . . . A few weeks after we surfaced, I made my first contact with A[dolf] Berman, after he had begun that work by himself. We decided to start assembling the remnants. We didn't reach most of the people either because the Jews couldn't find us or we couldn't find them.[4]

Zuckerman and Berman travelled to Lublin to meet other Zionist activists who had begun to assemble there and, in particular, members of the Hashomer Hatsa'ir movement and Emil Sommerstein (1883–1957)—a Zionist activist and member of the Polish parliament before the war.[5] However, rather than engage with a close reading of memoirs of Zionist activists such as Zuckerman, Zivia Lubetkin (1914–78), Berman, Tuvia Borzykowski (1914–59), and others, I turn to the ego documents produced by Polish Jewish survivors who were not involved in Zionist party politics before the war and for whom these imaginings were not simply continuities of pre-war allegiances and wartime underground activism.[6] Thus I am not concerned with ideological discussions among Zionist activists after the war, when Zionist parties and organizations were given a relatively free hand in Poland. Nor do I elaborate on the position taken by their opponents: Bundists and Jewish communists.[7]

In this chapter I seek to problematize the visions of a specific group of survivors, in both spatial and temporal terms. Having had little affiliation with Zionist concepts prior to the Holocaust, how did the survivors conceive of Palestine as a realm of their future revival, and how did the fantasy compare with Poland—the country they were to leave behind? I emphasize the notion that their perception of Palestine was, in fact, constructed in contrast to Poland. Poland was a tangible site of their past and loss—a place filled with concrete memories, tied to images of family life and social interactions with fellow Jews. But, after liberation, Poland was at the same time experienced as a profound void. On the other hand, Palestine was a fluid space full of possibilities, hopes not yet realized, and a future home to be filled and materialized.[8] Thus, both places and spaces evoked different emotions which were closely intertwined, with Poland as a site of emotional attachment and pain and Palestine as a site of intense but vague dreams.[9] As the survivors wrote their accounts without previous empirical evidence or detailed knowledge of the Zionist project, the early testimonies presented here were more likely to focus on general ideas and beliefs of how ideological convictions could be materialized in action, on the ground. In this context, Palestine carried connotations not only of being physically remote but also of being an 'abstract home' which was tied to exercising individual and collective Jewish agency and power, or even revenge.

In the idealistic minds of the survivors, it was an imagined motherland, away from territories which were familiar but linked to powerlessness, victimization, and the events of the Holocaust. Indeed, identifying the role of Palestine as a 'dream' in the early personal narratives involves paying attention to the geographies and spatialities of retelling their experiences during the war.[10] In what context was this dream formulated in the diaries, early memoirs, and testimonies? Similarly, what time-frame did the survivors set for themselves in order to realize their dream? To answer these questions I take inspiration from the monograph *Time and Revolution*, in which Stephen E. Hanson argues for the centrality of 'charismatic time' to an understanding of ideologically driven visions of the future: 'By defining new principles of legitimacy in times of social breakdown, charismatic leaders convince their followers that they are, in effect, beginning time anew.'[11] While there is no charismatic leader in the personal documents articulating the desire of leaving for Palestine, the survivors placed themselves in the 'in between time': after their liberation and before their departure.

While Adela Hilzenrad devoted much space in her diary to musing about her future in Palestine, most survivors wrote about their plans economically. Notably, they were not encouraged to do so in the testimonies deposited with the Central Jewish Historical Commission. Rather, these documents focused on their experiences during the Holocaust, identifying perpetrators and documenting Jewish responses to persecution. As a result, there is no question listed on the instruction pertaining to survivors' future plans.[12] For some, it may have also seemed a matter in flux, as they searched for their relatives or information about their fate, sought to recover property, and faced anti-Jewish violence.[13] In her close reading of survivor interviews conducted in Lithuania, Israel, and the United States, Hannah Pollin-Galay found striking differences that she credited to 'the ecologies of witnessing': that is, the shaping effect of each country's ambient post-war politics, social myths, regard for Jews, and other cultural influences on how individuals framed their personal experiences.[14]

Considering this, what role did Palestine play in the ecology of witnessing of the Polish Jewish survivors? Hilzenrad's dreams about the future drew on the past. While she cherished the memories of intimate encounters with nature, open spaces, and past happiness, she imagined herself returning to these happy times. In June 1944 she wrote in her diary:

With closed eyes, I imagined what life would be in the future. I allowed myself to dream about anything I wanted because I was the author of my dreams. The people are the way I want them to be. I am different too. I am the way I wanted to be. Nothing ugly or unpleasant can sneak into this film. All things happen as they used to. It is a wonderful summer in the mountains. I swim in a river and the sun shines. I sunbathe on the shore ... I walk on a path in the woods and inhale the balsamic scent of resin. I see a small glade where forget-me-nots are growing. I drink clear water from a mountain spring, which has a wonderful taste. I see the foamy waterfall and mountain peaks that hide in the clouds.[15]

Such memories provided Hilzenrad with hope for what the future could hold for her and her family. They helped her bear the challenges of life in hiding on the outskirts of the town, as her family negotiated their situation with those who had agreed to shelter them, who, as *Volksdeutsche*, had briefly considered fleeing west before the arrival of the Red Army. Together with her husband and son she looked for the clear signs of the German retreat from the town.

Prompted by the possibility of 'quickly approaching freedom',[16] Hilzenrad tied her image of the future to the experiences of the Holocaust and in particular to the betrayal of her neighbours, Ukrainians and Poles. And her hope took on a communal as well as a personal form: she wished for collective Jewish retribution and revival. Optimistically, she predicted that, upon leaving the shelter,

the Poles and Ukrainians would be ashamed to look us in the eye because of their behaviour toward us in those terrible times. Those who have actively co-operated with the Germans in murdering Jews will escape and they will be condemned to wandering in the world. Those who will not be able to run away or hide will surely receive their due punishment.[17]

In addition, Hilzenrad anticipated international support for the rehabilitation of the remaining Jews who would seek to rebuild their lives and regain equal rights. Together with her husband, she made plans for after liberation. It was as much about what happened to them in their country of birth as about the country of their future. Poland, in her eyes, symbolized both rejection and hatred of the Jews in the past and their ultimate victimization. She and her husband, for their part, rejected Poland in order to ensure the safety of their only child:

If our child would be saved from this massacre, in which hundreds of thousands of children perished, we have no right to risk his life again. Realistically it was clear to us that no matter in which country we would settle, we would still be Jews. Our thoughts turned to a different homeland, the one true, faraway homeland; about which we heard so much but never thought about settling there. In our real homeland we would never know senseless and terrible fear of death. There, if we would be attacked, we would defend it because it is our land, our country. There we would never hear the word 'Jew' in a derogatory way. We would never be hurt or denigrated just because we were Jews. If we would have to defend ourselves, we will fight. We will either win or die like human beings, not like animals.[18]

Thus, as was the case for many others, Palestine offered a promise of safety and dignity juxtaposed with the destruction, danger, and immanent humiliation of Jewish life in the diaspora. In this context, Hilzenrad tried to find meaning in the suffering and loss as a much-needed corrective to the illusions Jews harboured about their being at home in the diaspora:

It was necessary to go through this bloody war with mountains of victims, with a sea of tears and blood to come to the realization that all people deserve to have their land, their country. We should not be dispersed all over the world and we should not allow ourselves to be assimilated. We need to concentrate and join forces for the freedom of our people. We were demoralized by thousands of years of wandering. It turned us into slaves. We have gotten so used to slavery and we stopped worrying about it. We have to shake off this feeling; we have to desire freedom to fight for it. Only then, we will become a nation like all other nations of the world.[19]

As my research has shown, writing about one's future in Palestine was a spatial strategy, something that is central to a number of testimonies. Hilzenrad's diary expressed her shifting spatial awareness: from her familiar landscape of Drohobycz and, by extension, Poland to her future home in Palestine. She vividly described her home, but this familiar narrative lost its geographical concreteness when she envisioned the future. Rather, this place became a vague site of safety, dignity, and meaning. While Drohobycz was the place she knew, Palestine emerged a space of imagination in which she was to make new meaning. And thus Palestine became a way to reject a former home as too deeply scarred by violence and hatred and an intention to move from one to the other as an act of spatial agency.[20] In these dreams, then, Palestine is a void to be filled.

In terms of time, Palestine juxtaposed the vexing present filled with danger, mourning, and difficult decisions. Having celebrated the 'happy moment' embodied by the arrival of a Russian soldier, Hilzenrad and her family struggled with the decision whether or not they should retreat east with the Soviets. Assured by their host that the fight for the town was over and that it was full of Soviet troops, Hilzenrad and her husband noted:

We decided that we were free. We could open the window in our room. We could finally leave this place. Our leaving, however, did not happen as we planned. This was to be expected. As it happens, dreaming is 99 per cent different from reality. Our host still had to consider that the Germans might return in addition to shame in front of the neighbours for hiding Jews in his house. He asked us to leave his house so that no one would see us. On Sunday morning Marek left for town. We did not leave all together since we did not have a place to go to.[21]

Having learned that their former apartment in the ghetto was free, and as her husband was being encouraged by the Soviets to return to his work in a local clinic, Hilzenrad eventually left her hiding place in early August 1944. Yet her encounter with reality proved painfully disappointing. In contrast to her dream of feeling the grass under her feet, she struggled with walking on the terrain overgrown with tall vegetation. But, more importantly, she discovered her non-Jewish neighbours were neither ashamed nor afraid as she had expected. On the contrary, as Hilzenrad concluded: 'They pretended to be friendly but inside they would prefer that fewer Jews survived. Now, they could do nothing about it.'[22] She struggled with the sight of the empty Jewish houses, whose inhabitants she had known before the Holocaust. 'I passed a one-storey house where my relatives used to live. The same curtains hang in the windows. As if nothing has changed. I do know that the owners are not there. Their curtains remain but they died in the gas chambers of Bełżec.'[23] She encountered a ghost town and a cemetery, as the return made her realize the irrevocable loss not only personally but also as a sense of permanent loss of security: 'I cannot be happy since I was robbed of my faith in God and faith in people. The world around me is not the same. People in this world have a sleeping beast in them. Any moment, that beast could awake and would take me.'[24] The most concrete realization of the impossibility of rebuilding, of the loss of future in Drohobycz came when she encountered her home—a place she had left in November 1942, having gone into hiding. But, despite the memories, this very home turned out to be no longer habitable.

I approached the house. There was an apple tree in the backyard. Józio climbed the tree and I sat down, tired. It is quiet, peaceful and sunny. The place around me calmed me down. I will have a home and a normal life again. I have to start all over, from the ground up. My old life was completely destroyed. We cannot build our new life here, where everything reminds us of the tragedy and all that we went through. Here, all my efforts will be for nothing. We will leave from here to our homeland. We will live and work there.[25]

Hilzenrad went on to imagine her future home. But it was hardly a concrete dwelling. What she imagined was not a place but an ideological space of rebuilding and revival, not only of her own family, as she turned her voice to a collective Jewish voice:

I could imagine my life in my new home. The essence of my new home would be work and a burning love of freedom. That freedom has to become as common for us as daily bread. Nobody would ever be able to chase us away from our home. This is the only path that we should take. This is the only way we can ensure that our future generations will not go through what we went through. If we could not achieve that, then our lives were not worthy of being saved.[26]

In a similar context, Baruch Milch also survived in hiding in a small village near Tłuste. Born in Podhajce (Pidhaitsi) in 1907, Milch returned to his home town after liberation. His response closely resembled that of Hilzenrad:

I recalled the Podhajce that was, a town full of life. Now all was dust and ashes. Jewish Podhajce and her people had been extinguished in the ghetto, the cellars, the bunkers, the deep pits, the forest, the camps, and the mass graves. Seemingly hearing the voices of the people who had lived here, I was seized by a strange urge: to run away.[27]

Where was Milch planning to run away to? He did elaborate on his immediate plans in his post-war memoir. Yet when he reminisced about the happy life before the war, he recalled not only the blue and white box of the Jewish National Fund at his parents' home in Podhajce but also his own excited participation in the activities of Hashomer Hatsa'ir.[28]

Other early accounts give similar, mostly general, contours of the imagined promised land. Born in 1925, Kurt Lewin was the son of Jecheskiel Lewin, the rabbi of the Progressive Tempel in Lwów (Lviv). He survived in hiding, assisted by the metropolitan archbishop of the Ukrainian Catholic Church, Andrey Sheptytsky, and his brother Klymenty. In his memoir, published in 1946, Lewin recalled that in July 1945 he was recovering in a sanatorium in Krynica, where he met a Jewish communist, Daniel Kraus. Kraus had travelled through Palestine on the way from North Africa to the Soviet Union, and told him about orange groves and Jews who toiled on the soil and who were workers there. Lewin wrote:

I forgot about everything and in my soul transplanted there. I had long decided to go to Palestine and begin a new life there. But then, on this glorious July morning, I decided to put my decision into practice as quickly as possible. Return to the motherland. Turn a dream into reality. While the war was over, there was no opening of the gates of Palestine. But this did not terrify me. I had had enough of Poland, a terrible cemetery, full of hatred at every step. One needs to get out of the diaspora and begin to live the life of a Jew.[29]

Having returned from the sanatorium to the army, Lewin left again at the first opportunity and began looking for contacts who would enable him to emigrate.[30] His account ended as the ship *Elijahu Golomb* approached Tel Aviv, when Lewin noted enthusiastically that it was bringing him and other Jewish refugees 'to the motherland'.[31] Similarly, another survivor, Mietek Pachter, born in Warsaw in 1923, recalled his feelings after liberation in his post-war memoir, written in Davos in 1946. Together with his brother, he envisioned one meaningful future:

We had no intention of staying in Poland; we wanted to emigrate to Palestine. Is there a point in entering the military for two years? During that time we could already be in our country and building our future there. The decision was taken. We needed to leave for the recovered territories and search for means of temporary existence there to wait for a moment when it is possible to emigrate.[32]

For the survivors who testified about their wartime experiences at the local branches of the Central Jewish Historical Commission, the juxtaposition of Poland and Palestine was implicit. Thus, both adults and children who mentioned Palestine in their accounts did so at the very end of their narrative, turning it into a key framework not related to the specific events of the war or to their planning for their still vague future. Chaim Wittelson survived the Holocaust in the vicinity of Złoczów (Zolochiv), where he hid and passed as a non-Jewish farm hand. Testifying in his home town, Sosnowiec, he declared at the very end of his account: 'Only in March did I return to Sosnowiec. I count myself among the individuals who still have family members, and those are in Palestine.'[33] His testimony was documented with an additional note clarifying that he was a person of 'rather low intellectual level but a sincere and honest Zionist. His only desire now is to leave for his family in Erets (Yisra'el), in whatever way. Probably, in the next few days, he will leave Sosnowiec.'[34]

Children's testimonies reflect the distinction between the concrete memory of wartime suffering and the vague dream of a happy and safe future. The majority of children had not been initiated into Zionist ideology before the war, and thus were probably introduced to the idea by the adults whom they encountered after liberation. Accordingly, their stated desire for a future to be realized in Palestine is as vague as it is fervent. What does the promised land look like in the eyes of these children? In his testimony recorded in Kraków in the spring of 1945, a young Emanuel Kriegel recalled in great detail his fate during the Holocaust. Kriegel lost his father during the Soviet occupation, while his older brother, uncle, and cousin were murdered in the massacre of the Jewish intelligentsia at the very beginning of the German occupation.[35] In great detail, the boy recalled hiding together with his mother in a nearby village, being blackmailed together with other Jews hiding in a hospital, and witnessing the mass shooting of Jews from his hiding place in an attic.[36] He went on to recall what happened during almost a year hiding with a peasant woman, Szewczykowa. Barely able to walk, he was evacuated to Zbaraż, where he was found by his sister, while their mother perished in Buczacz. His account of his life after liberation was brief: 'With my sister, I travelled to Lwów and then to Łódź. I want to study as quickly as possible and even sooner I want to leave for Palestine.'[37]

Similarly, Jankiel Cieszyński inscribed his wartime experiences in the chronicle of the Jewish orphanage in Otwock, near Warsaw, which opened in 1945 under the auspices of the Central Committee of the Jews in Poland.[38] He had fled the ghetto a month before the deportation. 'I am now in a horrible situation, because I have been left alone like a stone in the world. For now, I thank God that I am alive and that I am well because I find myself in the orphanage. And I live with the hope that I will return to my motherland, to Palestine.'[39] Another child survivor, Dunia Berman, testified in Katowice about her experiences during the Holocaust in Horodenka and Tłuste, painfully describing the loss of her parents. She completed her testimony with a programmatic statement: 'I want to be in our land as soon as possible and with all my strength help build it. It should be as strong as possible so that we can take revenge on the murderers of our parents, sisters, and brothers.'[40]

It is interesting to consider, then, how these child survivors became aware of the Zionist dream land that awaited them. Some of the early accounts reveal how young survivors were made aware of the promise of their future in Palestine. Franciszka Oliwa worked in the Otwock orphanage as an educator and was in charge of a group of older children, with whom she developed a close relationship. She recalled:

Various Zionist organizations sought to influence our children and organized events close to our home and invited our wards to play together and partake in the treats, during which propaganda discussions about motherland, leaving for Israel and new kibbutzim took place. Our children were happy to participate in the camping. Zionist activities intensified and had a tremendous influence on the children, so much so that eventually the older group decided to emigrate to Israel.[41]

At the end of 1946 and beginning of 1947 these plans materialized and the majority of the older children left for Israel.

Ultimately, Palestine remained a vague motherland, whose status was a direct result of replacing old home towns. All its qualities, both explicit and implicit, stemmed from this shift, a transference of loyalty from one place to the other in the wake of the Holocaust. Szujka Ehrlihman from Lublin wrote on her way to Palestine to her sister, the only surviving member of the family:

I am on my way to Marseilles. I bid you farewell, beautiful Paris. I part from you without sorrow, your old face does not attract me. I crave youth, I want Palestine! Poland, where I was born, is not now my motherland. One cannot build a home on a cemetery. The blood of our dear ones calls to us from mass graves. Europe has not had enough of the innocent blood of our brothers. Now we want to fertilize with our sweat and if need be with our blood the soil of our country. All bridges are burned. There is no other path. Behind us is the huge army of the six million Jews murdered, gassed, and burnt in crematoria ovens. Their death shows us the path to life.[42]

Conclusion

As Polish Jewish survivors emerged from hiding or returned from camps under the German occupation or from the Soviet Union, they began to envision their future. As part of this emotional process, Palestine began to play a major role as both a personal and collective promised land—a space for national rehabilitation. However, these survivors continued to associate their spatial thinking about Palestine and its positive meaning with the place they were intimately familiar with: Poland. Thus, envisioning the future remained closely tied to evading death during the Holocaust. As the accounts discussed in this chapter demonstrate, their personal hopes were often expressed in collective terms, and their loss as a shared destruction. As they declared their allegiance to the new motherland, they referred to Poland both in terms of a state and in terms of their home town becoming a 'cemetery' after the war. Conclusively, in this juxtaposition, it appears that they did not need a detailed knowledge of the new land or Zionist ideals, or even a concrete geographical understanding. Rather, notions of life, light, youth, and security marked these imaginary borders, which provided a sense of hope for their future—both as individuals and as Jews of the diaspora.

Notes

I am grateful to Maria Ferenc and Hannah Wilson for their comments on an early draft of this chapter.

1 United States Holocaust Memorial Museum, Washington DC, 2011.287.1: 'Hilzenrad Family Papers', 'Diary 1941–1944': Adela Hilzenrad, 'Kiedy bestja się budzi...: Przeżycia z okresu okupacji niemieckiej. Czerwiec 1941 – sierpień 1944 r.', June 1944.

2 Ibid. The White Paper issued by the British government in May 1939 rejected the partition of Palestine, called for the establishment of a Jewish national home in an independent Palestinian state within ten years, limited Jewish migration to Mandatory Palestine to 75,000 for five years after which further immigration would be determined by the Arab majority, and restricted Jews from buying Arab land (*Palestine: Statement of Policy*, British Command Paper 6019 (May 1939)).

3 Y. Zuckerman, *A Surplus of Memory: Chronicle of the Warsaw Ghetto Uprising* (Berkeley, Calif., 1993), 568. Zuckerman was surprised that Berman rejected the notion of illegal Zionist activities. Zuckerman doubted that the Soviet-controlled authorities would give their support to Zionists. On the basis of his experience in the early months of the Soviet occupation in 1939, Zuckerman envisioned building a Hehaluts Zionist underground (ibid. 568–9).

4 Ibid. 565.
5 Ibid. 567.
6 See ibid.; T. Borzykowski, *Between Tumbling Walls* (Lohamei Hagetaot, 1976); Z. Lubetkin, *In the Days of Destruction and Revolt* (Lohamei Hagetaot, 1981); A. Berman, *Biyemei hamaḥteret* (Tel Aviv, 1971); see also H. Folman-Raban, *They Are Still with Me* (Ghetto Fighters' House, 2001).
7 On Zionist activities among survivors, see N. Aleksiun, *Dokąd dalej: Ruch syjonistyczny w Polsce, 1944–1949* (Warsaw, 2002); D. Engel, *Bein shiḥrur liveriḥah: nitsolei hasho'ah bepolin vehama'avak al hanhagatam, 1944–1946* (Tel Aviv, 1996); see also D. Slucki, 'The Bund Abroad in the Postwar Jewish World', *Jewish Social Studies*, 16/1 (2009), 111–44; id., 'Here-ness, there-ness, and everywhere-ness: The Jewish Labour Bund and the Question of Israel, 1944–1955', *Journal of Modern Jewish Studies*, 9 (2010), 349–68; A. Grabski, 'Kształtowanie się pierwotnego programu żydowskich komunistów w Polsce po Holokauście', in G. Berendt, A. Grabski, and A. Stankowski, *Studia z historii Żydów w Polsce po 1945 r.* (Warsaw, 2000), 67–102.
8 Y.-F. Tuan, *Space and Place: The Perspective of Experience* (Minneapolis, 1977).
9 See D. Engel, 'Palestine in the Mind of the Remnants of Polish Jewry', *Journal of Israeli History*, 16 (1995), 221–34.
10 T. Cole, '(Re)Placing the Past: Spatial Strategies of Retelling Difficult Stories', *Oral History Review*, 42 (2015), 30–49.
11 S. E. Hanson, *Time and Revolution: Marxism and the Design of Soviet Institutions* (Chapel Hill, NC, 1997), 11.
12 See *Instrukcje dla zbierania materiałów historycznych z okresu okupacji niemieckiej*, ed. J. Kermisz (Łódź, 1946), 12–21. For the activities of the commission, see L. Jockusch, *Collect and Record! Jewish Holocaust Documentation in Early Postwar Europe* (Oxford, 2012), 84–120.
13 See D. Engel, 'Patterns of Anti-Jewish Violence in Poland, 1944–1946', *Yad Vashem Studies*, 26 (1998), 43–85; J. T. Gross, *Fear: Anti-Semitism in Poland after Auschwitz* (Princeton, NJ, 2006); Pol. edn.: *Strach. Antysemityzm w Polsce tuż po wojnie: Historia moralnej zapaści* (Kraków, 2008); J. Tokarska-Bakir, *Pod klątwą: Społeczny portret pogromu kieleckiego*, 2 vols. (Warsaw, 2018).
14 H. Pollin-Galay, *The Ecologies of Witnessing: Language, Place, and Holocaust Testimony* (New Haven, Conn., 2018), 208–12, 216–18.
15 Hilzenrad, 'Kiedy bestja się budzi…', June 1944.
16 Ibid.
17 Ibid.
18 Ibid.
19 Ibid.
20 See Pollin-Galay, *The Ecologies of Witnessing*, 208–12, 216–18.
21 Hilzenrad, 'Kiedy bestja się budzi…', June 1944.
22 Ibid.
23 Ibid. For more of such accounts, see N. Aleksiun, 'Regards from the Land of the Dead: Jews in Eastern Galicia in the Immediate Aftermath of the Holocaust', *Kwartalnik Historii Żydów*, 246 (2013), 257–71.
24 Hilzenrad, 'Kiedy bestja się budzi…', Aug. 1944.
25 Ibid.
26 Ibid.
27 B. Milch, *Can Heaven Be Void?* (Jerusalem, 2003), 242.

28 Milch, *Can Heaven Be Void?*, 240. He recalled: '[we] usually met twice a week, mostly in the evenings, either outdoors or at the "den". We held fascinating discussions or heard lectures on relevant issues such as Jewish history, national uprisings, and collective living. We all longed to be in Eretz Israel—Palestine—even if it was far away. In fact, young Zionists already began emigrating to Eretz Israel to build a new life' (ibid. 44–5).

29 K. I. Lewin, *Przeżyłem: Saga Świętego Jura spisana w roku 1946 przez syna rabina Lwowa* (Warsaw, 2006), 179.

30 Ibid.

31 Ibid. 182.

32 M. Pachter, *Umierać też trzeba umieć*, ed. B. Engelking (Warsaw, 2015), 655.

33 Archiwum Żydowskiego Instytutu Historycznego, Warsaw (hereafter AŻIH), 301/531: Chaim Wittelson, testimony (Pol.), recorded by A. Laufer, 14 July 1945, p. 4. Born Sosnowiec, son of Leib and Maria, née Rosenberg.

34 Ibid. 6.

35 AŻIH, 301/196: Emanuel Kriegel, testimony (Pol.), recorded in Kraków, 22(?) May 1945, p. 1. Born Buczacz, 25 July 1930, son of Naftali Kriegel, merchant, and Anna Rosenstock.

36 Ibid. 2–3.

37 Ibid. 3.

38 See B. Zawada, 'Żydowski Dom Dziecka w Otwocku 1945–1948', *Kwartalnik Historii Żydów*, 213 (2005), 69–82; see also J. B. Michlic, 'The Raw Memory of War: Early Postwar Testimonies of Children in Dom Dziecka in Otwock', *Yad Vashem Studies*, 37 (2009), 11–52. On the Central Committee of the Jews in Poland, see D. Engel, 'The Reconstruction of Jewish Communal Institutions in Postwar Poland: The Origins of the Central Committee of Polish Jews, 1944–1945', *East European Politics and Societies*, 10 (1996), 85–107.

39 AŻIH, 302/289, pt. 2: 'Z przeżyć Jankla Cieszyńskiego, Otwock, Księga wspomnień', 3.

40 AŻIH, 302/515: Dunia Berman, testimony (Yid.), recorded by Dr Józef Weitz, 16 July 1945, p. 3. Born Horodenka, 1929.

41 AŻIH, 302/289, pt. 1: Franciszka Oliwa, 'Dom ocalonych dzieci w Otwocku, cz. 1: Wspomnienia', 33–4; see also ead., 'Dom ocalonych dzieci w Otwocku (1945–1949): Wspomnienia', *Biuletyn Żydowskiego Instytutu Historycznego*, 1986, no. 3–4, pp. 88–105.

42 AŻIH, 302/313, fo. 188: Szujka Ehrlihman, letter to her sister, Paris, 23 Aug. 1945. Born in Lublin and trained as a nurse, Erlihman survived the ghettos of Lublin and Warsaw.

Between Hostility and Intimacy
Christian and Jewish Polish Citizens in the USSR, Iran, and Palestine

MIKHAL DEKEL

IN EARLY NOVEMBER 1942, the New York-based Jewish aid organization the American Jewish Joint Distribution Committee (JDC) dispatched a representative to Iran to report on Polish Jewish refugees who had recently been evacuated there from Soviet central Asia and on those who were still stranded in the USSR, and in particular on the state of roughly 800 Jewish children who had been evacuated to Iran and awaited transport to Palestine. The purpose of the report was to assess what kind of aid was needed, and how much. The representative, Harry Viteles, an American based in Jerusalem and general manager of the Central Bank of Cooperative Institutions in Palestine, left Palestine on 1 November 1942, stopping in Baghdad for a week and continuing on to Tehran. There, over three weeks, he interviewed ninety individuals—American and British diplomatic and military personnel, Jewish Agency of Palestine workers, members of the Iranian Jewish community, and the refugees themselves—in order to get a clear picture of the situation. The result was a forty-seven-page report, as damning a document of Polish–Jewish relations as exists.[1]

Roughly one and a half million Polish Jewish citizens found themselves within Soviet borders early in the Second World War, whether because they escaped to the USSR or their towns fell under Soviet occupation. Of these, up to a third were exiled to labour settlements and gulags in the Soviet interior. Those who survived were released as a result of the amnesty for Polish citizens of August 1941, and by early 1942 they were mostly concentrated in the five Soviet republics of central Asia: Uzbekistan, Turkmenistan, Tajikistan, Kazakhstan, and Kyrgyzstan. Of these, a small minority of Jewish refugees, including members of the Anders Army—the military force of Polish exiles set up in the Soviet Union under General Władysław Anders —and several thousand civilians, were evacuated alongside Christian Poles to Iran, India, and Palestine. These Polish Jews were, as it is often said, 'saved by their deportation'.[2] Yet theirs was not exclusively a Jewish fate: they were exiled alongside ethnic Poles and other minority Polish citizens, amnestied as Polish citizens, and continued to Iran, India, and Palestine along with Christian Poles. Their ordeal, therefore, is not just a Jewish survival story, but a story of wartime relations between Jewish and Christian Polish citizens outside Nazi-occupied Poland.

These relations can be observed along a timeline that includes roughly four periods and four locations: exile to and incarceration in Soviet labour settlements (1940–1); mass migrations to and life in the central Asian republics (1941–5); life in

Iran (1942–3); and life in Palestine (1943–7). In all four locations, the lives of Jewish and Christian Polish citizens were governed and shaped by the laws and policies of empire (the Soviet empire in the labour colonies and central Asia; the British empire in Iran and Palestine). In all four there were differences between individuals, families, and host communities that greatly affected Polish–Jewish relations. Nonetheless, testimonies given by Jewish and Christian Polish refugees collected by the Polish government-in-exile, memoirs of Jewish and Christian refugees, wartime reports like that of Harry Viteles and others, bystander testimonies, and other sources offer a fairly consistent portrait of Polish–Jewish relations in each period and each location. In general, it is a picture of a progressively deteriorating relationship—until the arrival in Palestine. There—the final destination for many Polish Jews and the place where many Christian Poles remained the longest—some diminution in hostility occurred. While for most Polish Jews—whether Zionist or not—the Land of Israel became their homeland, for most Christian Poles, it was a largely agreeable, hospitable place of refuge and a centre of Polish culture outside Poland.[3]

Relations between Jewish and Christian Polish Citizens in Soviet Exile

One of the most useful sources available for understanding the mammoth journey Polish citizens undertook during the war years are the testimonies collected by the Polish Information Centre for the East (Centrum Informacji na Wschód; CIW), an arm of the London-based Polish government-in-exile. While the centre's official purpose was to document the living conditions of and the abuses against Polish citizens in the USSR, with the hope that this would help thwart the future creation of a Bolshevik Polish state, the testimonies (*protokoły palestyńskie*) it collected reveal much more than that.[4] On relations between Christian and Jewish Polish citizens, the testimonies, which were collected in Iran, India, Jerusalem, and other places of evacuation, suggest that during the initial period of exile there was, alongside some strife and even violence, a degree of 'heartfelt' co-operation between Jews and Poles in the labour camps and gulags. 'Jews and Poles helped each other in anything they could', 15-year-old Hannania Teitel recounted in the testimony he gave to the CIW in 1943.[5] It was a sentiment repeated in numerous testimonies and with regard to multiple settlements, especially those that were predominantly populated by Jews. Jewish refugees described bonding over a common language and a common desire to return to Poland, where both Jewish and Christian Polish citizens were repeatedly told by camp commanders they would never return. A Jewish child, testifying before the CIW, reported that, 'In the *posiolok* [settlement] were many Poles who were friendly to us, helped us settle in, and gave us useful advice'; another stated that, 'in our *posiolok* there were thirty Poles and six hundred Jews, and relations with them were very good. Among them was a high Polish official—a devout Catholic and an anti-semite—who became friendly with my father. They would have long conversations and became convinced that religion was the only consolation in that terrible situation.'⁶ Such testimonies reveal that, while incarcerated in labour settlements and gulags and oppressed by a common Soviet enemy (and by Ukrainian kulaks as immediate supervisors), relations between Jewish and Christian Poles were reasonable and at times even good and co-operative.

After the amnesty for Polish citizens, the mass migration south, the creation of the Anders Army, and the arrival of aid from the United States and elsewhere, Polish–Jewish relations began to deteriorate. Polish Jewish citizens who flocked to the Anders Army were eventually largely prevented from enlisting or were dismissed after enlistment (whether because of Soviet law, antisemitism in the military's ranks, or both); aid, paid for by Jewish and Polish charities, was distributed unequally among Jewish and Christian Polish refugees; an initial co-operation between the JDC and the Polish government-in-exile in a joint attempt to aid the refugees was eventually halted. Despite an 'official assurance' by the Polish ambassador in Washington that 'the Jews are to be given the same treatment as other Polish nationals now on Soviet soil', the distribution of aid, which was administered by delegates of the Polish government, did not, by and large, reach many Jewish refugees. This was why Harry Viteles was dispatched to Iran to assess the situation.[7]

Polish–Jewish Relations in Iran

In March and August 1942 roughly 75,000 Anders Army soldiers and 41,000 Polish civilians were evacuated from the USSR to Iran. The number of Jews among them was minuscule: roughly 3,500 soldiers and 2,500 civilians, including 871 children who would become known in Israel as *yaldei teheran*, the 'Tehran children'. In addition to the official count were several hundred stowaways, women who had entered into marriages of convenience with Anders Army soldiers in order to be allowed to leave the USSR, and recent Jewish converts to Catholicism.[8] These lived mostly in Tehran while official Jewish evacuees were for the most part lodged in larger Polish refugee camps across Iran. Unaccompanied Jewish children were brought from these camps into what became known as 'Beit Hayeladim Hayehudim Beteheran', the Jewish Children's Home of Tehran, a building and four tents located at the edge of the Polish camp at Dushan Tappeh, inside a former Iranian airforce base.

Viteles reported that refugees from 'all classes' of Jewish society in Tehran—Labour, Zionist, Bundists, and even nationalists who were 'staunch supporters of close co-operation and collaboration with the Polish Government'[9]—attested to the unequal distribution of aid between Jews and non-Jews. Iranian and British soldiers testified that during the March–April 1942 transports from Kranovodsk (now Turkmenbashi in Turkmenistan) to Iran, Polish children had arrived in Pahlavi with boxes of Manischewitz matzos and wearing clothing with Hebrew trademarks, allegedly sent from Palestine for Jewish children. Members of the American Red Cross in Tehran, who routinely visited Polish refugee camps in Iran, testified that 'the Polish administration was less concerned with the welfare and comfort of the Jewish refugees than they were with that of non-Jews'; that non-Jews were given 'better housing facilities', while the children in the children's home 'lived under canvas'; and, in addition, that non-Jews, particularly children, had 'better food', 'more blankets', and 'more suitable clothing' than Jews.[10] They also cited rampant 'dishonesty, unfairness, inefficiency, waste and extreme selfishness' in the administration of Polish refugee camps and rampant black-market dealings.[11] Viteles' report also found evidence of antisemitism in the Anders Army; anti-Jewish bias with regard to the number of Polish Jews who were allowed to join the army and to be evacuated from Soviet central Asia to Iran; and reports of bullying of Jewish children.

In turn, the Polish embassy in Tehran submitted to the Polish Foreign Ministry in London a report on its treatment of Polish Jews, in which it continued to maintain that the law of the Republic of Poland did not differentiate between Polish citizens on the basis of ethnicity, religion, or race. It alleged that any such discrimination had been the responsibility of the Soviet authorities, who had prevented Jews from enlisting in the Anders Army and from being evacuated to Iran. It highlighted an order from General Anders of 10 November 1941, in which he instructed his commanding officers to combat antisemitism. It claimed that the Polish embassy had tried to facilitate the evacuation to Iran of 400 additional Jewish refugees, but this had been blocked by the Soviet authorities, and also cited the names of prominent Jews it had nonetheless managed to include in the evacuations. It pointed to its efforts to intervene on behalf of Polish Jews who had not been released from camps and prisons, and of others who had been arrested, and also cited examples of attempts to appoint Polish Jews as welfare delegates in the USSR which were prevented by the Soviet authorities.[12]

Anders went still further. In a meeting of 27 October 1942 with General Henry Maitland Wilson, commander-in-chief of the British forces in Persia and Iraq, he claimed that those responsible for corruption, shortages, price gouging, and the sale of supplies earmarked for refugees on the black market were NKVD agents and civilians, 'Jews in particular', who had been evacuated from the USSR with the convoys but were now living in Tehran.[13]

The squalid living conditions of the Polish Jewish child refugees in Iran were noted by many observers and by the children themselves. When, in late October 1942, Zipora Shertok (Sharett), wife of the head of the Foreign Department of the Jewish Agency Moshe Shertok, arrived in Iran to visit the children, she reported miserable living conditions and children ill with scabies, eye disorders, and other infectious diseases. 'The children eat their bread portion at breakfast and are left without bread all day', she wrote. 'Less than a quarter of them have more than one set of underwear; two hundred are barefoot and the rest wear dilapidated shoes; no one has sweaters.' She described them as 'half naked', waiting for their only shirt or undershirt to return from the laundry.[14]

Emil Landau, a Warsaw-born Jewish teenager who kept a travel diary, described 'bread portions' that 'disappeared already after breakfast' and altercations with 'Polish antisemites':

The food is brought from the relatively distant camp kitchen. On its way it passes through several barracks of Polish antisemites who tend to block the way. At six a.m., a whole battalion is needed to march there and fetch the food for 700 people. The fetchers sometimes have no shoes, no socks, and no warm shirts. They walk with chattering teeth, freezing.[15]

Meanwhile, photographs and testimonies showed unaccompanied Christian Polish children living in villas, convents, and the vast estate of the pro-British former governor of Isfahan, Prince Sarem od-Doleh. Isfahan became known as the 'city of Polish children'.[16] They lived, as Iranian documentary photographer Parisa Damandan describes it, 'behind closed doors in a Polish environment... The "Poland of Isfahan" was an independent state within Iran.'[17] Polish children were taught a Polish curriculum by Polish teachers; studied Polish language, history, geography, and religion; listened to Polish radio and read Polish magazines; and celebrated Catholic festivals with the assistance of Catholic priests. According to a former 'Isfahan child': 'We had whatever we needed... we were happy in Isfahan.'[18] But beyond the disparity in living conditions, what developed in Iran were disparate Polish and Jewish national identities. In the larger Polish camp in Dushan Tappeh, eagles with crowns and shields—the Polish coat of arms—were carved into the ground and built out of rocks and candles. Meanwhile, in the Jewish children's camp, a banner bearing the words 'Beit Hayeladim Hayehudim Beteheran' was hung at the entrance. Zionist counsellors, most of them members of Hashomer Hatsa'ir, taught the children Hebrew songs. Rabbis, Zionist-leaning Iranian Jews, Zipora Shertok, and others visited and told stories of the Land of Israel. 'I was no longer a hapless refugee... but belonged to a nation', camp director David Lauenberg (Laor), a former Polish army officer cadet, wrote in his testimony.[19]

And so, in Iran, as is clear from film and testimonies, the two identities, Polish and Jewish, split off from each other and clashed even more strongly than in the pre-war period. Iran, with its decentralized, multi-ethnic, multi-lingual make-up, so radically different from the homogeneous European nation-states, tolerated the development of a Polish and to an extent also a Jewish independent state-in-exile within its borders. Shortly after the arrival of the Polish Jewish refugees, members of Mosad Le'aliyah Beit, the clandestine immigration arm of the Jewish Agency, arrived and eventually made contact with the local Jewish population. In Tehran, Hamadan, Isfahan, and Abadan, Hebrew study groups were established and Zionist booklets were translated into Persian.[20] 'Tehran', a Mosad Le'aliyah Beit agent wrote, 'was the beginning of Zionism as a "movement of the masses". Like all youth movements we spoke about "the masses"... but our notion was of an anonymous mass... The real meaning of the masses, just regular Jews, we saw for the first time in Tehran.'[21]

Jews and Poles in the Land of Israel

In early 1943 the Tehran children, their caregivers, and some other individuals were evacuated to Palestine. The Iraqi government, which supported the Arab cause in Palestine, refused them passage to Tel Aviv by land, and so they travelled by sea, on a harrowing voyage through the Persian Gulf, the Indian Ocean—full of mines—and the Suez Canal. In addition to the Jewish refugees, approximately 70,000 Anders Army soldiers and family members and hundreds of Polish civilians, including orphaned children, were also transferred to Palestine. Civilians travelled by car through Iraq and Syria. The army transferred from Iran to Khanakin in Iraq, then continued on a month-long trek to Palestine. Yehuda Pompiansky, a Jewish soldier in the Anders Army, testified that, en route to Palestine, Polish commanders referred to their destination as 'the Land of Israel' and the 'country of the Jews'.[22] Once they were in Palestine, Anders Army soldiers joined other Polish refugees who had been evacuated there earlier. In a news dispatch of 18 February 1942, Joseph Levy, the *New York Times* correspondent, reported that 30,000 Polish Jews and non-Jews had been admitted to Palestine since the war began two and a half years earlier, and that Palestine stood to become the 'principal centre for the absorption of Polish refugees'.[23]

In Palestine, the Jewish and Polish children immediately embarked on very different trajectories. The Tehran children, who were greeted ecstatically by the Yishuv, were entrusted to the care of Henrietta Szold and Youth Aliyah, and were eventually settled in kibbutzim, agricultural villages, and religious institutions (mostly Mizrachi) across the land.[24] Meanwhile, orphaned Christian children were lodged in Catholic boarding schools, while the adults lived in Haifa, Gedera, Rehovot, Castina, Tel Aviv, Nazareth, Jerusalem, and other cities. Soldiers, civilians, government officials, and Polish Red Cross workers now constituted the largest concentration of Poles in the east. As Valentina Brio has shown, this was where they built their largest cultural centre outside Poland. 'Palestine was the meeting of political, cultural, and social minds. It was the place of exile in the East where the Poles stayed the longest.'[25]

In Palestine, the Anders Army prepared for its subsequent engagement in what would become known as the Battle of Monte Cassino: in a large-scale drill they 'conquered' Mount Sinai, Nazareth, and other locations. Here they also lived a cultural life, with meetings of authors and journalists and poetry readings, such as the one organized by the Hebrew poet Saul Tchernichowsky with the Polish poets Władysław Broniewski and Marian Czuchnowski.[26]

A flourishing Polish-language press emerged in Palestine: *Gazeta Polska*, a daily paper for Poles in the Middle East; a soldiers' journal; a women's paper; a youth magazine; and a fortnightly literary review, *W drodze*.[27] Books of poetry, anthologies, and textbooks were published, and the Hebrew University assisted Polish publishing houses in producing new editions of Polish books already in its library:[28] local Polish-born Jews and Catholic refugees collaborated. Polish articles thought to be of interest to the local population were immediately translated for the Hebrew newspapers. Articles about Hebrew poets, including Tchernichowsky, who had ties to Polish literature, were translated and published in Polish journals.[29] Local Polish-born musicians played in Polish orchestras and in the jazz band of Henryk Wars, a Jewish pioneer of Polish jazz who had arrived with the Anders Army.[30] Gatherings of authors and artists were often a way for Anders Army soldiers to secure leave. 'Never in the history of Poland were there so many painters, journalists, and writers in such vicinity to armed force', one wrote.³¹

Polish poets went to kibbutzim. Marian Czuchnowski took classes at an agricultural school in Kibbutz Givat Brenner and wrote a book about Degania. Władysław Broniewski held readings in a kibbutz, most likely Ein Harod; once, when a generator failed and he had no light by which to read, a young kibbutz member continued, reciting Broniewski's poem by heart.³² In Tel Aviv and Jerusalem, contact between Poles and Jews bore a resemblance to the relations of urban Poles and Jews in the large cities of Poland in the interwar period. Local nightlife, and especially the brothels of Tel Aviv, was very popular with Polish soldiers; yet quarrels between Jewish and Christian high-school students in Tel Aviv were documented by the police; and some inter-ethnic tensions 'migrated' from the old country to the place of refuge and survived in the big-city environment. The Jewish press reported two murders by Polish soldiers, a fistfight at a technical school, and an attempted arson at Beit Ha'am, the largest auditorium in Tel Aviv.³³ Alexander Zawisza, writing for the anti-semitic London-based Polish newspaper *Myśl Polska*, warned of 'the Jews of Palestine' who possessed 'no pro-Polish feelings' but awaited 'the opportunity of returning to Poland'.³⁴ Yet to some degree the tensions and nationalism that characterized the lives of Jewish and Christian Poles in Iran and before in central Asia subsided. The Polish commandant of the Tel Aviv regiment, Major Wróblewski, categorically denied that Polish soldiers been responsible for any murders, and attributed the unrest to 'a drunk Polish soldier' who provoked an argument that had been blown out of all proportion. He claimed that, in fact, it was a Polish soldier who had been murdered in Tel Aviv.³⁵ Certainly, throughout the land, members of the Yishuv and the Polish refugees collaborated. Much of the cultural collaboration rested, it seems, on the shared Polish language. The *Jerusalem Post* reported on articles in *W drodze*; according to its editor, 'most of the people involved in the *Jerusalem Post* know Polish better than English'.³⁶

At a makeshift theatre in Jerusalem's Edison House, Polish Jewish actors from Palestine performed alongside Christian ones; Polish Jewish journalists like David Lazar and Paulina Appenszlak, editor of a pre-war feminist paper, *Ewa*, a supplement of *Nasz Przegląd*, wrote for Polish papers; dozens of memoirs and diaries, such as that of the poet and Anders Army officer Bronisław Brzezicki, were written; 842 Polish-language books (out of 947 in the entire Middle East) were published, 340 volumes being donated to the central library in Jerusalem when the Polish refugees left.³⁷

Dr Stanisław Kot, who had served as the Polish government-in-exile's ambassador in Moscow and Kuibyshev and then in Tehran, was in Palestine as well. A former member of the Polish Peasant Party which had opposed Piłsudski's rule in Poland before the war, he now resided in Jerusalem, serving as minister of state for the Middle East. Upon arrival from Iran, Kot spent weeks in recovery at Carmel sanatorium, a 12-acre hilly resort in Haifa overlooking the Mediterranean, which was founded by Dr Wilhelm Bodenheimer, a German Jewish refugee. It was there that he met Moshe Shertok and hinted at the possibility of additional evacuations from the

USSR, which triggered a frenzy of rumours that thousands of Polish Jewish children would soon be arriving in the Land of Israel.[38]

In the wake of the exposure of the murder of Polish officers by the Soviets in Katyń, Polish–Soviet relations were broken off, secret evacuation talks were halted, and the additional Polish Jewish children did not arrive. At the beginning of 1944 the Anders Army departed for Italy, but Polish civilians and military and government administrators remained in Palestine, many until the end of the British Mandate in 1947. The CIW remained active as well, continuing to interview Polish citizens in Palestine, including the Tehran children. Its questionnaire, whose main focus was on refugees' lives in the Soviet Union, was expanded to include questions on resistance, religious life, the experience of women, and Polish–Jewish relations. Testimonies had been taken from Polish Jews before, but it was in Jerusalem that identification of religious affiliation began to be documented.[39]

At the CIW, Jewish and Christian Poles—including a Polish aristocrat, Teresa Lipkowska, and the journalists David Glazer and Dovid Flinker—worked together to collect the testimonies of both Jewish and Christian Polish refugees in Palestine. Flinker, a Warsaw-based journalist, descendant of a Ger hasidic family, and former editor of the Warsaw-based Polish-language Jewish daily *Echo Żydowskie* and the Yiddish *Dos yudishe togblat*, conducted some of the interviews in Yiddish. 'Testimony 26', for example, is full of Yiddish idioms, such as *es helft vi a toytn bankes* ('it helped like applying cupping glasses to a corpse') and the like.[40] It is unclear whether the turn from Polish to Yiddish was done for pragmatic or political reasons or both.

In Palestine, Jews and Poles lived relatively harmoniously. This seems to have been predicated on the fact that the Jews in the Land of Israel now had their own aims, separate from Poland, and on Polish admiration for the technological and agricultural innovations in Palestine.[41] The relative thaw in the relationship extended elsewhere. In Iran in March 1943 the Jewish Agency of Palestine in Tehran threw a Purim party and invited Polish and British officials. A year later, in late 1944, Jewish Agency representative Dr Moshe Yishai sat side by side with the Polish consul in Tehran at a memorial service for Jews killed in the Warsaw ghetto. The speeches at the memorial, which was held at a Tehran synagogue, were given in Yiddish, and Yishai translated them for the consul. He had visited Palestine, Yishai writes in his memoir, and admired the 'different Jew'—not the 'merchant or a pedlar'—that the Land of Israel had produced. He respected the 'enterprise' but emphasized that his 'change in thinking [about Jews] only applied to the Jews of the Land of Israel'.[42]

In addition to serving as a place of refuge, Palestine became a centre from where aid was shipped to Polish refugees in central Asia and Africa. The Polish government-in-exile commissioned the production of typhus vaccines in Palestine, which were then sent to other places of exile, and bought vitamins and medicines. In Tel Aviv, a sweater-knitting circle provided clothing, and a soup kitchen collected food for shipment. Doctors—Poles, Jews, and non-refugees—were enlisted to care for Polish refugees in Nairobi. School supplies, textbooks, notebooks, pencils, pens, Polish books, prayer books, song books, records with Polish songs, dictionaries, typewriters with Polish typeface, and national symbols to be hung at cultural centres were bought. These efforts, according to Polish sources, were undertaken jointly with the Jewish Agency, which contributed £250,000 for relief that was sent to the refugees in central Asia.[43]

At a meeting of the Zionist Agency's Executive Council on 25 April 1942, Moshe Shertok, who had met Prime Minister Sikorski and the Jewish Polish government council member Ignacy Schwarzbart in London, praised the Polish government-in-exile for its report 'Mass Extermination of Jews in German Occupied Poland'.[44] This was based on the reports of Jan Karski, who undertook clandestine missions out of Poland and informed the Polish government-in-exile and others about the extermination of Jews in Nazi-occupied Poland. According to Shertok:

We had already received news of the slaughter in Poland ... of the systematic extermination, of the transport by trains ... from eye-witnesses who have made it to Palestine. But, until the official declaration of the Polish government there was a pact of silence between the British government and the British press ... What has elevated the urgency of the matter was the Polish dispatch ... I do not analyse the Polish motives, what they are thinking or not thinking ... But [Anthony] Eden's declaration [in the House of Lords about the extermination of Jews] would not have happened without the dispatch. It is a historical fact, the first international act to place the slaughter on the global agenda.[45]

In 1943 the Hebrew University in Jerusalem invited Stanisław Kot for a tour and a meeting of its general assembly.[46]

During this time, two-thirds of the Jewish soldiers in the Anders Army deserted, many joining the Yishuv's main paramilitary group, the Haganah. 'Why should we have stayed in the Polish army given how we were treated?', Yehuda Pompiansky wrote.[47] One-third of the Jewish soldiers nonetheless remained and fought at Monte Cassino, and at least one Polish-born Jewish man who had not been among the refugees joined the troops as well.[48] General Anders did not oppose Jewish soldiers leaving the army ('only the British searched for us', Pompiansky wrote in his testimony).[49] In the wake of the battle, when the song 'Red Poppies on Monte Cassino' was released, it was sung by the Polish Jewish singer Adam Aston.

Throughout this period, Polish schoolchildren studied in Catholic schools in Nazareth and Jerusalem and in schools established by the Anders Army.[50] In addition, Polish adult civilians and military administrative staff studied in various institutions. The Polish Institute and Sikorski Museum at Princes Gate, London, is filled with traces of their lives: expense books; lists of flowers, dresses, and typewriters bought; tuition bills for the Hebrew University in Jerusalem; courses and training programmes; receipts for rooms at the Julian Hotel in Jerusalem; recommendation letters for Polish students at the Jerusalem Conservatory of Music; lists of leisure and self-improvement items and activities; and so on.

In the Sikorski archive there are lists of Polish refugees in Palestine classified by city of residence, marital status, military or civilian, and religion. There are details of financial support, either recurring or one-off payments. There is a report of the soup kitchen in Tel Aviv and the quantities of sugar it required. There is a letter from a physician regarding the health of Polish refugees: those who needed urgent dental care, glasses, and orthopaedic treatment. There are the bylaws of the Association of Polish Lawyers in Jerusalem. There are reports on the activities of the Association of Lawyers, the Association of Technicians and Engineers, the Society of Biologists, and the Polish Red Cross in Tel Aviv. There is a report on a higher education lecture series, with lists of specialists in the fields of health care, education, farming, engineering, accounting, and translation, and lists of available English-language courses and lectures.[51]

'These were the best years of my life', Krystyna Orłowska, a former Polish refugee who now lives in Denver, stated in a 2017 interview. Evacuated to Palestine in November 1943, Orłowska remained there until October 1947, studying and boarding at the School of Young Volunteers in Nazareth.

I studied with Poles and Jews and Arabs and on weekends and breaks we would travel together to Tiberias and Tel Aviv to see movies . . . Once my friends and I walked all the way to the Carmelite Monastery in Haifa. The priests were so friendly, and the Arab boys so polite . . . The father of one of the Arab boys had a car and would drive us to the beach. We'd get ice cream, play ball, tan . . . I don't know what happened between Jews and Arabs, in those days everyone got along.[52]

And yet in Kibbutz Ein Harod, less than 20 miles away from Nazareth, twenty Tehran children were actively experiencing the simmering Arab–Jewish conflict, some of them already enlisted in the Haganah, living in run-down, swelteringly hot shacks, studying Hebrew, and working in the fields. Strict work and study schedules, lack of funds, and the tense political situation meant that they could rarely travel to the beach or to Tel Aviv to watch movies, let alone live, like some of the Polish refugees, in Baka, Katamon, or Rehavia, Jerusalem's loveliest neighbourhoods. But they now belonged to a nation-in-becoming. On the day of their arrival in Ein Harod, they were welcomed with music and singing and a banner that read, 'You are no longer Tehran children or refugee children but Ein Harod children like us.' Asked to choose a name for their group, they decided on Ets, the Hebrew word for 'tree' and the acronym for *olim tse'irim* (young *olim*, those who have 'ascended' to the Land of Israel).

'We are all hopeful', their teacher said, 'that this tree will become entrenched within us and grow deep roots and abundant branches.'[53] Indeed, nearly all Tehran children became Israeli citizens and grew abundant family branches in Israel, many fighting and several dying in Israel's wars. Two of them—Janusz Ben Gal and Hayim Erez—became generals; Emil Landau, the boy who had documented his journey in a travel diary, would receive one of Israel's first medals of honour, posthumously.

Most Christian Poles—the Polish children who had been studying in Nazareth and Jerusalem, the Polish civilian refugees, the non-combatant personnel, and the workers at the Government Delegation for Poland, the Polish Red Cross, and the CIW —would leave Palestine with the end of the British Mandate. If their Jewish peers had 'ascended' homeward, to the Land of Israel, the Christian Polish refugees would not be returning home to what was now the People's Republic of Poland. Many left for the UK, some ending up in displaced persons camps in England and Wales; some went to New Zealand, where the children of Isfahan, who remained in Iran for the duration of the war, were eventually transferred.

In the end it was Palestine that would be the most hospitable and longest-lasting place of refuge for Christian Polish citizens. Yet this is a chapter in Jewish and Polish history that seems to have been erased from both Jewish and Polish cultural memory ('I never understood and no one ever told me how come my mother's birth certificate was issued in Tel Aviv', Dr Asia Stefano, a scientist at MIT whose parents are Polish, said in a 2018 interview. 'No one would explain to me.'[54])

Some Christian Poles who collected Jewish testimonies for the CIW stayed in Palestine and then in Israel. Teresa Lipkowska became a mathematics teacher in a school in Haifa.[55] Some Polish artists, such as the filmmaker Josef Lejtes, continued coming and going to Israel. Lejtes made the first English-language feature drama in the Land of Israel, *My Father's House*. His next two films were also made in Israel: *Ein bererah* and *Faithful City*, a film that IMDb describes as depicting 'some of the courage, patience, bravery and understanding that attended the birth of Israel as a free and independent nation'.[56]

Traces of Polish lives—a plaque at a Catholic church in Ein Karem with 'Here in Ain Karem, children from the Polish school offer their thanks to God for deliverance from exile in Soviet Russia' carved on it in Polish; 340 Polish-language books, printed in Palestine, housed in the National Library in Jerusalem; an archive of Polish soldiers' memoirs; books about the Land of Israel written during their stay; a neatly manicured section allotted to Polish soldiers and refugees at the Catholic cemetery in Jerusalem; Polish graves in Jaffa, Ramallah, Haifa, and Jerusalem; plaques on the Via Dolorosa in Jerusalem and in a monastery in Tiberias; and spontaneous engravings on stones in Latroon and elsewhere, where the Anders Army trained—these remain in plain sight in today's Israel, but are looked at vacantly by the many who see them as undecipherable signs.

Notes

1 JDC Archives, New York Office, 1933–1944, file 712: Harry Viteles, 'Report on Visit to Bagdad (2.XI–9.XI, 1942) and Tehran (11.XI–2.XII, 1942)', 31 Dec. 1942; see also file 713.

2 M. Edele, S. Fitzpatrick, J. Goldlust, and A. Grossmann, 'Introduction: Shelter From the Holocaust: Rethinking Jewish Survival in the Soviet Union', in eid. (eds.), *Shelter From the Holocaust: Rethinking Jewish Survival in the Soviet Union* (Detroit, 2017), 1–27: 20.

3 See M. Dekel, *Tehran Children: A Holocaust Refugee Odyssey* (New York, 2019).

4 Copies of over 10,000 of the testimonies are stored in the Hoover Institution, Stanford University ('Poland: Ministerstwo Informacji i Dokumentacji Records, 1939–1945', 'Reports of Polish Detainees, 1941'); forty Yiddish testimonies, including four by Tehran children, are stored in Ginzakh Kidush Hashem, Benei Berak; and some Hebrew translations of testimonies are held by the Moreshet Archive, Mordechai Anielevich Memorial

Holocaust Studies and Research Center, Givat Haviva. See also H. Grynberg, *Dzieci Syjonu* (Warsaw, 1994); Eng. trans.: *Children of Zion*, trans. J. Mitchell (Evanston, Ill., 1997); Dekel, *Tehran Children*; E. Adler, *Survival on the Margins* (Cambridge, 2020); M. Siekierski and F. Tych (eds.), *Widziałem Anioła Śmierci: Losy deportowanych Żydów polskich w ZSRR w latach II wojny światowej* (Warsaw, 2006), 30–1.

5 Ginzakh Kidush Hashem, Benei Berak, David Flinker papers: 'Testimony of Hannania Teitel, 15 years old, born in Ostrów Mazowiecka, son of Zindel Teitel, co-owner of the Ostrów Maz. brewery. Arrived in Israel from Russia through Tehran in 1943' (Yid.); see Dekel, *Tehran Children*, 104.

6 Grynberg, *Children of Zion*, 89.

7 JDC Archives, New York Office, 1933–1944, file 421: minutes of the meeting of the JDC Executive Committee, 10 Dec. 1941; see Dekel, *Tehran Children*, 172–210.

8 After the amnesty, the Polish government-in-exile put the total number of Poles in the USSR at 1.2 million, with at least a quarter of them Jewish. The Soviet government declared the number of 'Polish citizens deprived of freedom', which it had released, to be 345,511. Jewish sources estimated the number of Polish Jews in central Asia to between 350,000 and 500,000 (Dekel, *Tehran Children*, 235).

9 Viteles, 'Report on Visit to Bagdad (2.XI–9.XI, 1942) and Tehran (11.XI–2.XII, 1942)'.

10 Ibid.

11 Ibid.; see J. Aldridge, 'Abuses by Poles in Tehran Reported: Correspondent Says Refugees even Sold Relief Goods Supplied by Americans', *North American Newspaper Alliance*, 13 Mar. 1943.

12 United States Holocaust Memorial Museum Archive, Washington DC (hereafter USHMM), KOL-25-33A: Polish embassy, Kuybyshev, 'Sprawa Żydów obywateli polskich w świetle oficjalnych dokumentów oraz praktyki władz radzieckich, Kujbyszew 11 VIII 1942'.

13 Polish Institute and Sikorski Museum Archive, London, AXII.65/1: 'Meeting at Tehran on 27 October, 1942 between the C.-in-C. and General Anders. Lt. Colonels Szymański and Hulls were also Present'.

14 Central Zionist Archive, Jerusalem, A245\121-23: Zipora Shertok, letter to her children, 14 Nov. 1942.

15 Emil Landau, diary. Courtesy of Ilana Landau; translated from the Polish by Uri Orlev.

16 P. Damandan, *The Children of Esfahan. Polish Refugees in Iran: Portrait Photographs of Abolqasem Jala, 1942–1945* (Tehran, 2010); see also K. Sinai (dir.), *The Lost Requiem*, documentary (Islamic Republic of Iran Broadcasting, 1983).

17 Damadan, *The Children of Isfahan*, 274.

18 Sinai (dir.), *The Lost Requiem*.

19 G. R. Ben-Michael, interview with David Laor (Lauenberg), in 'Yaldei teheran', *Biton forum lishemirat zikaron hasho'ah*, 33 (2010), 92–114: 108; on daily life in the Tehran camp, see G. Shamir, *Yaldei teheran* (Yaron Golan, 1989).

20 See M. Yishai, *Tsir beli to'ar: rishmei shelihut umasa beparas* (Tel Aviv, 1950).

21 Moreshet Archives, Mordechai Anielewicz Memorial (hereafter MAMAM), A.1584.14: Efraim Shiloh, testimony (Heb.), 28 Apr. 1980.

22 MAMAM, A.1492.02: Yehuda Pompiansky, testimony (Heb.), 2 Mar. 1966.

23 J. Levy, 'Palestine Serves as Refugee Haven', *New York Times*, 21 Feb. 1942, p. 4.

24 See Dekel, *Tehran Children*, 307–56.

25 V. Brio, *Pol'skie muzy na Svyatoi Zemle: Armiya Andersa: mesto, vremya, kul'tura (1942–1945)* (Moscow, 2017), 15.

26 Ibid. 63.
27 Ibid. 258.
28 Ibid. 72.
29 Ibid. 63, 277.
30 Ibid. 66, 120.
31 See ibid. 64.
32 M. Krutikov, 'When Polish Intellectuals Thrived in Pre-State Israel' (29 Mar. 2017): Forward website, visited 19 Oct. 2021.
33 'Poles attack Jews in Palestine: Polish Paper Questions Jewish Loyalty to Poland', *Jewish Telegraphic Agency*, 7 Feb. 1943.
34 Ibid.
35 USHMM, KOL-25-39A, fos. 214–15: Major Wróblewski, report on the distribution of funds by the Polish Refugee Aid Office in Jerusalem, 30 Aug. 1942. In the report were also hundreds of typed documents detailing funds allotted for each person and institution, perhaps as a response to allegations of misuse of funds in Iran.
36 Brio, *Pol'skie muzy na Svyatoi Zemle*, 262.
37 Ibid. 2, 75–6.
38 Moshe Sharett (Shertok), 'Yeshivat hanhalat hasokhnut yerushalayim, 25.4.1943. Aḥarit davar', ed. Y. Sharett (11 Nov. 1942): Moshe Sharett and His Legacy website, visited 13 May 2021.
39 See Siekierski and Tych (eds.), *Widziałem Anioła Śmierci*, 30–1.
40 'Testimony of Hannania Teitel' (Yid.).
41 Brio, *Pol'skie muzy na Svyatoi Zemle*, 75–6.
42 Yishai, *Tsir beli to'ar*, 90; see also MAMAM, C.54.02.01: Mosad Le'aliyah Beit, secret memo, 29 Sept. 1942. In his memoir, Yishai described how the Polish consul came to bid him goodbye at the airport upon his return to Palestine (Yishai, *Tsir beli to'ar*, 326).
43 Polish Institute and Sikorski Museum Archive, London, A19II/116, 'Palestine'; Wróblewski, report on the distribution of funds by the Polish Refugee Aid Office in Jerusalem, 30 Aug. 1942.
44 Kenyon College, Bulmash Family Holocaust Collection, 2012.1.98: Edward Bernard Raczyński, *The Mass Extermination of Jews in German Occupied Poland*, brochure printed by the Polish government-in-exile's Ministry of Foreign Affairs to foreign ministers, 10 Dec, 1942.
45 Shertok, 'Yeshivat hanhalat hasokhnut yerushalayim'.
46 Brio, *Pol'skie muzy na Svyatoi Zemle*, 227.
47 Polish authorities blamed Jewish Agency representatives for encouraging Jewish Anders Army soldiers to desert and for conducting interviews to prove that they had deserted due to bad treatment of Jews in the army (Yehuda Pompiansky, testimony (Heb.)).
48 18-year-old Julian Bussgang enlisted in the Anders Army in Tel Aviv on 10 November 1943 (USHMM, Museum Photo Archive, #73240: group portrait of students, both Catholic and Jewish, in the Polish high school in Tel Aviv, Mar. 1942).
49 Yehuda Pompiansky, testimony (Heb.).
50 Brio, *Pol'skie muzy na Svyatoi Zemle*, 68.
51 'Meeting at Tehran on 27 October, 1942 between the C.-in-C. and General Anders. Lt. Colonels Szymański and Hulls were also Present'.
52 Krystyna Orłowska, phone interview with author, 10 Oct. 2017.

53 Ein Harod Archive: 'Yomanei ein harod', 21 May 1943; quoted in Dekel, *Tehran Children*, 341.
54 Asia Stefano, interview with Peter Tsvetkov, Cambridge, Mass., 12 Apr. 2018. This was one of a series of interviews I arranged with descendants of Christian Poles who had spent the war years in Tel Aviv.
55 That negative accounts of the treatment of the Tehran children by Poles were not edited out of their testimonies is credited to Teresa Lipkowska (see Siekierski and Tych (eds.), *Widziałem Anioła Śmierci*, 30).
56 'The Faithful City (1952)': IMDb website, visited 9 Sept. 2021.

Mordecai Tsanin
Yiddish Orphanhood in Israel and Afterlife in Poland

MONIKA ADAMCZYK-GARBOWSKA

Fighting for the Yiddish Word

Soon after the end of the Second World War various Jewish organizations, institutions, and newspapers sent their representatives to Poland to examine the situation of the Jewish survivors. Of those travellers, some were journalists or professional writers, others political and social activists. Most of them were members of official delegations and stopped in Warsaw at the Hotel Polonia, the only decent hotel left in the ruined city. Usually, as well as visiting Warsaw and, especially, the ruins of the ghetto, they would visit Łódź and Lower Silesia—the parts of the country where most Jews were settling in the post-war period—and in case of visitors born and raised in Poland, their native towns. An obligatory part of the itineraries was the former concentration and death camps of Auschwitz-Birkenau, sometimes also Majdanek.[1] Among the best-known travellers were Jacob (Yakov) Pat, Shmuel Leib Shneiderman, Chaim Shoshkes, and Joseph Tenenbaum.[2]

A neglected traveller through Poland is Mordecai Tsanin, whose *Through Ruins and Ashes: A Journey through a Hundred Destroyed Jewish Communities in Poland* has never been translated into English and the Polish translation of which came out only in 2018, almost seventy years after its publication in Yiddish.[3] The difference between Tsanin and the other travellers is that, although he worked as a correspondent for the New York-based *Forverts*, he lived in Israel, while they lived in the United States. What is more, his report is the most detailed and the most distressing. Readers of the time were probably more interested in synthetic reports, without excessive details and obscure references or the extremely gloomy image Tsanin produced. Research on the reception of the Holocaust reveals that, soon after the war, some optimism was welcome. For example, at the beginning of his book, Tenenbaum set out the ideas that informed his trip: 'I go to Poland as an American Jew of Polish descent, on a mission to the heroic survivors of Polish Jewry in the new, liberated Poland', and expressed his hope that his book, which aimed at giving an honest presentation of facts and conditions at work in Poland at that time, 'may offer a modest educational contribution towards a better world'.[4]

Besides, the very titles of the other travelogues—Pat's *Ashes and Fire: Through the Ruins of Poland*, Shneiderman's *Between Fear and Hope: A Journey Across the New Poland*, Shoshkes' *Poland 1946: Impressions of a Journey*, and Tenenbaum's *In Search of a Lost People: The Old and the New Poland*—sounded more universal and did not focus only on the situation of the Jews but on the destruction of the whole country, while in the title of Tsanin's book a strictly Jewish perspective was obvious.

Tsanin made a few trips to Poland in 1946 and 1947. Usually in his contacts with Poles he presented himself as a non-Jewish, English-speaking journalist or even as an Englishman, which allowed him to get a better insight into the general sentiments, prejudices, and attitudes towards Jews prevalent in Poland at the time. His reports were originally published in *Forverts*, and most were later incorporated into *Through Ruins and Ashes*. A number of them found their way into the *yizker bikher*, memorial books, of the various cities, towns, and villages that he visited. It was actually in the memorial book of Kuzmir (Kazimierz) on the Vistula that I first came across his report, and it immediately struck me with its unique literary and documentary value.[5]

Mordecai Tsanin was born on 1 April 1906 as Mordecai Yeshayahu Cukierman in Sokołów Podlaski, where his father David Cukierman ran an office which assisted people with legal matters. He had five siblings. The eldest brother Herman (Henryk) left with his wife and his father for New Zealand in the late 1930s and then went to Australia, while his mother, Tova Malka, left for Palestine with the eldest daughter, Felicia. Another sister, Ester (Elsa), married the Polish Jewish writer Stanisław Jerzy Lec. Together with another sister, Rywka (Rysia), they survived in Poland on false papers. The eldest sister, Batya, died after a kidney operation at the age of 30.[6]

In Sokołów, Tsanin attended *ḥeder* and yeshiva. In 1920, when the family moved to Warsaw, he went to a Polish gymnasium. He supported Bundist ideas and was rather critical of Zionism. He made his debut in Warsaw in 1929 with stories and feuilletons in the Yiddish press. At that time he assumed the pen name Tsanin, which gradually started functioning as his actual name. Among other things, he wrote for *Oyfgang* and *Naye folkstsaytung*, Yiddish newspapers published in Warsaw. He published two books before the war: a collection of stories, *Viva Life!*, and a novel, *On Swampy Ground*.[7] Melech Ravitch, secretary of the famous Yidishe Literatn un Zhurnalistn Farayn, the association for writers and journalists at 13 Tłomackie Street, who first met him in Warsaw before the war, described him as a reporter through and through, as if the art of reportage popularized at that time in Europe by Egon Kisch were designed especially for him, 'for his looks, temperament, and character', and as a 'fighter', very energetic and fully involved in whatever he did while at the same time quite sensitive to the gloomy side of the human condition: 'an assertive personality, but in spite of all this assertiveness very sentimental.'[8] Many years later, Jack Kugelmass described him as 'a *shtarker*—he was afraid of no one.'[9]

Mobilized into the Polish army in September 1939, Tsanin found himself in a division headed by General Bortnowski. After the surrender of Poland he returned for two months to Warsaw and then via Białystok he reached Vilna, where he remained until the occupation of Lithuania by the Soviets in 1940. Thanks to the visa he received from the Japanese consul in Kovno,[10] he reached Japan via Vladivostok, and from there via Shanghai, India, and Egypt he arrived in Palestine in 1941. First he did manual work and then returned to journalism and writing fiction, remaining faithful to the Yiddish language until the end of his long life. From 1947 to 1956 he was an official correspondent for *Forverts* in Israel. He also wrote for other newspapers and periodicals published in various countries, including *Tsukunft, Di goldene keyt*, and *Davar*. He edited *Ilustrirte veltvokh*, and in 1949 initiated and became editor-in-chief of *Letste nayes*, the first Israeli daily in Yiddish. That is where his monumental historical novel *Artopanos Comes Home* appeared in instalments. It was later published in six volumes: *Jerusalem and Rome, Foreign Skies, Love in a Storm, The Rebellion of Mezhibozh, The Jordan Flows into the Dead Sea*, and *The Verdict*.[11] This enormous work, unsurpassed in Yiddish literature in terms of its size, covers the history of the Jews from the conquest of Judea by the Romans until modern times, describing the vicissitudes of the protagonists against the background of the stormy history of Jews in the diaspora, marked with persecutions and constant wandering. It is one of the neglected classics of Yiddish literature. As with numerous other writers in Yiddish, the shrinking readership contributed to this lack of recognition.

Tsanin published collections of his journalism: *Where Is Japan Going?, Sabbath Chats, The Paths of Jewish Fate, Decadence of a Messiah*; an autobiography: *Borders up to the Sky*; collections of stories: *Keys to Heaven, Snow in Summer, Don't Sleep, Mamma*; and a biography of the theatrical actor Herz Grosbard. He also contributed substantially to lexicography as the author of a great Yiddish–Hebrew and Hebrew–Yiddish dictionary.[12]

Mordecai Tsanin lived in Tel Aviv, initiating and getting involved in various activities aimed at preserving and developing Yiddish culture. He was a co-founder of the Beit Leyvick Center for Yiddish Language and Culture (named in honour of the Yiddish writer H. Leyvick). In 1973 he received the Itzik Manger Prize (another laureate in the same year was Isaac Bashevis Singer).[13] For many years he was president of the Association of Yiddish Writers in Israel (Farayn fun Yidishe Shrayber in Yisroel). He died on 4 February 2009 in Tel Aviv at the age of 103.

In the first years of Israeli statehood, the Yiddish language was treated with a good deal of reservation by the authorities as emphasis was placed on the development of Hebrew. When, in 1949, Tsanin wanted to transform *Letste nayes* from a weekly into a daily he had to obtain special permission. It was granted for only three issues a week. However, Tsanin found a way out: he created another paper, *Hayntike nayes*, also published three times a week, alternating with the other one. The authorities tolerated that stratagem, and finally, in 1957, they gave their permission for *Letste nayes* to be published as a daily (at the end of 1991 it was turned into a weekly again). In 1977 Tsanin left the editorial board and devoted all his time to writing and social work. *Letste nayes* was published until 2006, when it stopped appearing as a result of the shrinking readership.

On various occasions Tsanin stressed the sense of orphanhood he shared with other Yiddish writers. 'Yiddish Writers are Orphans' is the title of a short essay he published in a Polish literary supplement in the early 1990s.[14] In it he recalled his childhood in Sokołów Podlaski, the traditional education he received there, and learning Polish from a primer. He mentions that, after the family moved to Warsaw and he started writing, he also wanted to write in Polish, but realized that he did not know the language well enough, so he decided to write only in Yiddish. He deplored the fact that when the State of Israel was created it was necessary to get rid of the culture of the diaspora. He stated that therefore, when a book was published in Yiddish in Israel, there was almost no one to give it to: 'Those who know Yiddish in Israel now have bad eyesight, they grew old . . . Here, in Poland, a nation without a state grew but with a great culture. When they gained a state, it turned out that Yiddish literature did not belong to it.'[15] He expressed similar feelings in conversation with Agata Tuszyńska. Interestingly enough, he called himself a Zionist, but a Zionist writing in Yiddish, not Hebrew, which made him a stranger in Israel.[16]

Because of his tenacity in pursuing activities on behalf of Yiddish culture Tsanin could not avoid conflicts with the Israeli establishment. It is not therefore surprising that in an essay, *The Seventh Million*, published in book form by the Association of Yiddish Writers in Israel, Tsanin was critical of the attitudes of David Ben-Gurion and other members of the Israeli government (he called them 'der tsyonistisher establishment', 'the Zionist establishment') towards Yiddish language and culture, as well as of the attempts—in his opinion insufficient—of Jewish organizations in Mandatory Palestine to rescue Jews in Europe during the Second World War.[17]

Tsanin was generally known as a sharp critic on political and social issues as well as on literary matters. Like a number of other Yiddish writers and literary critics, he spoke with reservation about Isaac Bashevis Singer, especially compared with his brother, Israel Yehoshua, Sholem Asch (whom he considered the greatest Yiddish writer[18]), or David Bergelson, not to mention Sholem Aleichem, for whom 'it was worth creating the Yiddish language'.[19] And yet he admitted that Bashevis Singer was a talented storyteller: 'Singer is toilet pornography. That's how I could call it in Yiddish. Perverse literature, but beautifully told. This is dangerous, a God-given talent. As far as its values are concerned, I don't value it highly. But when you start reading, you cannot stop.'[20]

Photographs of Tsanin reveal his elegant looks. Always in a stylish three-piece suit, with a pipe: no wonder that while travelling to Poland in the 1940s he could easily play the role of an English gentleman. But he had little of the proverbial English reserve: his prose and the controversies he raised among both Jewish communists in Poland and Zionists in Israel testify to his strong individualism, fiery temperament, commitment to the ideals he cherished, and sensitivity, but also to a sense of humour and irony, an ability to observe details, and an excellent ear for the linguistic nuances of Polish and Yiddish. The title of a collection of essays published in 1997, *Dos vort mayn shverd* ('The Word is My Sword'), aptly renders his years-long struggles, his passion, and his uncompromising nature.

Jeremiad on the Ruins of the Earlier World

The title of Tsanin's report from Poland is very difficult to render, because the Yiddish idiom *iber shteyn un shtok* implies a long journey across country, and in this case the country is marked with the stones and rubble left after the destruction of the Jews in Poland.[21] Therefore I decided to give to the Polish translation a less ambiguous title: *Przez ruiny i zgliszcza*, which literally means 'through ruins and ashes'.

Tsanin's perspective in his report from Poland is dramatic. In spite of some humorous elements and descriptions resembling the plot of an adventure novel—for example, his failed attempt to get to Bełz and Bełżec by train because a Polish officer, believing he was an Englishman, warned him he might be taken for a spy trying to cross the Soviet border, not to mention the particularly dangerous situation in those regions due to skirmishes with scattered Ukrainian units—his book is one great jeremiad,[22] a lamentation, a threnody, and at the same time a detailed report written with the hope that sometime in the future it would attract the attention of historians. The book is dedicated to his wife Dora Tsanin (1912–96), who accompanied him. However, in the text itself there are no references to their common experiences, reflections, or feelings, although among the shtetls visited, apart from Tsanin's birth town Sokołów Podlaski there was also Wolbrom, where Dora was born. This might be a conscious literary device to strengthen the tone and significance of the jeremiad: in a number of testimonies in *yizker bikher* a similar position is taken by authors presenting themselves as the only Jewish visitors, although usually this was not the case.

Like other Jewish travellers to post-war Poland, Tsanin started his report with a description of Warsaw, devoting three chapters to the city: the ruins of the ghetto, the old Jewish cemetery at Okopowa Street, and the evening before Yom Kippur. He juxtaposed memories from before the war with the present: the entire book, except chapters devoted to visits to former concentration and death camps, is constructed in such a way that images from the past are confronted with the post-war reality. In Warsaw he saw no sign that Yom Kippur was coming; only in the vicinity of the Nożyk synagogue did Jews pass, as if furtively (religious Jews hiding their beards and sidelocks is a recurring motif). Tsanin stressed that he was most afraid of the visits to Warsaw and Łódź, since he realized that the contrast with the situation before the war, when huge and vibrant communities had existed there, would be the most painful. He recalled the richness of cultural life in Łódź and compared it with its present state. He described attempts to revive the Jewish theatre, stating that there was almost no audience for it because the majority of Jews inhabiting the city had little in common with the refined audiences before the war. Although this was the largest Jewish community after the war, he only heard children speaking Yiddish once, at a school performance when a choir sang a cheerful song.

In Łódź, Yiddish was not heard in the street either; if at all, then at 66 Zachodnia Street, where the post-war life of the Jewish community was concentrated. While there, he wondered if perhaps not everything was lost, if perhaps Jewish life could be revived, but after a few conversations he concluded that the majority of Jews wanted to leave Poland anyway. It was in Łódź where he actually admitted openly to his interlocutors that he came from the Land of Israel, first in his encounter with a droshky driver who half-jokingly asked if he could take his horse to Palestine, and then with a larger group in the courtyard of the heart of the local Jewish community. However, this encounter was marked with bitterness and irony, like most encounters with Jewish survivors:

They see an unfamiliar face so they surround me. 'Sholem aleikhem, where does the Jew come from?' 'From Erets Yisro'el.' 'From Yisro'el?' Even more people approach me to say 'Sholem aleikhem.' Their eyes light up. A Jew from Yisro'el. They want to know how things are in Yisro'el. And I say: 'I want to hear how things are here. At your place': 'And how can they be? Haven't you seen Łódź yet? So have a look and you will see how things are.'[23]

The only other mention of Israel in the book is in a chapter on the eve of Yom Kippur in Warsaw where Tsanin recognized near the Nożyk synagogue some Jews familiar to him from Tel Aviv. He guessed that they had returned from Palestine to Poland to start a new life as 'Poles of Mosaic faith', and he noted ironically that some Jewish women who in Tel Aviv associated with Poles and 'wore golden crosses on white necks'[24] now, after their return to Poland, came to Kol Nidrei.

In Kraków, where 6,000 Jews resided, it seemed to him that Jewish life had ended. He found it only in private apartments: for example, at the painter Manuel Rympel's, or in a cafe where the Jewish intelligentsia gathered. But 'the street belongs to the non-Jews. Kazimierz, the Jewish town, the narrow streets of Kazimierz, where in the past such a colourful Jewish life went on, today belong to the non-Jews.'[25] There was no Jewish press, no Jewish associations, clubs, or salons.

Tsanin's visit to Kraków took place at the beginning of the school year. In the street he saw crowds of children hurrying to school but did not notice any Jewish children among them: 'Here, in the street, I see the scope of our misfortune. Among so many thousands of children I don't notice even one pair of Jewish eyes.'[26]

He gets a strange impression in Tarnów, where approximately 350 Jews were trying to revive their earlier lives:

They are building from scratch. Three hundred and fifty Jews are building their community again. They have a rabbi and a ritual slaughterer. They established, when it was still allowed, political parties: General Zionists, Bundists, Po'alei Tsiyon Right and Left, and Hashomer Hatsa'ir, and the Polish Workers' Party (communists), and a party of religious Jews. Altogether three hundred and fifty people, including children and non-party members. The communist party (the Jewish section) consists of *two* members; one of them entered the board of the *kehilah* as a representative of the 'masses', that is, of his only party comrade.[27]

At the Tarnów *kehilah* there was a large library with books in Yiddish, a sports association, a Bundist choir, and a Po'alei Tsiyon theatrical circle: '"For whom is all this?" I ask. "For the masses" . . . God alone knows how stubborn and romantic Jews are', comments Tsanin.[28]

As one of very few foreign journalists, he visited most of the former death camps: Chełmno, Majdanek, Sobibór, Treblinka, and Auschwitz-Birkenau. The last chapter of the book bears the title 'The Gold Rush' and sums up what he saw during his travels. While writing about people searching through human ashes in and around the former death camps for gold and other valuables, he stated that writing about all this was 'too much for a Jew'. At the same time he expressed his hope that perhaps at some time when 'this nightmare will be further away, in coming generations a writer, a historian, will appear who will be able to research this chapter and describe it as a document of the terrible downfall of humanity in the twentieth century'.[29] While following discussions of Jan Gross's *Fear*, on the Kielce pogrom, and *Golden Harvest*, on scavenging the areas around Treblinka and other former death camps, I would often recall these words. Gross and a group of historians from the Polish Center for Holocaust Research in Warsaw undertook a number of the themes that Tsanin left for future scholars to consider.[30]

The end of the book is clearly pessimistic; nothing is left except ruins and ashes:

A Jew is travelling now across the destroyed cities and shtetls, wanders around ruins and rubble and cannot find a single untouched grave that has remained after the annihilated life. Only when you see a field grey from ashes will you know, Jew, that these are the ashes of your people. And only there can you cry out your 'Yisgadal veyiskadash'.[31]

Although Tsanin noted positive attitudes from some Poles—an antique collector in Lublin, a station-master in Treblinka, priests in Mława and Wolbrom, a farmer from the village of Wierbka—his general opinion of Polish behaviour was very critical. While asking why survivors were being settled in Lower Silesia,[32] where each stone was a cursed testimony to the earlier presence of Germans, instead of being enabled to return to their own homes or native towns, he concluded that such a return was rarely possible because of the hostile reaction of Polish neighbours. One of the results of the German occupation was a wall between two peoples that had coexisted for centuries. This wall was marked with permission to murder Jews and loot their possessions. In Tsanin's opinion, contact was hindered by the deeply hidden sense of guilt among Poles:

When a Pole in a shtetl talks to a Jew he does not look into his eyes and remains silent. Why cannot he tell him that he hid his father or brother, that he took care of his house, that he saved his sacred objects, that he helped a Jewish partisan by offering him a sip of water? Nothing like this. He is silent. Because in order to be able to speak freely with a Jewish survivor and look straight into his eyes, hundreds of thousands of Poles would have to carry out Jewish possessions from their houses, collect them in one place, and say:

'Jews, take away your things that we rescued from the hands of our common enemy. Germans murdered you and enslaved us, we helped as well as we could, take everything that has remained from your possessions. Go back to your homes, return to your work, and let's build together our lives as we did for long generations. Perhaps we didn't behave properly when you were being murdered; perhaps we did wrong persecuting your partisans in the forests. The enemy was cruel, terrible, he demoralized us. He humiliated us in our own eyes, and we no longer behaved like people and we let them demoralize us.'[33]

While there were almost no Jews in the little towns, their traces were visible everywhere: cupboards and tables in appropriated apartments and houses, candleholders and chandeliers in inns, peasant women in blouses made of Jewish prayer shawls, fragments of tombstones used for construction purposes, destroyed and desecrated cemeteries, and synagogues adapted for storehouses.

And yet for many years Poland played an essential role in the lives of Jews, for it was their home:

There was once Jewish Poland, an inn on the route of Jewish wandering. This was where they unpacked their bundles, the inn became their home. Under the Polish sky, generation after generation continued a chain of customs and traditions, spun a tale about holidays and sabbaths, embroidered life with the same tenderness, with which Jewish brides embroidered bags for phylacteries and parochets. And it seemed that the beautiful sky over Poland was also embroidered with the longing of Jewish hearts. The Jewish sky on which sunrises were mixed with the wine of Kiddush and sunsets burnt with *havdalah*.

And although Jews wept so many tears on the Polish land, there was also a sea of joy in their lives. A joy from working and creating, from living and persisting. But the German Amalek brought a storm of fire and death on Jewish life in Poland. And everything was destroyed and annihilated.[34]

However, although Tsanin was a more critical observer than his fellow travellers, sometimes his political naivety came to the fore. In spite of his critical view of communists, he thought that from the Jewish perspective their regime was a better solution than the regime of 'reactionary' Poland. Registering statements of simple people in little towns about the government consisting of 'Bolsheviks' and Jews, he did not try to understand their comments or reflect on them. As a socialist he was surprised that in Białystok a number of Poles behaved dishonourably towards Jews: such behaviour did not surprise him in little towns, for his opinion of Polish peasants was basically very low and not devoid of stereotyping. He presented them as an ignorant and primitive mob, while he associated the big city with the working class, from which he expected different attitudes.

Tsanin was also critical of Jewish institutions for insufficient involvement in commemorating the victims of the Holocaust. In an article published in *Forverts* in January 1948, soon after he left Poland, he wrote about his growing conflict with them, which resulted in them detaining him on the Polish–Czech border and confiscating some of his notes.[35] He was asked to leave the train at the border town of Zebrzydowice, when he was leaving the country after a half-year stay. Interestingly, Tsanin stressed the friendly attitude of the Polish authorities. He did not have any problems with extending his visa, and even when his articles started being published in the American press he did not encounter any criticism. As he states: 'the Polish authorities gave me the possibility of visiting all the places and looking at whatever my heart desired . . . I talked a number of times with important members of the government about my articles, and each time I met with friendly interest and understanding.'[36] Surprisingly, he was detained because of numerous complaints and denunciations from the Central Committee of Jews in Poland. Tsanin did not blame the whole committee but the communists within it who, in his opinion, made all possible efforts to prevent an objective look at the Holocaust, including the various attitudes of Poles.

He quoted a conversation with a Polish officer at the border who treated him very courteously and apologized for what happened but explained that he could not do anything about it. Supposedly the officer was very embarrassed and explained that he cared a lot about the reputation of his motherland and was afraid that arresting a foreign journalist might make a bad impression abroad. He tried to get in touch by phone with his superiors and the authorities in Katowice, 80 kilometres from Zebrzydowice, but it was impossible at 2 a.m. He managed to get in touch with them only several hours later.

They had to wait for a commission from Katowice that had left the city at 8 a.m. but whose arrival was delayed because of a snowstorm. As a result its members arrived at the border at 4 p.m. The commission consisted of two Jews, who, in response to Tsanin's question about the reason for his detention, responded that he 'wrote about things that should not be brought to light'.[37] They were not convinced by his argument that he was writing the truth. Even if it were true, it would still be harmful for the Jews, for, in their opinion, it was hostile propaganda against Poland. In the end, Tsanin was subjected to a thorough search which lasted until late at night and ended with the confiscation of his notes:

My arguments that the material was engraved in my memory and it was ridiculous to confiscate my notes on the destroyed Jewish communities did not help.

The commission explained that they did not find enough evidence on the harmfulness of my activities and they announced that I was free and I could cross the border by the earliest train.

At one o'clock at night I found myself, released, abroad.[38]

This report confirms Tamar Lewinsky's claim that Tsanin's critical perspective on the Central Committee of Jews in Poland, and, especially, as he believed, their insufficient interest and concern about the victims and what remained of the Jewish heritage, made him *persona non grata* with the committee.[39] Perhaps if it had not been for that intervention he could still have returned to Poland and covered more cities and towns in his reports.

The report on his detention on the border and his other articles on the topic of commemoration constitute valuable material on the shaping of the official memory about the Holocaust in the early post-war years.

The Polish intelligence service in Israel had its eyes on Tsanin in the 1960s. In a note from 12 March 1962, *Letste nayes* is described as 'the most anti-Polish paper in Israel'. The reason for such a description was the fact that it published a series of articles in which the hostility of a large part of the Polish population towards Jews during the Holocaust was discussed. The note ends with a comment that the editor-in-chief and co-owner of the paper was 'a Jew from Poland, Jeshayahu Mordekhai

CANIN, generally known as a "communist- and Soviet-baiter".[40] Also in another note, undated, referring to a meeting about the book *Siódmy wilk* by Henryk Dankowicz, a journalist from the Polish-language Israeli daily *Nowiny i Kurier*, it is stated that Tsanin spoke in Polish to a crowd of 400 people, expressing his 'anti-communist' and 'anti-Polish' feelings and claiming that 'the communist system breaks people down'. 'It is no secret who Tsanin is', the author of the note concluded.[41]

Tsanin's travelogue is written in a variety of styles and registers. Next to journalistic parts aptly rendering conversations with Jews and Poles there are highly emotional and lofty fragments full of rhetorical figures. On the one hand, they are stylistically reminiscent of biblical texts; on the other, they abound in socialist rhetoric. Moreover, since these reports were published in the press in instalments, Tsanin could not avoid some repetition, not all of which was removed from the book version. Therefore readers may find the frequent paeans on idealistic and altruistic Jewish youth fighting for freedom for the whole world, or exaggerated descriptions of the cultural significance of little towns in Podlasie, monotonous.

Comparing Tsanin's book with other travelogues, it seems that he predicted most accurately the course of Jewish existence in Poland after the war. Also, his individual point of view, the richness of his emotional states—from despair through lyrical reflection to irony and the grotesque—and its literary values render his report particularly interesting, albeit difficult, reading for the contemporary Polish audience.

Reception in Poland

The Polish edition of Tsanin's book appeared at the end of 2018, the same year as the controversial Holocaust law was announced, triggering a diplomatic crisis and various fierce and bitter debates. Soon afterwards, the monumental two-volume edition of *Dalej jest noc* came out, stimulating discussion and generating both favourable and very critical reactions. It could have been expected that Tsanin's book would be exposed to similar criticism, and yet the reception so far has been surprisingly positive, and the book seems to have hit the Polish reading audience at the right time. A number of reviews[42] and scholarly articles[43] were published, and meetings promoting the book in various cities and towns (among others, Warsaw, Lublin, Łódź, Kutno, Olkusz, and Kazimierz Dolny) were very well attended. I cannot think of any other book translated from Yiddish into Polish that has attracted so much attention. In her review, Anna Bikont, the author of an important book on Jedwabne,[44] notes that what Jan Tomasz Gross showed to Poles in his *Neighbors* in 2000 had already been described by a Jewish journalist fifty-three years earlier. She also refers to the memorable scene in Claude Lanzmann's *Shoah*, in which the director talks to the station-master from Treblinka and observes that Tsanin conducted a similar conversation thirty years earlier.[45] Yet Gross's book was met with a great deal of criticism (as was Lanzmann's film in communist Poland), while Tsanin's was not, although one can easily find exaggerations and simplifications in his report. The decisive factor in its favourable reception might have been the fact that it was written soon after the war by an independent journalist, making it difficult to raise the same accusations against him as have been raised against contemporary scholars: of distorting facts, manipulation, ignorance, and courting publicity or even financial gain. Furthermore it is a first-hand account, and these are always difficult to contradict.

The publisher Krystyna Bratkowska and I received a number of letters from readers with personal comments. The most moving letter came from Ryszard Szczepaniak from the town of Zielonka near Warsaw, who as a young boy was a witness of a deportation from his home town:

I cannot find the right words to properly acknowledge the great significance of publishing the book by Mr Mordecai Tsanin *Przez ruiny i zgliszcza*. I was for a short time, for only about one hour, a witness of the Holocaust and in spite of my 86 years I am still accompanied by horrible images and I hear very clearly the terrible crying of people who are being deprived of dignity, hope, childhood, old age, family, God and motherland. Yes, and motherland. The author's work grants him the nobility of righteousness and honour. I am turning my thoughts to Nature and God who gave him a long life.[46]

I have no doubt that Mordecai Tsanin would be deeply touched reading these words and feel that the prayer expressed in the introductory chapter to his book had been heard:

God Almighty, give me the strength so that I can describe with my poor words what my eyes saw and my heart felt during my wandering across the rubble and ruins of the life that is no more, and so that I could uncover at least a small piece of that great epic poem that was called Jewish life in Poland.[47]

Notes

1. See J. Kugelmass, *Sifting the Ruins: Émigré Jewish Journalists' Return Visits to the Old Country, 1946–1948* (Ann Arbor, Mich., 2014); M. Adamczyk-Garbowska, 'Krajobraz po Zagładzie: Relacje dziennikarzy żydowskich z powojennej Polski', *Midrasz*, 2012, no. 1, pp. 16–20.

2. Y. Pat, *Ash un fayer: iber di khurves fun poyln* (New York, 1946); Eng. trans.: *Ashes and Fire*, trans. L. Steinberg (New York, 1947); S. L. Shneiderman, *Tsvishn shrek un hofenung: a rayze iber dem nayem poyln* (Buenos Aires, 1947); Eng. edn.: *Between Fear and Hope* (New York, 1947); C. Shoshkes, *Poyln 1946: ayndrukn fun a rayze* (Buenos Aires, 1946); J. Tenenbaum and S. Tenenbaum, *In Search of a Lost People: The Old and the New Poland* (New York, 1948).

3. M. Tsanin, *Iber shteyn un shtok: a rayze iber hundert khorev-gevorene khiles in poyln* (Tel Aviv, 1952); Pol. trans.: M. Canin, *Przez ruiny i zgliszcza: Podróż po stu zgładzonych gminach żydowskich w Polsce*, trans. M. Adamczyk-Garbowska (Warsaw, 2018).

4. Tenenbaum and Tenenbaum, *In Search of a Lost People*, p. viii.

5. M. Tsanin, 'Kuzmir', in *Pinkes kuzmir*, ed. D. Shtokfish (Tel Aviv, 1970), 270–8. This was the first fragment that I translated and included in my anthology of texts on Kuzmir (see *Kazimierz vel Kuzmir: Miasteczko różnych snów*, ed. M. Adamczyk-Garbowska (Lublin, 2006), 269–73). Later I translated and published his chapters on Kielce, Zamość, and

Janowiec (M. Canin, 'Kielce', trans. M. Adamczyk-Garbowska, in *Tam był kiedyś mój dom…: Księgi pamięci gmin żydowskich*, ed. M. Adamczyk-Garbowska, A. Kopciowski, and A. Trzciński (Lublin, 2009), 451–3; id., 'Zamość', trans. M. Adamczyk-Garbowska, *Midrasz*, 2011, no. 2, pp. 15–16; 'Janowiec', trans. M. Adamczyk-Garbowska, *Midrasz*, 2012, no. 1, pp. 24–5).

6 See A. Tuszyńska, D. Barczak-Perfikowska, G. Latos, E. Strzałkowska, and W. Wejman, *Bagaż osobisty po marcu* (Warsaw, 2018), 94–6.

7 M. Tsanin, *Vivat lebn!* (Warsaw, 1933); id., *Oyf zumpiker erd* (Warsaw, 1935).

8 See M. Ravitch, *Mayn leksikon*, 5 vols. (Montreal and Tel Aviv, 1945–82), iii. 350–1.

9 Kugelmass, *Sifting the Ruins*, 7.

10 Chiune Sugihara, sometimes called the Japanese Schindler, issued Japanese visas to thousands of Polish and Lithuanian Jews in the summer of 1940, enabling them to escape from Soviet-occupied Lithuania.

11 M. Tsanin, *Artopanus kumt tsurik aheym*, i: *Yerusholayim un roym* (Tel Aviv, 1966); ii: *Fremde himlen* (Tel Aviv, 1968); iii: *Libshaft in geviter* (Tel Aviv, 1972); iv: *Di meride fun mezhibozh* (Tel Aviv, 1976); v: *Der yardn falt arayn in yam hamelekh* (Tel Aviv, 1981); vi: *Der gzar-din* (Tel Aviv, 1985); Eng. trans.: *Artopanus Comes Home*, trans. I. M. Lask (South Brunswick, NJ, 1980).

12 M. Tsanin, *Vuhin geyt yapan* (Tel Aviv, 1942); id., *Shabesdike shmuesn* (1957); id., *Oyf di vegn fun yidishn goyrl* (Tel Aviv, 1966); id., *Der dekadents fun a meshiyekh* (Tel Aviv, 1967); id., *Grenetsn biz tsum himl* (Tel Aviv, 1969/70); id., *Shlisl tsum himl* (Tel Aviv, 1979); id., *Zumershney* (Tel Aviv, 1992); id., *Shluf nit mameshi* (Tel Aviv, 1996); id., *Herts grosbard* (Tel Aviv, 1995); id., *Fuler yidish-hebreisher verterbukh* (Tel Aviv, 1982); id., *Fuler hebreish-yidisher verterbukh* (Tel Aviv, 1983). For more biographical information, see J. C. Frakes, 'Tsanin, (Yeshaye) Mordkhe', *Encyclopaedia Judaica*, 2nd edn., 22 vols. (New York, 2006), xx. 163–4; C. L. Fuks, 'Tsanin (Shaye) Mortkhe', *Leksikon fun der nayer yidisher literatur*, ed. S. Niger and J. Shatzkhy, 8 vols. (New York, 1956–81), vii, cols. 532–4; see also Z. Tsanin, 'From the Desk of Mordkhe Tsanin: My Father Worked on Letste Nayes, a Yiddish Newspaper in Tel Aviv' (31 Oct. 2018): YouTube website, visited 14 May 2021. I am grateful to Mr Ze'ev Tsanin for his helpful comments and some biographical information.

13 See Dr H.R., 'Nobilitacja języka żydowskiego', *Przegląd* (Tel Aviv), 1 May 1972, p. 27.

14 See M. Canin, 'Pisarze żydowscy są sierotami', *Ex Libris* (literary supplement to *Życie Warszawy*), 40 (1993), 4.

15 Ibid.

16 See A. Tuszyńska, *Kilka portretów z Polską w tle: Reportaże izraelskie* (Gdańsk, 1993), 55.

17 See M. Tsanin, *Der zibeter milyon: der khurbn un der tsyonistisher establishment in erets yisroel* (Tel Aviv, 1996).

18 Canin, 'Pisarze żydowscy są sierotami'.

19 Ibid. It is worth noting that at a time when most Yiddish writers and critics were boycotting Asch as a result of the publication of *Der man fun natseres* and other works with Christian themes on religious and national grounds, and *Forverts*, to which Asch had earlier contributed regularly and in abundance, would not publish his novels, Tsanin never joined the boycott, and *Letste nayes* was open for the writer. Melech Ravitch stresses this in his reminiscences about Tsanin as an illustration of his independence of mind (Ravitch, *Mayn leksikon*, iii. 353).

20 See A. Tuszyńska, *Singer: Pejzaże pamięci* (Gdańsk, 1994), 167.

21 Kugelmass translates the title literally as 'Over Stone and Branch', explaining that it is 'an expression referring to stumbling' (Kugelmass, *Sifting the Ruins*, 6, n. 22); *Encyclopedia*

Judaica has 'Through Thick and Thin' (Frakes, 'Tsanin, (Yeshaye) Mordkhe', 163); Wikipedia has 'Of Stones and Ruins' ('Mordechai Tsanin' (n.d.): Wikipedia website, visited 2 June 2021).

22 Kugelmass also mentions the 'jeremiad-like' quality of Tsanin's book (Kugelmass, *Sifting the Ruins*, 6).
23 Tsanin, *Iber shteyn un shtok*, 80; Canin, *Przez ruiny i zgliszcza*, 147.
24 Tsanin, *Iber shteyn un shtok*, 20–1; Canin, *Przez ruiny i zgliszcza*, 59.
25 Tsanin, *Iber shteyn un shtok*, 264; Canin, *Przez ruiny i zgliszcza*, 412.
26 Tsanin, *Iber shteyn un shtok*, 264–5; Canin, *Przez ruiny i zgliszcza*, 413.
27 Tsanin, *Iber shteyn un shtok*, 271; Canin, *Przez ruiny i zgliszcza*, 423.
28 Tsanin, *Iber shteyn un shtok*, 271; Canin, *Przez ruiny i zgliszcza*, 424.
29 Tsanin, *Iber shteyn un shtok*, 307; Canin, *Przez ruiny i zgliszcza*, 484–5.
30 J. T. Gross, *Fear: Anti-Semitism in Poland after Auschwitz* (Princeton, NJ, 2006); Pol. edn.: *Strach. Antysemityzm w Polsce tuż po wojnie: Historia moralnej zapaści* (Kraków, 2008); J. T. Gross and I. Grudzińska-Gross, *Złote żniwa: Rzecz o tym, co się działo na obrzeżach zagłady Żydów* (Kraków, 2011); Eng. edn.: *Golden Harvest: Events at the Periphery of the Holocaust* (New York, 2012); see also B. Engelking and J. Grabowski (eds.), *Dalej jest noc: Losy Żydów w wybranych powiatach okupowanej Polski*, 2 vols. (Warsaw, 2018). This monumental edition contains studies by nine scholars on the fate of Jews during the Second World War and after in various counties in Poland. Some of these places, for instance Łuków, Węgrów, and Miechów, were visited by Tsanin in 1947, and the last chapter of his book is devoted to the pillaging of the areas around former death camps.
31 Tsanin, *Iber shteyn un shtok*, 313; Canin, *Przez ruiny i zgliszcza*, 491. 'Yitsgadal veyitsadash' are the opening words of Kaddish, the prayer for the dead.
32 Tsanin, who visited many more places than other travellers, did not visit, or at least he does not mention in his book, the Jewish communities in Lower Silesia. As this region suffered less destruction in the war, it probably didn't fit into the pattern of confronting the present situation with reminiscences from the past.
33 Tsanin, *Iber shteyn un shtok*, 310; Canin, *Przez ruiny i zgliszcza*, 487–8.
34 Tsanin, *Iber shteyn un shtok*, 313; Canin, *Przez ruiny i zgliszcza*, 491.
35 M. Tsanin, '"Forverts" korespondent dertseylt, vi azoy er iz arestirt gevoren baym aroysfaren fun poylen', *Forverts*, 16 Jan. 1948, pp. 2, 7.
36 Ibid. 2.
37 Ibid.
38 Ibid. 7.
39 See T. Lewinsky, 'Polish-Jewish Displaced Persons in Occupied Germany', in F. Tych and M. Adamczyk-Garbowska (eds.), *Jewish Presence in Absence: The Aftermath of the Holocaust in Poland, 1944–2010* (Jerusalem, 2014), 95–124.
40 See Instytut Pamięci Narodowej, Warsaw, BU 01681/106: Sprawa ewidencyjno-operacyjna 'Parias'. Tsanin is listed there as 'Tsanin vel Canin, Jeshayahu-Mordekhai'. The case was closed in May 1969 due to the liquidation of the residency of the Polish intelligence service in Israel. I am grateful to Dr Łukasz Krzyżanowski for bringing these documents to my attention.
41 Ibid.
42 See e.g. A. Bikont, 'Raport z popiołów piekła', *Książki: Magazyn do czytania*, 2018, no. 5, pp. 46–8; H. Bortnowska, 'Przez ruiny i zgliszcza: Kto się boi tej książki?', *Gazeta Wyborcza*, 25–6 Jan. 2020, pp. 28–9; Ł. Krzyżanowski, 'Była kiedyś żydowska Polska', *Newsweek: His-*

toria, 2019, no. 3, pp. 12–23; P. Smoleński, 'Każdy miał kuferek, a w nim coś po Żydach', *Gazeta Wyborcza*, 16–17 Feb. 2019, p. 30; R. Sendyka, 'To, co było' (May 2019): Dwutygodnik website, visited 14 May 2021; P. Kieżun, 'Skarga i oskarżenie: O książce "Przez ruiny i zgliszcza" Mordechaja Canina' (29 Jan. 2019): Kultura Liberalna website, visited 14 May 2021; A. Kopciowski, '"Zgłębiłem tę czarną otchłań do samego dna..."', *Akcent*, 2019, no. 3, pp. 113–18.

43 See e.g. H. Datner, 'Epitafium Mordechaja Canina', *Kwartalnik Historii Żydów*, 270 (2019), 511–20; M. Dubrowska, 'Klagelied und Aufschrei: Zum Problem des polnischen Antisemitismus in Mordechai Zanins literarischer Reportage "Iber sztejn un sztok" (1952)', in W. Brylla and C. Lipiński (eds.), *Im Clash der Identitäten: Nationalismen im literatur- und kulturgeschichtlichen Diskurs* (Göttingen, 2020), 283–99; M. Kawa, 'Przez ruiny i zgliszcza: Społeczne i kulturowe zmiany powojennej rzeczywistości widziane oczyma Mordechaja Canina', *Language–Culture–Politics*, 2019, no. 1, pp. 93–103; K. Kijek, 'Istotność marginesu, czyli wyparte wątki w historiografii Żydów i studiów żydowskich w Polsce: Uwagi wokół polskiego wydania książki Mordechaja Canina "Przez ruiny i zgliszcza"', *Studia Judaica* (Kraków), 22 (2019), 337–53.

44 A. Bikont, *My z Jedwabnego* (Wołowiec, 2004); Eng. trans.: *The Crime and the Silence: Confronting the Massacre of Jews in Wartime Jedwabne*, trans. A. Valles (London, 2015).

45 Bikont, 'Raport z popiołów piekła', 47; see J. T. Gross, *Sąsiedzi: Historia zagłady żydowskiego miasteczka* (Sejny, 2000); Eng. edn.: *Neighbors: The Destruction of the Jewish Community in Jedwabne, Poland* (Princeton, NJ, 2001); C. Landsman (dir.), *Shoah*, documentary (Les Films Aleph, 1985).

46 Ryszard Szczepaniak, e-mail to Krystyna Bratkowska, 20 Feb. 2019.

47 Tsanin, *Iber shteyn un shtok*, 6; Canin, *Przez ruiny i zgliszcza*, 37.

4. FROM ISRAELI INDEPENDENCE TO THE END OF COMMUNISM

Art and Society between Poland and Israel
The Life and Work of Henryk Hechtkopf

HANNA LERNER

Introduction

In 1995, at the age of 85, Henryk Hechtkopf walked into the Tel Aviv office of the art periodical *Arba al ḥamesh* holding a poster for *The Dybbuk*, the smash-hit play of 1920s Poland. The poster had been published by the magazine a few weeks earlier with no mention of the designer's name. Hechtkopf wished to correct the editors' negligence and to credit the artist, Henryk Berlewi, who had been Hechtkopf's first art teacher in Warsaw during the 1920s. That visit led to an interview with Israeli writer Nava Semel, who emphasized Hechtkopf's persistent efforts to retrieve the links between contemporary Israeli art and the forgotten glorious past of European Jewish art before the Second World War. 'He wished to save the hundreds of artists active at that period from oblivion', she wrote.[1]

This chapter traces the extraordinary and rich life and work of Henryk Hechtkopf, whose journey began in 1910 Warsaw and continued in post-war Łódź, then Bat Yam, and finally Zikhron Ya'akov, where he died at the age of 94. He spent exactly half of his life in Poland and half in Israel, and contributed to both Polish and Israeli cultures, constantly seeking innovative artistic media through which he could present his unique perspective on and sensitive testimony to the historical events in which he participated. 'Hechtkopf's creative competence and audacity are rare', argued Galia Bar Or, who defined his post-war work as 'a prominent example of a true *avant-garde*, one which does not repress and does not forget'.[2]

The goal of this chapter is twofold. First, it seeks to present the central phases of Hechtkopf's life story and set the chronological and historical foundations for further investigations into his art and legacy. While particular aspects of his work are well known, such as his documentation of the ruins of the Warsaw ghetto, his graphic designs, and his influential illustrations of children's books in Israel, this chapter aims to present the full scope of Hechtkopf's art and life, not only as a painter, book illustrator, graphic designer, and animator but also as a film director, stage- and film-scenery designer, art teacher, social activist, and artists' community organizer.[3]

The second goal of the chapter is to identify new trajectories for future research on the often neglected story of the Polish Jewish artistic heritage and its impact on

Israeli culture. Hechtkopf participated in some of the most significant moments in Jewish, Polish, and Israeli history of the twentieth century. Some of these milestones were shared by other artists who travelled, like him, from Poland to Israel. While the chapter focuses on Hechtkopf's personal journey, it raises general questions which call for further research and discussion on issues ranging from Polish Jewish identity and the integration into Israel of the Gomułka Aliyah—the mass migration of Jews from Poland to Israel between 1955 and 1960 made possible by the breakdown of the Stalinist system in Poland—to the influence of Jewish artists on Polish art, cinema, and graphic design before and after the Second World War. These and other questions will be discussed in the concluding part of the chapter.

Parts of Hechtkopf's story are revealed here for the first time. The research for this chapter is based primarily on his private archive and estate, which includes his vast collection of paintings, drawings, and illustrations, as well as books, catalogues, newspaper clippings, and letters from the 1930s until his death in 2004.

The chapter is organized chronologically, following Hechtkopf's activities in Poland and then in Israel, and highlights aspects of his accomplishments and artwork, which span different media, genres, time periods, and countries. These materials require further discussion and analysis from both historical and comparative perspectives. The concluding section proposes some pathways for such future multidisciplinary research, exploring the historical, artistic, and cultural significance of Hechtkopf's contribution to, and impact on, both Polish and Israeli societies.

Poland (1910–1957)

Henryk (Hayim) Hechtkopf (Figure 1) was born at 3 Żelazna Street, Warsaw, on 5 April 1910. He described his family as being of 'long Jewish heritage, with roots in Spanish and Dutch Jewry on one side, and rabbinical leaders on the other side'.[4] His father, Izaak, was a merchant, who died when Hechtkopf was only a year old. He was raised by his mother, Ita (née Rosenman), a midwife, and had an elder sister, Sara. Growing up in the bustling streets of Jewish Warsaw, he was grounded in Jewish tradition and culture but also received a general secular education. He learned Hebrew as a child, at Hayim Kaplan's kindergarten, and then at the Hinukh Gymnasium, where Hebrew classes were mandatory.[5] In 1933 he received his MA in law (in Poland a first degree) from the University of Warsaw.

His interest in art began in childhood. At the age of 10, his schoolteacher Jacob Shatzky[6] introduced him to Henryk Berlewi, one of the leading Polish Jewish artists of the time. Berlewi became Hechtkopf's first art tutor and opened the doors of Polish and international art circles and the Jewish and Yiddish culture of 1920s and 1930s Warsaw. Berlewi studied art in Paris and Antwerp, and was a seminal figure in the Polish *avant-garde* and the renaissance of Jewish culture.[7] He was also a leading illustrator of Yiddish books in 1920s Warsaw, designing poetry books and journal covers for the prominent poets of the Khalyastre group, which included Uri Tsevi Grinberg, Perets Markish, and Melech Ravitch.[8]

Figure 1 Henryk Hechtkopf, self-portrait (1950)
Henryk Hechtkopf archive

In 1925, when he was only 15, Hechtkopf was awarded a prize for young artists by the municipality of Warsaw. Berlewi left for Paris in 1928, and Hechtkopf continued studying art with Władysław Weintraub, a painter, graphic designer, and stage designer for Jewish theatres in Warsaw, who had been educated in Warsaw, Paris, and Switzerland.[9]

Simultaneously with his legal studies, Hechtkopf also attended the Warsaw Art Academy and participated in the annual exhibitions organized by the Jewish Society for the Promotion of Fine Arts (Żydowskie Towarzystwo Krzewienia Sztuk Pięknych; Yidishe Gezelshaft tsu Farshproytn Kunst), which was based in Warsaw. In 1932, for example, he presented an aquarelle in the group exhibition at the Winter Salon organized by the society[10] and other paintings in an exhibition at 11 Wierzbowa Street in January 1935.[11] None of these works survived the Second World War. During those years he also began developing his skills as a graphic designer and stage designer, which would be especially helpful after the war.[12]

Hechtkopf spent the war years in the USSR, partly as a prisoner in labour camps, and returned to Poland following the repatriation agreement in late 1945. Upon his return, he discovered that his mother, sister, and the rest of his extended family had been murdered. Because of his legal education, Hechtkopf was offered a senior position in the reconstructed Polish judicial system; however, he preferred to pursue his career in art. In the next decade he devoted his life to documenting the destruction of Jewish life in Poland and attempting to revive Jewish culture. He played a primary role in several important initiatives to restore Jewish artistic life in Poland after the war, yet also contributed significantly to the renewal of Polish cultural life in general. Pursuing novel avenues of expression, in 1946 he successfully integrated himself into the emerging film industry of post-war Łódź. 'At a time of such great disaster, only a man with a resilient, vibrant and youthful spirit is able to make such a transformation', explained Bar Or, who recently curated an exhibition of Hechtkopf's drawings from this period.[13] In her words:

He was 36 at the time, an 'old man' in terms of that period, and in terms of his personal experience. Yet he continued to search for innovative contemporary paths of creation and documentation of his surroundings. He thus contributed to the formation of new infrastructure for future cultural development, as illustrated for example in his work in filmmaking.[14]

Documenting the Ruins

Hechtkopf's most monumental project during the spring of 1946 was the meticulous documentation of the ruined streets of the Warsaw ghetto in several dozen pen-and-pencil drawings, often risking his life to produce them (Figure 2).[15] 'I rushed to draw it feverishly', he said in a later interview, 'because I knew that even these meagre remains of the largest Jewish community in Europe would soon disappear.'[16] On the back of each drawing he punctiliously identified the exact location of the ruins, the buildings or street corners which had been turned into unrecognizable piles of rubble. These works, which, beginning in 1948, were presented in group exhibitions across Poland, received wide attention. The Yiddish writer Efraim Kaganowski described the 'great emotions and devotion' embedded in the drawings of the ruined ghetto, which 'managed to mirror the distinctive and honourable atmosphere hanging over these places, where death reigned. These works deserve a special album which should be exhibited around the world', he wrote. Twelve years later, in 1960, an album containing twenty-four of the drawings was published in Israel by Yad Vashem.[17]

In the late 1940s Hechtkopf also created a series of portraits of over eighty Holocaust survivors, many of them children, whom he came across in the streets of Warsaw or Łódź. Many were drawn on random pieces of paper or cardboard he found in the street. He called the series Nitsolim, and added a few words describing the person or the location of their encounter on the back (see Figure 3).[18]

Yet documenting the destruction, the lost urban life, and the survivors' faces was only part of Hechtkopf's major effort in the post-war years. During the late 1940s and early 1950s he played a leading role in the extraordinary attempt to revive Jewish culture in Łódź, Warsaw, and across Poland. Under the increasingly oppressive Stalinist influence on communist Poland, he undertook several initiatives intended

Art and Society between Poland and Israel 267

Figure 2 Henryk Hechtkopf, *Warsaw ghetto, Nalewki Street, even-numbered side* (1946)
Warsaw Ghetto Museum

Figure 3 Henryk Hechtkopf, from the Nitsolim series (1946)
Henryk Hechtkopf archive

Figure 4 Members of Sztuka marching in a parade celebrating the end of the Second World War, 9 May 1948. On the back of the photograph Hechtkopf listed the names as 'Bogen, Gryner, Wajnsztok, Muszka, Racanosk, Fogelman, Hechtkopf'. There are seven names but only six people in the third row
Henryk Hechtkopf archive

to preserve and renew Jewish artistic life, including through visual art, Yiddish and Hebrew publications and film-making; organizing conferences and exhibitions; and providing financial assistance to Jewish artists.

Resurrecting Jewish Art in Post-War Poland

Hechtkopf was a board member of the Jewish Association for Culture and Art (Żydowskie Towarzystwo Kultury i Sztuki), and chaired the artistic section of the association between 1947 and 1951. He was also one of the founders and a board member of Sztuka, a co-operative of Jewish artists in Łódź established in 1946 (Figure 4). After the war, the largely intact city of Łódź became Poland's de facto capital and soon replaced Warsaw as the centre of Jewish life, drawing in those Jewish artists, writers, and intellectuals who had survived the war (Figure 5).[19] Many of them, like Hechtkopf, returned from the USSR penniless. The goal of Sztuka was to assist Jewish artists to continue creating and to preserve and revive the tradition of pre-war Jewish art life. The co-operative organized exhibitions and provided Jewish artists with a means of earning a living by contracting design services to Jewish organizations, such as the Central Committee of Jews in Poland (Centralny Komitet Żydów w Polsce; CKŻP) and the Jewish theatre. In a major article in *Opinia*, celebrating the opening of the first exhibition of Jewish artists in Poland, Efraim Kaganowski praised the co-operative:

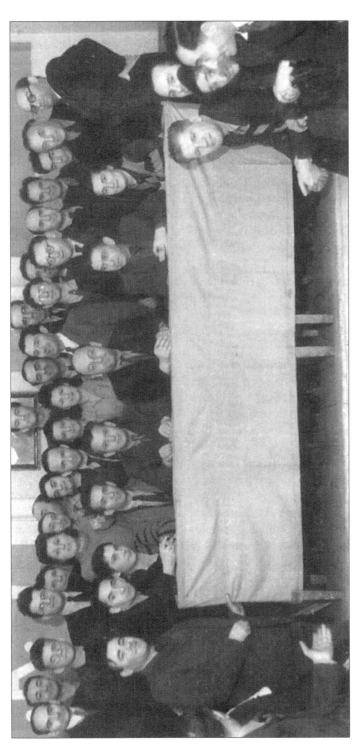

Figure 5 Hechtkopf attached a note to this photograph: 'A group photograph of authors, intellectuals, artists and officials of Jewish organizations in Poland in the 1950s. (I don't remember the exact year). Photo taken in Łódź'. He also listed the names of some of the others present: Adam Beckerman (painter), Pesach Binetzki (poet), Yossef Feingold (sculptor), Yitzhak Guterman (author published with Yidish Bukh), S. Lastik (journalist and author published by Yidish Bukh), Ber Mark (director of the Jewish Historical Institute in Warsaw), Mirski (head of the Central Committee of Polish Jews in Łódź) Aaron Mishka (painter), Leyb Morgentoy (writer and poet), Leyb Olitski (author published by Yidish Bukh), Benjamin Pazanovski and his wife, David Sfard (founder of Yidish Bukh), Yeshayahu Shpigl (author published by Yidish Bukh), Zigmund Valdmand (painter), Elhanan Wegler (poet), Weinstock (painter), Wolf Yasani (writer and journalist), Avrom Zak (author published by Yidish Bukh). Unfortunately it is not possible to assign the names to the individuals with any certainty.

Henryk Hechtkopf archive

in contrast to other artists who lived in Warsaw and Kraków and other places in Poland, and who did not declare their national association, the Łódź group unequivocally defined itself as a Jewish group and collaborated with the Jewish theatre, Jewish publishing houses and Jewish institutions. This collaboration allowed the opening of the exhibition ... which was hailed in the Jewish and non-Jewish world.[20]

The first exhibition of post-war contemporary Jewish artists in Poland opened on 11 January 1948 at the Gong Theatre, 11 Południowa Street, Łódź. Twenty-three artists presented 157 works, including paintings, sculptures, and graphic designs. The exhibition, organized under the auspices of the Jewish Association for Culture and Art, was accompanied by a detailed catalogue and was covered by the Polish and Yiddish press.[21] Hechtkopf chaired the opening ceremony and opened the event with a request for the audience to stand for a minute's silence.[22] The mayor of Łódź and prominent Jewish intellectuals participated. By the end of the exhibition, many of the works had been sold to Jewish institutions in Łódź and Warsaw.[23] In that exhibition, Hechtkopf presented five aquarelles and fourteen of his drawings of the Warsaw ghetto ruins, which attracted much attention from the press. Tadeusz Grygiel, chair of the Association of Polish Artists and Designers (Związek Zawodowy Polskich Artystów Plastyków) in Łódź, for example, wrote that 'the technique of the drawings is perfect ... the artist immortalized symbolic corners of the ghetto. I think the fourteen Warsaw ghetto drawings are worth significantly more when presented together ... serving as an invaluable document illustrating the reality of those times.'[24]

In 1948 Hechtkopf won two competitions organized by the CKŻP and the Jewish Society for the Promotion of Fine Arts, as part of the fifth anniversary of the Warsaw ghetto uprising.[25] In the first competition, the poster he designed was selected for the commemoration of the fifth anniversary of the uprising.[26] Thousands of survivors attended a ceremony on 19 April 1948, at which Natan Rapoport's Monument to the Ghetto Heroes was unveiled. The event was covered by international media and was widely covered in Polish newspapers, several of which published Hechtkopf's poster and other drawings he made on the subject.[27] His poster also appeared on the first Polish stamp commemorating the Holocaust.[28] The second competition was for portraits of five classic authors of Jewish literature—Mendele Moykher Sforim, Sholem Aleichem, Yitskhok Leybush Peretz, Hayim Nahman Bialik, and Sholem Asch. Sixty-one works were submitted.[29] On 25 February 1948 the prize committee announced that Hechtkopf would receive the highest prize awarded, of 50,000 zlotys.[30]

Hechtkopf closely collaborated with the Jewish Historical Society and the Central Committee of Jews in Poland on various projects. For example, in 1947 he was commissioned by the society to design the exhibition for the Jewish Pavilion in Auschwitz, which was to become part of the state museum that had opened on the site of the former death camp that year.[31] He was also an active speaker at conferences of Jewish artists organized by the Jewish Association for Culture and Art. In October 1948 he spoke at the Łódź conference, discussing the challenges faced by Jewish artists in Poland. He described the approach taken by the Sztuka group, promoting what he defined as 'practical art'. While seeking to preserve Jewish culture, such a pragmatic approach was mainly intended to ensure financial support for the artists, some of whom were living in poverty.[32] He also took part in an organized ten-day visit of artists to Lower Silesia, intended to forge connections with Jewish communities there and to imbue them with the historical and social importance of art and of the need to make it accessible to the surviving Jewish population.[33]

Another conference was organized by the Jewish Association for Culture and Art in Wrocław in October 1949, with the participation of 300 delegates from Jewish communities and cultural organizations from Poland, Romania, the United States, Canada, Mexico, and France. Representatives of local Jewish committees included leading writers, artists, and teachers, and the conference was accompanied by a group exhibition of Jewish artists. Hechtkopf's speech stirred much excitement and was cited by several newspaper reports, as he claimed that 'gradually, we are overcoming the formalistic approach, which is poisonous for artists. The motives that are close to us are those of rebuilding the world destroyed in the war.'[34]

In addition to his participation in exhibitions of Jewish artists in Łódź, Wrocław, Katowice,[35] and other places across Poland, Hechtkopf often participated in group exhibitions organized by the Association of Polish Artists and Designers. Between 1947 and 1956 he took part in at least seven of the association's annual exhibitions and was one the few Jewish artists who were officially members, alongside Aleksander Bogen.[36]

In addition to painting, Hechtkopf was often engaged in other artistic projects, including designing posters and logos for Jewish institutions and illustrations for newspapers.[37] Yet two areas of artistic expression particularly drew his interest: book illustration and film-making. Maintaining his connections with Yiddish literary figures from pre-war Warsaw,[38] Hechtkopf was closely involved in the establishment of David Sfard's Yiddish publishing house Yidish Bukh in Łódź in 1947, which was intended to revive Yiddish language and culture in post-war Poland.[39] Hechtkopf created the logo for it and designed the covers for over half of the books it published between 1947 and 1949.[40] He also illustrated *Majn idisz buch*, probably the first post-war Yiddish school textbook.[41] Published by Yidish Bukh in 1948, the book contained a collection of pre-war poems, stories, and fables by nearly seventy Yiddish authors, including Mendele Moykher Sforim and Y. L. Peretz. Overall, out of about forty Yiddish writers who survived the war and lived in Poland at the time, Hechtkopf's illustrations decorated the books and book covers of at least thirteen of them.

At the same time he began illustrating children's books in Hebrew. In 1947 he illustrated *Ḥaveri: alfon leyaldei yisra'el*, a textbook for the study of Hebrew published by the Halutz Centre in Poland to be used in their schools,[42] and several other Haveri booklets edited by Aharon Raszal.[43] A decade later, this would turn into his main occupation, entering the bookshelves of generations of Israeli children, both secular and Orthodox.

Hechtkopf and the Polish Film Industry

Hechtkopf was fascinated by the emerging film industry in post-war Poland. He worked closely with some of the leading Polish film-makers and was involved in several milestones of Polish cinema. In 1946 he was assistant director on one of the first films produced in Poland after the war, *Zakazane piosenki*, directed by Leonard Buczkowski, who had been an eminent film director before the war.[44] The film premiered at the Bałtyk cinema in Łódź, in 1946.[45] It was seen by 10.8 million people in Poland during the first three years of its release, and is still considered one of the most popular Polish films.[46] Hechtkopf also worked as assistant director, alongside Natan Gross, on *Dwie godziny*, which told the story of traumatized ex-prisoners who returned from their camps to Poland at the end of the war. Initially filmed in 1946, it was released only in 1957 due to political censorship.[47]

Another important film to which Hechtkopf contributed artistically was *Ulica Graniczna* (1949), the first film on the Warsaw ghetto uprising. It was directed by Aleksander Ford, one of the chief figures in Polish cinema, head of Film Polski (a government-controlled production company), and a teacher at the Łódź Film School.[48] Hechtkopf created the scenery paintings for the film, which received various awards, including the gold medal at the Venice Film Festival in 1948. The visual aspect, to which Hechtkopf's contribution was crucial, was a central factor in the film's international success, as noted by Marek Haltof, who observed that 'the straightforward and realistic (although studio-made) *Border Street* [*Ulica Graniczna*] shows the Germans' partitioning of Warsaw into Jewish and Aryan Quarters and gives a vast panorama of Jewish and Polish characters living in a building on the street that became the border of the ghetto'.[49]

As Jewish organizations declined in the 1950s, Hechtkopf was increasingly drawn into the world of film-making. He was credited as assistant director of *Żołnierz zwycięstwa* (1953). 1956 saw the release of two of his films: *Nikodem Dyzma*, on which he worked alongside Jan Rybkowski (Figure 6), and *Podhale w ogniu*, which tells the story of a seventeenth-century farmers' revolt against Polish landowners. Hechtkopf wrote the screenplay and directed the film together with Jan Batory.

Hechtkopf also joined one of the 'film units', a system of managing film production under state auspices which facilitated the revival of Polish cinema in the late 1950s. Each unit was composed of directors, screenwriters, producers, and other collaborators and assistants and was supervised by an artistic director with the help of a literary director and a production manager.[50] Hechtkopf was a member of Rytm unit, together with Jan Rybkowski, Stanisław Lenartowicz, and Stanisław Różewicz.

Despite his established position in the art and film circles in Łódź, in 1957 Hechtkopf left Poland and emigrated to Israel, together with the 60,000 others who made up the Gomułka Aliyah.[51]

Figure 6 On the set of Nikodem Dyzma. Hechtkopf is on the right
Henryk Hechtkopf archive

Israel (1957–2004)

In Israel, Hechtkopf and his wife, Alicja Zielińska,[52] settled in Bat Yam, an immigrant city on the Mediterranean shore, just south of Tel Aviv, the cultural centre of Israel. His arrival was celebrated in the local newspapers by acquaintances who knew him from Poland. The Polish Israeli author Anda Amir, for example, published an article in *Davar* welcoming the arrival of 'the new immigrant, the painter Henryk Hechtkopf, who brought with him a large part of his rich and diverse artistic production'.[53]

With the help of friends from Poland, he tried to establish connections with local film-makers, but he soon discovered that the film industry in Israel—ten years after independence—was virtually non-existent. Accordingly, he turned his attention back to painting, illustration, and the establishment of artistic institutions.

A year after his arrival, in 1958, Yad Vashem included a number of his drawings of the ruined Warsaw ghetto in the first Israeli exhibition of Holocaust artists from camps and ghettos. The album containing twenty-four of these drawings published two years later was highly praised by the Hebrew, Yiddish, and Polish press.[54]

In 1963 Hechtkopf held his first individual exhibition in Israel, presenting over sixty paintings at the Tel Aviv Artists House on Elkharizi Street. Two years later he was awarded the prize of the Israel Painters and Sculptors Association for 1965. Most of his paintings at the time were described as surrealist (see Figures 7 and 8), and he was identified with a group of emerging artists who imported surrealism into Israel,

Figure 7 Henryk Hechtkopf, *Dam va'esh vetimrot ashan* (Blood and Fire and Smoke), Sidrat Hasho'ah series (1964)

Henryk Hechtkopf archive

Figure 8 Henryk Hechtkopf, *Mul* (Against) (1963)

Henryk Hechtkopf archive

which included Yigal Tumarkin, Uri Lifshitz, Samuel Bak (who later settled in the United States), and Mordecai Moreh.[55]

He continued to paint, and exhibited his work across the country on an almost annual basis both individually and collectively, mainly in Tel Aviv, at the Tel Aviv Museum and Beit Dizengoff, and in Bat Yam, where he was heavily involved in the establishment of the Bat Yam Art Institute, working with a community of immigrant artists, mostly from eastern Europe, including, among others, Jacob Epstein, Aba Finkel, Aharon Alcalay, Chaim Kiewe, and Eliyahu Gat.[56]

In addition, he continued his efforts to document the changing landscape of urban life which he had begun in Warsaw, with several series of aquarelles and pen-and-pencil drawings of neighbourhoods in Tel Aviv, Jerusalem, Bat Yam, and Safed. In the immediate aftermath of the Six Day War, he created a collection of drawings carefully documenting street corners and ruined buildings in the Old City of Jerusalem that had been under Jordanian rule before the war. The collection was exhibited at Beit Ha'am in Jerusalem in 1973 on the fifth anniversary of Jerusalem Day. Between 1964 and 1976 he also created a collection of over a hundred paintings of Tel Aviv streets, concentrating particularly on the immigrant areas of Neve Tzedek and Manshiya in the southern part of the city. In a note he left attached to the drawings, he included detailed instructions for a future exhibition he planned to be held after his death, requesting that the drawings be presented on the one-hundredth anniversary of Tel Aviv. This wish was fulfilled when the exhibition Rehovot Tel Aviv took place in 2009 as part of the city's anniversary events at Beit Dizengoff.[57]

Although he participated in over forty exhibitions during his years in Israel, Hechtkopf's most significant influence on Israeli culture was achieved in another field in which he had worked professionally in his post-war years in Poland: the illustration of children's books. Fluent in Hebrew from childhood, soon after his arrival in Israel Hechtkopf became one of the most prolific and cherished illustrators of Hebrew and Jewish children's books in Israel and abroad.

'A child remembers paintings from his childhood for the rest of his life'

The first children's book Hechtkopf illustrated was Rafael Saporta's *I Once Had a Grapevine*, published by Masada in 1962.[58] 'This was the beginning of my career in Israel', he explained in one of his last interviews.[59] His influence on children's book illustration was immediate. The books he illustrated received glowing reviews from distinguished writers and critics, including Binyamin Tene, Shulamit Lapid, Bina Ofek, Meir Bareli, and Hamutal Bar-Yosef, who praised the beauty, the colours, the liveliness, and the educational and aesthetic value of Hechtkopf's drawings, and complimented the illustrator, who often 'understood the child's soul and needs even better than the author'.[60]

Over the next three decades, Hechtkopf illustrated more than 370 books, including schoolbooks and kindergarten books, working with the leading authors and publishing houses in Israel, such as Masada, Yavne, Cherikover, Ofer, Zimon, and Tapuach, and Orthodox publishers, such as Sharsheret and Mahanaim, among others. Some of the books he illustrated became canonical and many were published in multiple editions. Some are still in print four decades after their original publication. To give only a few examples, Hechtkopf illustrated books by Rafael Saporta[61] and Levin Kipnis.[62] In 1964 he illustrated *36 Legends from Passover to Passover* by David Cohen, the 'father' of the Federation of Working and Studying Youth (Hano'ar Ha'oved Vehalomed),[63] and Yehoram Ben Meir's *My Israel: From Dan to Eilat in Colour*.[64] In 1965 he illustrated Asher Barash's collection of stories *The Golden Menorah*, for which he received an award from the Ministry of Trade and Industry. The book was translated into English and Finnish.[65] He also illustrated children's books by Yemima Avidar-Tchernovitz,[66] Uriel Ofek,[67] Tzvia Vilenski,[68] Nathan Perski,[69] Binyamin Tene,[70] Shlomo Tanai,[71] Ester Kashti,[72] Rachel Shafir,[73] Ester Shtrait-Wurzel,[74] Anava Kantor,[75] Menucha Fuchs,[76] Irena Liebman,[77] Menucha Bekerman,[78] Dina Levin,[79] and many others. Often authors would write books inspired by his drawings.

One of the most successful series of illustrations he produced was for the famous *Temunot mesaperot lefaotot* (Figure 9), a large, colourful book of 120 pages intended to enhance the linguistic skills of pre-school children, created in collaboration with Nitza Naftali, chief supervisor of pre-schools in the Ministry of Education, and

Figure 9 Henryk Hechtkopf, illustration from *Temunot mesaperot: legil 5–7* (Stories for Children Aged 5–7), 16th edn. (Tel Aviv, 1986), 25

All rights belong to Henryk Hechtkopf and Yavne Bonus Press Ltd

Naftali Melumad, a senior educator.[80] The first book appeared in 1966 and became an immediate best-seller, highly praised especially for its bright, colourful, and intelligent drawings which served as the basis for organizing the child's educational activity. Over half a century later the book is still used by kindergarten teachers in Israel and has been published in over twenty editions. It was followed by a series of similar books for various pre-school age groups, published in the late 1960s and the 1970s, focusing on a variety of topics such as nature and science in everyday life; basic mathematical concepts for toddlers; domestic animals; algebra for early childhood; voices and sounds; and Israeli holidays.[81] Several of these books remained at the top of the best-seller lists of children's literature for many months.[82]

Reviewers frequently commented on the illustrations' distinct success in capturing Israeli nature and landscape. As one critic noted in 1966:

On his arrival in Israel, as a professional illustrator, [Hechtkopf] was disappointed as he flipped through the existing children's literature . . . the most immediate flaw he recognized was the foreign landscape, the borrowed atmosphere. And so, it was he, the newly arrived immigrant, who embarked on a journey of exploration and rediscovered the Israeli scenery . . . Every detail is typical Israeli, the 'tembel' hats, 'Eilat sandals', the t-shirts, the kitchen cabinets' structure, and above all the landscape. There is no shred of foreign view. The trees, the flat fields, the white blocks, common to Kiryat Malakhi, Kiryat Shmona, and Dimona.[83]

Similarly, Shulamit Lapid observed:

H. Hechtkopf points in his drawings to what exists beyond the room, the classroom or the neighbourhood . . . His drawings are realistic and reflect the world of experiences and concepts most familiar to the child. There is no doubt that the painted landscape is Israeli, with the cube-like houses, TV antennas, the window shutters, the standard apartments, the furniture, and so on.[84]

Hechtkopf's fame as an illustrator reached the Jewish community in the United States, and he received invitations to illustrate Jewish children's books published in English. Awarded the Israel–US Cultural Foundation Prize in 1974, he was also mentioned in the 1979 edition of the illustrators' biographical volume *Something About the Author: Facts and Pictures about Authors and Illustrators of Books for Young People*, published in the United States.[85]

One of the most distinctive topics in Hechtkopf's illustrations was stories from the Bible, a collection of which was exhibited in 1996 at the Mishkan Museum of Art in Ein Harod, followed by exhibitions in another four museums in Israel. The exhibition included only a small collection out of hundreds of biblical scenes he had painted over the years, published in eighteen books in Hebrew and in English. Hechtkopf was fascinated by Bible stories, a topic he considered 'most intriguing and difficult'.[86] Indeed, as Heli Govrin, curator of the Ein Harod exhibition, acknowledged, 'generations of students in Israel have been exposed to H. Hechtkopf's paintings, illustrating the Torah books for children . . . His point of departure is mostly didactic', she explained.

Hechtkopf felt the paintings must be precise in depicting the historical details and hence visited historical and archaeological museums and delved into research books. The artist was compelled to accurately represent the archaeological details, the cloths, and the heroes' material culture. His painting mirrored 'the spirit of the time'... The viewer will surely feel the love by which these paintings were created, the sense of mission and the artist's great talent.[87]

Among the best known of these books were *Torah layeled* (1974 and multiple editions; see Figure 10), *Sipurei hatorah liyeladim* (1982), *Sipurei ha'agadah liyeladim* (1983), *Giborei hatanakh* (1985), and *Nevi'im rishonim latalmid* (1985), published by Yavne Press, S. Zimon, and Orenstein Press. Additional books have been published in Israel and in the United States. Some are still currently printed in new editions, such as Levin Kipnis's *Min hatorah*.

Many of the books Hechtkopf illustrated targeted a young, secular, Hebrew-speaking, Israeli audience and included some of the most popular schoolbooks, studied by almost two decades of secular elementary school pupils. Most notable are *Torah layeled*, mentioned above, and particularly *Mikraot Yisra'el* and *Hamikra'ah Sheli*, which were series of school textbooks for first- to fifth-graders, published in several editions in the 1960s and 1970s. These books enjoyed widespread use in state schools, constituting the central textbooks in the field of literature and reading

Figure 10 Henryk Hechtkopf, 'Moshe bateiva', *Torah layeled* (Torah for the Child), ii: Shemot vayikra, ed. N. Gavrieli, B. Avivi, and A. Minkovitz, 23rd edn. (Tel Aviv, 1974), 9

instruction. Their wide distribution and extensive use made them a 'significant and influential tool' among these generations of Israeli youth.[88]

Notably, Hechtkopf had a similar impact on the visual culture of children in the Israeli Orthodox community, where he is often recognized as the 'most beloved illustrator'.[89] One series of books for Orthodox children was especially popular: Sipurei Tsadikim, which contained 120 books, based on Midrash, aggadah, and traditional stories of Jewish communities from around the globe. Beginning in the early 1980s, the series was published by Mahanaim Press. The books soon became common in Orthodox and ultra-Orthodox homes, and are still being reprinted and distributed after more than four decades. Many have been translated into a variety of languages, including Yiddish, Russian, English, French, and Spanish. 'Everyone agrees', it was reported, 'that a significant part of the books' success is due to the colourful paintings which illustrated the stories.'[90]

Yet the bright colours and cheerful faces that are so distinctive of Hechtkopf's illustrations covered a dark shadow in his heart—memories of a lost life and culture—which he carried with him for the rest of his life.

Remembering the Lost Culture

In 1979 he wrote about his work as an illustrator:

I feel and think that to work and create for children, to take a part and have influence on the education of children, is one of the most important tasks, because the future and image of the world depends on it. I am lucky that I can take my modest part in that . . . And yet a weighty reason for me personally—as an Israeli—to work especially for my Israeli young people, is one million Jewish children who were murdered in the Holocaust in the years 1940 to 1945.[91]

In contrast to the familiar rosy cheeks and smiling eyes so common to the thousands of cheerful illustrations Hechtkopf produced over the years, the horrors of the Holocaust were a central theme in his surrealist paintings, which he continued to create until his very last days.

Moreover, throughout all his years in Israel he maintained his life-long project of immortalizing the lost Jewish civilization and artistic life of pre-war Poland. For over four decades, he meticulously created a series of nearly seventy black ink drawings titled Yidishe Parnuse, depicting various occupations held by Jews in pre-war Poland (see Figure 11). In a Hebrew handwritten note he left in his archive, dated 2000, he described his plan:

The Yidishe Parnuse series which I gradually created over the years following my immigration in 1957 is based on my memories of life before the outbreak of the Second World War. It now includes fifty black-and-white drawings and I do not yet feel the collection is complete, for many lively images are within me of wonderful Jewish people busy in their various occupations, the vast majority of which were massacred by the Nazi beast, including nearly my entire family, including my mother, sister, and grandmother. These drawings are carved

Figure 11 Henryk Hechtkopf, *Yom shishi aḥar hatsohorayim: eifoh hakonim?*, (Friday Afternoon: Where Are the Customers?), Yidishe Parnuse series (n.d.)
Henryk Hechtkopf archive

from the blood of my heart, and I have created them to counter the false opinion that Jews did not work but rather exploited the labour of others. I strongly suggest publishing an album of these drawings to serve as a memorial for this wonderful Jewry.[92]

In addition, Hechtkopf continued his efforts to commemorate the Jewish artists who did not survive the Holocaust. His archive is filled with long lists of artists he knew in pre-war Warsaw. Often, he managed to secure their paintings or publish their forgotten names, as happened in the case of Berlewi's *Dybbuk* poster. Another example was the salvation of a self-portrait by Abraham Behrman, a Polish Jewish artist born in 1876 and murdered by a Nazi soldier in the Białystok ghetto in 1943. Hechtkopf, who knew the artist, bought the painting from a Polish art collector in Łódź in 1948. When he moved to Israel in 1957, he brought the painting with him, and in 1968 donated it to Tel Aviv Museum, to be presented at a special memorial exhibition of Jewish artists who perished in the Holocaust that took place in the Helena Rubinstein Pavilion.

Art and Memory: Concluding Remarks

Henryk Hechtkopf continues to inspire contemporary Israeli art and provoke philosophical and political discussions concerning the role of artists in the face of crisis. Most recently, in 2018, a collection of his drawings of the ruins of the Warsaw ghetto were presented in a special exhibition curated by Galia Bar Or, under the title *Forgetting Does Not Erase a Thing: Henryk Hechtkopf and the Warsaw Ghetto Ruins*.[93] Hechtkopf's drawings were presented alongside a large group exhibition, also curated by Bar Or, at the Pyramida Contemporary Art Centre in the Wadi Salib neighbourhood of Haifa, surrounded by massive rebuilding projects. In that particular context, the sketches were meant to raise broader questions concerning urban reconstructions, lost communities, and memories. In the words of Bar Or:

Hechtkopf's drawings illuminate the intriguing and historically recurring phenomenon of regimes' ban on the documentation of ruins. Often, a destroyed area becomes attractive as a ruin only years later, when viewed retrospectively, and it no longer seems threatening. But why do governments feel threatened by such documentation and often forbid it? This question was at the focus of the Pyramida exhibition. Hechtkopf was completely aware of the historical moment and his significant role as a witness leaving a testimony as a man and as an artist. He had the foresight to act against such repression of memory.[94]

Shaul Seter celebrated the 'humanistic artistic' message of the exhibition, which represented the 'fervent belief in the social role of art'.[95]

Memory, forgetting, urban destruction and renewal, but especially the immortalization of lost cultures and communities, were central driving forces behind Hechtkopf's life and work. This chapter has presented the chronological and historical framework of his life, introducing the great variety and richness of his personal story and creations. Yet many aspects of this story call for further investigation by historians, art critics, and sociologists. To begin with, his drawings, paintings (in various styles), illustrations, graphic designs, and film and theatre work require further thematic and comparative analysis within the context of their time and place. Hechtkopf's complex approach to Jewish culture and art also raises fascinating questions: he was a secular artist married to a Polish Catholic woman, yet he devoted large parts of his work to celebrating Jewish heritage and tradition through his drawings of Bible stories and traditional Jewish legends from across the world. Similarly, his role as an influential illustrator of children's books demands further study, given his equal popularity in secular and Orthodox communities, his distinctive involvement in the emergence of private publishing in Israel during the 1960s and 1970s, and his central engagement with school textbooks for the developing public education system in these years.

Hechtkopf embodied in his life and work the tight connection between the cultural heritage of Polish Jews and Israeli culture. The biographical sketch presented in this chapter only scratches the surface of the multilayered and multifaceted activities undertaken by Hechtkopf in over eight decades of artistic creation. His private archive is in itself a rare and fascinating collection of evidence of the rich and diverse Jewish art world that existed in the two interwar decades and the first post-war decade in Poland, which requires further cataloguing and research. What explains Hechtkopf's success in integrating into Israeli society and to what extent does he exemplify the Gomułka Aliyah? The extent to which he and other Jewish artists of his time embodied the bridge between the Polish, Yiddish, and Hebrew languages and cultures deserves further analysis. These are merely a few examples of topics and questions waiting to be discovered and explored by future curators, students, and scholars of Jewish art history, of Polish Jewish history, and of Israeli culture and society.

Notes

I am grateful for the invaluable comments and generous advice I received from Galia Bar Or, Yael Darr, Zuleika Rodgers, and Assaf Likhovski, and to Ela Bauer, Havi Dreifus, Alissa Dvir, Dorit Gani, Rotem Ruff, and Scott Ury, for their helpful suggestions. I would also like to thank the participants of the Sixth Bi-annual Israel–Poland Workshop for Early Career Scholars of the History and Culture of Polish Jews (25–7 June 2018) and the editors of this volume for their careful suggestions. I am especially grateful to my mother, Rachel (Kristina) Postawski, for working together with me on this project.

1 N. Semel, 'Kitsur toledot hazeman shel henrik hekhtkopf', *Arba al ḥamesh*, 68 (July–Aug. 1995), 29–31: 30.
2 Galia Bar Or, interview with author, 7 Sept. 2020.
3 For Hechtkopf's art, see 'Gallery': Henryk Hechtkopf Art website, visited 25 May 2021.
4 Henryk Hechtkopf archive, private collection: Henryk Hechtkopf, 'H. hekhtkopf: korot ḥayim', biographical note, 25 Nov. 1996.
5 S. Netzer, 'Yehudei varsha bein shtei milḥamot-olam', in G. Grief (ed.), *Toledot yehudei varsha: mireshitam ve'ad leyameinu* (Jerusalem, 1991), 87–160: 121.
6 Shatzky later emigrated to the United States and became a historian (B. D. Weinryb, 'Review: The History of the Jews in Warsaw by Jacob Shatzky', *Jewish Quarterly Review*, 40 (1950), 417–21).
7 A. Pietrasik, 'Re-staging the Avant-Garde: Henryk Berlewi's Return to Abstract Art', *View*, 3 (2013): View: Theories and Practice of Visual Culture website, visited 13 Dec. 2021.
8 D. Mazower, 'On Henryk Berlewi', *Mendele Review*, 9 (19 Apr. 2005): University of Haifa website, visited 13 Dec. 2021.
9 R. Piątkowska, 'Weintraub, Władysław' (n.d.): Polin: Virtual Shtetl website, visited 20 May 2021. Weintraub died in Treblinka in August 1942.
10 Henryk Hechtkopf archive: 'Otwarcie "Salonu Zimowego" – zbiorowej wystawy prac w Żyd. Tow. Krzewienia Sztuk Pięknych', *Nasz Przegląd Ilustrowany*, Jan. 1935 (newspaper clipping). Includes photos of nine paintings from the exhibition by A. Guterman, B. Rolnicki, F. Frydman, Łucja Welczer, S. Puterman, S. Fajgenbaum, S. Centnerszwerowa, Izrael Tykociński, and Henryk Hechtkopf. Except for Hechtkopf, none survived the war.
11 Henryk Hechtkopf archive: 'Wystawa zbiorowa Żyd. Tow. Krzewienia Sztuk Pięknych (Wierzbowa 11)', *Nasz Przegląd Ilustrowany*, Jan. 1935 (newspaper clipping). Includes

photos of seven paintings from the exhibition by Łucja Welczer-Szwajgerowa, Izrael Tykociński, Boaz Dulman, Maksymilian Eljowicz, Henryk Hechtkopf, Wincent Brauner, Henryk Rabinowicz. Except for Hechtkopf, none is known to have survived the war.

12 In 1934 and 1935 he worked as an assistant stage designer at Polish Acoustics, Warsaw; between 1936 and 1939 he was a graphic designer and illustrator at Rekino, Warsaw ('Hechtkopf, Henryk, 1910–', in A. Commire (ed.), *Something About the Author: Facts and Pictures about Authors and Illustrators of Books for Young People*, xvii (Detroit, 1979), 79–81).

13 '"Lishko'aḥ lo moḥek davar": henrik hekhtkopf verishumei geto varshah' (July–Dec. 2018): Pyramida website, visited 21 May 2021.

14 Bar Or, interview with author.

15 The Polish authorities' ban on documenting the destruction in Warsaw and the lawless atmosphere of that period often made the work on the drawings dangerous. In later years, in order to receive permission to transfer the drawings out of Poland, Hechtkopf had to change the date on some of them.

16 Henryk Hechtkopf archive: A. Amir, 'Hatsayar hekhtkopf', *Davar*, 28 Mar. 1958 (newspaper clipping).

17 H. Hechtkopf, *Warsaw: 24 Paintings of Warsaw Ghetto and Its Surroundings, from the Archives of 'Yad Vashem'/Varshah: 24 tsiyurim migeto varshah usevivotav miginzei yad vashem* (Jerusalem, 1960).

18 The paintings of the ghetto ruins and survivors are included in the collections of the soon-to-be-opened Warsaw Ghetto Museum, the Jewish Historical Institute in Poland, Yad Vashem, and the US Holocaust Memorial Museum.

19 Polonsky, *The Jews in Poland and Russia*, iii: *1914 to 2008* (Oxford, 2012), 627–8.

20 E. Kaganowski, 'Impresje z Wystawy Żydowskich Artystów Plastyków', *Opinia*, 1948, no. 30, p. 9.

21 See e.g. Henryk Hechtkopf archive: 'Otwarcie Wystawy Łódzkiej Grupy Żydowskich Artystów Plastyków', *Dziennik Łódzki*, 13 Jan. 1948 (newspaper clipping). Polish newspapers that reported on the exhibition included *Głos Robotniczy*, *Solidarność*, *Słowo Młodych*, *Mosty*, and *Opinia*; Yiddish ones included *Palkas stima*, *Yidisha shripman*, *Folks sztyme*, *Das nye laben*, and *La senda der veg* (Buenos Aires).

22 'Otwarcie Wystawy Zbiorowej Grupy Plastyków-Żydów w Łodzi', *Mosty*, 15 Jan. 1948, p. 4.

23 M. Maneli, '"Sztuka" Spółdzielnia Artystów Malarzy', *Solidarność*, 3–4 (Feb.–Mar. 1948), 28–30.

24 T. Grygiel, 'Wystawa Zbiorowa Grupy Plastyków Żydów w Łodzi', *Nasze Słowo*, 1948, no. 2, pp. 6–7. A set of these drawings was bought by the Jewish Historical Institute in Warsaw.

25 See R. Piątkowska, 'Jewish Society for the Encouragement of Fine Arts (Yidishe Gezelshaft tsu Farshproytn Kunst): An Attempt at the Continuation of Jewish Artistic Life in Postwar Poland, 1946–1949', in E. Grözinger and M. Ruta (eds.), *Under the Red Banner: Yiddish Culture in the Communist Countries in the Postwar Era* (Wiesbaden, 2008), 77–95.

26 'Projekt plakatu, wydanego przez Centralny Komitet Żydów w Polsce, z okazji piątej rocznicy powstania w getcie. Proj. – Henryk Hechtkopf', *Tydzień Robotnika*, 18 Apr. 1948, p. 11. A copy of the poster can be found in the Israeli National Library: 'Warsaw Ghetto Uprising Anniversary Poster, 1948', National Library of Israel, Digital Library website, visited 9 June 2021. See also M. Tarnowska, 'Żydowskie środowisko artystyczne w Warszawie w latach 1945–1949', *Pamiętnik Sztuk Pięknych*, 9 (2015), 33–59.

27 See e.g. 'Wieczna pamięć męczennikom i bojownikom Narodu Żydowskiego', *Nasze Słowo*, 1948, nos. 6–7, p. 1.

28 P. V. Polak, 'Bulim lezekher korbanot maḥanot hahashmadah', *Haaretz*, 24 Sept. 1959, p. 3.

29 'Rozstrzygnięcie konkursu na plakat poświęcony piątej rocznicy powstania w Getcie Warszawy', *Nasze Słowo*, 1948, no. 3, p. 13.

30 The prize committee decided that the first prize would not be awarded. Hechtkopf was awarded the second prize. Three artists shared the third prize and received 30,000 zlotys each: Tadeusz Gronowski from Warsaw, Dora Szenfeld from Łódź, and K. Gleb from Paris. Seven other artists from Poland and France received 10,000 zlotys each ('Komunikaty', *Przegląd Artystyczny: Organ Związku Polskich Artystów Plastyków*, 1948, no. 3, p. 8).

31 A. Rosenblum, 'Time in the Museum, the Museum in Time: The History of the Auschwitz-Birkenau State Museum', *Anthropology of East Europe Review*, 19/1 (2001), 42–55: 43; see also J. Lachendro, 'Auschwitz Museum in the First Years of Its Operation: Designing the Museum' (n.d.): Auschwitz-Birkenau State Museum website, 'E-learning', visited 22 May 2021.

32 Other speakers at the conference, which discussed various ways of promoting Jewish culture and art in Poland, included Efraim Kaganowski, David Sfard, Aleksander Bogen, S. Lastik, and H. Safrin ('Konferencja plastyków żydowskich w Łodzi', *Mosty*, 30 Oct. 1948, p. 10).

33 Henryk Hechtkopf archive: 'Obrady plastyków żydowskich', *Prasa*, 25 Oct. 1948 (newspaper clipping).

34 Henryk Hechtkopf archive: 'Wystawa plastyki żydowskiej: Odrzucenie formalizmu', *Słowo Polskie*, 16 Oct. 1949 (newspaper clipping).

35 Henryk Hechtkopf archive: M.P., 'Wystawa Zbiorowa Żydowskich Artystów-Plastyków w Katowicach', *Trybuna Robotnicza*, 20 Jan. 1950, p. 6 (newspaper clipping). The painting he presented at the Katowice exhibition, *Stary rolnik*, was bought in Israel in 1958 by the Executive Committee of Histadrut (Israeli Workers Union) (Henryk Hechtkopf, handwritten note attached to M.P., 'Wystawa Zbiorowa Żydowskich Artystów-Plastyków w Katowicach').

36 Henryk Hechtkopf archive: Association of Polish Artists and Designers exhibition catalogues, 1947, 1948, 1949, 1951, 1953, 1955, 1956. He presented between one and four paintings at each exhibition.

37 For example, he was invited by the CKŻP to design a logo for a new school in Warsaw. Examples for newspaper illustrations include a portrait of Bolesław Bierut ('Święto Odrodzenia Polski Świętem Żołnierza Polskiego', *Dziennik Łódzki*, 22 July 1947, p. 1) and for a story by Yeshayahu Shpigl (Y. Szpigel, 'Niebo wuja Teodora', *Opinia*, 1949, no. 59, p. 10).

38 Including Melech Ravitch, who emigrated to Montreal before the war and in 1948 sent Hechtkopf a copy of his latest book with a personal dedication (M. Ravitch, *Towards a Book of Books of Jewish Thought and Deed in the Last 2000 Years* (Buenos Aires, 1948)).

39 J. Nalewajko-Kulikov, 'The Last Yiddish Books Printed in Poland: Outline of the Activities of Yiddish Bukh Publishing House', in Grözinger and Ruta (eds.), *Under the Red Banner*, 111–34.

40 Hechtkopf designed and illustrated the two first books it published in 1947: *Malkhes geto*, a collection of stories about the Łódź ghetto by Yeshayahu Shpigl, and Chaim Grade's book of poetry, *Oyf di khurves*. He also designed and illustrated the cover of David Sfard's *Shrayber un bikher* published in 1949. Other authors whose books he designed and illustrated include Leyb Olitski, Shloyme Diamant, Yosef Okrutni, Yitzhak Guterman, and the poets Gute Guterman, Leib Kupershmidt, Leyb Morgentoy, and Yeshayahu Shpigl.

41 Y. Shpigl and S. Lastik (eds.), *Majn idisz buch* (Warsaw, 1948).
42 A. Raszal (ed.), *Ḥaveri: alfon leyaldei yisra'el. dargah beit* (Łódź, 1947).
43 A. Raszal (ed.), *Ḥaveri: iton leyaldei yisra'el*, 2 vols. (Łódź, 1947).
44 M. Haltof, *Polish National Cinema* (New York, 2002), 49–51.
45 Henryk Hechtkopf archive: invitation to premiere of *Zakazane piosenki* [8 Jan. 1947].
46 Haltof, *Polish National Cinema*, 81.
47 Ibid. 80; see also T. Lubelski, 'Polish Cinema: A History. Lecture 5 (1945–1954)' (25 Feb. 2016): YouTube website, visited 22 May 2021.
48 Haltof, *Polish National Cinema*, 51.
49 Ibid. 88.
50 Ibid. 120.
51 E. Węgrzyn, 'Reasons for Emigration of the Jews from Poland in 1956–1959', in M. Gerstenfeld and F. S. Ouzan, *Postwar Jewish Displacement and Rebirth, 1945–1967* (Leiden, 2014), 171–84.
52 The two met and married in Łódź after the war.
53 Amir, 'Hatsayar hekhtkopf'.
54 Hechtkopf, *Warsaw*.
55 R. Berman, 'Gedolei hasure'alistim bemuse'on tel aviv', *Yediot aḥaronot*, 30 Dec. 1966.
56 'Hamakhon le'omanut vehagaleryah haḥadashah' (n.d.): Bat Yam website, visited 22 May 2021. In 1985 Hechtkopf received an honorary Yakir Ha'ir award from the Bat Yam municipality for his many years of artistic activity in the city.
57 E. Armon Azulai, 'Sidrat tsiyurim shel tel aviv shetsayar henrik hekhtkopf tutsag larishonah baḥodesh haba', *Haaretz*, 16 June 2009, p. 13; E. Datz, 'Hakhinoti merosh', *Time Out Tel Aviv*, 25 June 2009, p. 18.
58 R. Saporta, *Hayoh haytah li gefen* (Tel Aviv, 1962).
59 M. Weinstock, 'Pa'am hatsayarim ahavu yeladim', *Mishpaḥa*, 1 Aug. 1996, pp. 32–3.
60 H. Bar-Yosef, 'Arba'ah sifrei yeladim', *Lamerḥav*, 16 Feb. 1968, p. 6; see also B. Tene, review of *Tsipor pela'im* by Aneva Kantor (Heb.), *Mishmar liyeladim*, 20 Mar. 1972; S. Lapid, 'Shirim lefaotot shemehem notsar hafolklor', *Maariv*, 25 Aug. 1972, p. 39; M. Bareli, 'Shirim lema'akhal', *Davar*, 3 Apr. 1972, p. 10.
61 e.g. R. Saporta, *Bayit kat va'aliyah* (Tel Aviv, 1961); id., *Pli-plah hoplah vekhol heḥai* (Tapuach, 1961); id., *Hatanin vehashemesh* (Tapuach, 1963); id., *Ido ufarato* (Tapuach, 1963); id., *Tevah ketanah basuf* (Tel Aviv, 1963); Eng. trans., *A Basket in the Reeds* (Minneapolis, 1965).
62 e.g. L. Kipnis, *Shabat: nurit meḥakah leyom hashabat* (Tel Aviv, 1976); id., *Sodot min haḥeder* (Tel Aviv, 1977); id., *Min hatorah: sipurim liyeladim* (Tel Aviv, 2002); id., *Shishah besakit eḥad* (Tel Aviv, 2009).
63 D. Cohen, *36 agadot mipesaḥ ad pesaḥ* (Tel Aviv, 1964). He also illustrated id., *She'arim niftaḥim* (Tel Aviv, 1966).
64 Y. Ben Meir, *Yisra'el sheli: entsiklopedyah liyediat hamoledet bitseva'im* (Tel Aviv, 1964); Eng. version: *My Israel: From Dan to Eilat in Colour* (Tel Aviv, 1965).
65 A. Barash, *Menorat hazahav: sefer ma'asiyot* (Tel Aviv, 1962); Eng. trans.: *A Golden Treasury of Jewish Tales*, trans. M. Roston (New York, 1966).
66 Y. Avidar-Tchernovitz, *Hayonah shel savta* (Tel Aviv, 1963).
67 U. Ofek, *Ashan kisah et hagolan* (Tel Aviv, 1974); id., *Dani ve'ester holekhim el hadodah* (Tel Aviv, 1980).

68 Hechtkopf illustrated around twenty-eight books by Tzvia Vilenski, including T. Vilenski, *Ma'aseh be'anan katan* (Tel Aviv, 1979); ead., *Hasefer sheli: sefer habayit shel yaldei kitah alef* (Tel Aviv, 1975); ead., *Hataba'at shel ruti* (Tel Aviv, 1979); ead., *Ha'agadot sheli: agadot uma'asiyot liyeladim bagil harakh* (Tel Aviv, 1979).
69 N. Perski, *Mikraot yisra'el* (Tel Aviv, 1975).
70 B. Tene, *Alef beit shel yeladim* (Tel Aviv, 1973); id., *Alef beit shel ḥayot* (Tel Aviv, 1973); id., *Mizmor laḥag* (Tel Aviv, 1973).
71 S. Tanai, *Mi rotseh sipur? sipurim veshirim liyeladim* (Tel Aviv, 1987).
72 E. Kashti, *Kokhav ohev yeladim* (Tel Aviv, 1965); id., *Hamenumeret ve'efroḥeiha* (Tel Aviv, 1966).
73 R. Shafir, *Eikh tsomeḥot hapitriyot?* (Tel Aviv, 1972).
74 E. Shtrait-Wurzel, *Haberiḥah* (Tel Aviv, 1973).
75 A. Kantor, *Tsipor pela'im: sipurim leyeladim* (Tel Aviv, 1972).
76 M. Fuchs, *Mah shekarah ba'ayarah: sipur alilati meḥayei ha'ayarah* (Jerusalem, 1998).
77 I. Liebman, *Partizan ushemo tsutsik* (Tel Aviv, 1971); ead., *Haḥevrah mehanaḥal* (Tel Aviv, 1972).
78 M. Bekerman, *Hasifriyah hagedolah* (Jerusalem, 1990); ead., *Shalvah baḥavah* (Jerusalem, 1996).
79 D. Levin, *Ha'efro'aḥ hasakran* (Benei Berak, 1976); ead., *Taltali* (Benei Berak, 1976); ead., *Simḥatah shel rivki* (Benei Berak, 1976); ead., *Gibor hageto* (Benei Berak, 1976).
80 N. Naftali and N. Melumad, *Temunot mesaperot lefaotot* (Tel Aviv, 1966).
81 N. Naftali, *Kolot utselilim: musegei mada beḥayei yom-yom lagil harakh* (Tel Aviv, 1967); ead., *Galgalim bitenuah: musegei mada beḥayei yom-yom lagil harakh* (Tel Aviv, 1967); ead., *Misparim vetsurot: pituaḥ musagim matematiyim* (Tel Aviv, 1969); N. Nir-Yaniv, *Ḥagei yisra'el: lagil harakh* (Tel Aviv, 1972); N. Naftali, *Teva umada beḥayei yom-yom: lagil harakh* (Tel Aviv, 1973); F. Goldschmitt, *Ḥapes oti: hitmatsut bamerḥav: pituaḥ musagim matematiyim* (Tel Aviv, 1975); N. Naftali, *ḥayot babayit: legil 5–8* (Tel Aviv, 1975); ead., *Galeh umetsa: pituaḥ musagim matematiyim: musegei yaḥas* (Tel Aviv, 1978); ead., *Ḥashev umetsa: pituaḥ musagim matematiyim* (Tel Aviv, 1978); S. Borek, *Sefer hahandasah sheli: handasah lagil harakh* (Tel Aviv, 1983).
82 For example, Naftali and Melumad's *Temunot mesaperot lefaotot* remained number one best seller for at least eleven months in 1971 and 1972, according to *Maariv* newspaper (see Y. Ha'elyon, 'Ravei hamekher shel detsember', *Maariv*, 26 Jan. 1973, p. 38).
83 G. Naomi, 'Temunot mesaprot', *Hatsofeh*, supplement, 11 Nov. 1966, p. 8.
84 S. Lapid, 'Bikurim lagil harakh', *Maariv*, 20 Oct. 1972, p. 39.
85 'Hechtkopf, Henryk, 1910–'. His name was also included in *Who's Who in World Jewry: A Biographical Dictionary of Outstanding Jews* (New York, 1972).
86 Cited in *Hatanakh betsiyur: mivḥar tsiyurim lesipurei hatanakh*, exhib. cat. Beit Rybak Museum (Bat Yam, 1996).
87 Cited ibid.
88 O. Zegen, '"Mikraot yisra'el" kikheli ḥinukhi me'utsav', *Dor ledor*, 31 (2007), 227–42.
89 Weinstock, 'Pa'am hatsayarim ahavu yeladim', 33.
90 M. Zigelbaum, 'Sipur ḥayim al tsiyurim "ḥayim"', *Kfar ḥabad*, 29 Aug. 1996, pp. 16–21.
91 'Hechtkopf, Henryk, 1910–', 81.
92 Henryk Hechtkopf archive: Henryk Hechtkopf, handwritten note (Heb.), 2000.

93 "'Lishko'aḥ lo moḥek davar'".
94 Bar Or, interview with author; see L. Barbo, 'Yesh poh ayin mibaḥuts shemiteḥilah lehitvade'a' (17 July 2018): *Erev Rav* website, visited 22 May 2021.
95 S. Seter, '"Ḥeifah matsigah: teguvah tsiyonit humanistit holemet' (25 July 2018): *Haaretz* website, visited 16 Dec. 2021.

Yom-Tov Levinsky, Jewish Ritual, and Exile in Israeli Culture

ADI SHERZER

Introduction

In recent years several studies have shed new light on the complex relationship between Israeli culture and the culture of the Jewish diaspora, especially that of eastern Europe.[1] In contrast to the dominant approach that stresses the Zionist break with and contempt for the exilic past, these studies have shown that, alongside the negation of Jewish life outside the Land of Israel, Zionism often used popular culture and diaspora rituals to deepen and authenticate the Zionist narrative. Thinkers, politicians, and cultural activists in Israel created delicate (and not always consistent) dialectics between rejection and preservation and between criticism and romanticization of Jewish culture. They assumed that stressing the continuity between past longing and present realization and the selective choice of episodes from the exilic past were essential to creating a new culture.

In this context, Hebrew culture in Israel was not very different from other attempts to create a modern Jewish culture that took place in eastern Europe and North America. As Israel Bartal has argued, 'secular Hebrew culture in Palestine and secular Yiddish culture in Eastern-Europe... were more similar than dissimilar', since they shared the same conceptual world.[2] This notion can be illustrated in the interaction of education and folklore. Like many of the Jewish schools in interwar eastern Europe, the pre-state education system of the Yishuv had a 'secular and traditional' nature, which was deeply influenced by the ideas of cultural Zionism.[3] As a result, although school textbooks criticized the exilic lifestyle, they stressed the value of east European Jewish rituals and customs, which they interpreted as folklore and not as religious praxis.[4] In addition to the education system, this was also manifested in the establishment of popular folklore organizations and journals in the Land of Israel that followed the work of Jewish folklorists in eastern Europe and aspired 'to collect the pieces' of exilic life so that they could contribute to the culture of the future Jewish state.[5] As Adam Rubin noted, this idea and the basic existence of Hebrew folklorism question the unequivocal place of *shelilat hagolah* (usually translated as 'negation of the exile') in Zionist and Israeli historiography.[6] This becomes even more obvious in the light of popular Hebrew anthologies, which, according to Bartal, sought to 'embody the historically continuous national existence to which Zionism laid claim'.[7] The continuous narrative was indeed selective and guided by the national perspective, yet it referred not only to ancient periods of sovereignty but also to the recent exilic past.

This chapter seeks to examine Zionism's complex relationship to the Jewish past through the case study of Yom-Tov Levinsky (1899–1973). Levinsky was a folklorist and editor of anthologies who established a reputation as an 'expert on the Jewish festivals' and tried to shape a unique Israeli culture based on the Jewish (mostly east European) exilic past. He was born in Zambrów in Suwałki province, in what is now the north-east of Poland, to a traditional family that was open to the Haskalah. He studied at the Łomża yeshiva, and when he came of age he relocated to Vilna and completed his studies at the Hebrew gymnasium and the Tarbut Teachers' Seminary. He studied for a year at the University of Vilna and finally completed his doctorate in Belgium. In 1935 he emigrated to Palestine, and, although he had difficulty integrating at the Hebrew University, he was recognized as an expert ethnographer and to a large extent founded the field in Israel. He worked mainly as part of Yeda Am, a society for folklore research founded in Tel Aviv during the Second World War which he headed until his death.

Dani Schrire situated Levinsky's work within the context of east European Jewish folklorism but argued that, unlike his predecessors, he adapted a unique technique of 'montage' that connected different pieces of folklore into a new integral whole.[8] Bartal has suggested that Levinsky's work is similar to the *kinus* (gathering) project of Ahad Ha'am and Hayim Nahman Bialik, which sought to preserve selected parts of the Jewish heritage for future generations.[9] Either way, Levinsky should be seen as an Israeli manifestation of ideas which developed in eastern Europe, mostly in the Odessa circle of Hebrew writers, folklorists, and cultural activists.

As was the case with many folklore researchers, and most of those involved in the *kinus* project, Levinsky's motivation was not purely academic. As Bartal notes, the basis of his endeavour was not 'the gathering of the old for the purpose of erecting a glorious monument to a sealed past and probing it exclusively from a scientific-"objective" distance, but rather clarification and sifting, reworking and extraction, in order to pass it on to future generations'.[10] One of his critics characterized his project as a 'memory of the heart' and explained that 'his soul was not cut off from its people. His heart still wanders there and remains connected to the land of the people, the place where the nation's soul and the nation's folklore was created.'[11] The author did not specify the location of the 'there' where Levinsky's soul wanders, but, from the context, it is clear that he meant the destroyed Jewish civilization of eastern Europe. Levinsky saw this civilization as vivid and relevant for the new Israeli reality. In this spirit, he lectured to various audiences, initiated seminars, broadcast on the radio, wrote articles, and edited popular anthologies for the general public and teachers.

Levinsky often used the Jewish festival cycle as an opportunity to evoke interest in the Jewish culture of eastern Europe. Direct evidence of this can be found, for example, in an article by the radio critic for the newspaper *Davar* in May 1950:

Radio listeners associate Dr Yom-Tov Levinsky's name with the Jewish festivals. Before each and every one, he broadcasts . . . common-sense explanations of its contents and customs. . . In attempting to redesign our holidays and festivals so they will suit the spirit of the generation, it is important to examine the tradition and ancient customs for inspiration and new ideas. Yom-Tov Levinsky's study of the Jewish festivals has made a significant contribution.[12]

Levinsky's radio broadcasts, his lectures to the general public, and his articles in the press before the festivals presented a coherent narrative that began with the ancient origins of a festival, continued with its celebration in the diaspora, and ended with how it is observed in present-day Israel. Levinsky devoted considerable energy to the study of the festivals, which culminated in the publication of *Sefer hamo'adim*—an eight-volume anthology collecting various sources relevant to each one.[13]

Below I examine five characteristics of Levinsky's attitude to the Jewish festival cycle that emerge from *Sefer hamo'adim* and his articles in the press from the founding of Yeda Am in 1942 until the Folklore Congress 1959 which marked a change in his activities.[14] The reason for choosing to rely specifically on these sources is primarily their wide distribution. Levinsky usually published his articles in *Davar*, which represented the ruling party, Mapai. *Sefer hamo'adim* appeared in numerous editions and became a regular feature on the bookshelves of many middle-class Israeli homes. It was aggressively marketed as a barmitzvah gift, sold by newspapers at a discounted price to subscribers, and was still being reprinted twenty years after its first appearance.[15]

Festivals as Part of the Continuing History of the Jewish People

The first and most prominent characteristic of Levinsky's writing is his treatment of the Jewish festivals as part of a history beginning in ancient Israel, continuing through the years of exile, and ending with new 'traditions' together with his proposals for the creation of new Israeli rituals. This framework was typical of Zionist thought which tended to begin and end discussions in the Land of Israel. But Levinsky also filled the gap between these two periods, extensively addressing life in the diaspora. His approach was thus continuous, although the story was not linear—Levinsky did not order his thoughts chronologically. Rather, he constantly integrated historical layers and connected persons, ideas, and customs from different times and places. In contrast to the Zionist tendency to 'return to history' and tell the story of the Jews in a methodological way, Levinsky created a mythical chronology based on associative connections that bring to mind the talmudic attitude to time.

This is clearly reflected in the way *Sefer hamo'adim* is arranged. Although the treatment of each festival almost always begins with its biblical source, the subsequent discussion mixes different sources: biblical, talmudic, halakhic, folkloric, and Zionist. For example, the volume for Sukkot begins by citing verses related to the festival in the Bible but later introduces a mixture of halakhic passages, academic studies, sources on its celebration in the diaspora, Zionist interpretations, and literary works by east European maskilim.[16] There are only two chapters in the book which are limited geographically or chronologically—'In the Homeland' and 'In Our Diasporas'. However, Levinsky also includes in other chapters passages referring to the practices of the Yishuv and those of the diaspora. An extreme example of Levinsky's conception of time can be found in an article he wrote in 1952 for Shavuot that illustrates his tendency to explain later Jewish customs through the creative interpretation of ancient sources.[17] He began by connecting the custom of eating dairy foods to the bringing of first fruits to the Temple and argued that the priests' focus on first fruits did not leave them time to slaughter the daily sacrifices and eat meat. This link is forced, since the scholarly consensus dates the custom of eating dairy products to the Middle Ages, and there is no trace of it in the literature of the ancient sages.[18] However, Levinsky did not stop there. When discussing other reasons for the custom, he linked the sacrifices in first-century Jerusalem to a Yiddish folk saying according to which Shavuot signifies the beginning of summer, when meat spoils quickly in the heat. Thus, a direct connection is established between the priests in the Temple and Yiddish speakers, as if hundreds of years and thousands of kilometres had not separated them, as if the Polish summer was similar to that of the Land of Israel.

This is a far-reaching conception of Jewish folklore that unites its various elements and completely blurs the unique anthropological characteristics that usually stand at the heart of ethnographic work. At the same time, however, Levinsky tended to describe diasporic Jewish life in full, providing extensive references to historical events, personalities, and institutions. All the volumes of *Sefer hamo'adim* include a detailed description of the customs of the festival in different communities, accompanied by the thoughts of major diasporic figures. Thus, for example, the volume for Shavuot includes texts by Rabbi Isaiah Horowitz (Prague), Rabbi Jacob Emden (Altona), the Dubner Magid (Dubno), Levi Isaac of Berdichev (Pińsk, Berdichev), Naphtali Herz Wessely (Berlin), Isaac Benjacob (Vilna), and others. A critical examination of the diasporic sources chosen by Levinsky reveals that, apart from the Talmud, most originated in the eighteenth century and therefore had no position regarding Zionism or a Jewish state. As for the nineteenth and twentieth centuries, Levinsky systematically ignored non-Zionist thinkers. Moreover, as I will show later, he often read diasporic reality through nationalist eyes and thus those pre-Zionist thinkers were retrospectively seen as proto-Zionists.

In any case, the sustained connection between the ancient past, the recent past, and the contemporary era makes the diaspora present in Israel, and makes it relevant to national culture. By neutralizing chronology and geography, Levinsky's associative approach ensured that the diaspora would not be seen as a closed chapter in the past but would instead be incorporated into the present.

Jewish Folklore as Shtetl Folklore

Another key characteristic of Levinsky's writing is the way he derived Jewish folklore from an imagined east European shtetl while marginalizing and exoticizing other Jewish traditions. As Dani Schrire notes, in most cases, Levinsky treated the Ashkenazi traditions as the common custom, while marking Sephardi traditions as peripheral.[19] This is also reflected in the organization of Yeda Am's journal: its main section dealt mostly with eastern Europe, while a separate section was devoted to 'oriental Jewish folklore'. Similarly, in *Sefer hamo'adim* and Levinsky's newspaper articles, the Ashkenazi traditions are usually presented as the prevalent custom, and the customs of communities in Islamic countries and the periphery of eastern Europe are presented separately. Accordingly, accounts of the practices of specific communities are provided in the 'In Our Diasporas' chapters of the volumes for Passover, Shavuot, and Sukkot. While customs, stories, and traditions throughout these volumes ostensibly reflect those of the entire Jewish people, in practice they almost always originate in the limited area of the former Pale of Settlement. Moreover, Levinsky did not represent the non-European communities according to their actual population size and thus marginalized them in another way. The large Jewish communities of North Africa, where more than half a million Jews lived in the 1940s, are accorded the same space as the small Jewish communities in Aden, Bukhara, and Ethiopia (each of which numbered only several thousand), while the large Jewish community in Iraq (which numbered about 100,000) is barely mentioned.[20] Furthermore, he often quoted proverbs and sayings in Yiddish while seldom including those in Ladino, and, as far as I have found, did not draw at all on Judaeo-Arabic or other Jewish languages.

The result is a stereotypical map of east European Jewish civilization occasionally supplemented by the exotic customs of Jewish communities—some inside eastern Europe and some outside it. This can be seen as representative of Jewish demography in the years leading up to the Holocaust and as a reflection of the ethnic structure of the Yishuv, but it seems that Levinsky did not devote any thought to this. East European dominance expressed first and foremost his own self-perception, his desire to continue the path of previous folklorists, and his desire to immortalize the Jewish world that had been destroyed in the Holocaust. Furthermore, this understanding matched the expectations of Levinsky's target audience, which was composed mostly of old and new immigrants from eastern Europe. In those years, this audience gradually internalized the consequences of the Holocaust and began to commemorate and document the communities that had been destroyed.[21] The focus of *Sefer hamo'adim* on these communities became part of these activities: in many ways it created a monument for a bygone world.

However, Levinsky's treatment of east European Jewish culture was also quite stereotypical and characterized by a clichéd image of the shtetl. Like that of many Jewish writers and intellectuals of the time, Levinsky's shtetl was usually a stereotype of Jewish existence not situated in time or space.[22] Following Dan Miron, this shtetl can be seen as no more than a literary 'myth', which 'rested upon one basic infrastructure and revolved around fixed principles'.[23] In the words of Or Rogovin, Levinsky carried out a process of 'shtetlization' that incorporated vernacular east European Jewish culture in order to make it more accessible to the Israeli reader.[24] Thus, the specific became symbolic, and the realistic became mythical.

In the passages of *Sefer hamo'adim* written by Levinsky himself, he often used the vague phrases 'the custom is . . .' or 'it is accepted that . . .': formulations that were meant to describe widespread Ashkenazi rituals, but which left their specific times and places obscure. In addition, while quoting others, Levinsky did not give the reader any background about the writer or his quoted text. Thus, for example, the average reader encountering Asher Barash's vivid description of shtetl children preparing for Shavuot had no way of knowing he was describing a specific shtetl, Łopatyn (Lopatyn) in eastern Galicia.[25] Likewise, of those reading Meir Wilensky's memories of the Hanukah games he used to play as a boy, only those who knew his background would recognize that these games were prevalent in the late nineteenth century in his shtetl of Ejszyszki (Eišiškės) in Lithuania.[26] These two shtetls, hundreds of kilometres apart and embodying two quite different Jewish cultures, have been merged for the average reader into one invented shtetl.

Even when Levinsky made reference to a specific geographical location, he usually left it general. A 1942 article dealing with the customs of the seventh day of Passover illustrates this through its reference to a series of unusual customs, among them 'a custom in Ashkenazi communities' of leading a stuffed figure of a man wrapped in rags through the city streets; 'a widespread custom in Poland' to denounce and mock the 'misers' who refuse to donate to charity; and a custom 'in Ukraine and Bessarabia' of wearing wooden 'postoli sandals'.[27] None of these was widespread. There is no record of them in the books of halakhah and custom, and it is clear that they cannot be attributed to all of the millions of Jews who lived in the Ashkenazi communities of Poland, Ukraine, or Bessarabia. In the light of their anomaly, Levinsky had to locate them somewhere, but the reader still obtains a general and nebulous picture rather than clear ethnography about a custom that was practised in a specific place in a specific period. Only in Levinsky's late folkloric studies, from the 1960s and 1970s, did things become concretized, as the shtetl received a name and the custom or story was placed in a historical context. The change can be attributed to Levinsky's transition to a more scholarly approach after completing *Sefer hamo'adim*. It is linked to the greater change that took place in Israeli society following the Eichmann trial in 1961, which affected not only the memory of the Holocaust but also the memory of Jewish life in the years preceding it. In Anita Shapira's view, the trial set in motion a transition from 'public memory' characterized by large masses and a general story (Auschwitz, extermination, six million) to 'private memory' linked to the 'private Holocaust' of the survivors and their families.[28] As part of this change, the concrete stories of Holocaust survivors began to be heard, and the general story of eastern Europe or the shtetl was broken down into specific stories about certain areas and communities. In this historical context, Levinsky also changed his method of operation. In the 1940s and 1950s he tried to implant the shtetl in Israeli culture as a general prototype so that it would be integrated into public memory. In the following years, with the transition to private memory, the symbol of the shtetl also had to undergo privatization and concretization in order to remain relevant.

Exile as the Relevant Past of the National Present

Despite the change described above, one feature characterized Levinsky's writings about diasporic Jewish folklore throughout his career, the painting of the exilic past in proto-nationalist colours and the retrospective reading of that past through a Zionist lens. Like Ben-Gurion and other Zionist leaders, Levinsky transformed the traditional expectation of redemption into one of national liberation, but he did so in a more direct way.[29] A typical example can be found in an article he wrote for Tu Bishevat in 1950, asserting:

> Two revolutionary changes have taken place in the festival's customs over the past five hundred years: the fixing of the day for eating the fruits [of the Land of Israel] by those dreaming of redemption, the kabbalists in fifteenth-century Safed; and the fixing of the day for the planting of new trees by those fulfilling and realizing the vision of redemption, the returnees to Zion in the twentieth century.[30]

With this formulation, Levinsky minimized the distance between the mystical vision of messianic redemption and the secular ideal of Zionist pioneering. Thus he erased the Zionists' revolt against exile and reinterpreted mystical longing through nationalist eyes. Another aspect of the same tendency can be found in the volume of *Sefer hamo'adim* for Tu Bishevat, which includes many texts relating to east European Jews' longing for the fruits of the Land of Israel. For example, Levinsky cites a satirical passage by Mendele Moykher Sforim describing the excitement that took hold of a shtetl with the arrival of a date from the Land of Israel.[31] In a characteristic act of interpretation, he removed the author's critical sting and turned the story into a didactic text that reveals the diasporic Jew's longing for the Land of Israel and hence the importance of the modern State of Israel. Likewise, the volume for Sukkot includes a series of stories about diasporic longing for an 'etrog from the Land of Israel'. One of the stories (by Yehoshua Margolin) describes the four species characteristic of the festival from the point of view of a boy in the diaspora, who sees them as 'emissaries' from the Land of Israel and addresses them with admiration.[32] The message of the story is decidedly Zionist, and in the end the boy declares: 'Every year when emissaries from the soil of the Land of Israel arrive at our *sukah*, my heart aches with longing, and in my heart I swear: "When I grow up, I will make *aliyah*."'[33]

As one of the critics of *Sefer hamo'adim* remarked, the presence of the diasporic longing for the land was intended to resound in sabras' ears and to infuse the grey reality of life in Israel in the early 1950s with meaning. He added: 'the present-day Israeli cannot sense what a child [in the diaspora] felt when the exotic fruits were served in the middle of the snowy winter . . . It is the force of this romantic feeling that led to the foundation of the State of Israel.'[34] Thus only by means of the exilic past could the full meaning of the establishment of the State of Israel be grasped, and festival customs became signifiers of this meaning.

This presented Jewish life outside the Land of Israel as a partial existence, but at the same time it portrayed it vividly, with no trace of criticism or contempt. Most of the passages in *Sefer hamo'adim* treat Jewish life in the shtetl empathetically and express a deep appreciation for the exilic longing for national life despite the difficult conditions. This subtle version of *shelilat hagolah* is clearly embodied in the text; however, only a critical analysis reveals how important it is for Levinsky's narrative. The texts he assembled do indeed portray the shtetl, but many of them focus on the Land of Israel.

Levinsky's understanding of the festivals was, however, very different from the common Zionist view. In accordance with the prevailing Zionist approach, he systematically transformed the religious significance of each festival into a nationalist one, but he did so indirectly, by way of anthropologization and relying on a folkloric perspective. This is especially noticeable in the volume of *Sefer hamo'adim* for Hanukah.[35] In a similar way to his treatment of other festivals, Levinsky devoted most of his attention to describing the rituals, songs, and foods that characterized the festival in eastern Europe, focusing on the experiences of the shtetl. The direct reference to the heroism of the Maccabees and their aspiration for freedom that characterized Zionist thinkers remains marginal. Levinsky, however, emphasized the preservation of this myth throughout the years of exile and thus gave it increased strength. In this way, the nationalist message is reinforced through the continuous reading of Jewish history and the focus on the diaspora.

Levinsky rarely reflected on his scholarly approach, but an analysis of his writings shows that he attached great importance to the articulation of a continuous line of Jewish history while stressing its national meaning. This was described in an article on Levinsky's work by Ben-Zion Dinur, who shared this world-view and developed an entire thesis about the Jewish festival cycle and its national significance:

The importance of *Sefer mo'adim* is that it has gathered the best of all the generations . . . There is a need to shed more light on the festivals in order to adjust them to the world of the new generation . . . We find ourselves in a situation where the foundations have been shaken, where the shape of the festivals has been blurred . . . to the extent that doubts arise as to our ability to cultivate a feeling of solidarity in the public, which is a condition for the existence of any social collective. There is therefore an urgent need to introduce the world of our festivals—with all their layers of thought and emotion, with all the experience of generations and the life's wisdom they contain—into the cultural life of this generation.[36]

Dinur wrote these words upon the completion of the eight volumes of *Sefer hamo'adim*. He believed that Levinsky's approach was essential to create cohesion in a young country composed of immigrants. In his opinion, only the presence of the diasporic past in Israel could bridge the gap between Jewish and Israeli cultures and initiate processes of socialization.

In this context, Pinchas Azai characterized Levinsky's world-view by comparing its continuous narrative with the fragmented narrative of the kibbutz festivals, which (ostensibly) skipped the diasporic chapter and focused on biblical myth.[37] An examination of *Sefer hamo'adim* does reveal that, despite extensive attention given to the observance of festivals in the Yishuv and the young State of Israel, the kibbutz festivals are afforded only a fairly marginal place. Thus, for example, despite the inclusion of many sources relating to Passover in the Yishuv, no kibbutz Passover Haggadah was included in *Sefer hamo'adim*. The only reference to such *hagadot* appears in two short passages which attempt to provide an ethnographic study of Passover in the kibbutz and appear alongside the description of Passover elsewhere in the country.[38] Moreover, these passages focus on the similarities between the kibbutz *seder* and the traditional *seder* and obscure its inherent radicalism. *Sefer hamo'adim* also marginalized kibbutz Shavuot rituals and only mentioned them alongside other traditional customs, such as all-night Torah study and the eating of dairy foods.[39] When talking about Tu Be'av, a day that had no real presence in the diaspora, Levinsky is much more forgiving of kibbutz culture.[40] Yet even here, most attention is paid to Rishon Letsion and the non-radical rituals its founders created.

Hence, it seems that Levinsky, who documented the new folklore arising in Israel and even initiated a number of new Israeli festivals, was ambivalent about kibbutz festivals and did not accept their attempts to replace the traditional rituals of Passover and Shavuot. Here he followed in the footsteps of Bialik, who, as early as 1930, rebuked the members of Kibbutz Ginegar, saying: 'festival [rituals] should not be invented' and advised them to 'celebrate the feasts of your ancestors and add a little of your own . . . but don't get too smart'.[41] As I will show below, Levinsky did not object to the creation of new festival rituals, but he believed that they should be developed in an evolutionary, not a revolutionary, way from existing diasporic festival customs. While the kibbutz festivals stressed the relevance of the distant biblical past, Levinsky emphasized the relevance of Jewish exilic life, a full and colourful culture that existed in the shadow of the longing for Zion. In this way, he gave east European Jewish civilization a proto-nationalist framing which could even be seen as the basis of a 'nation in the making' and essential for understanding the Israeli present.

Between Halakhah and Folklore

A fourth characteristic of Levinsky's work is the replacement of halakhah with folklore and the 'folklorization' of halakhah. Baruch Karu (Krupnik), who participated in the editing of *Sefer hamo'adim* and published several articles on it, focused on this point. He emphasized the subordination of halakhah to folklore proposed by Levinsky: 'The novelty . . . is that [*Sefer hamo'adim*] merges the old and the new, not only in the combination of new national festivals and memorial days but also in the composition of the materials and their selection.'[42] In his editing, Levinsky did not distinguish between halakhah, established customs, and popular folklore. Thus he turned the religious festival cycle into an expression of ethno-nationalism and focused on anthropology rather than theology. Levinsky did not explain the rationale for this approach, but Karu, like many others in Levinsky's circles, believed that the situation after the Holocaust years made it necessary:

[The focus on] ethnography and folklore these days is like an act of rescue from a flood or conflagration. The extermination [of the diasporic communities], on the one hand; and the ingathering of the exiles [in the Land of Israel], on the other, fundamentally changed [Jewish] life . . . We must remember the past. It is not up to us today to decide what was important and what was not important then.[43]

Levinsky did not limit himself to describing the prevailing halakhah and the accepted tradition. Rather, he repeatedly mentions extra-biblical and Hellenistic sources (especially Philo and Josephus), refers to customs that contradict halakhah (including Sabbatian ones), and points to foreign (mostly Christian) influences on Jewish rituals. As demonstrated in his writings, Levinsky saw halakhah as only one nonbinding expression of Jewish folklore. Like the editors of other ethnographic anthologies and unlike the authors of Orthodox books describing customs, Levinsky referred more to the way Jews in fact behaved and less to the way the law instructed them to act.[44] This approach recalls the talmudic principle of *puk ḥazei mai ama davar* ('go out and see what people do'), according to which the halakhic decisors must reflect the day-to-day conduct of the people.[45] Levinsky, however, took this idea to extremes, as Karu observes: while the tendency in descriptions of customs in Orthodox literature is to halt the flow and to fix the tradition at a certain point, Levinsky's approach is characterized by a 'positive attitude towards any tradition that has a creative element, without stopping at the *Kitsur shulḥan arukh*'.[46]

This approach is seen, for example, in the structure of the volume of *Sefer hamo'adim* for Hanukah.[47] The treatment of the halakhic layer is concentrated in a short chapter of only eleven pages (out of 208) and its discussion comes only after three long chapters treating the conceptual foundations of the festival, its historical origins, and the way it was celebrated in antiquity. This implies that, for Levinsky, halakhic literature was no more than one layer among many and not even a particularly important one at that. In many other chapters, there are references to various halakhic traditions (mainly those originating in eastern Europe), but they are presented as popular customs and not as rabbinic tradition.

More extreme examples of minimizing the place of halakhah can be found in Levinsky's articles in the press. For example, commenting on the separation of meat and milk in a discussion of Shavuot, he noted that 'there were many religious groups in Israel that did not accept this conclusion, and to this day the Karaites eat meat with milk'[48]—despite the fact that the laws of *kashrut* in this context are quite clear and have been accepted throughout the whole Jewish world. In an article on Tishah Be'av, Levinsky quoted Rabbi Hayim Joseph David Azulai (Hida), who determined that mourning and fasting should not be stopped after midday, in order to emphasize the 'custom of the people' of cleaning the house, wearing festival clothes, and even eating to prepare for the coming of the messiah.[49] The phrase 'custom of the people' is here misleading—Levinsky did not mention that these practices are rather marginal customs among the Ashkenazim, and he conflated the widespread Sephardi custom of cleaning the house and cooking with the extremist custom of eating on Tishah

Be'av, which is of Sabbatian origin. His view was determined by his ideology—he believed that after the establishment of the state and the partial realization of messianic hopes, it was appropriate to modify custom and 'celebrate the second part of Tishah Be'av with the joy of redemption'. Moreover, in his opinion, the authority to carry out such change did not belong to the rabbis but to the 'elected representatives of the nation'—the members of the Knesset.[50]

This proposal and the use of normative language are two of many examples of Levinsky's attempts to create binding Israeli folk rituals based (ostensibly) on centuries of Jewish customs. Since he saw the festivals as human creations, he did not hesitate to modify rituals so that they would conform to a nationalist perspective, or even to create new festivals. From Levinsky's perspective, the main feature of the festival cycle was that each generation created new customs suited to its way of life, and that now Israelis must act in the same way, while making sure to add to existing customs and not to annul them.

In this context, Levinsky's approach clearly differed in purpose from that of Orthodox authors who in these years wrote books about festival customs, among them the British rabbi Tzvi Hirsch Ferber and the Habad rabbi Shlomo Yosef Zevin.[51] Like Levinsky, Ferber and Zevin worked in the shadow of the Holocaust and felt that the new times had undermined the continuity of tradition. Like his, their world-view was formed in eastern Europe between the wars, and, like him, they also sought to fully describe the Jewish festivals with their various customs. However, while the practice they proposed was based on halakhah, the practice shaped by Levinsky was based on folklore.

The Ruined Diaspora and the Developing State

A fifth and particularly interesting feature of Levinsky's writing is his attitude to the Holocaust and the establishment of the State of Israel and his attempt to mark these events by emphasizing a connection between them and the Jewish past. Throughout *Sefer hamo'adim*, Levinsky included many references to the disasters that had befallen the Jewish people because of antisemitism and the Holocaust itself. The volume of *Sefer hamo'adim* for Passover includes a long chapter dealing with blood libels throughout history;[52] the volume for Shavuot includes a surprising chapter titled 'Day of Slaughter', which discusses a series of pogroms that took place during the festival;[53] the volume for Hanukah includes episodes of Jews' military heroism and partisan stories from the Holocaust;[54] the volume for Purim includes a series of local festivals (Purim Sheni) in which various communities marked their rescue from pogroms;[55] and the volume dedicated to the four fasts commemorating the destruction of the Temple (10 Tevet, 17 Tamuz, Tishah Be'av, and the Fast of Gedaliah) includes a large number of allusions to the Holocaust and features a picture of the Ghetto Heroes' Monument in Warsaw at the beginning.[56] All of these appear as part of the story of each festival, although Levinsky devoted half of the eighth volume of *Sefer hamo'adim* to riots and pogroms.

As in other contexts, here too Levinsky focused on the tragedy of the Jews of eastern Europe, and rarely mentioned antisemitic riots in other parts of the world. The discussion of decrees and disturbances in a specific chapter does not place the entire diasporic experience in a negative light, yet the reader feels the bitter fate of the Jews in exile and the constant destruction of their communities. Levinsky's logic for this structure can be found in an article he published in 1947 calling for the institutionalization of the commemoration of the Holocaust. He noted that 'Hitler and his henchmen sought to destroy the entire Jewish people and to eliminate its festivals. And most of the operations and exterminations were deliberately conducted on Saturdays and the major festivals.'[57] Thus, extermination and persecution are part of the heritage of the festival, and he therefore could not avoid the issue in *Sefer hamo'adim*.

Moreover, as reflected in the rest of this chapter, Levinsky did not conceive of the Holocaust as an event that should eliminate the joy of the festival. He proposed commemorating the Holocaust with a few days of mourning but also establishing two new festivals alongside them: the first, 'a memorial for a people whose spirit was not broken by the many troubles laid upon them'; the second, 'a day for Jewish culture in the lands of exile', in order to preserve the memory of the 'perished wise men of Israel'.[58] Levinsky was fully aware of the terrible significance of the Holocaust, in which he lost relatives and friends, but, as Schrire stresses, he also found in those events a powerful expression of the Jewish national spirit that remained 'unified, strong, and vital'.[59] In this context, the model that guided him was the diasporic model of Purim Sheni—a local day of thanksgiving celebrated by specific communities to mark rescue from a disaster, even if the disaster had not been completely averted.[60]

Concurrently, Levinsky proposed adopting a traditional model of mourning and establishing 20 Sivan, which in eastern Europe was already a fast day in memory of the Jews killed in the massacres of 1648 and 1649, as a memorial day. According to his proposal, the main mourning customs of Tishah Be'av would be followed on this day, with the dimming of synagogue lights and the reading of a newly composed scroll recounting 'the terrible massacre in the language of the Bible', thereby integrating contemporary content into a traditional framework.[61] Thus, Levinsky sought to use diasporic tools of memorialization to introduce the Holocaust, a symbol of the destruction of the diaspora, to the Israeli public. In so doing, he referenced a long historical sweep rather than a concrete event.

This tendency is clear from the poem that opens the eighth volume of *Sefer hamo'adim*, which is dedicated to Holocaust Day and Israeli Independence Day, a didactic and little-known work by Yehuda Karni, which states that 'all our fires for two thousand years were anticipated by the fire of Jerusalem'.[62] Moreover, the volume includes the 'Scroll of Calamities', in which riots and persecutions are arranged according to the calendar. It is divided into 'Calamities of Exile' and 'Calamities of Recent Generations'.[63] However, the 'Calamities of Recent Generations' mixes dates directly related to the Holocaust with those of other examples of anti-Jewish violence from the twentieth century, including the riots of the Palestinians against the Yishuv in the 1930s. As the committee that published *Sefer hamo'adim* stressed, Levinsky 'assumed that the recent Holocaust of the Jewish people is nothing but the most terrible and shocking latest link in the chain of horrors and annihilations, evil decrees, and humiliations that befell our people during the days of exile and alienation'.[64] Hence the Holocaust undergoes de-concretization, and its specific context and the extreme racist ideology that distinguishes it are minimized.

Later in the volume, Levinsky applied the same approach to the establishment of the State of Israel, which is taken out of its actual context and presented as part of the expectation of two thousand years in exile. Levinsky devoted only seventeen pages to the War of Independence, in comparison with forty-eight pages on pre-Zionist messianic ideas from the Middle Ages and the beginning of the modern era. He wove together the various sources in such a way that the establishment of the State of Israel is presented as a direct continuation of exile and not a rebellion against it.

In addition, throughout the first half of the 1950s, Levinsky attempted to shape Independence Day according to the model of diasporic Jewish festivals and not just as a 'national festival with flags and parades'.[65] He proposed celebrating the day with a series of rituals including lighting candles, a family meal, baking a special challah, eating symbolic foods, and reading from a scroll—all of which are taken from the repertoire of traditional festival celebrations.[66] His descriptions of the ideal Independence Day recall more than anything the atmosphere of a festival eve in the shtetl: 'Before dusk, people cease working, traffic stops, shops and cafes close, and the sabbath descends on the country. In every house, candles are lit in sabbath candlesticks . . . [and] people gather in synagogues and public places to hear the scroll.'[67] Thus, Independence Day, a symbol of Israeli sovereignty, is synthesized with exilic culture.

Levinsky's way of associating Holocaust Remembrance Day and Independence Day in the eighth volume of *Sefer hamo'adim* attempted to supplant the association that had been made between the memory of Israel's fallen soldiers and Independence Day. Nevertheless, it emphasized Levinsky's Zionist approach and his adherence to the accepted schema of 'destruction and redemption' or 'Holocaust and rebirth'. The volume's unambiguous message is the futility of Jewish existence in exile and the extraordinary historical significance of the establishment of a Jewish state. This point is also expressed in the other volumes of *Sefer hamo'adim*, each of which begins with sources from biblical Israel describing the basis of customs and ends with Israeli sources describing the celebration of festivals in the young country.[68] At the same time, however, Levinsky, continuing in the path of Ahad Ha'am and Bialik, proposed a different relationship between the diaspora and the state or between the shtetl and the state. He 'nationalized' exilic life by de-concretizing it and creating a mythical chronology.

Conclusion

In this chapter I have sought to shed light on the work of Yom-Tov Levinsky, who, through Jewish festivals, made exile and shtetl life present in the sovereign State of Israel. I have stressed his organic and associative presentation of the Jewish past; his preference for east European Jewish folklore; his revisionist reading of the diasporic past using a nationalist lens; how he replaced halakhah with folklore; and, finally, how he synthesized the great events of his time, the Holocaust and the establishment of the State of Israel, using a traditional ritualistic approach.

The question remains to what extent Levinsky's perspectives were publicly accepted and whom they represented. There is no simple answer to this question, but Levinsky's popularity in the 1950s and the very widespread circulation of *Sefer hamo'adim* do not allow him to be dismissed as a marginal figure. Levinsky's acts and world-view call for a rethinking of the Yishuv and the early State of Israel. I have emphasized the complex relationship between Israeli culture and diasporic Jewish culture and rejected the idea that it was characterized only by negativity and contempt. The uniqueness of Levinsky is that his writings express not a liminal subculture, such as the one raised recently in the discussion of Israeli Yiddish culture, but a deeply rooted alternative Zionist conception that sought to influence national culture.[69]

This cultural Zionist alternative originated with Ahad Ha'am and the Odessa circle, and so far it has been assumed that this was no more than 'a road not taken', mainly in the American Jewish context.[70] This chapter has sought to challenge this assumption and to describe the presence of this option in Israel as well. Further research will be needed to examine other figures associated with this approach (such as Ben-Zion Dinur, Avraham Broides, Emanuel Harussi, and Eliezer Steinman, all of whom also studied folklore and edited popular ethnologies), the connections between them, the institutions they founded, and the impact they had.

In recent years, Yaacov Yadgar has stressed the importance of traditionalism (rather than secularism and religiosity) as a core concept in Israel.[71] At the heart of this hybrid concept lies a sympathetic attitude to custom and tradition alongside reservations about the coerciveness of religious dogma. In addition, Yadgar emphasized the traditionalist instinctive support for Zionism that does not contradict a deep nostalgia for the diasporic past. He described the ethnic context of this identity and connected it to Jews from Islamic countries. However, it can also be cautiously attributed to Levinsky and his circle and suggest that, alongside traditional Sephardi identity, there also existed a traditional Ashkenazi identity. Be that as it may, Levinsky demonstrates how far the reality of 1950s Israel was from the superficial description of it as an autochthonous society that 'came from the sea', and how much the east European exilic past was a part of the national present.

Translated from the Hebrew by Sharon Levinas

Notes

The research for this chapter was conducted during a stay at Max-Weber-Kolleg, Universität Erfurt, as a guest fellow at the Research Centre, Dynamics of Jewish Ritual Practices in Pluralistic Contexts from Antiquity to the Present.

1 e.g. A. Saposnik, *Becoming Hebrew: The Creation of a Jewish National Culture in Ottoman Palestine* (Oxford, 2008); O. Shiff (ed.), *Galuyot yisre'eliyot: moledet vegalut basiah hayisre'eli* (Sde Boker, 2015); I. Bartal, *Tangled Roots: The Emergence of Israeli Culture* (Providence, RI, 2020).
2 I. Bartal, 'Yishuv and Diaspora in Changing Perspectives', in I. Gutman and A. Asaf (eds.), *Major Changes within the Jewish People in the Wake of the Holocaust* (Jerusalem, 1993), 373–81: 377.
3 Z. Tsameret, 'Ahad ha'am ve'itsuv hahinukh hahiloni beyisra'el', *Iyunim*, 16 (2006), 171–93: 189.
4 O. David, *Pislei paneiha shel umah* (Tel Aviv, 2012).
5 D. Schrire, *Isuf shivrei hagolah* (Jerusalem, 2018).
6 A. Rubin, 'Hebrew Folklore and the Problem of Exile', *Modern Judaism*, 25 (2005), 62–83.
7 I. Bartal, 'The Ingathering of Traditions: Zionism's Anthology Projects', *Prooftexts*, 17 (1997), 77–93: 78.
8 Schrire, *Isuf shivrei hagolah*, 82–4, 256.
9 Bartal, 'The Ingathering of Traditions', 79–82.
10 I. Bartal, 'Tarbut le'umit veyeda am', *Moznaim*, 37 (1973), 54–7.
11 'Yeda am: bamah lefolklor yehudi', *Herut*, 6 Feb. 1959, p. 5.
12 B. Ron, 'He'arot shel ma'azin', *Davar*, 19 May 1950, p. 30.
13 Levinsky was the editor of the last six of the eight volumes and co-edited the second. The series was published during the 1940s and 1950s: *Sefer hamo'adim*, i: *Rosh hashanah veyom hakipurim*, ed. Y. L. Baruch (Tel Aviv, 1946); ii: *Pesah*, ed. Y. L. Baruch and Y. Levinsky (Tel Aviv, 1948); iii: *Shavuot*, ed. Y. Levinsky (Tel Aviv, 1950); iv: *Sukot*, ed. Y. Levinsky (Tel Aviv, 1951); v: *Rosh hodesh, hanukah, tu bishevat*, ed. Y. Levinsky (Tel Aviv, 1954); vi: *Purim, lag ba'omer, tu be'av*, ed. Y. Levinsky (Tel Aviv, 1955); vii: *Yemei mo'ed vezikaron*, ed. Y. Levinsky (Tel Aviv, 1955); viii: *Yemei mo'ed vezikaron*, ed. Y. Levinsky (Tel Aviv, 1956). Some editions did not include vol. vii, and others included *Sefer hashabat*, ed. Y. L. Baruch (Tel Aviv, 1947).
14 For the change in Levinsky's work, see Schrire, *Isuf shivrei hagolah*, 305.
15 '"Hanokh lana'ar lefi darko', *Davar*, 18 May 1948, p. 3; '8 kerakhim mefo'arim be-27 lirot yisre'eliyot', *Haaretz*, 9 Dec. 1955, p. 11; 'Kedai likro', *Maariv*, 9 Aug. 1957, p. 17; 'Shai lahanukah', *Maariv*, 29 Dec. 1967, p. 53; 'Haluah hehadash', *Davar*, 7 Feb. 1975, p. 6.
16 *Sefer hamo'adim*, iv.
17 Y. Levinsky, 'Ma'akhalei halav beshavuot al shum mah?', *Davar*, 29 May 1952, p. 16.
18 D. Golinkin, 'Why Do Jews Eat Milk and Dairy Products on Shavuot?', *Responsa in a Moment*, 10/7 (June 2016): Schechter.edu website, visited 2 Oct. 2021.
19 Schrire, *Isuf shivrei hagolah*, 292.
20 The numbers are based on S. DellaPergola, 'Demografyah ve'amiyut yehudit', in N. Tzabar Ben-Yehoshua, G. Shimoni, and N. Chemo (eds.), *Amiyut yehudit* (Tel Aviv, 2009), 59–87: 74.

21 See J. Baumel, '"In Everlasting Memory": Individual and Communal Commemoration in Israel', *Israel Affairs*, 1/3 (1995), 146–70.
22 On the mythologization of the shtetl, see I. Bartal, 'Imagined Geography: The Shtetl, Myth, and Reality', in S. Katz (ed.), *The Shtetl: New Evaluations* (New York, 2006), 179–92; J. Shandler, *Shtetl: A Vernacular Intellectual History* (New Brunswick, NJ, 2014); J. Veidlinger, 'Everyday Life and the Shtetl: A Historiography', *Polin*, 30 (2018), 381–96.
23 D. Miron, 'The Literary Image of the Shtetl', *Jewish Social Studies*, 1/3 (1995), 1–43.
24 O. Rogovin, 'Chelm as Shtetl: Y. Y. Trunk's *Khelemer Khakhomim*', *Prooftexts*, 29 (2009), 242–72.
25 *Sefer hamo'adim*, iii. 261–3.
26 Ibid., v. 23–1.
27 Y. Levinsky, 'Minhagei yom tov aharon shel pesah', *Davar*, 7 Apr. 1942, p. 5.
28 A. Shapira, *Yehudim hadashim, yehudim yeshanim* (Tel Aviv, 1997), 86–103.
29 See A. Sherzer, 'The Jewish Past and the "Birth" of the Israeli Nation State: The Case of Ben-Gurion's Independence Day Speeches', *Middle Eastern Studies*, 57 (2021), 310–26.
30 Y. Levinsky, 'Al hag ha'ilan ufiryo', *Davar*, 2 Feb. 1950, p. 2.
31 *Sefer hamo'adim*, v. 354; see Mendele Moykher Sforim, *Masot binyamin hashelishi* (Tel Aviv, 1950); Eng. trans.: *The Travels and Adventures of Benjamin the Third*, trans. M. Spiegel (New York, 1949), ch. 1.
32 *Sefer hamo'adim*, iv. 125–37.
33 Ibid., iv. 126.
34 B. Karu, 'Mo'adim ketanim', *Haboker*, 25 June 1954, p. 6.
35 *Sefer hamo'adim*, v. 93–303. On the Zionist approach to Hanukah, see F. Guesnet, 'Chanukah and Its Function in the Invention of a Jewish-Heroic Tradition in Early Zionism, 1880–1900', in M. Berkowitz (ed.), *Nationalism, Zionism and Ethnic Mobilization of the Jews in 1900 and Beyond* (Leiden, 2004), 227–45.
36 B. D. Dinur, 'Hagei yisra'el vehasbaratam', *Haaretz*, 9 Dec. 1955, p. 11.
37 P. Azai, 'Entsiklopedyah shel shabat vehag', *Haaretz*, 9 Dec. 1955, p. 11.
38 *Sefer hamo'adim*, ii. 465–7.
39 Ibid., iii. 201–20.
40 Ibid., vi. 517–32.
41 H. N. Bialik, *Igerot*, 5 vols., ed. P. Lahover (Tel Aviv, 1939), v. 54.
42 Karu, 'Mo'adim ketanim'. On Karu's role in the editing process, see *Sefer hamo'adim*, v, p. iii.
43 B. Karu, 'Reshumot', *Haboker*, 10 Apr. 1953, p. 4; cf. G. Kressel, 'Kitvei-et', *Davar*, 28 Dec. 1962, p. 7.
44 N. Deutsch, 'From Custom Book to Folk Culture: Minhag and the Roots of Jewish Ethnography', in A. Kilcher and G. Safran (eds.), *Writing Jewish Culture: Paradoxes in Ethnography* (Bloomington, Ind., 2016), 273–90.
45 See A. Tennenbaum, 'Al hokhmat hatsibur ukeviat hahalakhah', *Mishpat ivri alon shevu'ei*, 338 (2009): Daat website, 'Mishpat ivri', visited 24 May 2021.
46 B. Karu, 'Sefer hamo'adim: sukot', *Haboker*, 14 Oct. 1951, p. 4.
47 *Sefer hamo'adim*, v. 93–301.
48 Levinsky, 'Ma'akhalei halav beshavuot al shum mah?'
49 Y. Levinsky, 'Hanivkeh bahodesh hahamishi?', *Davar*, 4 Aug. 1949, p. 2.
50 Ibid.

51 T. H. Ferber, *Sefer hamo'adim* (London, 1950); S. Y. Zevin, *Hamo'adim bahalakhah* (Jerusalem, 2000).
52 *Sefer hamo'adim*, ii. 262–308.
53 'Yom tibuaḥ', ibid., iii. 168–85.
54 Ibid., v. 288–302.
55 Ibid., vi. 297–322.
56 Ibid., vii. 12.
57 Y. Levinsky, 'Yemei zakhor lasho'ah', *Davar*, 27 July 1947, p. 2.
58 Ibid.
59 Schrire, *Isuf shivrei hagolah*, 289.
60 The phenomenon of Purim Sheni was partly discussed in E. Horowitz, *Reckless Rites: Purim and the Legacy of Jewish Violence* (Princeton, NJ, 2006), 279–315.
61 Levinsky, 'Yemei zakhor lasho'ah'.
62 *Sefer hamo'adim*, viii. 3.
63 Ibid., viii. 59–77, 78–90.
64 Ibid., viii. 4.
65 Y. Levinsky, 'Masekhet ḥagigah', *Davar*, 13 Apr. 1949, p. 9.
66 A. Sherzer, 'Itsuva shel tarbut mamlakhtit yehudit-yisra'elit: yom ha'atsmaut 1948–1958/ The Implementation of a Jewish-Israeli Civil Culture: Independence Day, 1948–1958', Ph.D. thesis (Beer Sheva, 2019), 246–9, 252–6.
67 Levinsky, 'Masekhet ḥagigah'.
68 I extend my thanks to Dr Tsafi Sebba-Elran for this insight.
69 See R. Rojansky, *Yiddish in Israel: A History* (Bloomington, Ind., 2020).
70 See N. Pianko, *Zionism and the Roads Not Taken: Rawidowicz, Kaplan, Kohn* (Bloomington, Ind., 2010).
71 Y. Yadgar, *Secularism and Religion in Jewish-Israeli Politics: Traditionists and Modernity* (London, 2011); id., 'Traditionism', *Cogent Social Sciences*, 1 (2015): Taylor and Francis Online website, visited 2 Oct. 2021.

Israel Expunged
Communist Censorship of the Polish Catholic Press, 1945–1989

BOŻENA SZAYNOK

THIS CHAPTER has two protagonists, the Catholic Church in Poland and the communists. It was their attitudes to Israel that decided the content of pieces published in the Catholic press. Catholic journalists wrote the articles, and the communist censors gave them their final form. It is essential, therefore, to recall how both bodies viewed the Jewish state.

For the Catholic Church, Palestine was the Holy Land, a place linked to the life and work of Jesus and known as the 'fifth gospel': it had always been a destination for Christian pilgrimage. It also had a political aspect. In the view of the Church, one solution to the 'Jewish question' in pre-war Poland, alongside 'assimilation by baptism' and segregation, was the emigration of Jews from Poland,[1] and Palestine was one of the destinations mentioned in this context. Although Jews' desire for a state of their own was viewed positively,[2] some Church representatives were negatively disposed towards the realization of the Zionist ideal in that part of the Middle East: 'a Catholic believer views a flood of Jews into the Holy Land and sacred places with reluctance', wrote *Przewodnik Katolicki* in 1935.[3] Attitudes of this kind were in line with the papal position,[4] as illustrated by Pius X's statement during a meeting with Theodor Herzl in 1904: 'It is not pleasant to see the Turks in possession of our holy places. We must put up with it. But to support the Jews in acquiring the holy places— *non possumus*.'[5] After the Second World War, the protection of the holy places, retaining the Church's rights to them, and peace in the region were important elements in the Holy See's policy. When it came to the UN decision concerning the division of Palestine, the Holy See became involved 'in the implementation of [UN] Resolution 181 concerning religious freedoms, which the Arab invasion of . . . Israel and the subsequent Arab–Israeli war had rendered politically, if not legally, doubtful'.[6]

In 1948 and 1949 Pope Pius XII issued three encyclicals which touched on the subject of Palestine: *Auspicia quaedam*, *In multiplicibus curis*, and *Redemptoris nostri*. They appealed, among other things, for prayers for world peace, expressed fears for the holy places, and postulated an international character for 'Jerusalem and its outskirts, where are found so many and such precious memories of the life and death of the Saviour'.[7] *Redemptoris nostri* referred directly to the 'Holy Places of Palestine'. It was promulgated in April 1949, after the first Arab–Israeli war, which is why it included words of 'emphatic approval [for] those [who] have contributed towards the re-establishment of peace'. Also mentioned were the destruction and 'profanation of sacred buildings . . . the devastation of peaceful homes of religious communities', and refugees of war 'prey to destitution, contagious disease and perils of every sort'. It appealed for assistance for refugees, for the protection of sacred sites, and for the rights of Catholics and pilgrims to be guaranteed.[8] In 1956 another encyclical, *Laetamur admodum*, requested prayers in connection with the situations in Poland, Hungary, and the Middle East.[9] During the Six Day War, the Holy See again demanded an international guarantee for the holy places and also sought to assist the victims of the conflict.[10]

In May 1948 a new development had occurred: the founding of the State of Israel. Until the beginning of the 1990s the Holy See had no formal diplomatic relations with Israel. However, sporadic meetings were held between Pope Paul VI and Israeli politicians, for example with Abba Eban in 1969, Golda Meir in 1973, and Moshe Dayan five years later. After 1967 the holy places important to Christians, such as the Church of the Holy Sepulchre, passed from Jordanian into Israeli hands and 'became more accessible to pilgrims of all confessions than in previous centuries'.[11]

A unique event during this period was the visit of Paul VI to Israel and Jordan in January 1964, but, as before, in the media of the Holy See, Israel was presented as the Holy Land ('Pilgrimage to the Holy Land, 1964').[12]

The other influence on information about Israel in the Catholic press in Poland was the communist censors. Their attitude to the Jewish state reflected Moscow's policies on the Middle East,[13] and their position therefore shifted between 1945 and 1989. After the war Stalin's anti-Jewish policies, as illustrated by the dissolution of the Jewish Anti-Fascist Committee and the execution of most of its leaders,[14] were accompanied by support for the Zionist idea of creating a Jewish state in Palestine. This support was also evident in the extensive discussions of Palestine at the UN forum in 1947, in the creation of training camps in Poland and Czechoslovakia for volunteers to the Haganah, and in the decision to recognize the State of Israel *de jure* three days after its proclamation. Moscow's position, however, changed quickly: in the divided Cold War world, Israel and the Jews found themselves on the side of the enemies of the communist bloc. In the countries of eastern Europe where Jews were living, 'the battle against Zionism' resulted in internal policies which included antisemitic purges, the termination of the activities of Zionist parties and the institutions they ran, and the repression of Jewish activists.[15]

New policies hostile to the Jewish state included the curtailment or complete suspension of emigration to Israel and the surveillance of Israeli diplomats, with some of them being declared *personae non gratae*. In the show trial of Rudolf Slánský, general secretary of the Czechoslovakian Communist Party, two citizens of Israel were among the accused. Anti-Israeli propaganda also became an element of the new Eastern bloc stance towards the Jewish state. For example, the communist press in both Polish and Yiddish stated that 'Zionism is a tool of American imperialism'[16] and that 'the Zionists are leading Israel towards catastrophe'.[17] Events reached their apogee with the USSR's decision to break off diplomatic relations with Israel in February 1953. As documents from the Ministry of Foreign Affairs in Warsaw reveal,

Poland had been ready to take a similar step earlier, but had been restrained by Moscow.[18] After Stalin's death, despite the renewal of diplomatic relations in July 1953, the State of Israel continued to be perceived as part of the hostile 'imperialist' world. It is not without significance that in Middle Eastern politics, communist Europe chose to ally itself with some Arab countries. Following another Arab–Israeli war, in June 1967, the majority of communist states (including Poland) broke off diplomatic relations with Israel, retaining only sporadic contacts, above all with the Israel Communist Party and in some cultural fields, until the end of the 1980s.

In addition to these issues, which were crucial in shaping the attitude of the Church and the United Polish Workers' Party towards Israel, articles were also published on topics which linked the history of Jews in Poland with developments in Israel and on the Holocaust, in particular the trial of Adolf Eichmann in Jerusalem in 1961.

There were moments when the positions of the Church and communists in Poland towards Israel were identical: for example, the Jewish state was recognized just after its proclamation by the government in Warsaw and the party paper *Głos Ludu* wrote about the 'just war' that the Jews were waging 'on the Palestinian front'.[19] Meanwhile, the Catholic press declared, through the title of one of its articles, 'to Israel our brother ... brotherhood'.[20]

Operation of the System of Censorship

Analysis of the interventions of communist censors in articles about Israel in the Polish Catholic press reveals not only what the Church wished to convey to its readers about Israel but also what elements of this did not appear as a result of decisions taken by the censors.

The censorship records illustrate communist policies regarding Israel, and show how these were realized in practice and how the communist authorities wished to influence what society thought about the Jewish state. Censorship in communist Poland was preventative: that is, the final form of a text was decided prior to publication. The most important body dealing with what appeared in the public sphere between 1945 and 1989 was the Central Office for the Control of Press, Publications, and Entertainment (Główny Urząd Kontroli Prasy, Publikacji i Widowisk; GUKPPiW).[21]

The press linked with the Catholic Church was diverse[22] and, despite state repression,[23] continued to appear throughout the whole communist period. That part of the Catholic milieu which co-operated with the authorities also had its own publications; however, this chapter does not cover publications not approved by the Church hierarchy or secular publications. Nor does it provide a comprehensive overview of Israeli issues covered in the Catholic press, although the articles removed or modified by the censor do, of course, illustrate, to some degree, the nature of this coverage. Furthermore, the analysis of censorship of material concerning Israel is not comprehensive, as many of the documents have not been preserved.[24] It does, however, show the issues regarding Israel to which the censors were 'sensitive' and the themes which they did not wish to be discussed in the public sphere.

The changing situation in Palestine, the establishment of the State of Israel, and the first Arab–Israeli war were all acknowledged in the Catholic press. Extensive pieces appeared,[25] and the censorship records reveal few interventions concerning these topics. What is more, the reports are clearly pro-Israeli in character. In autumn 1947 the conservative *Tygodnik Warszawski*[26] wished to publish a short article, 'The War with Zion', which described the 'repetition of a situation from two thousand years ago, when Rome stood face to face with Jewish fanaticism'. 'There are Englishmen', it claimed, 'who would prefer, following in Pilate's footsteps, to wash their hands of this affair', and concern was expressed that 'this should not end in a new destruction of Jerusalem'. The author of the piece expressed surprise that 'after such terrible bloodletting, the Jews did not embark on a path of political realism, which today even the Poles have adopted'. The censor did not permit the article to end with the sentence: 'Or perhaps they have allowed themselves to be used as a tool of foreign interests?'[27] That was deleted.

Another example of a pro-Israeli intervention is in a short article on events in Palestine, which *Tygodnik Katolicki* intended to publish in January 1949.[28] The piece mentions 'an unexpected exacerbation' of the situation in the region and Israel's protest at the UN regarding the actions of the British. The censor struck out the sentence: 'Israeli fighter pilots brought down five British planes making reconnaissance flights to check if the Israeli armies had crossed the Egyptian border', justifying his decision by claiming the description was inconsistent with 'the version from the official agency. The editorial board's presentation of the facts justifies the actions of the imperialists.'[29] In the new version, the piece reported only Israel's protest regarding the landing of British troops in Aqaba. The nature of the intervention reveals that the censor took the Israeli side, and did not allow the reader to learn (even in so short a text) that Israel undertook anything more than diplomatic action in the conflict.

These were not the only examples of pro-Israeli interventions on the part of the censor. In autumn 1949 a note concerning the publication of *Redemptoris nostri* was excised from *Wiadomości Duszpasterskie*.[30] The comment justifying the excision lists a lack of acquaintance with the 'contents of the encyclical' and comments that 'the note implied that the State of Israel threatened the freedom of the Church in Palestine'.[31] In this intervention too, the State of Israel was defended. These examples of a pro-Israeli position on the part of communist censors are noteworthy, since the situation was to change very quickly.

Certain deletions did not directly concern the State of Israel itself. For example, in March 1949, two paragraphs were removed from an account of the Stations of the Cross in Jerusalem which the periodical *Msza Święta*[32] had intended to publish. The author of the piece, describing parts of the service, had written: 'Just as before, the locals are like the perpetrators of the Lord's Passion. The latter are sleeping in the valley of Jehoshaphat, crushed under boulders, but their hatred remains.'

The fragment was removed, like another concerning the Arab women he met: 'with hatred in their faces. If Christ were to pass by here today, they would not weep. "Crucify him", they would cry, as they did once before.' The censor explained that intervention was prompted by opposition to 'the promotion of religious fanaticism' which 'conflicts with the freedom of religion and conscience as enshrined in the constitution'.[33]

Different again in character was the deletion in its entirety of an article which *Rycerz Niepokalanej*[34] had intended to publish in May 1949. It included the statement that the Israeli authorities wished to 'review the trial of Christ' and 'lift the death sentence imposed on the Saviour'.[35] According to the article, this directive had come from the Israeli minister for justice and also mentioned that the Israeli press had stated that 'it was not the Jews, but a minority with the Sanhedrin and Roman colonial law that had brought about Jesus' death by crucifixion'.[36]

The activities of the Church in Israel were also liable to censorship. In October 1949 *Rycerz Niepokalanej* planned to publish a one-page article, 'The Heroic Guard of the Holy Land', on the work of the Franciscans. Apart from a short introduction on the history of the Franciscan order in Palestine, the piece described in detail the realities of the first Arab–Israeli war. Since the censor rejected the entire text, the reader had no opportunity to learn that during the fighting the friars had remained in place, despite 'the wish to remove them'. However, nowhere in the article did the author mention who wished to remove them, the nationality of the army besieging Galilean Cana, or with whom the local priest attempted to 'mediate' to 'protect the surroundings and their inhabitants from certain catastrophe'. Nor is it stated whose military was being referred to in a description of the situation in Nazareth: 'the Franciscans courageously defended the orphans, convents, nuns . . . against military abuses'. The text states that, despite the war, work continued and mentions 'certain places from which all the faithful had fled'. The article also includes information about the dangers of bombardment. Friars are mentioned who 'at the price of hardship and sacrifice saved the unfortunate, regardless of their religion or nationality, above and beyond all the frictions that divide the Palestinian nations'.[37] Help supplying food and rescuing the wounded was mentioned, as was that 'in Jerusalem, Bethlehem, Nazareth . . . all the buildings of the order took in displaced families, providing them with sustenance'. The piece gave detailed information concerning the state of the populace ('Jerusalem . . . has no water or light') and of the order ('the material losses . . . are significant'). As mentioned above, the decision was taken to delete the entire article. This could have been due to censorship policies regarding information on the charitable and missionary activities of the Church, topics which were systematically removed by the censor.[38]

After 1949 the attitude of the communist states towards Israel began to change: their goodwill turned to hostility. An example of this new attitude from the censorship documents is the history of texts on a topic as ostensibly neutral as archaeological digs. In August 1949 it was not a problem for the first page of *Tygodnik Powszechny*[39] to include a substantial piece on the discoveries in Qumran;[40] two decades later, in May 1968, the journal *Ruch Biblijny i Liturgiczny* [41] wanted to include a review of an exhibition on the archaeological discoveries near the Dead Sea.[42] The piece was completely removed, and the Kraków censor's office, to which the periodical 'answered', consulted with the central office in Warsaw. A letter to Warsaw mentioning the 'short review' of the London exhibition, notes that it contained information about the 'great contribution' of Israeli archaeology and a photograph of the director of one of the academic institutions.[43] Three days later, the reply came that the piece was to be 'removed in its entirety'.[44]

One topic which interested the censors was Arab–Israeli conflict. The Six Day War meant that this issue was monitored closely in June 1967. The involvement of the communist states on the Arab side had resulted in most of them breaking off diplomatic relations with Israel. The first issue of *Tygodnik Powszechny* after the outbreak of the war contained a significant number of censor's interventions. Citing the central office recommendation of 6 June 1967, 'deletions and revisions were made' to eliminate 'seemingly objective, but in fact pro-Israeli overtones in the case in question'.[45] A few examples will illustrate this principle in practice. The reader of *Tygodnik Powszechny* would not discover that war had broken out in the Middle East, because the introductory sentence describing the conflict was removed. The censor's pen replaced 'military action' with 'an attack by Israel', and the statement 'both sides give conflicting information regarding the course of events' was deleted. There were also interventions in the descriptions of the internal situation in Israel (for example, the creation of a coalition government), assessments of the effectiveness of the Security Council ('the helplessness of this body appears obvious'), and the activities of the Soviet Black Sea fleet.[46] In subsequent articles, the adjective 'violent' disappeared from 'the violent defeat of the Egyptian air force and army', and the decisions of the censor reinforced the notion of who was responsible for the conflict: the expression 'battle on the Israeli–Syrian front' was changed to 'Israeli attacks'. Regarding President Nasser of Egypt, the censor deleted such sentences as: 'His personal standing, however, was shaken.'[47]

Despite the ending of the war, Middle Eastern topics remained subject to censorship. In February 1968, for example, the editors of *Tygodnik Powszechny* mentioned the activities of a Swedish diplomat. The censor permitted the statement that 'he circulates unsuccessfully between Middle Eastern capital cities' but removed 'attempting to bring about talks between Israel and the Arab states'.[48] The paper was also accused of 'misleading readers' by stating that 'Israel was striving for peace talks' without mentioning that it was doing so 'from a position of strength'.[49] Also deleted was the information that the Israelis had permitted the International Red Cross to search for missing Egyptian soldiers.[50] By the end of June 1967 the editors were constantly being accused of 'inappropriate comments on political events'. The censor took care that the reader should learn that the president of the USA and the prime minister of the USSR had not held a 'meeting' but only 'talks'.[51] A month later, the censor deleted a phrase about 'peace' in the Middle East as being 'objectively untrue'.[52]

In addition to the facts reported and the information transmitted, the censors also paid attention to vocabulary. One example was replacing the term 'Israeli passengers', in a piece about a plane detained by Algeria, with the word 'Israelis'. In another sentence, which in its first version read: 'Arabic communiqués report the seizure [of Syrian planes] by the Israelis', the censor replaced 'Arabic communiqués report' with 'agencies are reporting' and 'the Israelis' with 'Israel'.[53] As an intervention of June 1968 demonstrates, in articles on the Middle East, the censor consistently replaced the word 'conflicts' with 'Israeli aggression'.[54] During the Yom Kippur War in October 1973 the censor deleted the adjective describing the conflict as 'murderous' as well as information on missiles supporting Egypt which were 'paralysing' the Israeli airforce.[55]

It was not only the wars but also the Middle East peace process, which began in the 1970s, that interested the censor. In 1979, for example, readers of *Tygodnik Powszechny* were allowed to learn from an article on President Jimmy Carter's visit to the Middle East that 'we may be close to signing an Egyptian–Israeli agreement'.[56] Two weeks later, however, the contents of the Israeli–Egyptian agreement were removed from the weekly review section, along with an account of the document-signing ceremony.[57]

The pro-Arab attitude of the communist states meant certain information concerning the Arab states and their populations would disappear from articles about Israel. For example, entire paragraphs concerning military operations planned by Egypt were deleted from Władysław Bartoszewski's report 'On the Red Sea and the Dead Sea' in May 1948,[58] as well as the statement that, in Beer Sheva, 'groups of Bedouins with camels were constantly conducting their business on the squares in front of hotels'.[59] In May 1968 the following sentence was deleted from a piece in *Tygodnik Powszechny*: 'The twentieth anniversary of the founding of the state of Israel was marked in Arabic countries as the "painful anniversary of the loss of Palestine"', in which the censor claimed to perceive 'anti-Arabic overtones'. The accompanying incidental explanation remarked that they did not wish to recall this anniversary 'since Poland had been one of the first countries to recognize Israel twenty years ago'.[60]

Censors' interventions in Middle Eastern matters were not limited to Arab–Israeli questions. In 1967 the July issue of *Tygodnik Powszechny* planned to include some reports on the reaction of the Holy See to the Six Day War in its 'Kronika religijna' column. The first of these covered the trip, made at the pope's bidding, of the president of Caritas Internationalis to Israel. At a press conference on his return, he reported on the help given by the Holy See and Caritas Internationalis to all 'who had suffered on account of the war in the Middle East, regardless of their nationality, race, or creed'. Details on the situation of the civilian population, presented at the conference, concluded with the information that 'in recent days, seven aeroplanes have left Europe with the first aid organized by . . . Caritas and the Vatican Relief agency'. 'Kronika religijna' also included an account of the activities undertaken by another organization: the Pontifical Mission to Palestine, which had focused on providing aid to Palestinian refugees from 1948. It increased its aid from 1967 in response to the war. The piece reported that Paul VI had assigned $50,000 to the cause, and that an aeroplane with medicine and food was being dispatched to Amman 'on the pope's instructions'. The final entry on the Middle East in 'Kronika religijna' concerned the holy places, including assurances from the Israeli army spokesman that they would be defended by special units, and that old Jerusalem would be open to 'all believers'. None of these items was published. All were withheld by the decision of the GUKPPiW.[61] The editors attempted to place the deleted items in the following issue, this time in the 'Ze świata' column, but once again, they were removed in their entirety by the censor.[62]

As the above examples show, the subjects of Israel and the Church overlapped at times, provoking unequivocal reactions from the censor. The same was true for reports on the Holy See's efforts to ensure the internationalization of Jerusalem. The reader of *Tygodnik Powszechny* would not learn that 'the Church appeals for an international administrative body which, based on the principles of the UN and the Declaration of Human Rights, would guarantee full freedom for Catholics, Orthodox, Jews, and Muslims'. The deleted note had also included a sentence on the Church's desire that 'the holy city should become a meeting place accessible to all believers of the three great monotheistic religions'.[63]

The censor took action regarding some topics related to the Holocaust. In autumn 1964 two texts were removed in their entirety from *Gość Niedzielny*.[64] The first concerned the Israeli premiere of Rolf Hochhuth's play *Der Stellvertreter* at the Habima Theatre in Tel Aviv, which the Israeli president, prime minister, and minister for foreign affairs did not attend, despite receiving complimentary tickets. The justification for withholding this report and the other one concerning the Holocaust was their 'tendentious' character and 'whitewashing of Pius XII', which was deemed 'undesirable'.[65]

The case of the Nazi war criminal Adolf Eichmann was undoubtedly one of the major political events of the 1960s. After the war Eichmann had fled to Argentina, where he was captured in May 1960 by Israeli agents and brought to Israel. A year later, his trial in Jerusalem was watched by the whole world. The censor's records are full of often quite surprising material concerning the case. For example, in autumn 1960 the information that an Argentine film studio had proposed that Andrzej Munk, a Polish director, make a film about Eichmann in which the commander of the Israeli forces was to have been played by the popular Polish actor Zbigniew Cybulski was completely deleted.[66] Of course, there were also more serious interventions in texts concerning Eichmann. In February 1961 the entire first and second pages of *Tygodnik Powszechny* were taken up by Bartoszewski's 'Eichmann'. The censor removed the part mentioning Israel, citing 'Provision no. 25', the details of which are unknown. The contents of one of the subsections deleted are indicated by its subtitle: 'Identified and Captured'. The reader had no opportunity to read about the action of the Israeli commandos, described in detail in two columns, or a fragment of the next subsection 'On Jewish Soil', outlining what happened to Eichmann after he was brought to Israel.[67] In the version submitted to the censor the author was given as Teofil Cichocki, although the actual author, as acknowledged in the publication itself, was Władysław Bartoszewski. This shows how the editorial board played the censors, well aware that Bartoszewski was not a favourite with the staff of the GUKPPiW.

In April 1961 the report which *Tygodnik Powszechny* wished to publish from the Eichmann trial was at first withheld. The Kraków censors explained to the central office that, in their opinion, the article could be 'run' in the subsequent number, but they awaited the response of their superiors, again with reference to 'Provision no. 25'.[68] The piece was published in mid-April 1961, and its author signed himself 'Bart', presumably Bartoszewski.[69] A few statements by the Israeli minister for justice were removed from the article.[70]

In April 1961 the first page of *Tygodnik Powszechny* carried an article by Stanisław Stomma, 'A New J'Accuse'. This piece drew attention not only because of its title, which alluded to Zola's famous letter, but also because of the identity of its author, a Catholic member of parliament. The article did not only refer to Eichmann's trial; a significant section was dedicated to the history of Jews as Polish citizens and the future of the Jewish nation in Israel. Here, in agreement with the central office, the censor's pencil crossed out a sizeable section concerning the Jewish state. The reader in the Polish People's Republic was not to learn that 'the State of Israel is surrounded by enemies on almost every side' or that 'the restitution of statehood is taking place in unusually difficult circumstances on only a small scrap of territory'. Stomma wrote, and the censor struck out, a striking comparison of Israel to a 'pine, clinging with difficulty to a cliff, but into which it sinks its roots' and the surprise expressed 'at the heroic effort of the nation and its fidelity to itself, fidelity to its own past'.[71]

Kibbutzim were a particularly sensitive topic for the communist censor. In Bartoszewski's reports from Israel,[72] which attracted attention both because of their content and their author, the censor's greatest interventions were precisely around this theme. Almost four columns were removed from one piece, as a result of which the editorial board decided to withdraw it.[73] It eventually appeared in a significantly redacted form.[74] The Polish reader was deprived of information on the history of kibbutzim and Jewish settlement in Palestine and on the interesting mosaic of Israeli parties and ethnicities. The censors' deletions removed information about everyday life and problems in the kibbutzim, about both famous and ordinary citizens of Israel, and also about the Polish journalist Ksawery Pruszyński.[75] In another piece, by Father Paul Gauthier, the adjective 'socialist' was removed from the account of kibbutzim, on the grounds that 'their activities are supported by American Jewish capital'.[76]

The archival material unequivocally shows that much information regarding the development of Israel was forbidden. The reader had no right to learn, for example, that there was an 'excellent' highway running from Beer Sheva to Eilat; that factories were 'large', hotels 'luxurious, European through and through'; or that an airline 'served all routes within the country'. Another sentence removed by the censor mentioned the 'enormous input of labour on the part of young Jews'.[77]

The censors' decisions were based on a communist perception of international politics, which is why, in one piece, a whole paragraph was deleted concerning the competition for a project for the new city of Tel Aviv, which was won by architects from West Germany. According to the author, the rules of the competition had not laid down any national restrictions, and therefore, despite protests, 'both architects, whose pasts were held to be above reproach, would apparently be carrying out the project'.[78]

Alongside the examples above, commonplace information would also often attract intervention. In 1961, for example, two notes concerning Israel were deleted from *Msza Święta*: the first mentioned the growth of tourism, and the second a drop in the number of road accidents. The justification was that they had 'nothing to do with religious matters, and constitute[d] a kind of promotion of the Israeli authorities'.[79] In another article, the censor's attention was caught by the proximity of information on an Israeli military parade and the Labour Day parades. The editorial board was advised to inform the readership of why the Israeli army was parading and to separate the two articles.[80] The description of the celebration of the Jewish New Year was also censored. There is no indication of why a Polish reader could not learn that 'the verandas of single-storey houses and the streets . . . swarmed with people . . . The residents . . . wished each other a happy new year.'[81]

Israel was also mentioned in the Catholic press in connection with the history of the Jews in Poland. In 1960, for example, the press wished to report on the presentation of gifts by the Israeli Ministry of Religious Affairs to the Jewish Museum in Kraków. It is unclear how to interpret the censor's explanation that the piece on this subject was removed 'for infringing a provision concerning the matter'.[82] There are no such doubts in the case of a text on a Zionist congress in Jerusalem which *Tygodnik Powszechny* wished to include. One of the questions discussed during the congress was 'attracting Jews from the diaspora to Israel'. This article was removed in its entirety; the censor's decision was justified by a lack of interest in 'promoting either the links between Zionists or the State of Israel'.[83] Links with Poland also appeared in a piece that *Tygodnik Powszechny* wanted to publish in 1961. The censor struck out mention of 'Israeli Parliament members of Polish descent', citing 'the political situation'.[84] From Bartoszewski's report on his visit to Israel a section was removed concerning a Pole living in the United States whose family, which was also given a few sentences, had helped Jews during the war. Reference to an account in the Israeli press of a Jewish woman whom the family had helped was also removed.[85]

The censor was particularly interested in religious questions and Israel. In the autumn of 1961 a short report was deleted on a motion submitted to the Knesset by the Aguda representative concerning the 'prohibition of all Christian propaganda', since, in his opinion, 'this compromises national identity and weakens the Jewish state'. The motion was sent back to the commission and the government representative opposed public discussion of the subject. The censor did not allow the Polish reader to learn that the Israeli authorities 'did not hinder the Christian mission' or that Christians 'enjoyed full freedom and were treated benevolently'. The final section of the text concerned Jewish converts who 'are treated by the whole of society as national traitors. They are not persecuted, but . . . isolated politically and socially.' Addressing all the interventions in 'Kronika religijna'—the note on Israel was one of nine rejected—the censor stated that they concerned the social and political activities of the Church.[86] In the autumn of 1967 the report 'New Tasks for the World Council of Churches' discussed a meeting of the Faith Commissions held by the World Council of Churches. New questions arising in the course of the proceedings were mentioned which were to be the subject of 'in-depth studies', including the role of the Church Fathers, the first ecumenical councils, and the exposition of the Bible 'today'. The final question listed was: 'What are the current relations between the Israeli people and the Church?' The censor ordered the sentence to be reformulated, since it placed 'equal emphasis on the people of Israel, the Jewish religion, and the State of Israel'.[87]

The censor deemed other religious topics 'dangerous' to a reader in the Polish People's Republic. For example, in an extensive article from 1960, 'Catholics in Israel' by the Carmelite convert Father Daniel Rufeisen, a sentence disappeared stating that many people arriving from Poland who had converted to Catholicism in Israel 'might not . . . have done so in Poland'.[88] A year later, in October 1961, the editorial board of *Tygodnik Powszechny* wished to include a piece on a Bible competition taking place in Israel. Representatives from the host country and Brazil reached the final. An additional question to determine the winner concerned verses mentioning the return of Israel to Zion and the diaspora. It was therefore no surprise that the winner should turn out to be the host country's representative. The member of the jury representing the Catholic side was a Pole, Father Professor Ludwik Semkowski, a Jesuit and rector of the Pontifical Biblical Institute in Jerusalem. None of the details so far aroused the interest of the censor. A sentence was struck out, however, concerning the honorary guests present at the event: the prime minster and president of Israel and representatives of the diplomatic corps. The intervention was explained thus: 'We are not interested in promoting Prime Minister Ben-Gurion, all the more so since the event had no political dimension.'[89]

In November 1967 the reader of *Tygodnik Powszechny* would have no opportunity to learn that Christians from Arab countries were able to celebrate Christmas in Bethlehem, Nazareth, and Jerusalem. This was made possible by a one-week permit issued by the Israeli authorities.[90] The censors consistently removed this kind of information. A month later another note on the subject, which also contained information about the opening of a bridge in Jordan and a mention of followers of Islam whom the Israeli authorities had permitted to travel to Jerusalem for the end of Ramadan, was removed.[91]

Directly before Christmas, the editors again attempted to include a piece on how the holiday would be celebrated in Bethlehem. They wrote about the expected number of pilgrims, about 20,000, and how the Israeli authorities had provided 'every possible facility'. It was noted that Jews and Muslims were not permitted to enter Bethlehem during that period. It was also reported that a solemn mass would be filmed in the Basilica of the Nativity and that a recording of the service would be 'flown to Rome from where it would be broadcast to the whole world via satellite'. The article also mentioned that 'the Israeli postal service would issue a special postage stamp at midnight' to mark the occasion. The whole article was deleted.[92] The question of Christians in Israel was not the only subject under the watchful eye of the censor: in February 1968 information was removed about the World Congress of Rabbis in Jerusalem.[93]

Israel was only one of the Jewish themes of interest to the communist censors. All kinds of information was deleted from the Catholic press, including the history of the Jews in Poland, the Holocaust, antisemitism, outstanding figures, the anti-Zionist campaign of 1968, and relations between Poles, the Church, and Jews.[94] Each of these interventions had its own justification based on the state of foreign or internal Polish politics, but at the same time, they constituted a distinct catalogue of Jewish issues.

The censor's interventions in texts concerning Israel varied in scope, from individual words and sentences, to whole paragraphs or columns, to entire articles. The GUKPPiW could influence the editors of Catholic papers: for example, removing 'neutral' information about tourism in Israel sent a clear message that the Jewish state was not a desirable subject for the public sphere.

Israeli topics were covered to varying degrees by the Catholic press, appearing most often in *Tygodnik Powszechny*. This was an important opinion-forming newspaper in Poland and experienced most difficulties with the censor. Catholic journalists writing on Israel not only described a young Middle Eastern state but also touched on relations between the Jewish state and religious issues or on the history of Jews in Poland. The censors' interventions 'amputated' consciousness of these connections. It was a similar matter in the case of international relations, such as the position of the Holy See with regard to the Middle East. Censorship policy in postwar Poland deprived the reader not only of important information but also—as illustrated by the number of participants at Bartoszewski's lectures on Israel, for example—of information which interested them.[95] On the subject of Israel, hostile references to Jews on the part of Catholic journalists were only infrequently removed by the censor. An analysis of Jewish questions as a whole in the Catholic press reveals more interventions of this kind.[96]

Israel was a marginal subject in the Catholic press, and the pro-Israeli narrative of *Tygodnik Powszechny* was overwhelmed by the Communist Party's anti-Israel message, but it is worth asking which of these narratives most influenced the citizens of Poland. According to a report by the Centre for the Study of Public Opinion of September 1967—that is, after the Six Day War—in response to a question about the marriage of a relative to a foreigner, almost 52 per cent expressed 'absolute opposition' in the case of an Israeli. Citizens of Israel[97] took fifth place, after Chinese, African, West German, and Japanese citizens.[98]

Another study by the centre in January 1974—that is, following a subsequent conflict in the Middle East—showed that a significant percentage of respondents (42 per cent) who had declared that they acquired their knowledge on the region from television or the press (around 60 per cent), considered the Arab countries to be in the right. Only 3 per cent were behind Israel, 15 per cent considered both sides responsible for the conflict, and 40 per cent had no opinion.[99] This polling shows clearly that the attitude of a sizeable group of citizens of the Polish People's Republic towards Israel was in line with what was 'proposed' by the communist censorship.

Analysis of the censorship material from post-war Poland which has survived, despite the destruction of documents, illuminates important topics such as the history of Poles and Jews and the relationship between the communist bloc and the State of Israel. It is important also to stress that every text produced in the Polish People's Republic was subject to censorship (whether by the GUKPPiW or by the author), which inhibited the free exchange of opinion and free discussion. The incompleteness of the information available to the public inevitably impoverished discussion of important topics, among them the attitude of the Church to the State of Israel, the subject of this chapter.

Translated from the Polish by Anna Zaranko

Notes

Research on the position of the Catholic Church on Jewish subject matter after the Second World War (1945–89) was carried out as part of a project financed by the Narodowe Centrum Nauki in Kraków (grant no. DEC-2013/09/B/HS3/00619).

1 D. Pałka, *Kościół katolicki wobec Żydów w Polsce międzywojennej* (Kraków, 2006), 301–29.

2 Z. Trębacz, *Nie tylko Palestyna: Polskie plany emigracyjne wobec Żydów 1935–1939* (Warsaw, 2018), 312–15.

3 See ibid. 315.

4 R. Modras, *Kościół katolicki i antysemityzm w Polsce w latach 1933–1939*, trans. W. Turopolski (Kraków, 2004), 285–6; Eng. edn.: *The Catholic Church and Antisemitism: Poland, 1933–1939* (Amsterdam, 1994).

5 See J. Liszka, 'Ziemia Święta wczoraj i dziś', *Ruch Biblijny i Liturgiczny*, 5/4 (1952), 353–9: 357.

6 G. Weigel, *Świadek nadziei: Biografia papieża Jana Pawła II*, trans. M. Tarnowska, J. Piątkowska, D. Chylińska, J. Illg, and R. Śmietana (Kraków, 2000), 886–7; Eng. edn.: *Witness to Hope: The Biography of Pope John Paul II* (New York, 1999).

7 Pius XII, *In multiplicibus curis* (24 Oct. 1948): Vatican website, visited 25 May 2021.

8 Pius XII, 'Encyklika "Redemptoris nostri": O miejscach świętych w Palestynie', *Ruch Biblijny i Liturgiczny*, 3 (1949), 155–7.

9 Pius XII, *Laetamur admodum* (1 Nov. 1956): Vatican website, visited 25 Oct. 2021.

10 Archiwum Narodowe, Kraków (hereafter ANK), 29/722, 'Wojewódzki Urząd Kontroli Prasy Publikacji i Widowisk' (hereafter WUKPPiW), 9: 'Tygodnik Powszechny: Protokoły ingerencyjne', 19 Apr. – 7 July 1967, fos. 491, 493 (30 June 1967).

11 Weigel, *Świadek nadziei*, 888.

12 'Paolo VI: Viaggi' (n.d.): Vatican website, visited 25 May 2021.

13 B. Szaynok, *Poland–Israel, 1944–1968: In the Shadow of the Past and of the Soviet Union*, trans. D. Ferens (Warsaw, 2012).

14 See e.g. *War, Holocaust and Stalinism: A Documented Study of the Jewish Anti-Fascist Committee in the USSR*, ed. S. Redlich (Luxembourg, 1995); *Stalin's Secret Pogrom: The Postwar Inquisition of the Jewish Anti-Fascist Committee*, ed. J. Rubenstein and V. P. Naumov, trans. L. E. Wolfson (New Haven, Conn., 2001); A. Lustiger, *Stalin and the Jews. The Red Book: The Tragedy of the Jewish Anti-Fascist Committee and the Soviet Jews*, trans. M. B. Friedrich and T. Bludeau (New York, 2003).

15 See e.g. B. Szaynok, 'The Anti-Jewish Policy of the USSR in the Last Decade of Stalin's Rule and Its Impact on the East European Countries with Special Reference to Poland', *Russian History*, 29 (2002), 301–17.

16 M. Mirski, 'Syjonizm – narzędzie amerykańskiego imperializmu', *Nowe Drogi*, 1953, no. 1, pp. 82–91.

17 I. Lechter, 'Di tsyonistn firn di yisroel melukhe tsu a katastrofe', *Folkshtime*, 1 Sept. 1950, p. 1.

18 Szaynok, *Poland–Israel*, 234.

19 Ibid. 124.

20 J. Zawieyski, 'Izraelowi, bratu naszemu…: Braterstwo', *Tygodnik Powszechny*, 20 June 1948, p. 3.

21 Z. Romek, 'System cenzury w PRL', in T. Strzyżewski (ed.), *Wielka księga cenzury w PRL w dokumentach* (Warsaw, 2015), 9–27: 12.

22 The press was diverse both in character (local, monastic, diocesan, theological, academic) and frequency (weeklies, monthlies).

23 The communist authorities influenced the content of publications through censorship, paper allocation, and permitted print-runs. Catholic journalists were subject to repression, including arrest and imprisonment. Between 1945 and 1956 some publications were liquidated or had their editorial boards replaced.

24 For a few examples, see *Główny Urząd Kontroli Prasy 1945–1949*, ed. D. Nałęcz (Warsaw, 1994), 18. Daria Nałęcz writes that, apart from one briefing, the records concerning the period to 1948 disappeared after 1989 (*Główny Urząd Kontroli Prasy*, 18). With the exception of individual documents, there is no censorship material in the Wrocław State Archive. The records of the GUKPPiW in the National Archive, Kraków only contain the censors' interventions in *Tygodnik Powszechny* for the 1960s.

25 For example, in *Tygodnik Warszawski* and *Tygodnik Powszechny*, both hostile to the communist authorities, but also the weekly *Dziś i Jutro* which accepted the new political order in Poland.

26 *Tygodnik Warszawski* (1945–48) was 'a Catholic paper dedicated to questions of national life' created by Christian Democrat and nationalist activists. 'Its founding premises, in the spirit of the Church's social teaching . . . were polemical and oppositional with regard to the authorities.' The paper was liquidated by the communist authorities in 1948 and its journalists arrested, including editor-in-chief, Fr Z. Kaczyński, who died in prison in May 1953 (see E. Kristanova, *Książka na łamach katolickich czasopism społeczno-kulturalnych w Polsce w latach 1945–1953* (Łódź, 2012), 197–8).

27 Archiwum Akt Nowych, Warsaw (hereafter AAN), 2/1102, 'Główny Urząd Kontroli Prasy Publikacji i Widowisk' (hereafter GUKPPiW), 1415, 'Ingerencje cenzorskie GUKPPiW w czasopiśmie "Tygodnik Warszawski" w okresie 5 I – 25 XII 1947 r. Sprawozdania z kontroli prewencyjnej', fo. 34: L.K., 'Walka z Syjonem' (n.d.).

28 *Tygodnik Katolicki* was a 'religious paper for the recovered territories', published from May 1946 until October 1953. The paper's editorial policy was 'public betterment for the good of Poland — the more Catholic we are, the more Polish we are', and it maintained that 'institutional transformation . . . should be preceded by the internal transformation of the individual' (Kristanova, *Książka na łamach katolickich czasopism*, 223–4).

29 APP, WUKPPiW 214, 'Ingerencje dotyczące "Tygodnika Katolickiego"', 1949, fo. 11: 'Sytuacja w Palestynie' (31 Jan. 1949).

30 *Wiadomości Duszpasterskie* was published from 1945 by the diocesan curia of Poznań for its clergy and included, for example, drafts of sermons.

31 APP, WUKPPiW, 226, 'Ingerencje dotyczące prasy wyznaniowej 1945–1961', fo. 46: 'Papież Pius XII wydał…', *Wiadomości Duszpasterskie* (31 Oct. 1949).

32 *Msza Święta* was a biblical and liturgical monthly published by the Society of Christ for Polish Migrants. It published one issue in March 1936 and then had a hiatus of ten years, resuming publication in March 1946. Between 1953 and 1957 the authorities prevented its publication.

33 APP, WUKPPiW, 206, 'Cenzura prewencyjna dotycząca miesięcznika "Msza Św."', 1946–50, fo. 17: X.P., 'Droga krzyżowa w Jerozolimie' (28 Feb. 1949).

34 *Rycerz Niepokalanej* was a Catholic monthly founded by the Franciscan friar Maksymilian Kolbe, which appeared from 1922. Publication was resumed after the war. The authorities banned it from 1952 to 1981.

35 In 1948 the Supreme Court of Israel received requests to review the trial of Jesus. The court found that the Italian court, as the legal successor of the Roman authorities, was competent to hear the case. See P. Święcicka, *Proces Jezusa w świetle prawa rzymskiego: Studium prawno-historyczne* (Warsaw, 2012).

36 AAN, GUKPPiW, 1479, 'Ingerencje cenzorskie GUKPPiW w czasopismach w 1949 r. Sprawozdania z kontroli prewencyjnej', fo. 87: *Rycerz Niepokalanej* (May 1949; no author or title).

37 'Ingerencje cenzorskie GUKPPiW w czasopismach w 1949 r. Sprawozdania z kontroli prewencyjnej', fo. 123: Fr J. Zanelia, 'Bohaterska Straż Ziemi Świętej', *Rycerz Niepokalanej* (Oct. 1949).

38 B. Szaynok, '"To nie jest firma do tego, żeby puszczać, tylko do tego, żeby zatrzymywać": Cenzura po II wojnie światowej wobec tematyki żydowskiej na łamach czasopism katolickich', in J. Olaszek, A. Dudek, Ł. Kamiński, K. Kosiński, M. Przeperski, K. Rokicki, P. Sasanka, R. Spałek, and S. Stępień (eds.), *Yesterday. Studia z historii najnowszej: Księga dedykowana prof. Jerzemu Eislerowi w 65. rocznicę urodzin* (Warsaw, 2017), 900–16: 902–3.

39 *Tygodnik Powszechny* was a Catholic social and cultural weekly published in Kraków from March 1945. From 1953 to 1956 the authorities imposed their own editorial board. According to its editorial policy 'the paper is open to all Catholic journalists regardless of their political beliefs, as long as their views are in accordance with Catholic orthodoxy' (Kristanova, *Książka na łamach katolickich czasopism*, 129).

40 O. J. Tournay, 'Największe odkrycie biblijne współczesnej doby', *Tygodnik Powszechny*, 21 Aug. 1949, p. 1.

41 *Ruch Biblijny i Liturgiczny* was published every two months then quarterly from 1948. It was dedicated to biblical and liturgical issues.

42 ANK, WUKPPiW 23: 'Czasopisma katolickie: Protokoły ingerencyjne', 1967–8, fos. 213–15: Z. Kapera, 'Wystawa odkryć archeologicznych znad Morza Martwego', *Ruch Biblijny i Liturgiczny* (30 May 1968).

43 ANK, WUKPPiW 11, 'Tygodnik Powszechny: Protokoły ingerencyjne', 6 Apr. – 28 June 1968, fo. 397: M. Kaniewski, head of WUKPPiW, letter to I. Krutikow, GUKPPiW, 25 May 1968.
44 'Tygodnik Powszechny: Protokoły ingerencyjne', 6 Apr. – 28 June 1968, fo. 395: I. Krutikowa, GUKPPiW, telegram to M. Kaniewski, head of WUKPPiW, 28 May 1968.
45 'Tygodnik Powszechny: Protokoły ingerencyjne', 19 Apr. – 7 July 1967, fo. 365: 'Ze świata' (10 June 1967).
46 Ibid.
47 'Tygodnik Powszechny: Protokoły ingerencyjne', 19 Apr. – 7 July 1967, fo. 353, 355–6: 'Ze świata' (15 June 1967).
48 Tygodnik Powszechny: Protokoły ingerencyjne', 6 Apr. – 28 June 1968, fo. 163: 'Obraz tygodnia' (25 Apr. 1968).
49 'Tygodnik Powszechny: Protokoły ingerencyjne', 19 Apr. – 7 July 1967, fo. 439: 'Obraz tygodnia' (23 June 1967).
50 'Tygodnik Powszechny: Protokoły ingerencyjne', 19 Apr. – 7 July 1967 (23 June 1967).
51 'Tygodnik Powszechny: Protokoły ingerencyjne', 6 Apr. – 28 June 1968, fos. 463, 465: 'Obraz tygodnia' (30 June 1967).
52 ANK, WUKPPiW, 10, 'Tygodnik Powszechny: Protokoły ingerencyjne', 12 July – 31 Aug. 1967, fo. 163: 'Obraz tygodnia' (29 July 1967).
53 ANK, WUKPPiW, 11, 'Tygodnik Powszechny: Protokoły ingerencyjne', 3 July – 28 Aug. 1968, fo. 281: 'Obraz tygodnia' (21 Aug. 1968).
54 'Tygodnik Powszechny: Protokoły ingerencyjne', 6 Apr. – 28 June 1968, fo. 511: 'Obraz tygodnia' (12 June 1968).
55 'Obraz tygodnia', *Tygodnik Powszechny*, 21 Oct. 1973, p. 1. I am grateful to Aleksander Kardyś, president of Fundacja Tygodnika Powszechnego, Kraków, for providing access to the foundation's records.
56 'Obraz tygodnia', *Tygodnik Powszechny*, 18 Mar. 1979, p. 1.
57 'Obraz tygodnia', *Tygodnik Powszechny*, 1 Apr. 1979, p. 1.
58 W. Bartoszewski, *Moja Jerozolima, mój Izrael: Władysław Bartoszewski w rozmowie z Joanną Szwedowską* (Warsaw, 2004), 173.
59 Ibid. 174.
60 'Tygodnik Powszechny: Protokoły ingerencyjne', 6 Apr. – 28 June 1968, fo. 367: 'Obraz tygodnia' (22 May 1968).
61 'Tygodnik Powszechny: Protokoły ingerencyjne', 19 Apr. – 7 July 1967, fos. 491–3: 'Kronika religijna' (30 June 1967).
62 'Tygodnik Powszechny: Protokoły ingerencyjne', 19 Apr. – 7 July 1967, fos. 525, 257: 'Ze świata' (7 July 1967).
63 'Tygodnik Powszechny: Protokoły ingerencyjne', 12 July – 31 Aug. 1967, fos. 119, 121: 'Kronika religijna' (19 July 1967).
64 *Gość Niedzielny* was a conservative Catholic weekly, which first appeared in 1923 and after the war from February 1945. From 1953 to 1956, the authorities imposed their own editorial board. It was suspended under martial law from December 1981 to March 1982.
65 AAN, GUKPPiW, 2620, 'Ingerencje cenzorskie GUKPPiW, WUKPPiW w Bydgoszczy, Katowicach, Poznaniu w czasopismach w okresie I–XII 1964: Sprawozdanie z kontroli prewencyjnej', fo. 67: 'Premiera *Namiestnika* w Tel-Avivie', *Gość Niedzielny* (6 Sept. 1964).
66 ANK, WUKPPiW, 5, 'Tygodnik Powszechny: Protokoły ingerencyjne', 8 Aug. – 29 Dec. 1961, fo. 311 (4 Sept. 1961).

67 ANK, WUKPPiW, 4, 'Tygodnik Powszechny: Protokoły ingerencyjne', 5 Jan. – 5 May 1961, fo. 273 (10 Feb. 1961).
68 'Tygodnik Powszechny: Protokoły ingerencyjne', 5 Jan – 5 May 1961, fo. 305: Bart., 'Przed procesem Eichmanna' (6 Apr. 1961).
69 Bart, 'Proces Eichmanna', *Tygodnik Powszechny*, 16 Apr. 1961, p. 2.
70 'Tygodnik Powszechny: Protokoły ingerencyjne', 5 Jan. – 5 May 1961, fo. 305, 338: 'Proces eichmanna' (6, 12 Apr. 1961).
71 'Tygodnik Powszechny: Protokoły ingerencyjne', 5 Jan. – 5 May 1961, fo. 517: S. Stomma, 'Nowe: Oskarżam' (18 Apr. 1961).
72 Bartoszewski visited Israel in September 1963 'to broaden his knowledge, hold conversations, read documents, visit the country' and 'in order for [his] visit to Israel to be crowned by the planting of a tree for the Council for Assistance to the Jews—Żegota. And that's what happened.' During the visit, Bartoszewski also recorded a several hours long account concerning the work of Żegota (Bartoszewski, *Moja Jerozolima, mój Izrael*, 51–2). Six reports from Israel by Bartoszewski, of several pages each, appeared in *Tygodnik Powszechny* in 1964.
73 ANK, WUKPPiW, 6, 'Tygodnik Powszechny: Protokoły ingerencyjne', 8 Jan. – 10 June 1964, fo. 119: W. Bartoszewski, 'Źródło sędziego i źródło oracza' (12 Feb. 1964).
74 W. Bartoszewski, 'W En Hashofet i gdzie indziej', *Tygodnik Powszechny*, 23 Feb. 1964, pp. 4–5.
75 'Tygodnik Powszechny: Protokoły ingerencyjne', 8 Jan. – 10 June 1964, fo. 119: W. Bartoszewski, 'Źródło sędziego i źródło oracza' (12 Feb. 1964).
76 'Tygodnik Powszechny: Protokoły ingerencyjne', 8 Jan. – 10 June 1964, fo. 463: P. Gauthier, 'Dziennik z Ziemi Świętej' (8 Apr. 1964).
77 Bartoszewski, *Moja Jerozolima, mój Izrael*, 157, 174, 178.
78 Ibid. 166.
79 AAN, GUKPPiW, 2595, 'Ingerencje cenzorskie GUKPPiW, WUKPPiW w Katowicach, Krakowie, Łodzi, Olsztynie, Poznaniu', n.p.: *Msza Święta*, Poznań (21 Jan. 1961).
80 'Tygodnik Powszechny: Protokoły ingerencyjne', 6 Apr. – 28 June 1968, fo. 257: 'Obraz tygodnia' (8 May 1968).
81 Bartoszewski, *Moja Jerozolima, mój Izrael*, 154.
82 ANK, WUKPPiW, 3, 'Tygodnik Powszechny: Protokoły ingerencyjne', 5 Jan – 20 Apr. 1960, fo. 383: 'Z dnia' (20 Apr. 1960).
83 'Tygodnik Powszechny: Protokoły ingerencyjne', 5 Jan – 5 May 1961, fo. 89: 'Obraz tygodnia' (3 Feb. 1961).
84 'Tygodnik Powszechny: Protokoły ingerencyjne', 8 Aug. – 29 Dec. 1961, fo. 85: 'Obraz tygodnia' (7 Sept. 1961).
85 Ibid.
86 'Tygodnik Powszechny: Protokoły ingerencyjne', 8 Aug. – 29 Dec. 1961, fos. 173, 177: 'Kronika religijna' (4 Oct. 1961).
87 'Tygodnik Powszechny: Protokoły ingerencyjne', 8 Sept. – 20 Dec. 1967, fo. 179: 'Kronika religijna' (6 Oct. 1967).
88 'Tygodnik Powszechny: Protokoły ingerencyjne', 20 Apr. – 1 Sept. 1960, fo. 683: D. Rufeisen, 'Katolicy w Izraelu' (7 July 1960).
89 'Tygodnik Powszechny: Protokoły ingerencyjne', 8 Aug. – 29 Dec. 1961, fo. 339: 'Międzynarodowy konkurs biblijny' (28 Nov. 1961).

90 'Tygodnik Powszechny: Protokoły ingerencyjne', 8 Sept. – 20 Dec. 1967, fo. 131: 'Ze świata' (29 Nov. 1967).
91 'Tygodnik Powszechny: Protokoły ingerencyjne', 8 Sept. – 20 Dec. 1967, fo. 1058: 'Kronika religijna' (13 Dec. 1967).
92 'Tygodnik Powszechny: Protokoły ingerencyjne', 8 Sept. – 20 Dec. 1967, fos. 389, 391: 'Kronika religijna' (20 Dec. 1967).
93 ANK, WUKPPiW, 12, 'Tygodnik Powszechny: Protokoły ingerencyjne', 3 Jan. – 27 Mar. 1968, fo. 299: 'Światowy kongres rabinów' (22 Feb. 1968).
94 See e.g. Szaynok '"To nie jest firma do tego, żeby puszczać, tylko do tego, żeby zatrzymywać"'; ead., 'Zatrzymane w archiwach: Wojewódzki Urząd Kontroli Prasy Publikacji i Widowisk w Poznaniu wobec tematyki żydowskiej na łamach czasopism katolickich (1945–1950)', *Zagłada Żydów: Studia i materiały*, 14 (2018), 354–86.
95 The records of the security service monitoring Bartoszewski refer to the lectures he gave on returning from Israel. The documents mention that over a hundred people attended a meeting organized by the Catholic Intelligentsia Club in Poznań. The report from Kraków mentions a full hall: 'those present included many people with semitic features'. In Warsaw, the number of participants was described as 'several hundred', the secret collaborator also recording a notable group ('they dominated') of 'citizens of Jewish descent' (Bartoszewski, *Moja Jerozolima, mój Izrael*, 67–73).
96 Szaynok, '"To nie jest firma do tego, żeby puszczać, tylko do tego, żeby zatrzymywać"', 904, 910; ead., 'Zatrzymane w archiwach', 362–7.
97 In the same questionnaire, when asked about the nation 'which you like least', the Jews came eighth (4%), after the Germans (66%), the Czechs and Slovaks (17%), Chinese and Russians (13% each), Americans (11%), the English (6%), and the Ukrainians (5%) (J. Szacki, 'Wstępne opracowanie wyników ankiety "Polacy o sobie i innych narodach"' (Sept. 1967): Public.kantarpolska.com website, 'Archiwum raportów społecznych', visited 2 Nov. 2021).
98 Ibid.
99 Komitet do Spraw Radia i Telewizji, Ośrodek Badania Opinii Publicznej i Studiów Programowych, 'Sytuacja międzynarodowa w kontekście wydarzeń na Bliskim Wschodzie w opinii społeczeństwa polskiego' (Jan. 1974): Public.kantarpolska.com website, 'Archiwum raportów społecznych', visited 2 Nov. 2021.

Homeland, State, and Language
The Integration of Polish Jews into Israel

ELŻBIETA KOSSEWSKA

'PEOPLE TODAY long for their homeland, but instead they are granted only a state', Czesław Miłosz wrote of those who migrated from eastern Europe to the West.[1] According to Miłosz, a coincidence of matters and events might determine a migrant's affiliation to a state, but the identity moulded by the legacy of *małe ojczyzny* ('little homelands') remained indelible, because 'one's homeland is organic, rooted in one's past, always rather small, heart-warming, close as one's own body'.[2]

The year 1948 saw the establishment of a Jewish state. It was flooded by waves of culturally diverse immigrants. A wealth of types, as though lifted from the paintings of Marc Chagall or Maurycy Gottlieb, plucked from these little homelands, from cities, towns, and shtetls, appeared on the streets of Israeli towns. David Ben-Gurion saw in them a mass which, given the appropriate cultural policies, could become a single nation. The need to unify the Jewish part of Israeli society demanded the rejection of the legacy of the east European diaspora, which, its diversity and richness notwithstanding, did not foster integration with Jews from other countries. The leaders of the State of Israel anticipated changes in the hierarchy of aspirations in Jewish life. The general conditions after the war were conducive to this, above all the confusion of emigrants en route between the world they had left behind and the new world to which they wished to belong. Changing identities, just like citizenship or passports, was a feature of post-war reality, emigration, peregrination, and resettlement. Adapting to the new conditions of life in Israel inevitably gave rise to contradictory reactions: oscillating between preserving the culture of the country of origin in some instances and rejecting it in others, thereby accepting the creation of a new persona. During the transitional period, Jews who had been integrated into Polish culture accorded themselves the status of wanderers between cultures; despite the prevailing ethos of the State of Israel, they considered themselves citizens of two motherlands.[3]

During this preliminary stage of adapting to the new conditions in Israel, the immigrants from Poland suffered painful social isolation; they were slow to form contacts with the Yishuv, the Jewish community already in the Land of Israel, and also with ethnically distinct communities. The disparate cultures of the different immigrant groups made an approach which could, at least temporarily, accommodate these cultures necessary. Without this, the immigrants' sense of being alien would persist. An important role in the process of adjustment to the new reality was played by newspapers in the languages of the countries of origin. This press was intended for the period when the immigrants were beginning to use Hebrew and to find a place in

Israel, of which they were now citizens, a state whose essence—its strong national identity—seemed to many of them very distant, if not downright alien.

This chapter covers the first two decades of the State of Israel. It was during this time that most Jews from Poland arrived and the majority of Polish-language publications emerged.[4] The particular characteristics of the new arrivals determined how they adapted to Hebrew society and also the profile and content of the press produced for them. The cultural integration of Polish Jews into Israel was a dynamic process, with its own tempo and idiosyncrasies. Tracing its progress through the prism of the press produced for them by Israeli political parties seeking supporters has proved a fruitful approach to describing their cultural adaptation. The acclimatization of the new immigrants to the conditions in Israel was determined to a large extent by their wartime experiences and memories of the past, particularly in the case of Polish Jews.[5] For this reason, this chapter deals with the problems of memory intrinsic in the process of adapting to the Hebrew majority and taking on new personal models of identity.

The Polish-Language Press

The foreign-language press in the newly established State of Israel emerged in response to waves of immigrants from a number of countries. The Israeli political parties frowned on the use of the languages of immigrants' countries of origin as non-Zionist but, at the same time, saw newspapers in those languages as an essential vehicle for assimilation and were mainly responsible for their production, although there were some independent initiatives. Mapai, the General Zionists, the Progressive Party, the Israeli Communist Party (Maki), and Mapam all produced newspapers in foreign languages that reflected their ideals and promoted their causes.[6]

The parties sought to make contact with newly arrived immigrants in the transit camps in order to draw them into their sphere. While it was easy to maintain control over the new arrivals in the camps, it became markedly more difficult once they had left. Party activists were thus enjoined to make lists of individuals, families, and relatives, being told that 'unless you continue your work with them, we will lose them'.[7] A foreign-language press was one way to achieve this. In the first decade of its existence, Israel's political system resembled that of a multi-party state in which political parties exerted enormous influence over the lives of its citizens, and the foreign-language press was part of this phenomenon. It was part of the process of assimilation and closely linked with the political parties which created it and sought to use it to enlist the support of the new immigrants. The longevity of the foreign-language press was thus the result of its political importance rather than a sign of its prestige or the strong support of its readers.

At the founding of the State of Israel, Jews from Poland constituted a third of all Jews in the country;[8] however, there is little evidence of any attempts to produce newspapers in Polish. Those who survived the Holocaust did not usually feel any attachment to Polish; quite the opposite, many wished to distance themselves from it as quickly as possible.[9] Jews from Poland who arrived in Israel after the war initiated only three Polish-language publications.[10] The majority of newspapers in Polish, particularly in the early years of the Jewish state, stated in their first issue that they were using the language solely because it was a practical means of communication. The immigrants had already begun to learn Hebrew in the transit camps, alongside hearing lectures on Zionism and the Jewish state, political indoctrination, and mobilization for battle and the building of the state. The promotion of Hebrew increased after the establishment of the State of Israel in intensive language schools, the army, workplaces, kibbutzim, hostels, youth movements (usually affiliated with a political party), schools and universities, and on the radio.[11] The exaltation of Hebrew was accompanied by the simultaneous denigration of Polish and, on the face of it, a rejection of the experiences of wartime and the diaspora, a resistance to the multiculturalism of a scattered nation, and a readiness to adopt the values of the inhabitants of the Land of Israel.

This adaptation to the conditions in the independent state proved difficult. The contribution of former, particularly older, Zionist activists in the diaspora was no match for the 'sabra' ideal of those born in the land—strong, self-reliant, and confident—and they felt superfluous and rejected after their arrival in Israel. A person's value, and with time that of whole groups of immigrants, was measured according to their usefulness to the state: youth and grit were extolled; old age was equated with life outside Israel, which had been both literally and ideologically unproductive. Hence the comment of Yohanan Bader, a Jew from Poland and a member of the Knesset from the Herut party, who, when discussing the problems of adapting to Israeli conditions, said of Holocaust survivors: 'they will never be true, full, carefree sabras for whom their own country, their own state, their own home, their own culture, and their own language are so natural, that they do not even know how strange, how joyful, how great a happiness it is to be part of them'.[12] In this way, he exposed the illusions of those who believed that by abandoning the language of their country of origin, adopting Hebrew, and collectively forgetting the past they would be able to adapt to Israeli society.

The nature of the Polish-language press changed with the arrival of migrants between 1948 and 1950. By 1956 there were eighteen newspapers in Polish in Israel. The Gomułka Aliyah, the wave of immigration from Poland between 1955 and 1960 following a period when emigration from Poland to Israel was banned, not only swelled the Polish-speaking community and the readership of such newspapers but also increased the number of journalists writing in Polish. In this period, not counting the infrequent Polish-language versions of Hebrew papers, the Friday supplements, and party bulletins which resembled information leaflets rather than regular newspapers, twenty-one titles appeared in Polish, some of which were duplicated on mimeographs and appeared irregularly.[13] The Gomułka Aliyah differed from its predecessors because of the higher educational and professional status of those of whom it was made up and their specific sense of cultural and social identity. All this affected how its members assimilated and the difficulties they encountered.

The Gomułka Aliyah was also strongly left-wing. Its members were Polonized and politically active, some of them having consciously rejected Zionism in favour of a different ideological alternative, communism, which they felt gave them a greater chance of the assimilation that many of them desired. The requirement that their exit petitions state that they had no intention of returning to Poland represented for this group, or at least for a significant part of it, the bankruptcy of an ideal, of the dream that assimilation was possible, along with a belief in communism as the means through which it was to be accomplished. After unsuccessful attempts at assimilation in the diaspora, having loosened their ties with the Jewish people, in Israel they found themselves in a cultural desert. The Polish-language press became an important tool in the process of the national 'reclamation' of these new arrivals. They forged bonds with the state both on the basis of their new experience of living in it and through the Zionism some of them had imbibed in their countries of origin in their native languages.

In Israel, the alienation felt by Polonized Jews was further reinforced by the need to adopt unfamiliar patterns of conduct, values, and a lifestyle strongly connected with the culture of a state that from the very beginning was defined as a state for Jews. Their contact with the Middle East revealed how hard it would be for them to base their identity on its culture and traditions; instead they emphasized their individuality; they felt Polish, particularly as in Israel there was nothing to deny that Polishness. But coming to Israel and adapting to conditions there entailed accepting that their children would speak Hebrew; that they would celebrate Jewish festivals which they had not celebrated for a long time, if at all; and that they would have to reject what had hitherto been dear to them—Polish culture.[14] They did not have long to make this change in their identity, merely the time it took to travel from Poland to Israel—in the former they felt themselves to be Poles, in the latter they were awaited as Jews. In Israel, Polonized Jews were expected not only to profess Jewish identity but to manifest it and to demonstrate their rejection of their Polish identity.[15] The need for immigrants, striving to assimilate with the majority, to adopt a new sense of identity forced them, most often involuntarily, to accept the stress on the national state and national values imposed by the Israeli state. In Israel, the confrontation between the national consciousness of the Jews of the Gomułka Aliyah with social expectations provoked frustration at their inability to meet them. The struggle with the otherness and foreignness of Israel, consequently, led to a sense of rejection, alienation, and hesitancy when confronted with the need to conform.[16] Those who could not adapt, who did not understand the values of the *vatikim* (veteran citizens of Israel), remained aloof. Others, in their first encounters with what was supposed to be their own nation, resorted to criticism of Israeli society albeit based on their own lack of identification with it rather than the actual reality. Wiktor Cygielman wrote in *Od Nowa*:

They're so loud these Jews, so ill-mannered, and so typical! It's unbearable. 'Are these the words of a Polish antisemite in Warsaw?' asks the journalist. 'No, of a Jewish antisemite in

Tel Aviv.' Unfortunately, the current *aliyah* from Poland has provided us with that kind too. Quite a few, in fact . . . But to have Jewish chutzpah and pose as a Polish nobleman —that doesn't quite work.[17]

In one anecdote, a newly arrived immigrant from Poland, observing Israeli society, asked in disbelief: 'And all those who don't speak Polish, are they Jews too?'[18]

The status of new immigrants from Poland, which was better in fact than that of other ethnic groups, plus an ongoing reckoning with the past, was not enough to make them feel at ease. As a result, they felt the need for literature in Polish, which helped them to lose the sense of being 'former people' and of being strangers in their new country.[19]

The Jews who arrived from Poland during the Gomułka Aliyah, depending on their past, experiences of the diaspora, level of Polish acculturation, attitudes to Zionism, openness to a new way of life, and above all familiarity with Hebrew, either adapted to their new conditions and integrated with the rest of Israeli society or swelled the poorly developed market of the press for Polish-speakers while enriching its content with their own writings. 'I Have Become More Polish in Israel', recalls one reader of *Nowiny*:

We found ourselves in Israel with crates full of Polish books and folk textiles from Cepelia, records of Chopin, and the 'Mazowsze' and 'Śląsk' [folk troupes] . . . In the evenings, we still catch the evening news from Warsaw on 'Beethovens' or even on 'Pioneers' [radio sets]. We exchange Polish books from our personal collections. We talk—to the indignation of the *vatikim* and their children—all day—in shops, cafes, on the street—only in Polish.[20]

On the one hand, the intellectual level of the members of the Gomułka Aliyah and their need to satisfy their cultural requirements and to participate actively in public and intellectual life; and, on the other, their limited grasp of Hebrew, led to greater demand for works in Polish. They continued eagerly to use Polish, which they regarded as a literary language and not only a symbol of antisemitism. As one of them explained:

It was in Polish that we attacked the world of evil and iniquity. In Polish, the language of Mickiewicz, Słowacki, and Prus, that we dreamt of the future happiness of humanity. Finally, it was in the language of Sienkiewicz and Tuwim, Orzeszkowa and Reymont, that we began to speak, cry out, and shout of Jewish injustice, of the Jewish nation, of the Jewish state. This is the language in which we described the charms of Hebrew.[21]

Many immigrants, suffered from nostalgia for Poland. It was said: 'Hebrew is for the high holidays and festivals; Polish is for memories'.[22] Hebrew was certainly still promoted but 'for the moment' spiritual assimilation was seen as the goal, in the belief that it would be followed by linguistic assimilation. Adaptation to conditions in the State of Israel and the temptation to leave meant that, for many, Polish became a cultural refuge. The culture of the country of origin seemed like merely another piece of 'baggage' brought from the diaspora and, in the eyes of Zionists, unnecessary. For the Jews of Poland, alongside the books, clothes, and radios in their possession, this was the principal thing they brought with them. In an article on Anita Wolfstein, a Polish-speaking poet who began to write in Polish only after coming to Israel, R. L. Sawin described her community's attitude to the language: 'they knew this language, it was their mental anchor, and in it they expressed the overwhelming shock of finding themselves in a new country, its harsh climate, strange new human, social, and cultural structures, burdened with the necessity of quickly absorbing the Hebrew language—and with a clear longing for the world they had left behind.'[23]

Polish consulates were flooded with requests for books, publications, and literature in Polish. However, the provision of such books and periodicals was not a high priority in the framework of the trade agreement between Poland and Israel. Thus, for example, publications ordered in November 1951 did not reach Israel until the following April. Polish bookshops appeared, mainly in Tel Aviv, and new shipments were announced on the first pages of the Polish-language press. Cultural events— lectures on Polish literature and audiences with writers, scholars, and artists from Poland—were eagerly anticipated.

There were also many requests for the Polish émigré monthly *Kultura*, published in Paris.[24] *Kultura* provided a locus for discussion of Polish Jewish issues from both sides, arousing considerable emotion, particularly when the national values of Poles and Jews clashed. The periodical remained a platform for many viewpoints, creating a transnational discourse in which the arguments of people who thought about Polish matters could meet, though in the case of Polish Jews, their significance was exclusively historical. The debate on the subject of Poland's future, however, which took as its starting point a Polish state based on right-wing values, quashed any joint initiatives on the part of Poles and Jews. Poles of Jewish origin, after experiencing antisemitism from both the left and the right, scaled down their activities within every Polish political option. After Poland broke off diplomatic relations with Israel in 1967, demand for Polish-language publications plummeted amid a general social aversion to the subject of Poland and its perceived antisemitism. Polish–Jewish relations became mired in the politics of remembrance and issues related to the martyrology of the Jewish people, which stymied any engagement with contemporary problems. In Israel, members of the intelligentsia with Polish backgrounds turned to publications in Hebrew.

The aims of the foreign-language press in Israel were above all to integrate new citizens into Israeli society. The convergence of a culturally and linguistically diverse European hotchpotch with Middle Eastern culture that marked the first generation of the State of Israel lost its diasporic colour and became more markedly centred on Hebrew in the next generation. By the end of the 1960s, the foreign-language press had become obsolete: the new voter was a young voter who read the newspaper in Hebrew. The generational shift was important: it was part of the process of removing the reins of leadership from the elderly and contesting paternalistic democracy. This is clearly visible in the erosion of state structures dominated by parties, the crisis of values in the *vatik* world and their system of hegemony. Furthermore, another aspect of the general shift was connected not only with age but also with ethnicity: a predominance of Mizrachi Jews from the Middle East and North Africa was predicted by the end of the 1960s. A culmination of cultural and political changes surrounding Polish-language publishing determined its decline and disappearance.

Narrow Tracks

David Ben-Gurion saw the masses of Jewish people flowing into Israel as a force indispensable to the building of the state, which could be harnessed if they were moulded into a culturally cohesive nation, which he understood at the time as the body which had the power to create and mould the new Jewish state. At the beginning of 1949, after barely a year, the population of Israel had increased by 36.4 per cent,[25] that is, a third of Jewish society was made up of new immigrants, on top of earlier immigrants still not fully integrated into Israeli society.[26] Before the founding of Israel, the influx of new inhabitants was regulated by certificates issued according to the demand and the economic possibilities of Palestine—first of all came people with capital and Zionist ideologies. The almost doubling of a largely non-Zionist and non-pioneer Jewish population in less than a decade raised questions about the future character of the state. The local Jewish community was also a problem: before the founding of the State of Israel, 85 per cent of the Yishuv came from a European background. From 1948 the 'colour and typology of the Yishuv began to change', according to Ben-Gurion, with the arrival of Mizrachi Jews. The leaders of the Yishuv began to be concerned that, given such a large influx of immigrants, Israeli society might lose its pioneer character, that the Yishuv leadership might lose its hegemony, and that there might be a permanent shift in values. Were the new immigrants bringing anything that could provide a cultural foundation for future action? Following the Holocaust, would the new immigrants be able to manage their trauma and, more importantly, would they be useful in building the state? The problems of migration seemed urgent and important enough for Ben-Gurion, in the middle of the War of Independence, to call two meetings of Hebrew writers. They took place in Tel Aviv on 27 March and 11 October 1949. Thirty-five writers were involved, including Lea Goldberg, Martin Buber, Natan Alterman, Uri Tsevi Grinberg, Abraham Shlonsky, Avigdor Hameiri, Ben-Zion Dinur, and Samuel Hugo Bergmann. Missing from this circle was S. Y. Agnon, whose absence can be explained by the fact that his work was addressed to Jews in a general sense, beyond party or geographical divisions. Ben-Gurion had something completely different in mind, namely literary creation in Hebrew, making it a tool for the social and political integration of the Jewish masses and Israel a world centre of Hebrew life.

The meetings were devoted to national integration; nevertheless very different positions were maintained with a sharp division between the Yishuv and the new immigrants. The former were carried away by the euphoria of the victorious battle for independence, the talk was of the revolutionary transformation of the nation's identity in which they had participated—they felt like history's victors. The new immigrants were depicted as an inchoate mass, on whom they would bestow a form in the future and before whom they would open up new possibilities. Lea Goldberg, for example, depicted the new immigrants as overwhelmed and paralysed by fear, speculators active in a black market: 'it will be a difficult love, but people could emerge from this material', she said.[27] The evaluation of the usefulness of the new immigrants in the rise and rebirth of the nation was low, whereas Israeli society owed them its existence, as many of them had fought in the War of Independence. In April 1948 the Haganah consisted of 21,775 soldiers, in July that year 63,586, and in October over 96,699, whereas in March 1949 there were over 130,000.[28] Each of them had experienced war, they knew what it meant to fight for their life and existence. Highlighting the Yishuv's role in the victory was a manifestation of the anti-diaspora attitude inherent in the state ideology. Furthermore, the new immigrants constituted personnel required by the state. The majority of them hailed from European countries, they were well educated, multilingual, and contributed cultural elements of their own little homelands to Israeli culture. Those in power created a hierarchy of state values, with new immigrants—regardless of their situation or achievements, other than very obvious service to the state—at the bottom of the social pyramid.

Some writers rejected the heritage of the diaspora, but others were worried that this would limit the character of the new state. For example, Martin Buber and Samuel Hugo Bergmann both felt that the train of Jewish history was turning onto the narrow track of 'Israelism', a new form of provincialism which could not draw on the Jewish past. Bergmann feared that young Israelis would replace Jewish humanism with nationalism or xenophobia and become isolated from the world. In his opinion, the state could not contain the history of a nation which had prophetic visions of the world and a wide influence on civilization: a Jewish state had to have something more, something spiritual and moral, opening it to the sphere of what was beyond the state.[29]

'The most honest-to-goodness blondes'

In Israel, the creation of a common identity required newly arrived immigrants to reject the diaspora, abandon the language of their country of origin in favour of Hebrew, and often change their surname. The heroic sabra became the model Israeli Jew: an individual filled with Zionist zeal, who through their behaviour and culture expressed their affiliation to the Land of Israel, its climate, nature, and customs, and their attachment to the Middle East rather than to Europe. Admiration for the sabra dominated the press. The sabra style was emulated: the tanned, khaki look, wearing a tembel hat. A sabra was a strong Jew, self-reliant, and confident, with nothing of the tired, sad, anxious Jew of the diaspora.

The collective memory of the Holocaust was conformed to the social and political expectations of the State of Israel. Adapting to the sabra ideal on the part of new immigrants from Poland required a selecting of experiences, introducing incomplete memories and 'half-truths' into the public sphere. There was a departure from martyrological thinking in favour of the cult of heroism. Competition between various groups of Jews regarding their diasporic fortunes encouraged people to record mainly extraordinary events on their part.[30] The biographies of Polish Jews were part of a constant game between the past and the present, perceived through the prism of political interests which shifted depending on the context of the state ethos. The debate over how to remember or whether to remember at all was played out in both the Hebrew- and the Polish-language presses: diffidently, according to tendencies typical of the time; a battle between silence and a protest against it, transposing the memory of the heroes of the ghetto onto the Israeli ethos of martial prowess while simultaneously marginalizing other Jewish experiences of the war. The fate of Jews far from the battle front or ghetto uprisings was not visible. The helplessness of Holocaust victims grated with the sabra's ethos of strength, and individual experiences were thrust aside by the imaginary mass armed feats of Polish Jewry, blurring the truth about the Holocaust on the personal level, about private tragedies which could not break through to Israeli public perception due to the lack of spectacular battle scenes.[31] Polish-language newspapers, regardless of political affiliation, acquiesced in this and even encouraged it, willingly taking up the theme of the Holocaust on the anniversary of the ghetto uprisings. Articles from that time contain half-truths and understatement, with a blend of exhilarating emotion, creating an essentially shallow narrative of the Second World War.[32] There was no audience for the tragic memories of the survivors. Their perceived apathy and passivity provoked distaste. In the words of one reader of *Kurier Powszechny*:

To the Editor! Could you please explain to me why such documents [accounts of the Holocaust] are dragged from the fireproof coffers of hellish archives into the light of day. As far as I am aware, those who 'survived' are very unwilling to return to the realms of those experiences. In those monstrous years, each of them faced head on the necessity of one or another tragic compromise, the memory of which haunts them in nightmares. Why disturb people's hard-regained joy of life with this kind of memoir? . . . I think it is easier to forget for those 'who lived through' it than for us, who are still haunted by the echo of screams dying away from ghettoes engulfed by flames. Why then reawaken once again our horror and suspicion of those who 'survived' (at what price?) or our doubt in ourselves (who knows if I would have been any better?). Nor do problems of this kind create a bridge between the past and future. The 'sabra' generation, amongst whom I include all those children whose language is currently Polish—will soon look at the cited extract with reluctance, disdain, and a complete lack of understanding—based on the correct assumption that the tears evoked by such memories should be shed without witnesses, behind tightly closed doors.[33]

It was signed Cypora of Bat Yam, who referred to herself as an old immigrant. No voice of protest appeared in the Polish-language press opposing this forgetting. The paper lacks debate—if only a record of a different account or personal experience. The Holocaust isolated that part of the Jewish nation who had survived it from those who had barely heard of it. Among the Polish Jews, knowledge of the Holocaust was complete, but blocked; in Israeli society it was present, but rejected. In family accounts, the Holocaust was a taboo theme. Children were protected from it, in the attempt to weld them to another world, of the Jewish state. It took a third generation to desire to learn what the generations of their parents and grandparents strove to forget.

The Jewish state was meant to be like a non-Jewish state, and the Jews to all intents and purposes, from employability to appearance, like any other nation.[34] The 'new' Jew emerged against the background of the images of Jews prevalent in the diaspora. Polish Jews were concerned with 'good looks': the ability to pass for a non-Jew. In Israel, Jews from Poland wishing to free themselves from the stereotype of the timid, feeble Jew opted for the strong sabra ideal, taking the opportunity to bury the past:

Not only do our children not understand the implications of the swastika; they also do not understand the qualified and complicated Jewry of their peers overseas. A Jew is an Israeli. A Jew who is not an Israeli is something very vague and strange, something from that hazy domain in which there is room for a swastika and for that difficult word 'antisemitism'.[35]

As a result, they cultivated an Aryan appearance, an 'un-Jewish' face; their free life in Tel Aviv was the antithesis of the ghetto. In an account of socializing with Jews from the Middle East, the appearance of Jews from Egypt or Morocco was favoured because 'they were the most honest-to-goodness blondes!'[36]

Maintaining the 'correct' appearance had its roots in historical attempts to assimilate, to conform to the privileged majority who were not persecuted for their appearance. The Holocaust made this more imperative, with the need to obtain 'Aryan papers', but those who survived were unable to liberate themselves from this wartime way of thinking. The trial of Eichmann only served to strengthen the significance of the 'right look'. In an article on the trial, one judge was characterized as follows:

The Jewish judge, [Yitzhak] Raveh, has a long face, a high forehead, a brick-red complexion and calm grey-blue eyes. He looks like a Norwegian. The ideal 'Nordic' type, according to Nazi classification. May the reader forgive me for returning stubbornly to these matters. I do so consciously, since I consider that the 'right look' of the Jews, and the not-at-all-right one of the accused, is one more nail in Eichmann's symbolic coffin.[37]

In Israel, the triumph of the 'new Jew' rested on the fact that their appearance could be more Aryan than that of those for whom this appearance was pivotal: the Germans: 'Of course, it is complete coincidence that the policemen guarding Eichmann are a hundred times more "Aryan" in appearance than the accused. Sabras as a rule, with blue eyes, snub noses, tawny heads of hair.'[38] The 'right look' had little to do with aesthetics, but decidedly a lot to do with acceptance and a sense of security. This is why the reference points for immigrants changed depending on the environment in which they happened to live: sometimes it was the appearance of a non-Jew, and at other times that of a sabra. And sometimes these two prototypes merged and the sabra looked like a non-Jew.

The Eichmann trial slowly brought the plight of Jews during the Second World

War to the awareness of Israeli society. But the usefulness of tragic memories still depended on the extent to which they legitimized the state. In the public sphere, the human catastrophe that was the Holocaust emerged, slowly freeing memories from the 'hero's straitjacket' and creating space for other private experiences to be expressed. After Eichmann's trial, it was written: 'however inhuman, brutal, and cynical it sounds, when one picks up a paper on the days when Eichmann disappears from its columns, it feels like returning from the cemetery along the road back to the house from which one accompanied a family member to be buried.'[39] Until 1961 the Jewish hero of partisan warfare occupied the columns of the Polish-language press; after the trial, more individual war experiences begin to filter through, tentatively at first but building to a flood of testimonies from Holocaust witnesses.

At the foundation of the State of Israel, the present dominated the past; from the moment of Eichmann's trial, the past took precedence.[40] Knowledge of the Holocaust became widespread and was employed as a force for national cohesion, a framework within which to express emotions and a connection with the state, especially in the context of threats and the need for defence, which intensified strongly during the Six Day War of 1967. The mythic power of the victory in the Six Day War was built on the catastrophe of the Holocaust. The victorious Israeli army was contrasted with the helplessness of the Jewish diaspora. A certain type of mentality was created: the victorious Jew. Israeli political discourse leaned towards the right, in a debate permeated with xenophobic and nationalistic values.

Victory in the Six Day War greatly increased the prestige of Hebrew. The Israeli forces in the War of Independence were multilingual; those who took part in the Six Day War spoke Hebrew. Older people became more willing to learn the language; children more embarrassed to speak Polish. The foreign-language press began to suffer the stigma of being foreign. Given the sense of social solidarity and patriotism awakened by the war, it seemed to highlight division and the absence of a national ethos. For the survivors of the Holocaust, the sight of an tight-knit state that was able to defend itself provided the strongest argument for aligning themselves with it, ending the phase of hesitation and doubt and questions of where to go next.[41]

Conclusion

The large number of Polish-language publications in the first two decades of the State of Israel should not be seen as an attempt to promote Polish culture or as an issue in the history of Polish–Jewish relations. The language used was Polish, but the subjects were almost exclusively Israeli. Had the foreign-language media become the guardians of the culture and language of their countries of origin, they would also have provided a creative impulse and would have had a chance for a long existence, something the Israeli authorities badly wanted to avoid. The Polish-language press in Israel was solely an instrument of communication on the path to complete integration into Israeli society. Every step forward in assimilation brought its demise closer:

dying with the generation of Jews who had arrived in Israel from Poland. Sociopolitical conditions, the reception of this minority by the Hebrew sector of society, and the antisemitic associations of Polish meant that children did not wish to speak Polish with their parents. In turn, the political provenance of the press meant that the parties lost motivation when the costs of publication were disproportionate to the political gains to be made. The Polish-language press was the product of political interests and the existence of a group of journalists from Poland for whom Polish was an integral part of their identity and a readership whose limited professional activity provided little impetus to learn Hebrew more quickly.

It would seem that a study of the early memories of the Holocaust published in the Polish-language press in Israel would be of fundamental importance, but this was not a full or true record. In the first years after the Second World War, Holocaust narratives in Israel were essentially superficial. The process of imparting memory in a multi-ethnic society striving to create a common identity inhibited the expression of positions which—at any given moment—were not felt to be desirable by the establishment. The creation of a collective consciousness demanded that each group's fate be inscribed into the history of the state, which fostered a rivalry between the heroism and achievements of east European Jews and Jews from other countries. Tracing the changes in the collective memory of Polish Jews reveals the history of their fears and anxieties, from fears concerning 'the right look' (the still desirable Aryan or sabra look) to the fundamental terror and trauma experienced in the daily lives of people surviving the Holocaust.

Translated from the Polish by Anna Zaranko

Notes

1 C. Miłosz, 'La Combe', *Kultura*, 132 (1958), 26–38: 34.
2 Ibid.
3 J. Bader, '1000 numerów i więcej', *Nowiny Poranne*, 1000 (1956), 3.
4 See E. Kossewska, *Ona jeszcze mówi po polsku, ale śmieje się po hebrajsku: Partyjna prasa polskojęzyczna i integracja kulturowa polskich Żydów w Izraelu (1948–1970)* (Warsaw, 2015), 65–89; Eng. trans.: *Polish Jews in Israel: Polish-Language Press, Culture and Politics*, trans. S. Gilroy (Boston, Mass., 2021), 46–60; see also ead., '"Ona jeszcze mówi po polsku, ale śmieje się po hebrajsku": Prasa polskojęzyczna a integracja językowa polskich Żydów w Izraelu', *Kultura i Społeczeństwo*, 2010, no. 4, pp. 59–75.
5 'Nowe życie w Ramle', *Przegląd Wydarzeń w Izraelu*, 2 (1949), 6.
6 In 1952 there were 104 foreign-language newspapers in thirteen different languages published in Israel (Israel State Archives, Jerusalem, 717/7 ג, 'Kisilov': document attached to Moshe Goldstein, director of *hasbara*, letter, 1 June 1950).
7 Massuah Institute for the Study of the Holocaust, Kibbutz Tel Yitzhak, 10/9 עין: meeting of the welfare board for new *olim*, 3 Apr. 1949; cf. Archive of Mifleget Ha'avodah, Beit Berl, 2/929/1958/8: Moshe Kitron, letter to Gior Yoseftal, 17 Mar. 1958.
8 In 1945 Jews from Poland constituted 20.7 per cent of the Jewish population of Palestine. Three years later, at the founding of the State of Israel, this figure had grown to 33.8 per

cent. In 1950, 26,485 people left Poland for Israel; the following year, 2,657; and in the period 1952–5, 1,179. Many were without a trade; others were craftsmen, merchants, or clerks; and a small percentage were members of the intelligentsia. Jewish emigration from Poland to Israel in the period 1955–60 numbered 42,569 people. The profile of readers of the Polish-language press can therefore be determined on the basis of the professional make-up of people departing Poland for Israel in the years 1955–6. Following a period of restricted emigration and the repatriation of the Jewish population from the Soviet Union, people arrived who had previously been unable to leave Poland, but also workers from the party and state apparatus, demobilized officers of the Polish army, former functionaries of the security forces and police, members of the intelligentsia, and workers from the agricultural sector. See A. Stankowski, 'Nowe spojrzenie na statystyki dotyczące emigracji Żydów z Polski po 1944 roku', in G. Berendt, A. Grabski, and A. Stankowski, *Studia z historii Żydów w Polsce po 1945 r.* (Warsaw, 2000), 104, 117–21.

9 'Od Redakcji', *Kronika Tygodniowa*, 1 (1950), 1.
10 *Głos Ludu, Przegląd Wydarzeń w Izraelu*, and *Gazeta Tymczasowa*.
11 'Niema [sic] Marokańczyków i Polaków – są tylko Żydzi', *Przegląd Wydarzeń w Izraelu*, 33 (1949), 1.
12 Bader, '1000 numerów – i więcej', 1.
13 *Kurier Powszechny* and *Kurier Niezależny*, which were published alternately, merged with the two versions of *Nowiny* and became *Nowiny i Kurier* (Progressive Party and Mapai); *Po Prostu* (the Bund); *Echo Tygodnia* (General Zionists); *Echo Izraela, Fakty* (Mapai); *Siedem Dni: Aktualności Tygodnia, Przegląd Miesiąca, Rimon, Przekrój Izraelski, Od Nowa* (left-Zionist party, Mapam); *Walka* (communist party, Maki); *Głos Informacyjny, Digest po Polsku*.
14 E. Pel, 'Spór o Tanach', *Od Nowa*, 10 (1959).
15 H. Szwarcman (W. Cygielman), 'Myśli oderwane', *Od Nowa*, 10 (1959), 3.
16 M. Chalamisz, 'Od burzenia ołtarzy do nihilizmu', *Od Nowa*, 7 (1958), 1.
17 Szwarcman, 'Myśli oderwane', 3.
18 A. Chciuk, *Wizyta w Izraelu* (Paris, 1972), 96.
19 '282x "Od Nowa"', *Od Nowa*, 24 (1965), 1.
20 J. Markiewicz, 'Dopolszczyłam się w Izraelu', *Nowiny Izraelskie*, 66 (1958), 3.
21 S. Lebenbaum-Drzewożycki, 'Dziwny czar izraelskiej polszczyzny', *Nowiny Izraelskie*, 14 Dec. 1957, p. 3.
22 Chciuk, *Wizyta w Izraelu*, 113.
23 R. L. Sawin (Ryszard Löw), 'Anita Wolfstein', *Kontury*, 14 (2003), 107–8.
24 'Debit "Kultury" w Izraelu', *Od Nowa*, 32 (1960), 4; Association Institut Littéraire Kultura, Maisons-Lafitte: Jerzy Giedroyć, letter to Leo Lipski, 17 Dec. 1956; Jerzy Giedroyć, letter to N. Nieświski (Filip Ben), 19 Oct. 1952; Jerzy Giedroyć, letter to David Lazar, 20 Sept. 1960.
25 Yad Yaari Archive, Givat Haviva, 18461, 'Divrei soferim bifegishah shezimen rosh hamemshalah' (27 Mar., 11 Oct. 1949), p. 19: speech by David Ben-Gurion, 11 Oct. 1949; p. 20: speech by Ben-Zion Dinur, 11 Oct. 1949.
26 Speech by David Ben-Gurion, 11 Oct. 1949; speech by Ben-Zion Dinur, 11 Oct. 1949.
27 'Divrei soferim bifegishah shezimen rosh hamemshalah', p. 10: speech by Lea Goldberg, 27 Mar. 1949; pp. 23–4: speech by Lea Goldberg, 11 Oct. 1949.
28 *Hahistoryah shel erets yisra'el, milḥemet ha'atsma'ut*, ed. Y. Ben-Arieh, 10 vols (Jerusalem, 1983), x. 128.

29 'Divrei soferim bifegishah shezimen rosh hamemshalah', pp. 6–7: speech by David Ben-Gurion, 27 Mar. 1949; see also speech by David Ben-Gurion, 11 Oct. 1949; speech by Ben-Zion Dinur, 11 Oct. 1949.
30 D. Harten, 'Na marginesie zjazdu Żydów polskich', *Nowiny i Kurier*, 15 (1961), 2.
31 H. Joffe, 'W lasach i puszczach: Saga rodu bohaterów', *Nowiny i Kurier*, 181 (1961), 2.
32 'Saga rodu bohaterów', *Nowiny i Kurier*, 174 (1961), 2; 'Saga rodu bohaterów', *Nowiny i Kurier*, 177 (1961), 2; 'Saga rodu bohaterów', *Nowiny i Kurier*, 181 (1961), 2–3.
33 Cypora of Bat Yam, letter to editor, *Kurier Powszechny*, 55 (1958), 4.
34 'Chopin i sabra', *Nowiny Izraelskie*, 47 (1960), 3.
35 T. Hatalgi, 'Nasze dzieci a swastyka', *Nowiny i Kurier*, 13 (1960), 2.
36 Meta, 'Zbliżenie "polsko-egipskie"', *Nowiny i Kurier*, 112 (1960), 2.
37 S. Lebenbaum, 'Niemiecki język, eichmanowskie poty i żydowska ciotka', *Nowiny i Kurier*, 174 (1961), 3.
38 S. Lebenbaum, 'Sekretarka p. Mecenasa, "Polacy" i policjanci (Notatnik jerozolimski)', *Nowiny i Kurier*, 171 (1961), 3.
39 M. Mariańska, 'Okno na świat', *Nowiny i Kurier*, 125 (1960), 3.
40 M. Mariańska, 'Sąd już się rozpoczął', *Nowiny i Kurier*, 125 (1960), 3.
41 U. Kejsari, 'U progu nowej aliji', *Nowiny i Kurier*, 170 (1967), 4.

The Polish Exodus of 1968
Antisemitism, Dropouts, and Re-emigrants in *Nowiny i Kurier*

MIRI FREILICH

The Antisemitic Campaign in Poland

In 1968 an anti-Zionist and antisemitic propaganda campaign resulted in the departure of 12,927 Jews from Poland. The Jewish population of Poland had been shrinking since the end of the Second World War. According to various estimates, some 50,000 Jews survived the Holocaust on Polish soil, and about 140,000 Jewish refugees returned from the Soviet Union. In June 1946, 220,000 Jews were registered in Poland. During the Kielce pogrom of July 1946, forty-two of the city's remaining Jews were killed. The pogrom was the culmination of a series of incidents of Jews returning to their homes and being attacked, robbed, and murdered. After the Kielce pogrom, some 130,000 Jews fled Poland. In 1956 Władysław Gomułka was appointed party secretary and permitted Jews to emigrate to Israel: about 35,000 left. By the end of the 'Gomułka Aliyah', between 25,000 and 30,000 Jews remained in the country. Of these, about 4,600 emigrated to Israel between 1961 and 1967.[1]

The day after the outbreak of the Six Day War between Israel and the Arab states, 6 June 1967, Poland notified the Israeli government of the severance of diplomatic and economic relations.[2] This move was also marked by an antisemitic campaign in the local media and at public gatherings of the ruling Polish United Workers' Party (Polska Zjednoczona Partia Robotnicza; PZPR) and its institutions. The Polish government took steps that led to the removal of Jews from the centres of political power. Among the first to be dismissed were those with senior positions in the party. Later, professionals, such as university lecturers, journalists, actors, directors, musicians, and others, were fired.[3] There was also a marked increase in the number of antisemitic incidents throughout Poland.[4] The remaining Jews of Poland realized that they were not welcome in the country and began to leave.

The Jews who left Poland were forced to give up their Polish citizenship. As the State of Israel no longer had an official representative in Poland, the Dutch embassy dealt with issuing exit visas. The Polish government doubled the price of the visas, which most Polish Jews could not afford, so the Jewish Agency paid for them.[5] However, only 3,084 of those leaving Poland went to Israel. The rest scattered between the countries of western Europe and the United States.[6] The choice not to move to Israel engendered harsh criticism of the expellees in the Israeli press.[7]

Władysław Gomułka, leader of the PZPR from 1956 to 1970, characterized the Jews of his country as a treacherous group that had no place in the Polish state. At a trade union convention in Poland on 19 June 1967, he called the Jews a 'fifth column' and compared the conquest of Arab territory by Israel during the Six Day War to the German invasion of Poland.[8] In a speech delivered to members of the PZPR on 19 March 1968, he divided the Jews of Poland into three groups. The first, he claimed, was composed of Jews who ideologically and emotionally identified with the State of Israel. This group expressed its world-view during the Six Day War when its members showed a willingness to fight alongside the State of Israel. They were in his words 'Jewish nationalists' and would sooner or later leave Poland. The second group was made up of people who 'do not feel themselves to be either Poles or Jews. One cannot object to this. No one can impose a sense of national identity on those who do not feel it. Because of their cosmopolitan feelings, such people ought to avoid areas of work where the affirmation of national sentiment is essential.' The third group consisted of people for whom 'Poland is their only homeland ... many of whom, through their work and struggle, have faithfully served People's Poland and the cause of building socialism in our country'.[9] With this blatant antisemitism the party leadership sought to distract Polish citizens from the dismal economic situation and from demonstrations by students and workers across the country. But mainly the Jews served as a scapegoat in the internal struggle between two rival factions at the highest level of the Communist Party. By means of the anti-Jewish campaign, Gomułka wanted to signal to his political rival, the interior minister, Mieczysław Moczar, that he too would not shy away from using antisemitism to maintain his position. Moczar sought to strengthen his own position by removing Jews from their posts within the party and replacing them with his supporters. However, since Moscow continued to support Gomułka, there was not much chance for Moczar to realize his ambitions.[10] The antisemitic campaign went into high gear in March 1968 when students from the University of Warsaw demonstrated against the government for banning the production of Adam Mickiewicz's play *Dziady*. The main argument behind the ban was that the play had anti-Soviet tendencies, even though it had been written in the first half of the nineteenth century. According to the authorities, Jewish lecturers and students initiated the demonstrations. Gomułka could have opposed Moczar's media campaign against the Jews but instead allowed it to continue.[11] Among the leaders of the campaign was Bolesław Piasecki,[12] one of Moczar's supporters. Piasecki had been a leader of the National Radical Camp (Obóz Narodowo-Radykalny), an antisemitic nationalist organization in independent Poland, which sought to expel the Jews in the second half of the 1930s.[13] After 1944 he attempted to work with the new authorities.

While the Jews of Poland were facing this wave of antisemitism, Israeli society was focused on the aftermath of the Six Day War. The victory and subsequent conquest of Arab territories gave Israel confidence in its military capabilities and created a sense of euphoria in the country, brought an end to the recession in which the economy had been mired before the war, and strengthened diaspora Jewry's feelings of identification with Israel.[14] About 350,000 Jews from Western countries emigrated to Israel between 1967 and 1971.[15] The Israeli press was mainly concerned with the ramifications of the victory for Israel's international status and the economic consequences of the Six Day War. The severance of diplomatic relations between countries in the communist bloc and the State of Israel did not cloud their feelings of security and pride. The great changes experienced by Israel following the Six Day War meant that the major newspapers, *Maariv*, *Yediot aharonot*, and *Haaretz*, were not free to cover the events in Poland on a daily basis. In contrast, the newspapers published by the various parties paid more attention to the events in Poland. *Davar*—the newspaper of Mapai, the ruling party at the time—*Lamerhav*, and *Al hamishmar* were attentive to what was happening in Poland and devoted quite a few articles to the exodus of Jews.[16]

Daily newspapers in foreign languages were also published in Israel following the immigration of Holocaust survivors from central and eastern Europe in the 1950s and 1960s.[17] The first issue of the Polish-language newspaper *Nowiny i Kurier* appeared in 1957 following the merger of the two Polish-language newspapers—*Nowiny*, the organ of the Progressive (Liberal) Party, and the *Kurier*, owned by Mapai—which had competed with each other in the 1950s for the declining audience of Polish readers. *Nowiny i Kurier* initially had two editors: one from the Progressive Party and one from Mapai, but a legal battle led to Mapai taking exclusive control of it.[18]

The Gomułka Aliyah had increased the demand for a newspaper written in Polish, and these immigrants became its largest readership. Mapai's leaders saw *Nowiny i Kurier* as a means to deliver social and political messages and to help integrate the new immigrants into Israeli society. Along with presenting life in Israel in a positive light, *Nowiny i Kurier* also addressed the difficulties experienced by the new immigrants in the absorption process in Israel.[19] It was a small newspaper limited in scope and containing no more than six pages a day. The main part was devoted to events in Israel and around the world, and it contained few opinion pieces. In every issue the editor published a commentary on the main events of the day, and most of these short articles dealt with Israel's status in the world. Friday's issue had sixteen pages and included opinion pieces, a women's section, and a supplement for cultural matters, cinema, and theatre. Many articles in *Nowiny i Kurier* were published simultaneously or slightly earlier in Hebrew-language newspapers such as *Davar* or *Maariv*, although sometimes the Polish version of these articles was shorter.

Prior to the severance of diplomatic relations between Poland and Israel, the newspaper avoided criticism of the Polish United Workers' Party or relations between Jews and Poles in the past or the present. This trend expressed a deliberate policy of Israel's leadership that sought to maintain a normal relationship with Poland and therefore refrained from discussing issues that were 'problematic' for Poles. Poland was an important diplomatic conduit for maintaining relationships with the countries of the communist bloc. In the 1960s relations between Poland and Israel were good, and the Israeli foreign minister, Abba Eban, was even invited to visit Warsaw by Adam Rapacki, the Polish foreign minister.[20] However, the anti-Zionist and antisemitic campaign of 1968 changed this, and the restrictions on articles criticizing Poland or Polish–Jewish relations were lifted.

Apart from the editor-in-chief of *Nowiny i Kurier*, Shalom Yedidya, a native of Lwów (Lviv) who fled Poland at the outbreak of the Second World War and arrived in Palestine in 1940, all of the journalists on the newspaper were part of the Gomułka Aliyah.[21] One of the senior members was Aleksander Klugman, whose articles were also published in Mapai's Hebrew newspapers, especially *Davar*, *Lamerḥav*, and *Al hamishmar*. Klugman analysed the events in Poland in 1968 and did not spare the past and present Polish leadership. A native of Łódź, Klugman was a Holocaust survivor, and after the war he had held senior positions in the PZPR's official organs, including *Głos Pracy* and *Trybuna Mazowiecka*, where he served as secretary of the newspaper's party cell. Although he supported Gomułka's rise in 1956, he and his family experienced antisemitism. He emigrated to Israel in 1957 and was hired to work for a newspaper as soon as he arrived.[22]

After the severance of relations between Israel and the countries of the communist bloc, articles and news items were published almost daily that dealt with the anti-Zionist and antisemitic campaign of the Gomułka regime. Most of the news about what was happening in Poland reached the newspaper through foreign news agencies and the American press, because Israeli journalists were not allowed to enter Poland. Anti-Jewish measures and the political struggles at the top of the Polish government in 1968 and 1969 were also discussed.[23] *Nowiny i Kurier* charged Gomułka and Moczar with joint responsibility for the antisemitic campaign.[24]

The paper often emphasized the human aspects of the campaign and pointed to similarities between it and Nazi policy towards the Jews. Thus, the headline on 4 July 1968 read 'Mass Arrests, Suicides of Polish Jews and Drastic Orders against Those Intending to Leave Poland'. The article claimed that hundreds of Jews had been arrested. It also reported that the parents of university students were worried that their children had disappeared, fearing that they had been arrested or worse. About 5,000 elderly and disabled people of Jewish descent ceased to receive the subsistence allowance, effectively sentencing them to starvation, because the government banned the transfer of JDC funds to the Jewish population. The article emphasized that even American senators maintained that the Polish campaign recalled the antisemitism of the Nazi period.[25] The campaign did in fact lead to many imprisonments and personal tragedies.[26] The Ministry of the Interior prepared lists of people of Jewish ancestry who had been fired from their jobs, despite the fact that officially there was no obligation to disclose such information. People whose ancestors had converted to Christianity a generation or even two earlier were also harmed by the move and were forced to leave Poland.[27]

After restrictions were lifted, *Nowiny i Kurier* published articles analysing Poland's antisemitic policies, comparing them to the laws enacted between 1935 and 1939 that discriminated against Jews economically and socially, a period when various nationalist groups initiated acts of violence against Jews, and to the attitude of the Poles during the Holocaust.

In an article titled 'The Jew Is Out of the Bag', Klugman accused the Polish authorities of once again using Jews as a scapegoat in their internal political struggles.

He claimed that in Poland all the characteristics of the period of Nazi rule now existed except for the gas chambers and crematoria.[28] Drawing on Leon Pinsker, who in his pamphlet *Auto Emancipation* defined 'Judaeophobia' as an incurable mental illness,[29] Klugman described 'żydofobia', Poles' fear of Jews, as a disease that usually appeared in times of political and economic crisis in Poland. The Polish government's pointing a finger at the Jews in response to the student demonstrations in March 1968 was conclusive proof of the existence of this illness. The Poles were 'really sick people', Klugman wrote, 'and even a court would have excused them on the grounds of insanity'.[30] Gomułka's statement that Polish Jews were complicit in crimes against humanity allegedly committed by soldiers of the Israel Defense Forces during the Six Day War testified to the intensity of the disease.[31]

The writer and poet Teodor Hatalgi (Schneeberg) also presented Polish antisemitism as an incurable mental illness 'that follows no logical pattern'.[32] Hatalgi focused on physical violence as the main symptom of the disease, mentioning the pogrom in Przytyk in 1936, when Jewish stallholders were attacked by Polish rioters in the town's market square. He also mentioned the *numerus clausus*, the 'ghetto benches', and other policies implemented against Jewish students in institutions of higher learning in Poland between the two world wars, which also led to violence against students. During the Second World War the hatred was expressed in the murders perpetrated by the Narodowe Siły Zbrojne, a nationalistic and antisemitic organization founded in September 1942.[33] Hatalgi downplayed the help Poles gave to Jews during the Holocaust, claiming that, compared to the hostile treatment meted out by the Polish population to the Jews, such manifestations of help were meaningless. In the antisemitic policy of 1968 he saw the tragic culmination of a thousand years of Jewish existence in Poland.[34]

Yohanan (Jan) Bader, a Knesset member for the opposition Herut movement, shared these views concerning the reasons for antisemitism, and added that it also arose because Jews looked different. According to Bader, in the 1930s the Polish authorities attacked Jews because of their prominent presence among the population; however, the outbreak of antisemitism in 1968 testified that even when there was a minimal Jewish presence in Poland, hatred could still erupt.[35]

Nowiny i Kurier thus did not classify the outbreak of antisemitism in 1968 only as a political tool in the struggle for control of the Communist Party leadership. The policy was evidence that the Polish people were infected with an incorrigible antisemitism, and the history of Jews and Poles was proof of this.

Dropouts

Apart from discussing political developments in Poland, the reasons for antisemitism, and the sense of the tragic end of Jewish history in Poland, *Nowiny i Kurier* focused on the process of 'absorbing' immigrants into Israel, which was the responsibility of the Ministry of Aliyah and Immigrant Absorption, established in 1948. It helped immigrants from the moment they arrived in Israel, assisting them in finding jobs and housing. Hebrew courses were established in various places throughout the country, and university studies were made possible for young immigrants free of charge. The Organization of Polish Expatriates in Israel also tried to facilitate the social absorption of immigrants by creating social ties between families of immigrants and Israeli families of Polish descent.

Despite such efforts, there was the problem of 'dropouts': almost all of those leaving Poland passed through Vienna but did not end up in Israel. The Israeli press cited a number of reasons for this. Inter-married couples, for example, feared the complicated conversion processes of the Orthodox establishment in Israel. The requirement to enlist in the army also deterred many. In addition, the slanted coverage in the Polish press influenced the decision not to go to Israel. The Israeli press across the spectrum was unsparing in its criticism of those Jews who chose to go elsewhere. Critics used harsh words and the sense of insult was great: 'The news of the last remnants of Polish Jewry arriving in the West and refusing to immigrate to Israel sows salt in our wounds and reveals one of the tragic episodes of contemporary Jewish history', the leading Hebrew newspaper *Davar* wrote.[36] *Maariv* criticized those Jews leaving Poland for accepting large sums of money from Israel for their exit visas but then not coming to Israel.[37] It was suggested that Israel cut ties with them and stop courting them to come. One journalist wrote: 'they do not deserve to be taken care of—let them take care of themselves'.[38] *Haaretz* even speculated that 'most immigrants from Poland provided certain services for which they may have hoped to receive distinctions and rewards from Moscow, but they are afraid to come to Israel because they co-operated with the communist regime'.[39] Józef Muszkat, a jurist who emigrated to Israel in 1957, responded to these accusations, explaining that although the Jews served in the party apparatus during the Stalinist period, many of them changed their occupations in the 1960s and became an integral part of the Polish intelligentsia. *Nowiny i Kurier* found it difficult to deal with the Israeli public's criticism of Jews who did not come to Israel. The newspaper hoped that the latest wave of antisemitism had made it clear to Jews who remained in Poland that there was no other place in the world for them except Israel. But when it became apparent that most of them had chosen not to emigrate to Israel, an attempt was made to understand their motives. In a series of articles from Europe appearing under the headline 'An Israeli in Europe', Aleksander Klugman described complex encounters with Poland's remaining Jews. Klugman left for Vienna in autumn 1969 on behalf of the newspapers *Davar* and *Nowiny i Kurier* to meet with those leaving Poland.[40] His encounters with them were of personal significance and reminded him of the trauma he experienced during the Holocaust. Those in Vienna who had left Poland were compared to the Jews in the period of mass deportations from the Nazi ghettos: 'I did not think that I would see another deportation of Jews', he wrote from Vienna. 'Although this time it was a luxurious deportation . . . but the same frightened and scared eyes, the same feeling of terror, the same big question mark.'[41] As someone who emigrated to Israel in 1957, Klugman had a hard time understanding the Jews who chose not to go there. On the one hand, he reluctantly referred to the argument that the shaky security situation deterred them. On the other hand, he appreciated the claim that they had difficulty believing that life in Israel proceeded 'normally'. The Holocaust survivors and their children with whom he spoke feared that they would not be able to cope with the problematic security situation and many were afraid of another war.[42]

Together with the criticism, there was agreement among the journalists who covered the exodus of Jews from Poland that the activities of the Hebrew Immigrant Aid Society (HIAS) in Vienna was one of the main reasons why Jews preferred to migrate to European countries or the United States. Klugman shared this view, maintaining that HIAS encouraged Jews leaving Poland to stay in Europe.[43] 'In Vienna there was a fierce competition between HIAS and the Jewish Agency', he wrote. 'Who authorized this organization to compete with the Jewish Agency?'[44] He maintained that if HIAS had been active in Vienna when he left Poland during the Gomułka Aliyah, then many of those Jews would also not have emigrated to Israel.[45] Despite all the difficulties at home and abroad, the State of Israel was obliged to continue to do everything in its power to bring them to Israel and to facilitate their successful absorption.

Following tensions between the Jewish Agency and HIAS over the processing of Jews who had left Poland but remained in Vienna, it was agreed that HIAS would only deal with those who announced that they did not want to go to Israel. HIAS also undertook to remove those who did not want to emigrate to Israel from Vienna quickly in order that they not influence others.[46] In retrospect, it is difficult to determine whether HIAS's activity influenced the decisions of those leaving Poland.

Klugman was in favour of the economic assistance that immigrants from Poland received from the State of Israel and hoped that the benefits would persuade them to immigrate and facilitate their absorption in Israel.[47] At the same time, he was attentive to the criticism of readers of *Nowiny i Kurier* of the benefits given to the immigrants. An article entitled 'Who Is Eating Whose Bread?' tried to convince those who experienced economic and social difficulties after immigrating to Israel in the Gomułka Aliyah that they should accept the privileges given to the new immigrants because the State of Israel was now able to make available resources that were not available between 1956 and 1957.[48]

Re-emigrants

There were also immigrants who could not acclimatize to Israel and emigrated not long after arriving: they 'came, peeked, and turned their backs'.[49] In 1968 the State of Israel had only about two and a half million inhabitants. Professionals sometimes had a hard time finding a suitable job. The possibilities for absorbing academics into institutions of higher learning were limited as there were only three universities in Israel, the Hebrew University, which was founded in 1925, and Tel Aviv and Bar Ilan universities, which were founded in the mid-1950s. White-collar professionals, artists, and theatre and film professionals also had difficulty finding jobs suited to their skills and qualifications.[50]

Among the famous immigrants who left after a short stay were the historian Szymon Szechter (1920–83) and his secretary Nina Karsov (b. 1940); the sociologist Zygmunt Bauman (1925–2017) and his family; and the actress Ida Kamińska (1899–1980). Szechter and Karsov and Bauman and his family left Israel for England, while Ida Kamińska tried her luck in New York.

They all arrived in Israel in late 1968. When they landed at the airport, journalists were waiting to interview them, and expected to hear statements condemning Polish antisemitism. However, the newly arrived seemed to be afraid to speak openly, possibly so as not to harm those they had left behind. Bauman and Szechter emphasized that the Polish people were not antisemitic and that only the leadership had harassed the Jews. Szechter explained that the measures against the Jews were an expression of the political struggle between Gomułka and Moczar. According to him, the Poles opposed the Polish government's policy towards Jews.[51] Kamińska said that antisemitism was present everywhere in the world and stressed that her many friends in Poland were very upset about her departure.[52] Zygmunt Bauman openly stated that 'it was not Israel's force of attraction that brought [immigration] but the force of repulsion of people's disappointed hopes and expectations for the elimination of antisemitism under the communist regime. Most of the immigrants know why they left Poland but are not so sure why they came to Israel.'[53]

The departure of the historian Szymon Szechter and Nina Karsov from Poland received attention from the world media. Szechter had fought in the Red Army between 1941 and 1943 and was seriously wounded and lost his eyesight. He remained in the Soviet Union until 1957 and returned to Poland as part of the repatriation agreement between the two countries. In the 1960s he taught history at the University of Warsaw, where his specialism was the history of the Polish peasants' movement between the wars. His studies of the peasant strikes of 1937 to 1939 were refused publication. Karsov had jumped from the train carrying her to Treblinka and was seriously injured but rescued by Polish farmers, who adopted her. Until her arrest she did not know that she was Jewish, and upon her arrival in Israel a tree was planted on the Avenue of the Righteous Among the Nations at Yad Vashem for the woman who saved her life.[54] Szechter and Karsov were arrested in August 1966 following a search by the Polish security police of Karsov's apartment, which uncovered the draft of a book dealing with political trials in Poland between 1965 and 1966. Szechter was put under house arrest, and in October 1967 Karsov was sentenced to three years in prison. Following her imprisonment, the philosopher Bertrand Russell and Amnesty International fought for her release. The authorities allowed Szechter to go to Israel with his family. Szechter, however, refused to leave Poland while Karsov was still in prison. He divorced his wife, who had meanwhile emigrated to Israel with their children, and married Karsov in prison. After the release of Karsov on 5 September 1968, the two left for Israel. There they met Szechter's first wife and children.[55]

After a short time in Israel, Szechter and his family and Karsov left for London.

There, Szechter divorced Karsov and remarried his wife. In 1970 they founded Kontra, a publishing house for books in Polish. They first published an account of their experiences, *Monuments Are Not Loved*, and then a number of books by the anticommunist writer Józef Mackiewicz, including *The Road to Nowhere*.[56]

Over the years, Zygmunt Bauman became one of the most influential sociologists in the world. Immediately upon his arrival in Israel, Bauman told reporters at the airport: 'I was wrong, I am at the beginning of the road again.' He also added that 'I will never again live in any country in the world where I will belong to a national minority.'[57] In later interviews, he said he decided to leave Poland after seeing antisemitic propaganda films on Polish television on the eve of the 1968 calendar year.[58] Bauman was one of the professors at the University of Warsaw who were accused of subversive activities, including the student demonstrations in March 1968.[59] He was fired on 25 March 1968 and was then harassed over the telephone by former colleagues, who made use of antisemitic slurs and called on him to leave Poland. In the elevator of his building hung a notice stating that the Bauman family were 'enemies of the Polish people'.[60]

Bauman and his family decided to emigrate to Israel because family members had already emigrated there in 1957. Bauman emphasized when he arrived that he had chosen to live in Israel even though he had received tempting job offers from academic institutions around the world.[61] Upon arriving in Israel, he told reporters about his life: he was born in Poznań before the Second World War, and during the war his family fled to the Soviet Union. In 1944 he enlisted in the first Polish army organized in the Soviet Union during the war; he was wounded, but later returned to the army and was among the conquerors of Berlin. He joined the Polish Communist Party in 1945. As a young man he was a staunch communist and believed that communism would bring equality and an end to antisemitism.

Bauman did not tell reporters that during his military service he had served in the Political Education Department of the Polish Ministry of Internal Security, which followed Poles suspected of 'subversive activity' against the regime.[62] When confronted with the revelation of this in 2007, he explained that he had been naive and had believed in the righteousness of the things he did for the communist regime. Among other things, he said:

I bear full responsibility for that. At that time it seemed to me the right thing to do . . . Some choices in everybody's biography can be looked upon as wrong choices, except that it didn't seem to be a wrong choice at that time. When I was 19 years old I didn't know as much as I know now that I'm 82.[63]

He also claimed:

If the author of this lampoon [Bogdan Musiał, who alleged in a right-wing journal that Bauman had collaborated in the political cleansing of opponents of the regime] had really worked in the archives he'd probably discover that the files dedicated to me as the enemy are much thicker than the files dedicated to me as a collaborator. But I wouldn't expect balance from him . . . I feel more like a victim, really, in this case.[64]

He was dismissed from the Polish security services in 1953 after his father applied to the Israeli embassy for a visa. Bauman, consequently, severed ties with his father for a period of time.[65]

When he came to Israel, Bauman emphasized that, although he was a communist, he had never hidden his personal views. He said that during the 'Polish October' riots of 1956 he took an active part in organizing the student protest at the University of Warsaw.[66] After being appointed head of the Department of Sociology at the University of Warsaw in 1964 he became much sought after and was frequently invited to lecture at Western universities. He called for greater freedom of expression and supported colleagues who sought to attend international conferences but were refused by the university administration, and students who were reprimanded for their opinions. Thereafter, his articles and books were censored.[67]

Bauman quickly learned Hebrew and began teaching at Tel Aviv University. During his time in Israel, he gave lectures to the general public and published articles in the Israeli press on the social characteristics of Polish Jewry between 1957 and 1968.[68] However, in 1970 he decided to leave the country, because he found it difficult to connect with life in Israel. He opposed the continued control over the territories occupied during the Six Day War and argued: 'It is difficult to recuperate from the consequences of nationalism in a different nationalist atmosphere.'[69] In September 1970 Bauman moved with his family to England, where he worked at the University of Leeds until his death.

Hence, deportation from Poland did not interfere greatly with Szechter's or Bauman's professional and academic development. In contrast, for Ida Kamińska leaving Poland led to the decline of her career despite her continuing to act in Israel and the United States. The daughter of the Yiddish actress Ester Rachel Kamińska, Ida began her acting career at the age of 6, performing with her mother. During the Second World War she fled to the Soviet Union, returning to Poland in 1946. She then established a Jewish theatre in Łódź, which later became the Jewish State Theatre of Poland. She received many awards from the Polish authorities for her work in the arts.[70] Kamińska had run the Yiddish theatre in Warsaw for many years; 1967 was an important year for her, because she celebrated fifty years on the stage and the theatre moved to a new building which had just been completed. However, following the severance of diplomatic relations with Israel, the attitude of the authorities towards the theatre and its actors changed. They were under surveillance and banned from leaving Poland. The authorities even began interfering in the theatre's repertoire, which had previously comprised mostly Jewish and Israeli works, including such pieces as Ephraim Kishon's *Haketubah*.[71] Kamińska's turning point was the demand to stage an 'anti-Zionist' play.[72] She refused, thus ending her decades-long career as an actress and theatre manager. Except for the Yiddish theatre, all Jewish educational and cultural institutions in Poland were closed.

Kamińska left Poland on 23 August 1968. She stayed for a short time in Vienna and arrived in Israel on 8 September 1968. She said that without her engagement in the Yiddish theatre in Warsaw she could not find a reason to live in Poland and that therefore she had renounced her Polish citizenship. 'The fact that I am here speaks for itself', she told reporters who greeted her at the airport.[73] When asked what her plans were, she replied that she wanted to continue performing in Yiddish plays. And indeed, shortly after her arrival, she acted in leading roles in Yiddish plays in Israel.[74]

Kamińska's arrival was widely reported in the Israeli press. Cultural institutions and government officials expected her to remain in Israel and provide impetus to the Yiddish theatre in Israel.[75] After the establishment of the State of Israel, the Committee for the Review of Films and Plays imposed an official ban on performances in Yiddish. Despite this, the Yiddish Goldfaden Theatre was established in February 1951 in Tel Aviv. A conditional order prohibiting the staging of performances was issued against the theatre, which closed a few months later, mainly for economic reasons. When one of the theatre's founders, Nathan Wolfowitz, violated the order and staged Moshe Gershenzon's *Hershele ostropoler* he was sued. At the same time, despite the ban, up to half a million people watched the Yiddish actors Shimon Dzigan and Yisroel Schumacher in Israel in the early 1960s.[76]

Upon Kamińska's arrival, an evening of reading and acting was held by the Public Culture and Arts Council of the Ministry of Education in Habima Hall.[77] At a festive reception held in her honour about a week later in Tel Aviv, Kamińska said that she did not feel like a guest in Israel and that Israel was her home. She added: 'the wounds that have been inflicted on me recently will heal faster here than anywhere else'.[78] The Jewish Agency and government officials promised to help her create a Yiddish theatre and to let her use the Nachmani Hall in Tel Aviv, which had previously been the location of the Kameri Theatre and now stood empty.[79] The cultural correspondent of *Davar* hoped that Kamińska's presence would cause any opposition to plays in Yiddish being performed in Israel to be forgotten and that she would be able to gather around her Yiddish actors who had difficulty finding their place in Israeli culture. 'Times have changed', wrote *Davar*, 'the nation is growing up and does not need zealous protection of the revived national language.'[80] The expectation was that Kamińska would be able to 'erect a monument to the culture of the people who perished in the Holocaust'.[81] But, after it became known that she had also explored the possibility of performing in New York, the press began to criticize her, and some actors boycotted her reception because she did not explicitly say that she intended to stay in Israel.[82] Journalist Tamar Avidar resented that 'we [Israelis] have to compete with the Americans',[83] adding that Kamińska was 'nothing more than an elderly actress who desperately needs the love of the audience'.[84] 'She was offered three halls and financial support in Israel and she's still vacillating.'[85] At the same time, there were those who understood the quandary:

There is not enough of an audience for a great actress like Kamińska ... She knows very well that there is no place in Israel for a high-level artistic theatre [in Yiddish] ... What do you want from Ida Kamińska? That at her age she should go to *ulpan* [an institute for intensive Hebrew-language courses] and learn the language? ... She would not do so.[86]

Despite the criticism, or perhaps because of it, Kamińska decided to move to New York. However, the Jewish American audience was not enthusiastic, and reviews were quite reserved.[87] *Nowiny i Kurier* shared the view that Kamińska had made a 'mistake' in moving to New York.[88] The paper also drew conclusions from the way Kamińska was received in New York: Israel was indeed a small country, but it was home. Kamińska's story proved once again that the Jews' place was in Israel even though the big world beckoned to the talented.[89]

In 1975 Kamińska decided to return to Israel. She tried to establish a new Yiddish theatre called Yidish Kunsteater with the actor Joseph Buloff. It was supported by the Ministry of Education and the Jewish Agency, and most of the actors were immigrants from the Soviet Union. However, the attempt did not succeed, and the theatre closed its doors not long after it was established. The local media chose not to forget her decision not to establish a Yiddish theatre in Israel in 1968. According to *Davar*:

> Her immigration from Poland to Israel has taken seven years and she has been granted immigrant rights to housing and employment and more . . . but we do not resent the benefits she will be given . . . she deserves everything . . . she deserves it for keeping the embers alive in the years since the Holocaust and the destruction of Polish Jewry . . . When we lovingly offer you a flower at the 'premiere' and you are honestly told: 'Welcome'—please say at least one word: 'Sorry'.[90]

Conclusion

Nowiny i Kurier presented to its readers various aspects of the antisemitic campaign in 1968 and its consequences. In contrast to the early years of its existence, when it avoided discussing the charged issue of Polish–Jewish relations, the paper presented the exodus of Jews in 1968 as a tragic end to a thousand years of Jewish existence on Polish soil and described Polish antisemitism as an incurable mental illness comparable to Nazi antisemitism. On the personal plane, *Nowiny i Kurier* found it difficult to cope with the choice of most Polish emigrants not to go to Israel, as well as the criticism of this choice in the Israeli press. The complex personal dimension of emigration to Israel is reflected in articles about the well-known Jewish immigrants who were forced to interrupt successful careers in Poland and start a new life. Unlike the Hebrew-language newspapers, the Polish newspaper refrained from using harsh words against the Jews who chose not to emigrate to Israel. But its conclusion that Israel was the only place in the world where Jews could be safe was identical to that of the Hebrew newspapers.

Translated from the Hebrew by Sharon Levinas

Notes

1 When the communist regime collapsed in 1989, between 5,000 and 10,000 Jews remained in Poland, some of whom concealed their Jewish origins. In March 2018, at a ceremony marking the fiftieth anniversary of the persecution and deportation campaign of 1968, the

Polish president, Andrzej Duda, apologized on behalf of his country for the events of that time (A. Stankowski, 'How Many Polish Jews Survived the Holocaust?', in F. Tych and M. Adamczyk-Garbowska (eds.), *Jewish Presence in Absence: The Aftermath of the Holocaust in Poland 1944–2010* (Jerusalem, 2014), 205–16; D. Stola, 'Jewish Emigration from Communist Poland: The Decline of Polish Jewry in the Aftermath the Holocaust', *East European Jewish Affairs*, 47 (2017), 169–88; J. Eisler, 'Jews, Antisemitism, Emigration', *Polin*, 21 (2009), 37–61).

2 This move was dictated to Poland and the countries of the communist bloc by the Soviet Union (Y. Govrin, *Yaḥasei yisra'el im artsot mizraḥ eiropah me'et nitukam bishenat 1967 ad ḥidusham bashanim 1989–1991* (Jerusalem, 2009), 80–7).

3 Stola, 'Jewish Emigration from Communist Poland', 181–2.

4 A. Plocker, 'Artsot moledet: nituk hayaḥasim bein yisra'el lepolin, yuni 1967', *Yisra'el*, 20 (2002), 181–97; ead., 'Yehudim kegayis ḥamishi: hamasa ha'anti-tsiyoni bepolin, 1967–1968', *Zemanim*, 116 (2011), 90–101.

5 A. Dolev, 'Ad hayehudi ha'aḥaron', *Maariv*, 13 June 1969, p. 11.

6 Stola, 'Jewish Emigration from Communist Poland'.

7 A. Klugman, 'Lamah hem lo rotsim la'alot', *Davar*, 1 Jan. 1969, p. 3. In an interview with a Jewish student who came to Vienna, Klugman asked: 'If you want to get to Denmark, why did you take Israeli money in the Dutch embassy?' He claimed he did not receive a satisfactory answer (A. Klugman, 'Yetsiat polin 1969', *Lamerḥav*, 30 Nov. 1969, p. 3).

8 'Przemówienie na spotkaniu z warszawskim aktywem partyjnym wygłoszone 19 marca 1968' (8 Apr. 2013): mPolska24 website, visited 18 Jan 2022; see D. Stola, *Kampania antysyjonistyczna w Polsce 1967–1968* (Warsaw, 2000), 29–46.

9 'Przemówienie na spotkaniu z warszawskim aktywem partyjnym wygłoszone 19 marca 1968'; see Stola, *Kampania antysyjonistyczna w Polsce 1967–1968*, 115–35. See 'Żydowscy studenci odegrali ważną rolę w demonstracjach', *Nowiny i Kurier*, 20 Mar. 1968, p. 1; 'Mashkifim bevarshah gomulka ne'evak al ma'amado bashilton', *Lemerḥav*, 21 Mar. 1968, p. 1; 'Hatsharto shel gomulka', *Lemerḥav*, 27 Mar. 1968, p. 1; Y. Gutman, 'Perek aḥaron: hayehudim bepolin aḥarei hamilḥamah', *Yalkut moreshet*, 33 (1982), 62–102; 34 (1982), 121–50; J. Eisler, *Marzec 1968: Geneza, przebieg, konsekwencje* (Warsaw, 1991), 360–3.

10 D. Stola, 'Fighting against the Shadows: The Anti-Zionist Campaign of 1968', in R. Blobaum (ed.), *Antisemitism and Its Opponents in Modern Poland* (Ithaca, NY, 2004), 284–300; M. Mushkat, *Philo-Semitic and Anti-Jewish Attitudes in Post-Holocaust Poland* (New York, 1992), 225–30.

11 D. Stola, 'Anti-Zionism as a Multipurpose Policy Instrument: The Anti-Zionist Campaign in Poland, 1967–1968', *Journal of Israeli History*, 25 (2006), 284–300.

12 On Piasecki, see M. Kunicki, 'The Nationalist Right under Communism: Bolesław Piasecki and the Polish Communists, 1944–1979', in D. Kusá and S. Moses (eds.), *Aspects of European Political Culture* (Vienna, 2005), 59–76.

13 A. Klugman 'ONR – co to znaczy', *Nowiny i Kurier*, 12 July 1968, p. 4; M. Goldfarb 'Polityczne tło najnowszych wydarzeń w Polsce', *Nowiny i Kurier*, 14 Feb. 1969, p. 7.

14 S. Della Pergola, 'Ukhlusiyat yisra'el ba'asor hashelishi: megamot veheksherim', in A. Halamish and O. Shif (eds.), *Yisra'el 67–77: hemshekhiyut umifneh* (Beer Sheva, 2017), 185–220.

15 Ibid.

16 On the history of the Israeli press, see D. Caspi and Y. Limor, *Hametavekhim: emtsa'ei hatikshoret beyisra'el 1948–1990* (Tel Aviv, 1995).

17 M. Naor, 'Hatikshoret', in H. Yablonka and T. Tsameret (eds.), *Ha'asor hashelishi 1968–1978* (Jerusalem, 2000), 401–15.

18 'The Two Polish-Language Newspapers Merged', *Davar*, 16 Nov. 1958, p. 4. In October 1971 a four-page Hebrew supplement was added to *Nowiny i Kurier* and other Mapai newspapers in Yiddish, Hungarian, French, and Romanian.
19 E. Kossewska, 'Mapai and the Polish-Language Press in Israel: The Brief Life of Kurier', *Gal-ed*, 23 (2012), 77–96. On Mapai's control of foreign-language newspapers in Israel, see 'Hakeisarut halo'azit shel mapai', *Haaretz*, 20 Feb. 1958, p. 2.
20 Kossewska, 'Mapai and the Polish-Language Press in Israel'.
21 Ibid.
22 See 'Itonai yisre'eli meshiv legomulka', *Davar*, 21 May 1968, p. 6; K. Shabtai, 'Hayehudi she'ala lakotrot', *Davar*, 14 June 1968, p. 11. Klugman published a number of books dealing with Polish–Jewish relations. In 1968 he published *Obrachunki z Polską*, which was banned from distribution in Poland.
23 'Wszystkiemu winni znów syjoniści', *Nowiny i Kurier*, 15 Sept. 1968, p. 3.
24 A. Kowalski, 'Trzy porażki Mieczysława Moczara', *Nowiny i Kurier*, 10 Jan. 1969, p. 9; id., 'Partyjny awans Moczara', *Nowiny i Kurier*, 11 July 1969, p. 3.
25 'Masowe areszty i samobójstwa Żydów polskich', *Nowiny i Kurier*, 4 July 1968, p. 1.
26 'Trudności emigrantów żydowskich w Polsce', ibid., 26 Jan. 1969, p. 3.
27 Gutman, 'Perek aharon'. Polish students questioned by the police were coerced into cooperating with the argument that it was not proper for a true Pole to associate with or protect Jews and that contact with Jews was forbidden.
28 A. Klugman, 'Wyszło żydło z worka', *Nowiny i Kurier*, 17 July 1969, p. 4.
29 L. Pinsker, *Autoemancipation! Mahnruf an seine Stammesgenossen von einem russischen Juden* (Berlin, 1882); Eng. trans.: *Auto-Emancipation: An Appeal to His People by a Russian Jew*, trans. D. S. Blondheim (New York, 1906).
30 Klugman, 'Wyszło żydło z worka'.
31 Ibid.
32 T. Hatalgi, 'Epilog tysiąclecia', *Nowiny i Kurier*, 4 July 1969, p. 9.
33 Ibid.
34 Ibid.
35 Y. Bader, 'Żydzi i Polacy', *Nowiny i Kurier*, 6 July 1969, p. 8.
36 Y. Pninger, 'She'erit yehudei polin vehitlabetutam', *Davar*, 7 Nov. 1969, p. 10.
37 A. Dolev, 'Ad hayehudi ha'aharon', *Maariv*, 13 June 1969, p. 11.
38 Y. Mikhalski, 'Yotse'ei polin einam geru'im yoter', *Lamerhav*, 5 Dec. 1969, p. 9.
39 N. Lavi, *Haaretz*, 7 Nov. 1969.
40 A. Klugman, 'Czy machnąć ręką na Żydów polskich?', *Nowiny i Kurier*, 21 Nov. 1969, p. 7.
41 A. Klugman, 'Słoń w składzie porcelany', *Nowiny i Kurier*, 7 Dec. 1969, p. 3; see also Klugman, 'Yetsiat polin 1969'.
42 Klugman, 'Czy machnąć ręką na Żydów polskich?'; id., 'Słoń w składzie porcelany'.
43 A. Klugman, 'HIAS, czyli utrwalenie galutu', *Nowiny i Kurier*, 26 Oct. 1969, p. 3; see also id., 'Alilot al aharonei hayotse'im mepolin', *Davar*, 25 Nov. 1969, p. 5.
44 Klugman, 'Alilot al aharonei hayotse'im mepolin'.
45 Ibid.
46 A. Klugman, 'Hias mehabel ba'aliyah leyisra'el', *Lamerhav*, 3 Dec. 1969, p. 3.
47 A. Klugman, 'Kto czyj chleb zjada', *Nowiny i Kurier*, 14 Feb. 1969, p. 4.
48 Ibid.

49 A. Dolev, 'Ad hayehudi ha'aḥaron', *Ma'ariv*, 13 June 1969, p. 11.
50 'Ha'aliyah bein milḥemet sheshet hayamim lemilḥḥemet yom hakipurim': Jewish Agency Archive website, 'Aliyah behistoryah', visited 13 June 2021.
51 'Gizanut omer profesor shekhter', *Davar*, 24 Jan. 1969, p. 5.
52 'Ida kaminska: bekarov ehyeh beyisra'el', *Lamerḥav*, 27 Aug. 1968, p. 2.
53 H. Landau, 'Be'ayot habitaḥon veha'aliyah bekenes anshei ruaḥ "betsavta"', *Al hamishmar*, 16 Jan. 1969, p. 3.
54 'Nina Karsow chce zasadzić drzewo imienia swej przybranej matki', *Nowiny i Kurier*, 22 Jan. 1969, p. 2; 'Profesor Szechter o Ninie Karsow', *Nowiny i Kurier*, 9 Jan. 1969, pp. 3, 6.
55 'Profesor Szymon Szechter i Nina Karsow przyjechali do Izraela', *Nowiny i Kurier*, 20 Jan. 1969, p. 1; 'Nina Karsow chce zasadzić drzewo imienia swej przybranej matki', *Nowiny i Kurier*, 22 Jan. 1969, p. 2; 'Hateragedyah bemishpaḥat prof shekhter ba'ah lesiyumah hatov', *Davar*, 29 Apr. 1970, p. 3.
56 N. Karsov and S. Szechter, *Nie kocha się pomników* (London, 1970); Eng. trans.: *Monuments Are Not Loved*, trans. P. Stevenson (London, 1970); J. Mackiewicz, *Droga donikąd* (London, 1981); see Wydawnictwo Kontra website, visited 13 June 2021.
57 D. Goldstein, 'Zbłądziłem, jestem znów na początku drogi', *Nowiny i Kurier*, 19 Sept. 1968, p. 3.
58 M. Burzyk and M. Jędrzejek, 'Wszystkie życia Zygmunta Baumana', *Znak*, 2018, no. 1, pp. 6–17. The couple were invited to a dinner with friends to celebrate the Christian New Year. During the meal, the television was switched on to watch a series of skits usually shown on Polish television at that time of year (*szopka noworoczna, kabaret noworoczny*). One of these skits involved a monstrous doll with a 'Jewish' nose, which climbed onto a globe of the world and stuck its hands into it (ibid.).
59 'Iton polani ma'ashim et prof bauman be'aḥarayut lamehumot', *Lamerḥav*, 9 Feb. 1970, p. 2.
60 T. Kwaśniewski, 'Bauman: Dałem się uwieść', *Magazyn Wyborczej Wolna Sobota*, 28 June 2013: *Gazeta Wyborcza* website, accessed 16 Dec. 2021.
61 Burzyk and Jędrzejek, 'Wszystkie życia Zygmunta Baumana'.
62 'Sztandar Młodych atakuje prof. Zygmunta Baumana', *Nowiny i Kurier*, 17 Sept. 1968.
63 Kwaśniewski, 'Bauman: Dałem się uwieść'.
64 A. Edemariam, 'Professor with a Past' (28 Apr. 2007): *The Guardian* website, visited 18 Jan. 2022.
65 Following the opening of Poland's national archives after the fall of communism, documents were revealed that testified to his tenure in the Polish Ministry of Internal Security, where he was responsible for exposing and denouncing those who were considered opponents of the regime.
66 Edemariam, 'Professor with a Past'.
67 Goldstein, 'Zbłądziłem, jestem znów na początku drogi'.
68 A. Magen, 'Sotsyologyah vesotsyalism beḥayei yom yom', *Lamerḥav*, 31 Jan. 1969, pp. 4, 10; Z. Bauman, 'Hapitron hasofi, 1968', *Lamerḥav*, 14 Feb. 1969, p. 6; S. Gal, 'Ha'antishemiyut bepolin neshek bama'avak al hashilton', *Al hamishmar*, 10 Feb. 1969, p. 3; Landau, 'Be'ayot habitaḥon veha'aliyah bekenes anshei ruaḥ "betsavta"'.
69 S. Plocker, 'Re'ayon im bauman al nose'im shonim', *Al hamishmar*, 2 Apr. 1969, p. 11. During his last visit to Israel, in an interview with Avner Shapira, he claimed that 'there is not much difference between my feelings today and, alas, the feelings I felt more than forty years ago' (A. Shapira, 'Aḥarei shedaḥah peniyah palestinit lehaḥrim et yisra'el zigmunt bauman tokef et hakibush' (17 Feb. 2013): *Haaretz* website, visited 16 Dec. 2021).

70 'Yovelah shel ida kaminska', *Lamerḥav*, 19 Sept. 1967, p. 2.
71 The Polish government's interference in the repertoire of the Jewish theatre in Warsaw was revealed in late 1967 when Henryk Grynberg, one of the theatre's actors, sought political asylum in the United States ('Saḥkan yehudi bikesh miklat be'artsot haberit', *Davar*, 31 Dec. 1967, p. 1).
72 B. Adler, 'Ida kaminska: hamasakh yarad al yahadut polin', *Hatsofeh*, 22 Sept. 1968, p. 21.
73 'Ha'uvdah she'ani poh medaberet be'ad atsmah', *Davar*, 8 Sept. 1968, p. 4.
74 Advertisement for Jacob Gordin, 'Mirele efros', *Nowiny i Kurier*, 18 Sept. 1968, p. 6.
75 E. Rostal, 'Pomyłka Idy Kamińskiej', *Nowiny i Kurier*, 12 Dec. 1969, p. 3.
76 See R. Rozhanski, 'Ha'omnam "safah zarah vetsoremet"? lishe'elat yaḥaso shel ben-guryon leyidish le'aḥar hasho'ah', *Iyunim bitekumat yisra'el*, 15 (2005), 463–82: 468.
77 Adler, 'Ida Kaminska'.
78 'Ida kaminska: beiti beyisra'el', *Al hamishmar*, 17 Sept. 1968, p. 6.
79 'Ulam naḥmani huvtaḥ le'ida kaminska', *Al hamishmar*, 13 Oct. 1968, p. 12.
80 H. Novak, 'Levateya shel saḥakanit', *Davar*, 20 Sept. 1968, p. 11.
81 Ibid.
82 T. Avidar, 'Habayit kan avodah bamakom shebo yutsu hatena'im hatovim beyoter', *Maariv*, 18 Sept. 1968, p. 10.
83 Ibid.
84 Ibid.
85 Ibid.
86 D. Lazar, 'Haniḥu le'ida', *Maariv*, 26 Sept. 1968, p. 9.
87 Ibid.
88 Rostal, 'Pomyłka Idy Kamińskiej'.
89 Ibid.
90 A. Canarti, 'Ida kaminska ḥazerah ke'olah', *Davar*, 14 Mar. 1975, p. 20.

5. FROM THE END OF COMMUNISM TO TODAY

Home as a Place of No Return
Journeys to Poland in the Writings of Child Survivors and the Second and Third Generations

EFRAIM SICHER

Tancred's Wound

In her rereading of Freud's and Lacan's psychoanalytical theories of trauma, *Unclaimed Experience*, Cathy Caruth proposed that the meaning of trauma—which is literally a psychic wound—should be sought in the memory of the wound, through which the voice of the victim speaks, thus going further than Freud in his exposition of what he called, in *Beyond the Pleasure Principle*, 'traumatic neurosis'.[1] Analysing the traumatic experience of battlefield survivors, Freud illustrated the compulsive repetition of painful events, sometimes in an uncanny or seemingly fated manner, with the story of Tancred in Tasso's *Gerusalemme liberata*, who unwittingly kills his beloved, Clorinda, and then wounds her spirit, which then speaks out in pain. For Freud, the story illustrated the repetition of trauma that occurs passively, rather than actively.[2] Caruth contentiously extended the parable of Tancred's wounding of his beloved to a necessary wounding that enables the voice of the victim to emerge in a secondary traumatic memory. Since Clorinda is dead, it is now, in a sense, Tancred's wound. To revisit the traumatic past, whether voluntarily or unconsciously, is to feel the pain and suffering through a second wounding which makes available previously inaccessible knowledge. 'For while the story of Tancred, the repeated thrusts of his unwitting sword, and the suffering he recognizes through the voice he hears represents the experience of an individual traumatized by his own past—the repetition of his own trauma as it shapes his life—the wound that speaks is not precisely Tancred's own but the wound, the trauma of another.'[3] It is the voice of the Other within the psychic revisiting of trauma that speaks out in pain. This is an encounter with the revenant haunting the psyche since the original wound, which paradoxically gives voice to the trauma and inflicts renewed pain, although the traumatic event occurred many years earlier, since when time has transformed the landscape and obliterated the past.

This chapter looks at such returns to the traumatic past as they are narrated in memoir and film or imagined in fiction and art. Passing from lived memory to history and literature, the transmission of the traumatic past revisits the scene of the wound, at the risk of repeating the pain of the wound, in order to work through trauma and to complete the process of mourning for relatives, whose story may sometimes be fragmentary or unknown but who hold the key to the narrator's personal biography and sense of self. Proceeding from child survivors to the second and third generations after the Holocaust, I will show how the motivation to go back 'there', to the place of the wounding, has not diminished. On the contrary, this impossible return raises topical questions of individual and collective identity, the instability of narrative, and the unreliability of memory. In postmodern novels such as Jonathan Safran Foer's *Everything Is Illuminated* (2002), the story of an assimilated American Jew's quest for his family's past in Ukraine, the truth is elusive and can perhaps never be fully known. However, the exhaustive telling and questioning of the story, as in Claude Lanzmann's *Shoah* (1985), is itself a purposeful return that gives the past meaning, even if the 'place' which the camp survivor Szymon Srebnik identifies in the opening of the film is for many returnees blank or erased, a non-place of memory.

Child survivors of the Holocaust imagine 'going back' to Poland and sometimes do indeed return, as Shimon Redlich has done in his historical investigation of his home town, *Together and Apart in Brzezany*, which is also an intimate childhood memoir, and Katke Reszke's film *Shimon's Returns*, which documents Redlich's return trips to Poland.[4] As a historian, Redlich investigated his own story of being hidden as a child together with his family by a Ukrainian woman and a Polish man, who (thanks to Redlich) were recognized as Righteous Among the Nations by Yad Vashem. The historical research meant going back to Eastern Galicia and confronting local Ukrainian villagers (including some who may have collaborated in or witnessed the massacre of Jews). In *Together and Apart in Brzezany*, Redlich emphasizes the delicate multi-ethnic composition of the local population before the war—Poles, Jews, and Ukrainians (in that order). 'Eastern Galicia was at a crossroads of peoples, cultures, religions, and civilizations.'[5] The Ukrainians felt oppressed by the official policies of Polonization and colonization; the Jews were largely assimilated. Redlich was brought up speaking Polish, although the adults spoke Yiddish among themselves. In *Shimon's Returns*, Redlich is seen being welcomed by the descendants and relatives of the villagers who sheltered his family and those who remembered his family. Returning to his old haunts in Łódź, where his family lived after the war before migrating to Israel in 1950, Redlich locates his family's former apartment. He interviews passers-by to get an impression of the city's cosmopolitanism, and re-enacts his love for a woman during his years in Łódź by riding in a horse-drawn carriage with her. The message is a positive one, of pre-war multi-ethnic coexistence and post-war adjustment, rather than a flat picture of antisemitism and trauma.

Return is an act of repetition, which can have both debilitating and therapeutic effects. Redlich previously re-enacted his wartime trauma in the film *Undzere kinder* (1948), featuring the well-known Jewish comedians Shimon Dzigan and Yisroel Schumacher, in which he played not his own story but that of a boy who hides during a round-up, a role for which he had to learn to speak Yiddish. Yet in *Shimon's Returns* there is a further repetition of traumatic memory when Redlich encounters some men in Nazi stormtrooper uniforms who turn out to be local enthusiasts displaying their Second World War motorcycle and sidecar on a busy street. Although not identified as neo-Nazis, these men in their thirties and forties claim they are representing a history that must not be forgotten. At one point Redlich puts on a helmet and tries out the seat on the motorcycle. Later he says that he does not know what made him do this, but it seems to me pretty obvious that the former victim is fascinated by the empowered position of his father's murderers. He needs to return to the place of traumatic memory in order to mourn his father, although his burial place in the unmarked mass grave can only be known by an act of divination, which a Jewish friend does in the Jewish cemetery, where a goat is calmly grazing and children are happily playing football. Returning completes the work of mourning, even though personal memory may be incomplete or fragmentary. Yet at the same time the return establishes a *lieu de mémoire* to which the return is made and which enables the transmission of memory.[6] Returning allows Redlich to reclaim subjecthood as a carrier of memory, an Israeli historian who experienced a history in which he was marked for annihilation. Nobody was supposed to survive to tell the story: this was meant to be a history (as Dori Laub points out) to which there were no witnesses.[7]

Searching for the Lost *Symbolon*

In Aleida Assmann's analysis of autobiographical memoirs, the reflexive *mich-Gedächtnis*, 'me-memory', brings together the memory externalized in objects and places in a process of re-identification with self that is triggered by such return journeys when the lost object or place is reunited in embodied memory with the bereaved. This is similar to the Greek term *symbolon*, which refers to two halves of a token that are brought together.[8] Here the *symbolon* is fractured in the total destruction of the Holocaust and given wholeness when reunited with the lost memory object, a corporealized metaphor for the child's loss of his father and recovery of his story together with his father's corpse. In Paweł Łoziński's film *Birthplace*, the Polish Jewish writer Henryk Grynberg returns to Radoszyna, where he grew up before the family was forced into hiding, in order to confront the local villagers and to search for where his father is buried.[9] While some of the older residents appear ready to talk, they are mostly locked in fear and shame, still afraid of retribution, though one or two openly denounce the greed and selfishness of their neighbours' betrayal and treachery during the German occupation. Digging in a field, Grynberg finds a milk bottle, the lost *symbolon* which is the object identifying his father, a milkman killed by a Polish acquaintance who coveted his two cows. Grynberg (who defected to the United States in 1967 and has no nostalgic regrets for leaving the country which effectively disowned him and his writing) returned to post-communist Poland and to his memories of hiding in the Polish countryside in a dark, lice-infested pit in the woods. Unlike Redlich's experience of going back and being recognized by those who helped save his family, Grynberg gets a cold, sometimes hostile, reception. Grynberg is the interlocutor from outside, but also the revenant silently indicting the villagers, who clearly thought the past was safely buried. The distance of the camera only intensifies the disturbing lack of empathy of the witnesses towards the victims. Exceptionally, one woman cries when she recognizes Henryk and calls him by his childhood name, 'Heniuś'. She remembers, word for word, what Grynberg's mother said while in their house one night during the war—hers is the only kind face in the film. Whether the interviewees are lying or telling the truth, Grynberg remains impassive, not showing any emotional reaction. Some knew his family very well, both before and during the occupation, and relate in detail what he (as a small boy of 6 or 7) could barely remember, but they are unwilling to tell the whole story, preserving their community of silence and showing little compassion for their former Jewish neighbours. They defend their behaviour by repeating again and again how risky it was to help Jews.[10] A few villagers help locate the burial place of Grynberg's father and excavate the frozen ground as if they were digging for potatoes. The film's title, *Birthplace*, refers to the father's tomb, which is also the womb from which the son literally emerges holding his father's skull, thus giving birth to his memory and identity as he returns to his biological and geographical origins. Now the source of traumatic memory, the psychic wound, is laid open.

Grynberg has recorded his mixed feelings about making the film, which he feared would be too painfully personal, yet he decided: 'I had a duty to fulfil towards my father who lay there in a field while his murderer sneered and defiled the place.'[11] Yet he realized also that the young film director and his crew could help him work through the loss of a dear friend and help him bury his father in a Jewish grave.[12] The film was unscripted, and Grynberg simply followed the directions he was given, unaware of whom he was going to meet and what they were going to say.[13] He relates that at one point he was asked to speak to someone off-camera so that nobody could hear:

An unshaven man my age came and said he had seen as a child my father lying there killed and next to him a one-litre bottle stained with milk and he remembered that when they buried him they threw the bottle in. 'When you find the bottle you'll know it's there.' And we found it, with a white smudge of the milk still in it.[14]

After re-burying his father in the Warsaw Jewish cemetery, Grynberg took the bottle home with him to America, the last thing his father held and the only object from the past he had. The film makes for difficult viewing, but it was screened around the world, putting the murderers on public trial.[15] Grynberg concludes his book-length essay, *Inheritance*, with: 'I cannot forgive. I'm not entitled to. Let the murderers forgive, if they could . . . I sensed a chilly shudder facing evil. However, in some eyes, I find some warmth as well. It is essential for life.'[16]

'Like Orpheus', comments Katarzyna Jerzak, Grynberg 'turns back—against the prohibition to look back. "Do not turn around," say not the gods but the living, for whom the past is too terrible—why dwell on it, why raise ghosts?'[17] Yet like an inverse Cassandra, Grynberg's prophetic gaze is fixed on the doomed past.[18] In the Israeli French psychoanalyst and artist Bracha Ettinger's Eurydice series (1992–2006) and her exhibition *Facing History* (Pompidou Centre, 2010), the victim's face becomes a non-face, and our facing of a traumatic history becomes a de-facing.[19] Ettinger based her artwork on a Nazi photograph of naked women at Mizocz, near Równe (Rivne), in 1942, herded into a pit before being murdered by the Einsatzgruppen. Ettinger transforms this perpetrator's view of the mass killing of naked women into the gaze of Eurydice, which Ettinger uses to present both the absent and present trauma in her visual return to Poland, a return which is also a wounding, as in Caruth's interpretation of the Tancred parable: after Orpheus travels to Hades to get a reprieve for Eurydice, he looks back at his wounded beloved whom he thus condemns to the underworld for eternity.[20] As Marianne Hirsch observes, 'the underside of return [is] the fear that violence will be repeated', that is, as in Orpheus's backward look, 'return will prove to be deadly'.[21] The horrific images are the opposite of a 'home' to which one wishes to return. Yet a blurred image of the baby held by one of the victims going to their death is also a mirror-image of the artist's embodied return to her prenatal past (the artist's own portrait as a baby is superimposed on the photograph of her family walking in a Łódź street in 1937). This superimposed image, like many of the grainy faces washed over in ink and charcoal, reproduced as interrupted photocopies, are the imprints of the psyche's wounds in Ettinger's parents' untold story. Ettinger explores what she calls a 'matrixial' sphere outside the phallus, at and beyond a borderline, free of the opposition of male and female, that addresses the traumatic violence and restores subjectivity, as well as compassion.[22]

These washed-out, overlaid images are disturbing reminders of the shadows of the archive. These are traces of events that collapse the safe distance between the present and the past, to which one cannot return without fear and guilt, and they resist the collusion in erasure of both Jewish and sexual difference. This is the wound of what Ettinger calls the 'm/Other.' By cutting and enlarging these photographs that have become iconic in collective memories of the Holocaust, then having scarlet dyes bleed through them, Ettinger works against their painful nudity, their reduction to non-corporeal non-being, and relocates the aesthetic in trauma. She invites us to return to the traumatic scene and, through affectivity, reclaim these mothers as the artist's and our own.[23]

The Beautiful Green Killing Fields

Nostalgia, according to Svetlana Boym, is a sentiment of loss and displacement, but it is also a romance with one's own phantasy.[24] It is a double exposure or superimposition of two images—of home and absence, of past and present, of dream and everyday life. The return to Poland results from a complex and deeply troubled nostalgia for a lost homeland, for a buried birthplace. Many survivors undertake the unending odyssey to that place of origin in their minds until it grows into a mythical landscape of a fairy-tale childhood in a destroyed world that can never be revisited. The Israeli novelist Aharon Appelfeld imagined a fictional childhood in his native

Bukovina in several of his novels before actually returning there. Speaking of Bukovina as a 'buried homeland', Appelfeld explains one reason he delayed making the trip home:

I didn't want to put the work of my imagination to the test of reality. Over the years, I had built a village of my own, with peasants and Jews of my own devising, and I was afraid that reality would come and slap me in the face, by showing me that I had made many errors. True, a few survivors from the area had flattered me by praising the precision of my descriptive details, but I didn't believe them. I knew the power of imagination, but I also knew that it could be deceptive.[25]

Unlike the fictional dreamscape that projects a lost childhood in Appelfeld's early fiction, his novel *Poland the Green Land* projects the estrangement of going back to a barely recognizable land in the story of a son of survivors who travels to his parents' native village in Poland.[26] In the novel, Jacob becomes involved in a love affair that prevents him going back to his home and family in Israel. It is as if the return to the land of his parents and grandparents becomes an emotional trap, as if it were possible to undo history and continue a fantasy life in the luxuriant Polish countryside, as if nothing had happened. Moreover, the desire for a Polish woman transgresses taboos but also fulfils a fantasy wish, not just to overcome the gulf of animosity between Poles and Jews but to possess the past, to know it carnally, and to be possessed by the family's ghosts standing invisibly in the pastoral verdant landscape of Poland (as in contemporary Israeli artist Ilana Ben-Israel's painting, *Green Poland and Its Buried Treasures*).

Like Bracha Ettinger, Appelfeld moves between the competing spaces of memory and loss that give meaning to multiple traumatic ruptures across unbridgeable divides. They are haunted by spectral figures. When drawn by nostalgia for a lost home, memory embarks on the impossible return to a vanished place that exists only as the imagined (not lived) time of before: before the catastrophe, before the traumatic loss of family and of cultural identity. Brought to the Land of Israel as a youth in 1946, Appelfeld went through the forced remaking of identity experienced by many young Holocaust survivors who had been in the camps or spent the war in hiding. Like them, Appelfeld developed a sense of displacement and alienation from a culture that reinvented itself as Israeli and secular and that wiped the slate of the past clean. Appelfeld, however, was interested in his roots and the destroyed culture of eastern Europe. Having grown up in a secular, acculturated, German-speaking family, Appelfeld recalls that assimilation was already a way of life, a heritage not an aspiration.[27] For Appelfeld only a return to Jewish identity and values could alleviate the alienation of his generation and restore a sense of identity that would sustain the Zionist enterprise of Israel as home for the Jewish people.[28] Appelfeld's return to the east European past both metaphorically and literally is a Jewish journey, rather different from Shimon Redlich's rediscovery of a complex pre-war coexistence of Poles, Ukrainians, and Jews.[29]

Yet Appelfeld's Poland is entirely mythical and transhistorical and bears little relation to a real place. It is as if, in his fiction, Appelfeld is constantly making an imaginary return to bring his characters home to an Israeli literature that was for a long time reluctant to admit them.[30] Appelfeld abandoned his earlier aborted journeys into the remembered sights and sounds of the traumatic past and instead returned to lost cultural paradigms that anticipate the demise of those who animated them. The Jews in his *Badenheim 1939* seem unaware they are living through the last days of a doomed deluded belief in cultural symbiosis and assimilation.[31] Retrospective knowledge of their imminent fate invests the novella with foreboding, not to mention horror at their inadequate responses to their helplessness. The dirty train that will take them away breaks any symbolism of a magic realism.

The peregrinations of the Jewish people between Europe and Israel do not reach a goal, but their literary representation recovers the past by recreating a lost sociogeographical space that can only be imagined.[32] In the view of Sidra Dekoven Ezrahi, 'return' is not so much going back as repetition, an 'acting out' that seeks to come to terms with trauma but also repeats previous literary journeys to an effaced landscape.[33] As in Isaac Bashevis Singer's Polish stories, Europe before the catastrophe is always an ambivalent point of origin, but, unlike the imaginary Al-Andalus of pre-Expulsion Spain, it cannot be so easily reimagined.[34] When, in Appelfeld's earlier fiction, returning to a European childhood left the protagonist feeling dislocated both in his city of origin and in Jerusalem, it was not so much returning home as compulsive repetition.[35] Appelfeld's later fiction and autobiographical writings turned from this endemic restless homelessness to a search for roots in a mythopoeic Jewish journey, a metaphorical pilgrimage to the past that establishes the author's identity as an Israeli writer.

In Appelfeld's *Poland the Green Land*, the Jewish return is symptomatically generational: traumatic memory is embodied by a son of Jewish Holocaust survivors, Jacob Fein, who rejects his parents because their memories and their Jewish past have no meaning for him. Driven by a midlife crisis, Jacob, now a successful businessman, feels the need to confront his mother's repressed memory of her traumatic experience in the Holocaust and he travels to his parents' native village (an imaginary place in Poland that is strangely detached from any credible grounding in history or nature), where, paradoxically, he feels at home. He ignores the suspicious looks of the villagers, who are anxious that the return of the Jews might lead to retribution or restitution of property, and realizes he is emotionally estranged from his wife and children. He meets a local Polish woman, Magda, who holds the key to the memory of his parents' past, but who also serves as a refuge from modern Israel, which has lost its connection with its roots in Jewish history. Magda reveals to him the story of his family, and they develop a passionate relationship as she acts out his fantasy of a desirable woman who is the Other in Jewish culture (rather like the relationship of Jacob and Wanda in Bashevis Singer's historical novel *The Slave* (1962)). The Poles remind the Israelis that they are Jews who need to recover their faith and must reconnect with the traditions of their forefathers. Jacob discovers desecrated Jewish tombstones and takes upon himself the sacred mission to redeem the memory of his ancestors, but fails.

Shoshana Ronen has suggested that the Hebrew terms *shuvah* and *teshuvah* point to return as a form of repentance, a spiritual return in Appelfeld's novel to Jewish identity or religiosity.[36] For that reason, it makes more sense for a sabra of the second generation, a reserve army officer, to return in Appelfeld's novel to the land of yeshivas and *tsadikim* in Poland, not to the acculturated secular past of Appelfeld's own German-speaking Czernowitz (Chernivtsi). The journey proves to be a cathartic passage to a state where Jacob can come to terms with an unknown past to which he has been reconnected not by the Israeli Ministry of Education, Yad Vashem, or his family, but by a warm, loving Polish woman. Only after his journey to Poland can Jacob repair the rift between the generations, between Israel's secular break with its diasporic past and an ancient Jewish tradition of which he is a part.

In Appelfeld's novel, a fellow passenger tells Jacob on the way back to Israel that the green fields of Poland conceal destroyed Jewish cemeteries and make it impossible for him to pray there.[37] Both men have gone back to Poland to seek forgiveness from the dead, but the healing of the rift between the generation of survivors and their children is not successful. Like his biblical namesake, Jacob has to find love in an ancestral birthplace and struggle with the arch-foe, his brother Esau, before he can recognize his heritage and identity. Yet after the Holocaust there is no reuniting with parents and family, no closure.

The Next Generation

There is a similar generational rift in writers of the second generation, who seek repressed knowledge of their own stories in the journey to Poland but find no closure, only identification and empathy. The Israeli novelist Michal Govrin was one of the first children of survivors from Israel to travel to Poland, long before the renewal of diplomatic relations. Govrin made the trip in 1975, while studying theatre and Jewish mysticism in Paris. In her account, 'The Journey to Poland', a travelogue and a dialogue with her mother, the trip made a tremendous impact on her emotionally and artistically. Yet, as for the fictional Momik in David Grossman's novel *See Under: Love* (1985), the journey had begun many years previously, during her childhood growing up in Tel Aviv in the 1950s, not comprehending that what had happened in the dark, mysterious land 'over there' was called the Holocaust, that her mother had a different husband and a son before the war, who did not survive: 'But there was the other "knowledge", that knowledge of pre-knowledge and of pre-language, transmitted in the thousand languages that connect a child and his parents without words. A knowledge that lay like a dark cloud on the horizon. Terrifying and seductive.'[38] Poland and Kraków were not 'real' places for her, as she only began to understand at the age of 10 what it meant to grow up in a community of survivors. There were, however, secret bridges between the zone of silence at home and the world outside, where the Eichmann trial was taking place and the children learnt about the Holocaust at school and at memorial meetings.

The separation stage of individuation and leaving home left Govrin estranged from her mother, but her travels in Europe and her awakening to sexual love forced her to confront the dark abyss of the past herself, where death lurked behind desire, where Eros touched Thanatos. She was ready to go to Poland to explore the hidden knowledge that had formed her as she was, but she was not ready for the sheer animal fear that gripped her in her mother's native city of Kraków. She 'was especially not ready for the complexity of [her] responses, for their force . . . The contradictory burst of fascination and revulsion, alienation and belonging, shame and vengeance, of helplessness, of complete denial.'[39] The 'return' to Poland allowed Govrin to forge a new relationship with her parents, one of understanding and compassion but also identification with the solidarity and suffering of the women in the Płaszów labour camp and on the death march. The journey to Poland is a one-way trip to the loss of innocence. But there can be no closure, as shown in the travel diary accompanying her narrative that Govrin wrote for her parents. The transformative journey to her family's secret past is both a real journey that connects her to her parents' past and a metaphorical and metaphysical journey within herself.

Second-generation American Jewish novelist Barbara Finkelstein's 'Return to Poland' (1998) is by contrast a conventional, non-literary travelogue of a daughter of survivors who joined her parents after they decided to make the trip despite fifty-three years of vowing not to set foot in Poland again. Finkelstein's mother is still afraid they might be killed if they return, so strong is the constant terror that has remained within her from the years of hiding from Nazis and local collaborators. But when one of their daughters goes on the March of the Living they decide it is time to make the trip. They are curious to see their home towns of 'Uchan' (Uchanie) and Hrubieszów and want to track down the Poles who saved some of their family.

Yet, while Finkelstein's parents wish to thank the Poles who saved members of their family and are overwhelmed by the generous and unexpected hospitality awaiting them, she finds it hard to get over her generation's desire to brandish their survival as proud Jews and to adjust to the bourgeois consumerism of post-communist Poland, which she had only known from her parents' stories as a country of fear and betrayal or of post-war shortages. Poland is not the vast graveyard she imagined but a land in the throes of burgeoning capitalism, only lacking the Jewish middle class to make it work. In the end, Finkelstein forges a new link with her parents and their past. Nevertheless, the traumatic memory is still safely contained: she will never know what her mother used to be, will never understand the full story, but then, as her mother tells her, she does not have to understand.[40]

There has been a generational shift in the ritual of return, so that in a way the return to Poland has become an institutionalized feature of Jewish life in both the diaspora and Israel, which inevitably distorts the image of Poland as an exceptional site of memory, outside the framework of normality.[41] Hannah Herzig's *Pictures Seeking Captions* presents a paradigm for the second generation's writing of the journey to Poland, where she searches for knowledge of her family's story and her own history in order to understand herself and the personal feelings that stayed so long inside her. Herzig knows she was born in a displaced persons camp in Germany in 1946 to a family from Drohobycz, but the family pictures are missing names and captions that would give her an understanding of who she was and what happened to her family in the 'wojna'—the war that somehow explained everything that had gone wrong. To understand it was not enough to find answers to questions: 'To know a name, a chronology, a place, even if the details don't lead anywhere. The main thing here is the location itself and not the results.'[42] The search led to Sława Wołczyńska, who together with her husband hid a number of Jewish families, including the Herzigs, in their basement for twenty-two months until liberation.

Hannah Herzig returned to Frenwald, near Munich, the childhood home in the pictures, and found knowledge—of her father and of her childhood as 'Ania'. Then she travelled to Drohobycz, to fill in the dots on the mental map of her identity but also to match the map of Eastern Galicia to the history of the Holocaust. The struggle to obtain scraps of information (not all of them reliable) in the austere conditions of run-down, poverty-stricken, post-communist Ukraine, with little help from her broken Polish, leads eventually to painful knowledge: the world is not comfortably divided into Jews and Aryans, good and bad, rescuers and betrayers. The little that is left of the basement where thirty-nine Jews once hid is barely recognizable, and the neighbours had only moved in recently, so they knew nothing of the history of the place. There was no memory of Drohobycz's Jews. Only the wooden cathedral and the painted houses reminded Herzig of the splendid town that was her parents' home. She did not find her relatives' graves and did not know which of her family were shot in the forest, but she connected with the countryside of the Carpathians, her parents' pre-war Polish landscape, which gave her more knowledge of her family's past than any archival documentation. The picture had not come into focus, but by being 'there', where her parents came from, Herzig had managed to restore in her mind the moment before it all happened, when her parents led ordinary lives, when they might just have fled across the Carpathians to Romania from the disaster that erased their world.[43] The symbolic object is elusive, but the loss is made real.

The search for the lost object that gives identity in a second generation journey to Poland is met again in Daniel Mendelsohn's *The Lost*, a 'post-memorial autobiography' of his attempt to retrieve six relatives who went missing during the Holocaust in Eastern Galicia by collecting evidence around the world, travelling to the area of Bolechów (Bolekhiv) and interviewing surviving witnesses.[44] This example of return bridges generational distance by recovering a narrative of what Mendelsohn could not possibly remember as someone born in the USA fifteen years after the end of the Second World War. Mendelsohn wondered if it was a story which wasn't his '"property," so to speak, except in the most abstract sense'.[45] Certainly, he was intimidated by the responsibility and daunted by the impossibility of representation.[46] By committing this return to writing, Mendelsohn makes the past his own through interrogating the stories he hears, resisting the refusal or inability to tell him what he needs to know in order to understand, a resistance matched by the uninterrupted asyntactic flow of narrative which cuts across the reported dialogue; much as in W. G. Sebald's *Austerlitz* (2001), the circuitous, digressive discourse reflects the eddying web that sucks the narrator into a void together with the reader. Mendelsohn likewise inserts photographs that both document and interact with what he calls the 'Chinese boxes' of his narrative.[47]

Marianne Hirsch has spoken of the photograph of a lost relative, like the photograph of the author's dead brother in Art Spiegelman's *Maus* (1980–91), as an example of mourning in postmemory, a vicarious presence of the absent Holocaust victim in the present who connects the generations.[48] Here the 'photograph seeking a caption' is that of Mendelsohn's great-uncle Shmiel, to whom he bears a striking resemblance. Shmiel, whom Mendelsohn always knew as 'Shmiel who was killed by the Nazis', similarly serves as a mute witness to trauma in postmemory: 'For a long time there were only the mute photographs and, sometimes the uncomfortable ripple in the air when Shmiel's name was mentioned.'[49] Mendelsohn comes to understand that what torments his grandfather most of all is not knowing, and the boy accepts his grandfather's reason for rebutting his persistent enquiries about lost relatives. But there are other reasons too. Mendelsohn wants to give the man in the photograph a time and place more real than the stories of an idyllic spot in the mountains, where it was possible to live and live well. Yet he does not suspect how much his grandfather is implicated in feelings of guilt, although even he feels the discomfort he is causing when he touches the forbidden territory of the past. His grandfather's brother, his sister-in-law, and their four girls seemed 'not so much dead as lost, vanished not only from the world but—even more terrible to me—from my grandfather's stories'.[50] That word 'lost' relates, Mendelsohn recalls, not just to their being killed but to the remoteness of a world and a history to which they belonged. His search is driven by guilt for his own self-centred negligence in having ignored their abandonment.[51] The two pairs of unidentified eyes that appear in the first part of the book are presumably those of Shmiel and Daniel, a double looking at the unknown past that is nevertheless a single witnessing.[52]

The dark hole in which the author's family was hidden before they were taken away and shot is the symbolic object of the author's quest, although it is revealed only at the end, when the narrator thought the search was over. The black box in his grandfather's story (*kestel* in Yiddish), which the boy had imagined was a fairy-tale castle, turns out to be a black hole in a metaphysical sense as well.[53] Yet the grandfather has passed on to the author his guilt for abandoning his brother and his family and his impotence in being unable to help. In this way, the story of the six lost relatives symbolically tells the story of the lost six million; it completes a family album as well as placing the album in a biblical cycle (the stories in Genesis of fratricide, universal calamity, and trial, but also of a tree of forbidden knowledge). The search begins on the day of the narrator's barmitzvah, when he marked his entry into adulthood by publicly reading from the biblical stories, thus confirming his own entry into the traumatic history of his family and of his people, but, Mendelsohn is at pains to point out, also into a universal history of genocide.[54] Yet not all the stories are reliable, nor is the narrator (the *kestel*/castle misunderstanding is only one example of the narrator's mistakes and false leads).[55] The haunting of the past stretches across generations and so the 'not knowing' or incomplete knowledge leads to an almost voyeuristic fascination with the unspeakable details of what is not known but which makes us feel we were there (such as the explicit and voyeuristic description of the sadistic torture and massacre of the Jews of Bolechów).

The narrator finds the hiding-place in the end, but never identifies the betrayer, and the saviour of the Szedlak family remains unidentified.

I was standing on the place . . . It is one thing to stand before a spot you have long thought about . . . It is another to be standing in a place of a different sort, a place that for a long time you thought was hypothetical . . . [but] it was not so much the *place* that seemed to matter as the *it*, the terrible thing that had been done, because you weren't really thinking of the place as anything but a kind of envelope, disposable, unimportant. Now I was standing in the place itself, and I had no time to prepare. I confronted the place itself, the thing and not the idea of it.[56]

Now that the place which had existed only in imagined possibilities is real, Mendelsohn understands the limits of human knowledge and acknowledges the fallacy of believing that details and specifics would tell the entire story. The place which he has found is, after all, a non-place of memory, not a place of return.

As in Herzig's search for her family's hiding place, the black box turns out to be empty, and both the lost six and the six million have disappeared into a void that is also a void of language which becomes the 'all-informing principle' of *The Lost*.[57] Mendelsohn's imagining of Shmiel's death by gassing or shooting turns out to be pure fiction, but it is his only way of narrating the unimaginable. It is, as Marc Amfreville avers, nevertheless true to what Freud called in his essay 'The Wolf Man' 'psychic reality', which reflects the haunting of the past in phantasies. The black box can never contain full knowledge of the Holocaust archive: there will always be something stored away that is inaccessible.[58] Nevertheless, even though Mendelsohn fails to gain much knowledge about Shmiel and his family, there was something that could not be obtained from encyclopaedia entries: the sheer experience, the specificity, of being there in the proximity and intimacy of people who knew his family.[59]

Challenging Assumptions, Breaking Taboos

The imaginary return of the second and third post-Holocaust generations to Poland reveals something about the contemporary narrative in Israel which questions the blanket stereotype of antisemitic Poles and Poland as the largest Jewish cemetery in Europe. Some survivors vowed never to return because of their negative views of Poland and Polish hostility towards Jews during the Holocaust, as well as what they perceived as pervasive and still persistent antisemitism. These prejudiced views were reinforced by the Kielce pogrom of 1946 and by the removal of Jews from Polish public life in 1968 but were also carried over to collective historical and cultural discourses.[60] For Poles, the Holocaust was one episode of the German occupation during the Second World War, and many resented claims for restitution of nationalized private property to Jews, which were stalled and finally blocked by an amendment to Polish law in August 2021. However, the fantasy that the retaliatory object (the Jews) will return to Poland (a literal return of the repressed) might be a kind of surreal trauma therapy of the uncanny presence of dead Jews that has served contemporary Polish artists in their challenge to Polish nationalist narratives. Contemporary Polish art resurrects the 'spectral Jew' in religious images of crucifixions and gravestones, making the Jewish dead a real presence in the troubled memory and politics of villages where Jews were murdered by their Polish neighbours, such as Jedwabne, as in Władysław Pasikowski's film *Aftermath* (2012).[61]

The first part of Israeli video artist Yael Bartana's trilogy *And Europe Will Be Stunned*, *Nightmares* (2008), is a provocative intervention that imagines a call for the return of the Jews to Poland forty years after their expulsion, projecting both Polish and Jewish nationalism. In this parody of diasporism, which recalls Philip Roth's novel *Operation Shylock* (1993), the inversion of Zionist tropes of return to the Land of Israel from the 1920s and 1930s undoes the notion of an ancestral homeland. However, the movement for a renaissance of Jewish life in Poland fails, and its leader Sławek is assassinated.[62] No less subversively, Rutu Modan's graphic novel *The Property* (2013) critiques the discourses of Polish–Jewish relations and stakes out a resistance to heritage tours and restitution of property, which are portrayed as ritual returns that do not take account of the complexity of Polish–Jewish relations or for that matter any relations between mythic foes. Instead, in the pastel colours and candid wit that she made her hallmark in *Exit Wounds* (2007), Modan offers a love story with a Polish man—the survivor grandmother's secret that is the real legacy of her Polish past. The granddaughter Mika likewise has a sexual relationship with a Pole which enacts her ambivalent feelings about Poland and also serves as a platform for her to assert her sexuality, as when she draws erotic pictures of him. And yet she too is re-enacting the Holocaust, albeit in a film set that intrudes into the daily life of a Warsaw street, as if the past and the present run in parallel. In a sense, she is living her grandmother's past despite trying to break away from the hold of that past.

Mika travels to Poland with her elderly and cranky grandmother and recovers not the family property but Polish–Jewish romance on two generational levels. Mika discovers the secret of her father's birth as the illegitimate son of a Pole and her grandmother, who was whisked off in disgrace to Mandatory Palestine and lost touch with her lover. The family apartment was sold to Grabowski, whom Mika would have liked to leave in the apartment to spite her cousin Tzilla, whose fiancé Yagodnik has been stalking her in the hope of getting his hands on the property himself. The property is a heritage disputed by Poles and Jews, neither of whom wish to acknowledge that love can bring them together. There is no resolution, but grandmother and granddaughter have each come to terms with the past.[63]

Journeys to Poland by members of the third post-Holocaust generation lead to an uncanny discovery of a land they know but have not previously visited.[64] If, since Alex Haley, African Americans have been looking for their roots, grandchildren of Holocaust survivors feel a special need to return to Poland and overcome stereotypes in order to see Poland as it is today, in all the complex range of attitudes they encounter, from welcoming the Jews back to resurgent antisemitism. What many diaspora Jews discover in contemporary Poland, as Jérémie Dres does in his graphic novel *We Won't See Auschwitz* (2012), is, as Alan Berger notes, a clue to their own identity which holds them to the past, to affinity with Jewish history and traditions, even if they are not religious, because Poland exists in the present as a continuum of Jewish life, not just death.[65] Dres chooses not to see Poland through the gates of Auschwitz but to engage with real live Poles and Polish Jews, including the 'returning Jews', who have discovered their Jewish origins and have come back to Judaism.

Unending Closure

The present return to Poland began shortly before the restoration of diplomatic ties between Israel and Poland in 1988. After the fall of communism, the trip to Poland, not just to the concentration camps but also to the sites of a thousand years of Polish Jewish history, became a major event in many Israeli schoolchildren's and students' lives and a commonplace journey in search of roots. Poland became a destination for pilgrimage to sites of cultural tourism.[66] The literary traveller to Poland after the Holocaust, however, is no ordinary tourist but comes loaded with preconceptions and expectations, cultural attitudes, and stereotypes, yet finds something familiar, almost uncanny.[67] Poland has for the descendants of survivors a fairy-tale aura that is superimposed onto the parents' narratives, as they embark on the journey to bring back their family's lost lives as something real.[68]

Such journeys do not and cannot end in reconciliation with the past. This is because in the Holocaust the natural life cycle was violently disrupted and the past completely cut off. In Hebrew, Poland is called *polin*, for, according to the legend of the migration of Ashkenazi Jews from Germany in the fifteenth century, birds told the refugees, 'po-lin', 'here we stay for the night'. In other words, in retrospect, Poland could not be a permanent home for the Jews. However, the other Hebrew name for Poland, *polanyah*, has popularly been interpreted as the dwelling-place of God, recalling a thousand years of Jewish religious life. Either way, Avi Sagi has argued that, unlike the Bakhtinian chronotope of the journey as a space between home and destination, the return is disrupted. Using Homi Bhabha's terms in *The Location of Culture*, Sagi distinguishes *homeless* from *unhomed*. Home is what one is uprooted from, reflecting a postcolonial disposition of transnational migration. For this reason, in Appelfeld's novels, arriving at a destination leaves his protagonists alienated.[69] I would disagree with Sagi's conclusion that Appelfeld's imaginary journeys to the past in his novels lack an existential dimension since they did not bring resolution. There cannot be resolution because memory of the past is not direct or experiential.

Appelfeld's novels become a surrogate memory of what he can barely remember as a child wandering the forests of occupied Europe and which he could not describe as literal reminiscences.[70] Memory, he writes in his memoir, *The Story of a Life*, is allied with imagination. It comes in vivid shards of dreamlike scenes which hold significance for who he is, like the image of the last vacation in the Carpathians before the war. Afterwards he was a small animal in the forests and only occasionally would splintered images rise out of the mist. Then came the oblivion induced by forced absorption in Israel.[71] Only his body, he has said, remembers clearly, where memory has its deep roots.[72]

What is the pull of the vanished past and what do writers and artists seek in a country that is not their birthplace? Poland has a prominent place in the Jewish imagination and particularly in Hebrew literature. The *locus classicus* of the return to a lost east European past is Nobel prize-winner S. Y. Agnon's imaginary recreation of Buczacz in *A Guest for the Night* (1938), but these were also his earlier stories about Jewish life in Poland before its destruction.[73] However, since the Holocaust Poland has been imbued with a sense of incommensurate and total loss—and not only because it was the major centre of east European Jewish life before the war and the location of the most notorious Nazi death camps. As Ronen explains, the first wave of return journeys in post-Holocaust Hebrew fiction described a void, a huge cemetery where identity was constructed through mediated images of the Holocaust. In such a non-place (what Marc Augé has called *non-lieux de mémoire*), literary or essayist journeys could not be more loaded.[74] The second wave, including children of survivors, sought dialogue with a new, democratic Poland and discovered that the past, however complicated, was real and populated by real people, some of whom helped save Jews and held the key to their family history.[75] Returning speaks to a need for closure but also of a search for an irretrievably lost other self.

The pilgrimages and cultural heritage treks, as Erica T. Lehrer has shown,[76] have yielded therapeutic effects for some of those who cut all ties with their former native land, or have resulted in nostalgia for those who kept their Polish Jewish cultural identity. Returning to the place where the victims had walked, but their children and grandchildren had never been themselves, makes the individual and collective trauma real. At the end of *Poland the Green Land*, Jacob says he found nothing in Poland. There is a similar feeling of vacuity and futility in Aharon Appelfeld's own return to his childhood landscape in Czernowitz in the film *All That Remains* (1998), an emptiness familiar from other returns of refugees and exiles to the land of their birth which rejected them. Here that feeling of emptiness is accentuated by a hostility and total erasure: Appelfeld's existence is only acknowledged by one local man, a former schoolmate. Survivors have been writing about their return journeys since the liberation of Poland in 1944, and often report encountering a surreal vision of unrecognizable streets, empty houses, and non-existent synagogues in their former home town. The *yizker bikher* (memorial books) relate that they found no family or friends to greet them, and they were not always recognized or welcomed.[77] Appelfeld was looking for a mass grave but his search ended with a sense of nothingness:

'For years that village lay within me, and now I was approaching it. I couldn't find anything recognizable about it.'[78] Redlich comments on Appelfeld's estrangement from his native village and alienation from the hostile stares of local peasants by noting that, while feelings of dislocation and displacement are to be expected, returning may evoke different attitudes, depending on the survivor's outlook, personal circumstances, and the extent of the traumatic experience.[79] Yet the search for the past is driven not only by the urge to bury the dead, to stand at the graves, and to face the place of trauma (as Redlich and Grynberg did) but also by the necessity of creating memory in order to give meaning to the future, to create normal lives, as well as to see life in the past, not only death.[80] Or as Helen Epstein explains in her account of her journey to her mother's native Bohemia, we all need a place to which to return in order to know who we are, to undo the annihilation that would destroy our identity, especially if, as she did, one grew up without memories of the traumatic past.[81]

Like Dres giving a name and place to his deceased grandmother, Nancy K. Miller, in her memoir *What They Saved*, felt the need to keep the strange, mysterious relics of family memory left by her father in order to create 'signposts' on a journey, like dots on a map she had to follow, which led to lost family graves in Ukraine.[82] The return, to some extent as unwilled as the original deportation, re-embodies a geographical space from which Jews were expelled and erased, leaving behind total absence.[83] For Marianne Hirsch, in her own vicarious return to her parents' Czernowitz, imagined returns to eastern Europe, as in Assmann's *mich-Gedächtnis*, recover some lost object that has become detached from its previous existence. Her postmemory work attempts to do what working through the suffering by the victims should have done, to come to terms with the past and to start again. Yet there is no going back; in Hirsch's words: '"Home" becomes a place of no return.'[84]

Notes

I am indebted to Shimon Redlich for comments on a previous version of this chapter, and to Katarzyna Jerzak for her assistance and encouragement. I also benefited from conversations with the late Aharon Appelfeld at his home at Mevaseret Zion.

1. C. Caruth, *Unclaimed Experience: Trauma, Narrative, and History* (Baltimore, Md., 1996); S. Freud, *Beyond the Pleasure Principle*, trans. J. Strachey, Standard Edition of the Complete Psychological Works of Sigmund Freud, 28 (London, 1961).
2. Freud, *Beyond the Pleasure Principle*, 22.
3. Caruth, *Unclaimed Experience*, 8.
4. S. Redlich, *Together and Apart in Brzezany: Poles, Jews, and Ukrainians, 1919–1945* (Bloomington, Ind., 2001); K. Reszke and S. Grunberg (dirs.), *Shimon's Returns*, documentary (LogTV Ltd, 2014).
5. Redlich, *Together and Apart in Brzezany*, 38.
6. See P. Nora, 'Between Memory and History: *Les Lieux de Mémoire*', *Representations*, 26 (1989), 7–24.
7. D. Laub, 'An Event Without a Witness: Truth, Testimony and Survival', in S. Felman and

D. Laub, *Testimony: Crises of Witnessing in Literature, Psychoanalysis, and History* (New York, 1992), 75–92.

8   A. Assmann, *Der lange Schatten der Vergangenheit: Erinnerungskultur und Geschichtspolitik* (Munich, 2014), 122–3; Eng. trans.: *Shadows of Trauma: Memory and the Politics of Postwar Identity*, trans. S. Clift (New York, 2016), 100. Assmann's example is Günter Grass, who was a member of the Waffen-SS, someone who was trying to forget, unlike victims who presumably try to remember. The details of Grass's participation in the Waffen-SS emerged only later.

9   P. Łoziński (dir.), *Miejsce urodzenia*, documentary (Studio Filmowe Kronika, 1992); for a general introduction to Grynberg's writing, see K. Jerzak, 'Henryk Grynberg: The Loneliness of Living for the Dead', *Journal of Modern Jewish Studies*, 4 (2005), 49–53.

10 K. Sokołowska, 'Problemy z empatią: *Miejsce urodzenia* Pawła Łozińskiego i *Dziedzictwo* Henryka Grynberga', in T. Sucharski and M. Murawska (eds.), *'Rozliczanie' przeszłości: Relacje polsko-żydowskie w tekstach kultury XX i XXI wieku* (Słupsk, 2016), 97–112.

11 H. Grynberg, 'Obowiązek', in *Monolog polsko-żydowski* (Wołowiec, 2003), 104–24: 104; translated by Katarzyna Jerzak.

12 Ibid. 105.

13 Ibid. 112.

14 Ibid. 113–14; translated by Katarzyna Jerzak.

15 Ibid. 121.

16 H. Grynberg, *Dziedzictwo* (London, 1993), 90; trans. in S. Redlich, 'Returning to the Shtetl: Differing Perceptions', *Polin*, 17 (2004), 267–76: 272.

17 Jerzak, 'Henryk Grynberg', 52.

18 Ibid.

19 See A. Kisiel, 'Aesth/Ethical Bodies: Bracha Ettinger's *Eurydices* and the Encounter with the Other's History', in J. Jajszczok and A. Musiał (eds.), *The Body in History, Culture, and the Arts* (London, 2019), 149–60.

20 B. Ettinger, 'Woman-Other-Thing: A Matrixial Touch', in *Bracha Lichtenberg Ettinger: Matrix-Borderlines* (Oxford, 1993), 11–18; ead., 'Art as the Transport Station of Trauma', in *Bracha Lichtenberg Ettinger: Artworking, 1985–1999* (Ghent, 2000), 91–115; C. Buci-Glucksmann, 'Eurydice and Her Doubles: Painting After Auschwitz', in *Bracha Lichtenberg Ettinger*, 71–90.

21 M. Hirsch, *The Generation of Postmemory: Writing and Visual Culture after the Holocaust* (New York, 2012), 218. For a critique of Hirsch's use of Caruth's reading of Freud in her interpretation of Ettinger's paintings, see M. Roca Lizarezi, *Renegotiating Postmemory: The Holocaust in Contemporary German-Language Jewish Literature* (Rochester, NY, 2020), 16–21.

22 Ettinger, 'Woman-Other-Thing'.

23 D. Glowacka, *Disappearing Traces: Holocaust Testimonials, Ethics, and Aesthetics* (Seattle, 2012), 182–94.

24 S. Boym, *The Future of Nostalgia* (New York, 2001).

25 A. Appelfeld, 'Buried Homeland', trans. J. M. Green, *New Yorker*, 23 Nov. 1998, p. 49. On the imaginary landscape of Appelfeld's early fiction, see A. S. Hübner, 'Buried Homeland: The Bukovina in the Works of Aharon Appelfeld', *Revue européenne des études hébraïques*, 11 (2005), 21–32.

26 A. Appelfeld, *Polin erets yerukah* (Jerusalem, 2005); see also Hübner, 'Buried Homeland'.

27 A. Appelfeld, *Beyond Despair: Three Lectures and a Conversation with Philip Roth*, trans. J. M. Green (New York, 1994), 7–8.

28 Aharon Appelfeld, conversation with the author, 2009.
29 Redlich, 'Returning to the Shtetl', 273–4.
30 Appelfeld, 'Buried Homeland'; see A. Mintz, *Hurban: Responses to Catastrophe in Hebrew Literature* (New York, 1984), 12–13, 203–38.
31 A. Appelfeld, *Badenhaim ir nofesh* (Benei Berak, 1978); Eng. trans.: *Badenheim 1939*, trans. D. Bilu (Boston, Mass., 1980).
32 S. D. Ezrahi, *Booking Passage: Exile and Homecoming in the Modern Jewish Imagination* (Berkeley, Calif., 2000), 179–81.
33 Ibid. 181; see also S. D. Ezrahi, 'The Jewish Journey in the Late Fiction of Aharon Appelfeld: Return, Repair or Repetition', *Mikan*, 5 (2005), 47–55.
34 Ezrahi, 'The Jewish Journey in the Late Fiction of Aharon Appelfeld', 49.
35 Ibid. 50. On Poland in Bashevis Singer's work, see C. Shmeruk, 'Polish–Jewish Relations in the Historical Fiction of Isaac Bashevis Singer', *Polish Review*, 32 (1987), 401–13; M. Adamczyk-Garbowska, 'Ziemia Święta w Biłgoraju: O polskich aspektach twórczości Izaaka B. Singera', *Więź*, 1 (1991), 95–107.
36 S. Ronen, 'A Journey to Poland—A Return to the Self in *Poland, a Green Country* by Aharon Appelfeld', *Yod*, 19 (2014), 201–9; see Y. Schwartz, *Appelfeld: From Individual Lament to Tribal Eternity*, trans. J. M. Green (Hanover, NH, 2001).
37 Appelfeld, *Polin erets yerukah*, 215.
38 M. Govrin, 'The Journey to Poland', trans. B. Harshav, *Partisan Review*, 66 (1999), 555–73: 556; ead., 'Hamasa lepolin, mikhtav mimeḥozot aḥizat einayim', in M. Govrin, J. Derrida, and D. Shapiro, *Guf tefilah* (Tel Aviv, 2012), 91–119.
39 Govrin, 'The Journey to Poland', 562.
40 B. Finkelstein, 'Return to Poland', in P. Kafka (ed.), *'Lost on the Map of the World': Jewish-American Women's Quest for Home in Essays and Memoirs, 1890–Present* (Frankfurt am Main, 2001), 25–85: 82.
41 See J. Feldman, *Above the Death Pits, Beneath the Flag: Youth Voyages to Poland and the Performance of Israeli National Identity* (New York, 2008).
42 H. Herzig, *Temunot meḥapeshot koteret* (Tel Aviv, 1997), 54.
43 Ibid. 151–2.
44 D. Mendelsohn, *The Lost: A Search for Six of Six Million* (New York, 2006); see R. Slodounik, 'Postmemorial Autobiography in Daniel Mendelsohn's *The Lost: A Search for Six of Six Million*', *Shofar*, 35/1 (2016), 29–50.
45 Quoted in A. Rigney, 'Scales of Postmemory: Six of Six Million', in C. Fogu, W. Kansteiner, and T. Presner (eds.), *Probing the Ethics of Holocaust Culture* (Cambridge, Mass., 2016), 113–28: 113.
46 See V. Aarons and A. L. Berger, *Third-Generation Holocaust Representation: Trauma, History, and Memory* (Evanston, Ill., 2017), 67; Ezrahi, *Booking Passage*, 106.
47 Mendelsohn, *The Lost*, 33; see Rigney, 'Scales of Postmemory'; P. Lévy, 'Storytelling, Photography, and Mourning in Daniel Mendelsohn's *The Lost*', in V. Aarons (ed.), *Third-Generation Holocaust Narratives: Memory in Memoir and Fiction* (Lanham, Md., 2016), 57–72.
48 M. Hirsch, *Family Frames: Photography, Narrative, and Postmemory* (Cambridge, Mass., 1997), 17–40.
49 Mendelsohn, *The Lost*, 7.
50 Ibid. 15.

51　Ibid. 73.
52　Slodounik, 'Postmemorial Autobiography in Daniel Mendelsohn's *The Lost*', 35.
53　Mendelsohn, *The Lost*, 482.
54　See W. Kansteiner, 'Interview with Daniel Mendelsohn, Author of *The Lost: A Search for Six of Six Million*', in Fogu, Kansteiner, and Presner (eds.), *Probing the Ethics of Holocaust Culture*, 129–40.
55　See M. Amfreville, 'Family Archive Fever: Daniel Mendelsohn's *The Lost*', in S. Onega and J.-M. Ganteau (eds.), *Contemporary Trauma Narrative: Liminality and the Ethics of Form* (London, 2014), 159–71: 167.
56　Mendelsohn, *The Lost*, 501 (emphasis original).
57　Amfreville, 'Family Archive Fever', 167–8.
58　Ibid. 171.
59　Mendelsohn, *The Lost*, 124–5.
60　See R. D. Cherry and A. Orla-Bukowska (eds.), *Rethinking Poles and Jews: Troubled Past, Brighter Future* (Lanham, Md., 2007).
61　See E.-R. Baker, 'Memorialising the (Un)dead Jewish Other in Poland: Spectrality, Embodiment and Polish Holocaust Horror in Władysław Pasikowski's *Aftermath* (2012)', *Genealogy*, 3 (2019): MDPI website, visited 3 Dec. 2021; U. Blacker, 'The Return of the Jew in Polish Culture', in S. Bird, M. Fulbrook, J. Wagner, and C. Wienand (eds.), *Reverberations of Nazi Violence in Germany and Beyond: Disturbing Pasts* (London, 2016), 125–40; E. Lehrer and M. Waligórska, 'Cur(at)ing History: New Genre Art Interventions and the Polish-Jewish Past', *East European Politics and Societies*, 27 (2013), 510–44; T. Łysak, 'Artistic Interventions: From Commemorating Post-Holocaust Losses to Carving a Space for Jewish Life in Poland', in J. W. Boyer and B. Molden (eds.), *EUtROPEs: The Paradox of European Empire* (Chicago, 2015), 162–82; see also M. Waligórska, 'Healing by Haunting: Jewish Ghosts in Contemporary Polish Literature', *Prooftexts*, 34 (2014), 207–31; Z. Dziuban (ed.), *The 'Spectral Turn': Jewish Ghosts in the Polish Post-Holocaust Imaginaire* (Berlin, 2019).
62　Y. Almog, 'Europe Will Be Stunned: Visualization of a Jewish Return', in A. Eshel and R. Seelig (eds.), *The German–Hebrew Dialogue: Studies of Encounter and Exchange* (Berlin, 2017), 197–210. On this and other interventions in Polish collective memory of the invisible Jews, see S. Frosh, *Those Who Come After: Postmemory, Acknowledgement and Forgiveness* (Cham, 2019), 103–4; Lehrer and Waligórska, 'Cur(at)ing History'; Waligórska, 'Healing by Haunting'.
63　On the transfer of traumatic memory to the third generation in *The Property*, see M. Reingold, 'On the Limits of Trauma: Postmemories in the Third-Generation Holocaust Graphic Novels *Flying Couch* and *The Property*', *History and Memory*, 33/2 (2021), 135–57.
64　A. L. Berger, 'Life After Death: A Third-Generation Journey in Jérémie Dres's *We Won't See Auschwitz*', in Aarons (ed.), *Third-Generation Holocaust Narratives*, 73–87: 74.
65　Ibid. 78.
66　See Feldman, *Above the Death Pits, Beneath the Flag*; R. Gruber, *Virtually Jewish: Reinventing Jewish Culture in Europe* (Berkeley, Calif., 2002).
67　S. Ronen, *In Pursuit of the Void: Journeys to Poland in Contemporary Israeli Literature* (Kraków, 2001), 46–7.
68　M. Grimwood, 'Imagined Topographies: Visions of Poland in Writings by Descendants of Survivors', in D. Glowacka and J. Zylinska (eds.), *Imaginary Neighbors: Mediating Polish–Jewish Relations after the Holocaust* (Lincoln, Neb., 2007), 187–204: 190–1.

69 A. Sagi, 'Polin erets yerukah—minikur lezehut', in A. Lipsker and A. Sagi (eds.), *Esrim ve'arba keriot bekhitvei aharon apelfeld* (Ramat Gan, 2011), 237–60; see H. Bhabha, *The Location of Culture* (New York, 1994).
70 Appelfeld, *Beyond Despair*, 68–9.
71 A. Appelfeld, *Sipur ḥayim* (Jerusalem, 1999), 5–6; Eng. trans.: *The Story of a Life*, trans. A. Halter (New York, 2004), pp. v–vi; see E. Miller Budick, *Aharon Appelfeld's Fiction: Acknowledging the Holocaust* (Bloomington, Ind., 2005), 153–79.
72 Appelfeld, *Sipur khayim*, 49; id., *The Story of a Life*, 50.
73 See N. Ben-Dov, 'Poland as a "Promised Land" in Agnon's *Tales of Poland*', in A. Molisak and S. Ronen (eds.), *Polish and Hebrew Literature and National Identity* (Warsaw, 2010), 98–105; D. Laor, 'Polish History, Jewish Memory: Some Observations on the Writings of S. Y. Agnon', in Molisak and Ronen (eds.), *Polish and Hebrew Literature and National Identity*, 106–11; Redlich, 'Returning to the Shtetl'.
74 M. Augé, *Non-Places: Introduction to an Anthropology of Supermodernity* (London, 1997); see J. Hassoun, M. Nathan-Murat, and A. Radzynski, *Non lieu de la mémoire: La Cassure d'Auschwitz* (Paris, 1990); S. Ronen, 'Post-Holocaust Representations of Poland in Israeli Literature', *Polish Review*, 60 (2015), 3–20.
75 Ronen, 'Post-Holocaust Representations of Poland'.
76 E. T. Lehrer, *Jewish Poland Revisited: Heritage Tourism in Unquiet Places* (Bloomington, Ind., 2013).
77 M. Adamczyk-Garbowska, *Patterns of Return: Survivors' Postwar Journeys to Poland* (Washington DC, 1997); J. Kugelmass and J. Boyarin (eds.), *From a Ruined Garden: The Memorial Books of Polish Jewry*, 2nd exp. edn. (Bloomington, Ind., 1998), 243–66.
78 Appelfeld, 'Buried Homeland', 50.
79 Redlich, 'Returning to the Shtetl', 275.
80 Ibid.
81 H. Epstein, *Where She Came From: A Daughter's Search for Her Mother's History* (Boston, Mass., 1997), 17.
82 N. K. Miller, *What They Saved: Pieces of a Jewish Past* (Lincoln, Neb., 2011), 4–5.
83 See J. Walker, 'Moving Testimonies: "Unhomed Geography" and the Holocaust Documentary of Return', in J. Lothe, S. Rubin Suleiman, and J. Phelan (eds.), *After Testimony: The Ethics and Aesthetics of Holocaust Narrative for the Future* (Columbus, 2012), 269–88.
84 Hirsch, *The Generation of Postmemory*, 212.

Israelis? Poles?
Blurring the Boundaries of Identity in Contemporary Israeli Literature

SHOSHANA RONEN

IN THIS CHAPTER I would like to point to a change of paradigm in contemporary Israeli literature concerning the perception of Poland and Poles. Literature is not written in a cultural and social vacuum,[1] so I argue that this paradigm change is rooted in cultural and social changes that Israeli society has been going through in recent years. The typical Israeli Zionist approach to Poland and Poles is constructed from a mixture of a few components, among them the collective memory of the Holocaust and of the Polish land as a huge Jewish cemetery, the perception of Polish antisemitism, and the Israeli Zionist identity concentrated, on the one hand, on Jewishness, in spite the fact that Zionism is mostly a secular ideology, and, on the other, on the 'negation of the diaspora'.

Identity

Although more than seventy years have passed since the founding of the State of Israel, Israelis' 'passionate interest in re-examining their collective identity has not diminished'.[2] The late Israeli writer Ronit Matalon wrote that Israelis are preoccupied by and even obsessed with the question of constructing their identity. This is understandable in an immigrant society where the Zionist narrative is overwhelmingly dominant. Identity politics, boundary-marking, and self-definition are survival strategies for certain groups in their relation with the state, its coercive power, and its dominant narratives. Matalon asserted that Hebrew literature needs a home, in the sense of a place and a language. In Israel, where two narratives collide, the major Zionist-nationalist one and the minor migratory one, questions regarding identity are burning issues, which are dealt with intensively in Hebrew literature. The dominant narrative in Israel created the image of the sabra, an ideal type—a native Israeli, authentic, rooted in the land, courageous, tilling the soil, a new kind of Jew. Regarding *olim*—immigrants to the Land of Israel—the belief was that they would become natives in a short time.[3] Matalon described this as 'the brutal blurring of the Israeli melting pot'. The second, minor, narrative is that of immigration. This narrative, according to Matalon, involves those who came to Israel from parts of the Levant, where different cultures existed side by side. This narrative is at odds with the Zionist ethos, which demands one national-cultural identity obligatory for all, a monolithic culture that suppresses and stifles diversity. Matalon claimed that a significant moment in Israeli discourse was when the word *aliyah* (ascent) was replaced by the word *hagirah* (immigration). This shift reflected the abandonment of the Zionist illusion that immigration is a kind of a childhood disease cured by Zionism.[4]

Zygmunt Bauman claimed that constructing a rigid identity is an unfeasible task that requires a lifetime. He wrote: 'Identity seekers invariably face the daunting task of "squaring a circle": that generic phrase . . . implies tasks that can never be completed in a "real time", but are assumed to be able to reach completion in the fullness of time—in infinity.'[5] Bauman stressed that the incomplete identity which people might attain is not inborn but formed and transformed throughout an entire life: '"Belonging" and "identity' are not cut in rock, they are not secured by a lifelong guarantee . . . they are eminently negotiable and revocable . . . one's own decision, the steps one takes, the way one acts—and the determination to stick by all that—are crucial factors of both.'[6] Accordingly, the creation of identity is a constant creative struggle.

In my view, some of the literary works written in Israel recently reveal a weakening of the homogeneous Zionist identity and a readiness to cope with a more complex and heterogeneous self. This complex self, which wants to be rooted in authentic ground in order to be broader and stronger, must also acknowledge the past and, in Israel, the diaspora. I argue that the power of 'the negation of the diaspora' is fading. Therefore, Israelis today do not need a 'rigid identity' or the illusion that 'I know who am I by defining precisely what I am not' but are much more prepared to accept the elastic and liquid definition given by Bauman. Another reason for the change in Israeli literature regarding Poland might be the overcoming of the taboo associated with the Holocaust that prevailed in Hebrew literature for many years. A good example is *The Memory Monster* by Yishai Sarid, which I will discuss later.

Encounter with Poland

I have described the encounter of Israelis with Poland in Hebrew literature on a number of occasions. In a recent article I came to the conclusion that the 'difference of generations' viewpoint in Holocaust studies and post-Holocaust literature— which holds that the first generation comprises the survivors, the second generation is made up of their children, and the third generation the survivors' grandchildren— is inadequate, and suggested, rather, the use of the term 'wave'.[7] My use of 'wave' instead of 'generation' does not stem only from the chronological issue, the age of the writers, which does not always fit the division of generations, but is mainly the result of the fact that changes in the perception of Poland in Israeli literature are a result of major changes in Israel and Poland and among both Poles and Israelis, and thus are not merely a question of the age of the writer.

At present, I see two waves. The first occurred during the 1980s, when Israelis were finally allowed to travel to Poland,[8] and the 1990s, when Poland was in a state of transition from communism to democracy. The second wave took place in a different Poland, a capitalist country and member of the European Union. A remarkable new phenomenon that Israeli travellers encounter in Poland after the peaceful transition of 1989 is the great interest of Poles in Jewish history and culture in the Polish lands. In fact, this trend is a part of Poles' search for their own neglected and forgotten history.[9] In addition, not only is Poland different but so too are Israeli travellers to Poland, at least as they are portrayed in literature. It seems that authors and narrators, even if they still retain stereotypes, are at least aware of them and can, therefore, question and even mock them in their writings. For the writers of the first wave, Poland is primarily a huge Jewish cemetery, and Poles merely exist in the background, not as partners for dialogue but as symbols of the 'Other', clearly distinct from 'us'. In contrast, writers of the second wave are not afraid of entering into dialogue and interaction with Poles, whom they treat as subjects. 'The second-wave travellers have all this in the back of their minds, but they are also distant from themselves, and they have a sense of irony as they observe the Polish reality around them.'[10] The second-wave narrators have a flexible identity, an openness to multiple ethnic belonging or at least complex identities, and are free of fears of the uncanny and unknown.

The encounter with Poland in Israeli literature is not identical in all literary works. Poland has changed, and Israelis have changed too. As I have pointed out, after the systemic change of 1989 and even more so since 2004 when Poland joined the European Union, the common stereotypes of Israelis regarding Poland could no longer persist. The grey, gloomy, dark, and poor communist Poland was the perfect background for the stereotypes Israelis had regarding Poland and Poles.[11] However, Poland today looks similar to other European countries, and Europe for Israelis has a different image from Poland under communism. Europe, for Israelis, is the cradle of culture, wealth, and freedom; it is the object of dreams of a better, more peaceful and comfortable way of life. How surprising it is for them to discover that Poland is located in Europe.

I believe that a crucial change in Israeli society, which enables Israelis to be more open-minded in relation to Poles and Poland, is the diminishing power of taboos and myths and, to a large extent, the undermining of the Zionist idea of 'the negation of the diaspora'. Israeli literature of the last few years reveals a growing curiosity concerning the diaspora.[12] Zeev Sternhell shows how negative the attitudes of Zionist leaders in Palestine were towards it. They criticized Jewish life there in a manner similar to that of the most zealous antisemites. In their view, the diaspora had no life or culture. For A. D. Gordon, diaspora Jews were parasites not only in the sphere of the economy but also spiritually;[13] Ben-Gurion had a similar opinion, maintaining that Jews could not develop a normal culture in the diaspora because they were entirely dependent upon local cultures.[14] There could be no compromise with the diaspora; its rejection was total.[15] Consequently, 'all hopes, and efforts focused on Palestine. The country was regarded as the sole center of not only Jewish existence but also Jewish history, the source of inspiration and the elixir of life.'[16] Yael Zerubavel shows that with the passing of time descendants of the mythological sabra began to express more interest in and identification with their exilic past.[17]

One of the reasons for this could be the enduring Palestinian–Israeli conflict. The burden of permanent conflict perhaps results in the feeling that Jews in the diaspora in the past and Jews in Israel today face a similar threat to their survival. Zerubavel argues that Israelis should seek to achieve a balance between rejection of the diaspora and nostalgia for it.[18] In a lengthy two-part article in the periodical *Teoria uvikoret* in 1994, Amnon Raz-Krakotzkin claimed that a historical consciousness founded on the rejection of the diaspora excludes the feasibility of a definition of Jewish identity which could include recognition of the Palestinian perspective. By contrast, a historical consciousness that includes the concept of diaspora opens the door for a pluralist definition of the Jews in Israel and for a universal ethical standpoint. This universal standpoint makes possible not only the inclusion of the Palestinian perspective but also that of Sephardi Jews, who have been discriminated against and repressed. Accepting the concept 'diaspora' enables denied voices to be heard and the rights of various religious and ethnic groups in Israel to be acknowledged.[19] Twenty-five years later, Raz-Krakotzkin revisited his essay and argued that the concept 'diaspora' provides the groundwork for binational and multi-ethnic projects. Diaspora, he claimed, is a fundamental concept in Jewish consciousness, and he therefore sought to undermine the antithesis between diaspora and sovereignty and suggested the idea of an exilic stance in the Land of Israel, exile within sovereignty.[20] Such voices point to the fact that radical thinking concerning the basis of Zionist ideology is a part of the Israeli discourse.

Another shift in Israeli society is the weakening of taboos regarding the Holocaust. Critical opinions concerning collective memory in Israel and the commemoration of the Holocaust are increasingly present in public discourse. An interesting and powerful example of this trend in Israeli literature is *The Memory Monster* by Yishai Sarid.[21] It takes the form of a letter to the chairman of Yad Vashem from an ambitious young historian and guide of Israeli high-school students, soldiers, and politicians on what are called 'Shoah trips' to Poland. The narrator addresses the chairman with great respect as 'the official representative of memory' and recounts how he was drawn to become a historian of the Holocaust and a guide of Shoah trips. As he writes: 'I am ready to harness myself to the memory carriage, to instil the memory in students.'[22]

However, over time his 'labour of memory' blows up in his face. It becomes a monster that devours his soul. He understands that memory, so successfully imprinted in the minds and souls of young people, in fact poisons them and himself. It becomes a virus, an evil deity, that replaces empathy, compassion, and morality. On one of his visits to Auschwitz he came to realize that 'in a place of hatred hate grows'.[23] The endeavour of imprinting memory through Shoah trips creates young people who really hate. They hate the Poles, they hate the miserable Jewish victims, they hate the Palestinians, but they admire the German perpetrators. The Germans were beautiful, clean, impressive, relaxed, self-assured, unrestricted, so 'cool' that the teenagers appreciate their power, cruelty, daring. The Germans were abominable heroes, but heroes.[24] 'I was a diligent and loyal agent of memory', he writes, when he comes to understand the results of his well-performed task. The result of the enterprise of memory-engineering in Israel is to create confused ethical monsters.[25] He realizes that in these pilgrimages to the death camps no one dares to truly face the atrocities and their ethical outcomes. Therefore the virus of memory which is instilled in the minds of Israelis is dangerous.[26] From this virus derives the conclusion, expressed by one of the teenagers, that in order to survive one should be a little bit like the Nazis. The lesson one learns from the memory monster is the supreme importance of power: without it a person is entirely helpless, and anything can be done to them. Thus, the message is imprinted: only power, no conscience, no doubts; these only damage the soul and make it difficult to function.[27]

The pilgrimage to Auschwitz (or to any death camp) has its rituals and performances. During this excursion young Israelis offer up a sacrifice to the memory monster, the new God, which they are called upon to worship. The sacrifice is the souls of the teenagers, their humanity, and their compassion for the victims. Their conclusion seems to be that 'never again' means to return to Israel with a Nazi, not a Jewish, consciousness. The judgement expressed in the book might be perceived as radical and exaggerated or, on the contrary, as articulating a deep truth about the collective memory of the Holocaust in Israel. What is significant is that it could be written and published in Israel in 2017 and not cause a scandal. In addition, it echoed ideas that have been articulated in academic studies in recent years.[28]

The Property

The Property, by Rutu Modan, is a graphic novel that tells the story of two women, a grandmother, Regina Segal, and her granddaughter, Mika, who travel to Warsaw, Regina's birthplace.[29] The goal of the trip is ostensibly to reclaim an apartment that belonged to Regina's family before the Second World War. However, as the story unfolds, it appears that Regina has a hidden reason for this journey, a reason that is the underlying motif of the novel.[30] Regina feels an urge to travel to her birthplace after the death of her son, Mika's father. She wants to go on her own, and it takes some effort by her family to convince her that she should take Mika. The hidden reason for the journey is Regina's desire to find her pre-war Polish lover. It turns out that, as a young woman, Regina became pregnant by her Polish boyfriend, but her father, who could not accept this, decided to marry her to a Jew who worked for him and to send her to Palestine before war broke out. Regina was too young and weak to oppose her father, and the broken-hearted girl had to leave her lover in Warsaw. In Palestine she gave birth to their son. This is the dark secret that Regina has carried for many years, although it seems that for Mika this story is not completely unknown. Like her grandmother before the war, during her stay in Poland, Mika has an affair with a Polish man, Tomasz, a tourist guide and graphic artist. She tells him Regina's story but also adds that she is not sure whether it is true or a family legend. In this graphic novel there are two love relationships between Jewish women and Poles. The first, an old affair before the war and the second in the present, when it seems to be more socially acceptable.

Regina meets Roman Górski, her ex-lover and the father of her son, who lives in Regina's family's old apartment and who does not immediately recognize her. The story turns into a kind of melodrama, with stormy scenes, misunderstandings, and a sort of happy ending, although Modan adds a sense of humour, irony, and distance. In this way she is able to point to many features of Jewish–Polish relations and the power of mutual stereotypes. Humour not only mocks and disarms stereotypes, it also helps in lessening tension and confronting the exclusive perspectives which characterize Polish and Jewish perceptions of the war.[31] Stereotypes and different perspectives are expressed above all in mutual suspicion. Roman is sure that the only reason for Regina's visit is her desire to reclaim the apartment in which he has lived since the war. He tells Regina 'I thought you came because of memories but you came for money.'[32] The stereotype of Jews and money is so strong that even Roman, the lover of a Jewish girl, is not free of it. Modan admitted that working on the book she wanted to play with this stereotype.[33] Regina also expresses doubts about Poles. When Mika tells her that Tomasz is a tourist guide who offers tours for Jews, Regina refuses to believe her. She is sure that Mika cannot trust him, certain that he has some hidden goal and wants to take advantage of her. She warns Mika not to go to his place, because he might kill her; perhaps his grandfather slaughtered Jews.[34] With time, Mika also feels suspicious of Tomasz when she finds his notebook with illustrations, which show he knows Regina's secret. She loses her trust in him, and thinks that he flirted with her only to obtain material for his book. Regina was thus correct: one cannot trust the Poles. Eventually, Roman understands that Regina came to Warsaw not for the property but to tell him about the death of their son, and Mika accepts Tomasz's apology and clarifications. Mika is not surprised or shocked by the fact that she has just met her grandfather or that she is a quarter Polish. She does not experience any crisis of identity. Ethnicity, which creates a sharp distinction between Poles and Jews, is blurred. Moreover, the painful distrust characteristic of Jewish–Polish relationships turns in the novel into conventional complicated relationships between men and women. In this way, the relationship between Poles and Jews with its unique load is portrayed as banal melodrama.

Regina and her granddaughter return to Israel, but the hope that the two couples can keep in touch and meet in the future remains:

Modan makes use of the cliché of Israelis going to Poland to reclaim their property. What for Israelis is an act of seeking justice is for Poles a nightmare. The question of reclaiming property is complicated, as it involves other interests and emotions as well. In one way or another, such a framework is the best background for a story of suspicion, fear, hatred, and conflict. However, Modan turns it into a story of love, affection, and longing. Instead of fighting and hating one another, Jews and Poles in the novel make love.[35]

Modan also deals with the clichéd and shallow way in which Israelis view Poland and the 'industry of Shoah tourist trips'. On the flight to Warsaw the aeroplane is full of teenagers on a high-school students' trip to Holocaust sites in Poland, whose behaviour on board is carefree, lively, and mischievous. They do not reflect on what awaits them, do not read about or discuss the historical, moral, or psychological issues which are indispensable to understanding the brutal past. The students treat their educational trip to Poland simply as a holiday. Other passengers compete over whose family had more wealth in pre-war Poland or a more noble ancestry, with important and famous rabbis. Death camps are treated as Disneyland sites: each day is dedicated to another death camp, and the guide says that he prefers Majdanek to Auschwitz because it is much more frightening, like someone who looks for a chilling experience in an amusement park. The Israeli collective memory of the Holocaust is as composed of stereotypes as Sarid showed in *The Memory Monster*. Modan seeks to subvert these clichés of the Israelis' collective memory of the Holocaust. Not only are the patterns of remembering ironized (the patterns of youth delegations to Poland, the search for roots, reclaiming property, mythologizing the personal family past) but so too is the strict separation of us—the Jews—and them—the Poles—who are perceived as two different groups with totally separate histories and roles in the Holocaust. We, the Jews, are the victims and they, the Poles, are not mere bystanders but persecutors who betrayed their neighbours through the long years of the war. Modan suggests that this strict separation might be blurred, that Jews and Poles can fall in love with each other and might even have a child, a human being who is neither pure Jew nor pure Pole but a mixture of both, and this fact is not a cause for unease but just a simple fact. Reingold proposes that *The Property* 'introduces the idea that for Jews, too, Poland can offer a space to reconnect to the living past and present and not just to the dead past'.[36] Moreover, rather unusually for Israeli literature, Modan gives a place to the Polish narrative, which is different from the Jewish narrative regarding Poles.[37] Tomasz is working on a graphic novel about the Warsaw uprising in 1944, a central event in the Polish collective memory of heroism during the war. In addition, the cemetery that appears in the novel is not a Jewish cemetery, a typical destination on journeys to Poland in Israeli novels, but a Polish Catholic cemetery on All Saints' Day, when Poles visit their family graves.[38] This is a holiday with which Israelis are rather unfamiliar. Moreover, the sites Mika and Regina visit on their trip are not typical of Shoah trips (cemeteries, ghettos, concentration and death camps) but imply normality: cafes, offices, stores, and a Polish cemetery.[39] Modan also deconstructs Polish stereotypes, such as that Jews are greedy or do not acknowledge the victimhood of the Poles.[40] She shows that the (hi)story of the Polish–Jewish relationship and the memory of the Holocaust is a complex one and not, as sometimes both sides want to see it, black and white. The Jewish and Polish narratives of the Second World War are divergent. Modan says that this is an important issue in her book: 'When I went to Poland, I think my biggest surprise as an Israeli was to find out that Poles have a very different story about the past from what I was taught . . . Their story, for them, was true, just like mine. We have to accept that they have a different narrative.'[41] Concerning the two diverse narratives, I think that Assaf Gamzou's conclusion regarding Modan's novel is accurate:

> *The Property* . . . deconstructs common Israeli assumptions concerning World War II. In place of national conception, another history is revealed, one in which Poles and Jews had much more intricate and nuanced relationships . . . we discover a different history, one not motivated by conflicting national identities, but by personal memory, love, and tragedy.[42]

Thus Modan suggests that a way for Poles and Jews to reconcile their differences is to acknowledge their common but divisive past through a full awareness and knowledge of it.[43]

Bandit

Bandit, by Itamar Orlev, tells a story of brutal and painful relationships between fathers and sons.[44] Until the son resolves his inner conflict about his complex, love/hate relationship with his father he cannot be a good father to his own son. The book shows the search for identity and understanding and does not offer a definite solution. However, this important issue is not the topic of the present chapter, and I will concentrate on Jewish–Polish relations in the novel. In *Bandit*, Jewish–Polish relationships are signified by father–son relations. In order to exorcise the shadow of his abusive father, Tadek (Tadeusz) Zagórski travels to Poland, although he goes without fully understanding his motives.[45]

Tadek is a Polish-born Israeli, 36 years old, a writer who hardly writes, and the father of a little boy. His life is in crisis, since his wife and son have left him because he has failed in his roles as husband and father. Tadek feels emotionally crippled. He cannot build bonds with his son and is paralysed in his contact with him. 'I could not be the father I wanted to be; I did not want to be the father I was.'[46] His failings as a father derive from his complicated relationship with his own father, Stefan, during his childhood in Poland. Tadek was brought to Israel in 1964 with his two sisters and brother by his mother Ewa when he was 12. He is the youngest child and the only one who has remained in Israel with his mother. His siblings, all of whom suffered at the hands of their father, live in North America. The father remained in Poland. Stefan was supposed to join his family later, but Ewa prevented his immigration. She has in fact escaped to Israel with her children to get away from him. She was probably able to block Stefan's immigration because she is Jewish and he is Catholic. Ewa tells Tadek openly that she immigrated with her children to Israel to save them from their abusive father and give them the prospect of a better future than the one they could expect in Poland. She emphasizes that her actions were not motivated by support for Zionism but were a pragmatic decision. Tadek, abandoned by his wife and son, decides to travel to Poland and to encounter his father, who lives in Warsaw in an old-age home for partisans and war heroes. Stefan's personality is multifaceted. He is extremely violent, and used to beat his wife and children cruelly and constantly. He was always drunk: Tadek remembers that the smell of vodka was his father's smell.

He used to disappear from home for long periods, once for two whole years. While in Warsaw, Tadek discovers that his father had, at the same time, a second family with two children. Stefan often took the money earned by Ewa's hard work and spent it on drink. However, Tadek also remembers magical moments when Stefan was charming, sang, played musical instruments, and danced. At such times he could be a sparkling, affectionate character. These rare moments sometimes overshadowed the constant petrifying fear that accompanied Tadek during his childhood.

Tadek, like Mika, shows that the dichotomy of 'us Jews' and 'them Poles' cannot be maintained. Yet with Tadek the inadequacy of this dichotomy is much more obvious. Mika was born in Israel, is totally Israeli in her culture and ways of thinking, and is only a quarter Polish, while Tadek was born in Poland and lived there until the age of 12. He speaks Polish, he knows Poland and its culture, he is an immigrant in Israel, and he is half-Polish. He spent his childhood on a state farm and his holidays with his beloved Catholic grandmother in her village, and was unaware that he was Jewish. The only religious experience he had was Catholic prayers with his grandmother before going to sleep. These places in the countryside are the lost paradise of his childhood. Tadek's memories of the village are pastoral and nostalgic. For years he has longed to return there, to see again the landscape, to breathe its air. He remembers many scenes from it, such as praying to the guardian angel with his grandmother before going to sleep and the warmth of her protecting body when they slept in the same bed. His grandmother was a tough, hard-working peasant, the only person his father was afraid of. After a few years, the family moved to a slum in Wrocław, where there was no beautiful nature or loving grandmother but only the bare brutality of the poor urban environment and his destructive father. This period is portrayed as impoverished and brutal. Tadek remembers real hunger, violence, alcoholism, and fights between gangs of street children.

On his journey to his birthplace, Tadek discovers many details about his father that were unknown to him. However, these do not solve the complexity of Stefan's personality. This violent drunkard is, to some extent, a victim of the war, whose fate was even more atrocious than that of his mother, the Holocaust survivor. Orlev, like Modan, gives a place to the narrative of the Other, and in *Bandit* it is the main narrative, something unknown to the Israeli reader.

The case of *Bandit* is intriguing. On the one hand, it was published in 2015 and its spirit belongs entirely to the second wave; on the other, the action takes place in 1988, in the twilight of poor, murky communist Poland which was the backdrop of the first wave. Yet Tadek travels to Poland not as to a huge cemetery of Jews, but to post-war Poland, to his homeland, and to visit his living Polish family. The Polish communist background, the poor urban landscape, do not play a major role in the book, since Tadek is looking for the living, for his father, and for his own identity. His father's life is the Polish narrative, especially during the war. And it is multifaceted, not black and white; it cannot therefore fit the Israeli narrative. Like Tomasz in *The Property*, who gives the Polish story a place, for instance in describing the Warsaw uprising, so Stefan in *Bandit* has his own Polish narrative. His life story is a confirmation neither of the Israeli stereotype of the murderous, antisemitic Pole nor of the Polish narrative of the unblemished heroism and suffering of a righteous nation. Orlev abandons the Israeli perspective in favour of a more complicated one that gives space to the Polish viewpoint but is not a reflection of the present Polish politics of memory. The plot unfolds in three different time periods. The first is Tadek's present, the 1980s, his life with his wife and son until they leave him, his voyage to Poland, and his encounter with his father and his family in the village. The second is Tadek's childhood in Poland in the 1950s and the beginning of the 1960s, and the third is the Second World War, as described by Tadek's parents, mainly his father, recounting their different experiences during the war.

In an interview, Orlev admitted that in his family the Polish story had not been completely resolved. His interest in Polish culture and Poland was not a new one; he had had it since childhood:

[In our family] there has always been some kind of weakness for Poland, not the Poland of *gefilte fish* but that of the non-Jews, of culture. When I discovered the Polish poets, for example, it was a marvellous discovery. I read them one by one, Herbert, Miłosz and Szymborska, I learned to know the filmmakers in Poland. My acquaintance was far away from the image of the Poles in Israel. I remember being in India, every once in a while I'd meet some guy from Poland: straight away I'd sing him the only song I know in Polish. We cheered on the Polish national team in the Olympics. That is how it was. It is not that from morning till evening I dream in Polish, but I definitely have a weakness.[47]

Stefan's life is a different Polish story from the one Israelis usually know. Tadek, as an immigrant in Israel, points to Israeli society as a mirror of Polish society. Both are intolerant of outsiders. The figure of the vulgar and violent Polish antisemite is well known and shows up in the novel in some images from the war and, especially, in the use of Polish expressions: for example, 'Don't be stingy like the Jews.' Tadek learns that he is Jewish only a short time before the family emigrates to Israel. His brother tells him that they are going to Palestine, the country of the Jews, and warns him not to pee in the company of other children. Tadek promises, although he does not understand that this is so that they will not realize he hasn't been circumcised. And then his brother tells him: 'If anyone there calls you a *goy*, break his teeth.' Tadek asks, 'What is a *goy*?' and his brother answers 'I do not know, but there in Palestine, it is the coarsest curse you can use.'[48] In Poland, the coarsest curse is still 'Jew'. When Tadek first meets his father in the old-age home, the latter asks him to pretend to come from America and not Israel because the other residents might think that he is a Jew. The position of Jews in Poland of the 1980s is not comfortable. When Wojciech, Stefan's friend in the old-age home, tells him that his son looks Jewish, he is so offended that he assaults him. The same Wojciech has never married because he is mourning his Jewish girlfriend, whom he planned to marry, but she was killed in the war. Stereotypes are deeply rooted in both societies. In Poland Tadek is a Jew, and in Israel he is a *goy*. It turns out that Tadek, after emigrating to Israel, decided to be circumcised because the kibbutz children picked on him. The lack of tolerance towards the other is similar to that in Poland, only in Israel it is the Jews who are intolerant. Stefan tells him that his Jewish friend emigrated to Israel with his Polish wife and discovered that 'there they [the Jews], sons of bitches, hate the *goyim* almost as much as here they hate the Jews'.[49]

As mentioned, Stefan is a victim of the war. Tadek takes his father from the old-age home for a trip to the latter's birthplace. During the trip Tadek meets other family members, like his cousin Halina, who is dear to him, and her charming family in Chełm. In fact, Tadek has a larger family in Poland than in Israel: his non-Jewish Polish side is numerous. His grandmother is dead, but in the village, which arouses pleasant memories in Tadek's mind, his aunt Irena—Stefan's sister—is still alive. In the few days of travelling from Warsaw to eastern Poland, Stefan tells Tadek for the first time about his experience during the war. It is not a coherent story: the plot is fragmented, the tale is full of silences. Nonetheless, Tadek and the reader can fill in the gaps and have the whole story before their eyes.

Stefan's life story is painful and crude. He experienced horrific episodes, but did he pass the moral test? Orlev's story points to the fact that to be a hero it is not necessary to be pure and moral. What is perceived from one perspective as heroism can be perceived from another as wrongdoing. During the war Stefan was a partisan in the Polish underground, which subsequently became the Home Army. At the beginning, his activity was typical for the resistance: bombing bridges, shooting Germans, or escaping from them. In his fragmented story Stefan also speaks about Jews in the villages. How they were treated by the Germans, how some Poles helped Jews, and how some Poles deceived them—handed them over to the Nazis or killed them. Stefan also mentions that the local police collaborated with the Nazis.[50] *Bandit* shows how complicated the relations between Jews and Poles were during the war. Jewish suspicion of Poles was so overwhelming that even when a Pole (Tadek's uncle) had no intention of handing a Jewish woman who was hiding in his barn over to the Germans, she was so afraid that he intended to betray her that she tried to escape and got shot. Poles also denounced partisans to the Nazis; that was how Stefan himself was caught. Stefan describes informing as a regular and common practice, a law of nature. But what annoyed him particularly was the passivity of the Jews. How could a few soldiers take thousands into the forests and kill them? Why did they not fight back? They were unarmed, but they were numerous. If they had fought, maybe some would have been saved.[51] Stefan loved to fight, and fear was not an emotion with which he was familiar. He could not understand inaction or fear for one's own children, or that people might have had enough and lose their will to live.

Yet the most horrendous experience for Stefan was the torture and cruelty he suffered in the Gestapo headquarters in Lublin and during the subsequent two years imprisoned in Majdanek. In Majdanek he also saw Jews. The difference between the Jews and the Poles, according to Stefan, was how they were killed: the Nazis fought the Poles, but they slaughtered the Jews.[52] He managed to escape from Majdanek together with a group of partisans through sewage channels and forests. After some months of convalescence, he returned to the headquarters of the Home Army in Warsaw, and there he was assigned a new role—as executioner for the underground. Stefan tells Tadek that in Majdanek the Germans had taught him to kill without remorse. He now had to implement death sentences imposed on collaborators and informers, but also sometimes on his own initiative he killed robbers and rapists who abused Poles and Jews.[53] Sometimes he killed them in front of their children, but only ever after they had confessed their crimes. In order to carry out his role successfully, he had to learn two things: to hate and to drink a lot of liquor. He obtained special permission to drink 'at work'. Usually members of the Home Army were not allowed to drink, but his superiors knew that otherwise he would not be able to perform his role. After the war he was sentenced to death by the communists on the charge that, as a member of the Home Army, he had murdered innocent people. However, a partisan friend who had been with him in Majdanek and who became a communist official after the war arranged an amnesty for him. Did his wartime experience justify Stefan's later behaviour, the cruel and brutal way he treated his family? Not according to Ewa: others who experienced terrible things during the war remained good people who did not abuse their families.

Tadek looks at his old, pathetic father and thinks: 'This man who is my father, a Polish hedonist who has screwed and hit and murdered . . . in some sense he is a Polish bandit . . . but when I look at him, there is no aura above this miserable figure who lies on the bed.'[54] He concludes that he does not care anymore what his father did; what matters is the pain caused by his father to his family. He mourns for himself, his mother, and his siblings, who had to suffer for so many years because of Stefan's uncontrolled urges.

On his return to Israel, at his father's request, Tadek gives his son a book documenting the stories of his grandfather as a partisan. In this way, Stefan's Jewish grandson is also bound to his Polish family's history.[55]

Is Tadek a Pole or an Israeli Jew? Is he a victim or a bystander? Orlev blurs the boundaries of identity. Tadek is both a Pole and a Jew, and in the private sphere he might be the victim of his father and the torturer of his son. Orlev crosses the boundaries of black/white, right/wrong, sacrificing/sacrificed. While Modan does something similar but in a light way, full of irony and distance, Orlev takes the tragic path and shows that the Jewish and Polish roles in the relationship are not fixed and determined but far more multifaceted than either Jews or Poles think.

Conclusion

In both *The Property* and *Bandit* not only does fear of the diaspora have no role in the self-identity of the protagonists but also the 'Jewishness' of the Israeli no longer has to satisfy the requirements of pure Jewish ethnicity. Tadek also feels at home in Poland, and Mika is a citizen of the world. Their self-identities do not need the exclusive Zionist narration of national-ethnic state—'the Land of Israel for the people of Israel'. Both novels also broaden the narrative of the Holocaust, embracing the Polish narrative within the Jewish one.

Poles and Israelis both want to construct a positive image of the past, although for different motives. Poles have not yet worked through the trauma of war and their guilt at being passive bystanders or collaborators. Furthermore, to be the perpetual victim (as both groups perceive themselves) is a heavy burden that conceals the complexity of history. The narrative of 'not all the Poles were antisemites, murderers, and collaborators with the Nazis, there were some noble and righteous Poles' can also heal Israeli paranoia. It is perhaps much easier for both groups to live in the present, embracing and embedding not totally accurate historical narratives. However, expanding their historical horizons might heal some wounds.

Notes

1 G. Shaked, *Hasiporet ha'ivrit 1880–1970*, 5 vols. (Tel Aviv, 1977–98), i. 19–34. Shaked claimed that Israeli literature in Hebrew corresponded to what he called 'the Zionist metanarrative', either by propagating and reflecting it or by rejecting and criticizing it (see ibid. v. 19–105). Although I believe that this does not cover the full spectrum of Hebrew literature written in Israel, it does show that it is not created in a vacuum.

2 Y. Zerubavel, 'The "Mythological Sabra" and Jewish Past: Trauma, Memory, and Contested Identities', *Israel Studies*, 7/2 (2002), 115–44: 115.

3 A. Shapira, 'Hamitos shel hayehudi heḥadash', in id., *Yehudim ḥadashim, yehudim yeshanim* (Tel Aviv, 2003), 155–74; Zerubavel, 'The "Mythological Sabra" and Jewish Past', 116–18.

4 R. Matalon, *Kero ukhetov* (Tel Aviv, 2001), 41–9.

5 Z. Bauman, *Identity: Conversations with Benedetto Vecchi* (Cambridge, 2004), 10–11.

6 Ibid. 1.

7 S. Ronen, 'Post-Holocaust Representations of Poland in Israeli Literature', *Polish Review*, 60 (2015), 3–20. The 'second generation' is well known in the literature; in recent studies the term 'the third generation' has also been widely accepted (see e.g. V. Aarons (ed.), *Third-Generation Holocaust Narratives: Memory in Memoir and Fiction* (Lanham, Md., 2016); E. Jilovsky, J. Silverstein, and D. Slucki (eds.), *In the Shadows of Memory: The Holocaust and the Third Generation* (London, 2015); J. Budzik, '"Erec szam" – "kraj tam": Strategie konstruowania obrazów Polski w literackich i pozaliterackich tekstach kultury o Zagładzie, izrealskich autorów trzeciego pokolenia', Ph.D. thesis (Adam Mickiewicz University, 2019)).

8 In fact, from 1983 for the commemoration of the fortieth anniversary of the Warsaw ghetto uprising.

9 This trend is also present in *The Property* by Ruto Modan, which will be discussed below. It includes Poles who work as tourist guides of Jewish Warsaw, who want to reconstruct the ghetto, or organize re-enactments of the liquidation of the ghetto. There are many literary works written in Poland relating to Jewish culture and history. See e.g. O. Tokarczuk, *Księgi Jakubowe* (Kraków, 2014).

10 Ronen, 'Post-Holocaust Representations of Poland in Israeli Literature', 7.

11 See S. Ronen, *Polin, a Land of Forests and Rivers: Images of Poland and Poles in Contemporary Hebrew Literature in Israel* (Warsaw, 2007).

12 e.g. M. Hermoni, *Hebrew Publishing Company* (Or Yehudah, 2011); Y. Itskovits, *Tikun aḥar ḥazot* (Jerusalem, 2015); B. Mer, *Smots'ah: biyografyah shel reḥov yehudi bevarshah* (Jerusalem, 2019); E. Nevo, *Neuland* (Or Yehuda, 2011); Y. Pinkus, *Hakabaret hahistori shel*

profesor fabrikant (Tel Aviv, 2008). I call the trend in these and other books 'neo-diasporism in modern Hebrew literature'. This is a project I am currently working on.

13 Z. Sternhell, *The Founding Myths of Israel: Nationalism, Socialism, and the Making of the Jewish State*, trans. D. Maisel (Princeton, NJ, 1966), 47–8.

14 Ibid. 48.

15 'Negation of the diaspora' was not typical of all Zionist thought: for example, that of Yehoshua Thon (S. Ronen, *A Prophet of Consolation on the Threshold of Destruction: Yehoshua Ozjasz Thon, an Intellectual Portrait* (Warsaw, 2015), 189–202).

16 Sternhell, *The Founding Myths of Israel*, 49.

17 Zerubavel, 'The "Mythological Sabra" and Jewish Past', 138.

18 Ibid.

19 A. Raz-Krakotzkin, 'Galut betokh ribonut: levikoret "shelilat hagalut" batarbut ha'isre'elit', *Teoria uvikoret*, 4 (1993), 23–55; 5 (1994), 113–32.

20 A. Raz-Krakotzkin, 'Mi ani lelo galut?', *Teoria uvikoret*, 50 (2018), 61–74.

21 Y. Sarid, *Mifletset hazikaron* (Tel Aviv, 2017).

22 Ibid. 9–11.

23 Ibid. 31.

24 Ibid. 73.

25 Ibid. 32.

26 Ibid. 74.

27 Ibid. 102–3.

28 J. Feldman, *Above the Death Pits, Beneath the Flag: Youth Voyages to Poland and the Performance of Israeli National Identity* (New York, 2008); id., 'Israeli Youth Voyages to Holocaust Poland: Through the Prism of Pilgrimage', in A. M. Pazos (ed.), *Redefining Pilgrimage: New Perspectives on Historical and Contemporary Pilgrimages* (Farnham, Surr., 2014); I. Yaron, *Masaot benei no'ar le'atarei hamavet bepolin: yomano shel antropolog* (Petah Tikva, 2019).

29 R. Modan, *Hanekhes* (Tel Aviv, 2013); Eng. trans.: *The Property*, trans. J. Cohen (New York, 2013).

30 I do not discuss the visual aspects of the novel. Gamzou has shown how the colourful, manufactured graphics ensure that the novel is perceived as pure fiction (A. Gamzou, 'Third-Generation Graphic Syndrome: New Directions in Comics and Holocaust Memory in the Age after Testimony', *Journal of Holocaust Research*, 33 (2019), 224–37: 232, 234; see also B. Gasztold, 'Of Love and War: Poles and Jews in Rutu Modan's *The Property*', *Scripta Judaica Cracoviensia*, 15 (2017), 141–52: 143–4).

31 Stereotypes have a double function: on the one hand, they reinforce prejudices; on the other hand, 'they facilitate cross-cultural awareness' (Gasztold, 'Of Love and War', 141–2, 150).

32 Modan, *The Property*, 118; see ead., *Hanekhes*, 118.

33 In an interview with CBR.com, she said: 'when I was writing I liked the idea of playing with the stereotype of Jews and money' (A. Dueben, 'Rutu Modan Explores Post-WWII Poland in "The Property"' (1 Oct. 2013): CBR.com website, visited 14 June 2021).

34 Modan, *The Property*, 85–6; see ead., *Hanekhes*, 85–6.

35 Ronen, 'Post-Holocaust Representations of Poland in Israeli Literature', 20.

36 M. Reingold, 'Israeli and Polish Holocaust Commemoration in Rutu Modan's *The Property*', *Journal of Holocaust Research*, 33 (2019), 175–90: 179.

37 It was not the first time that Israeli literature had expressed the Polish narrative alongside the Jewish one (see e.g. H. Herzig, *Temunot mehapeshot koteret* (Tel Aviv, 1997); see also

S. Ronen, 'Masaot lepolin basifrut hayisre'elit ke'emtsa'i lehavnayat zikaron vezehut', in *Meḥkarim belashon, sifrut vetarbut ivrit: divrei hakinus hamada'i ha'ivri ha'esrim be'eiropah* (Toruń, 2013), 109 23).

38 Gamzou, 'Third-Generation Graphic Syndrome', 234.
39 Reingold, 'Israeli and Polish Holocaust Commemoration in Rutu Modan's *The Property*', 182–3.
40 I refer only to stereotypes presented in the novels, not the whole complex of Jewish–Polish mutual perceptions. On the current political Polish dominant narrative and its contra-narratives, see Reingold, 'Israeli and Polish Holocaust Commemoration in Rutu Modan's *The Property*', 184–6.
41 Dueben, 'Rutu Modan Explores Post-WWII Poland in "The Property"'.
42 Gamzou, 'Third-Generation Graphic Syndrome', 235.
43 Reingold, 'Israeli and Polish Holocaust Commemoration in Rutu Modan's *The Property*', 189.
44 I. Orlev, *Bandit* (Tel Aviv, 2015). Itamar Orlev is the son of Uri Orlev, the Holocaust survivor and Israeli children's author.
45 J. Rotem, 'Madua hasefer hazeh maḥats et libi gam bikeriah sheniyah ushelishit' (17 Sept. 2015): *Haaretz* website, visited 16 Dec. 2021.
46 Orlev, *Bandit*, 349.
47 A. Rubinstein, 'Selaḥ li, avi, ki katavti' (29 May 2015): Yisra'el hayom website, visited 14 June 2021.
48 Orlev, *Bandit*, 147.
49 Ibid. 106.
50 Ibid. 116.
51 Ibid. 164.
52 Ibid. 166.
53 Ibid. 290.
54 Ibid. 337–8.
55 Rotem, 'Madua hasefer hazeh maḥats et libi gam bikeriah sheniyah ushelishit'.

Other Family Stories
The Third Post-Holocaust Generation's Journey to Poland

JAGODA BUDZIK

In this chapter I examine the trope of the journey to Poland in texts by Israeli authors of the third post-Holocaust generation, especially in comparison with how Poland appears in narratives widely accepted by the Israeli public. The authors discussed below focus on their families' personal experiences of Poland, which differ from how it is perceived in the Israeli national imagination. As I hope to demonstrate, a shift occurred between the second and third post-Holocaust generations, which influenced how authors conceptualize the motif of the journey to Poland. This change not only grants the author a deeper understanding of their family history but also challenges the official Holocaust narrative and the clichés in the Israeli national imagination.

In literature by second-generation authors, one of the most prominent motifs is that of families reliving their Holocaust experiences from the perspective of a child. Interestingly, not only has this strongly influenced works by actual children of Holocaust survivors but it has also become a durable literary figure in itself, elevated to the rank of a paradigm by David Grossman's novel *See Under: Love*.[1] Silent families travelling to Poland in the 1970s and 1980s, a country which has nothing more to offer them than a sense of emptiness, is one of the themes that stands out most prominently in these texts. The third-generation writers also use the motif of returning to one's roots. However, in the texts I have selected for discussion that quest has changed its meaning, as have the authors' generational affinities and the circumstances in which they employ the theme of going back to Poland. By introducing ambiguity into the solidified narrative schemata or by modifying them altogether, these authors turn their family experience into a statement. Each of the texts under consideration here distances itself from what it considers to be the 'memory mainstream' with the use of different means of expression: generic, formal, and narrative.

Nonetheless, describing Israeli authors' confrontations with Holocaust memory in terms of post-Holocaust generations has its roots in the distinctive nature of their experience,[2] which can sometimes be perceived as too narrow to truly express its actual complexity.[3] Visual artist Hadas Tapouchi, in the introduction to her project 'Third Generation', expresses similar concerns: 'The term that gives this project its title, "Third Generation", refers to individuals who are now a third generation from the Holocaust. "Generation" is a symbolic concept that suggests that people of the same age share a similar social experience and collective memory.'[4] Tapouchi tries to break down this unifying, and thus sometimes oppressive and simplifying, categorization by juxtaposing portraits of young Israeli Jews, Palestinians, Poles, and Germans, particularly with regard to their fixed placement within national frames. The characters' confrontation unequivocally leads to questions about whether belonging to a particular national community of memory is what defines their identities as captured in the pictures. I believe this proves that the generational concept, when approached critically rather than dogmatically, can serve as a useful tool with numerous applications. On the one hand, immanently inscribed with the sense of transience, the third generation locates the author's experience in the context of changes which have taken place within the Israeli Holocaust narrative and its impact on how Poland tends to be conceptualized. On the other hand, it allows reflection on individual and collective identity and, more generally, on the mechanisms of memory.

In works by third-generation authors, Poland is particularly conducive to reflections on collective remembrance and personal identity. I therefore agree with Shoshana Ronen, who argues that Poland is never perceived as neutral: 'A journey to Poland, in Israeli literature, is not typical. A person who decides to travel to Poland is not simply a tourist who wants to explore unknown places, climates, customs, works of art, etc. A journey to Poland in Israeli literature is very loaded.'[5] Elsewhere she has stated:

Poland is perceived by the Israeli traveller as a huge Jewish cemetery. The place is known mostly through the prism of testimony from Holocaust survivors. These testimonies about the atrocious past are sometimes the stories of people who were close relatives or neighbors, but sometimes stories are read at school and during Holocaust Remembrance Day ceremonies.[6]

From this perspective, Poland provides the background for historical narratives and also remains solidly present in contemporarily constructed memory discourses, formed to a great extent through school pilgrimages.[7] Jackie Feldman argues that 'the trip to Poland has become a central rite in what Charles Liebman and Eliezer Don-Yehiya have termed Israel's "civil religion". The objective of civil religion is the sanctification of the society in which it functions, and it can only be successful insofar as the individual fuses their identity with that of the collective.'[8]

Such pilgrimages create conditions that are conducive to the search for a historical, genealogical, and cultural continuity, in which Poland serves as a link between the past and the present. From an institutional perspective, the dichotomy between the categories of 'the Holocaust' and 'rebirth' is projected, in the institutionally created collective imagination, onto national and geographical planes, which juxtaposes Jews with non-Jews, and Poland—the land of the Holocaust—with Israel —the land of Jewish rebirth. The latter sequence and its spatial dimension perhaps most adequately represents one of the many functions performed by the Holocaust in creating the official narrative of Israeli identity, transformed, reproduced, and deconstructed by culture. Its constant presence indicates the extent to which Holocaust memory is a major element in describing events from the past and how directly they are linked to the state's origins.

However, third-generation authors more and more often distance themselves from this scheme. The image of Poland they construct is often significantly different from the images constructed by the second generation and the official narrative. In their narratives, Poland ceases to be only a place marked by the Holocaust, a testimony to a void, and 'the country of death'. It becomes, in Michel Foucault's terms, a scene of 'counter-memory'. Applying this term to the Israeli context, Yael Zerubavel explains that:

Countermemory is essentially oppositional and stands in hostile and subversive relation to collective memory. If the master commemorative narrative attempts to suppress alternative views of the past, the countermemory in turn denies the validity of the narrative constructed by the collective memory and presents its own claim for more accurate representation of history.[9]

This is likely to be the case in a situation where a family journey to Poland, conditioned by individual family burdens, becomes an alternative to the collective experience of a school pilgrimage. As a result, the representational schemata undergo further developments, and the experience of Poland, though apparently solidified in well-established cultural frames, seems to slip out of the official narrative of Holocaust memory, by means of which it deconstructs the categories which that discourse typically applies.

The Property and the Subversive Use of Clichés

Such a vision is conjured up by Rutu Modan in her graphic novel *The Property*,[10] which recounts the journey of a young Israeli, Mika, and her grandmother, Regina, to Warsaw, where the latter spent her childhood and youth. The images the journey evokes, though engaging with some familiar themes (such as school journeys to Holocaust memory sites in Poland and restitution of Jewish property), are eventually set apart from the clichés of the Israeli journey to Poland. As the narrative unfolds, this becomes increasingly apparent, as the following three scenes clearly demonstrate.

The putative reason for the visit is to reclaim an apartment that belonged to the family and was appropriated during the war. From the first scenes it seems clear that Regina's war experience has left her with an immense resentment of Poland and the Poles. Because of that she incessantly tries to distance herself emotionally from the journey. When still on the plane, she says: 'Warsaw is of no interest to me. It's one big cemetery.'[11] Yet it turns out that the real motive behind Regina's journey is not to reclaim the lost apartment, which it seems does not exist, but to find her pre-war lover, a Pole, in the light of which her resentment of Poland proves to be a facade. Modan hence uses the motif of Poland as a 'big cemetery' and constructs one situation after another typical of that motif: a trip to a world in which 'there's nothing to search for',[12] a school trip with a predetermined schedule: 'Monday: Treblinka; Tuesday: Majdanek, along with gas chambers.'[13] Each of the tropes, however, is gradually deconstructed, exposed as a mere distraction, and discarded.

On the plane from Tel Aviv to Warsaw, the protagonists meet a group of Israeli high-school students, who are on a pilgrimage to memorial sites. Modan distances Mika from the experience, as, during a conversation with the group's guide, Mika admits that she never visited Poland as a high-school student.[14] From the very beginning this separates her experience from those of most of her peers. It also clearly indicates that *The Property* is a different story, in which the family journey of Regina and Mika is marked as distinct from the national phenomenon of school pilgrimages.

Modan also refers to the emotions that underpin Israelis' encounters with Polish spaces, but instead of replicating the common experience and practice of grieving Holocaust victims, she shows how wide the actual range of emotions which an individual might experience when visiting Poland is and how diverse the reasons behind them might be. In the scene where Mika first meets Tomasz, a Polish guide to Jewish Warsaw, he is able to guess her origins: 'Let's see . . . You're sitting in a café in the ghetto, you look sad.'[15] His attempt to approach ironically the clichéd emotionality of Israeli Jewish visits to Poland proves a failure. Mika's sadness is not caused by the Holocaust but by the recent death of her father. In this way the concepts of death and mourning change their context: they extend beyond the collective, nationally determined, and politically charged trauma cemented by Israeli confrontations with Poland.

The ultimate fracturing of the cliché of Poland as a Jewish cemetery takes place in the climactic scene, set during the Catholic holiday of All Souls' Day in a Christian cemetery, most probably Powązki Cemetery. On the one hand, the decision to set the action in this location interrupts the automatic chain of associations which limit the use of the words 'cemetery' and 'Poland' exclusively to the context of the Holocaust; on the other hand, it opens a way to formulate the central conclusion of the novel: that an Israeli confrontation with Poland may have more than just one manifestation, and that the division between the Polish and the Israeli is not always a clear one. It is in this scene that all the Polish and Israeli characters from *The Property* meet and where Regina introduces Mika to her Polish ex-lover, who is, most likely, Mika's grandfather.

In this way, the frames of an individual and intimate narrative in a sense turn out to be wider and more inclusive than those marking the collective vision of the past. The motif of the cemetery slips out of the symbolic field traditionally ascribed to it by Israeli literature and the national imagination. It becomes a space where the boundaries between national perspectives and nationally determined experiences are blurred. Thus represented, Warsaw, apart from its identity as a cemetery, also acquires other meanings: it becomes, in accordance with Michael Rothberg's theory, a field where multidirectional memory operates, within whose frame 'the overlaying and interferences of memory help the process of constituting the public sphere as well as the various individual and collective subjects searching for a space where they could express themselves'.[16] Modan's use of the motif of a family journey to deconstruct the collective memory schemata is not limited to criticizing the patterns solidified in the national narrative; it also questions the exclusive and unequivocal character of the national perspective that is usually imposed.

This points directly at another of Modan's contestations in *The Property*: the inadequacy of the post-memory category in cases where memory discourse is based primarily on clichés. That contestation clearly reverberates in the exceptionally powerful scene where Mika meets a re-enactment group staging the events of the Warsaw ghetto. Faced with actors wearing uniforms with swastikas, Mika involuntarily puts her hands up as if she has known from the start what role she has been assigned in that situation. Her reaction could be a case of post-memory, which would suggest that the experience of the Holocaust, and the position in which it placed the Jews, has been inherited by Mika as a result of a transgenerational transfer. However, the grotesque context in which the gesture happens should be read as a negation of the reality, at least of the actuality, of those mechanisms. Mika's uncontrolled and immediate act of putting her hands up, as Modan seems to suggest, is as much a legitimate proof of the transgenerational transfer as is the scene of the liquidation of the ghetto, staged by Polish history-lovers.

A Silent Biography Reoccupied

A change in attitude towards Poland as the setting for family biographies, for writers of the third generation, not only accentuates the growing distance from the events of the Holocaust but is also related to the deaths of increasing numbers of those who experienced it at first hand and could share their memories of it. This, along with the institutionalization of such memories in the official Israeli Holocaust narrative, generates a durable divide between the perception of Poland as a place where one's ancestors lived and the increasingly popular view of Poland as a universal symbol of the whole nation's suffering. In accordance with Jeffrey Alexander's observation, the Holocaust has been transformed into 'a generalised symbol of human suffering and moral evil';[17] Poland has inevitably become a reference point for the institutionalized rituals of memory, and as such it has taken root in the Israeli national imagination.

In the case of authors whose family members survived the Holocaust, the deaths of those relatives has meant losing the possibility of asking questions and learning about a crucial part of their family history. A special attempt to fill such an identity void has been made by Yuval Yareach in his novel *The Silences*, which seeks to transform that monumental narrative, one functioning at a collective level, into an individualized one.[18] In an interview, Yareach admitted that the only way to at least partially know about his grandmother Manja's experiences was to retrace her life from an everyday perspective, by describing it day by day and almost obsessively recreating all its details.[19] As a result, Yareach accepted the challenge of producing a total narrative—a historical novel recreating wartime events from his own family's history, in particular those from his grandmother's life, which he diligently documented, in a very detailed manner, from the day of her birth in 1916, through her time in the Kraków ghetto, from which she briefly escaped and managed to entrust her newborn baby daughter to a Polish family, her imprisonment in the Płaszów concentration camp, and finally Auschwitz-Birkenau. The last part of the novel describes the post-war years of the family: the moment when Manja is reunited with Lala, who survived hidden by the Polish family, and when together they leave for Palestine. A note which prefaces the text describes how writing the family history was preceded by extensive research in Polish and Israeli archives: what is particularly significant is that the author was constantly accompanied by the granddaughter of the Polish family who had saved his newborn mother by hiding her throughout the war.

However, what draws the reader's attention is the obsessive particularity. Each sub-part of the 500-page text starts with information about the date, the weather, and sometimes even Manja's actual weight. These compulsive attempts to recreate the details of that reality, which were irretrievably lost with Manja's death, and the recurring cruel and detailed descriptions of camp life, the hunger, cold, and fear, are supposed to bring the author, and the reader, closer to understanding that reality. The history, which was first hidden in Manja's silences evoked in the title of the novel, and which after her death was apparently lost forever, engenders the experience that lies at the heart of the author's identity, and that of many of his peers: 'This book is based on the life of my grandmother, the late Manja Wolfgang, but almost nothing of what I wrote have I heard from her. Over all those years she said very little herself and always left questions on this subject unanswered ... This is why I searched for myself.'[20]

A partial answer to why Manja Wolfgang remained silent may be found on the pages of Yareach's novel, but her silence was also a consequence of how the Holocaust has been remembered in Israel over the decades. In this context, the story of Manja Wolfgang's life and silence, as told by her grandson, turns into a story of double exclusion from the Israeli collective narrative she experienced—both as a Holocaust survivor (who were often excluded from Israeli public discourse in the first decades after the proclamation of the state[21]) and as a woman. The latter might be particularly significant with regard to Manja's inability to apply her experience to the collective patterns of remembering the Holocaust, since, according to Efraim Sicher, 'gender discourse of the Holocaust has been muted, partly because it was not until the seventies that women told their stories as the women's experience of the Holocaust, but also because psychology and sociology alike ignored gender difference'.[22] Thus, all the numerous references to Manja's body, physiology, sexuality, and other characteristics seem to play a significant role in the author's attempt to create a narrative which could fill the void left by the Holocaust narrative he grew up with.[23]

Indeed, one of the factors that made Yareach write *The Silences* was his inability to identify himself with the narratives that surrounded him as he was growing up:

Despite the school lessons devoted to the Holocaust, articles, newspapers, and TV programmes, Holocaust Memorial Days celebrated every year, stories and testimonies, a lot of things remained unclear for me. After my grandmother's death it started to nag me even more; because of that I was reading even more and more and finally I started my own book, which you see in front of yourselves, and even a few times, because of it, I visited Poland.[24]

As he admitted in one interview, his work on the book was supposed to help him recreate, step by step, his grandmother's experiences. Furthermore, Poland, understood on his own terms and not those dictated by the official narrative, promised to become the place that held the identity that he was searching for.

Poland as a Wound upon One's Own Skin

An especially interesting, though different, version of visiting Poland in search of answers to one's identity is Itamar Orlev's *Bandit*, whose starting point was the authentic story of Ami Drozd, though loosely interpreted by him.[25] The novel is set in the late 1980s. The main protagonist is the son of a Jewish woman Holocaust survivor, who left for Israel in the 1960s, and a Polish man, who sheltered her during the war while active in the resistance. The hero, Tadek (Tadeusz), arrives in Poland to look for his father, Stefan, with whom he has not been in touch since moving to Israel. He finds him in an old-age home for veterans in Warsaw, where he is spending his last years, in the hope of explaining why his family's complicated life followed the path it did. Finally, though initially reluctantly, *Bandit* adopts the conventions of a quest novel as Tadek goes with his father to the place of his birth. As they travel, Tadek listens to his father's stories about his wartime experiences: his participation in the resistance, his imprisonment in the Majdanek camp, from where he escaped, and the final years of the war in the Polish underground. He also learns the story of Stefan's hiding of the Jewish woman, Ewa, who later became his wife and Tadek's mother. The gradual discovery of these facts shapes Tadek's perception of his father, earlier seen as the main cause of all his childhood traumas, anew.

The fact that the novel is set in Poland in the 1980s inevitably generates associations with earlier Hebrew texts about that period, such as the reportage of Yehudit Hendel and Michal Govrin, which describes Poland as dead and empty.[26] The genres and perspectives are not, paradoxically, the most significant differences between these narratives. The very identity of the protagonist—the son of a Polish man and a Jewish woman, with a Polish name and speaking Polish—defies the traditionally accepted national divisions and avoids the usual story of an Israeli traveller confronting a place charged only with memories of the Holocaust. Wrocław, Warsaw, and Lublin—the cities Tadek visits are familiar to him. More than being just sites of Holocaust memory, they embody painful, though sometimes nostalgic, memories of his childhood.

In addition, the events that set the story in motion are related to the historical conditions to a lesser degree than might be expected: they are almost entirely subjected to the psychological dimension of the novel. Only when it influences the characters' actions and becomes important to the plot does the historical context come to the fore—what the father did during the war, the reality of the People's Republic of Poland—whereas the rest of the time it is kept in the background—the mother's Holocaust experiences, the events of March 1968. Even though the author —despite a few mistakes—describes the communist reality in great detail and goes beyond the stereotypical greyness, the characters' motives and the seemingly universal mechanisms, such as the dynamics of family relations, that stand behind their decisions constitute the novel's main focus. At the same time, communist clichés are a pretext to make further and deeper enquiries into the personal relationships of the characters: for example, the omnipresence of vodka leads to a discussion of Stefan's alcoholism and its effect on the family.

Thanks to its extensive family subplot and meticulous analysis of the characters' psyches, there are numerous reasons to think that one of the most important goals of *Bandit* was to create new possibilities, which arise from setting the action in the Polish landscape, rather than relying on those from the Israeli collective memory:

Outside I felt a pleasant chill. A night in the countryside, which I had been dreaming of for years, embraced me with the smell of fields, a light breeze and a starry sky. From a distance you could actually hear sounds of the city, but they were far away. I lit a cigarette. My breath was back. I tried to think about something else, for example, that I am standing here in the courtyard of Halina's house, that I am smoking the cigarette, and that it all seems so normal. In no way could I imagine it earlier but this time it looks like one of a million similar moments.[27]

Although Tadek is the son of a Holocaust survivor, he never looks at Poland through the prism of his mother's Holocaust experiences. They are always present in the background, but it is his father's story that becomes the key to Orlev's description of the Polish experience. Tadek fails to replicate the unequivocal and nationally conditioned division into Polish and Israeli or Polish and Jewish, which he nonetheless becomes aware of on more than one occasion:

I didn't know Warsaw, I didn't know anyone there, yet the Polish language, which had surrounded me since the moment I landed, was like music in the background that was supposed to accompany me my entire life. Suddenly I realised how irritating was the unwavering harshness of Hebrew, its dryness, which, like sand on the tongue and in the teeth, had been filling up my mouth for over two decades.[28]

Orlev's story thus reverses the usual direction of Israeli constructions of Poland.

The author's decision to set the plot in the 1980s and the fact that the characters do not fit neatly into the recognized generational arrangement reveal in an interesting way the critical potential of the 'generation' category. The main protagonist, Tadek, was born shortly after the war, and as such he should obviously be treated as a representative of the second generation. However, the fact that he emigrated to Israel with his mother and his siblings as a teenager means that his identity was largely influenced by his life in Poland. From that point of view, the protagonist becomes a hybrid with different experiences and multiple perspectives, so that his, and by proxy the reader's, perception of Poland is more diverse and less shaped by the clichés rooted in Israeli imagination.

Conclusion

Israel's official narrative and national mythology present themselves as an ascent, as encapsulated in the expression *misho'ah litekumah* (from the Holocaust to the national revival). Even the Yad Vashem complex is designed so that at its lowest point lies the memory site for those murdered in the diaspora and at its highest is the military cemetery on Mount Herzl.[29] The authors discussed in this chapter seem to move in the opposite direction. Having grown up in a period when the Holocaust was a key element in the national imagination, in their works they transfer the confrontation with Poland to an individual level. Instead of replicating the clichés in the national imagination, they see Poland through the prism of individual family experiences and think critically about the generally accepted patterns of memory. In so doing, they have turned Poland into a space in which ambiguities, alternative versions of the apparently known stories, new perspectives, and relational memory can coexist. Rutu Modan's use of common clichés turns out to be subversive, and eventually helps create a more inclusive and ambiguous narrative. Yuval Yareach, by reconstructing his grandmother's silenced past, points to the inadequacy of the official Holocaust narrative. The reality created by Itamar Orlev eludes nearly all the categories which construct the collective way of thinking about the past, including the generational approach.

The third generation's perception of Poland is strictly related to ways of thinking about Israel's political situation and the stormy, though short, history of the state. The strategies of using clichés about Poland or intentionally defying them often mirror the authors' world-views. However, when the authors refer to their own lives, the reference frequently becomes an ideological, ethical, or aesthetic statement made in response to the Israeli Holocaust narrative. More than of Poland, they speak of the challenges that the Israeli national imagination itself has to face. Therefore, to paraphrase the title of Nathan Englander's *What We Talk About When We Talk About Anne Frank*,[30] the question 'What do they talk about when they talk about Poland?' should be answered: 'First of all about themselves.'

Notes

1 D. Grossman, *Ayen erekh: ahavah* (Tel Aviv, 1991); Eng. edn.: *See Under: Love*, trans. B. Rosenberg (London, 1999).

2 Alan L. Berger sees 'a cognitive darkness that was not present among the survivors and their children' as the main determinant (A. L. Berger, 'Unclaimed Experience: Trauma and Identity in Third Generation Writing about the Holocaust', *Shofar*, 28/3 (2010), 149–58: 151).

3 See E. Jilovsky, J. Silverstein, and D. Slucki, 'Introduction: The Third Generation', in eid. (eds.), *In the Shadows of Memory: The Holocaust and the Third Generation* (London, 2016), 1–12.

4 H. Tapouchi, 'The Third Generation': Hadas Tapouchi website, 'Other Projects', visited 5 Nov. 2021.

5 S. Ronen, *Polin, a Land of Forests and Rivers: Images of Poland and Poles in Contemporary Hebrew Literature in Israel* (Warsaw, 2007), 17–18.
6 S. Ronen, 'Post-Holocaust Representations of Poland in Israeli Literature', *Polish Review*, 60 (2015), 3–20: 4.
7 See J. Feldman, *Above the Death Pits, Beneath the Flag: Youth Voyages to Poland and the Performance of Israeli National Identity* (New York, 2008), 4.
8 J. Feldman, 'Marking the Boundaries of the Enclave: Defining the Israeli Collective Through the Poland "Experience"', *Israel Studies*, 7/2 (2002), 84–114: 85; see C. S. Liebman and E. Don-Yehiya, *Civil Religion in Israel* (Berkeley, Calif., 1983).
9 Y. Zerubavel, *Recovered Roots: Collective Memory and the Making of Israeli National Tradition* (Chicago, 1995), 10; see M. Foucault, *Language, Counter-Memory, Practice: Selected Essays* (New York, 1977), 113–98.
10 R. Modan, *Hanekhes* (Tel Aviv, 2013); Eng. trans.: *The Property*, trans. J. Cohen (New York, 2013).
11 Ibid. 15.
12 Ibid.
13 Ibid. 10.
14 Ibid. 14.
15 Ibid. 42.
16 M. Rothberg, *Multidirectional Memory: Remembering the Holocaust in the Age of Decolonization* (Stanford, Calif., 2009), 202.
17 J. C. Alexander, 'On the Social Construction of Moral Universals: The 'Holocaust' from War Crime to Trauma Drama', *European Journal of Social Theory*, 5 (2002), 5–85: 6.
18 Y. Yareach, *Hashetikot* (Tel Aviv, 2016).
19 O. Horesh, *Hanekhed katav al hashetikah shel savto* (5 May 2015): Ynet website, visited 14 June 2021.
20 Yareach, *Hashetikot*, 7.
21 T. Segev, *The Seventh Million: The Israelis and the Holocaust* (New York, 1993).
22 E. Sicher, 'The Return of the Past: The Intergenerational Transmission of Holocaust Memory in Israeli Fiction', *Shofar*, 19/2 (2001), 26–52: 42–3. For an analysis of gender Holocaust discourse in Israel, see R. Lentin, *Israel and the Daughters of the Shoah: Reoccupying the Territories of Silence* (New York, 2000).
23 See Yareach, *Hashetikot*, 322.
24 Ibid. 7.
25 I. Orlev, *Bandit* (Tel Aviv, 2015). Ami Drozd told his story in a documentary (A. Drozd (dir.), *Australia sheli*, documentary (Transfax, 2011)).
26 Yehudit Hendel depicts Poland as empty and grey, features which are assigned to every single place that she wants to visit but never does, expressed through the constantly repeated phrase: 'I didn't go to Kałuszyn/Krasnystaw/Krosno. What should I look for in Kałuszyn/Krasnystaw/Krosno?' (Y. Hendel, *Leyad kefarim sheketim* (Tel Aviv, 1987), 47–64). Michal Govrin depicts the Poland of the 1970s through the prisms of greyness and neglect (M. Govrin, 'Mikhtevei mimeḥozot aḥizat ha'einayim', *Iton 77*, 209 (1997), 22–42: 42).
27 Orlev, *Bandit*, 329–30.
28 Ibid. 94–5.
29 As Jackie Feldman has argued, the discontinuity that characterizes Yad Vashem's landscape might be perceived as a reflection of 'the problematic *disjunction* between Shoah

victims and the earth of the State of Israel where they are commemorated' (J. Feldman, 'Between Yad Vashem and Mt. Herzl: Changing Inscriptions of Sacrifice on Jerusalem's "Mountain of Memory"', *Anthropological Quarterly*, 80 (2007), 1147–74: 1152; italics original).

30 See N. Englander, *What We Talk About When We Talk About Anne Frank* (London, 2012).

Neuland, or the Displacement of an Ideal
Israel in the Work of Eshkol Nevo

ALINA MOLISAK

The fact that it is invented won't make it any less real.
Alastair Bonnett, *Off the Map*

UTOPIAN THINKING and the desire to create an ideal community can lead to the creation of real places. In discussing the role of ideologies in this process, Alastair Bonnett points to an aspect of the migration involved, namely negative connotations of former places of settlement: 'What holds utopia in place is not just a vision of a perfect place but the experience of living in a bad one. Ironically, these bad places were often former ideal places, their failure provoking people to seek out more perfect alternatives.'[1]

The establishment of the State of Israel links both of these perspectives. Zionist dreams of a sovereign state had been a powerful ideological factor in the Jewish diaspora since the late nineteenth century, and the experience of anti-Jewish violence, the wave of pogroms before the Second World War, and the shock of the Holocaust all served to reinforce the conviction that it was crucial for there to be a separate place which could guarantee a secure Jewish existence.

Eshkol Nevo is one of the most highly regarded members of the new generation of Hebrew authors. From his debut novel, *Homesick*, which quickly attracted acclaim both within Israel and further afield, through his subsequent novels, *World Cup Wishes* and *Neuland*, his prose has consistently offered the reader a fascinating, often intertextual and intercultural, examination of important existential problems relating both to the individual and to contemporary society.[2] He is the recipient of awards in Israel (the Book Publishers Association Golden Book Prize, 2005) and abroad (FFI–Raymond Wallier Prize, France, 2008; Adei Wizo Prize, Italy, 2011). In 2012 *Neuland* won one of the most important Israeli literary accolades, the Steimatzky Prize for Book of the Year, which led critics to compare him to such leading Israeli authors as David Grossman, Abraham Yehoshua, and Amos Oz.[3] *Neuland* is to some extent autobiographical. Nevo was an officer in the Israeli army at the time of the First Intifada. After his military service, like many young people, he set out on an lengthy journey, partly—as he related in an interview[4]—in search of his own identity and partly in search of answers to questions about the functioning of contemporary post-Zionist Israeli society.

The narrative of Nevo's *Neuland* takes the postmodern form of an email exchange between its two main protagonists, Inbar and Dori.[5] It is significant that this correspondence, which is conducted after their return to Israel from Latin America, is interspersed with brief references to rocket strikes and ruined houses: the violence is incorporated into the rhythm of daily life. The personal and family experiences of past military action are separately described, mainly in retrospect: in the case of Dori's father, Menny Peleg, these concern the Yom Kippur War; in Dori's case, the First Lebanese War. Further historical context is provided by the experiences of Inbar and Dori's grandparents, emigrants from the European diaspora, and the enduring, ever-present 'long shadow of the Holocaust'.[6]

What I find particularly interesting in Nevo's narrative are the diverse expressions of translocation, which involve historical as well as geographical dimensions. The novel's title, *Neuland*, is a clear allusion to Theodor Herzl's utopian novel *Altneuland* (1902), in which he mapped out the establishment of the Jewish state.[7] As founding father of the Zionist movement and promulgator of the idea of a Jewish nation and state (especially in *Der Judenstaat*; 1896), Herzl and his vision are a constant point of reference in Nevo's intertextual narrative.

Altneuland was a means of propagating the Zionist cause through literature.[8] In Herzl's view the solution to the Jewish problem lay in the creation of an independent Jewish state, based on a novel synthesis of capitalism and socialism called 'mutualism'. The inhabitants of this ideal place would work for seven hours a day; other aspects of modernization were to include rail links and canal networks. It is notable that in his account of *Altneuland* Herzl considered different forms of spiritual life to be equally legitimate: it was possible to pray in a synagogue, a church, or a mosque or to have the same metaphysical experience in a concert hall. Of particular significance, however—especially when comparing the two narratives—is the presumed equality of all the inhabitants of *Altneuland* (it is worth adding that they were all to speak German). Furthermore the local 'Mohamedans' were assumed to be happy to accept these civilizational transformations, since the architect of the Jewish state did not take local emancipatory aspirations into account and took it for granted (as did many other politicians of the period) that the newcomers settling in the Land of Israel would establish order in accordance with the European model of modern society. Two of Herzl's ideas appear in *Neuland*: the equality of all inhabitants and the security of the Jewish nation.

Neuland revolves around two members of each of three generations. The first two are Lily, Inbar's grandmother, and Fima, Dori's grandfather. Lily and Fima leave Warsaw in the 1930s as part of a group of young Zionists and travel to Haifa, motivated by their faith in the Zionist cause, their experiences of antisemitism and increasing anti-Jewish violence, and 'the news coming from Germany, [which] gave their voyage the urgency of an escape from a snow avalanche growing more powerful as it thundered down a mountain'.[9]

The second generation is that of the 'state builders' and includes Lily's daughter, Hana, and Fima's son, Menny Peleg, the third central character. Menny disappears, leaving a document on his computer written as stream of consciousness without punctuation or capital letters, in which he appraises his generation:

we the generation that founded the state of israel are a fucked-up generation ... our parents had dreams and left us the hard work ... that's my generation the generation before it dreamed and the one after it dreams and that's my generation the founding generation both feet on the ground slowly slowly slowly sinking.[10]

The next generation includes Inbar, a journalist, Dori, a history teacher, and his sister.

The first translocation in the novel is Lily and Fima's journey from Poland to the Land of Israel. The retrospective account of their confrontation with the reality of the 1930s, their journey, and their arrival in Haifa provides the historical background. A second example of translocation is the choices made by some of the background characters: those leaving Israel to go to America, Australia, or—in the case of Inbar's mother—at least temporarily, to Berlin. Berlin is, as well as the site of the confrontation between her and her mother, also where the contemporary Israelis are confronted with the past of the German state, with the historical trauma of the Holocaust, and with a complex cultural heritage.[11]

The entire narrative structure revolves around the disappearance of Menny, his personal translocation, which is closely connected to the restorative thrust of *Neuland*. His journey to Latin America is not merely an escape or a search for consolation following the death of his wife. The most challenging experience for a member of the 'statehood generation' is war. A taboo subject within the family, it nonetheless appears powerfully and repeatedly in the dramatic battles in Sinai. The radical change Menny chose was dictated by the realization that his former location was 'lost', 'contaminated by fear' as his son puts it in conversation with his wife when they recall a favourite beach and the attack that took place there.[12] This metonymic description in fact applies to the whole of contemporary Israel and is amplified at the end of the story by the reference to the beginning of another war.

One characteristic feature of postmodern subjectivity is a state of nomadism, or transpositioning.[13] What distinguishes the global world is the fact that no one 'lives in the place where he was born. The Australians live in London. The Brits work in Spain . . . The French work in China. Or Singapore. And the Swiss have fallen in love with Ecuador and are already checking out the possibility of buying land near Quito and setting up an ecological farm on it.'[14]

Further characteristics of the postmodern subject are performativity, co-operation, activity, and an opposition to the status quo. They are not so much discernible attributes as ideal characteristics. As Ewa Domańska puts it, 'in this change-oriented world, a subject with the capacity for agency becomes extremely desirable. To effect changes, to be their catalyst and not their object—that is the most desirable model.'[15]

The radical choice made by Menny clearly demonstrates that his transformed identity combines all of these characteristics. He was 'the cool, level-headed, war hero. One of Israel's most successful strategy consultants for the management of business crises.'[16] In choosing to move to a completely different place, he achieves not only a translocation in the sense of a 'disappearance' from social or family circles, he also acquires a new name—Mr Neuland—creates an entirely novel space, and funds an existential project along the lines of the Zionist ideals of Herzl's age and the establishment of the State of Israel. His project is formulated as an invitation to others who wish to change the world, starting by living in a place called Neuland. It is not just the processes of globalization or nomadism which enable this, but above all Menny's critical attitude to reality and the power of his performative gesture.

Thanks to his change of location, Menny not only changes his name, he also crosses the extremities of existence, the border between life and death. At a certain point he realizes that his dead wife, who has started to reappear in his dreams, is sending him back to events in the past, to that 'forgotten story of a farm established in Argentina for East European Jews'.[17] But Menny becomes aware that the figure in his dreams, in uttering the name Baron Hirsch, is also propelling him into the future. As he himself says: 'It doesn't matter what Baron Hirsch intended to do with those farms; it matters what I can do with them.'[18] The moment of radical transformation takes place when he becomes convinced that he has 'received a calling' and sees his new role with absolute clarity—this time as someone who, in times of extreme crisis, is capable of finding a remedy, and who is impatient to fulfil his destiny. At that point Menny relinquishes his old life and enters a new form of existence: 'So I hurry. I don't take the potion any more [which had helped him regain the ability to dream]. I don't hear MiGs any more. I don't want to die any more.'[19]

The choice of Argentina as particularly well suited to the creation of a place such as Neuland is not accidental: it is a reference to an aspect of the history of Jewish migration. By the last decade of the nineteenth century Herzl had become convinced by the strength of antisemitism, which was rife in almost all circles of society in both the Habsburg monarchy and France—where he reported on the Dreyfus trial —that the only favourable prospect for Jews lay in their emigration from Europe and the establishment of their own state. In 1895, in the course of his efforts to develop the Zionist movement, Herzl met Baron Maurice de Hirsch and presented his plans to him. While Baron Hirsch did not entirely share Herzl's conviction, he began from then on to promote the Zionist cause. In his view it was essential to couple Jewish emigration from Europe with the establishment of (chiefly agricultural) settlements. In 1891 Hirsch founded the Jewish Colonization Association, the purpose of which was to fund new and secure places for the Jewish population to live. It was in Argentina that the colonies financed by Hirsch were established.

Dori touches on these historic events when (as a historian) he refers to the activities of Baron Hirsch and, in quasi-didactic mode, notes that 'Herzl himself considered two territories for his vision of the Jewish state: Palestine and Argentina.'[20] In Dori's analysis, the fact that the founder of Zionism chose contemporary Palestine as Erets Yisra'el means that 'he believed that the myth of the return to Zion had a better chance of persuading a critical mass of people to leave their homes for the unknown'.[21]

The reappearance of Fima illustrates the generation-spanning doubts about the likelihood of the ideal being realized. Fima, who decided on further emigration to America, declares, as if presaging Menny's actions: 'It's just going to get worse. They don't want us here, our neighbours. We'll have to face them with drawn swords for ever, and anyone who always has a sword in his hand can't play music, or write, or love.'²² Recalling the historical Zionist debates about the location of settlements, Fima adds: 'We should have gone to Uganda ... Or Argentina. Or we just should have kept wandering from place to place.'²³

It is Menny who undertakes a kind of dislocation of the Zionist ideal, who revisits the endeavour of redefining Herzl's concept in the present-day world. The place which he establishes in the barren Argentinian wilderness appears, on the one hand, to be a utopian enclave almost wholly cut off from the postmodern world (there are no mobile phones and other electronic media do not work); on the other hand, it can be viewed as a product of the imagination, an ephemeral place which brings together a transient ad hoc community, united by their common pursuit of an ideal.²⁴

In the course of one of the conversations with his son, Menny quotes from a book by the Argentinian writer Alberto Gerchunoff called *Los gauchos judíos*: 'Zion lies wherever peace and serenity hold sway.'²⁵ The invented or, more precisely, translocated Neuland of Nevo's novel is an 'anger- and violence-free' space,²⁶ a discreet place, and a uniquely 'therapeutic space', since its founder's premise was that 'life in the source country, in Israel, is an ongoing trauma. And everyone who comes from there is wounded to some degree or another.'²⁷ Viewed in this way, Neuland becomes a type of enclave which facilitates extended consideration and debate concerning Zionist ideals.

Sara, a long-time resident of Neuland, describes an important characteristic of it: 'It really means that we stop being the persecuted Jews of the Holocaust and start being "a light unto the nations", as Herzl envisioned. Do you know the blessing we say on Friday nights? "You have chosen us *together with* all the nations."' Inbar, who has come from Israel, accepts the change from the traditional form of words: 'Instead of "of all the nations"? Nice.'²⁸

As the new arrivals learn (and with them, the reader), Neuland is not a utopia and is not intended to replace the existing state. The point of Neuland's existence is to capture the old ideals of Zionism, of Herzl's great project. The translocation achieved by Menny becomes a kind of gesture of renewal, an invitation, or a 'reminder of the Athens that the State of Israel was supposed to be if it hadn't turned into Sparta'.²⁹ Explaining the logic of his own conduct to his sceptical son, Menny makes a firm diagnosis of the present: 'A country cannot exist only to survive . . . The original reason for the establishment of Israel was to gather all the Jews of the Diaspora in a place where they would not be persecuted. But that *was* the purpose, past tense. A country needs a vision.'³⁰

Despite the establishment of Israel, Herzl's vision remained unrealized, and Israel's greatest mistake was its departure from the ideal of equality. This is how Menny explains to his son the need to establish a new community: 'The way we treat people who are not us . . . that was one of the source country's greatest failures. And it's because we're extraterritorial that we can do it better.'³¹

The value judgements expressed by someone who has decided to act in such a radical way draw on the dreams of the preceding generation. The parents of the protagonists left the European diaspora declaring explicitly that their purpose was 'to build a new society. A better society. To establish new ways for people to live together ... Every generation makes the same mistakes as the generation that came before it, and our generation says—enough! Let us create something new!'[32] Yet another reference here is to the Israeli Declaration of Independence, one of the foundations of which is the principle of justice and equality:

> The State of Israel will be open for Jewish immigration and for the Ingathering of the Exiles; it will foster the development of the country for the benefit of all its inhabitants; it will be based on freedom, justice and peace as envisaged by the prophets of Israel; it will ensure complete equality of social and political rights to all its inhabitants irrespective of religion, race or sex; it will guarantee freedom of religion, conscience, language, education and culture.[33]

Menny's gesture of renewal combines both Herzl's vision of a Jewish state and the Declaration of Independence, when he states: 'Today, 22 April 2006, the name of the place flickered before me ... And I also knew that at the entrance to it, on the plain wooden gate, I'll write in huge letters the words that Herzl wanted to be written on the gates of his Jewish state: "Man, you are my brother"'.[34]

According to Menny, the translocation of the ideal which he has effected is not just a return to the ideals of the first Zionists but is also a type of transgression, a deliverance from the political paradigms laid down by history, a search for new cultural spaces. Inbar and Dori listen to how Menny gathered together the Israelis who now live in Neuland. They met while travelling through Latin America, in Bolivia at Passover (which also symbolically refers to the traditions of Judaism, commemorating as it does the emancipation from Egyptian slavery). When the spiritually transformed Menny 'started talking about Herzl's vision and about the gap between that vision and the way it's been realised in Israel, and said that this is a crisis, but definitely an opportunity too', he only had a small audience.[35] He said that he was on his way to Argentina and that 'anyone who was interested, who was attracted by the opportunity to make real changes in himself and society' should join him.[36] The concept of a dual transformation is clear here, the post-Zionist identity crisis as an opportunity for change, both for a renewal of social ideals and the individual establishment of a new subjectivity, a subjectivity in line with Jolanta Brach-Czaina's formulation, namely that this 'transformation concerns the creation of a broader identity which is more elastic than the previous one, a dynamic identity. Living in the midst of rapid change demands inner activity and an outlook which is open to the diversity of serial events.'[37] Such an entity, or rather its diverse phases and variants, is represented in the novel by different characters, not just by the radically altered Menny. They are represented by the ubiquitous nomadism and by physical topography (contemporary Israel, contemporary Latin America) and mythological topography (in the sense of literary topography, or, more broadly, the Jewish cultural heritage).

An additional feature of the novel is an awareness of locality. A separate thread links the accounts of Neuland as created in present-day Argentina and the historical heritage, the presence of Jewish emigrants in those regions. The space in which a place like Neuland came into being bears the hallmarks of the past. A type of translocation in time accompanies the repositioning of the ideal of the Zionist community. Although Dori ironically describes nearby Moisés Ville in fairly contemptuous terms: 'Just like a little shtetl', nonetheless he is referring to a real place which still retains visible traces of Jewish settlement.[38] One of those traces is a distinctive monument: 'At the main entrance to Moisés Ville stands the statue of a ship that looks like the ones that brought the illegal immigrants to Israel', under which a sign reads 'In Celebration of the Centennial Year of the First Jewish Colony in Argentina'.[39]

The whole account of the translocation of the ideal is woven around place, and this includes space for meeting or dialogue. The meeting of Inbar and Dori was accidental but also essential to the life of both, in the same way as relations between Lily and Fima had developed in the first generation. The family meetings referred to, the relations of women (grandmother–mother–daughter) and men (grandfather–father–son), are quite different. Dori, who initially rebels against his father, is unwilling to accept his transformation and his wholesale reappraisal of former ideals: 'Who does he think he is? The Messiah?'[40] He and Inbar, in the course of their quest, not only discuss the potential whereabouts of Menny but also, thanks to their conversation and actions, reassess their own personal lives to date. They also discuss alternative historical scenarios. Inbar, reflecting on the experience of migration by generations of Jews over many centuries, says: 'Maybe there's a kind of collective unconscious that remembers the road not taken . . . Maybe that's why the . . . why your dad's emotional upheaval brought him to Argentina'.[41] In turn Dori, as a teacher, 'loves to widen these cracks in official history for his students so that through them they can catch a glimpse of what is beyond the material they have to learn for their exams'. As he himself puts it: 'I don't teach history . . . I teach histories'.[42] Both Inbar and Dori, members of the next generation, contemplate (while still in Argentina, before they return to Israel) an alternative version of history; a dialogue which begins by contemplating 'what would've happened if we'd taken the Argentinian road' is tinged with idealistic visions: 'imagine if the Jewish state were in South America . . . maybe . . . maybe there wouldn't be an army'.[43]

While considering other, unrealized plans of action, they recall Robert Frost's important poem 'The Road Not Taken':

> Two roads diverged in a yellow wood,
> And sorry I could not travel both
> And be one traveler, long I stood
> And looked down one as far as I could
> To where it bent in the undergrowth;
>
> Then took the other, as just as fair,
> And having perhaps the better claim,
> Because it was grassy and wanted wear;
> Though as for that the passing there
> Had worn them really about the same,
>
> . . . . . .

> I shall be telling this with a sigh
> Somewhere ages and ages hence:
> Two roads diverged in a wood, and I—
> I took the one less traveled by,
> And that has made all the difference.[44]

The narrative concerning the place chosen by Menny relates on the one hand to historical dilemmas and on the other to Herzl's *Altneuland*, since in the vicinity there are memories and traces of the founders of Moisés Ville, late nineteenth-century settlers descended—just like the founding fathers of the state—from the east European diaspora.

In one of the email exchanges between Inbar and Dori shortly after their return to Israel, a question is posed concerning yet another form of displacement, this time not of space but of time:

Do you think that from now on all the wars will start to repeat themselves in reverse order? That we'll have a second Yom Kippur War? A second Six Day War? Do you see why there's something to be said for what Mr Neuland [Menny] is trying to do? True, his means are radical, but maybe only radical means can work when everything else is at a stalemate?[45]

Yet another translocation in time—in combination with the reformative impulse of ideals—appears to be the most fundamental overstepping of the confines of history. It is similar to the notion of the homeland in Józef Wittlin's essay on Joseph Roth, in which he deploys a definition framed by Ilya Ehrenburg. According to Wittlin, Ehrenburg 'juxtaposes the old and now somewhat trite concept of the territorial homeland, separated from other homelands of its type by trade barriers, bastions, border posts, mountains, rivers, traditions, prejudices, interests, differences of language, customs, uniform, and currency—with a new concept of the homeland in time, a homeland which is in constant motion'.[46]

Neuland is after all intended to direct the reader's attention to its distinctive non-territoriality, to the fact that the idea of the Argentinian Neuland is to be 'a wandering shadow camp',[47] or, as one of the characters metaphorically describes it: 'Think of us as *Futuro*, Herzl's visionary ship of wise men.'[48] Seen in this way, the existence of Neuland constitutes a type of ethical challenge, since 'the state already exists' and the only thing that is needed, according to Jamili—a newcomer to Neuland who turns out to be an incarnation of the Wandering Jew—is for a 'diaspora Sanhedrin to be re-established in a new place every time'.[49] This is the means by which this 'shadow camp' will influence the 'source country'.

In one of her somnambular monologues, Lily (also an emigrant from eastern Europe) reflects on the concept of having a place of one's own: 'And what about our country? So many Jews living in one place, but in their minds, they have another place they came from and another place they want to run away to tomorrow.'[50] The two main characters decide to return to Israel, despite the row between Dori and Menny, who points out that there is another war going on, 'an unnecessary war that won't change a thing, and there's no point in participating in it'.[51] In contrast to these two is a couple who never want to stay in one place, the surrealistic Nessia ('the girl inside you', as Jamili tells Inbar[52]) and Jamili himself.

The figure of the Wandering Jew accompanies the reader almost from the very beginning of the story. Inbar's mother is writing a doctoral thesis on the subject in Berlin, and she notes that the Wandering Jew can be seen as a universal traveller, 'traversing wide expanses and eras, symbolising the hardships of humanity as it treads the path of progress'.[53] She herself wonders about the fact that one of the characteristics of contemporary postmodernity is the peculiar disappearance of space described as a place: 'And perhaps, in the culture of the new millennium, there is no "there" or "here".'[54] As an admirer of the writer Stefan Zweig, as a detached student of the many derivations of historic and contemporary culture, and as an observer of reality, she also highlights a very significant transformation: 'Most researchers agree that since the establishment of the State of Israel, there has been a sharp decrease in the number of "appearances" of the Wandering Jew throughout the world. As if, with the establishment of the national home of the Jews, they no longer need that story to explain their eternal wandering to the world.'[55] She promptly adds, however, that the academic world always lags behind a little, that it needs time to read, to observe, and to write and publish—and so it has not (yet) noticed 'that the Wandering Jew has been resurrected over the last decade'.[56]

Translated from the Polish by Anna Zaranko

Notes

1 A. Bonnett, *Off the Map: Lost Spaces, Invisible Cities, Forgotten Islands, Feral Places and What They Tell Us About the World* (London, 2014), 186.

2 E. Nevo, *Arba'ah batim vega'agua* (Or Yehuda, 2004); Eng. trans.: *Homesick*, trans. S. Silverston (London, 2008); id., *Mishalah aḥat yaminah* (Or Yehuda, 2007); Eng. trans.: *World Cup Wishes*, trans. S. Silverston (London, 2010); id., *Neuland* (Or Yehuda, 2011); Eng. trans.: *Neuland*, trans. S. Silverston (London, 2014).

3 See O. Herzog, 'The Israeli Nomad in Search of the Promised Land' (14 Aug. 2011): *Haaretz* website, visited 14 Dec. 2021; C. Eller, 'Orgasmen im Kibbuz' (13 Jan. 2014): *Die Zeit* website, visited 14 Dec. 2021; U. Stolzmann, 'Irrlichternde Ferne' (28 May 2014): *Neue Zürcher Zeitung* website, visited 14 Dec. 2021.

4 Stolzmann, 'Irrlichternde Ferne'; see also P. Smoleński, 'Pisarz Eshkol Nevo: Izraelczycy kochają go za "Neuland" i są na niego wściekli' (24 Apr. 2014): *Gazeta Wyborcza* website, visited 14 Dec. 2021. Nevo's critical stance in respect of the Israeli left and other politicians is treated by some readers (in particular those associated with a traditional interpretation of Zionist thought) with considerable scepticism.

6 See F. Tych, *Długi cień Zagłady: Szkice historyczne* (Warsaw, 1999).

7 Literature played a prominent role in promoting the Zionist cause. In 1853 the Kovno-born Abraham Mapu published a novel entitled *Ahavat tsiyon* ('Love of Zion'), thus establishing the entire genre of Zionist literature.

8 There had been efforts in a similar vein which pre-dated Herzl and his convening of the First Zionist Congress in Basel. In 1864 Rabbi Tsevi Hirsch Kalischer had founded the Berlin Central Committee for the Jewish Settlement of Palestine, while in 1862

Moses Hess had published *Rom und Jerusalem: Die letzte Nationalitätenfrage* ('Rome and Jerusalem: The Last National Question').
9 Nevo, *Neuland*, trans. Silverston, 162.
10 Ibid. 355–6. According to conventional historiographical terminology, those who founded and built the state are known as the 'statehood generation'.
11 On Israelis settling in Berlin, see F. Oz-Salzberger, *Yisre'elim, berlin* (Jerusalem, 2001).
12 Nevo, *Neuland*, trans. Silverston, 70.
13 R. Braidotti, *Nomadic Subjects: Embodiment and Sexual Difference in Contemporary Feminist Theory* (New York, 2011), 73.
14 Nevo, *Neuland*, trans. Silverston, 114.
15 E. Domańska, 'Zwrot performatywny we współczesnej humanistyce', *Teksty Drugie*, 2007, no. 5, pp. 48–61: 56.
16 Nevo, *Neuland*, trans. Silverston, 28.
17 Ibid. 380.
18 Ibid.
19 Ibid. 381.
20 Ibid. 349.
21 Ibid. 49.
22 Ibid. 584.
23 Ibid.
24 Bonnett, *Off the Map*, 288.
25 Nevo, *Neuland*, trans. Silverston, 551.
26 Ibid. 506.
27 Ibid. 510.
28 Ibid. 547.
29 Ibid. 551.
30 Ibid.
31 Ibid. 548.
32 Ibid. 163.
33 'Hakhrazat Hatsma'ut shel medinat yisra'el', *Iton rishmi*, 1 (14 May 1948).
34 Nevo, *Neuland*, trans. Silverston, 381.
35 Ibid. 453.
36 Ibid.
37 J. Brach-Czaina, *Błony umysłu* (Warsaw, 2003), 121.
38 Nevo, *Neuland*, trans. Silverston, 499. Moisés Ville is a small town in the province of Santa Fe in Argentina, founded in 1889 by east European Jews.
39 Ibid. 499.
40 Ibid. 383.
41 Ibid. 384.
42 Ibid. 58.
43 Ibid. 350.
44 R. Frost, 'The Road Not Taken', in id., *The Collected Poems* (London, 2013), 105.
45 Nevo, *Neuland*, trans. Silverston, 12.
46 J. Wittlin, 'Na marginesie książek Josepha Rotha', *Wiadomości Literackie*, 7 June 1931, p. 2.
47 Nevo, *Neuland*, trans. Silverston, 557.

48 Ibid. 552.
49 Ibid. 557.
50 Ibid. 600.
51 Ibid. 563.
52 Ibid. 558.
53 Ibid. 191.
54 Ibid.
55 Ibid. 284.
56 Ibid.

Israel and Poland Confront Holocaust Memory

YIFAT GUTMAN AND ELAZAR BARKAN

Introduction

Historians and diplomats are not natural bedfellows. Governments do not usually incorporate historical expertise into their diplomatic negotiations and only rarely include historians in peace negotiations.[1] Nor are history or historians usually included in track II diplomacy, the practice of non-governmental, informal, and unofficial contacts between private citizens or groups of individuals. If it is considered at all, history is left to academics and the organizations of civil society. This stems from the belief that the past cannot be changed and therefore has to be accepted as given rather than addressed or negotiated. But while it is true that history refers to the past and, as such, cannot be changed, the manner in which the past is presented is malleable, and the memory of it changes often and continuously.[2] The premise of historical dialogue is that history and memory are a central source of ethno-national identity and hence can lead to coexistence or conflict between rival national narratives.[3] While nationalist governments often manipulate public opinion, exploiting and distorting memories of past violence, suffering, and injustices for domestic political goals, historians do possess professional integrity, and historical truth carries a weight that cannot be easily manipulated by political pressure.[4] However, aware that 'historical truth' is a contested term that may invoke notions of postmodern relativism, we tread lightly. We understand it as limited to a professional consensus or near-consensus shaped by dialogue. Within scholarly debates, while there is no hard demarcation between true and false, scholars even from polarized perspectives often agree on core narratives as separate from patently false claims. (The argument about the nomenclature of German/Polish concentration camps, which is discussed below, is an example of historical dialogue that changes what is viewed as historical truth.) Even outside scholarly debates, in the public space, historical truth is perceived and evaluated as derived from the academic study of the past. As historical narratives have an explicit and direct impact on group identities, historians can contribute to reconciliation among nations by playing an informal adjudicatory role in the creation of such narratives and ensuring adherence to scholarly and ethical norms in public debate.[5]

This chapter examines one historical controversy that was characterized by the political, social, and professional aspects of memory conflict—that provoked by the Polish memory law of 26 January 2018.[6] This case shows the many shortcomings of a political process that ignores professional scholars. Lack of transparency distorts historical narratives in the name of political and nationalist expediency. It also confirms that historical scholarship can serve as an independent channel to bridge a contested past, through historical dialogue—a discursive space and mode of persuasion in contrast to the brute force of politics.

The Polish memory law was an amendment to the Law on the Institute of National Remembrance (Instytut Pamięci Narodowej; IPN) that was passed by the Sejm, the lower house of the Polish parliament, on 26 January 2018. Although it aroused domestic and international controversy, it was supported by Poland's ruling Law and Justice Party (Prawo i Sprawiedliwość; PiS), and was enacted into law. The law has two parts: (1) criminalizing the use of the terms 'Polish death camps' and 'Polish concentration camps', which imply that Poland was responsible for the Nazi German camps, and (2) banning references to atrocities committed by Poles during the war, which are viewed as defaming the Polish people.[7] The law had no geographical boundaries and was intended to have global scope. Its first part was generally accepted, viewed as perhaps heavy-handed but legitimate (or as historical truth). The second part aroused an international controversy—not only did it seem to criminalize what was widely believed in Jewish collective memory, it also threatened well-publicized and serious historical research, such as that on the massacre of Jews in Jedwabne in July 1941. Under the law, any history that claimed that 'the Polish Nation or the Republic of Poland was responsible or co-responsible for Nazi crimes committed by the Third Reich' would become criminal.[8] It also criminalized victims' memories and testimonies. The harmonious bilateral relations between Israel and Poland created since the end of communism in 1989 quickly deteriorated into a diplomatic crisis. Israel froze its diplomatic relations pending a revision of the law. Nationalist Israeli politicians competed with each other over who could criticize Poland most harshly. The crisis led to negotiations, including a public visit by a Polish delegation to Israel (March 2018) and the announcement of the establishment of formal negotiations between officials of both ministries of foreign affairs. Three months later, a resolution of the dispute was announced (27 June 2018) which was the result of secret negotiations conducted between the offices of the Israeli and Polish prime ministers. The resolution included a decriminalization of the offences, making them subject to civil litigation. The new narrative included a joint statement that condemned both antisemitism and anti-Polonism, implying that anti-Polonism could be equated with antisemitism. The agreement led to intense public criticism in both countries directed at both governments, which was marked in both by domestic political and historical jockeying. For a few news cycles the controversy remained in the headlines, and it continues to inflame the discourse about the Holocaust and contribute to the tense relations between the two states, which is manifest in particular events, diplomatic and scholarly exchanges, and political statements.

The controversy provides a valuable opportunity to examine the role of historians, diplomats, politicians, civil society, and public intellectuals in negotiating reconciliation. The discourse was both formal and informal. Historians were members of the diplomatic missions on both sides of the conflict. Polish state-affiliated historians (members of the IPN) were appointed as the head and members of the Polish diplomatic delegation. Israeli historians from the Yad Vashem Holocaust Museum and Archive joined the Israeli delegation. It was clear that historical expertise was seen as critical in helping to negotiate a version of the past which was both historically accurate and acceptable to both countries.

Using interviews and discourse analysis, we examined the negotiations between Poland and Israel and the domestic public debates on the Polish memory law in both countries. We mapped the media coverage and the social agents who took part in these debates from its approval in January 2018 until August 2019. We held semi-structured interviews with fifteen of those involved, including members of the diplomatic delegations of both countries, public leaders and intellectuals, and members of civil society who protested against the law and its modification on both sides of the debate.

We found that when the historical truth is accepted by both sides, conflict dies. The first part of the law, discrediting the designation of the concentration camps as Polish rather than German, was generally accepted as historical truth. However, the second part, the prohibition of discussing Poles as Nazi collaborators or perpetrators, only aggravated the public discourse. Furthermore, the claim of parity between anti-semitism and anti-Polonism as presented in the reconciliatory statement of the two governments—the purported diplomatic resolution of the conflict—further inflamed the debate. The creation of what was seen as a false historical narrative sparked further domestic and international outcry and protest against the subordination of the historical narrative to political and diplomatic expediency. Instead, historians and civil society organizations in both countries demanded public recognition of crimes committed by Poles. Their stance came to dominate the public discourse and can be expected to remain a fixture in the history of Jewish–Polish relations.

This outcome suggests that, although historical truth is a controversial concept academically, and while objectivity has been challenged for over a century among scholars, in cases of memory conflict, the public recognizes the importance of historical truth over diplomatic expediency. Some historical truth is essentially non-controversial, such as the historical fact of the very existence of the concentration camps, which was validated and accepted domestically and internationally. In contrast, the Polish government's attempt to deny Polish complicity in the atrocities and the fate of Polish Jews met international criticism and domestic protest from civil society and intellectuals, which led to the decriminalization amendment of June 2018 and a wider acknowledgement of Polish complicity in Nazi crimes.

A collateral benefit of the exchange is the confirmation that historical truth operates within a partially shielded space that is shaped by expertise. In contrast, fake news, or the claim that everyone has their own truth regarding the past and that these truths cannot be mediated, is often not persuasive to the public, which can see beyond the professional disillusion with relativism. Furthermore, historical truth is perceived differently in dissimilar sociopolitical contexts. In the Israeli and the Polish contexts, the rival positions resemble each other: both are promoted by populist, nationalist governments, and both governments are quick to label any criticism, international or domestic, that betrays the national collective as treason (anti-Polonism or antisemitism). Yet such scare tactics do not work. Both sides were enmeshed in the public discourse, and when either side tried to challenge the professional historical truth, it was rebuked. This interdependence repeatedly undermined attempts to resolve the dispute by diplomacy.

Diplomats and Historians In and Out of Dialogue

Professional historians and those in the service of governments tend to produce accounts of the past that are influenced by their position. Professional historians ordinarily seek to reach the most accurate factual empirical record and interpretation of past events, and their success or failure is determined by the reception and validation of their work by their peers. In contrast, historians who work for governments are more likely to seek a version of the past that best promotes the national self-image and serves their country's foreign policy interests. The tension between professional historical truth and official state representation of the past has increased in recent years, with conflicts over contested violent pasts appearing around the globe.

Poland had the largest Jewish minority in Europe before the Second World War, and, notwithstanding everyday antisemitism, Jews had felt fairly secure in the country for centuries. David Engel has argued that the permanence of group memory is an obstacle to attempts to bridge the rival Polish and Jewish historical narratives. Further, he observes a similarity between the two nations, which both see themselves as chosen people and ultimate victims. This mirror-image has remained stable through two world wars, the physical extermination of 90 per cent of the Jewish population of the country, and the communist dictatorship, when most of the remaining Jews were pressured to emigrate. The antagonism has persisted until today.[9] However, in civil society in both Israel and Poland there are groups and individuals who try to overcome this enmity and work towards reconciliation. The current tension erupted precisely because the underlying antagonism was never addressed. A successful dialogue would be proof that neither narrative is promoted exclusively on the basis of the ethnic identity of the scholars involved, and that both professional historians and civil society can promote open-ended, evidence-based discourse.

In addition to national tensions, the dispute exposed professional controversies which reflected political divisions. One such conflict arose between historians and politicians in the domestic debates in both countries, and raised the question of who had the authority and the ability to determine the state's official version of the past. Each government adopted a fixed position, while historians split and expressed various views, serving both as legitimizers and opponents of state memory policy. State historians used their professional authority and legitimacy to uphold the state's official version of the past. When the Polish government was more liberal—as under the presidency of Aleksander Kwaśniewski—the IPN pursued an agenda that also investigated atrocities committed by Poles. Nationalist historians who opposed this approach attacked state officials and historians as traitors to Polish heroism. When the government changed, the official historians were replaced and historical truth was adjusted to serve nationalist goals. Nationalist politicians, with the support of state historians, attacked the self-critical Polish historians for their disloyalty in betraying and subverting their national moral heritage as martyrs and heroes. Truth and denial are key tropes of these exchanges in both the domestic and international dialogues.[10]

Memory laws are one of the tools states use to buttress the official version of the past in the face of critical histories, both domestic and international.[11] A variety of national laws address the historical record or the shared perception of the past— for example, hate-speech laws, memorial-day laws, and laws that establish national museums and archives.[12] Here we discuss illiberal memory laws—laws that criminalize critical perceptions of the national past which are deemed damaging to the good name of the nation. These laws, which have been increasingly promoted by populist governments and politicians, often elicit domestic resistance from historians, opposition politicians, and the organizations of civil society. In addition, such laws often spark international criticism and diplomatic censure or even sanctions from the countries that were involved in the historically contentious topic and view the new representation as offensive.[13]

Memory laws collide with critical, historical, truth-telling narratives, which flourish academically and publicly, having various impacts on society including in economic spheres such as tourism. Concurrently, increased attention to gross abuses in the past drives demands for redress. To state the obvious: that no government can control open discourse globally is an understatement, and most memory laws only amplify public attention and increase controversy.

Both Poland and Israel have passed memory laws that go beyond the specific legislation under examination here. The conflict that emerged in response to the Polish memory law of January 2018 illuminates the basic friction that can also be seen in other cases of memory laws, underscoring the tension when national narratives are confronted by historical truth.

Historical Background: The Polish–Israeli Memory Conflict

The aim of the PiS government of 'rising from our knees' after decades of what it deemed to be international humiliation involved the rewriting of the widely accepted narratives of two historical periods: the Holocaust and the 1989 transition to democracy. Both initiatives can be framed within the search for a new post-socialist national identity along two axes: one liberal, democratic, and European; the other populist, ethno-national, and Catholic.[14] Domestically, the PiS actively sought to reframe the legacy of Solidarity and the transition to democracy it spawned.[15] Internationally, the memory law that was approved on 26 January 2018 came after unsuccessful efforts to redeem Polish national honour through claims for reparations from Germany and Russia.[16]

The relatively non-controversial part of the law rejected (and criminalized) the use of the term 'Polish death camps' and 'Polish concentration camps', which were seen to imply that Poland was responsible for German crimes. Instead the law required that these be called 'German death camps and concentration camps in occupied Poland'. That the camps were misdesignated as 'Polish' has been largely accepted by the global community, governments, and scholars, recognizing that these were Nazi camps built in occupied Poland, and that 2 million to 3 million ethnic Poles were killed by the Nazis, many in the death camps. But the more controversial part related to the investigation of atrocities committed by Poles during the war. These included claiming that Poles collaborated with the Nazis and committed crimes against humanity. The law made supporting such narratives a criminal offence, and was intended to apply to the exposure of individual or mass crimes, including historical events that have been recognized and acknowledged as part of Polish and international historical discourse for at least a generation. The most infamous among these is the pogrom in Jedwabne in 1941, where the Christian population burned alive hundreds of Jews.[17] But there were many other instances of analogous mass violence and acts of daily personal violence against Jews during the Nazi occupation. The law sought to censor the exposure of such crimes: to place these histories off-limits.

This controversy came after two decades of 'Jewish revival' that celebrated Jewish culture and history and acknowledged some of the violent aspects of Polish–Jewish relations. Historians and social scientists were central in publicizing this violent past, while Jewish culture festivals, local memory activists,[18] Jewish studies programmes, and the POLIN Museum of the History of Polish Jews illuminated the new Polish Jewish 'restoration'. This duality provided space for a new Poland, but one that continued to be seen as a nation that had not fully acknowledged its violence to its Jews during and after the Holocaust.[19] Poland remained at the heart of the Holocaust, both geographically and as having had the largest Jewish community in Europe before the war. Many of the more than 300,000 Jewish survivors of the Holocaust in Poland had experienced Polish antisemitism at first hand, and those who are still alive six decades later played a central role in the historical dispute.

The law's approval one day before International Holocaust Remembrance Day sparked heated responses in the international arena, primarily from Israel and the American Jewish community. Israel, which had established good diplomatic relations with Poland since the end of communism, froze those relations, demanded a change in the law, and lobbied the Polish Ministry of Justice to suspend its implementation until its validity could be decided by Poland's Constitutional Court. Poland responded by initiating a diplomatic exchange to show goodwill and a desire for dialogue. A Polish delegation came to Israel in March 2018 to negotiate a resolution of the conflict with a delegation of officials from the Israeli Ministry of Foreign Affairs (MFA). In addition to professional diplomats, both delegations included historians, albeit as representatives of state history and memory institutes. The Israeli delegation was composed of three Yad Vashem officials: the director of governmental and external affairs, Yossi Gevir, and senior historians Dina Porat and David Silberklang, in addition to MFA legal and diplomatic staff, the Israeli ambassador to Poland, and two other senior MFA officials. The Polish delegation included the state secretary of the Polish Ministry of Foreign Affairs (Ministerstwo Spraw Zagranicznych, MSZ), the deputy president of the IPN, Mateusz Szpytma, the appointed director of the Museum of the Second World War in Gdańsk, Karol Nawrocki, the journalist and member of the IPN council Bronisław Wildstein, and legal experts. Both sides recognized that the construction of a historical narrative was at the heart of the dispute. Thus, while Poles tried to show empathy with and sensitivity to the concerns of Israel, they emphasized the need to stay in line with the official historical narrative of Poland. When the Israeli side raised the issue of criminalizing teachers, tour guides, and educators of Holocaust history, the Poles did not see how a different narrative could be an issue, as any teacher who diverted from the Polish narrative would betray their profession.[20] Israelis felt that there was no acknowledgement on the Polish side of different voices and narratives of the controversial history.

The meeting in March ended without a resolution and was not followed by another. The diplomatic dialogue seemed to have led to a dead end. It was not widely covered in the press, and the conflict disappeared from the headlines, yet the tension remained in the formal relations between the two countries. Within a short period of time, a secret channel of talks between the offices of the Israeli and Polish prime ministers replaced the MFA and the MSZ.[21] The talks culminated three months later in the Polish government decriminalizing the law and reducing the offences to the civil sphere, and a joint statement was issued on 27 June 2018 by both prime ministers condemning both antisemitism and anti-Polonism. However, this diplomatic resolution did not end the conflict. While the governments could agree on a false historical narrative in order to achieve short-term domestic political advantages, civil society objected.

The joint declaration was immediately subjected to extensive public critique in both countries. Yehuda Bauer, one of the most prominent Holocaust historians, accused Israeli prime minister Benjamin Netanyahu of betraying Israel by violating 'the historical truth, the memory of the Holocaust and the wonderful people in Poland who have researched the facts on which we base our criticism'.[22] These researchers, argued Bauer, would be the target of lawsuits. He accused Netanyahu of prioritizing Israel's transitory economic and political interests over the memory of the Holocaust. He suggested the statement was an immoral victory of short-term interests that would leave lasting damage.[23] As elaborated later, Bauer's view was widely supported, not only by groups of Holocaust survivors and civil society activists but also by historians from Yad Vashem and politicians from Netanyahu's government.

Instead of putting the past to rest, the joint statement brought further conflict, which continued to evolve around specific events and political remarks. At various stages, statements in the Polish and Israeli media regarding the law or the past at issue caused new crises. One of these was the appointment of an Israeli historian, Daniel

Blatman, in December 2018, as chief historian of the Polish-government-supported Warsaw Ghetto Museum.[24] From a Polish perspective, this was a reconciliatory gesture, opening up the historical dialogue, whereas there were those in Israel who suspected that Blatman's appointment was an attempt to advance a particular agenda. The debate in Israel evolved among historians, with Blatman criticizing scholars for taking a Judaeo-centric approach to studying the Holocaust, while his critics (such as Bauer) argued for a victims' perspective.

A new phase in the conflict began in February 2019 following a meeting between prime ministers Netanyahu and Morawiecki for the first time since the June 2018 agreement. In a press briefing, the Israeli prime minister, directing his comments to the Israeli public, said 'Poles co-operated with the Germans' during the Holocaust, and that he did not know anyone who got prosecuted for saying so.[25] There was an immediate rebuke by Poland, and although Netanyahu later issued a clarification saying that he was not referring to the Polish nation or to all Poles, the historical disagreement led to a new diplomatic crisis. The Polish government issued a critique, and in the following days Morawiecki decided not to attend the Visegrád Group meeting that Israel was eager to host. Suddenly, Poland had the ethical upper hand. Netanyahu's self-contradictions (June 2018 compared with February 2019) showed the fragility of the historical narrative when exploited by short-sighted politicians.

Mapping the Debate

This investigation is based on the media coverage of the law in Polish and Israeli print media and on the internet, as well as on semi-structured interviews with those involved in the domestic and binational debates. From the media publications, we mapped the variety of stances that appeared in public statements and political speeches, interviews, op-eds, and news coverage. We also mapped the rhetoric, narratives, repeated phrases, and social agents and organizations involved. In Poland, we examined a total of 262 articles in seven national newspapers and magazines and additional internet sources (Facebook and Twitter). These media sources were chosen to capture the variety of views on the law from its approval in January 2018 to July 2019. The printed press represented a variety of formats and audiences: the right-wing *Gazeta Polska Codziennie*, the tabloid *Fakt*, the liberal elite daily *Gazeta Wyborcza*, the centrist *Rzeczpospolita*, the left-wing weekly *Polityka*, the right-wing weekly *Sieci*, and the liberal weekly *Newsweek Polska*. The media focused on the main events: the approval of the law was debated from mid-January until mid-February and again in late June around the joint statement of the Polish and Israeli prime ministers and the resulting amendment of the law. Protest (petitions, demonstrations, and public statements) against the law remained on the margins of the debate in the printed press and was more visible on the internet and in social networks around the anniversary of the 1968 expulsion of Polish Jews by the communist government.[26]

In Israel, we examined more than 150 articles between January 2018 and July 2019. The media search included the dailies and news websites of *Haaretz* (liberal elite),

Yisra'el hayom (populist right), and *Yediot aharonot*/Ynet (centre), as well as the websites of organizations and agents who took part in the debate, such as Yad Vashem, the MFA, the Polish embassy in Israel, and the progressive website Siha mekomit. Similarly to Poland, the debate centred around specific events, including the approval of the law and the delegations' meeting, the joint statements of the prime ministers, Blatman's appointment, and Netanyahu's statement in February 2019. In May 2019 the Israeli media discussed the law once more in the context of a hostile encounter between an Israeli citizen and the Polish ambassador to Israel, as well as the issue of the return of Jewish property in Poland.

Studying recent events raises difficulties, among them the challenges of transcending dominant ideologies as well as analytically determining the start and end of a process that is still unfolding. We address these difficulties by presenting a multivocal public debate and a methodological and theoretical perspective that has been used in other case studies and periods.[27]

The domestic public debates in Poland and Israel involved historians, politicians and state officials, and civil society groups, each claiming the authority to determine the historical record. The discourse among governments, historians, and civil society is best visualized as a Venn diagram of three partially overlapping circles for each country. The dynamic between the circles in each country responded to statements and events initiated by the other country that invoked the conflicted memory. Informed by surges in media coverage, we reviewed the debate within and between Poland and Israel around five events that reflected the central points of friction: the approval of the law (January 2018); the anniversary of March 1968 (March 2018); the joint statement (June 2018); Blatman's appointment (December 2018); and Netanyahu's statement to the Israeli press during the prime ministers' second meeting in Poland (February 2019).

Each country presents a spectrum of views that covers everything from its official presentation of the past to its critics and protestors. In Israel, the spectrum lies between Prime Minister Netanyahu's June 2018 statement that equated antisemitism and anti-Polonism (from a diplomatic perspective the most accommodating to Poland) and the insistence of dozens of Holocaust historians, such as Yehuda Bauer, on Polish complicity in Holocaust crimes. As mentioned previously, Israeli politicians competed with each other to see who could offend Poland the most. Evidently, these politicians were not interested in historical truth and instead focused on their domestic audience.

Historians occupied different positions between these ideal types, as the controversy regarding the role of Dina Porat, chief historian at Yad Vashem, exemplifies. Porat was Netanyahu's consultant for the joint statement with the Polish prime minister. Other Yad Vashem historians (including a member of the MFA's March delegation, David Silberklang) and civil society groups criticized the statement, accusing Porat of colluding with a political compromise that contradicted historical truth. The drafting of the joint statement ignored Yad Vashem and specialist historians.[28] Although Netanyahu publicly thanked Porat 'from Yad Vashem' for seeing the process through, Porat stated in an interview with Kan TV that she acted in her private capacity as 'consultant' to the team appointed by Netanyahu, not as the chief historian of Yad Vashem.[29] She stood behind the resolution, stating that it could be 'lived with'. Shifting the focus, she argued that Poles were victims of the Nazi occupation: the entire Polish nation could not be blamed for organizing harmful actions against Jews.

The lack of clarity on the involvement of Porat in drafting the joint statement was one of the motivations behind a request by human rights activists that the identity of the historians and academic institutions Netanyahu had consulted in drafting it be made public. In a letter to the MFA, they argued that the joint statement was negotiated in secret channels including a meeting at a Mossad facility, contrary to best practice, which required that historical statements involve comprehensive discussions with experts and the public.[30] The MFA rejected the request, claiming that disclosing such information could damage Israel's foreign relations and would prevent academic experts from assisting the ministry in the future.[31] Interestingly, the historical consultants themselves preferred to remain anonymous out of concern for the damage to their academic careers which could result from assisting in drafting the contested, historically disputed, statement.[32] This behaviour suggests that the statement was viewed as compromised and false not by only its critics but by its authors as well.

Polish historians stood on both sides of the dispute, for and against the government's memory law and more general 'history policy'. Those employed by the IPN were obliged to support the government's policy. Liberal historians who had previously worked for the IPN under the more liberal regime and academics in general became the targets of this policy, especially those who had been investigating Polish complicity in crimes against Jews. Even before the memory law, the Polish government had attacked as enemies of the nation prominent Holocaust historians such as Jan Tomasz Gross, Jan Grabowski, Barbara Engelking, and Jacek Leociak, who had conducted research on Poles' complicity in actions against Jews.[33] Right-wing groups also protested against the international support for these historians and the institutions with which they were affiliated, and called for the cancellation of international conferences they wanted to attend because of their 'anti-Polish character'.[34] The IPN took part in these efforts through official statements calling for the dissemination of the history policy in universities and educational institutes.[35] The IPN also produced historical material that supported the official view for state-sponsored institutions, like the Museum of the Second World War in Gdańsk, and attempted to undermine the work of the self-critical historians, for example through the dissemination of scholarly reviews that criticized their work.[36]

These historians, most prominently Gross and Grabowski who are based in the West, were supported by domestic Holocaust historians, public intellectuals, and organizations of civil society, whose work for the past two decades has focused on studying and documenting negative Polish behaviour towards Jews during and immediately after the Holocaust. These individuals criticized the official policy as motivated by political interests rather than by its stated aim of fighting for historical truth. According to Jan Grabowski:

At a time when there is political pressure, the historical debate is transformed into a clash of two powers. Intellectuals, historians, and journalists have no chance against the state ... I wouldn't call this a dispute between opposing opinions; the aim is to suppress independent research and to impose a nationalistic interpretation on society.[37]

Gross gave a similar statement in an interview for *Newsweek Polska*: 'Since the propaganda about lifting Poland from its knees has not obtained universal support, the new law should be understood as the government's attempt to alter history.'[38] Barbara Engelking, however, focused her response on her professional expertise and provided historical facts to counter the government's efforts to stress that Poles saving Jews during the war was a common practice.[39]

The view of the law as a government attempt to silence the critical voices of historians and memory activists was shared by many who rejected the idea that research into the Jewish past could be harmful to the good name of the nation. Leftist politician and historian Tomasz Nałęcz said bluntly that 'the PiS takes revenge on scholars that expose its historical lies'.[40] This view was supported by the fact that the passage of the law was accompanied by threats, sanctions, and public incitement by government officials and supporters against critical voices in the Polish academy, museums, and NGOs. Scholarly work that exposed Polish crimes against Jews faced the most significant pressure; however, it continued to be published and circulated by public intellectuals.[41]

While historians wrestled to preserve their professional authority and academic freedom, politicians on both sides aggravated the conflict by distorting well-established historical truths. In rejecting the Polish law, Yair Lapid, the Israeli opposition leader and parliament member, rushed to his Twitter account to claim that 'there were Polish death camps and no law can ever change that'.[42] The assertiveness of this claim did not make it true or acceptable. Israeli foreign minister Israel Katz went even further, reviving a quotation from the late former prime minister Yitzhak Shamir that Poles 'suckled antisemitism with their mothers' milk'.[43] Both comments inflamed the conflict. Lapid's statement was thoughtless, as it contradicted the factual and widely accepted history that they were German camps. Katz's comment was racist, and resulted in diplomatic retaliation by Poland with its withdrawal from the Visegrád Group meeting in February 2019 in Israel. This was supposed to have been the first time the group met outside the Visegrád region.[44] Not for the first time did a politician snatch defeat from the jaws of victory. Israel, which had had the moral upper hand in the dispute, lost much of it as a result, and its Polish supporters could not justify such an offence, which the antisemites saw as proof of anti-Polonism. On the Polish side, Prime Minister Morawiecki compared Polish and Jewish collaboration with the Nazis in an interview in February 2018.[45] The statement evoked angry responses from the Israeli prime minister, the president, senior Yad Vashem historians,[46] and from the political left and some right-wing politicians in Poland. Even one of Morawiecki's close friends, lobbyist Jonny Daniels, called it a form of Holocaust denial.[47] The two countries remained at loggerheads.

Overcoming these statements proved a challenge. One attempt was the joint statement of June 2018, which ironically contained another distortion in constructing a symmetry between antisemitism and anti-Polonism. Morawiecki declared the joint statement a victory for historical truth.[48] Jarosław Gowin, minister of science and higher education, announced that the shared statement was 'an amazing weapon' that subsequent governments would be able to use effectively to fight 'the lie about the alleged co-responsibility of the Polish people for the Holocaust'.[49] At the same time, Gowin declared that the statement would advance reconciliation by creating a dialogue with the world's Jewish community.[50]

The framing of the joint statement was criticized by the left and the right in Poland. The far right was concerned with what it understood to be a weakening of the law and the PiS's policy, while the left responded with a mixture of complete rejection but also slight optimism that the joint statement could be a move towards reconciliation with Israel and the world. Thus, according to Władysław Kosiniak-Kamysz, leader of the agrarian Christian Democratic opposition party Polskie Stronnictwo Ludowe: 'It's a shame and scandal. The amendment and the way it was proceeded were a mix of stupidity and hypocrisy.'[51] The more optimistic view was expressed by Kamila Gasiuk-Pihowicz of the liberal party Nowoczesna, who argued that the statement was 'better late than never' but still condemned the damage the law had done: 'Why did you allow this cesspool of antisemitism to explode, why did Polish–Israeli, Polish–American relations have to be destroyed?'[52]

While civil society in Israel unanimously rejected the joint statement, as will be discussed below, Polish civil society was divided between the political left and right in its responses. Right-wing groups and conservative media outlets criticized the statement and the decriminalization of Polish complicity in Holocaust crimes as a sign of weakness by the Polish government. These views were repeated whenever Polish complicity was invoked by Israeli politicians or state officials. On the left, the views were mixed. Journalist and Holocaust survivor Daniel Passent expressed disappointment that the 'agreement was achieved at a cost: truth; scholarly research by Poles, Israelis and other scholars, as well as my personal memory.'[53] Szewach Weiss, former Speaker of the Israeli parliament and a former Israeli ambassador to Poland, a widely respected public figure in both countries, expressed satisfaction and the hope that 'Poland and Israel will walk the same path together. We don't need to forget about the past, but let's go forward together. I hope we'll return to the good relations of half a year ago.'[54]

Historians on the Other Side

In the controversy over the Polish memory law some historians took the other side to their nation. This was especially obvious with the appointment of Daniel Blatman, a senior historian at the Hebrew University of Jerusalem and a former student of renowned historian Israel Gutman of Yad Vashem, as chief historian of the Polish-government-supported Warsaw Ghetto Museum. Both Israeli and Polish Holocaust historians accused Blatman of crossing the boundary between scholarship and politics or between historical truth and nationalist manipulations of the truth; Blatman levelled the same accusation at his critics. The museum, directed by Albert Stankowski, who previously worked at the Polin museum, is dedicated to the Warsaw ghetto and will be located in a building that served as a children's hospital in the ghetto. It is seen by many Polish and Israeli historians as another step in the continued efforts of the Polish government to rewrite the Polish national narrative. Before approaching Blatman, Stankowski approached a number of Polish historians, but they declined to accept since they saw it as collaborating with the government's history policy.[55] Appointing an Israeli historian was perceived as showing that the museum was open to dialogue and to including new perspectives.

Others saw this as merely a fig leaf, an argument strongly rejected by Blatman. A heated debate followed his appointment in December 2018. 'Some of the critics are my colleagues who once were my friends and maybe no longer are', Blatman told *Haaretz*,[56] while continuing to publish opinion pieces in the newspaper which mixed criticism of Yad Vashem with justification of the Polish narrative (as evidenced by the exchange on 13 October 2019). Blatman had previously criticized Yad Vashem for the Zionist ideology which he claimed underlay its scholarship and had called for a more critical approach to Holocaust research.[57] After his appointment, in his criticism of Yad Vashem scholars, in particular Havi Dreifuss of Tel Aviv University, he asserted: 'Yad Vashem teaches the Holocaust in the same way that a totalitarian country teaches history.'[58] Dreifuss had earlier been offered a position at the Warsaw Ghetto Museum and declined. She did not, she asserted, want 'to serve an enterprise led by officials distorting the Holocaust and attacking historians.'[59] Four prominent Polish scholars of Jewish history who been targets of the PiS government since 2015, Jan Grabowski, Barbara Engelking, Jacek Leociak, and Agnieszka Haska, pointed to the irony inherent in Blatman's statement and his position as a historian under an increasingly authoritarian regime.[60]

In Blatman's terms, the dispute is between two historiographical approaches, one nationalist and the other critical: the nationalist approach is manifested by Yad Vashem's stress on the Jews as the central victims of the Holocaust. The critical approach within which he places himself tries to study the Holocaust in its European, national, or local context.[61] This notion is expressed in his vision for the new Warsaw Ghetto Museum: 'The Holocaust of Polish Jewry should be located in the Polish historical space, not in an exclusively Jewish space.' Similarly to the Polish narrative that compares Jewish and Polish suffering under Nazi occupation, he stated that 'the city of Warsaw and the Polish population . . . were under the same Nazi occupation and were also subjected to the terror'. He argued that he did not compare the fate of Jews and Poles during the war, because the former did not see themselves as Jews at that time, but rather as Poles. Blatman also compared the governments of Poland

and Israel as a way to reject the accusation of serving an anti-democratic government in Poland: 'Following that line, I should also not co-operate with Yad Vashem because it's under the aegis of a minister of whose policy I'm very critical', he said, referring to the education minister, later prime minister, Naftali Bennett.[62]

The four Polish historians and Dreifuss were not convinced by this argument, however, and saw Blatman as 'a figurehead for this pernicious project which seeks to whitewash history'. They viewed Blatman's appointment as a 'useful tool to break the resistance of underpaid and reluctant Polish historians, who—until now—have refused on principle to join this nationalistic project'.[63] Blatman, however, sees these Polish and Israeli Holocaust historians as justifying another nationalist project: the Israeli one.[64]

This dialogue is based on both sides agreeing that there is a historical truth and that it can be empirically verified. At the very least Karl Popper's criterion for falsification is generally embraced by professional historians. Furthermore, the need to maintain ethical standards is also shared. The dialogue over truth and ethics will no doubt change in the future, but it will continue to struggle over interpretation. Such disagreements do not challenge historians' professional legitimacy in public debate.

Both the Israeli and the Polish governments have a nationalist memory policy that excludes the other's claim to having suffered the most. Both are also pragmatic, trying to appease their different audiences. Yet the stress on martyrdom that works domestically is counterproductive in foreign policy. Both governments are willing to compromise their national narrative in order to create a diplomatic alliance to bolster international support and legitimacy. As a result, a nationalist statement directed at a domestic audience could create a crisis in relations with a rival state that has to be settled diplomatically. This need to speak to a polarized audience caused repeated crises.

Indeed, the substance of historical truth carries different implications depending on the political and cultural context. When Polish historians or civil society groups support the historical responsibility of Poles for antisemitic violence, they take on their own national narrative and face criticism as 'enemies' of the Polish nation. This requires courage in the face of public defamation and threats. But the same substantive claim of Polish complicity in crimes against Jews when voiced by Jews or Israelis plays to the Jewish nationalist narrative and benefits from populist and nationalist politics. It does not require intellectual or political courage. In Poland, and within the Polish diaspora, the anti-Polonism of Israelis and the Jewish diaspora gives comfort to Polish antisemites, who justify their hate by pointing to those Jews who hate Poles. In Poland, it validates their own victim narrative.

The historical dialogue has polarized both sides, yet there is substantial diversity within each group. There are those on the Israeli side who supported a 'Polish' narrative, including Blatman, Porat, and (at times) Netanyahu, each for his or her own historical or political reasons. On the Polish side, leading Holocaust historians and politicians from the opposition supported the Israeli narrative of Holocaust history. While the mainstream public in both countries has held to its respective national narrative, there were rifts in each country, with strong voices supporting the other position.

Memory Laws, History Policies, and the Limits of State Manipulation

Civil society in Israel, on both the left and the right, supported the general view—which was widespread in the West—that the Polish law was an attempt to whitewash responsibility and guilt and was doomed to fail. As the dispute unfolded, Holocaust survivors were quoted extensively, giving expression to their outrage and declaring that the law was proof that the Poles had committed crimes against the Jews. The denial evoked memories of hatred and suffering at the hands of the Poles; thus the dialogue became a crescendo of accusations. These grievances escalated into a survivors' protest at the Polish embassy in Israel, among other incidences of grassroots activism.

A similar spectrum of approaches—from legitimacy to denial of Polish complicity in crimes against Jews during and after the Holocaust—carried different political and moral meanings in Poland. While support for the first section of the law regarding the ban on calling Nazi concentration camps 'Polish' was found across the political spectrum—all were equally offended by Lapid's statement—the internal conflict divided those who supported the claim that Poles were never complicit in crimes against Jews and those who saw this as a form of Holocaust denial. The divide between these approaches primarily corresponded with the political divisions between the liberal left and the populist right in Poland and affected not only politicians and historians but also civil society. The responses clearly rejected unfounded claims and confined the debate to the veracity of core disagreements.

Public protest against the law vacillated, giving way to mass protests against other PiS policies. Jewish and non-Jewish historians and intellectuals continued to respond on social networks, expressing their views against the growing politicization of the academy and threats against scholars and memory activists by the right-wing media and the dominant political discourse. The Polish Jewish journalist Konstanty Gebert even violated the Polish law, challenging the prosecutor to sue him. The prosecutor never obliged.[65]

Liberal left-wing civil society united to express its objection to the memory law. For example, a petition urging the president not to sign the law sponsored by the Akcja Demokracja foundation was followed by an 'open letter addressed to international public opinion' signed by 108 civic NGOs. Under the hashtag #solidarityintruth, the multilingual statement in English, Polish, and Hebrew identified its writers and addressees as friends who cared about Polish–Jewish dialogue and 'the truth about our common history'. Addressing the memory law specifically, the statement critiques its whitewashing of the Poles' involvement in the Holocaust, as well as 'thoughtless actions by politicians that arouse antisemitic statements—all this is not being done in our name'. The statement calls for historical truth and solidarity between Poles and Jews as the foundation of coexistence and return to the path of reconciliation. 'We want the whole truth about the Holocaust, however painful it may be ... No to antisemitism. No to misrepresenting history.'[66]

The fiftieth anniversary of the campaign of the Polish communist government to expel Polish Jews in 1968 occurred in March 2018. The Polin Museum marked it with a critical historical exhibition, titled 'Estranged: March '68 and Its Aftermath'. The special historical exhibition ended with a presentation of contemporary statements from social media that contained antisemitic language similar to the political discourse of the communist regime against Polish Jews in 1968.[67] The exhibition made the museum a target for the PiS administration, and, after more contention, the minister of culture and national heritage, Piotr Gliński, delayed renewing the contract of the re-elected museum director, Dariusz Stola, in the spring of 2019, leaving the museum without a director.[68] In the end the conflict was resolved by the appointment in February 2020 of Stola's deputy, Zygmunt Stępiński.

The Polin Museum and the city of Warsaw, as well as other municipalities that have long been governed by mayors from the left, have tried to compensate for the state's efforts to control historical and civil voices through the use of budget cuts, job terminations, and bureaucratic sanctions. Municipalities helped NGOs survive once they no longer received state resources, such as subsidized rent, and supported conferences and artistic and activist events on the Jewish past. Together with civil society, such urban municipalities demonstrated the limits of the central government's ability to intervene in history and went against the abuse of history as a tool for political propaganda and manipulation.

However, the PiS government was able to realize its history policy in urban centres as well. In March 2017 Gliński fired Paweł Machcewicz as director of the Museum of the Second World War in Gdańsk after a long dispute over whether the museum should present a patriotic or a universalist narrative.[69] The PiS organized regular commemorative events in front of the presidential palace in Warsaw to mark the crash on 10 April 2010 of a Polish Air Force Tu-154 outside Smolensk, which caused the death of Lech Kaczyński, the fourth president of the Republic of Poland—whose twin brother, Jarosław, is the chairman of the PiS—and ninety-five government officials, intellectuals, and civil society figures. The creation of the Warsaw Ghetto Museum, despite the existence of the Polin Museum, meant that there would be a rival Jewish museum in the city. Gliński said that the new museum would highlight the mutual love between Poles and Jews.[70]

However, centre-left historians, including IPN historians under the previous government, continued to publish research that proved to the impartial observer (foreign historians and others) the complicity of many Poles (not all by any means) in the Holocaust. They investigated and publicized cases of mass violence of Poles against Jews, including Jedwabne and the Kielce pogrom of July 1946, that were followed by public debate, official memorial ceremonies, and even an official apology.[71] Denying what had already been publicly accepted as historical truth by the academy, former government, and the public was much more difficult. According to Agnieszka Haska of the Centre for Holocaust Research in Warsaw, 'the history of the Holocaust is not a buffet where you can choose which bits you want', emphasizing the wide-ranging research which had already been carried out on this problem in Poland.[77] Holocaust historians also continued to publish histories during this period, and these were added to the collective historical knowledge used by civil society to fight the memory law that denied these historical events and criminalized their being made public.

Conclusion

Past atrocities are receiving increased global attention, as victims and their descendants call for recognition and redress for their suffering. The Polish–Israeli controversy provides a rich and complex test case. It demonstrates that such controversies cannot be reduced to a simple conflict between governments, as there are many stakeholders who have a right to be heard. The various participants in both the formal and informal historical dialogues derive their authority from different sources. Professional historians are qualified experts whose authority is derived from their accepted methodologies and argumentation and their academic standing; politicians derive their authority from their government roles and from the relative strength of their governments. Professional historians do disagree with each other and may find themselves on the other side of the debate from their own government. However, politicians are often influenced by unrelated and tangential concerns, such as upcoming elections or international standing. Therefore, historians are seen as having a greater legitimacy, even in the official diplomatic sphere.

The nationalist position in the Polish–Israeli case was more assertive but less persuasive than the expert position of historians. This points to possible solutions to conflicts through giving historians roles in formal dialogues, including mapping areas of agreement and disagreement and creating narratives that respect the diversity of opinion on both sides. This is not risk-free: it is clearly possible for governments or NGOs to appoint nationalist members to such a dialogue, which could derail the whole process.[73]

One conclusion is that dialogue can offer new approaches to resolving conflicts if there is goodwill on both sides. Although its success is not assured, it is unlikely to aggravate the situation, as it is conflictual to begin with. Agreement is more likely if it is based on professional historical truth rather than on short-term political goals. This can be seen in the Polish demand that the concentration camps be described as 'Nazi' or 'German' but not 'Polish'. Japan's and Germany's approaches to their neighbours over the last seventy years also clearly display the difference between resolving and perpetuating historical conflict. While historical dialogue can exacerbate conflict, it is more likely to lead to a resolution of the disputed issues. It certainly does add a tool to the mechanisms for conflict resolution.

Demands for redress, fuelled by the growing prominence of human rights as the ethical framework for international relations, continue to occur even when those rights are under political pressure from governments and are in decline. Currently, human rights rhetoric is embraced by governments as a tool for criticizing other countries, and there are plenty of abusers to criticize. However, this discourse of demands for redress for past atrocities has evolved since the 1980s into a multi-layered historical dialogue which includes the formal and informal participation of officials, scholars, civil society organizations, and activists. This takes place both domestically and internationally, and activists and civil society organizations often push such demands into the public sphere. Yet historical dialogue as a shared method for resolving memory conflicts is not widely acknowledged. Those involved in conflict resolution and peace-building, including politicians, occasionally recognize the importance of history, but have no means of addressing it. Consequently, the topic is dealt with in an ad hoc manner, which often leads to failure and increased animosity.

Thus the policy conclusion of our study is that states should give more explicit recognition and resources to historical dialogue. Moreover, historical dialogue can create a framework for public debate when conflict threatens to emerge. Historical reconciliation is, almost without exception, agonistic,[74] and may seem like magical thinking in today's international relations. It is not a permanent solution and is always at risk of nationalist manipulation. Memory conflicts can re-emerge at any time, as long as they remain important to the victims and their descendants. The racial justice movement in the United States brought a new intensity to the questions of reparation and of constructing historical narratives and community memory.

This demand for redress is spreading globally. The Herero demands from Germany—after more than a hundred years—are an important example. Japan's relations with Korea and China provided a rich territory for historical dialogue in the last four decades that has defined the relations of these states. The break-up of Yugoslavia is an extreme case of manipulating history to incite a conflict. In our analysis of the Polish–Israeli historical dialogue over the last few years, we have shown how politicians created a crisis that could have been avoided with the help of historians and historical dialogue. Memory activism is a growing field, and governments are happy to leverage it to place new demands that play to their nationalist support and strengthen them domestically, even at the expense of foreign relations.

The memory conflict between Poland and Israel is ongoing, inflamed by political statements and court rulings. The impact is wider than bilateral. Israel contributed to the crisis in Poland's relations with Russia when it gave Russian president Vladimir Putin the stage at the 2020 Annual Holocaust Forum that Yad Vashem hosted in Jerusalem. Poland withdrew from the event when it was not offered an opportunity to respond to Putin's account of the Second World War, which was propagandist to the extent that Yad Vashem felt it had to issue a corrective statement after the event. Meanwhile, the Polish government continued its crusade against critical historiographical and journalistic research into alleged Polish participation in war crimes. In 2020 a right-wing anti-defamation NGO helped file a civil libel lawsuit against Grabowski and Engelking on behalf of the niece of a village mayor who was named by a Holocaust survivor as having betrayed twenty-two local Jews to the Nazis. The testimony appeared in *Dalej jest noc*, although the mayor was acquitted in a post-war trial.[75] In 2021 a Warsaw court ordered the historians to apologize. Yad Vashem called the case 'a serious attack on free and open research'.[76] Finally, the court decision was overruled by a higher court. Also in 2021, journalist Katarzyna Markusz faced police investigation for a story she published in *Krytyka Polityczna* in October 2020 about Polish participation in the Holocaust.[77]

The latest controversy seems to replicate the 2018 memory conflict and to undo its diplomatic resolution. At the centre is a new bill that was approved by the Polish senate and signed by the president that limits claims for redress for loss of Jewish property. In response to the bill, Yair Lapid, in his role as Israeli foreign minister, recalled Israel's diplomatic envoy to Warsaw and called the law 'antisemitic'.[78] Israeli state officials considered cancelling the June 2018 joint statement that amended the January 2018 Holocaust law. The Polish ambassador stayed in Poland under the directive of his Foreign Ministry, which threatened to limit the travel of Israeli youth delegations to Poland.[79] And so, tensions and contradictions over historical truth and official narratives continue to inflame the conflict. Diplomacy and governmental actions currently amplify the intensity of the historical dispute.

Our findings show that historical truth is not imperilled by diplomacy or state narratives. Although the Israeli–Polish case exemplifies how to conduct historical dialogue badly, it also shows the potential for advancing reconciliation by engaging history, although this must be done prudently. One conclusion is therefore to encourage peace-building and conflict resolution, to take history seriously as a means of preventing the exacerbation of national differences, and to develop policies to redress historical grievances. Certainly, politicians ought to accept that manipulating history has its limits, particularly when it is engaged in by rival parties. They would clearly advance their cause better by making use of qualified scholars and approaching the complex issues of the past more professionally.

After this article was completed, Russia invaded Ukraine, arguing that it was part of Russia historically. In the wake of the invasion, questions of historical identity surfaced quickly and played out similarly to the debate between Poland and Israel. Ukraine proposed to change the names of hundreds of public spaces named after Russians. The Israeli ambassador to Kyiv proposed the new names should include those of Ukrainians who saved Jews during the Second World War rather than adhering to the earlier practice of naming places after Ukrainian nationalists who often collaborated with the Nazis. Thus is the fluidity of historical dialogue displayed in the most horrific war in Europe for eighty years. There is much more of this to come as countries define themselves by choosing among their usable historical identities.

Notes

1 There are exceptions: one format for engaging historians in the service of reconciliation is a bilateral historical commission. Germany initiated several commissions with its

neighbours, including the German–Czech commission, which has become an ongoing initiative. Colombia presents a different example: a joint historical committee of the government and the FARC facilitated progress when the Havana talks seemed frozen. Another type is an education pact, like the one signed in 2018 between Burma and Israel. See E. Barkan, 'Memories of Violence: Micro and Macro History and the Challenges to Peacebuilding in Colombia and Northern Ireland', *Irish Political Studies*, 31 (2016), 6–28; J. Kopstein, 'The Politics of National Reconciliation: Memory and Institutions in German–Czech Relations since 1989', *Nationalism and Ethnic Politics*, 3 (1997), 57–78; N. Landau, 'Israel, Myanmar Sign Education Pact for Programs about "Holocaust and Its Lessons" and Xenophobia' (29 May 2018): *Haaretz* website, visited 14 Dec. 2021.

2 History is the record of past events as studied by historians in the present; collective memory is the symbolic representation of these past events by social groups in the present. The binary opposition that sees history as objective and scientific and memory as subjective, selective, and methodologically unregulated is less useful in this chapter than the dynamic relationship between past and present that both terms cover. See E. H. Carr, 'The Historian and His Facts', in *What is History?* (New York, 1961), 3–35; A. Confino, 'Collective Memory and Cultural History: Problems of Method', *American Historical Review*, 102 (1997), 1386–1403; A. Erll, 'Cultural Memory Studies: An Introduction', in A. Erll and A. Nünning (eds.), *Cultural Memory Studies: An International and Interdisciplinary Handbook* (Berlin, 2008), 1–15.

3 B. J. Shetler, 'Historical Memory as a Foundation for Peace: Network Formation and Ethnic Identity in North Mara, Tanzania', *Journal of Peace Research*, 47 (2010), 639–50.

4 E. Barkan, 'Historians and Historical Reconciliation', *American Historical Review*, 114 (2009), 899–913.

5 Ibid.

6 'Full Text of Poland's Controversial Holocaust Legislation' (1 Feb. 2018): *Times of Israel* website, visited 8 Dec. 2021.

7 There is much more complexity in the second part of the law, which made liable to criminal prosecution 'whoever claims, publicly and contrary to the facts, that the Polish Nation or the Republic of Poland is responsible or co-responsible for Nazi crimes committed by the Third Reich' (ibid.), but we focus here on how this part was understood in the media and public debate.

8 Ibid.

9 D. Engel, 'On Reconciling the Histories of Two Chosen Peoples', *American Historical Review*, 114 (2009), 914–29.

10 See E. Barkan, 'Historical Dialogue: Beyond Transitional Justice and Conflict Resolution', in K. Neumann and J. Thompson (eds.), *Historical Justice and Memory* (Madison, Wis., 2015), 185–201.

11 Y. Gutman, 'Memory Laws: An Escalation in Minority Exclusion or a Testimony to the Limits of State Power?', *Law and Society Review*, 50 (2016), 575–607; N. Koposov, *Memory Laws, Memory Wars: The Politics of the Past in Europe and Russia* (Cambridge, 2017); U. Belavusau and A. Gliszczyńska-Grabias (eds.), *Law and Memory: Towards Legal Governance of History* (Cambridge, 2017).

12 N. Tirosh and A. Schejter, '"I will perpetuate your memory through all generations": Institutionalization of Collective Memory by Law in Israel', *International Journal of Media and Cultural Politics*, 11 (2015), 21–35; E. Fronza, 'The Punishment of Negationism: The Difficult Dialogue between Law and Memory', *Vermont Law Review*, 30 (2005), 609–26;

J. J. Savelsberg and R. D. King, *American Memories: Atrocities and the Law* (New York, 2011); E. Zerubavel, *Time Maps: Collective Memory and the Social Shape of the Past* (Chicago, 2003).

13 Ongoing conflicts which are grounded in polarized historical narratives include Ukraine and Russia; Japan, South Korea, and China; and intrastate disputes with indigenous peoples and minorities, like the Rohingya in Burma.

14 K. Korycki, 'Memory, Party Politics, and Post-Transition Space: The Case of Poland', *East European Politics and Societies and Cultures*, 31 (2017), 518–44.

15 J. Kubik, 'Solidarity's Afterlife: Amidst Forgetting and Bickering', in A. Rychard and G. Motzkin (eds.), *The Legacy of Polish Solidarity: Social Activism, Regime Collapse, and Building of a New Society* (New York, 2015), 161–202.

16 K. Gebert, interview with Y. Gutman, 29 June 2018.

17 J. T. Gross, *Sąsiedzi: Historia zagłady żydowskiego miasteczka* (Sejny, 2000); Eng. edn.: *Neighbors: The Destruction of the Jewish Community in Jedwabne, Poland* (Princeton, NJ, 2001).

18 Memory activists are individuals or groups who, working outside state channels, use commemoration as a means of publicly targeting the official or dominant view of the past in their society. Their aims can be to change the official memory or to protect the dominant memory from change. See Y. Gutman, *Memory Activism: Reimagining the Past for the Future in Israel-Palestine* (Nashville, Tenn., 2017); Y. Gutman and J. Wustenberg, 'Challenging the Meaning of the Past from Below: A Typology for Comparative Research on Memory Activists' (10 Oct. 2021): Sage Journals website, *Memory Studies*, visited 3 Jan. 2022.

19 E. Lehrer, 'Bearing False Witness? "Vicarious" Jewish Identity and the Politics of Affinity', in D. Glowacka and J. Zylinska (eds.), *Imaginary Neighbors: Mediating Polish–Jewish Relations after the Holocaust* (Lincoln, Neb., 2007), 84–109.

20 According to one of the Israeli members of the delegation (off-the-record interview with Y. Gutman and E. Barkan, 4 June 2018).

21 The joint statement of June 2018 was secretly discussed by PiS members of the European Parliament, Ryszard Legutko and Tomasz Poręba (D. Passent, 'Handel historią' (9 July 2018): *Polityka* website, 'En Passant', visited 14 Dec. 2021), negotiating with the Israeli delegates led by former security officials Brigadier General (Res.) Professor Jacob Nagel and Advocate Dr. Yossef Chechanover.

22 Y. Bauer, 'Israel's Stupid, Ignorant and Amoral Betrayal of the Truth on Polish Involvement in the Holocaust' (3 July 2018): *Haaretz* website, visited 14 Dec. 2021.

23 Ibid.

24 O. Aderet, 'Warsaw's Controversial New Holocaust Museum to Present "Polish Narrative"' (14 Dec. 2018): *Haaretz* website, visited 14 Dec. 2021.

25 Associated Press, 'Israel Hosts East European Leaders after Summit Scrapped' (19 Feb. 2019): Ynet website, visited 14 Dec. 2021.

26 Stanisław Krajewski, interview with Y. Gutman, 14 June 2018.

27 U. Scott, 'Strange Bedfellows? Anti-Semitism, Zionism, and the Fate of "the Jews"', *American Historical Review*, 123 (2018), 1151–71; Engel, 'On Reconciling the Histories of Two Chosen Peoples'.

28 'Yad Vashem Historians Respond to the Joint Statement of the Governments of Poland and Israel Concerning the Revision of the 26 January 2018 Amendment to Poland's Act on the Institute of National Remembrance' (5 July 2018): Yad Vashem website, 'Yad Vashem

Press Releases', visited 15 June 2021; O. Aderet, 'Hata'ut hagedolah shel netanyahu: nisayon likhpof et hahistoryah litseraḥim mediniyim' (5 July 2018): *Haaretz* website, visited 14 Dec. 2021; E. Mack, 'Dina porat, sokhenet haḥeresh shel netanyahu hemilḥamto "antishemiyut haḥadashah"' (14 July 2018): Siḥa mekomit website, visited 14 Dec. 2021.

29 Dina Porat, interview with Yoav Krakowski, 'Kan News', Kan 11, 8 July 2018.

30 Advocate Eitay Mack, letter to MFA, 2 July 2018 (copy held by Yifat Gutman).

31 MFA, letter to Eitay Mack, 14 Nov. 2018 (copy held by Yifat Gutman); see also N. Landau and O. Aderet, 'Israel Refuses to Reveal Who Drafted Controversial Joint Holocaust Statement with Poland' (11 July 2019): *Haaretz* website, visited 14 Dec. 2021.

32 Landau and Aderet, 'Israel Refuses to Reveal Who Drafted Controversial Joint Holocaust Statement with Poland'.

33 In an op-ed in *Die Welt* Gross criticized Poland's reluctance to accept refugees and asserted that Poles killed more Jews than they did Nazis during the Second World War, which enraged the PiS and its supporters (J. T. Gross, 'Die Osteuropäer haben kein Schamgefühl' (13 Sept. 2015): *Die Welt* website, visited 14 Dec. 2021). The government's response was harsh: it attempted to take back the Order of Merit of the Republic of Poland that Gross won in 1996 and opened a libel investigation by Poland's general prosecutor, but faced criticism both national and international (A. Duval Smith, 'Polish Move to Strip Holocaust Expert of Award Sparks Protests' (14 Feb. 2016): *The Guardian* website, visited 14 Dec. 2021). The prosecutor noted that his office would consult historians, including those at the IPN. The investigation was ultimately closed without action being taken against Gross (O. Aderet, 'Poland Drops Case against Holocaust Scholar Who "Insulted the Nation"' (30 Oct. 2016): *Haaretz* website, visited 5 Jan. 2021). It showed the limits of the government's ability to rewrite history.

34 S. Sokol, 'Another Fight over Holocaust Memory Threatens Warming Ties between Israel and Poland' (18 Feb. 2019): Jewish Telegraphic Agency website, visited 14 Dec. 2021.

35 e.g. 'A Statement of the Council of the Institute of National Remembrance' (27 Feb. 2018): Institute of National Remembrance website, 'For the Media', 'Statements', visited 3 Jan. 2022.

36 For such reviews of B. Engelking and J. Grabowski (eds.), *Dalej jest noc: Losy Żydów w wybranych powiatach okupowanej Polski*, 2 vols. (Warsaw, 2018), see 'Nowe recenzje książki "Dalej jest noc: Losy Żydów w wybranych powiatach okupowanej Polski"' (21 Feb. 2019): Instytut Pamięci Narodowej website, 'Aktualności', visited 15 June 2021.

37 K. Czarnecka, 'Ukryte w niepamięci: Rozmowa z prof. Janem Grabowskim o faktach dotyczących Zagłady na terenach Polski', *Polityka*, 14–20 Feb. 2018, pp. 22–4.

38 J. T. Gross, 'Fałszowanie historii' (4 Feb. 2018): *Newsweek Polska* website, visited 14 Dec. 2021.

39 Ibid.

40 T. Nałęcz, 'Polityka bezwstydu', *Ale Historia* (supplement to *Gazeta Wyborcza*), 18 June 2018, p. 2.

41 Two recent examples are Engelking and Grabowski (eds.), *Dalej jest noc*, which sparked a heated debate in 2018 and 2019 over its finding that two out of three Jews who escaped Nazi deportation were killed due to Polish involvement, and J. Leociak, *Młyny boże: Zapiski o Kościele i Zagładzie* (Warsaw, 2018), on the Catholic Church's hypocrisy and demonization and rejection of Jews who sought rescue.

42 Yair Lapid, @yairlapid, 27 Jan. 2018, 3:07 a.m.: Twitter website, visited 15 June 2021.

43 N. Landau, 'Visegrad Summit in Israel Canceled after Poland Pulls Out Over Holocaust Row' (19 Feb. 2019): *Haaretz* website, visited 5 Jan. 2021.

44 Associated Press, 'Israel Hosts East European Leaders after Summit Scrapped'.
45 C. Liphshiz, 'Poland's Prime Minister Said Some Jews Collaborated with Nazis: Scholars Say He Distorted History' (20 Feb. 2018): Jewish Telegraphic Agency website, visited 14 Dec. 2021.
46 Dina Porat said then that comparing Jewish collaborators to Polish collaborators was morally and historically false because of the complex spectrum of collaboration (Liphshiz, 'Poland's Prime Minister Said Some Jews Collaborated with Nazis. Scholars Say He Distorted History'). Ironically, a few months later Porat assisted the Israeli prime minister in drafting the joint statement that compared antisemitism and anti-Polonism.
47 Passent, 'Handel historią'.
48 M. Kolanko, 'Legislacyjny ekspres', *Rzeczpospolita*, 28 June 2018, p. A4.
49 J. Dobrosz-Oracz, 'Liczą się skutki dalekosiężne', *Gazeta Wyborcza*, 29 June 2018, p. 6.
50 Ibid.
51 Kolanko, 'Legislacyjny ekspres'.
52 Ibid.
53 Passent, 'Handel historią'.
54 J. Nizinkiewicz, 'Wracamy na wspólną drogę', *Rezczpospolita*, 28 June 2018, p. A5.
55 Aderet, 'Warsaw's Controversial New Holocaust Museum to Present "Polish Narrative"'.
56 D. Blatman, 'Yad Vashem Teaches the Holocaust like Totalitarian Countries Teach History' (18 Dec. 2018): *Haaretz* website, visited 14 Dec. 2021.
57 D. Blatman, 'Yad Vashem is Derelict in Its Duty to Free the Shoah from Its Jewish Ghetto' (10 Apr. 2016): *Haaretz* website, visited 3 Jan. 2022.
58 Blatman, 'Yad Vashem Teaches the Holocaust like Totalitarian Countries Teach History'.
59 Aderet, 'Warsaw's Controversial New Holocaust Museum to Present "Polish Narrative"'.
60 J. Grabowski, B. Engelking, A. Haska, and J. Leociak, 'Why is this Israeli Jewish Scholar a Willing Poster Boy for Poland's Brutal Distortion of the Holocaust?' (24 Dec. 2018): *Haaretz* website, visited 14 Dec. 2021.
61 Aderet, 'Warsaw's Controversial New Holocaust Museum to Present "Polish Narrative"'.
62 Ibid.
63 Grabowski, Engelking, Haska, and Leociak, 'Why is this Israeli Jewish Scholar a Willing Poster Boy for Poland's Brutal Distortion of the Holocaust?'
64 D. Blatman, 'The Holocaust's Evasive History in Both Poland and Israel' (3 May 2019): *Haaretz* website, visited 5 Jan. 2021. Polish politicians and former diplomats have repeated this argument, focusing on the similarly conflicting interests of both Israeli and Polish leaders that result from their nationalist agendas. Radosław Sikorski, former head of the Polish Ministry of Foreign Affairs and the Ministry of National Defence, said to *Rzeczpospolita*: 'PiS and Likud [Israel's ruling party] are two similar nationalist parties. Both have a similar definition of the nation, that is, as an ideal being. Both formations believe that what gives them superiority over other nations is the suffering of their nation during the Second World War. And both nations suffered a lot. The only brutal truth is that 90 per cent of Polish Jews were murdered during the war, and 90 per cent of Polish Catholics survived. So PiS cannot outbid the Jews when it comes to martyrdom' (J. Nizinkiewicz, 'Sikorski: PiS nie wygra z Żydami licytacji na martyrologię' (19 Feb. 2019): *Rzeczpospolita* website, visited 14 Dec. 2021).
65 K. Gebert, interview with Y. Gutman.
66 'Solidarity in Truth: Open Letter of Polish NGOs Condemning Anti-Semitism' (9 Mar. 2018): Fundacja Liberté! website, visited 15 June 2021.

67 'Estranged: March '68 and Its Aftermath' (n.d.): Polin Museum of the History of Polish Jews website, visited 15 June 2021.
68 M. Kozubal, 'Wicepremier Gliński blokuje muzeum POLIN' (6 July 2019): *Rzeczpospolita* website, visited 14 Dec. 2021.
69 J. Michalska, 'Director of Poland's Second World War Museum Dismissed' (11 Apr. 2017): *Art Newspaper* website, visited 3 Jan. 2022.
70 S. Walker, 'Holocaust Historians Divided over Warsaw Ghetto Museum' (22 June 2019): *The Guardian* website, visited 14 Dec. 2021.
71 Former president Aleksander Kwaśniewski made a public apology to the Jews of Jedwabne during a memorial ceremony at the town on 10 July 2001.
72 Walker, 'Holocaust Historians Divided over Warsaw Ghetto Museum'.
73 For a collection that includes historians who do not accept that the Polish phrase *żydokomuna* (Judeo-communism) is an antisemitic trope rather than historical truth, see E. Barkan, E. A. Cole, and K. Struve (eds.), *Shared History—Divided Memory: Jews and Others in Soviet-Occupied Poland, 1939–1941* (Leipzig, 2008).
74 Anna Bull and Hans Hansen borrowed the concept of agonistic pluralism from Chantal Mouffe (A. C. Bull and H. L. Hansen, 'On Agonistic Memory', *Memory Studies*, 9 (2016), 390–404). Mouffe claimed that values conflict in public deliberations over consensus and proposed that an agonistic mode of remembering that includes multiple perspectives of a contested past can transform enemies into adversaries and engage them in dialogue (C. Mouffe, *On the Political* (London, 2005); see also S. Maddison, *Conflict Transformation and Reconciliation: Multi-Level Challenges in Deeply Divided Societies* (London, 2015)).
75 B. Engelking, 'O Esterze Siemiatyckiej, sołtysie Edwardzie Malinowskim i procesach sądowych' (26 Jan. 2021): Centrum Badań nad Zagładą Żydów website, visited 14 Dec. 2021.
76 'Polish Court Tells Two Holocaust Historians to Apologise' (9 Feb. 2021): BBC website, 'News', visited 15 Nov. 2021.
77 K. Markusz, 'Ambasador Niemiec mówi trudną prawdę o historii: Polska nadal kłamie' (9 Oct. 2020): *Krytyka Polityczna* website, visited 14 Dec. 2021; B. Cohen, 'Cops in Poland Question Editor of Jewish Website Over Article on Polish Complicity with Nazi Persecution' (5 Feb. 2021): *The Algemeiner* website, visited 14 Dec. 2021.
78 J. Lis, 'In Protest over Polish Restitution Law, Lapid Recalls Israel's Top Diplomat to Warsaw' (14 Aug. 2021): *Haaretz* website, visited 14 Dec. 2021.
79 O. Aderet, 'Poland Recalls Israel Envoy, Considers Downgrading Ties as Row Over Restitution Law Deepens' (16 Aug. 2021): *Haaretz* website, visited 14 Dec. 2021.

Index

A

Abdulmejid, Sultan 30
Ad Hoc Committee on the Palestinian Question 212, 214–18
Adamkiewicz, Jerzy 182
Adler, Nathan Marcus 58
Adler, Pinhas 96
Adler, Shoshana 102
Agnon, S. Y. 36, 367
Agudat Ha'itona'im Betel Aviv (Tel Aviv Journalists' Association) 141
Agudat Yisrael 88, 126, 127, 131–3
Ahad Ha'am 289
Aharon Moshe Migeza-Tsevi of Brody 37–8, 49 n. 84
Aharon the Second 36
Aharonovitz, Yosef 117
Akavia, Miriam 100, 102
Akcja Demokracja 424
Akiva 163
Al hamishmar 339–40
Al Hamishmar faction of General Zionists 124
Alcalay, Aharon 275
alcohol, merchants of in Israel 35
Alexander, Jeffrey 392
Alexander, Wolff 63
Aliyah, *aliyot* 80
  First 35, 43, 73
  Second 73, 108, 207
  Third 80, 108
  Fourth (Grabski) 80, 105–23, 128, 159, 172, 182
  Fifth 108, 172
  Gomułka 264, 272, 325–6, 327, 337–52
  Ministry of Aliyah and Immigrant Absorption 341–2
  see also immigrants, Polish
aliyah replaced by *hagirah* 373–4
All-Polish Youth 204
Alliance Israélite Universelle in Thorn (Toruń) 64
Alt Nay 148
Alterman, Natan 329
American Jewish Joint Distribution Committee (JDC) 235, 340
Amfreville, Marc 364
Amir, Anda 273
Amnesty International 344
Anders, Gen. Władysław 82, 235, 238
Anders Army 235, 237–8, 240, 242–3

Anielewicz, Mordechaj 81
anti-Jewish violence 90, 425
anti-Polonism 411–12, 418
antisemitism in Poland 204, 208–9, 212–13, 220–1, 257, 328, 382, 402, 411–13, 416, 420
  1968 337–52
  in military ranks 237–9
  in Sejm 130–1
  'żydofobia' 341
Appelfeld, Aharon 357–60, 366–8
Appenszlak, Jakub 97, 185, 192
Appenszlak, Paulina 241
Arba al ḥamesh 263
architects, Jewish 76
Arciszewski, Mirosław 180–1
Argentina, Jewish colonies in 402–7
Arlosoroff, Chaim 110, 151, 170–1
Asch, Sholem 252, 270
Asher Lemel of Galin 53–4
Ashkenazi community in Israel 52–8
assimilation 88, 97, 208–10, 212
  in the diaspora 326
  'passing' as non-Jewish 332
  and Zionism 100–2
Assmann, Aleida 355, 368
Association of Industrial and Trade Chambers 195
Association of Jewish Writers and Journalists (Yidishe Literatn un Zhurnalistn Farayn) 141–3
Association of Polish Artists and Designers (Związek Zawodowy Polskich Artystów Plastyków) 270–1
Association of Yiddish Writers in Israel (Farayn fun Yidishe Shrayber in Yisroel) 251
Aston, Adam 243
Auerbach, Meir 55
Auschwitz:
  museum 270
  pilgrimage to 376–7
  see also death camps; Shoah trips
Avidar, Tamar 347
Avidar-Tchernovitz, Yemima 276
avodat hoveh 127
Avraham Dov of Owrucz 33–4
Avraham of Kalisk 30, 41, 48 n. 69
Avraham Weinberg of Slonim 36
Avraham Ya'akov of Sadagora 38, 40
Azai, Pinchas 295
Azulai, Hayim Joseph David (Hida) 297

B

Ba'al Shem Tov, life 41
Bader, Yohanan (Jan) 149–50, 325, 341
Bak, Nisan 33–4, 38
Bak, Samuel 275
Bak, Yisra'el 33, 38
Bak family 38
Bak press 38–9
Bar Or, Galia 263, 266, 281
Bar-Yosef, Hamutal 275
Barash, Asher 276, 293
Bareli, Meir 275
Bartal, Israel 43, 288–9
Bartana, Yael 365
Bartoszewski, Władysław 312–14, 316, 321 n. 72, 322 n. 95
Baruch Mordechai Etinger of Bobruisk 42
Bat Yam Art Institute 275
Batei Nisan Bak (Kiryah Ne'emanah) 41
Batei Varshah 40
Batory, Jan 272
Bauer, Yehuda 416, 418
Bauman, Zygmunt 344–6, 374
Beck, Józef 212
Beckerman, Adam 269
Befrayung 163
Begin, Menachem 82, 130, 211
Behrman, Abraham 280
beit din in Jerusalem 39
Beit Ha'itona'im al Shem Sokolow, *see* Sokolow Journalists' House
Beit Hayeladim Hayehudim Beteheran 237–9
Beit Leyvick Center for Yiddish Language and Culture 251
Bekerman, Menucha 276
Ben-Avi, Itamar 140, 145–7
Ben-Gal, Avigdor 'Janusz' 82, 244
Ben-Gurion, David 140, 213, 252, 294, 315
  Hebrew writers convened by 329–30
Ben Hillel, Mordechai 145
Ben-Israel, Ilana 358
Ben Meir, Yehoram 276
Ben-Yehuda, Eliezer 140, 145
Ben-Zvi, Yitzhak 140
Bendori, Feivish 160, 164–6
  and Jewish immigrants 323
  negative view of diaspora 375
  as reader of Piłsudski 96
  secretary of General Federation of Labour 109
  and White Paper 105
  and Zionist Congress of 1933 158–79
Benei Berak 200 n. 69
Benisch, Abraham 59

Benjacob, Isaac 291
Bennett, Naftali 423
Bergelson, David 252
Berger, Alan 366
Bergmann, Samuel Hugo 329–30
Berkowitz, Yitshak Dov 118, 156 n. 95
Berlewi, Henryk 263–5, 280
Berman, Adolf 224–5
Berman, Dunia 231
Betar 164–6, 169, 211
  youth movement 129–30
Betar (magazine) 93
Bey Shukri, Hassan 180
Bialik, Hayim Nahman 80, 106, 270
  against invention of festivals 296
  and cultural life in the Yishuv 111–12, 129
  kinus project 289
  and Moriah Publishing House, Odessa 144
  negative attitude to Polish immigrants 118
Biderman, David Tsevi Shelomoh, founder of Lelov dynasty 40
Biderman, Elazar Menahem Mendel 40
Biderman, Moshe of Lelov 40
Biderman, Yitshak David 40
Bikont, Anna 258
Binetzki, Pesach 269
Birnbaum, Natan 73
Blatman, Daniel 416–18, 421–3
Bloch-Blumenfeld, David 186
Blok Erets Yisra'el Ha'ovedet (Bloc of the Working Land of Israel) 162
blood libel 298
B'nai B'rith 75
Bnei Zion in Rohatyn 76–7
Bobkowski, Aleksander 202 n. 108
Bocheński, Adam 207
Bocheński, Adolf 204, 207, 211
Bocheński, Aleksander 204
Bocheński, Józef Maria 204
Bocheński, Mieczysław 207
Bodenheimer, Dr Wilhelm 241
Bogen, Aleksander 271
Bolsheviks 206
Bonnett, Alastair 399
Bortnowski, Gen. Władysław 250
Borzykowski, Tuvia 225
boycott of German products and services 186
Boym, Svetlana 357
Brainin, Reuben 146
Bratkowska, Krystyna 259
Brill, Yehiel 39
Brio, Valentina 240
Brodzki, Józef 191

Broides, Avraham 301
Broniewski, Władysław 240
Brzozicki, Bronisław 241
Brzozowski, Stanisław 2
Buber, Martin 119, 329–30
Buczkowski, Leonard 272
Buloff, Joseph 348
Bund 88–9, 131–3
  sports clubs 79
Bunt Młodych 204, 207–8, 210
Bussel, Hayuta 211
Bussgang, Julian 247 n. 48

C

Cahan, Ya'akov 134
Canin, Jeshayahu Mordekhai 257–8
Caritas Internationalis 311
Carlebach, Ezriel 147–9
Caruth, Cathy 353
Cat-Mackiewicz, Stanisław 190, 205
Catholic Church in Poland, and communists 305–22
Catholicism:
  conversion to 315
  on Palestine 305–6
  Paul VI 306, 312
  pilgrimages to Israel 70–2
  Pius X, on the Holy Land 305
  Pius XII 312
Cel 96–7
cemeteries, Jewish 355–6, 360, 379
  in Jerusalem 39
Central Bank of Cooperative Institutions in Palestine 235
Central Committee of Jews in Poland (Centralny Komitet Żydów w Polsce; CKŻP) 231, 257, 268, 270
Central Jewish Historical Commission 226, 230
Central Office for the Control of Press, Publications and Entertainment (Główny Urząd Kontroli Prasy, Publikacji i Widowisk; GUKPPiW) 307
Centralny Komitet Żydów w Polsce, *see* Central Committee of Jews in Poland
Centre for Holocaust Research in Warsaw 426
Centrum Informacji na Wschód (CIW), *see* Polish Information Centre for the East
Chwila 89–90, 97, 147, 215
Ciesielska, Marta 97
Cieszyński, Jankiel 231
CIW, *see* Polish Information Centre for the East
Cohen, David 276
Commission for Religious Denominations and Public Enlightenment 55

communism 88, 214–15
  censorship of Polish Catholic press 305–22
Communist Party 131–2
Consistoire Central des Israélites de France 60
converts:
  to Catholicism 237
  Jewish 315
counter-memory 390
Cukierman, David 250
Cukierman, Herman (Henryk) 250
Cukierman, Mordecai Yeshayahu, *see* Tsanin, Mordecai
culture:
  Hebrew national proponents 106
  Hebrew and Yiddish 288
  Jewish, in Israel and outside 288–304
  Polish Jewish artistic 263–87
Cygielman, Wiktor 326–7
Czaina, Jolanta Brach 404
Czapski, Józef 213
Czas 205
Czernowitz, Shemu'el 117
Czuchnowski, Marian 240

D

Dąbrowski, Jan Henryk 94
Dalej jest noc 428
Damandan, Parisa 239
Daniels, Jonny 421
Dankowicz, Henryk 258
Dat Va'avodah 163, 166
Davar 146, 251, 273, 289–90, 339–40, 342, 348
Dayan, Moshe 306
death camps 255
Deiches, Eliyahu Yehudah 55
Den 144
Der fraynd 156 n. 95
Der jude 166 n. 100
Der moment 142–3, 146, 148–50, 163, 195, 201 n. 82
Der telegraf 149
Di goldene keyt 251
Di naye velt 156 n. 95
diaspora:
  rejection of 330–1
  Zionist attitude to 375–6
Dinur, Ben-Zion 295, 301, 329
Dizengoff, Meir 180
Do'ar hayom 145–6
Doktór, Jan 72
Domańska, Ewa 401
Domeyko, Ignacy 70
Don-Yehiya, Eliezer 389
donations:
  to Israel from Britain 58–61
  to the Yishuv 52–68; *see also ḥalukah* funds

Dos vort 170
Dos yudishe togblat 242
Dov Ber of Lubavitch 41
　daughter Menuhah Rachel 42
Dreifuss, Havi 422 3
Dres, Jérémie 366
Druck, Samuel 93
Dubner Magid 291
Dybbuk, The 263
Dziennik Narodowy 187
Dzierżyński, Feliks 206
Dzigan, Shimon 143, 347, 354

E

Eban, Abba 306, 339
Echo Żydowski 242
Eger, Akiva 62
Eger, Solomon 63
Ehrenburg, Ilya 406
Ehrlihman, Szujka 1, 231–2
Eichmann, Adolf 312
Eichmann trial 332–3
　and change in Israeli society 293
　reports on censored 312–13
Ein Zeitim 35
Einstein, Albert 114
Eldar, Ruth 97
Eliyahu Yosef Rivlin of Płock 42
Emden, Jacob 291
Endecja 204–5
Endeks 187–8
Engel, David 159, 413
Engelking, Barbara 419–20, 422, 427
Epstein, Helen 368
Epstein, Jacob 275
equal rights for Jews 74
Erez, Hayim 244
'Esther', autobiography 129
Ets Hayim institutions 40
Ettinger, Bracha 356–7
Ewa 241
Eybeschütz, David Shelomoh 33
Ezrahi, Sidra Dekoven 359

F

Fakt 417
Farayn fun Yidishe Shrayber in Yisroel, *see* Association of Yiddish Writers in Israel
Federation of Working and Studying Youth (Hano'ar Ha'oved Vehalomed) 276
Feingold, Yossef 269
Feldblum family 97
Feldman, Jackie 389
Ferber, Tzvi Hirsch 298

festivals:
　Jewish 290–1, 295
　kibbutz 295–6
feuilletons 146–8
film industry in post-war Poland 272
Film Polski 272
Finkel, Aba 275
Finkelstein, Barbara 361
Fleischman-Seidman, Rachel 101
Flinker, Dovid 242
Floyar-Rajchman, Henryk 199 n. 55
folklore, Hebrew 288–304
　see also halakhah, 'folklorization' of
Folklore Congress 1959 290
Ford, Aleksander 272
Forverts 249–51, 256
Frankl, Ludwig August 63
Franz Josef, Emperor 39
Freiheit (Po'alei Tsiyon) 163
Freud, Sigmund 353, 364
Friede, Maksymilian 188
Frishman, David 164 n. 55
Frost, Robert 405–6
Frumkin, Yisra'el Dov 40, 42
Fuchs, Menucha 276
Fuks, Marian 97
Fularski, Mieczysław 193
Fundusz Obrony Narodowej, *see* National Defence Fund

G

Gadomski, Romuald 83
Gai Oni 35
Galicia, Jewish community in 74–6
Gamzou, Asaf 379–80
Gasiuk-Pihowicz, Kamila 421
Gat, Eliyahu 275
Gauthier, Fr. Paul 313
Gazeta Polska 190, 240
Gazeta Polska Codziennie 417
Gazeta Wyborcza 417
Gebert, Konstanty 424
Gedud 97
General Zionists 58–9, 124–5, 141, 162, 164, 171, 324
Gerchunoff, Alberto 403
Gershenzon, Moshe 347
Gerson of Kitiv 32
Gevir, Yossi 416
Giedroyc, Jerzy 204, 207, 213
Giladi, David 148
Głąbiński, Stanisław 183–4
Glazer, David 242
Glickson, Moshe 106, 110–11, 117, 123, 125, 145
Gliński, Piotr 425

Głos Pracy 340
Główny Urząd Kontroli Prasy, Publikacji
    i Widowisk (GUKPPiW), *see* Central Office
    for the Control of Press, Publications and
    Entertainment
Godlewska, Joanna 97
Goldberg, Isaac Leib 164 n. 55
Goldberg, Lea 329–30
Goldfaden Theatre 347
Gomułka, Władysław 337–8, 340–1, 344
Gordon, A. D. 375
Gordon, Judah Leib 146
Gordonia (Mapai-Hever Hakevutsot) 163
Gość Niedzielny 312
Gottlieb, Yehoshua 124, 148, 163
Govrin, Heli 277
Govrin, Michal 360–1, 393
Gowin, Jarosław 421
Grabiec, Józef 100
Grabowski, Jan 419–20, 427
Grabski, Władysław 80, 107
Gramsci, Antonio 156 n. 93
Green, Abigail 58
Grinberg, Uri Tsevi 106, 113, 118, 264, 329
Grosbard, Herz 251
Gross, Jan Tomasz 258, 419
Gross, Natan 272
Grossman, David 360, 388
Grossman, Meir 161
Gruber, Henryk 202 n. 108
Grünbaum, Yitshak 79, 131, 124–8, 133–5, 159, 162,
    164, 188
Grupińska, Anka 101–2
Grygiel, Tadeusz 270
Grynberg, Henryk 355–6
Gush Ha'avoda, *see* Labour Zionist bloc
Guterman, Yitzhak 269
Gutman, Israel 422
Guttmacher, Elijahu 62–5, 73
Gwiazdowski, Tadeusz 192

H
Haaretz 106, 110, 123, 145–6, 150, 188, 339, 342, 417,
    422
Haboker 141, 147, 150
Hacohen, Mikhel 39
Ḥadashot ha'arets 164 n. 55
Hado'ar 115
Hador 164 n. 55
Haganah 82, 211, 243–4, 330
hagirah 374
Ha'igud Ha'artsi Shel Ha'itona'im Be'erets Yisra'el,
    see National Association of Journalists in the
    Land of Israel

Haikin, Shimon Menashe 41
Hakefir 97, 99
hakhsharah 163–4, 166–7
Hakohen, Hayim 56
halakhah, 'folklorization' of 296
Halberstam, Hayim 35
Halberstam, Israel, of Kraków 82–3
Halczak, Bohdan 100
Halevanon 39–40
Haltof, Marek 272
ḥalukah funds 28–30, 33–4, 36–7, 41, 52, 72
Halutz Centre 271
Hamakabi 97
Hamas 215
Hamashkif 149
Hameiri, Avigdor 329
Hamelits 145–6
Hano'ar 97
Hano'ar Ha'oved Vehalomed, *see* Federation of
    Working and Studying Youth
Hanson, Stephen E. 226
Ha'olam 107, 112, 164 n. 55
Hapo'el Hamizrahi 132
Hapo'el Hatsa'ir 160, 162
Hapo'el hatsa'ir 106
Hartglas, Apolinary 90, 92–3, 101, 126
Harussi, Emanuel 301
Hashilo'aḥ 112, 141, 164 n. 55
Hashomer Hatsa'ir 129, 134, 160, 162–3, 225, 229,
    239
hasidism:
    Bratslav 36
    communities in Israel 27–50
    First Aliyah 28
    Habad 36, 41, 42
    in Hebron 37–43
    in Jerusalem 37–44
    Karlin dynasty 36, 40
    Lelov dynasty 40
    Lithuanian 36
    Lubavitch 43
    Ruzhin 35
    in Sadagora 38–9
    in Safed 32–7
    Sanz hasidim 39
    in Tiberias 32–7
    women in hasidic society in Israel 29
    see also kolelim
Haska, Agnieszka 422, 426
Hatalgi (Schneeberg), Theodor 341
Hatsefirah 141–2, 144, 146
Hatsohar 161
Hausner, Bernard 180, 183, 197 n. 22, 198 nn. 25–7
Havatselet 40

Hayei Olam Yeshiva 40
Hayim of Sanz 38
Hayim Elazar Waks of Piotrków 40
Hayim Nathanson of Wreschen 63
Hayim Tyrer of Chernovits 33
Hayishuv 117
Haynt 88, 97, 142–3, 146–50, 156 n. 95, 162
Hayntike nayes 251
Hayom 116, 141, 164 n. 55
Hazamir 142
Hazan, Ya'akov 125
Hazeman 150
Hebrew 98, 102, 112, 327
   promotion of 325
   rising popularity of 79
   vs. Polish in Israel 325–9
   writers, convened by Ben-Gurion 329–30
Hebrew Immigrant Aid Society (HIAS) 343
Hebrew University of Jerusalem 106
Hechtkopf, Henryk 263–87
Heftman, Yosef 140–4, 148–9
Hehaluts 159–61, 163–73
Hehaluts Hatsa'ir 163, 224
Heller, Daniel 129
Heller, Shemu'el 34–5
Hendel, Yehudit 393
herem:
   against immigration to Israel 72
   call for against Ruzhin courts 35
Herschdörfer, Ozjasz 124
Hertz, Aleksander 96
Herut 149, 341
Herut 149
Herzig, Hanna 361–2
Herzl, Theodor 73, 75, 127–8, 305, 401–4
   Altneuland 140, 400, 406
Herzliyah 163
Hess, Moses 408 n. 8
Hevrat Yishuv Erets Yisra'el, *see* Society for the Settlement of the Land of Israel
Hibat Tsiyon 133
Hida, *see* Azulai
Hilzenrad, Adela 224, 226–9
Hinukh Gymnasium 264
Hirsch, Baron Maurice de 402
Hirsch, Marianne 357, 363, 368
Histadrut (General Federation of Labour) 147, 159–60, 162–3
Histadrut Erets Yisra'el Ha'ovedet (League for Labour Palestine) 160–1, 164, 168
historical truth, concept of 410–33
Hitahadut 162, 171, 173
Hitler, Adolf 205
Hochhuth, Rolf, *Der Stellvertreter* 312

Holocaust:
   censorship of reports on 312
   and emigration to Israel 84
   Holocaust Forum 427
   knowledge of in Israel 333–4
   memory of, in Poland and Israel 410–33
   and previous disasters 298–301
   remembrance of in Israel 331–2
   survivors 293, 325, 339, 343, 424
   survivors, child, and Poland 353–72
   survivors, portraits of 266–7
   taboos regarding 376
   trauma, aftermath of 353–72
Holtzman, Avner 111
Hońdo, Leszek 101
Hoofien, Siegfried 194
Horowitz, Isaiah 291
Hovevei Tsiyon (Lovers of Zion) 73
   in Rzeszów 77
Hütt, Pinchas 76

I

identity in contemporary Israeli literature 373–87
Ilustrirte veltvokh 251
immigrants to Israel 52, 108
immigrants, Polish, to Israel 72–87, 212–13, 338
   after the Holocaust 224–34
   attitude to Israel 105–22
   and a homeland 323–36
   on *Polonia*, 1933 180–202
   re-emigration to Poland 343–8
   viewed as solution to the 'Jewish question' 305–6
   see also Aliyah
immigration to US 107, 123
Institute for Emigration and Colonization Research 185
Institute of National Remembrance (Instytut Pamięci Narodowej; IPN) 411, 416, 418–19
Instytut Pamięci Narodowej (IPN), *see* Institute of National Remembrance
Iran, Polish Jewish refugees in 235–9
Irgun Tseva'i Le'umi 82, 130
Israel Painters and Sculptors Association 273
Israeli Communist Party (Maki) 324
Israeli Declaration of Independence 404
Israeli Editors' Committee 142
Israeli Ministry of Foreign Affairs (MFA) 415–16, 418–19
Israelis visiting Poland 374–5, 388

J

Jabotinsky, Ze'ev (Vladimir) 77–8, 105, 127, 145, 158, 161, 166, 168–9, 211

Jafe, Shlomo 187
JDC, *see* American Joint Distribution Committee
Jerusalem Post 241
Jerzak, Katarzyna 356
Jewish Agency 151
  aid to Polish refugees outside Israel 243
  competition with Hebrew Immigrant Aid
    Society 343
  establishment of 113–14
  in Iran 239
  payment of Polish visas 337
  and Polish commerce 184–6, 188, 193
  and 'status quo agreement' of 1947 132
  and Yiddish theatre 347–8
Jewish Anti-Fascist League 306
Jewish Association for Culture and Art (Żydowskie
  Towarzystwo Kultury i Sztuki) 268, 270–1
Jewish Colonization Association 402
Jewish Fighting Organization 224
Jewish Historical Society 270
'Jewish Hitlerism' 163
Jewish Legion 168
Jewish National Fund (Keren Kayemet Leyisra'el)
  75, 164, 229
Jewish orphanage, Otwock 231
Jewish–Polish relations in Israel 239–45
'Jewish question' 208–10, 212–13, 305
Jewish Society for the Promotion of Fine Arts
  (Żydowskie Towarzystwo Krzewienia Sztuk
  Pięknych; Yidishe Gezelshaft tsu Farshproytn
  Kunst) 265, 270
Jewish State Party (Mifleget Hamedinah Ha'ivrit)
  161, 171
Jewish State Theatre 346
Jewish Telegraphic Agency 182–3
Judah Hehasid of Siedlce 37, 38, 72
Justman, Moshe Bunem 150–1

K

Kaczyński, Jarosław 425
Kaczyński, Lech 425
Kaganowski, Efraim 266, 268, 270
Kalischer, Tsevi Hirsch 62, 64, 73, 407 n. 8
Kamińska, Ester Rachel 346
Kamińska, Ida 344, 346–8
Kantor, Anava 276
Kaplan, Hayim 264
Kapuściński, Ryszard 203–4
Karni, Yehuda 299
Karski, Jan 243
Karsov, Nina 344–5
Karu, Baruch (Krupnik) 296–8
Kashti, Ester 276
Katz, Benzion 150–1

Katz, Israel 420
Katznelson, Berl 146
Kefir (Zionist publication) 97
Keren Hayesod 114, 116, 160
Keren Hehaluts Hamizrahi 78
Keren Kayemet Leyisra'el, *see* Jewish National
  Fund
Keren Tel Hai 94
Kessary, Ouri 148
Khalyastre group 264
kibbutz movement 76
  festivals 295–6
  in Poland 78–9
kibbutzim:
  Degania 78
  Degania Alef 211
  Ein Harod 211, 244
  Hakibuts Hame'uhad 160, 163, 164, 166
  Lohamei Hageta'ot (Ghetto Fighters) 81
  reports on censored 313
  Yad Mordechai 81
Kiewe, Chaim 275
kinus project 289
Kipnis, Levin 276, 278
Kirschenbaum, E. J. 198 n. 33
Kirschenbaum, Menachem 184
Kiryah Ne'emanah (Batei Nisan Bak) 41
Kisch, Egon 250
Kishon, Ephraim 346
Klajnwajs, Henoch (Heniek) 102
Klausner, Joseph 106, 112
Klepfisz, Heszel 215
Klugman, Aleksander 81, 340–50
Kohan, Marek (Meir) 148
kolelim:
  Habad 42
  Hod (Holand Vedaytshland) 53–4, 62
  independent 51
  in Israel 28–9
  Karlin 36
  Kolelot Hasefardim 52, 54
  Kosov 35
  Lemberg 35
  Moldavyah Vevelakhyah 36
  Ostriyah 35, 38
  Perushim 31, 40, 54, 62
  Reisen 36
  Rosh Pina colony 35
  Varshah 3, 34, 36, 40, 51–8, 61–2
  Vizhnits 35
  Vohlin (Kolel Hahasidim) 30, 36, 38, 40, 43
  Zhitomir 36
Kolmevaser 144
Kontra 345

Kosiniak-Kamysz, Władysław 421
Kot, Stanisław 241, 243
Kraus, Daniel 230
Kraushar, Aleksander 91
Kressel, Getzel 151
Kriegel, Emanuel 230-1
Krytyka Polityczna 428
Kugelmass, Jack 250
Kultura 204, 328
Kurier Powszechny 331
Kurjer Poranny 101, 191
Kutchinsky (Kucyński), Dow 76
Kwaśniewski, Aleksander 413
Kwiecień, Kabina 91

L

Labour Zionism 158-60, 163, 166, 170, 172
Labour Zionist bloc (Gush Ha'avoda) 162, 165, 171
Ladino 292
Lämel School 38
Lamerḥav 339-40
Landau, Emil 238-9, 244
Lange, Oskar 215
Lanzmann, Claude, *Shoah* 258, 354
Lapid, Shulamit 275, 277
Lapid, Yair 420, 424, 428
Lastik, S. 269
Laub, Dori 355
Lauenberg (Laor), David 239
Laufbahn, Yitshak 106, 113, 115, 118
Law and Justice Party (Prawo i Sprawiedliwość; PiS) 411, 419-20, 423-5
Lazar, David 147-8, 241
Łazor, Jerzy 181, 198
League for Labour Palestine, *see* Histadrut Erets Yisra'el Ha'ovedet
League of Nations 187, 189
Lec, Stanisław Jerzy 250
Lehi 78, 82
Lehren (Dutch bankers) 54
Lehren, Akiva 62
Lehren, Tsevi Hirsh 29
Lehrer, Erica T. 367
Lejtes, Josef 245
Lenartowicz, Stanisław 272
Leociak, Jacek 419, 422
Letsion, Rishon 296
Letste nayes 251, 257
Levanda 60
Levant Fair 187, 194-5
Levi Isaac of Berdichev 291
Levin, Dina 276
Levin, Yitshak Meir 133
Levinsky, Yom-Tov 288-304
  Sefer hamo'adim 290-300

Levy, Joseph 240
Lewandowski, Józef 101
Lewin, Jecheskiel 229
Lewin, Kurt 229-30
Lewin Epstein, Lewi 195
Lewinsky, Elhanan Leib 146
Lewinsky, Tamar 257
Lewite, Leon 187
Leyvick, H. 251
Library Society of Law Students 204
Liebman, Charles 389
Liebman, Irena 276
Lifshitz, Uri 275
Lipkowska, Teresa 242, 245
Łódź Film School 272
Lohamei Hageta'ot (Ghetto Fighters) kibbutz 81
London Society for Promoting Christianity amongst the Jews 37
Łoziński, Paweł 355
Lubetkin, Zivia 81, 225
Lubomirski, Zdzisław 191-2
Ludvipol, Abraham 145
Łukaszewicz, Stanisław 199 n. 56
Luria, Hayim 64
Lurie, Joseph 145, 156 n. 100
Luxemburg, Rosa 206

M

Maariv 147-9, 339, 342
Maccabi 79
Maccabiah Games 79
Machcewicz, Paweł 425
Mackiewicz, Jósef 345
Magid of Mezritsh 33
Maitland Wilson, Gen. Henry 238
Maizlish, Moshe 41
Makarczuk, Janusz 201 n. 82
Malka, Tova 250
Mapai 158, 160, 162-4, 172-3, 290, 324, 339-40
Mapam 324
Mapu, Abraham 407 n. 7
March of the Living 361
Margaliot, Gershon 33-4
Margolin, Yehoshua 294
Maritime and Colonial League 191, 193
Mark, Ber 269
Markish, Perets 264
Markusz, Katarzyna 428
Marshall, Louis 114, 128
Matalon, Ronit 373
Mazur, Eliyahu 126
Meir, Golda 306
Melumad, Naftali 277
memorial books 81, 250

memory activists 430
memory of Holocaust 410–33
memory law (2018), Polish 410–33
Menahem Mendel 42
Menahem Mendel of Premishlan (Peremyshlany) 32
Menahem Mendel of Shklov 37
Menahem Mendel of Vitebsk 30, 36, 72
Mendele Moykher Sforim 115, 270–1, 294
Mendelsohn, Daniel 362–4
Mendelsohn, Ezra 128–9, 131, 135–6, 159
Menuhah Rahel, daughter of Dov Ber 42
Merminsky, Israel 160
MFA, *see* Israeli Ministry of Foreign Affairs
Mickiewicz, Adam 2, 128–9, 338
Mifleget Hamedinah Ha'ivrit, *see* Jewish State Party
Milch, Baruch 229
Miller, Nancy K. 368
Miłosz, Czesław 323
Ministerstwo Spraw Zagranicznych, *see* Polish Ministry of Foreign Affairs
Ministry of Aliyah and Immigrant Absorption 341–2
Ministry of Education 348
Miron, Dan 144, 292
Mirski, head of Central Committee of Jews in Poland 269
Mishka, Aaron 269
Mishkan Museum of Art 277
Mizrachi 161–2, 164, 170–1, 183
  youth movement 143
Mizrachi Jews 240, 329
Mizrachi Zionist Organization 133, 180
Młoda Polska 214
Mocarstwowa, Myśl 204, 207, 216
Moczar, Mieczysław 338, 340, 344
Modan, Rutu (Ruth), *The Property* 365, 377–80, 390–2, 396
Mohuczy, B. 190
Moisés Ville 405–6
Montefiore, Moses 29, 33–5, 37–8, 42, 58, 60–1
Morawiecki, Mateusz 417, 420–1
Mordekhai of Chernobyl 33
Moreh, Mordecai 275
Morgenstern, Arie 53
Morgentoy, Leyb 269
Moriah 144
Mosad Le'aliyah Bet 239
Moshe, youngest son of Shneur Zalman of Liady 42
Moshe Landsberger of Posen 62
Mount of Olives cemetery 39
Mozes, Yehuda 147
Msza święta 308, 314

Muhammad Ali 30, 34
Mühlstein, Anatol 207, 209–13
Munk, Andrzej 312
Muravev, Mikhail Nikolaevich 206
Museum of the Second World War, Gdańsk 419, 425
Musiał, Bogdan 345
Muszkat, Jósef 342
Myśl Polska 241

N
Nahman of Bratslav 37
Nahman of Horodenka 32
Nahum of Szadek 53, 62
Nałęcz, Tomasz 420
Nalewki and Dzika Streets as metaphor 6–7, 105–6, 110–19, 123–39, 143
Nałkowska, Zofia 192
Národ 96
Narodowe Siły Zbrojne 341
Nasz Głos 94–5
Nasz Przegląd 97, 99–100, 180, 185, 241
Nasza Palestyna 97
Nasza Prasa co-operative 148
Nasze Jutro 95
Natali, Nitza 276
National Association of Journalists in the Land of Israel (Ha'igud Ha'artsi Shel Ha'itona'im Be'erets Yisra'el) 140–4
National Defence Fund (Fundusz Obrony Narodowej; FON) 94
National Democrats 126
National Radical Camp (Obóz Narodowo-Radykalny) 94, 338
nationalism:
  Jewish 129
  Polish, influence on Jews 129–30
Nawrocki, Karol 416
Naye folkstaytung 250
Netanyahu, Benjamin 416–19, 423
Neufeld, Yosef 76
Neuland/*Neuland* 399–409
Neustadt, Melech 160, 162–4
Nevo, Eshkol, *Neuland* 399–409
Newsweek Polska 417, 420
Nicholas I, Tsar 59–60
Nieduszyński, Tadeusz 184
Nomberg, Hersh Dovid 143
Nowe Słowo 100
Nowiny 327
Nowiny Codzienne 92–3
Nowiny i Kurier 258, 337–52
Nowy Dziennik 75, 124, 147
numerus clausus 341
Nurock, Mordechai 126

O

Obóz Narodowo-Radykalny, see National Radical Camp
Obshchestvo dlya rasprostraneniya prosveshcheniya mezhdu evreyami v Rossii, see Society for the Promotion of Culture Among the Jews
Od Nowa 326–7
'Odessa journalism' 144–5, 147
Ofek, Bina 275
Ofek, Uriel 276
Olamenu 97
Olitski, Leyb 269
Oliwa, Franciszka 231
Opinia 99, 217, 268
Organization of Polish Expatriates in Israel 342
Orlev, Itamar, *The Bandit* 380–4, 394–6
Orlicz-Dreszer, Gustaw 191–2
Orłowska, Krystyna 244
Ossendowski, Antoni 192
Ostrowski, Gershon 160, 165
Oyfgang 97
Oz, Amos 117, 203, 214–15

P

5-ta Rano 99
Packter, Mietek 230
Pale of Settlement 209
Palestine:
  exports to Poland 189
  as an imagined motherland 224–34
  partition, British White Paper (1939) on 224, 232 n. 2
  trade with 182–202
  UN Ad Hoc Committee on the Palestinian Question 203, 211
  UN Partition Plan for Palestine 132
Palestine Bulletin 183
Palestine and Near East Trading House 191
Palestine–Poland Immigrant Bank 186
Palestine Post 187–8
Palestine Tribune 149
Palestyna i Bliski Wschód 186–7
Palestyna po raz trzeci 191, 203, 205, 210–17
Paprocki, Antoni 190
Paruch, Waldemar 198 n. 35
Pasikowski, Władysław, *Aftermath* 365
Paskevich, Count Ivan 52, 55
Passent, Daniel 421
Pat, Jacob (Yakov) 249
Pazanovski, Benjamin 269
Pekidim Va'amarkalim (Clerks and Administrators) 33–4, 37, 41, 54–7, 60–2
  in Amsterdam 29

Pereira Mendes, Henry 59
Peres, Shimon 136
Peretz, Yitskhok Leybush 115, 143–4, 149, 270–1
Peri, Eliezer 211
Perlu, Nathan 276
perushim 36–9, 53
Philipson, Ludwig 60
Piasecki, Bolesław 338
pilgrimages to Israel 70–2
Piłsudski, Józef 77, 129, 159, 181–4, 191, 206–7, 209–10, 212
  as model for Jews 95–6
Piłsudski, Rowmund 204
Pinkerfeld, Jacob 76
Pinsker, Leon 73, 341
PiS, see Law and Justice Party
Po'alei Agudat Israel Labour 132
Po'alei Tsiyon 160, 162, 168, 173, 224
Po'alei Tsiyon Left 162
Po'alei Tsiyon Right 158
pogroms 213, 215
  Jedwabne 415, 424
  Kielce 84, 337, 365, 424–5
  Kishinev 134
  Przytyk 341
  see also riots, anti-Jewish
Poland:
  changing view of 375
  as co-responsible for Nazi crimes 411
  distinctiveness, Polish, in 19th c. 51–68
  economic policy and the Yishuv 180–202
  film industry post-war 272
  as a huge Jewish cemetery 373–4, 389–91
  Jews returning to 354–72
  and Mandatory Palestine 71
  memory law (2018) 410–33
  and patriotism, Jewish 89–95
  Polish Jews in Israel 323–36
  Polish Jews and Israel before 1948 69–87
  Polish organizations in Israel 244
  Polish refugees in USSR 235–6
  schooling in 129
  see also antisemitism; immigrants, Polish
Polin Museum 425
Polish Information Centre for the East (Centrum Informacji na Wschód; CIW) 236, 242, 244–5
Polish Institute, London 243
Polish–Jewish Agreement (July 1925) 209
Polish–Jewish relations:
  in Iran 237–9
  in Israel 239–45
  in USSR 235–7
Polish–Lithuanian Commonwealth 204

Polish Ministry of Foreign Affairs (Ministerstwo Spraw Zagranicznych; NSZ) 195, 416
Polish Ministry of Industry and Trade 192, 195
Polish–Palestine Bank of Warsaw 191
Polish–Palestine Chamber of Commerce and Industry 195
Polish Peasant Party 241
Polish People's Republic 215
Polish Socialist Party (Polska Partia Socjalistyczna; PPs) 89, 206
Polish Transatlantic Shipping Company 180
Polish United Workers' Party (Polska Zjednoczona Partia Robotnicza; PZPR) 337–40
Polish Zionist Organization 159–60
Political Education Department of the Polish Ministry of Internal Security 345
Polityka 417
Pollin-Galay, Hannah 226
Polonia 193–4
Polonization 129
Polska Kasa Oszczędności; PKO, see Postal Savings Bank
Polska Mocarstwowa 207
Polska Partia Socjalistyczna, see Polish Socialist Party
Polska Zjednoczona Partia Robotnicza; PZPR, see Polish United Workers' Party
Polskie Stronnictwo Ludowe 421
Pomeranz, Mojżesz 204–5, 207–11, 214, 216–17
Pompiansky, Yehuda 240, 243
Popper, Karl 423
Porat, Dina 416, 418–19, 423
Pordes, Anis 102
Portman, Natalie 203
Posner, Avraham 62
Postal Savings Bank (Polska Kasa Oszczędności; PKO) 185
Prawo i Sprawiedliwość, see Law and Justice Party
press:
  communist censorship of 305–22
  east European Jewish, and Israeli journalism 140–57
  Hebrew 140–57
  'Odessa journalism' 144–5, 147
  Polish, in Israel 240, 324–9, 337–52
  Russian, in Odessa 144
  Yiddish 142, 149–50, 163, 170–1, 250–2
printing in Jerusalem 39–41
Progressive (Liberal) Party 324, 339
propaganda, anti-Israeli 306
Pro-Palestine Committee 191–2
Pruszyński, Ksawery 1, 190–1, 203–5, 217
Pruszyński, Mieczysław 204–5

Pryłucki, Tsevi 148
Przegląd Zachodni 93
Przewodnik Katolicki 305
Public Culture and Arts Council of the Ministry of Education, Israeli 347
Putin, Vladimir 427

R
Radek, Karl 206
Rahman, Abdul (the 'Black Rabbi') 42
Rapacki, Adam 339
Rapaport, Natan 270
Rassvet 144
Raszal, Aharon 271
Raveh, Yitzhak 332
Ravitsch, Melech (Zekharye Khone Bergner) 143, 250, 264
Raz-Krakotzkin, Amnon 376
Redlich, Shimon 354–5, 368
Reingold, M. 379
Reszke, Katke 354
Revisionist Zionism 129–30, 132, 148–50, 159–63, 165, 170–2
  youth groups 134
Richter, Bogdan 191
Righteous Among the Nations 354
riots, anti-Jewish, in Galilee 34
Rishon LeZion 200 n. 69
ritual as folklore 288
Rogovin, Or 292
Ron, Moshe (Dancygekron) 141–2
Ronen, Shoshana 360, 367, 389
Rosenberg, Shalom 166 n. 102
Rosenfeld, Shalom 148
Rotenstreich, Fishel 186, 188
Roth, Joseph 406
Roth, Philip 365
Rothberg, Michael 391
Rozenzweig, Michael 191
Różewicz, Stanisław 272
Rubashov, Shneur Zalman 170
Rubin, Adam 288
Rubin, Carl 76
Ruch Biblijny i Liturgiczny 310
Rufeisen, Fr. Daniel 315
Ruppin, Arthur 106, 112, 186
Russell, Bertrand 344
Russian ban on donations to Israel 52, 58–61
Russification 206
Rybkowski, Jan 272
Rycerz Niepokalanej 309
Rympel, Manuel 254
Rzeczpospolita 417

S

Sabbatai Zevi 72
Sabbatians 37
sabra:
 admiration for 330–1
 image of 373
Safed, printing press in 33
Safran Foer, Jonathan 354
Sagi, Avi 366
Salant, Samuel 54
Salomon, Yoel Moshe 39
Sanacja regime 181, 183–5, 190–1
Sanguszko, Prince Roman Stanisław 70
Saporta, Rafael 275–6
Sarem od-Doleh, Prince 239
Sarid, Yishai 374, 376–7
Sawin, R. L. 328
Schaetzel, Tadeusz 192
Scharf, Rafael 91
Schenirer, Tulo 102
Schipper, Yitshak 131
Schlanger, Maurycy 98
Schneersohn, Menahem Mendel 41–2
Schneersohn, Shalom Dov Ber 43
Schneersohn, Shemu'el 43
Schneiderman, Shmuel Leib 249
Schnitzer, Shmuel 148
Schrire, Dani 289, 291, 299
Schumacher, Yisroel 143, 347, 354
Schuss, Ze'ev (Włodzimierz) 82
Schwarzbart, Ignacy 243
Sebald, W. G. 363
Seer of Lublin 37
Selzer, Jakub 79
Semel, Nava 263
Semkowski, Fr. Ludwik 315
Sephardi community in Israel 52–8
Seter, Shaul 281
Sfard, David 269, 271
Shafir, Rachel 276
Shamir, Yitzhak 130, 420
Shapira, Anita 293
Sharon, Arie 76
Shatzky, Jacob 264
Shavit, Yaakov 106
shekel distribution 167–71
shelilat hagolah 288, 295
Sheptytsky, Andrey 229
Shertok, Moshe 184–5, 189, 238, 241, 243
Shertok (Sharett), Zipora 238–9
Shlonsky, Abraham 329
Shneur Zalman of Liady 30, 41–2
Shneur Zalman Fradkin of Lublin 39

Shoah trips 376, 378–9, 391
Sholem Aleichem 115, 118, 146, 252, 270
Shoshkes, Chaim 249
Shpigl, Yeshayahu 269
shtetl 291–3, 295
Shtrait-Wurzel, Ester 276
Shurer, Hayim 160, 165, 167
Sicher, Efraim 393
Sieci 417
Sikorski, Gen. Władysław 82–3, 216
Sikorski Museum 243
Silber, Marcos 159
Silberklang, David 416, 418
Singer, Isaac Bashevis 143, 252, 359
Six Day War 333, 341
 censorship of press on 310
 consequence for Jews in Poland 337–9
Skirmunt, Konstanty 197 n. 22
Skrzyński, Aleksander 182–3, 209–10
Slánský, Rudolf 306
Slonim, Ya'akov 42
Słowacki, Juliusz 70, 128–9
Slowes, Mia 101
Słowo 190–1, 205
Smooha, Sami 136
Socialist Zionists 124, 131
Society for the Promotion of Culture Among the Jews (Obshchestvo dlya rasprostraneniya prosveshcheniya mezhdu evreyami v Rossii) 144
Society for the Settlement of the Land of Israel (Hevrat Yishuv Erets Yisra'el) 62, 64
Society for Trades and Agricultural Labour 212
Sokolow, Nahum 140, 144, 149, 191–2
Sokolow Journalists' House (Beit Ha'itona'im al Shem Sokolow) 140–57
Sokołowski, M. 202 n. 108
Solta, Dariusz 424
Sommerstein, Emil 225
Spiegelman, Art, *Maus* 363
Srebnik, Szymon 354
Stankowski, Albert 422
State Export Institute 190–1, 193
Stefano, Dr Asia 245
Steinman, Eliezer 108, 301
Stendig, Samuel 180, 192, 194
Stępiński, Zygmunt 425
stereotypes, of Jews 2
Stern, Abraham 78
Sternhell, Zeev 375
Stola, Dariusz 425
Stomma, Stanisław 313
Stronnictwo Narodowe 191
Stroński, Stanisław 191

Strug, Andrzej 200 n. 76
Surdykowski, Jerzy 88–9
Świetlocki, Stanisław 195
synagogues:
  Avraham Avinu, Jerusalem 42
  Beit Menahem/Tsemah Tsedek, Jerusalem 42
  Hurva, Jerusalem 39
  Karlin, Safed 48 n. 69
  modelled on Temple 70
  Ohel Moshe, Jerusalem 40
  Tempel, Kraków 75
  in Tiberias 36–7
  Tiferet Yisra'el 39–1
Szaniawski, Jerzy 100
Szczepaniak, Ryszard 259
Szechter, Szymon 344–5
Szembek, Jan 192
Szold, Henrietta 240
Szpytma, Mateusz 416
Szteinke, Fr. Anzelm 70
Sztuka 268, 270
Szymel, Maurycy 98

T

Tabenkin, Yitshak 164
Tanai, Shlomo 276
Tapouchi, Hadas 388–9
Tawiow, Yisra'el Hayim 146
Tchernichowsky, Saul 129, 240
Teitel, Hannania 236
Tel Aviv:
  as allegory 109–10
  name 140
Tel Aviv Artists House 273
Temkin-Berman, Batya 225
Tene, Binyamin 275–6
Tenenbaum, Joseph 249
theatre:
  Jewish 268, 346
  Yiddish 346–7
Thon, Abraham Ozjasz 75, 77, 92, 125, 147
Tomaszewski, Jerzy 182
Trumpeldor, Berit 95, 128
Trybuna Mazowiecka 340
Trybuna Narodowa 96, 149–50, 156 n. 102
Tsanin, Dora 253
Tsanin, Mordecai (Cukierman, Mordecai Yeshayahu) 249–62
Tsukunst 251
Tumarkin, Yigal 275
Turov, Nissan 145
Turski, Marian 190
Tuszyńska, Agata 252
Tuwim, Julian 212

Tygodnik Powszechny 309–16
Tygodnik Warszawski 308

U

UN Ad Hoc Committee on the Palestinian Question 203, 211
UN Partition Plan for Palestine 132
Undzer leben 156 n. 95
United Religious Front 132
Ury, Scott 126
USSR, Polish refugees in 235–6

V

Valdmand, Zigmund 269
Vardi, Aharon 108
Victoria, Queen 59
Vienna, Jewish community in 74–5
Vilenski, Tzvia 276
Vilna Gaon 37, 53
Vincenz, Stanisław 98
Viteles, Harry 235–8

W

W drodze 240–1
Wandering Jew 406–7
Wańkowicz, Melchior 71
Wars, Henryk 240
Warsaw Art Academy 265
Warsaw ghetto:
  ruins 266–7, 270, 273, 281
  uprising 81; film on 272
Warsaw Ghetto Museum 417, 422, 425
Warsaw *kehilah* 131
Wegler, Elhanan 269
Weinberg, Shemu'el 36
Weinstock, Leon 215
Weintraub, Władysław 265
Weiss, Szewach 421
Weizmann, Chaim 105–6, 110–16, 118–19, 123–5, 140, 158–60, 172
Wessely, Naphtali Herz 291
Wiadomości Duszpasterskie 308
Wildstein, Bronisław 416
Wilensky, Meir 293
Wittelson, Chaim 230
Wittlin, Józef 406
Wodziński, Marcin 64
Wojstomska, J. 202 n. 108
Wołczyńska, Sława 362
Wolff, Joseph 37
Wolfowitz, Nathan 347
Wolfstein, Anita 328
Wołkowicz, Samuel 180
women:
  in hasidic society in Israel 29
  in the Yishuv 45 n. 21

World Association of Jewish Journalists 142
World Zionist Organization 158-9
Wróblewski, Major 241

Y

Ya'akov Dov of Roman 34
Ya'akov Shimshon of Shepetovka 33
Ya'akov Yehudah Leib Levi 54-6, 62-3
Ya'akov Yehudah Leib of Ślesin 53-4
Ya'akov Yitshak, 'Holy Jew' of Pshiskhe (Przysucha) 40
Ya'ari, Meir 125, 211
Yad Vashem 344, 354, 396, 412, 416, 418-20, 422-3, 427-8
Yadgar, Yaacov 301
Yareach, Yuval 395
  The Silences 392-4
Yasani, Wolf 269
Yeda Am (folklore research society) 289-90, 292
Yedidya, Shalom 340
Yedies 163, 170
Yediot aḥaronot 142, 147-9, 339, 418
Yehoshua, Israel 252
Yehoshua Trunk of Kutno 40
Yellin, David Tevia 54
Yiddish 97, 102, 209
  ban on performance in 347
  Hebrew preferred to 102
  language 102, 251, 292
  in post-war Poland 271
  press 142, 149-50, 163, 170-1, 250-2
  theatre 346-7
  see also Association of Yiddish Writers in Israel
Yidish Bukh 271
Yidish Kunsteater 348
Yidishe Gezelshaft tsu Farshproytn Kunst, *see* Jewish Society for the Promotion of Fine Arts
Yidishe Literatn un Zhurnalistn Farayn, *see* Association of Jewish Writers and Journalists
Yishai, Dr Moshe 242
Yishuv 43-4
  fundraising mission to Posen and Pomerania 62-3
  kolelim in 51
  Old Yishuv in Israel 27
  and Polish economic policy 180-202
Yisra'el hayom 418
Yisra'el Joffe of Kapust 41
Yisrael Perlov of Stolin 36
Yisra'el of Ruzhin 33-4, 38-9
Yisra'el of Shklov 33-4
Yitshak of Boyan 40
Youth Aliyah 240
youth movements 167-9
  Jewish 134-5, 162-4

Z

Zak, Avrom 269
Załęcki, Gustaw 185
Zaleski, August 192
Zarzycki, Ferdynand 194-5
Zawisza, Alexander 241
Zbyszewski, Titus 182-3, 197 n. 22, 198 n. 27, 200 n. 69
Ze'ev Wolf of Cherniostrov 33
Zeitlin, Hillel 148
Zerubavel, Yael 375-6, 390
Zevin, Shlomo Yosef 298
Zielińska, Alicja 273
Zilberberg, Eliezer 148
Zionism 71, 205, 207-8, 374
  in Argentina 403
  Et Livnot faction of General Zionists 97, 124, 129, 172
  and language 97-100
  as national project 190-1
  and neutrality 89-90
  and patriotism 90-5
  and popular culture 288-304
  in Poland 88-104
  in Poland before 1918 73-7
  in Poland 1918-39 77-81
  in Poland 1939-48 81-4
  in Poland post-Holocaust 224-34
  Polish 158-79
  and Polish Jews in Israel 123-39
  rejection of 326
  in Russia 126-7, 159
  see also Labour Zionism; Labour Zionist bloc; New Zionist Organization; Polish Zionist Organization; Revisionist Zionism; Zionist Organization
Zionist Agency 243
Zionist Congress (1933) 171
Zionist Organization 105, 132, 160, 167-8
Zuckerman, Baruch 160
Zuckerman, Yitzhak 81, 224-5
Zweig, Stefan 406
Związek Zawodowy Polskich Artystów Plastyków, *see* Association of Polish Artists and Designers
Żydowskie Towarzystwo Krzewienia Sztuk Pięknych, *see* Jewish Society for the Promotion of Fine Arts
Żydowskie Towarzystwo Kultury i Sztuki, *see* Jewish Association for Culture and Art
Żyndul, Jolanta 101